CERTAIN VICTORY

Books of Interest from the Series

Japan and the Modern World

Series Editor: Mark Selden, Binghamton University

The Atomic Bomb
Voices from Hiroshima and Nagasaki
Kyoko and Mark Selden, eds. and trs.
Foreword by Robert Jay Lifton, M.D.

The Atomic Bomb Suppressed
American Censorship in Occupied Japan
Monica Braw

The Japanese Monarchy, 1931–1991
Ambassador Grew and the Making of the "Symbol Emperor System"
Nakamura Masanori
Translated by Herbert P. Bix; Jonathan Baker-Bates; Derek Bowen

Living with the Bomb
American and Japanese Cultural Conflicts in the Nuclear Age
Laura Hein and Mark Selden, eds.

The Other Japan
Conflict, Compromise, and Resistance Since 1945
New Edition
Joe Moore, ed.

Re-Inventing Japan
Time, Space, Nation
Tessa Morris-Suzuki

CERTAIN VICTORY

Images of World War II in the Japanese Media

David C. Earhart

An East Gate Book

M.E.Sharpe
Armonk, New York
London, England

An East Gate Book

Library of Congress Cataloging-in-Publication Data

Earhart, David C., 1963-
Certain victory : images of World War II in the Japanese media / by David C. Earhart.
p. cm. — (Japan in the modern world)
"An East gate book"
Includes bibliographical references and index.
ISBN 978-0-7656-1776-7 (cloth : alk. paper)
1. World War, 1939-1945—Japan—Press coverage. 2. World War, 1939-1945—Japan—Mass media and the war. 3. World War, 1939-1945—Japan—Propaganda. I. Title.

D799.J3E37 2007
940.53'52—dc22 2006034584

Printed in the United States of America

The paper used in this publication meets the minimum requirements of American National Standard for Information Sciences Permanence of Paper for Printed Library Materials, ANSI Z 39.48-1984.

BM (c) 10 9 8 7 6 5 4 3 2 1

"I prefer the most unfair peace to the most righteous war."
—Lord Byron, *Childe Harold* (canto IV, line 177)

"Nothing is as good as peace, and nothing so frightening as war."
—Nagai Kafū, *Danchōtei nichijō* (*Danchōtei Diary*), 20 August 1945

CONTENTS

Map of the Japanese Empire and the Pacific Theater of World War II

- The Japanese Empire in 1910
- Expansion on the Asian Continent, 1931-1940
- Territorial Gains, 1941-1942
- Greatest Extent of the Japanese Empire, June 1942

PREFACE

The Japanese government of the 1930s was not the first to use the media to motivate and manipulate the citizenry in a time of national emergency. Nor was a streamlined, centralized modern state a Japanese invention, but in the years immediately preceding World War II, the Japanese Imperial State did achieve a degree of fusion of government, military, economy, and media, as well as the mobilization of the citizenry, rivaling that of the Soviet Union and Nazi Germany. Of course, the rule among all nations that fought World War II, including Great Britain and the United States, was the unity of the citizens and the war effort. In Japan, from the early 1930s, and particularly from 1941, this concentration of power and mobilization of society toward a single goal—total, permanent war—required an epic narrative, highlighting the positive results of the people's efforts and spiritually mobilizing them to make the necessary sacrifices for nation and emperor. The function of the media within the mass culture of a modern society at war is to produce images and texts orienting citizens within the national cause as participants in a glorious history-in-progress, one whose goals are lofty (in the case of Japan, freeing Asia from the grip of rapacious European colonial rulers and fulfilling the "destiny" of the Yamato race and their ancient imperial tradition) and above all else, one that leads ineluctably to victory. For the media to play the role of narrator of a national mission requires unity and coordination among the media, the government, and the military. When this dynamic is operating properly, a juggernaut of dazzling illustrations and inspiring stories bring together the home front and the battle front in a glorious and triumphant synthesis.

In the United States, World War II is still referred to as "the good war," although at the time it was often described as a crusade to save democracy. In Japan, too, the media gave several titles to this epic tale of conflict. From 1937 through 1940, this struggle was usually called "the China Incident, A Holy War," and in 1940 and 1941, "the Greater East Asian Co-Prosperity Sphere" or "Developing (or alternately, Constructing) Asia." In December 1941, this tale of national greatness evolved dramatically, and was anointed with an appropriately grand title: "the Great East Asia War." The shorthand for these titles was simply "Certain Victory" (Hisshō), the epic tale this book recounts through eight hundred images selected from over fifty thousand pages in two thousand five hundred Japanese publications, predominantly photodigests and newspapers published in Japan between 1937 and 1945. I have spent nearly twenty years amassing and researching these materials.

This book borrows analytical tools, more commonly applied to serially published novels, to deconstruct Japan's narrative of "Certain Victory." The rationale for doing so is found in the many parallels between the writerly practice of the archetypical serial novel and the method of producing weekly photodigests in wartime Japan: in both cases, the creator assumes an authoritative, omniscient stance toward the narrative, which traces a plot through its development and denouement. The story is uniquely the work of its author, who maintains close creative control over it. In other words, there was only one source for the story of the war's progress conveyed to the Japanese people. The corporate author of "Certain Victory" was the Cabinet Information Bureau (CIB), a branch of the Japanese government responsible for disseminating war information and serving as guardian of the imaging war on the home front, as well as supervisor and censor of the private media.

The multitude of Japanese citizens who voraciously consumed "Certain Victory" read it as enthusiastically as the devotee of the serialized social or adventure novel, because its pages reflected their ambitions and reconfirmed their values. Thus the literary analogy is further supported by parallels in readerly practice. As antagonists, protagonists, and scenes change through the process of a novel's creation and serialization, readers accordingly revise their interpretive strategies and refine theories of the resolution of the tensions presented in the narrative. The final resolution, that is, the end of the story, while presumed to be known only to the author, is constantly foreshadowed in the work. Indeed, the many elements of "Certain Victory," a massive *bildungsroman* in which Japanese society would evolve under the nurturing influence of a centralized, all-powerful state, and eventually meet the challenges to its becoming a master race, were all arranged as indications—signifiers—of the certain victory to come. Many of the idioms of "Certain Victory" are specific to Japan, but the master narrative at work—the assumption of racial or national invincibility and moral superiority—is as common to all nations engaging in modern warfare as is the hackneyed "happily ever after" that ends so many potboilers. Of course, this plot would lack dramatic tension, and not hold the audience's interest, if it lacked elements suggesting a counter-narrative with a completely different outcome. Simply put, the possibility that the war would end in failure was a constant subtext in "Certain Victory," one that gained momentum as the war progressed and the initial victories that extended Japanese power throughout the Asia Pacific region in early 1942 turned into a cascade of massive defeats leading from the colonies back to the home front.

My hope is that in deconstructing the CIB's mediation of the war, its re-presentation of a distant reality through the media products of intricately structured and polished texts and carefully crafted photographs and artwork, readers will find a comparative framework through which to analyze how other national medias have narrated other wars, not least those of the United States in World War II, Korea, Vietnam, Iraq, and particularly the global War on Terror being scripted by the Pentagon and disseminated through the US media as this book goes to press. The Great East Asia War and the War on Terror may not be morally or strategically analogous, but each should be read as a serialized novelistic narrative of triumph, carefully controlled and mediated by a corporate author who seeks to assume sole authority through the combination of military and government power and tight control over the media's dissemination of information regarding the conflict. While the military failure of Japan's quest for an Asian empire has been thoroughly scrutinized by historians, the media narrative of national triumph preceding and enabling the mass mobilization of Japanese society has received scant attention. The exact point at which Japan's remarkably resilient narrative disintegrated will be of particular interest to readers watching the US media's handling of the Iraq war and the War on Terror.

Each chapter of this book presents a story of its own. The first six chapters present a diachronic cross-section of the mobilization of Japanese society (especially in the years just prior to Pearl Harbor), borrowing the wartime model of the nation as one family under the emperor. These chapters establish the most immediate context in which to understand the media's presentation of the war against the Western powers. The last six chapters form a loose chronology of the Great East Asia War, from Pearl Harbor to Hiroshima and Nagasaki. My hope is that collectively, these overlapping and interconnecting chapters accomplish three things: First, deconstruct the contemporaneous official narrative of the denouement of Great East Asia War; second, identify iconic and ordinary images and thereby capture the "look" and "feel" of the war, demonstrating that wartime cultural production is anything but anomalous and establishing its rightful place within the larger context of twentieth century Japanese mass popular culture and the international wars that shaped the era; and third, provide a catalogue of primary resources in English translation for students, scholars, and everyone interested in the intersection of media, government, and war in mid-twentieth century Japan.

The selections include visual representations of every major aspect of World War II as presented to the Japanese home front. Admittedly, some topics have received rather short shrift. The Sino-Japanese War of 1937-1945 warrants an entire volume of its own. Due to space restrictions, it is treated as the prelude to the Great East Asia War, as it was so deemed by the government in 1941. Japan's Axis partnership could have filled a chapter, although Japanese media images relating to the Axis are heavily concentrated upon the months surrounding the conclusion of the Tripartite Treaty in October 1940. Once Germany was at war with the Soviet Union and Japan had its own war in the Pacific, the Nazis and Fascists quickly faded from the popular press. The absence of civilian men in the cross-section of Japanese society is deliberate. In the Japanese wartime media, men not in military service became nearly invisible.

This is not a history of the wartime media (which also included film, radio, and juvenile publications and textbooks) or of the wartime print media. Indeed, this book is not a history at all—it is intended to convey the wartime Japanese media's presentation of contemporary events, rather than to provide a comprehensive account or assessment of those events. It seeks to convey the logic and the content of Japan's "Certain Victory" as dissembled by the CIB, especially its visual representations. In a few instances, I have noted where the narrative of "Certain Victory" strays from the accepted historical record of the war. In general, however, I take for granted that the account of the war presented here is, by the nature of its creation, impossibly optimistic and at times radically distorted, and I encourage readers to do the same while trying to see the war through the eyes of contemporary Japanese.

The images herein deal primarily with the Japanese home front and the mobilization of the citizens. Nevertheless, this book, by definition, must leave unanswered some of the largest questions it raises, especially regarding public reception of the narrative of "Certain Victory" and the degree to which citizens willingly participated in the war effort. While "Certain Victory" was created and packaged by a large crew of photographers, writers, graphic artists, and illustrators, its pro-government bias precluded individual expression. "Certain Victory" provides one context in which to read, with greater appreciation and deeper understanding, personal narratives of the war written by Japanese who experienced it firsthand.

The CIB occasionally described its work (as well as the work of its bureaucratic counterparts in China, Nazi Germany, the United States, and elsewhere) as "propaganda" (*senden*), meaning the propagation among the citizenry of pro-government attitudes and actions in the pursuit of war and empire. Since the nuance of this word is so pejorative today, I avoid it in my analysis and discussion of "Certain Victory," allowing the graphics and text to speak for themselves.

A few bibliographical details need to be noted here. This book consciously imitates the layout of the CIB photodigest *Photographic Weekly Report* (*PWR*), the single most influential and authoritative of Japan's wartime news journals. As with most prewar Japanese publications, this magazine opens from right to left, and two-page spreads read sequentially from right to left. The Japanese layout of photographs and captions has been preserved in many cases, which will initially be counterintuitive for most Western readers. The variations in the citations of periodicals reflect stylistic changes over the course of time. For instance, *PWR* did not assign page numbers to its front cover and inside front cover when it was initially published, but when it abolished advertisements in 1941, it began numbering its front cover as its first page. All captions and news articles cited in this book are my own translations from Japanese, unless otherwise noted. Japanese names appear in Japanese order, with family name first, except where an author's name is cited exactly as it appeared in an English-language publication.

This is a selection of wartime images scanned from original wartime publications from my private collection, not a selection of artifacts per se. Although I have tried to capture the flavor of wartime publications, I felt it appropriate to remove minor imperfections (dust, specks of ink blotting, or loss) from the scanned images, insofar as the demands of this book's format could not preserve the original scale or color of the images. Flaws in the photographs themselves or flaws in the printing process affecting the entire print run were left intact.

Finally, there is the matter of the people who populate this book, *Certain Victory*. I would like to offer my assurances to everyone pictured here—as well as to their families, their descendants, and their loved ones—that I have the highest respect for their experiences, their suffering, and their loss. If this book provides even a small measure of nourishment to humanity's desire to end war, then may that provide comfort to the men, women, and children pictured in these pages, both the living and the dead.

ACKNOWLEDGMENTS

This book, the culmination of nearly twenty years of researching Japanese wartime publications, could not have been completed without the encouragement and assistance of several people, three to whom I owe a tremendous debt of gratitude.

Mark Selden, series editor, championed this project. He took me under his wing and tutored me in the process of producing a publishable manuscript. His mentoring honed my historical methodology and kept the manuscript on task, and his punctilious editing and indefatigable knowledge of Asian history greatly improved this book. Of course, any errors or omissions are my own.

My parents, Byron and Virginia Earhart, provided a sounding board as the manuscript evolved. My father, with over forty years of experience in Japanese studies, painstakingly read the first and second drafts of this book, making innumerable suggestions for revisions as well as recommending secondary sources.

Susumu Kamimura, my partner of many years, formatted the entire manuscript in the publisher's camera-ready template. The layout of every page of this book reflects Susumu's skill as a graphic designer and his meticulous, unerring eye for detail.

This is also an excellent opportunity to thank my many friends at Rissho Kosei-kai for allowing me to be, in an ideal sense, an independent scholar and thinker. I am truly grateful for their generous support throughout the process of writing this book, which was born of a shared desire to contribute to making the world a place of just and lasting peace. I believe that by thoroughly investigating the dark paths leading to war, we can gain a better understanding of how our species gives in to its aggressive impulses.

The staff of M. E. Sharpe, especially Makiko Parsons, has been wonderful to work with. I greatly appreciate Sharpe's agreeing to publish a much longer book than initially proposed, allowing me to include twice as many illustrations.

Chapter 12, "The Kamikazefication of the Home Front," is based in part on an article originally published in *Critical Asian Studies* (37:4), December 2005: "All Ready to Die: Kamikazefication and Japan's Wartime Ideology." My thanks to the publishers for permission to reprint portions of that article here.

Finally, I would like to thank everyone who has encouraged this project at different stages in its evolution: Laura Hein, Gennifer Weisenfeld, and Maggie Mudd helped this project take definition; anonymous reviewers recommended my book proposal be accepted for publication; and Kazuyuki Abe and Susumu Kamimura volunteered their time and energy in assisting me in the purchase of rare primary materials located in Japan. If I have forgotten to thank someone here, I hope s/he will accept my apologies.

CERTAIN VICTORY

INTRODUCTION:
A PICTURE WORTH A THOUSAND ARGUMENTS

In wartime Japan, an unprecedented event took place on 28 March 1945: a photograph of the Shōwa Emperor (better known in the West by his princely name, Hirohito) was printed in a magazine as an enormous centerfold. The emperor had hitherto been shown only in formal settings. With the exception of the austere official portrait (Chapter 1, figure 3)—a portrait intended for display in schools, offices, and homes—he was usually shown from a respectful distance at some state function. The emperor was the highest authority in the land and the commander-in-chief of the armed forces. The putative descendant of the Sun Goddess and titular head of State Shinto, he was revered as a living god (*arahitogami*) by his subjects. His closely guarded media image presented him residing in a flawless world of purity, calm, refinement, and order. This 23½-by-16½ inch poster-size centerfold shows him impeccably attired in full military dress with polished riding boots and riding crop, striding ahead of his advisers and generals (figure 2). He was not at the head of a victory parade, however. Instead, he was conducting a review, not of military might, but of the massive war damage in a neighborhood inhabited by working-class commoners. Indeed, the site had been littered with thousands of their twisted, blackened

1. *Present-Day Japan, Coronation Number, English Language Supplement of the Osaka Asahi and the Tokyo Asahi*, 1928. Frontispiece. The caption reads, in English, "His Imperial Majesty the Emperor of Japan in the Garments He Will Wear at the Coronation. Painted by the prominent artist, Eisaku Wada."

2. *Photographic Weekly Report* 364-365, 28 March 1945, pp. 4-5.

corpses just days before and hence was unfit to receive this living god, since in Shinto belief the dead were viewed as unclean and defiling. The photograph was taken at the Tomioka Hachiman Shrine in Fukagawa, an industrial district in southeast Tokyo. The caption described the event: "His August Majesty, in a show of great benevolence, condescended to bestow the auspicious honor of an hour-long imperial visit upon war-ravaged neighborhoods hit by an air raid on 10 March." History would later dub this "the Great Tokyo Air Raid."

This frequently reprinted photograph has become one of the emblematic images of World War II, appearing in books and films about the war six decades later. But unlike the 1938 Japanese flag-raising in the Chinese capital of Nanjing (figure 33 in Chapter 3) and the 1945 American flag-raising on Mount Suribachi, Iwo Jima (a staged photograph, we now know) or a major victory, like the British surrender of Singapore in 1942 (figure 37 in Chapter 7) or MacArthur wading ashore in his promised return to the Philippines in 1944, it is not celebratory. There are many "real-time" spontaneous World War II photographs that capture a turning point in the war, a decisive moment when the course of world history changed—Stalin's laughing face at Yalta, the mushroom cloud above Hiroshima. But this is not one of those photographs. The caption (and, indeed, the internal evidence of the photograph) tells us that it was taken eight days after the Great Tokyo Air Raid, and five months before the Japanese surrender.

What, then, accounts for the photograph's enduring appeal, and how should we assign meaning to it? Knowing that the Imperial Household Ministry carefully orchestrated the emperor's movements and closely guarded his privacy and his public image, can we discern in his facial expression compassion, anger, shock, or despair? Does he tread heavily or step lightly through the clutter of debris in what was, just days before, a bustling corner of Tokyo? Could this photograph convey the emperor's sympathy for his people, even show that he was as human and vulnerable as they were? Or was the opposite true: did this picture show that this god-emperor was so far removed from the reality of the war and had so little regard for his subjects that he was unfazed as he strode through the devastation? Was the photograph published as proof that the emperor himself was unhurt in the air raid?

Unfortunately, no first-hand observations about either the emperor's visit to Fukagawa or the taking of this photograph have come to light. The photographer is uncredited and the genesis of the photograph is shrouded in secrecy. We do know that this photograph was officially released to the press by the Cabinet Information Bureau (CIB), which coordinated and monitored all information during the war, and which reproduced it in the government's official weekly newsmagazine, *Photographic Weekly Report* ([*PWR*], *Shashin shūhō,* which the CIB edited).

The CIB's stated purpose in disseminating this photograph was to exhort people to do even more for the war effort. The short article accompanying the photograph concluded with an appeal to "repay the emperor's extreme kindness in showing deep concern for his subjects with a firm spiritual resolve to make every effort to shoot the despicable enemy and thereby protect this Land of the Gods." We wonder, though, whether this stated objective was achieved. Did the average reader who saw this photograph and read this article determine to work harder to win the war, to achieve the stated objective of the imaging war: the ultimate, final victory?

Like Nazi Germany's Propaganda Ministry and the United States Office of War Information, the CIB was an agency whose very business was drumming up morale and convincing people that the war was good and right and, above all else, winnable. War, after all, had to be "sold" to the people and they had to "buy" it, and this commodification of violence is equally true today. In modern society, this consumption of war is facilitated by imagery and image, that is, by an imaging war that is fought before and during a military engagement, and sometimes long after it ends.

World War II was the age of the still photograph, although the use of the photograph to sway public opinion in wartime can be dated to the Crimean War of 1854-1856.[1] Photographs dominate this book because they were the single most influential medium of the wartime press in Japan, as they were everywhere during the war. As a means of communication, the photograph served well because of its familiarity as a popular form, its interpretive immediacy, and its seemingly transparent verisimilitude; it also functioned effectively as image because it could be easily manipulated, readily disseminated, and potently persuasive. Perhaps most importantly, the camera was a modern, Western machine that, when placed in Japanese hands, produced pictures conveying a Japanese ethos.

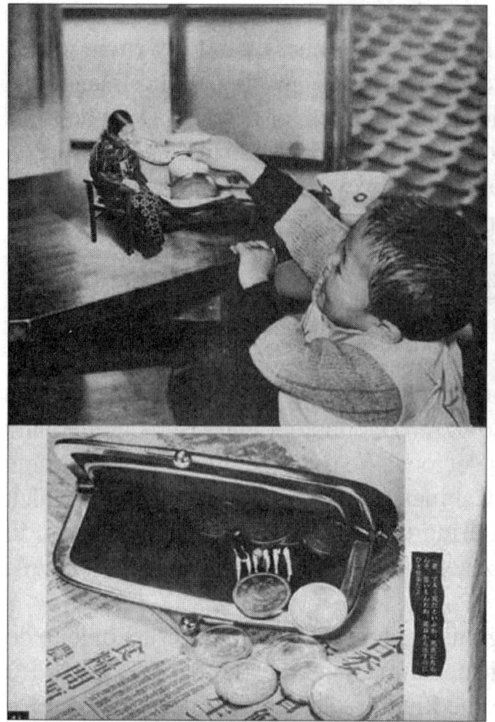

3. *PWR* 97, 3 January 1940, pp. 40-41. (Page 40 is on the right, page 41 on the left.) "If Big Things Were Small, and Small Things Weren't Small." A set of photomontages by Senba Tōru reverses the natural order, suggesting psychological truths: (top right) a dog appears to be master to his keeper, (bottom right) bicyclists climb the side of a smokestack in defiance of gravity, (top left) baby feeds grandmother, (bottom left) tiny people push aluminum one sen coins out of change purse. Given the aims of the Japanese government and the purpose of *PWR*, these photographs are surprising for their candor regarding the manipulability of the photographic medium and the subversive potential of their messages.

Photographic truths are hardly limited to documentation; the medium may arrive at an aesthetic truth or a psychological truth. Even *PWR* allowed such possibilities in a rare moment of levity, as seen in figure 3. This curious set of whimsical, surreal photographs by famed modernist photographer Senba Tōru, included in *PWR*'s New Year's 1940 issue, reversed the usual rules and relations of objects, suggesting psychological truths. This experiment in reality-defying photomontage was never repeated in *PWR*.

As documentation, that is, as photojournalism, the photograph tells many truths, but is also open to the manipulation of the photographer and the editor, such that it may generate many interpretations, even conflicting ones, among different viewers in different times and places. We have good reason today, with hindsight, to dismiss as mere "propaganda" the official explanation of the photograph of the emperor at Fukagawa's war-ravaged Hachiman Shrine: that the emperor's visit was an expression of his benevolence, his caring for his subjects. However, when we reject out-of-hand this contemporary context, the meaning initially assigned by the agency that created, edited, and disseminated this photograph, then we limit our ability to understand the full range of Japanese experiences of the war and fail to see the complexities surrounding media artifacts. And although at the present moment we may "receive" this photograph differently, as a document presaging the imminent destruction and defeat of Japan, and (because we know the outcome) as proof of the foolhardiness of trying to mobilize people to fight for a lost cause, or even as proof of the emperor's culpability in the war—it is well to recall the Japanese people and their reception of this situation in the spring of 1945. Despite the tremendous destruction and loss of life, the political status quo was hardly affected by the Great Tokyo Air Raid, and the Japanese government continued to prosecute the war for several months until the atomic bombings and the Soviet declaration of war led to surrender. If many Japanese were coming to recognize the futility of the war, there was very little insubordination.

Returning to the picture of the emperor, we can also analyze it as a photograph. We immediately notice the composition, which nicely frames the emperor between denuded tree trunks. The emperor is shown to advantage, squarely placed in the center foreground, and caught in mid-stride looking straight ahead, with his head held high, even as the members of his entourage have their eyes cast down at the ground. Surely the photographer was a seasoned professional. We also notice the contrasting elements of the picture. This godlike emperor in martial splendor is walking along a bombed-out, debris-strewn street, his commanders in tow, an act meant to bolster confidence in Japan's ultimate victory, even as enemy bombs had carved out a sixteen-square-mile moonscape in the heart of Japan's largest city, the Imperial Capital. This irony certainly conveyed a second message, one that subverted the official "victory" narrative, and we know from private diaries published after the war that an intelligent, objective reader was quite capable of reading the impending defeat "between the lines" of the official version of events, and realizing the necessity to prepare for an uncertain future.

This second, subversive message—that the emperor and the High Command had failed to protect the people from the devastation of this air raid—appears more plainly in *Asahigraph*'s use of the same photograph. Of course, the *Asahigraph* editors had wholeheartedly supported the war effort and marveled at Japan's military achievements up to this point, and the Asahi News Corporation, like all publishers, had to bow down before the CIB. Although the *Asahigraph* article about the emperor's visit to Fukagawa is, word-for-word, exactly the official version printed in *Photographic Weekly Report*, the placement and use of the photograph is substantially different, enough so to suggest that the editors deliberately (and at some personal risk to themselves) laid out the story-spread so that the reader could decipher this second, subversive message.

In *Asahigraph*, the photograph of the emperor at Fukagawa appeared on page 3 (the left page) of the publication, taking second place to the fate of air raid survivors on page 2 (the right page). In newspapers and periodicals, stories about the emperor had to be given the place of prominence, that is, the upper right corner of the front page of the newspaper or the first interior page of a magazine (technically, page 3 in the *Asahigraph*).[2] Because the emperor was considered sacred, the page opposite his picture was left blank in *PWR* (see figures 2 and 3 in Chapter 1) to prevent ink from soiling his august visage. When the *Asahigraph* magazine is closed, however, the dirty faces of common Japanese (the air raid survivors) rub against the emperor's face. The *Asahigraph*

4. *Asahigraph* (44:13), *Great East Asia War Report* 167, 28 March 1945, pp. 2-3.

layout surrounds the photograph of the emperor with his suffering subjects, whose absence is terribly conspicuous in the *PWR* layout. The *Asahigraph* editors all but point out that the emperor's benevolent concern for his subjects precludes his coming into contact with them.

Since the war's end, this photograph of the emperor surveying the air raid damage has remained an enigma. "A picture is worth a thousand words," to quote the hackneyed adage, and this one is worth a thousand arguments as well, since popular and scholarly debate about the war, especially surrounding the emperor's role and responsibility, has intensified in the sixty years since this photograph was taken. The secrecy cloaking the emperor before, during, and after the war largely shielded him and his actions from close scrutiny, thwarting any attempt to establish a definitive interpretation of this photograph. In the wake of Japan's defeat, the emperor renounced his divinity and was reborn as an apolitical "national symbol" of democratic Japan, a mortal man who loved "chocolate-covered peanuts, Mickey Mouse, baseball, and marine biology" according to *The Human Emperor*, a book published in Japan in 1947. The wartime image of the emperor as military and spiritual leader was quickly consigned to the rubbish heap of history. A comparison with a very similar photograph will help illuminate this point.

Consider the celebrated film footage of England's Queen Mother visiting the bombed-out areas in and around London during the 1940 blitz. There are some notable differences from the picture of the emperor in Fukagawa, in that the Queen Mum was shown in direct contact with survivors. We note certain remarkable similarities in the actions recorded and the meaning assigned to them at the time: despite this temporary setback, "our side" will emerge victorious and our national interest will be protected, and the highest authority in the land hereby consecrates the people's sacrifices and encourages their efforts to that end. Perhaps most striking is the great distance between the historic resonance of these two photographic artifacts since war's end. The Queen Mum was at the center of Blitz commemorations, placing a plaque at the rebuilt Coventry Chapel fifty years after it was bombed. She led nationwide British celebrations of the fiftieth anniversary of V-E Day, with news commentators replaying the stirring wartime footage of her.

In stark contrast, the Japanese and their wartime emperor never publicly joined in marking anniversaries of the war. In 1986, in commemoration of the sixtieth year of Hirohito's reign, a discreet memorial stone was erected at the Tomioka Hachiman Shrine with a poem on its obverse and a message on its reverse: "On the Eighteenth of March in 1945, in the final stage of the Great East Asia War, His Imperial Majesty the Emperor toured sections of Tokyo reduced to a charred wasteland by the great air raid, and stopped here in the grounds of Tomioka Hachiman. The emperor, whose heart was deeply pained by the brutality of the bombing campaign, afterward issued His Imperial rescript to end the war. On the obverse of this stone is the poem he wrote at that time. It is carved here in praise of and as a lasting tribute to His Imperial virtue by the Tokyo Metropolitan Committee to Celebrate the Sixtieth Year of His Imperial Majesty's Reign."

The images presented in this book constitute a mere fraction of over thirty thousand pages of contemporary Japanese wartime publications, predominantly periodicals, collected and examined over the course of two decades of research. Though small, this selection captures something of the "look" and the "feel" of the Great East Asia War by viewing it from the perspective of Japanese of the time. The CIB fashioned the image and set the tone of the war. Indeed, the CIB not only directed, censored, and consolidated the entire domestic publishing industry, it also produced its own newsweekly magazine, *Photographic Weekly Report*, which had a weekly circulation of ninety thousand in 1938, one hundred seventy thousand in 1940, and five hundred thousand in 1943.[3]

The CIB's primary work was "imaging" the war, providing pictures and stories for the home front that would fire the determination to fight. The CIB shared this goal with every government agency embroiled in the war, in Japan and elsewhere,[4] and remarkably familiar media images were produced on all sides of the conflict. What nation at war did not have its own version of GI Joe, Rosie the Riveter, the war-bond selling gamin, the patriotic schoolgirl donating her cherished doll to a scrap drive, the salt-of-the-earth Mom and Pop who stoically watch their boy come home in a box? These suggest the common denominator of the war effort everywhere in World War II, and such wartime images from Japan can be matched with images from most or all of the countries engaged in the war. Every government and mass media used visual "propaganda" to mobilize support for the war. Some of these parallels will be pointed out, but our focus is on the Japanese scene and particularly its most distinctive, revealing features.

5. *PWR* 100, 24 January 1940, p. 8. The first thirty-six covers of *PWR*, laid out like a sheet of postage stamps, with a simple line graph showing the increase, and decrease, in *PWR* readership between issues 38 and 100. The actual number of readers is not divulged; with issue 38 representing a unit of one hundred, issue 100 had a readership of one hundred forty, showing an increase of 40 percent in just over one year. The same issue contained a similar page (p. 17) of front covers and a bar graph providing a breakdown of *PWR*'s content in the first one hundred issues, as follows: emperor and imperial family, 1 percent; China Incident, 16 percent; explanation of national policy, 40 percent; conditions of the [Asian] continent, 11 percent; scientific information, 6 percent; women and family, 4 percent; overseas information, 13 percent. Such transparency in government-sponsored journalism underscored the close connection between its production and reception. The people themselves seemed to welcome having their government tell them what to think.

In boosting morale, the Japanese wartime media drew upon Japanese traditions: politics, history, society, culture. The CIB's selectivity, its determination about what to show (and what not to show) to the people, reflects the Japanese government's framing of social and aesthetic values projected as the nation's "unique" tradition. Individualism, selfishness, and decadence—diseases spread by the West—were Japan's sworn enemies in the "ideological war." Self-sacrifice, propriety, and adherence to group norms were the cure, and in countless articles, the government, through its CIB mouthpiece, explained and illustrated the virtues of obedience, sincerity, a perfect physique, and spiritual purity. The "look" of the war was characterized by minimalism and austerity and expressed graphically through realistic, mimetic art. Wartime chic emphasized the raw, rustic, unadorned, the native, and the powerful.

The images presented here were designed to propel the home front into experiencing the war vicariously, to feel it rush through their veins, to put themselves "in the picture." Above all, they were offered as photographic proof that the war was an expression of Japanese values and a means of fulfilling national and racial destiny. This goal never changed during the war, but the images did evolve. Their evolution is itself a peculiar narrative, one that consistently trumpets victory, even as it relates military retreats and devastating air raids, and calls for yet greater sacrifices to be made by the entire population. By war's end, much of the population of Japan that had been watching and supporting a distant overseas war would experience it directly, whether called up to fight or feeling it ravage their communities, their homes, their families, their lives.

These images of Japan at war present a world utterly alien today, even to the Japanese. The rapid postwar changes enacted by the Supreme Commander for the Allied Powers in Japan (SCAP) have already been mentioned. The CIB was dismantled by the occupying forces within weeks of the war's end. The SCAP labeled most wartime publications as contrary to the building of a new Japan and banned many of them. Paper was a precious commodity during the war and immediately thereafter, and wartime periodicals were the first to be pulped. Besides, much was lost in the burning of Japanese cities in the final months of the war, and few Japanese wanted to keep these reminders of defeat, so wartime periodicals are not common in Japanese libraries.

These images invite readers everywhere to pose a number of unsettling questions: Did all Japanese believe the misinformation their media fed them? Did other governments also lie to their people about this and other wars? Why did the Japanese government lead its own people and other Asian peoples into a maelstrom of death and destruction, and what parallels exist in other times and places? And what can we all learn about human nature in general from the experiences of the Japanese people during the war? In order to posit answers, we begin by retrieving these photographs and illustrations that formed vital pieces of the imaging war waged on the Japanese home front.

Ultimately, in assigning responsibility to other human beings and their social institutions, all of us make choices about how we lead our own lives and the social institutions to which we belong, wittingly or not. In judging these images and the people who first saw them, we judge ourselves. We live by what we choose to remember—and to forget.

Notes

1. In *The Indelible Image: Photographs of War, 1846 to the Present* (New York: Harry N. Abrams, 1985), Frances Fralin dates the first war photographs to 1846 daguerreotypes taken during the Mexican-American War (p. 12) and identifies the first photographs created and designed to influence public opinion regarding warfare as Roger Fenton's photographs that served as "photo-documentation to counter reports of inhuman conditions in the army camps that were being published in the British press, [which] neutralized perceptions of that conflict, whether in his contemporaries' eyes or in the eyes of historians" (p. 9).

2. The rule of imperial images appearing on the first inside page of publications was codified in the early 1930s. In the late 1920s, when Japan's photojournals were still in their infancy (and the CIB had yet to be formed), no such rule existed. For instance, the 4 January 1928 *Asahigraph* (10:2) placed two uncredited photographs of the emperor conducting military reviews on page 27 of a thirty-two page issue, facing a review of a kabuki production. This New Year's issue carried a large photograph of a beautiful "Mrs. Harrison, wife of Mr. Kay Harrison, an English businessman in Tokyo . . . at her home with an exquisitely beautiful tray-landscape of Mr. Fuji before her." The same issue printed, on page 30, photographs of Prince Kuni and his wife at an Osaka skating rink, decked out in stylish Western clothes and ice-skates.

3. Figures cited in Nanba Kōji, *"Uchiteshi Yamamu": Taiheiyō sensō to hōkoku no gijutsusha tachi* (Tokyo: Kodansha, 1998), pp. 54-55. The enormous influence wielded by *PWR* during the war is difficult to exaggerate. For instance, Kaneko Ryūichi states that since *PWR* was circulated within Neighborhood Associations, "its message can be said to have reached every Japanese citizen." See p. 192 in "Realism and Propaganda: The Photographer's Eye Trained on Society," in Anne Wilkes Tucker, Dana Friis-Hansen, Kaneko Ryūichi, and Takeba Joe, *The History of Japanese Photography* (New Haven, CT: Yale University Press, 2003), pp. 184-194.

4. Paul M. A. Linebarger's classic study, *Psychological Warfare* (Washington, D. C.: Infantry Journal, 1948), contains a useful diagram of the CIB and its organization (pp. 184-185). Gregory J. Kasza's study of prewar and wartime censorship provides an excellent overview of the CIB's establishment, evolution, and operations. See *The State and the Mass Media in Japan, 1918-1945,* (Berkeley: University of California Press, 1988), especially pp. 152-153, 157, 174-187, and 219-224.

1. EMPEROR SHŌWA

Emperor Shōwa (usually referred to in the West by his princely name, Hirohito [1901-1989]) combined in his person the aura of a head of state, commander-in-chief, and a living god (that is, a manifest deity, *arahitogami*). The degree to which the emperor himself directed and controlled the government, the military, and religious faith was shrouded in secrecy and remains a source of controversy.[1] His authority in all matters was, however, beyond question. By the time his photograph first appeared in *PWR*, three generations of Japanese had been taught to revere the emperor. The Imperial Rescript to Soldiers and Sailors (1882) and the Imperial Rescript on Education (1890), documents inspired by simplified Confucian ethics, emphasized obedience to the authority of the emperor and his "proxies" in the military and the government.

1. *PWR* 184, 3 September 1941, p. 17. "Citizens' Schools and Air Defense." The accompanying text says, "We patrol guards do our utmost to protect the vault containing the August Image (*goshin'ei*). Someday, we will become fine national defense warriors. A heavy sense of responsibility swells our breast." The chrysanthemum seal is directly above the vault doors.

The official portraits of the emperor and empress were usually kept in a small storehouse (*hōanden*) in the schoolyard, built specifically to house them. In the event of fire or earthquake, the teacher or person responsible on that day had to transport them to safety, even at the risk of his or her own life. The loss or destruction of the imperial portrait could result in dire consequences.[2] Photograph: Nakafuji Oshie.

The chrysanthemum seal of the imperial house adorning each sword and rifle carried into battle was a constant reminder that soldiers and sailors were agents of imperial will. When troops captured a fort, a city, or an island, they posed for the inevitable "banzai" photograph and gave the obligatory cheer of "Long Live His Majesty the Emperor!" (*Tennō heika banzai!*) And the press regularly reported that these were the final words of those who died in battle. When a man gave his life in the service, he became a warrior-god (*gunshin*) and a nation-protecting deity (*gokokushin*) enshrined at Yasukuni Shrine in Tokyo alongside the spirits of the imperial ancestors. This practice was inaugurated by Emperor Meiji in 1869 when he founded Yasukuni Shrine in the newly renamed capital, Tokyo.

In Japan, as in China, there was no custom of the emperor's profile serving as a symbol of the nation or the government. In Europe, from the time of the Romans down to the present day, monarchs adorn currency, but the Japanese did not adopt this custom. Indeed, money was considered vulgar and defiling, and the god-emperor himself never handled it. The chrysanthemum seal on currency, postage stamps, savings bonds and other governmental instruments, on the bow of imperial warships, and above the entranceway to government buildings was emblematic of the emperor. The emperor's person was synonymous with Japan, but his face was not. Consequently, although the entire war was fought in the emperor's name, and every military and civilian sacrifice

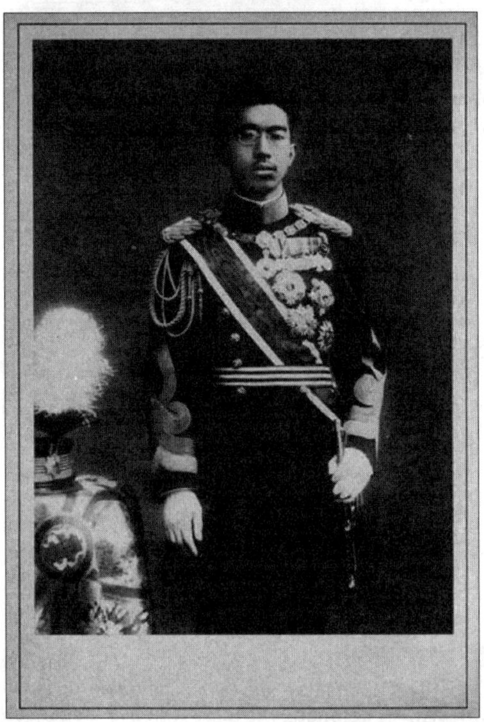

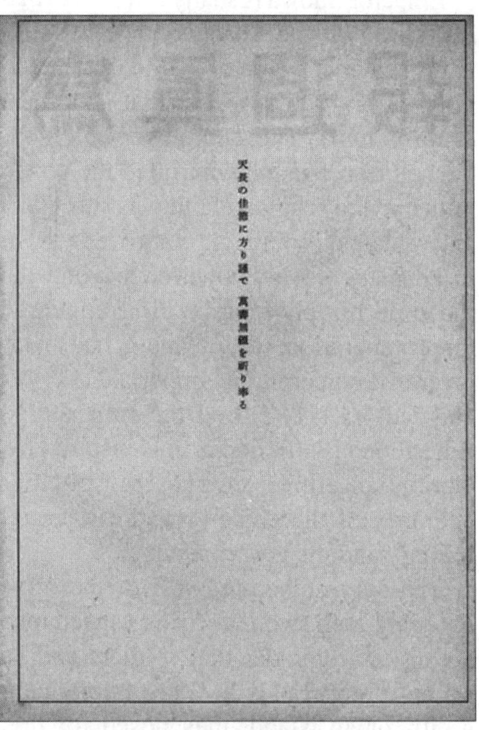

2 and 3. *PWR* 11, 27 April 1938, inside front cover and p. 1.

The first photograph of the emperor to appear in *PWR* was the formal portrait of him enshrined in government offices and schools throughout the empire at the time of his enthronement in 1928. It appeared in *PWR* a few days before 29 April, a holiday honoring his birthday.[3] The uniform he wears is that of the sovereign, largely unchanged since the time of his grandfather, Meiji, and patterned after the mid-nineteenth century military-inspired imperial dress then in fashion in Europe. The stiff portraiture also owes much to customs established in Meiji's day. The caption was something of a command: Offer prayers for myriad and unlimited blessings received through the benevolence of His Majesty.[4]

The page facing the emperor, the inside front cover (in later issues, numbered page 2), was left blank so that it would act as a tissue-guard protecting the imperial image. *PWR* usually left the opposing page blank whenever it contained a single-page photograph of a member of the imperial family. The magazine's title on the cover has bled through this blank page, but has not affected the emperor's photograph. This portrait was reprinted for New Year's 1939, along with the official portrait of the empress, in *PWR* 46, 4 January 1939, pp. 2-3. The photographer is unknown.

was ostensibly made for him, photographs of the emperor in the wartime press were few. Only thirty-three of 375 issues of *PWR* (about one of every eleven issues) contained an image of the emperor. The one hundredth issue of *PWR* contained a breakdown of coverage in the magazine up to that time (24 January 1940); only one percent of the magazine's coverage was devoted to the emperor and the imperial family.[5]

The thirty-five different photographs of the emperor within the approximately nine thousand pages of *PWR* provide examples of the official presentation of his image to the people. He appeared four times in 1938 and six times in 1939 (one of these being a repeat of the "official portrait" [figure 1]). During the same two years, Hitler appeared more frequently in *PWR*. In 1940, the emperor appeared seventeen times. Seven photographs of him were included in *PWR* 145, the special double issue commemorating the 2,600th anniversary of the founding of the nation, which centered on the imperial dynasty and its mythology. (Of these seven, four were repeat images from earlier in the year.) Photographs of the emperor were scaled back to three in 1941. The following year, there were six photographs, the same number as in 1939. But in the final three years of the Great East Asia War, his resplendent form was only pictured in *PWR* one time each year.

4. *PWR* 12, 4 May 1938, p. 1. "His Majesty the Emperor was pleased to attend the second day of the Grand Festival at Yasukuni Shrine on 26 April. His Majesty deeply prayed before the spirits of the 4,533 newly enshrined nation-protecting deities and ancestor deities."

His uniform here is that of the official portrait: sash and cordons, elaborate ribbed sleeves, shoes and pants, and doffed shako with pentacle mark. This is the only contemporaneous photograph of him in this attire to appear in *PWR*. At this time, the all-out war in China (the "China Incident") was ten months old and had not yet been declared a "long-term war" by Japan's military leadership.

For the remainder of the war, the emperor would always appear in what was evidently the field uniform of the commander-in-chief, which came in two colors, khaki for the army (with boots, jodhpurs, and brimmed military cap), and white for the navy.

The chrysanthemum seal on the raised curtain denotes the imperial patronage of the shrine, which was founded by decree of Emperor Meiji in 1869. The photograph is uncredited.

In the pages of *PWR*, no individual photographer was ever credited with capturing the imperial visage. Many of the photographs of the emperor are not credited at all, even to an agency or ministry. (Of course, *PWR* often did not credit photographs.) For those that are credited, the Cabinet Information Bureau (publisher of *PWR*) and the Imperial Household Ministry (in the postwar period, the Imperial Household Agency) were named as photographers. Photographs of the emperor on board navy ships are credited to the Navy Ministry.

All thirty-five of the photographs of the emperor appearing in *PWR* (with the exception of the official portrait, figure 1) show him performing some aspect of his official duties as head of state, commander-in-chief, or high priest of State Shinto. Of course, these roles were not strictly segregated, a fact borne out by the emperor's dress: in all *PWR* images of the emperor from mid-May 1938 until the end of the war, he appears in the uniform of commander-in-chief, even when visiting shrines. He donned

5. *PWR* 13, 11 May 1938, pp. 10-11. "Imperial authority shines at Emperor's Birthday Dress Review of Troops during the [China] Incident." The venue is identified as Yoyogi Field, 29 April 1938, the photographer is not. This is the first of nine photographs of the emperor presiding over military reviews to appear in *PWR*; such photographs had appeared before in the press. The imperial colors with the chrysanthemum seal show more prominently than the emperor astride his white steed White Snow.

the white naval commander-in-chief uniform for naval inspections. Nearly half of these thirty-five photographs—seventeen images—are devoted to the emperor's duties as commander-in-chief. Nine feature the emperor on horseback at outdoor military reviews, of which seven were taken at Yoyogi Field, most from an almost identical distance and vantage point. (Photographs like these had appeared in the press before the Manchurian Incident and the creation of *PWR*.) Two picture him conducting naval reviews, one aboard the battleship *Nagato* and the other aboard the destroyer *Hie*. One shows him saluting a graduating class of military students in the palace plaza, while another shows him saluting graduates of the Imperial Army Air Force. Two show him receiving congratulations from the people after important victories. The two most compelling photographs of the commander-in-chief show him reviewing captured war booty in 1942 and presiding over the Imperial High Command in 1943.

6. *PWR* 99, 17 January 1940, pp. 10-11. "New Year's Imperial Army Dress Review. 8 January, at Yoyogi Field." The emperor is more clearly visible in this Cabinet Information Office photograph. The layout places the caption between photographs of the imperial retinue and of the parade of tanks.

7 and 8. *PWR* 204, 21 January 1942. The first photograph of the emperor to appear in *PWR* after the outbreak of the Great East Asia War (bottom, pp. 4-5) showed him as commander-in-chief presiding over a military review at Yoyogi Field, Tokyo, the annual New Year's Military Review, which fell on the first-month anniversary of the war. This was the first of six photographs of the emperor to appear in *PWR* in 1942. The separate photograph on page 3 (top) showed airplanes flying over in formation and artillery as part of the military review. These two photographs are uncredited.

緒戦の初春を飾る
一月八日陸軍始観兵式 東京代々木原頭

緒戦の初春を飾る
一月八日陸軍始観兵式

9. *PWR* 320, 10 May 1944, pp. 4-5. "His Majesty the Commander-in-Chief at the Emperor's Birthday Dress Inspection of the Troops, Yoyogi Field." There is a second white horse in the photograph, but the rider cannot be clearly seen. The use of a white stallion was reserved for the emperor. This uncredited 16½ -by-23-inch centerfold, as large as a poster, was the only photograph of the emperor to appear in *PWR* in 1944. No other photographs of the inspection were included, such as that showing artillery and airplanes in the January 1942 inspection.

None of the nine *PWR* photographs of the emperor at military reviews place him in frame with artillery, tanks, or airplanes. When the machinery of war was shown, it appeared in a separate photograph. (Curiously, a photograph appearing in another government publication, Dōmei Tsūshin's *Great East Asia Photo Almanac*, did. See figure 9.) The ritual elements of these reviews were codified in Emperor Meiji's day, before tanks and airplanes were used in warfare. The emperor was always shown on horseback or on foot. The emperor's link to his troops, however, was not through the machinery of war but through authority received from his mythical ancestors, most notably the general-emperor Jinmu, subjugator of warring clans and founder of the Japanese nation, and through the imperial family's inheriting the shogun's ethos of Bushido during the turnover of power known as the Meiji Restoration. As commander-in-chief, the emperor carried a sword, a weapon resonant with the long tradition of Japanese warriors dating back to the mythological Jinmu (himself pictured carrying a sword, one of the three imperial regalia of the Chrysanthemum throne). A machine gun or a flame-thrower was a more effective weapon in combat, to be sure, but these brutal modern weapons were not made to be brandished by a god-emperor.

10 and 11. (top) This photograph of the emperor reviewing troops in full view of tanks was published in *Great East Asia Photo Almanac, 1942*, with the English caption, "A grand military review was held on April 29, 1941, in the presence of His Majesty the Emperor on the occasion of the Emperor's birthday." The publisher, Dōmei Tsūshin, was the official news agency of the Ministry of Foreign Affairs. The *Photo Almanac* printed captions in Japanese, Chinese, and English, and its intended audience was non-Japanese, especially in China and Southeast Asia.

(bottom) *PWR* 226, 24 June 1942, p. 3. On 8 May 1942, the emperor inspected war booty captured on the southern fronts and brought to the palace grounds. The text says that "His Majesty has been deeply satisfied by the many victories of the officers and troops of the Imperial Forces since the beginning of the Great East Asia War." There would be very few such imperial pronouncements after the first six months of the war drew to a close. The photograph identifies the weapon as a British army Vickers 9.4 centimeter (3.7 inch) antiaircraft gun from Singapore. This is the only photograph of the emperor in *PWR* that shows him in frame with modern weaponry. The same photograph, with different dimensions, appeared in Dōmei Tsūshin's *Photo Almanac for 1943* with the English caption, "His Majesty the Emperor, inspecting the booty captured on the Southern fronts on May 8, 1942, graciously thought of the men on the fronts."

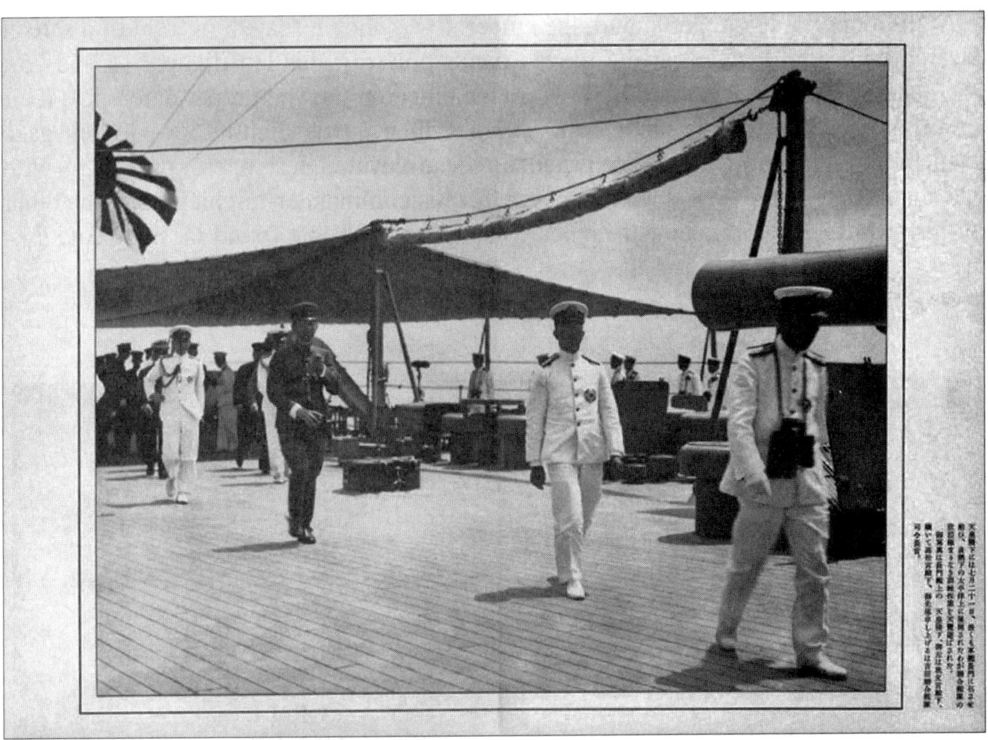

12 and 13. (top) *PWR* 76, 2 August 1939, pp. 11-12. "The emperor visits the battleship *Nagato*, where he reviewed the maneuvers displayed by our extremely brave Combined Fleet in the Pacific, where [the political situation] is heating up. This photograph was taken aboard the *Nagato*. [In the center is] the emperor, and to his left, His Imperial Highness Prince Chichibu, followed by His Imperial Highness Prince Takamatsu. Leading them is Admiral Yoshida [Zengō] of the Combined Fleet." One of only two *PWR* photographs of the emperor at a naval review, it is so dark that none of the faces are clear in the original magazine. This uncredited photograph shows the Taishō Emperor's three sons together, the only such photograph in *PWR*. The 42,850-ton flagship *Nagato* was commissioned in 1920 and refitted in 1934-1936. It was Admiral Yamamoto's flagship at Pearl Harbor, but only saw battle once, at Leyte in 1944, being held in reserve for the "final battle" for the Japanese Home Islands. The last active Japanese battleship of the Pacific War, its final use was in the US Operation Crossroads nuclear tests at Bikini Atoll, where it sank on 29 July 1946 after being severely damaged by an underwater blast.

(bottom) *PWR* 215, 8 April 1942, p. 3. The emperor salutes the graduating class of the Army Air Force Officers' School on 27 March, where he also watched a flight drill by graduating students. *PWR* included no photographs of either the students or the airplanes.

At the Imperial High Command, the emperor was shown seated, in front of a screen covered with gold leaf, his white gloved hands poised in his lap (figures 14 and 15). The generals and admirals gathered before the emperor showed proper deference: their uniforms were immaculate, their backs straight, their heads slightly bowed, their gaze fixed on the table before them. The ritualized scene elevated the emperor on a stage, with two small stands on either side of him, one for his commander-in-chief's hat, the other for his sword. This arrangement invites comparison with that found in many Buddhist

14. *PWR* 271, 12 May 1943, pp. 4-5. "His Majesty the Commander-in-Chief at the Imperial High Command." This Imperial Household Ministry photograph was the only photograph of the emperor to appear in *PWR* in 1943. The accompanying text says, "In this sixth year since the Imperial High Command was installed inside the palace, there has been no distinction between night and day, and we are in extreme awe just thinking that His Majesty's review of secret strategies inside this camp sometimes extends late into the night. All of us, from the officers and troops on the front lines to the subjects on the home front, are moved to tears by His Majesty's great consideration (*omikokoro*), and we pray for the long reign of the emperor and greater prosperity of the imperial family as well as for His Majesty's mind being eased by our striving toward complete victory in the Great East Asia War."

altars where the main deity is flanked by smaller attendant deities. The emperor and the emblems of his military authority are set centrally, at the place of honor in the center, in front of a blinding gold screen. There are resonances here to the central ritual space in many Japanese homes, the recessed alcove space known as the *tokonoma*, which may contain a work of art, a treasured object, and a vase of flowers. In this image of the Imperial High Command, the generals and admirals each have a stack of papers before them, while the emperor does not, suggesting that communication was unidirectional, perhaps taking the form of the emperor's instructions to them.

15. The photograph in figure 14 was the basis of this painting by Miyamoto Saburō,[6] "The Supreme Commander Holds an Audience with the Imperial High Command," plate 2 in *Great East Asia War Art, Second Series.*

The use of color in this rather somber painting highlights the imperial presence. The brilliant gold screen behind the emperor almost leaps from the surface of the canvas, restrained only by the lustrous colors of the fine silk cloth covering the table. The patterned silk is dyed in colors used in Japan for centuries, pastels from the Japanese spectrum representing the five elements (first identified by the Chinese): forest green, ochre, dull mustard yellow, madder red, white.

Japan had many victories in the seven and a half years of war covered in *PWR*, but only two days of national celebration were designated during the Pacific War: for the surrender of Singapore, on 18 February 1942, and for the unconditional surrender of all enemy forces in Indo-china (Vietnam) on 12 March 1942. Of the seventeen *PWR* photographs of the commander-in-chief, only two show him victorious. In these two photographs of the emperor accepting the masses' congratulations, there is some indication of what an ultimate Japanese victory might have looked like.

PWR published eight photographs of the emperor as head of state, representing the Japanese nation at events of national or international importance. Three of these show him in the royal box at the ceremony marking the 2,600th anniversary of the founding of the nation on 11 November 1940. Of the other five, one shows him paying a visit to the high court on the fiftieth anniversary of the establishment of the Imperial Japanese Court System in 1939. He is seen convening the opening of the 1940 Imperial Diet

16 and 17. (left) *PWR* 39, 9 November 1939, p. 1. "Shortly after 3 P.M. on 28 October, His Majesty the Emperor himself rode out upon the Double Bridge (Nijūbashi), pleased to receive the congratulations offered by the people who completely filled the palace plaza, there to celebrate the victory and to cheer His Majesty's supreme authority." The event is the fall of Wuhan, China. The citizenry were not pictured.

(right) *PWR* 210, 4 March 1942, p. 3. The emperor salutes a crowd that gathered in the plaza outside the imperial palace to offer congratulations on the surrender of Singapore on 18 February, which was declared a national holiday. Separate photographs are used for the emperor and his subjects. The text explains that the emperor appeared on the Double Bridge at 1:55 P.M. to receive the cheers of the crowd, which also sang the national anthem, "Kimigayo" ("May Thy Majesty's Reign Be Long"). At 2:10 P.M., Empress Nagako appeared with the crown prince and three of his sisters. The crown prince waved a Rising Sun flag. No photograph of the empress and her children appeared in *PWR* on this occasion.

on the fiftieth anniversary of its foundation. And he was photographed saluting the graduates of Tokyo Imperial University (today's Tokyo University) in 1940. The Imperial Court System, the Imperial Diet, and the network of imperial universities were "gifts" of the Emperor Meiji to the people. He was photographed in June 1940 greeting his fellow emperor Pu-Yi of Manchukuo upon his arrival at Tokyo Station, and in November observing a national athletic meet.

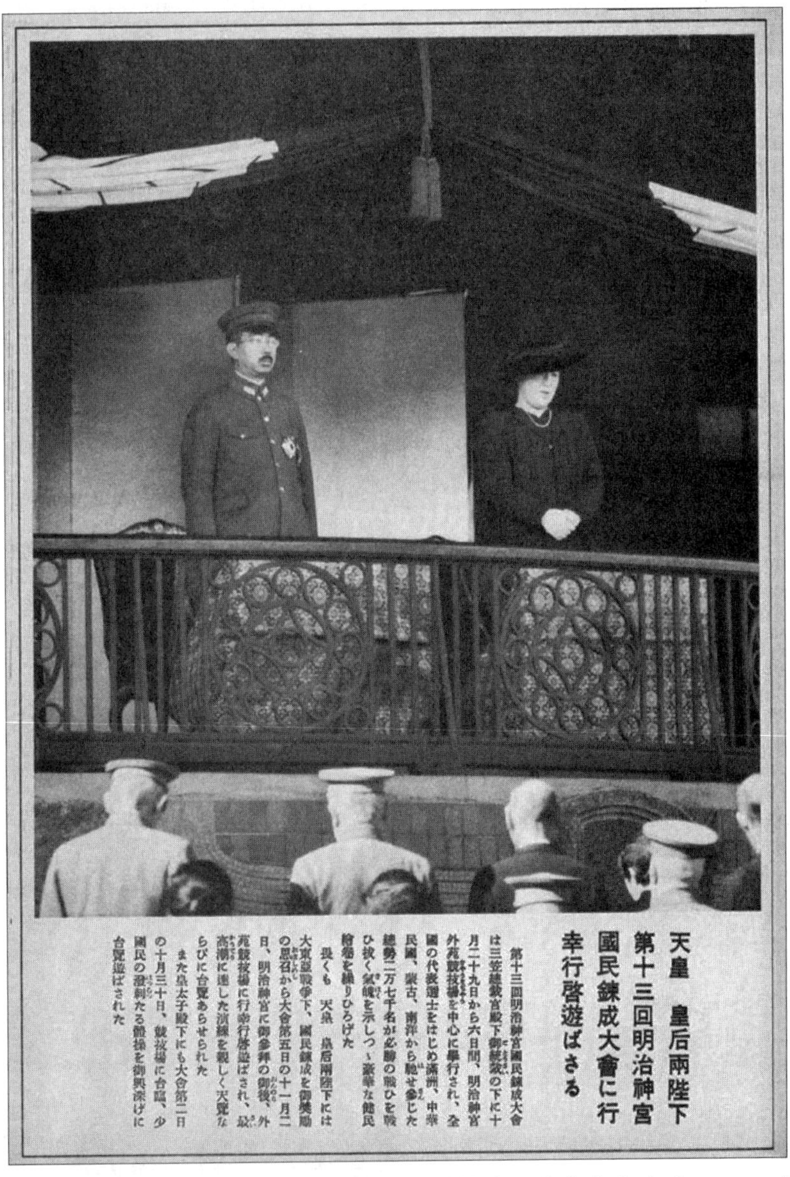

天皇　皇后兩陛下
第十三回明治神宮
國民錬成大會に行
幸行啓遊ばさる

第十三回明治神宮國民錬成大會は三笠總裁宮殿下御統裁の下に十月二十九日から六日間、明治神宮外苑競技場を中心に擧行され、全國の代表選士をはじめ滿洲、中華民國、蒙古、南洋から馳せ參じた總勢二万七千名が必勝の戰ひを戰ひ抜く氣魄を示しつゝ豪華な鍛民繪卷を繰りひろげた

畏くも　天皇　皇后兩陛下には大東亞戰爭下、國民錬成を御奬勵の思召から大會第五日の十一月二日、明治神宮に御參拜の御後、外苑競技場に行幸行啓遊ばされ、最高潮に達した演練を親しく天覽ならびに台覽あらせられた

また皇太子殿下にも大會第二日の十月三十日、競技場に台臨、少國民の溌剌たる體操を御興深げに台覽遊ばされた

18. *PWR* 246, 11 November 1942, p. 3. On 2 November 1942, from their desire to "encourage the physical training of the citizenry" the emperor and empress attended the fifth day of the Thirteenth Meiji Shrine National Physical Training Meet, which brought together "twenty-seven thousand contestants representing all of Japan, Manchukuo, the Chinese Republic, Mongolia, and the South Pacific."

19 and 20. (top) *PWR* 90, 8 November 1939, pp. 10-11. On 1 November 1939, the fiftieth anniversary of the establishment of the Imperial Judicial Court system, the emperor visited the Imperial High Court Building in Tokyo, pausing to look upon the bronze image of the eighth High Court Chief Justice, Kojima Iken.

(bottom) *PWR* 147, 11 December 1940, p. 1. The emperor, standing upon the stage reserved for his use, presides over a ceremony at the Diet marking the fiftieth anniversary of its founding. The deliberations of the Diet were thus construed as taking place under the imperial gaze and as an imperial dispensation.

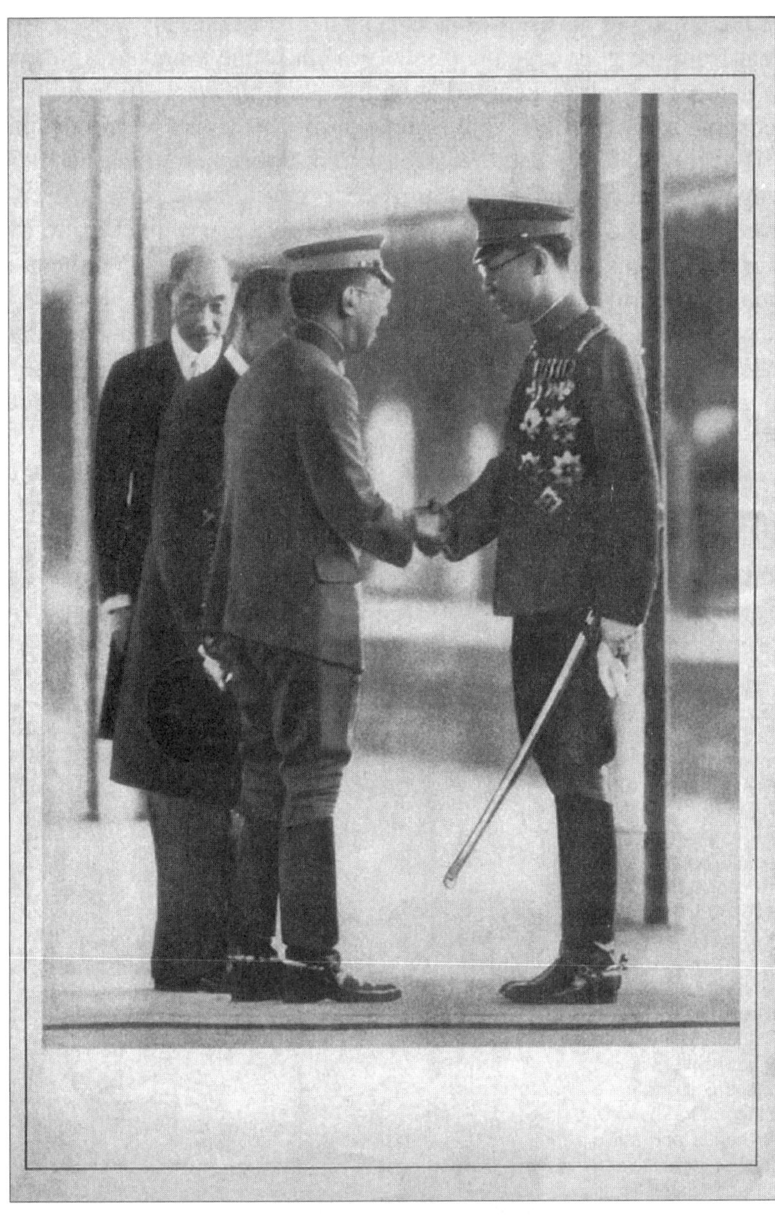

21. *PWR* 124, 10 July 1940, p. 1. Manchurian emperor Pu-Yi visits Japan, offering congratulations on the 2,600th anniversary of the founding of the Japanese empire. He arrived at Yokohama Harbor on 26 June and took a train specially reserved for him to Tokyo, staying at the Akasaka Detached Palace as a guest of the imperial family. "Warmly greeted at Tokyo Station by the emperor, their firm friendship is evident in their handshake." This very unusual (and uncredited) photograph is unique for *PWR* in a number of respects: it shows the emperor's back, the emperor is shaking hands (a Western custom), the emperor is directly interacting with another person, the emperor is standing on a plane level with another person, and the emperor is greeting a foreign dignitary. In postwar years, of course, there were many photographs of the emperor with various heads of state. Captions of photographs of the emperor rarely identified him; it was enough to indicate that he was astride his favorite horse, White Snow. Here, however, the text carefully identifies both emperors, noting that the Manchurian emperor is on the right, while the Japanese emperor is on the left.

Although the emperor was ostensibly Japan's head of state, his exalted position and direct descent from the gods precluded involvement in the mundane affairs of human beings. The hands-on work of interacting with the people was left to politicians, who also received more space in *PWR*. Tōjō Hideki, during his tenure as prime minister from October 1941 to July 1944, appeared in at least sixty-three photographs in *PWR*. He was tiny but recognizable in photographs of him addressing the Diet, and he even appeared multiple times in a single issue where an article covered one of his trips to Manchuria, Singapore, or the Philippines. He was frequently shown in interactive situations meant to bolster public support for the war, such as spending a day with miners or "production warriors." Three times he was on the cover of *PWR*: shortly after he became prime minister (*PWR* 192, 29 October 1941), when he took one of his predawn horseback tours of living conditions in the capital (*PWR* 215, 8 April 1942), and in a rare multicolored cover of the issue commemorating the first anniversary of the outbreak of the war (*PWR* 249, 2 December 1942; see figure 62 in Chapter 7). Coincidentally, in both *PWR* 192 and *PWR* 215, the emperor appeared on page three. (The emperor never appeared on magazine covers during the war, presumably because the exposed cover might be damaged in handling. Instead he appeared on the first inside page, that is, page 1 or 3 depending on the style of pagination.) In the case of *PWR* 249, a photograph of his subjects praying in the plaza of the imperial palace appeared on page 3.

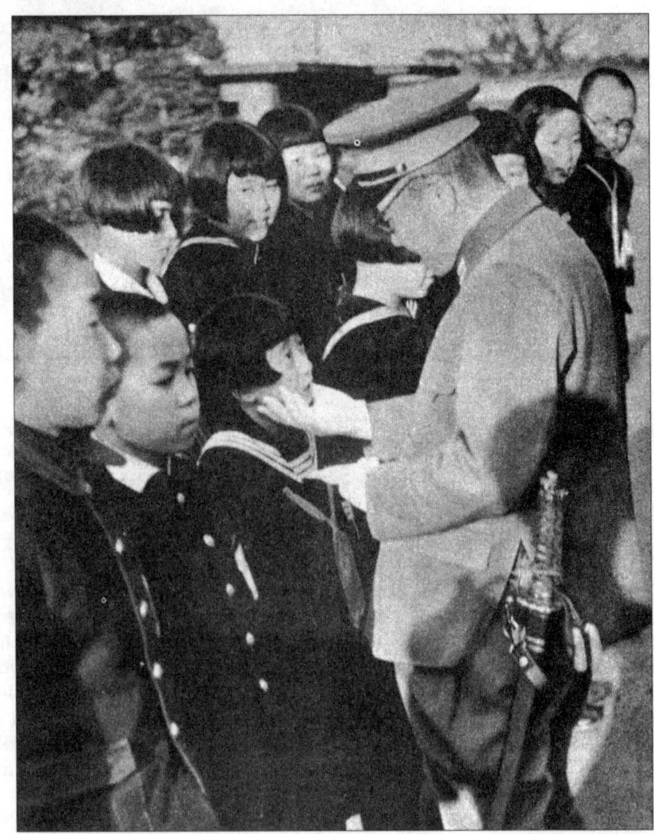

22. *PWR* 266, 7 April 1943, p. 3. "A Father's Loving Care for the Children of Yasukuni. Prime Minister Tōjō Gives Encouragement to War Orphans."

The caption reads, "Crossing over distant mountains and rivers to come to the capital, the Manchurian War Orphan Platoon arrived in Tokyo on the Twenty-sixth [of March] and on the same day greeted Prime Minister Tōjō at his official residence. Prime Minister Tōjō especially took time from his many government duties to put the orphans first and have this time with them. One by one, he patted their heads and put a hand on their shoulders, telling them, 'We will not bring shame upon your father's name.' The orphans were so moved by the consideration of Prime Minister Tōjō, who showed them kindness and fatherly compassion, that their cheeks were wet with tears."

These are presumably the children of Japanese settlers in Manchuria whose fathers were drafted and killed in the service.

Six *PWR* photographs depict the emperor's position as the highest priest of State Shinto. Four were shot at Yasukuni Shrine in association with either the Spring Grand Festival or Autumn Extra Session Festival enshrining warrior-gods. One shows him at Jinmu Shrine during his June 1940 visit to the Kansai region, and one shows him in December 1942 leaving Ise Shrine having asked his ancestor-gods to assure victory.

天皇陛下には　紀元二千六百年の御奉告と興亜聖業の完遂を御祈念のため　六月九日宮城御發輦　關西方面に行幸遊ばされ　皇大神宮豊受大神宮及び　神武天皇畝傍山東北陵　仁孝天皇後月輪陵　孝明天皇後月輪東山陵　明治天皇伏見桃山陵等に御參拜　御途次橿原神宮へも御參拜あらせられた

御寫眞は神武天皇畝傍山東北陵にて

謹寫　宮内省

23. *PWR* 121, 19 June 1940, p. 1. "In order to report to the imperial ancestors the 2,600th anniversary of the founding of the nation and accomplishing the sacred work of Developing Asia, on 9 June His Majesty departed the imperial palace and traveled to the Kansai region." He visited mausoleums devoted to four of his imperial ancestors: Jinmu, his great-great-grandfather Ninkō, his great-grandfather Kōmei, and his grandfather Meiji. Here he is seen at Jinmu's Mausoleum, Unebiyama no Ushitora no Sumi no Misasagi, in Kashihara, Nara Prefecture. Photograph: Imperial Household Ministry.

24 and 25. (top) *PWR* 63, 3 May 1939, pp. 8-9. The emperor and his entourage leaving Yasukuni Shrine on the occasion of the five-day Grand Festival, in which 10,389 new warrior-gods were enshrined.

(bottom) *PWR* 115, 8 May 1940, p. 1. A very similar photograph shows the emperor and his entourage leaving Yasukuni Shrine, having just presided over that year's ceremony enshrining 12,799 new warrior-gods. The limousine was not pictured in the spring 1940 imperial visit to Yasukuni (the opposing page was left blank). The white steed and the limousine were the best quality, traditional and modern royal conveyances. These nearly identical photographs of the emperor at Yasukuni underline the ritual nature of the event. Both photographs are credited to the Cabinet Information Office that published *PWR*, with no photographer named.

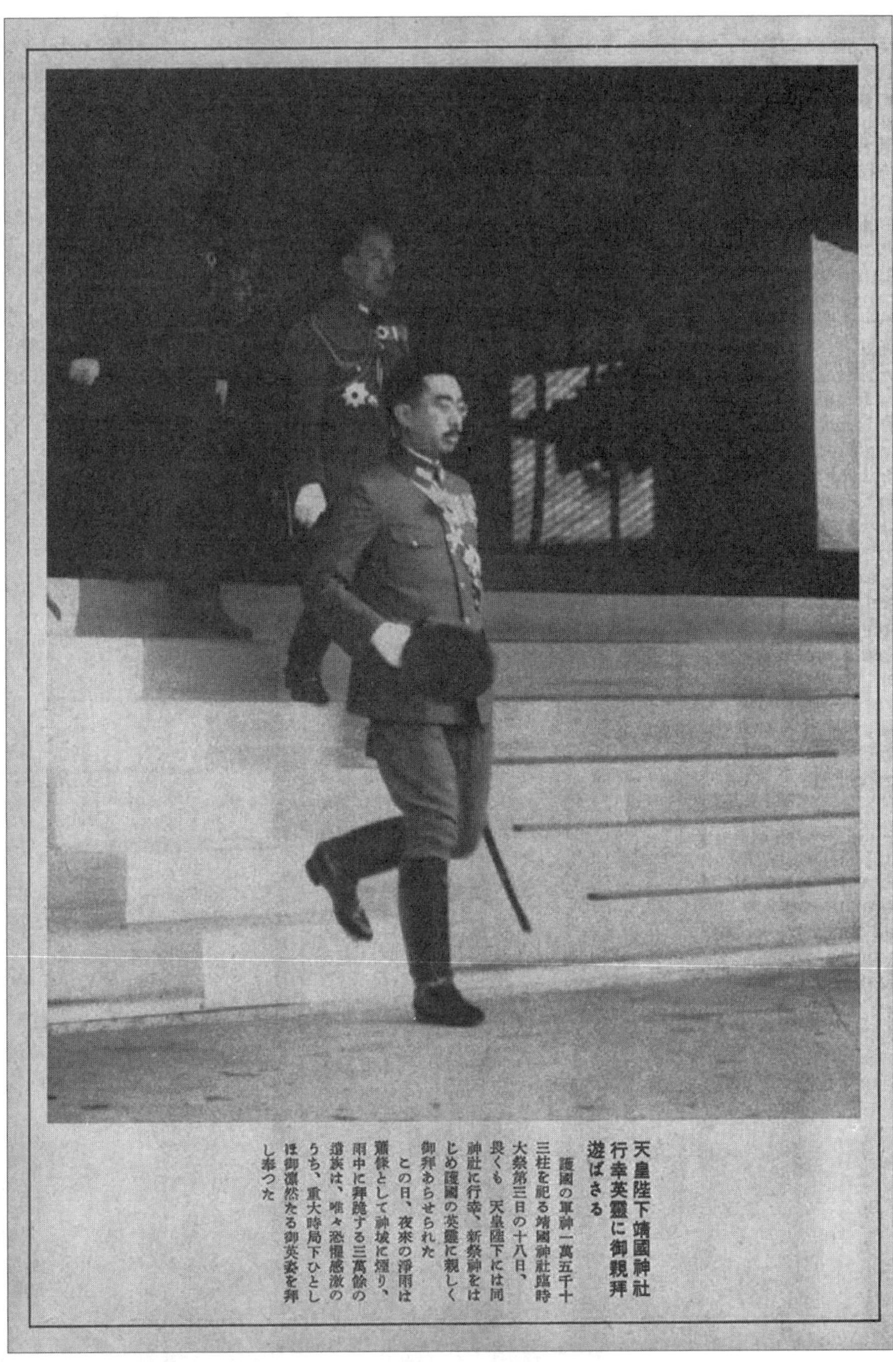

天皇陛下靖國神社行幸英靈に御親拜遊ばさる
護國の軍神一萬五千十三柱を祀る靖國神社臨時大祭第三日の十八日、畏くも天皇陛下には同神社に行幸、新祭神をはじめ護國の英靈に親しく御拜あらせられた
この日、夜來の淨雨は蕭條として神域に煙り、雨中に拜跪する三萬餘の遺族は、唯々恐懼感激のうち、重大時局下ひとしほ御凛然たる御英姿を拜し奉つた

26. *PWR* 192, 29 October 1941, p. 3. An uncredited photograph of the emperor leaving Yasukuni Shrine upon the conclusion of the enshrinement of 15,013 new warrior-gods. Some thirty thousand bereaved family members attended these services in the rain. The last photograph of the emperor at Yasukuni to appear in *PWR*, it focused on him from a closer range, with only one member of his retinue in frame. Photographs of the emperor at Yasukuni did not appear in *PWR*'s coverage of the enshrinement ceremonies of 1942, 1943, 1944, and 1945, even as they appeared in other publications.[7] His final visit to Yasukuni was in November 1975.

27 and 28. (top) "His Majesty the Emperor proceeded to the Ise Grand Shrines on December 12, 1942, to pray for the victory in the War before the Founder of the Empire" was the English caption to the photograph (top, credited to the Imperial Household Ministry) in Dōmei Tsūshin's *Great East Asia Photo Almanac, 1943*. The wartime press assigned great significance to the fact that the emperor himself undertook the trip to Ise to personally pray for victory before Emperor Jinmu, mythical founder of the Japanese empire. This was one of a handful of wartime events involving the emperor immortalized in a painting.

(bottom) When the same photograph appeared in *PWR* 252, 23 December 1942, p. 3, the unnamed official walking in front of the emperor was cropped from the frame, so that the emperor was squarely centered in the image. The cropped photograph also served as the basis of this painting by Fujita Tsuguharu,[8] "His Majesty the Emperor Prays at Ise Shrine," plate 1 in *Great East Asia War Art, Second Series*. During the war, paintings of the emperor were even fewer than photographs. Like so many wartime paintings, this one is meticulously faithful to a photograph already famous at the time of its creation.

Two photographs of the emperor in *PWR*, which do not fit neatly into any one category, come close to being "candid" shots. One shows the emperor leaving the High Command, Naval Section building, about to board his waiting limousine. The other shows him "taking a walk" to view race horses and war horses during a horse show and race in the spring of 1941. The one photograph that best brings together all three roles was also the last image of the emperor to appear in *PWR*, taken as he surveyed war damage in March 1945, leading the High Command through a bombed-out shrine dedicated to the god of war (Introduction, figure 2).

Although much wartime rhetoric described the emperor as the head of the "family" of citizens, no group photograph of the imperial family ever appeared in *PWR*. Indeed, *PWR* never showed the emperor together with his own children.[9] There were three occasions on which photographs of both the emperor and Empress Nagako were printed in *PWR*: New Year's 1939 (their separate official portraits being printed on facing

29 and 30. (left) *PWR* 114, 1 May 1940, p. 1. "On 28 April, His Majesty the Emperor paid his first visit to the Naval Section of the High Command since the [China] Incident, where he met with Navy Chief of Staff Prince Fushimi, Navy Minister Yoshida, and other officials. While partaking of the noon meal with them, His Majesty asked many questions about the conduct of the navy, which has achieved splendid military results since the Incident began." The sign just to the right of the emperor reads, "High Command, Naval Section." Otherwise, the photograph of the emperor about to board his limousine conveys little of the caption's sense of importance. Photograph: Cabinet Information Office.

(right) *PWR* 164, 16 April 1941, p. 1. "His Majesty the Emperor makes his way on foot from the royal box in the First Hall to the Second Hall, observing along the roadway a line of champion race horses, choice stud horses, model military horses, and working military horses." The venue was a horse race and show in Yoyogi Field, site of the imperial military reviews. Photograph uncredited.

pages), the 2,600th Anniversary of the Founding of the Nation Ceremony (11 November 1940), and the Thirteenth Meiji Shrine National Physical Training Meet (2 November 1942). He was occasionally pictured with other members of the imperial family, usually with one of his brothers, Prince Chichibu and Prince Takamatsu. Chichibu and Takamatsu appeared in *PWR* (with or without their wives) almost as often as the emperor did. Empress Nagako and Crown Prince Akihito appeared individually in *PWR* four and seven times. Akihito appeared in *PWR* twice in 1944, once more than the emperor.

The wartime photographs of the emperor display a carefully constructed persona—that of a living god. The only close-up photograph of him in *PWR* was the official portrait (figure 1). During the war, he was photographed from a distance, his features barely discernible, because "only photographers certified by the Imperial Household Ministry were permitted to record the emperor's image. And they had to use a telephoto lens from a distance of at least twenty meters [sixty-seven feet]."[10] No wonder, then, that *PWR* contains no family photographs of the emperor, and no shots of him relaxing, laughing, or smiling. The still photographs of the emperor are frozen in rigid formality, the facial expression is serene, impassive.[11] The emperor's power conveyed by these images is much less political than it is mystical, cultural, and historical authority, in other words, that of a living god. This power was demonstrated to the people through religious rituals and nationalistic ceremonies, and expressed through a system of symbols and signs: the imperial ancestor-deities, the chrysanthemum seal, the double phoenix, the three sacred objects of imperial rule (a mirror, jewel, and sword), the imperial seal on rescripts,

31-34. In wartime photographs, the emperor's posture was rigid and his expression set. A comparison of detail from four mid-stride photographs taken in 1939 (figure 24), 1940 (figure 25), 1941 (figure 26), and 1945 (surveying air raid damage, Introduction, figure 2) suggests that his movements were ritualized and his photographs carefully selected. These photographs were all taken from his right side as he stepped down on his right foot.

the white steed, the Double Bridge leading to the palace. His image and authority, disseminated through the education system and the mass media, were used to support a militarized state that suppressed and punished any questioning of imperial ideology.

If the press was silent about the role of the emperor in planning and directing the war, it projected well his role in boosting morale as guardian and sanctifier of national identity. He was the central force in a sacralized nation. The war was authorized in the name of the emperor, as the highest authority in the land, and it was anointed and consecrated by him as the highest priest of State Shinto. The "Incident" in China was a "Holy War" because the emperor decreed it so. As the divinized Japanese nation was waging war, State Shinto was locked in battle against the evil forces that damaged Japan's national prestige and hindered the Japanese version of manifest destiny that placed Japan—the Land of the Gods—above all other nations and made the Japanese race supreme. In terms of boosting war morale, the emperor's seal, his imprimatur, or the mere suggestion of his August person was synonymous with the entire history of Japan from its creation, through the present, and into the future; the spiritual well-being of the nation; and the very land of Japan. Official doctrine not only equated fighting for the emperor with fighting for the nation, but with fighting for everything that was sacred.

35. *PWR* 249, 2 December 1942, p. 3. Loyal subjects pray for victory in the plaza of the imperial palace on 8 December 1941. The photograph appeared in *PWR* on the first anniversary of the outbreak of the war. The opposing page reproduced the Imperial Rescript Declaring War against the United States and Great Britain because "they have obstructed by every means our peaceful commerce, and finally resorted to a direct severance of economic relations, menacing gravely the existence of Our Empire . . . a trend of affairs [that] would, if left unchecked, . . . nullify Our Empire's efforts of many years for the sake of the stabilization of East Asia."

Similar photographs of citizens praying before the palace appeared annually on the anniversary of the war's outbreak, making this a stock image of the war. This uncredited photograph highlights the symmetries of the arches of the Nijūbashi (Double Bridge), the arches of the split bamboo fence, and the arched backs of the kneeling figures, creating an image of harmony. The parallel between the bamboo fence and the closely huddled family-like group suggests that the people themselves will form a line of defense around the emperor, filling in the gaps in the bamboo fence. (Dōmei's *Photo Almanac for 1942* published a very similar photograph of a different group of praying citizens in the same plaza, with no gaps in the fence.) The photograph gains power through the emperor's physical absence, since the invisible bond between sovereign and subjects was one completed by the (Japanese) viewer's instant recognition of the same bond he or she shared.

Notes

1. The mainstream press (in Japan and in the United States) maintained this secrecy during the emperor's lifetime, and he himself died without ever having commented upon his role in the war. The Japanese wartime press provided few clues about what the emperor actually did during the war, and therefore speculation surrounding the emperor's role in the war and his wartime responsibility lies outside the scope of this study. Influential Americans writing in the late 1930s and early 1940s saw the emperor as a puppet of the military clique, a view promoted during the Occupation by Douglas MacArthur: see John Gunther, *Inside Asia* (New York: Harpers, 1939), p. 19; *New York Times* Tokyo correspondent Otto D. Tolischus, *Tokyo Record* (New York: Reynal and Hitchcock, 1943) pp. 78, 402; Joseph Grew (US ambassador to Japan from 1932 to 1942), *Ten Years in Japan* (New York: Simon and Schuster, 1944), p. 462. Two authors writing in English describe the emperor's direct involvement in the prosecution of the war: David Bergamini, *Japan's Imperial Conspiracy* (London: Heinemann, 1971), and Herbert P. Bix, *Hirohito and the Making of Modern Japan* (New York: HarperCollins, 2000). Both works examine a large body of documents, including many kept secret during and long after war. Bix in particular uses diaries and letters by court, government, and military insiders to make the case for the emperor closely monitoring war developments and directing that effort.

2. Several such incidents are described in the Japan Revolutionary Communist League publication, *Zenshin* 2129, 8 December 2003, p. 8. Viewable online at www.zenshin.org/f_zenshin/f_back_no03/f2129.htm.

3. The Meiji and Taishō Emperors' birthdays were also holidays. The Shōwa Emperor's birthday (29 April) remained a national holiday until his death in 1989, at which point this holiday was renamed "Greenery Day." In May 2005, the Diet voted to change "Greenery Day" to "Shōwa Day" beginning on 29 April 2006. "Shōwa Day" is meant to commemorate the people's overcoming the challenges and turmoil of the Shōwa era.

4. An extremely polite version of Japanese, with special verbs and nouns reserved for the imperial family, was employed in captions accompanying imperial images. Even in wartime English-language publications, the Japanese did not attempt to render literally such phrases as "honorable jewel-seat" (*gogyokuza*, the emperor's chair at an event or meeting). Bix notes that in 1928, "the Photography Department of the Imperial Household Ministry made preparations for 'bestowing' on the nation's schools the most important symbol of the new nationalism—the sacred photograph of Emperor Hirohito and Empress Nagako, he in his new supreme generalissimo's uniform, with decorations on his chest." See *Hirohito and the Making of Modern Japan*, p. 201.

5. For a breakdown of *PWR* coverage from 1938-1940, see Introduction, figure 5. While *PWR*'s coverage did change after the outbreak of the Pacific war, the one percent of coverage devoted to the emperor and the imperial family probably only decreased after 1940.

6. Along with Fujita Tsuguharu, Miyamoto Saburō (1905-1974) was probably the most accomplished of Japan's "war artists." Miyamoto's style was closer to German expressionism—singled out by Hitler as "degenerate art"—than to the grandiose, mimetic style preferred by the militarists commissioning war art. While Miyamoto, Fujita, and other artists adapted their styles to suit their clients during the war years, some of Miyamoto's war art is done in a more personal style that allows for multivalence in interpretation, as we shall see later. In the postwar years, he was one of Japan's finest modern artists. In recent years, anti-war drawings and paintings (some completed, but not shown, during the war, others done soon after) have been better known than his work completed during the war glorifying Japan's military. Today, two museums are devoted to his work, one in Setagaya, Tokyo, the other in Komatsu.

7. For examples, see the monthly *History Pictures* (*Rekishi shashin*), which published side-by-side photographs of the emperor and the empress at Yasukuni Shrine in November 1942 (issue 354, p. 3), June 1943 (issue 361, p. 10), and November 1943 (issue 366, p. 6). See figure 14 in Chapter 5 for the empress at Yasukuni.

8. The complicated life of Fujita Tsuguharu (1886-1968, also romanized Tsuguji) warrants mention as an illustration of the seemingly random yet highly effective nature of wartime mobilization. By many accounts Japan's premier war artist, Fujita was the Tokyo-born son of a prominent army doctor and protégé

of Mori Ōgai. Fujita graduated from Tokyo Art School in 1910. He settled in Montmartre in 1912, where he was befriended by the artists of the École de Paris, including Chaïm Soutine, Amadeo Modigliani, and Pablo Picasso. His innovation was the adaptation of Japanese techniques to oil painting. Several successful exhibitions in Paris, and in North and South America, established Fujita as one of the leading modern artists of the 1920s and 1930s. His second wife was a French woman, his first and third, Japanese. After living in Paris for more than twenty years and touring Europe and the Americas, Fujita made his home in Japan in 1937, in the midst of the China War. He was initially enthusiastic about the war and toured the front in China, producing some important works of war art. He returned to Paris in 1939, taking up residence near fellow artist Miyamoto Saburō, but moved back to Japan after the Germans occupied France. His artistic abilities were again put into the service of the militarists, and he was sent on assignment to Indo-china in 1941, which Japan had occupied in the name of the Axis powers. There, he produced watercolors of native scenery and people. He was sent to Indonesia the following year. His most famous war canvases show hand-to-hand combat between legions of Japanese and British or American soldiers, such as his "Attu Gyokusai" (Chapter 11, figure 15). In 1949, he left Japan for the United States and moved to France in 1950, where he became a citizen after renouncing his Japanese citizenship. In 1959, he was baptized as a Catholic and assumed the name "Leonard Foujita." He died in 1968 without having returned to Japan. When asked his thoughts about having been a war artist during an interview by Hashimoto Masatoku of the *Asahigraph* in October 1945, Fujita replied, "Technicians (*gijutsuka*) of my type are called artists. That is to say, for us, while the nation is at war, it is natural to paint war pictures, just as when there is peace, we draw those kind of [peaceful] pictures—and there is nothing unusual in that. I think that as an artist, I must be able to draw anything. I am a man like Hokusai in Japan, or Picasso in France. I must be able to draw, whether it be a landscape, a still life, or a female nude. I must be able to sketch anything, it's no good if there is something I can't paint. And I think that even if drawing from imagination, I must paint pictures that clearly connect to the truth" (*Asahigraph* [44:33], 15 October 1945, p. 14). Japanese art critics have been kinder to Fujita in recent years, no doubt wanting to claim for Japan this artist with such strong ties to some of the most renowned international artists and influential artistic movements of the twentieth century. Perhaps the greatest irony of Fujita's career is that, other than works produced during his student days, the only work he produced in Japan were war pictures, a genre he never worked in outside of Japan. In particular, his portraits of women are appreciated by collectors. For more on Fujita as a painter of war art, see Mark H. Sandler, "A Painter of the 'Holy War': Fujita Tsuguji and the Japanese Military," in Marlene J. Mayo and J. Thomas Rimer eds., *War, Occupation, and Creativity: Japan and East Asia, 1920-1960* (Honolulu: University of Hawai'i Press, 2001), pp. 188-211.

9. Informal photographs of the emperor from this time surely exist, perhaps within private collections of members of the imperial family or in the imperial archives. To my knowledge, none from the war years are available today, because during the war access to the emperor was carefully monitored and controlled.

10. Bix notes that official photographers "usually (though not always) show only the upper half of the emperor's body, and never his back because it was slightly rounded. He could not be shown smiling, for living gods were not supposed to smile. He could only be photographed standing motionless or at attention. Such photographers could be relied on not to use their photographic skills to undermine popular loyalty to the throne. Above all, they were expected to show their own personal feelings of reverence for their subject" (*Hirohito and the Making of Modern Japan*, p. 550). Bix does not name these photographers.

11. Of course, nineteenth century cameras, with their long exposure time, required holding a fixed expression and a motionless position, or the subject would be blurred. By the time of *PWR*, however, advances in technology allowed cameras to capture people in motion. Japanese camera magazines from the 1930s regularly held contests among amateur photographers on such themes as "sports events" or "portraiture," and in 1927, *Asahigraph* published a series of photographs showing Prince Takamatsu, described as "the sporting prince," playing tennis and skiing.

2. THE GREAT JAPANESE EMPIRE

On the eve of the Great East Asia War, Japan's print media presented the empire over which the Shōwa Emperor reigned as a land of paradoxes. This self-described "peaceful" nation was fighting a fierce war in China. On the one hand, Japan was a constitutional monarchy, a democracy with an elected Diet, but on the other hand, a string of political assassinations[1] had seriously weakened democracy. The judicial system guaranteed civil rights, but the militarized government openly embraced fascist ideas, maintained tight control over society and public discourse, and routinely arrested and indefinitely detained anyone who might question its authority. The cities grew with concrete and steel, hummed with jazz and neon, sported the latest foreign fashions and fads, but much of the countryside lacked electricity and plumbing, and looked unchanged since premodern times. The old-fashioned and the ultra-modern, the Japanese and the Western, the natural and the man-made, appeared side by side in the pages of *Photographic Weekly Report* and other Japanese periodicals. The Japanese people seemed to have had little difficulty accepting these oppositional elements of their national identity, but Japanese nationalism did not demand eschewing Western cultural products until armed conflict with the West was imminent.

1. *PWR* 147, 11 December 1940, inside front cover. Symbol of the Imperial Japanese Government, the Diet Building (constructed between 1930 and 1936) is still in use today. The columns cite ancient Greece, birthplace of democracy, and the ziggurat crowning the structure harkens back to Babylon and its kingdom. Although the political parties were temporarily disbanded in 1940 as part of the New Order, there were nationwide elections in 1942 and Japan remained a constitutional monarchy with a representational government throughout the war.

2. Japanese Government Railways Board of Tourist Information, *Japan Pictorial* (Tokyo: ca. 1937-38), wrap-around dustjacket illustration. This book, full of photographs of natural, manmade, historical, and staged anthropological tourist attractions, had captions in English, French, and German, and aimed at drawing tourists from the West to Japan for the events scheduled for 1940, the year when the 2,600th anniversary of the founding of the Japanese nation would be celebrated. In terms of subject, design, and technique, this photomontage juxtaposed the ancient and the modern, the native and the imported, the rural and the urban, the natural and the man-made, even nature as peaceful and serene (snow-capped Fuji) and nature as violent and awesome (the largest active volcano in Japan, Mount Aso in Kumamoto Prefecture). Natural beauty dominates the montage, with cityscape huddled around a bay beneath Fuji. Japan's illustrious past is found in the Kamakura Great Buddha (cropped out of the left margin, or back cover, due to space considerations), the Nara Deer Park, the cherry blossoms celebrated in song and poetry. A stone bridge links the natural beauty of the left side of the montage to the modern forms of travel hovering around Fuji: airplane, ocean liner, automobile. The kimono-clad women form a counterpoint to women in western attire riding in the auto (barely visible in the original). The unnamed artist[2] must have had a dark sense of humor: the erupting volcano is only visible when the dustjacket is unfolded (the volcano being on the inside front flap). Conspicuously absent in this photomontage are soldiers and the machines of war, but it does include all the other pieces of the narrative of Japan's miraculous modernization that made Japan the political, military, and cultural leader of Asia.

3. *PWR* 5, 16 March 1938, back cover. This advertisement for "new" Matsuda light bulbs and radio tubes incorporates a map of the Japanese empire and the Rising Sun Dawning on Asia. The slogan says, "The Light Illuminating Kokutai is Matsuda." Scholars claimed that kokutai ("national polity," roughly, "national destiny") began with the founding of the nation by the first emperor, Jinmu. This "ancient" concept, when coupled with modern Western technology (the light bulb) would conquer Asia. The text reads from left to right, the Western order, rather than from right to left, the traditional Japanese order, quite unusual for *PWR*. Matsuda is today's Toshiba Electronics Corporation.

By the time of the Russo-Japanese War of 1904-1905, Japanese industrialization had advanced rapidly and the nation had made remarkable strides in developing its military, economy, commerce, and educational system. In the late nineteenth century, Japan's leaders borrowed heavily from Western technology, setting up factories and developing a national system of universities that recruited scientists and scholars from Europe and America. Technology was the key to mass production and modern industry, as well as to modern warfare and empire-building. Indeed, military automobile, truck, and airplane production preceded commercial production in Japan.[3] And the military was a major investor in Japan's heavy industries.

Results of the 1940 census set the population of the Japanese Empire at one hundred five million, of which seventy-three million inhabited Japan proper. Most of the remaining thirty-two million resided in the Japanese colonies of Korea and Taiwan, with some overseas Japanese living in Manchuria and throughout the empire, and smaller numbers in Europe and the United States. The population of the Japanese Home Islands had doubled in the half century preceding the 1940 census. The majority of Japanese were engaged in agriculture, but the number of urban dwellers had more than doubled, from 12.2 million in 1920 to 27.6 million in 1940. The rapid increase in blue-collar labor was in part a product of expansive foreign trade, which reached a record volume in 1940: 3.97 billion yen in exports and 3.71 billion yen in imports.[4] Although the value of foreign trade fluctuated in the 1.5 to 2.5 billion yen range from 1920 to 1936, it jumped above three billion yen in 1937 and continued to climb steeply to nearly four billion yen in 1940, as Japan heavily imported steel, copper, rubber, petroleum products, and other raw materials necessary for manufacturing, heavy industry, and war.

4. *PWR* 21, 6 July 1938, p. 2. An advertisement for Isuzu trucks with the slogan, "Forward, Japanese-made (=Isuzu)! Protect the Home Front." The word "domestic" (*kokusan*, literally "nationally" or "domestically produced") has been given syllabary (*furigana*) reading "Isuzu." The images and slogans appealed to Japanese consumers to be patriotic and buy Japanese cars, the same brand used by the army.

5 and 6. (top) *PWR* 89, 1 November 1939, p. 1. "The *Nippon-gō* completes its Round-the-World Flight." A crowd awaits the return of the *Nippon-gō* at Haneda Airport, Tokyo, on 20 October after an epic fifty-six-day journey around the world.

Heavy industry was a necessity to the national defense of an advanced nation and its empire-building. Since the first Japanese flight in 1910,[5] Japan stayed apace of the latest technological developments. Photograph: *Tokyo Nichinichi Newspaper*.

(bottom) *PWR* 135, 25 September 1940, pp. 18-19. "There's No Limit to Japan's Wings," an article boasting of Japan's unlimited ability to produce airplanes. Photograph: Kokusai Bunka Shinkō Kai.

7 and 8. These *PWR* cover photographs convey power, preparation, and plenty.

(left) *PWR* 184, 3 September 1941. "Special Report: Urban Air Defense."

The arrangement into neat rows gives the impression that these gas masks are being mass produced on an assembly line. The caption explains that "International law prohibits the use of poison gas, but if a warring country ignores these laws and uses gas, the injuries incurred could be horrific. Our country has put its full steam into the manufacture of gas masks, preparing for any possibility." Photograph: Great Japan Manufacturing National Service Corporation.

(right) *PWR* 183, 27 August 1941. The caption reads, in part, "In order to win in modern warfare, there can be no doubt about the great number of bombs required." These were being manufactured under new legislation increasing munitions production.

9 and 10. Citizens were expected to conform to Japan's modern, streamlined social order and unite their energies in fulfilling Japan's kokutai, which was defined as "the life of the state, its clarification" being "the nation's mission."[6] Kokutai was the state seen as an organic being, a leviathan far greater than the sum of its constituents. Three ages of "clarifying" kokutai were identified: the first beginning with the founding of the nation by the mythological first emperor, Jinmu, purportedly in the year 660 BCE; the second with the founding of the Great Japanese Empire by Emperor Meiji in the 1870s; and the third to begin in 1941.

(left) *PWR* 141, 6 November 1940. "Robust shouts of 'one, two' echo across the clear autumn skies, their four limbs stretching to a healthy rhythm, their youth almost fragrant—these female students, participants in the Developing Asia Health Rally, practice calisthenics at Kōshien Field." Photograph: Tanaka Masachika.

(right) *PWR* 173, 18 June 1941. The caption takes the form of dialogue:

"They're looking good—what school uniform are they wearing?"

"Don't you know—from now on, they're making a new hat and uniform for all students of teachers' colleges and middle schools, and this is it. The hat is the army's short brim, that is, the combat hat, and the uniform is the maiden version of the Citizens' Uniform."

The caption identifies these students as belonging to Tokyo No. 1 Middle School.

The organizing concept of Japanese government and society in the late 1930s was *kokutai* (literally, "national polity"). Kokutai was an essentialist philosophy claiming that Japan's manifest destiny in Asia was predetermined by a sacred history, Japan being the only nation in the world created by the gods and still ruled by their descendant (the emperor). Kokutai theorists aimed at making Japan a theocracy in which the emperor was both the head of the official state religion (State Shinto) and the nominal head of the government, and they viewed Western culture as an invasive and corrosive force that was diluting and polluting the "Japanese spirit." The proof was found in Japanese imitating Western decadence and materialism and growing increasingly "selfish" and disinclined to make sacrifices for the sake of the nation and to unquestioningly accept government policies and directives. Nevertheless, the public had a seemingly insatiable appetite for Western cultural imports from Europe and especially from the United States, including film, jazz music, and the latest styles in clothing and fashion, even as kokutai scholar Tanaka Chigaku warned in 1936 that "America is another China, too, in its rotten spirit";[7] China being described as a country unfit to govern itself and therefore awaiting "Nippon's extension of the heavenly task," that is, the expansion of Japan's territorial aims.

11. *Asahigraph* (31:24), *China Battle Front Photographs* 73, 14 December 1938, p. 34. Among influences from the West, none was as pervasive (and deleterious to public morals) as American popular culture. "Bringing Up Father," by American cartoonist George McManus, was translated into Japanese and featured weekly in *PWR*'s main rival, the weekly *Asahigraph*, from 1923 until early 1940. Here, Jiggs makes a fool out of himself with a bowling ball.

Asahigraph (31:20), *China Battle Front Photographs* 69, 23 November 1938 (p. 44) reprinted a telegram sent by McManus to *Asahigraph* thanking and congratulating the publisher for fifteen years of "Bringing Up Father."

12. *Asahigraph* (31:21), 23 November 1938, pp. 30-31. Stills and reviews of the latest Japanese and foreign film releases appeared almost weekly in *Asahigraph*, connecting Japanese film fans to global culture. These publicity stills are of Katherine Hepburn and (inset) Ginger Rogers in "Stage Door," an RKO melodrama about aspiring actresses working on and off Broadway and living independently, sometimes at the expense of virtue.

Hollywood films played to enthusiastic audiences throughout the empire, even in Manchuria, in the year following the screening of the film-version of Pearl S. Buck's pro-China novel, "The Good Earth" (1937). The Asahi Corporation also published a monthly *Film News*, one of several magazines devoted to the cinema. The government understood that entertainment was a useful tool for disseminating values and motivating people, and gradually, but forcefully, took measures to curtail and direct leisure time and to replace "decadent" Western culture with indigenous cultural products (including those of the Manchurian Film Company) or those of Nazi Germany or Fascist Italy. Government measures effectively halved the number of foreign films shown in Japan in just one year, from 222 in 1937 to ninety-four in 1938.[8]

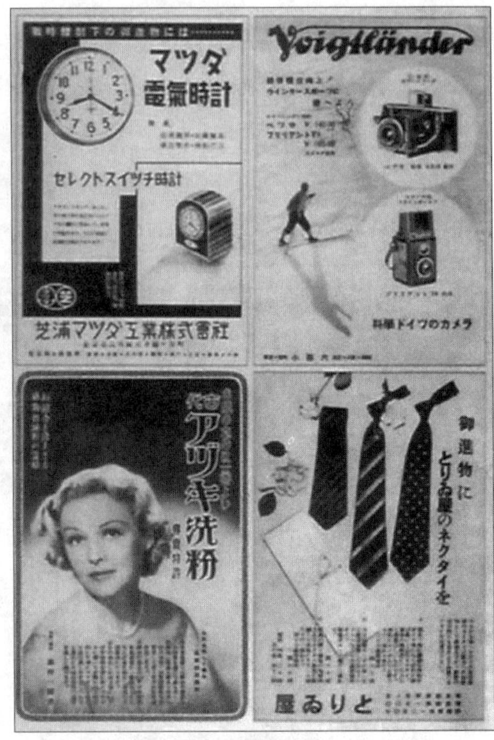

13 and 14. (left) *Asahigraph* (31:25), 21 December 1938, back cover. This Art Deco Brazil Coffee advertisement with its image of skiers would not have been out of place in any upscale American or European magazine of this time. The sophisticated leisure touted here was doomed by mobilization of the home front for the China war. Coffee could hardly be had at any price after 1941, and no one would wear the posh sweater with the large "B" on it once the "ABCD" (American, British, Chinese, and Dutch) powers became the enemy.

(right) *Asahigraph* (31:26), 28 December 1938, p. 34. A page of advertisements for luxury goods reflecting materialism, one of the evils emanating from the West: cameras, electric clocks, neckties, and cosmetics. All of these products (except the German-made Voigtländer cameras, retailing at the astronomical prices of 140 yen and 165 yen) were made in Japan for the Japanese market. Advertisements like these were never carried in *PWR* and would almost entirely disappear from *Asahigraph* after 1941. Items such as cameras would vanish from shop shelves during the Pacific War.

The Great Japanese Empire (Dai Nippon Teikoku), as it was called from 1883 until the end of World War II, was in important respects modeled on Western colonies that provided a location for resettling surplus population and providing a market for manufactured goods in exchange for raw materials.[9] As with Western empires, the Japanese Empire was maintained through a strong military presence. Japan's first acquisition was Okinawa (the Ryūkyū Islands) in 1879. China ceded Taiwan to Japan in 1895 as a result of the Sino-Japanese War, and half of Sakhalin, the Kuriles, and Port Arthur were incorporated in 1905 upon conclusion of the Russo-Japanese War. After defeating Russia, Japan annexed Korea in 1910. The Caroline Islands and Germany's Shandong concession in China were Japan's compensation for fighting with the Allies in World War I. By the 1920s, Japan had consolidated its position as a colonial power and the most powerful Asian nation.

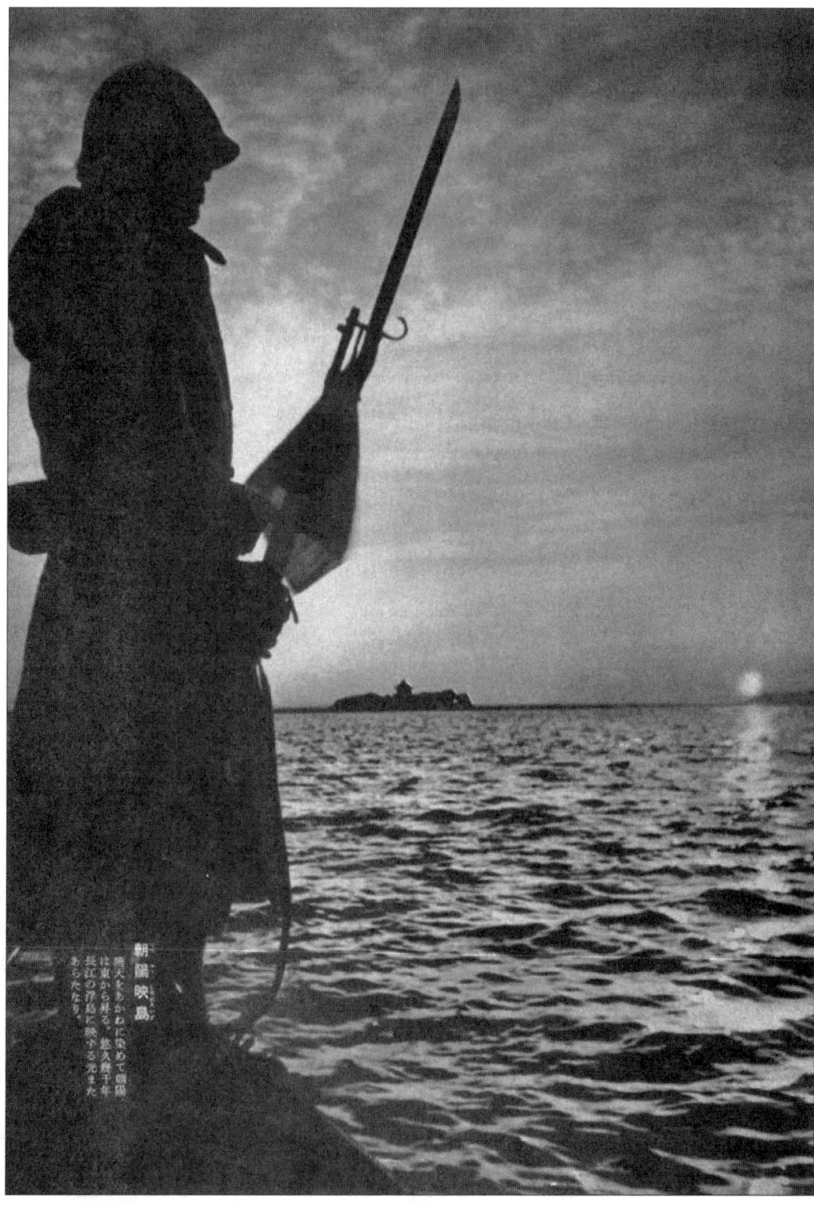

15. *PWR* 46, 4 January 1939, p. 1. "The Morning Sun Shines on the Island. The dawn skies are dyed red, the morning sun rises in the east. Since time eternal, thousands of years ago, its light has shone on this floating Island of the Yangtze, as it still shines today." Appearing in the New Year's issue, this photograph shows the rising sun, symbol of Japan, illuminating an unspecified floating island (*fudao*) of the Yangtze, a metaphor for Japan's bringing the light of civilization to China. The title is written in classical Chinese style (complete with Japanese syllabary [*furigana*] showing the proper reading), underscoring this message. Ironically, China had provided Japan with the essential tools of civilization, including these ideograms of written language, over the course of several centuries (ca. 500-800), but Japan, now master of Western technology, had reversed the "big brother, little brother" relationship—hence the claim that Japan's light had shone on the Yangtze "since time eternal." The sentry was a stock image of empire in the West, too. He conveyed a second message to the home front, especially during the New Year's celebrations: his sacrifices for the emperor and the nation allowed the home front to enjoy life.

16-17. *PWR* 41, 23 November 1938.

(top) "Civilizing the Savage Tribes" of Taiwan's mountainous interior. The extreme-angle cover photograph accentuates rugged facial features and makes the spear (a symbol of savagery) look longer and sharper. The contrast between Taiwan, receiver of civilization, and Japan, bestower, was a measure of Japan's greatness.

(bottom) The cover article (pp. 8-9) included this report illustrating progress in civilizing Taiwan. Below right, a Shinto shrine in the hinterland joins the savages spiritually to the Japanese Empire; below left, teaching adults to read and write Japanese. The two lower photographs are of the tribal chief, who serves as doctor, teacher, and policeman. Under Japan's tutelage, the savages have learned spinning and other cottage industries linking them to the Japanese economy. Photographs: Taiwanese Governing Authority.

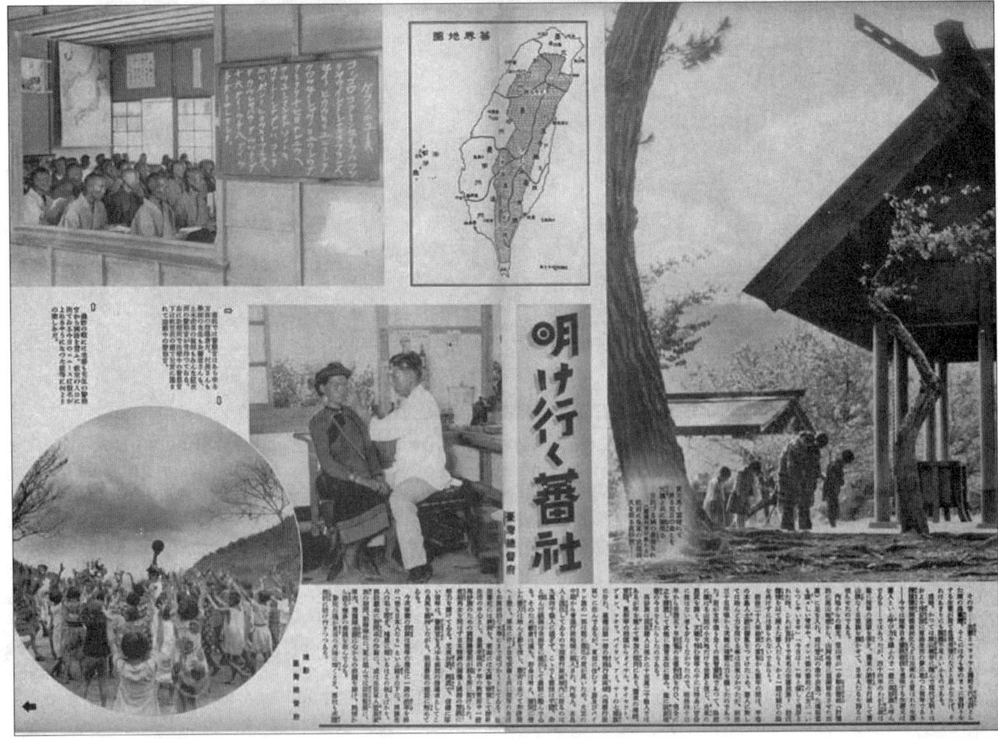

From the outset, Japanese colonization was not only political, military, and economic domination, but spiritual and cultural as well. The first structures the Japanese built on Taiwan were for the government and the military. Shinto shrines and schools—crucial elements in the inculcation of a Japanese national identity—quickly followed. Korea, a populous land with a longer history than Japan, proved more difficult to colonize than Taiwan. Japanese and Korean peoples had much in common historically, as their courts exchanged visits in the sixth through eighth centuries, and during a period of unrest on the Korean peninsula, the Yamato clan sent troops to bolster a faltering court.[10] Chinese civilization initially entered Japan through these exchanges. However, the late sixteenth century Japanese shogun Toyotomi Hideyoshi invaded Korea with catastrophic results. The Koreans repelled the invasion, which left much of Korea in ruins and thousands dead. In the modern era, a Korean patriot assassinated the first Japanese Resident-General of Korea, Itō Hirobumi in 1909, setting the stage for a ruthless regime with no tolerance

18 and 19. (left) *PWR* 80, 30 August 1939. A cover commemorating 30 August, the day in 1910 when Korea was annexed by the Japanese Empire. The beautiful young woman wears traditional Korean costume and holds the Rising Sun flag, which glows in her hands. With forced adoption of Japanese surnames, national costume was one of the few areas in which Koreans were allowed ethnic identity. This is probably the only *PWR* cover devoted to Korea. Attractive women and robust children, suggesting those needing protection and the potential of youth, were often used to represent the newest members of the Japanese Empire.

(right) *PWR* 64, 10 May 1939. "Japanese-Manchurian Youths Pledged to Technology." The accompanying caption says, "The flag of the Akita Prefectural Japanese-Manchurian Technical Training Institute symbolizes the oneness of Japan and Manchuria and the spirit of industrial cooperation. This young warrior will do everything in his power to put that spirit into practice. The flag is new, and the youth's efforts are just beginning. These powerful, dependable young souls will surely join hands to construct the East Asia of tomorrow." Photograph: Umemoto Tadao.

for dissent. When Koreans demonstrated peacefully for independence in 1919, thousands were killed. The Japanese program of Korean "assimilation" included forbidding the use of Korean language in schools. The most extreme act of erasure of racial identity came in 1938, when all Koreans were forced to adopt Japanese surnames.

When Japan's Kwantung Army seized the vast expanse of Manchuria after staging the coup the Japanese referred to as the "Manchurian Incident"[11] in 1931, a different model of rule was implemented. In light of strong international and Chinese criticism of Japan, Manchuria was proclaimed an independent country, "Manchukuo." The last Qing emperor, Henry Pu-Yi, was made emperor of Manchukuo, patterned after the Japanese model of constitutional monarchy. The Manchurian coup strained Japan's relations with the principal Western colonial powers in Asia—the United States, Great Britain, and the Netherlands. In 1933, the League of Nations adopted the Lytton Report condemning the Japanese seizure of Manchuria. The Japanese delegate, Matsuoka Yōsuke, stormed out of the assembly after announcing Japan's immediate withdrawal from the League. Subsequent Japanese overtures to the Western powers did little to assuage fears of Japanese intentions in Asia, and a series of "incidents"—armed skirmishes between Chinese and Japanese resulting in fatalities—led to heightened tensions between Tokyo and Washington, Paris, London, and Amsterdam. While few foreign countries recognized Manchukuo, hundreds of thousands of Japanese and Korean colonists established farms on its broad plains, often forcing indigenous landowners off the land. Manchurian, Mongolian, and Chinese insurgents harassed Japanese efforts to "civilize" and industrialize Manchukuo, from its inception until the end of the Great East Asia War.

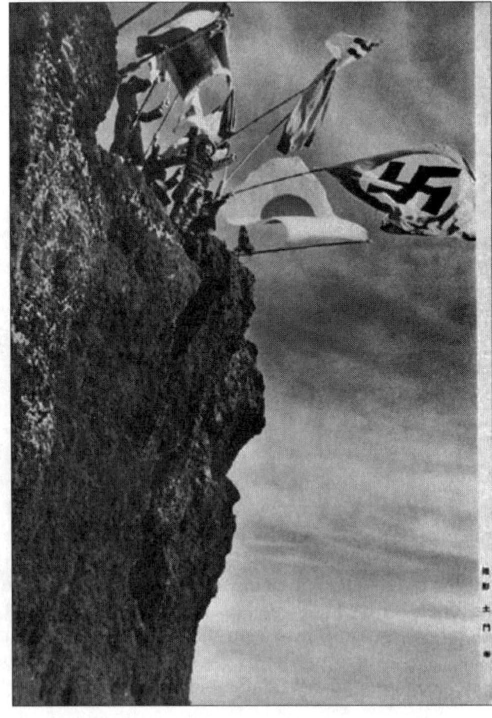

20. *PWR* 25, 3 August 1938, p. 7. "The Axis flags flutter on the summit of Mount Fuji." As part of a Japanese-German student worker exchange program, Axis youths climbed Fuji together and planted the Axis flags atop the sacred peak. Fuji is the highest point in Japan, and one of the most immediately recognizable symbols of Japan for Japanese and non-Japanese alike. This unfamiliar view of Fuji is perhaps appropriate to the new age of the Tripartite Treaty.

This dramatic photograph is credited to Domon Ken, one of Japan's foremost modern photographers.

Japan turned to rising powers with which it found an affinity: Nazi Germany and Fascist Italy. These three nations, in their modern form, had been founded within a decade of each other (1862-1872), and as latecomers to empire-building, resented having their ambitions reined in by older imperial powers, especially Great Britain and France, joined by the United States. The three nations also shared an antipathy toward democratic government. Japan entered into an Anti-Comintern Pact with Nazi Germany in 1936, which Italy joined the following year. The pact did not obligate Japan militarily until a new agreement, the Tripartite Pact, was reached in 1940.

21. *Asahigraph* (35:16), 16 October 1940. On 27 September 1940, Japan formed a military pact with Italy and Germany, the Tripartite Treaty. Here the young Axis is represented by children. For several months, the Axis flags were a vogue, but student exchanges, diplomatic visits, and Japanese interest in German statecraft and technology never produced close collaboration.

Even as animosities between Japan and the United States continued to flare up in the late 1930s, the two countries remained major trading partners. Japan depended on American exports, especially crude oil and iron ore. The Japanese government promoted tourism through various offices such as the Japan Board of Tourist Industry (today's Japan Travel Bureau), the Nippon Yūsen Kaisha (NYK) Line, and the Southern Manchuria Railway, which placed splashy advertisements in upscale American periodicals, describing Japan as a place of quaint beauty, ancient monuments, and modern conveniences. The Japanese Pavilion at the San Francisco International Exposition of 1939-1940 transplanted a corner of this tourist paradise in North America, featuring traditional Japanese architecture.

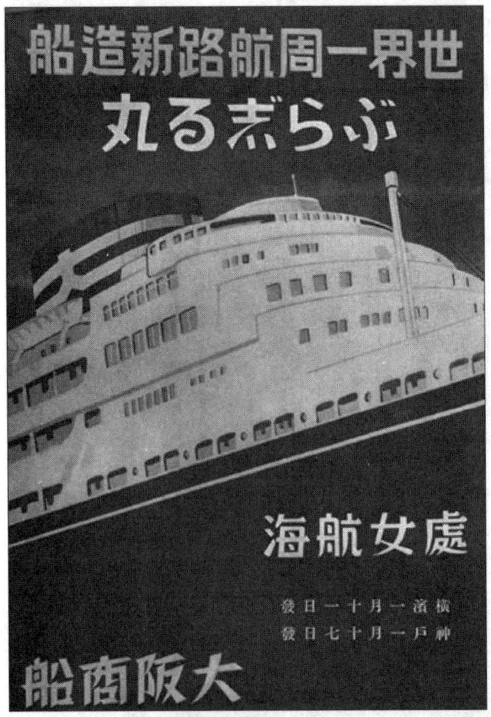

22 and 23. (left) *PWR* 59, 13 December 1939, inside front cover. A full-page advertisement (probably reproduced from a poster) announcing the January 1940 maiden voyage of the Osaka Commercial Line's 12.7 ton *Burajiru-maru* (in contemporary English-language publications, the *Brasil-maru*), a massive luxury liner named for a frequent destination of Japanese immigrants. Its first trip from Yokohama to Santos was completed in thirty-six days, and it sailed around the world in three months. After only a year of commercial service, the *Brasil-maru* was requisitioned by the navy and converted into an aircraft carrier. It was sunk by American torpedoes near Truk on 4 August 1942.

(right) *Glimpses of the East, 1937-1938*, p. i. Published by Nippon Yūsen Kaisha Lines, this complete guidebook for international steamship travelers publicized events commemorating the 2,600th anniversary of the founding of the Japanese nation and Olympics scheduled for 1940. This Board of Tourist Industry (today's Japant Travel Bureau) advertisement features the ancient-modern theme. The caption says, "Japan is indeed a 'Land of Incomparable Scenery, of Age-Old Culture and of Progressive Industry.' It is an ideal holiday-land, fit to visit at any season of the year and for all tastes and purses."

24. *Asahigraph* (32:14), 5 April 1939. Two women in kimono in front of the Japanese Exhibit Hall at the World Exposition in San Francisco. Beginning in September 1937, the weekly *Asahigraph* carried the subtitle *China Battle Front Photographs* (*Shina zensen shashin*) and devoted its cover photograph and lead story to the China war. While this issue is *China Battle Front Photographs* 89, the war is not the lead story and has left the cover for the first time in a year and a half. This issue downplayed the fighting in China (supposedly nearly over by this time) and promoted an image of international, cosmopolitan, peace-loving Japan.

In 1940, many of the paradoxical images of Japan were brought together in Japan's boldest enunciation of kokutai, the national destiny. Both an International Exposition and Olympiad were scheduled to be held in Tokyo to coincide with the 2,600th anniversary of the legendary founding of Japan. This was the opportunity to show the world that Japan was a modern nation with a highly evolved culture, justifying its claim to lead Asia. The plans for the Tokyo Olympics and International Exposition, as well as the solemn rituals marking the 2,600th anniversary of the founding of the nation, would showcase the "New" Japan against the backdrop of the island nation's distinctive culture and resplendent beauty. The celebrations and events would last an entire year, and the world was invited to witness these spectacles. At the center of the festivities were the emperor and the imperial palace grounds. The images created around these events remain strong statements of national identity.

Advisers from Nazi Germany were called in to assist in the planning of the 1940 Tokyo Olympics, patterned after the Munich Olympics of 1936. The sparse, severe look of the stadium, as well as the choreographed events emphasizing the unity and uniformity of the citizenry, were signs of similar national goals and philosophies. The

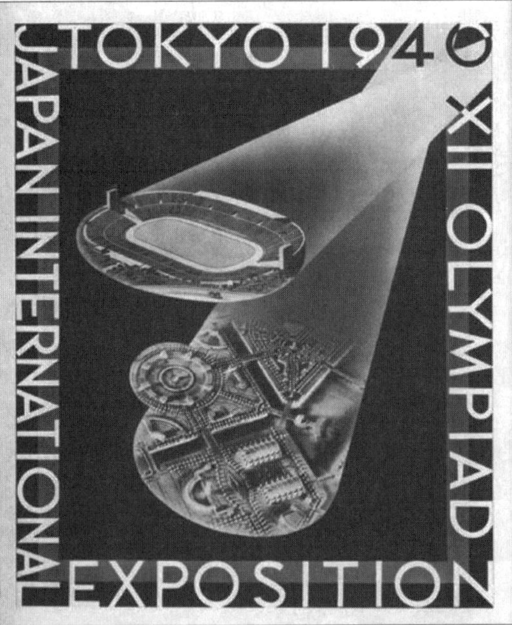

25 and 26. (left) The inside front cover of *Glimpses of the East, 1937-1938*, published for steamship travelers aboard NYK Lines, reproduced in full color a poster for the Tokyo International Exposition of 1940, with Japan represented by a young woman in traditional costume and Mount Fuji, the all-purpose icon of Japan. Modern technology is present in the radio tower, ships, and the dock protruding into the ocean. The colorful design juxtaposes these elements in a spare, but imaginative plane. An inside article (in English) discussed the XII Olympiad scheduled to be held in Tokyo in 1940.

(right) The Board of Tourist Industry publication *Pictorial Japan* (p. 72) reprinted this black-and-white poster for both major international events planned for 1940 showing the grounds for each, the Olympic Stadium at top and the International Exposition fairgrounds at bottom. The splendid art deco design, with its emphasis on geometric shapes and lines, places the event venues in two large spotlights, like two stars appearing alone on a darkened stage.

Tokyo Olympics were invoked in motivating the home front to "shape up." One lesson the Japanese did not need to learn from the Nazis was that physically fit citizens meant strong troops and a healthy home front; calisthenics had been introduced into school curricula after World War I. Japan's first bid to host the Olympics was a casualty of the Second Sino-Japanese War.[12] In its place, the Japanese went ahead with an "East Asian Sports Contest," putting to use the Olympic stadium and pool built in Yoyogi, Tokyo. The International Exposition became unfeasible. The Japanese military opposed the outlay of money and material, and the outbreak of World War II in Europe curtailed tourism. The Olympics would finally be held in Tokyo in 1964, and an International Exposition was held in Osaka in 1970, the two events signaling Japan's postwar recovery, international acceptance, and emergence as a major economic power.

27. *PWR* 121, 19 June 1940, p. 18. "The East Asian Sports Contest." The accompanying article states, "On 5 June at the Meiji Shrine Outer Garden Stadium, under the gaze of Their Imperial Highnesses Master-of-Ceremonies Prince and Princess Chichibu in the Royal Box, the solemn, gorgeous curtain was raised on the East Asian Sports Contest, the Olympia (*orinpia*) of the peoples of New East Asia celebrating the 2,600th anniversary of the founding of the nation. We recall that three years ago, the Tokyo Olympics (*orinpiku*) were abandoned in order to push forward at full-speed with the Sacred War [in China]. A long time has passed between this sports meet and the 'Far Eastern Olympics' (*Kyokutō orinpiku*) held ten years ago in 1930. This people's festival showed the world the vigor of East Asia's youth and that through sports, the two thousand young people gathered here from Japan, Manchukuo, the newly born Chinese Republic, the Philippines, Hawaii, and Mongolia can be better neighbors and firmer friends." The meet included Asian sports, such as judo and sumo, which were not yet a part of the Olympic games. Many of the same East Asian Sports Contest photographs appeared in both *PWR* 121 and *PWR* 145.

28 and 29. (top) *PWR* 145, 30 November 1940, p. 40. "The East Asian Sports Contest." The caption reads, "The spirited vigor of youth and their nation-building Calisthenics Corps in the opening ceremony." This parade of banner-bearing, barefoot, half-naked youth shows the Nazi influence in the planning of the East Asian Sports Contest. These are the virile young men who would build the Greater East Asian Co-Prosperity Sphere.

(bottom) *PWR* 121, 19 June 1940, p. 17. "Music of New Asia's Youth." The Army-Navy Band was joined by a chorus of one thousand female students.

30-33. *PWR* 145, 30 November 1940, p. 41. Four small photographs of "The East Asian Sports Contest." Top left and right, established Olympic sports: women's long jump and men's 100-meter dash. Bottom left and right, Asian sports: Chinese martial arts and the "very popular" Mongolian sumo wrestling.

Art also played a role in the celebrations. There was a rare public display of 146 eighth-century imperial treasures of the Shōsōin. A major exhibition of contemporary paintings, sculpture, and traditional crafts commemorating the 2,600th anniversary was shown in Kyoto in the spring and Tokyo in the autumn. The commemorative exhibition's catalogue of Japanese-style paintings (*nihonga*) included a statement that noted, "The organizing principle of this exhibition is the expression, through art, of the supreme ideal of kokutai, symbol of the unique existence of the Great Japanese Empire." Half of the two hundred forty works included in the Nihonga catalogue were devoted to staid themes of Japanese (and Chinese) painting: flora and fauna or unpeopled landscapes with water or mountain scenery. Another forty were pictures of women and girls, some in traditional kimono or peasant dress, others in modern Western fashions. One showed a girl in a checked dress on a bicycle, and "Seasonal Customers," by Kaneko Takanobu (figure 35), showed two stylish women in skirts and heels sitting on ottomans looking over fabrics in a haberdasher's art deco office, complete with standing ashtray, a scene remote from "the supreme ideal of kokutai." Village scenes, famous buildings and temples, and historical personages accounted for most of the remaining works.

Four of the exhibition works evoked the military, but set in the distant past, while only two works showed contemporary soldiers: "Wounded Soldiers' Morning" by Nakamura Hakui, with robust soldiers in hospital gowns practicing with longbows, and "Japanese Sword" by Kobayakawa Shūsei (figure 36). Conspicuously absent from this catalogue, as well as from the *PWR* article devoted to the exhibition, were works devoted to the war in China. Two major exhibits of war pictures devoted to the "Holy War" had already toured Japan, so certainly the genre was well established. Given the stated objective of the exhibition and the overtly militaristic nature of many of the national and local events surrounding the anniversary, the commemorative exhibition contained surprisingly little artwork highlighting Japan's military achievements. The exhibition artwork shows that as late as November 1940, the Japanese government was not dictating that artistic work must glorify the military or the state's totalitarian goals, although this degree of artistic freedom would all but disappear after war erupted in the Pacific.

34. *PWR* 138, 16 October 1940. The special exhibition of recent art commemorating the 2,600th anniversary of the founding of the nation was featured on this cover of *PWR* and in an inside article. This finely crafted terra-cotta statue, "Fulfilling the Way of Heaven," is by Naitō Noburu. The text tells us that this Kamakura warrior, with firm resolve, sincerely prays to the gods, showing the proper attitude of "we citizens of Japan, who must advance in our aim to construct a New World Order with ferocious courage and justice." These are the words of an unnamed *PWR* writer, not the artist.

35 and 36. (top) "Seasonal Customers," by Kaneko Takanobu was daringly modish with its Western interior and fashions. The prominent ashtray is particularly provocative, since civilians, especially women, were expected to forgo cigarettes so that men at the front had them.

(bottom) "Japanese Sword" by Kobayakawa Shūsei is typical of artwork featured in "Holy War Art" exhibitions, but atypical for the work included in the 2,600th Anniversary of the Founding of the Nation Commemorative Exhibition. Both are reprinted from the catalogue, *Exhibition of Nihonga Commemorating the 2,600th Anniversary of the Founding of the Nation*, p. 26 and p. 10, respectively.

The imperial review of the navy and the army in October constituted two major events of the anniversary year. The purpose of publicizing these imperial reviews was twofold. The display of military might sent a message of strength and determination to the home front, to Japanese forces and their enemies in Asia, and to the Western powers. The photographs of the emperor exercising his role as commander-in-chief conveyed to the nation and the world beyond his active role in military affairs.

紀元二千六百年奉祝

特別観艦式

謹寫海軍省

紀元二千六百年を寿ぐ特別大観艦式は秋晴れの十月十一日横濱港外において荘厳かつ盛大に挙行された

畏くも　天皇陛下には戦艦比叡に召させられ、先導艦高雄、供奉艦加古、古鷹を随へさせられ、参加の聯合艦隊旗艦長門をはじめ、舶艫相ふくむ艦艇百餘隻の精鋭が築く鐵の浮城、及び秋空を掩した海鷲五百機の大編隊が示した威容を親しくみそなはせられた

なほ、この日　天皇陛下には優渥なる勅語を賜ひ、複雑微妙な國際情勢の下に太平洋の波瀾く高まらんとして帝國の使命重大を加へるとき海軍将兵の益々奮励努力すべきことを御諭し遊ばされた

御召艦比叡の艦橋から畏くも双眼鏡御手に御観艦をみそなはせられる　天皇陛下

37. *PWR* 139, 23 October 1940, p. 3. "2,600th Anniversary of the Founding of the Nation Special Imperial Naval Review. The Emperor on the Bridge of the Destroyer *Hie*." The review took place off Yokohama Bay on 11 October and involved over one hundred ships. The text says in part, "On this day, the emperor conveyed his August remarks that in this complex and intricate international situation, with currents [i.e., tensions] running high in the Pacific and the mission of the empire increasing in importance, the Imperial Navy's officers and sailors must make their very best effort." Photograph: Navy Ministry. This full-page photograph appeared in *PWR* 145 in a reduced size.

38 and 39. *PWR* 145, 30 November 1940, pp. 14-15. The Commemorative Dress Review of the Army. The emperor reviewed troops and watched a drill of airplanes and tanks at the Yoyogi Training Grounds in Tokyo on 21 October 1940. *PWR* usually segregated the emperor and his subjects into separate photographs.

(top) The emperor, astride his steed White Snow, reviewing troops.

(bottom) A forest of rifle-bayonets held aloft by the troops being reviewed.

The grounds of the imperial palace were bedecked with banners commemorating the 2,600th anniversary of the founding of the nation. Celebrations and special events took place throughout the year in every region of Japan, from the largest cities to the smallest mountain hamlets. Precious festival carts were dusted off and taken out of storage, and famous treasures and special talents were put on display throughout the land. While most of the events reprised local and regional traditions, such as performances of folk music and dances, some incorporated the imagery and rhetoric of the Axis partners, the New Japan, the New Order in Asia, and the Greater East Asian Co-Prosperity Sphere.

PWR 145, the commemorative double issue, featured some fifty photographs showing local celebrations in every part of the empire, including Korea, Taiwan, Manchuria, and major occupied cities in China (Beijing, Shanghai, Nanjing, Guangzhou). Everywhere, crowds cheered "banzai!" Mass rallies with patriotic music were common, as were streetcars and buses decorated with flowers and ribbons in the manner of parade floats. A lantern parade in Hiroshima was led by three men made up to look like Konoe, Hitler, and Mussolini. A Japanese destroyer off Okinoshima fired its guns in salute. One photograph of prisoners at a special commemorative assembly inside Toyoda Prison, Tokyo, carried the caption, "even the incarcerated give heartfelt congratulations." Like festivals everywhere, these celebrations were an admixture of extraordinary elements: the mystical and the sensual, the serene and the raucous. All of these elements came together in an outpouring of patriotic sentiment paying homage to the emperor and the nation.

40. *PWR* 145, 30 November 1940, p. 22. This night scene of the commemorative banners erected in the imperial palace grounds conveys the serene, mystical, and ancient elements of the anniversary.

National unity was the common theme of these celebrations. After all, it was Emperor Jinmu, the founder of the nation, who was said to have used the phrase, "Hakkō ichiu" ("the eight corners [of the world] under one roof") to describe his unification of the known world under his sacred rule. The ancient phrase was an imperative to all Japanese subjects to bring the world together under imperial rule, a goal requiring the undivided energy and devotion of all members of the Greater East Asian Co-Prosperity Sphere.

41 and 42. (top) *PWR* 141, 6 November 1940, pp. 18-19. At the Eleventh National Athletics Competition at the Meiji Shrine grounds, members of the All Japan Athletics Association form the numbers 2,600. Coordinated demonstrations of patriotism were popular in 1940.

(bottom) *PWR* 145, 30 November 1940, p. 47. The Hakkō Pillar, constructed near Miyazaki City, Kyūshū on the legendary site of Jinmu's palace, "Points to the skies with its dignified form, 'Hakkō Ichiu' in Prince Chichibu's calligraphy carved in its center." Dedicated on 3 April 1940, the day of the Emperor Jinmu Festival, it quickly became a symbol of the New Order in Asia and the expansion of Japan's rule of Asia.

After the war, the 100-foot pillar was rechristened the "Peace Tower." The eternal flame was brought from the Peace Tower to Tokyo in 1964 for the Tokyo Olympics.

Of all of the events held in 1940, the most important was the imperial ceremony marking the 2,600th anniversary, which began on 10 November 1940, with ceremonial greetings exchanged between the emperor and Japanese and foreign dignitaries. The main ceremony was held the following day in the Outer Garden of the imperial palace at 2 P.M. with fifty-five thousand representatives of Japan and foreign dignitaries present. The program was reproduced in *PWR* 145. The attendees assembled prior to the arrival of the emperor and empress, and all stood when they entered. All sang the national anthem, "Kimigayo," after which unnamed foreign dignitaries were seated.[13] A message from the emperor was read. It stated that the anniversary celebration, with representatives from all of Japan and from around the world, would be observed with a special musical performance, and that the emperor hoped that, "despite the great upheaval the world was now experiencing, the day of peace would come soon so that all nations could share in Japan's joy." Next came a musical program by the Army-Navy Band, and an All-Japan Student Chorale sang. Prince Takamatsu then took the center stage and led all assembled in three cheers of "banzai!" Everyone then stood as the emperor and empress took their leave, signaling the end of the ceremony.

The 2,600th anniversary of the founding of the nation was an opportunity to show the people of Japan, Asia, and the world that Japan was a thriving "unique" culture with an ancient, sacrosanct history, a modern nation with the latest technology needed for running its empire in a time of peace as well as a time of war. The celebrations could not have taken place without the cooperation of thousands of volunteers, and their spirit of unity and their service to the nation were repaid in terms of a sense of purpose and proximity to power. The apotheosized image of national greatness and racial superiority thus created was reflected back to the people by their emperor, himself as pure and blank as a mirror, one of the three items in the imperial regalia.

43. *PWR* 145, 30 November 1940, pp. 24-25. "Taking the center of the stage, His Imperial Highness Prince Takamatsu leads the One Hundred Million in a chorus of three cheers of 'banzai!'" A corner of the drapery of the imperial box can be seen in the upper left corner of the photograph.

The "One Hundred Million" were the one hundred million subjects, the population reached by the Japanese Empire in 1937. During the war, the phrase expressed the unity of the people and was part of many slogans.

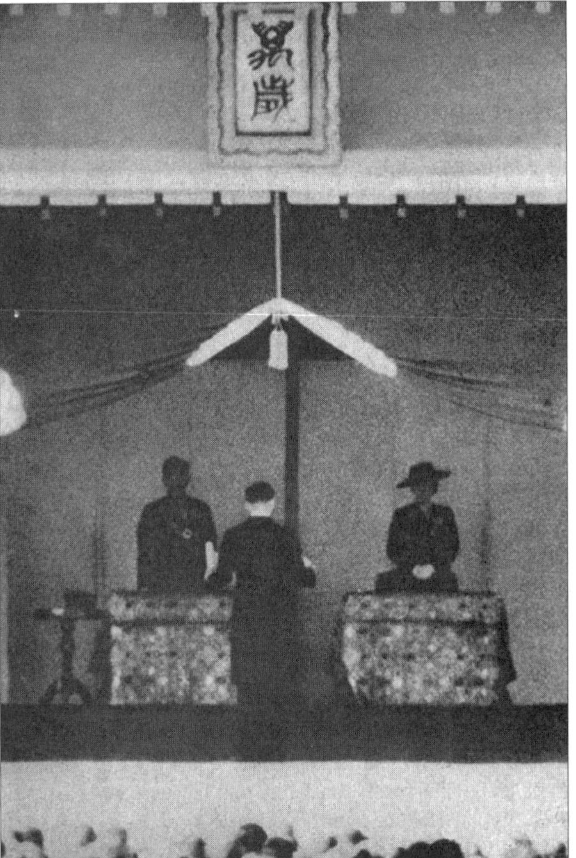

44 and 45. *PWR* 145, 30 November 1940.

(top, pp. 20-21) The emperor and empress receive the "banzai" cheers of the crowd of fifty-five thousand participating in the ceremony marking the 2,600th anniversary of the founding of the nation on 11 November. Surely the most significant and prestigious (and probably the largest) mass rally held in Japan up to this time, the sea of humanity was photographed as a wide-shot transversing four pages of *PWR* with overall dimensions of 5 inches by 32 inches. (The photograph has been cropped here.) The imperial couple (seated at the center of the shrine building beneath a tablet reading "Banzai") are very darkly shadowed and miniscule, barely discernible on the printed page.

(bottom, p. 19) *PWR* 145 also included this close-up of the emperor and empress at the ceremony, seated beneath the commemorative "Banzai" tablet with an archaic style of calligraphy (borrowed from ancient Chinese sources), which was also featured on a postage stamp commemorating the 2,600th anniversary of the founding of the nation.

Notes

1. On 14 November 1930, Sagoya Tomeo, a hired gun associated with the Black Dragon Society, shot Prime Minister Hamaguchi Osachi as he was about to board a train at Tokyo Station. He died after several surgeries on 26 August 1931. On 7 February 1932, former Finance Minister Inoue Junnosuke was shot to death in the street by Konuma Tadashi, a member of a paramilitary group called the Blood Brotherhood. On 5 March 1932, Baron Dan Takuma was shot to death at the side entrance of the Mitsui Bank by Hisanuma Gorō, also of the Blood Brotherhood. On 15 May 1932, a group of young army officers gunned their way into the prime minister's residence, where they assassinated Prime Minister Inukai Tsuyoshi. On 12 August 1935, Nagata Tetsuzan, director of the War Ministry's Military Affairs Section, was called upon in his office by Lieutenant-Colonel Aizawa Saburō, who ran him clean through with a sword, killing him. The largest assassination plot unfolded on 26 February 1936, when several hundred soldiers of the First and Third Regiments of the army, stationed in Tokyo, attempted a coup d'état and took over the center of Tokyo, site of the Diet Building and government offices. Their plot included the assassinations of several powerful members of the government. Eighty-one-year-old Finance Minister Takahashi Korekiyo was shot to death in his bed at home and died instantly. The seventy-seven-year-old former Prime Minister Viscount Admiral Saitō Makoto was shot to death in his bedroom. In all, forty-seven bullets entered his body. Grand Chamberlain Suzuki Kantarō was shot three times, but survived. Prime Minister Okada Teisuke was attacked in the prime minister's residence, site of the Inukai assassination. Matsuo Denzō, Okada's brother-in-law, pretending to be the prime minister, was machine-gunned and killed. The prime minister's maids passed off Matsuo's body as Okada's. Okada hid in a closet until he could escape by disguising himself as a mourner at his own wake. The press had already announced his death, and when he emerged alive, he was so reviled for such cowardly behavior that his political career soon came to an end. Lord Privy Seal Makino Nobuaki escaped to the hills behind an inn when a gun battle ensued between his body guards and the assassins. Police prevented the assassination of the *genrō* (senior advisor) Prince Saionji Kinmochi. Saionji had been targeted previously, in 1932. The last person to die in the 26 February mutiny was General Watanabe Jōtarō, the army's Inspector General of Education. Former Prime Minister Baron Hiranuma Kiichirō was shot on 14 August 1941, but recovered. On 18 September 1941, four unidentified men with pistols tried to attack Prime Minister Prince Konoe Fumimaro, but he escaped in his car.

2. This dustjacket is very similar to the work of Hara Hiromu displayed at the Paris Exposition of 1937. See Nanba Kōji, *"Uchiteshi yamamu": Taiheiyō sensō to hōkoku no gijustusha tachi* (Tokyo: Kodansha, 1998), p. 40. Both incorporate the same photographs of the car and the ash-belching volcano.

3. Automobile production had been linked to the army since its inception in Japan. The Foreign Affairs Association of Japan noted in *The Japan Year Book 1938-39* (Tokyo: Kenkyusha, 1938): "The first automobile to be manufactured in Japan was by the Tokyo Motor Car Works, under the management of Mr. S. Yoshida, in the year 1909, but until the present progress has been very slow. In 1910, several military motor cars were manufactured for the Army in the Osaka Arsenal" (p. 550). Commercial vehicle production began in 1911 with the DAT model. *The Orient Yearbook for 1942* (Tokyo: Asia Statistics, 1942) also commented: "The outbreak of the Sino-Japanese Hostilities in July, 1937 presented a strong impetus for the expansion of the domestic automobile industry. Especially remarkable was the advance made by the Nissan Motor Company and the Toyoda [today's Toyota] Motorcar Company, the two concerns sanctioned by the Government under the Motorcar Manufacturing Industry Law. These two companies were closely followed by the Tokyo Motorcar Industry Company, manufacturers of the Isuzu car, which is of standard size specified by the Minister of Commerce and Industry" (p. 294).

4. Asian Statistics, ed., *The Orient Yearbook for 1942* (Tokyo: Asian Statistics, 1942), p. 320.

5. *PWR* 135 (25 September 1940, p. 17) carried an article on Captain Tokugawa Yoshitoshi on the thirtieth anniversary of his flight of the first heavier-than-air machine in Japan at Yoyogi Field in Tokyo.

6. The quotation is from a book published serially in booklet form, translated from Japanese into English and printed in Japan. Chigaku Tanaka, "What Is Nippon Kokutai? Introduction to Nipponese National Principles," No. 8 (Tokyo: Shishio Bunkō, 1936), p. 211. After the war, Tanaka founded his own religion,

based upon the principle of Kotonarism. See H. Byron Earhart, *Japanese New Religions, A Bibliography* (Ann Arbor: University of Michigan Press, 1979), pp. 80-81 for Tanaka's religious tracts.

7. Chigaku Tanaka, "What Is Nippon Kokutai?" No. 8, p. 205.

8. Gregory Kasza, *The State and the Mass Media in Japan, 1918-1945* (Berkeley: University of California Press, 1988), p. 234.

9. At the same time, the Japanese Empire had its own distinct features: it was a contiguous empire, it actively developed new territories, and the colonized became citizens (albeit with fewer rights). Prasenjit Duara describes Manchukuo as the first example of "new imperialism rooted in the historical circumstances of the United States, the Soviet Union, and Japan. . . . The new imperialists espoused anticolonial ideologies and emphasized cultural or ideological similarities" because "the new imperialism reflected a strategic conception of the periphery as part of an organic formation designed to attain global supremacy for the imperial power." See his 30 January 2006 *Japan Focus* article, "The New Imperialism and the Post-Colonial Developmental State: Manchukuo in Comparative Perspective" available at http://japanfocus.org/article.asp?id=512.

10. Archeological evidence strongly suggests that the first emperors of Japan were, in fact, from a clan that originated in Korea. The current emperor has admitted as much, stating that "I, on my part, feel a certain kinship with Korea, given the fact that it is recorded in the Chronicles of Japan that the mother of Emperor Kammu was of the line of King Muryong of Paekche," quoted in the 28 December 2001 edition of the *Guardian*. See Jon Watt's article, "The Emperor's New Roots," available at www.guardian.co.uk/japan/story/0,7369,625426,00.html.

11. The Manchurian Incident took place on 18 September 1931 when soldiers of Japan's Kwantung Army blew up part of the track of the Japanese-run Southern Manchurian Railway and blamed Chinese bandits for the attack. This became the pretext for the invasion of Manchuria.

12. The ill-fated 1940 Olympics have a complicated history. Japan first participated in the Fifth Olympiad in Stockholm (1912), to which it sent five athletes. Japan won its first Olympic medals (bronze, men's tennis) at Antwerp. In 1931, as the city of Tokyo continued to rebuild following the devastating 1923 earthquake, it began to seriously consider making a bid for the 1940 Olympics. From the outset, the negotiations were riddled with economic and political maneuvering. On 31 July 1936, the International Olympic Committee (IOC) voted thirty-six to twenty-seven to award the 1940 Olympics to Tokyo. When all-out war broke out in China in September 1937, IOC member China was quick to object to Japan's hosting the Olympics. Over China's objections, the IOC confirmed Tokyo as the site on 16 March 1938. Joseph R. Svinth wrote, "When the Japanese and Soviet armies got into an undeclared war in Manchuria on July 11, 1938, the Japanese government panicked. Thus, four days later, the Ministry of Health and Welfare announced that Japan could not host the Olympic games in 1940. 'During the Emergency,' Yoshiaki Mitani explained in the *Japan Times* on July 18, 1938, 'physical activities should be hiking, etc., that build strong bodies' rather than simply amuse spectators." The 1940 Olympics were then assigned to Oslo, runner-up in the 1936 vote. The Finns also saw their Olympic dream postponed when the country was invaded at the outset of World War II. The Finnish Olympic facilities would be modified and used when the nation hosted the 1948 Olympics. See Joseph R. Svinth, "Fulfilling His Duty as a Member: Jigoro Kano and the Japanese Bid for the 1940 Olympics," *Journal of Competitive Sport*, May 2004, available at ejmas.com/jcs/2004jcs/jcsart_svinth_0504.htm

13. US Ambassador to Japan Joseph C. Grew was in attendance and delivered a speech on behalf of the diplomatic corps. For his firsthand account of the proceedings, see Joseph C. Grew, *Ten Years in Japan* (New York: Simon and Schuster, 1944), pp. 352-353.

3. MEN OF THE IMPERIAL FORCES

The 1930s witnessed a rapid rise in the political power of the Japanese military, ushering in new roles and a new image for the Japanese soldier. The decade began with a series of "Incidents"—military skirmishes in Manchuria and China,[1] brought to conclusion in a matter of weeks or months, resulting in the creation of Manchukuo—and ended with the military bogged down in a bloody, protracted conflict in China, the Second Sino-Japanese War. Japanese troops suffered sixty-two thousand combat deaths from the time of its outbreak (the Marco Polo Bridge Incident of 7 July 1937) through December 1938. In 1939, the number of deaths was half that of 1938, and in 1940, half that of 1939. Nevertheless, by the end of the government's three-year projection to conclude the Second Sino-Japanese War before December 1940, Japan had lost one hundred eight thousand men in combat. In addition, fifty thousand had perished from illness in China and Manchuria, and another thirty-five thousand were wounded during these three and a half years. The Russo-Japanese War, the deadliest in modern Japanese history before 1939, had claimed the lives of one hundred ten thousand Japanese, but reaped immediate gains of territory and international political clout. The China war had dragged on inconclusively for three times as long, cost one-and-a-half times as many lives,[2] and won only the ire and suspicion of Japan's neighbors and the great powers.

In the 1930s, Japanese were no less patriotic than in the past, but they did not enthusiastically welcome Japan's military exploits on the Asian continent.[3] When the government set out to sell the public on this latest war, it presented the soldier as a noble warrior engaged in a holy war against forces threatening Japan's national greatness and the destiny of the Yamato race. The noble warrior improved the image of the military man of the early 1930s. When the decade began, military service was a rite of passage for many of the young men of Japan, especially those from the countryside who filled the rank and file. They entered boot camp as boys, and exited as men. When they returned to society, their military experience was supposed to have made them more "masculine." In the media, all soldiers were loyal and brave, but some were also bunglers and braggarts. They were good-natured and hot-tempered, chivalrous and lecherous. In short, they were the embodiment of Japanese machismo. We will see in the media's depiction of soldiers in the late 1930s that this noble warrior would retain some of these characteristics, discard others, and add some new ones, as he increasingly became both the agent of Japanese foreign policy and the embodiment of home front ideals.

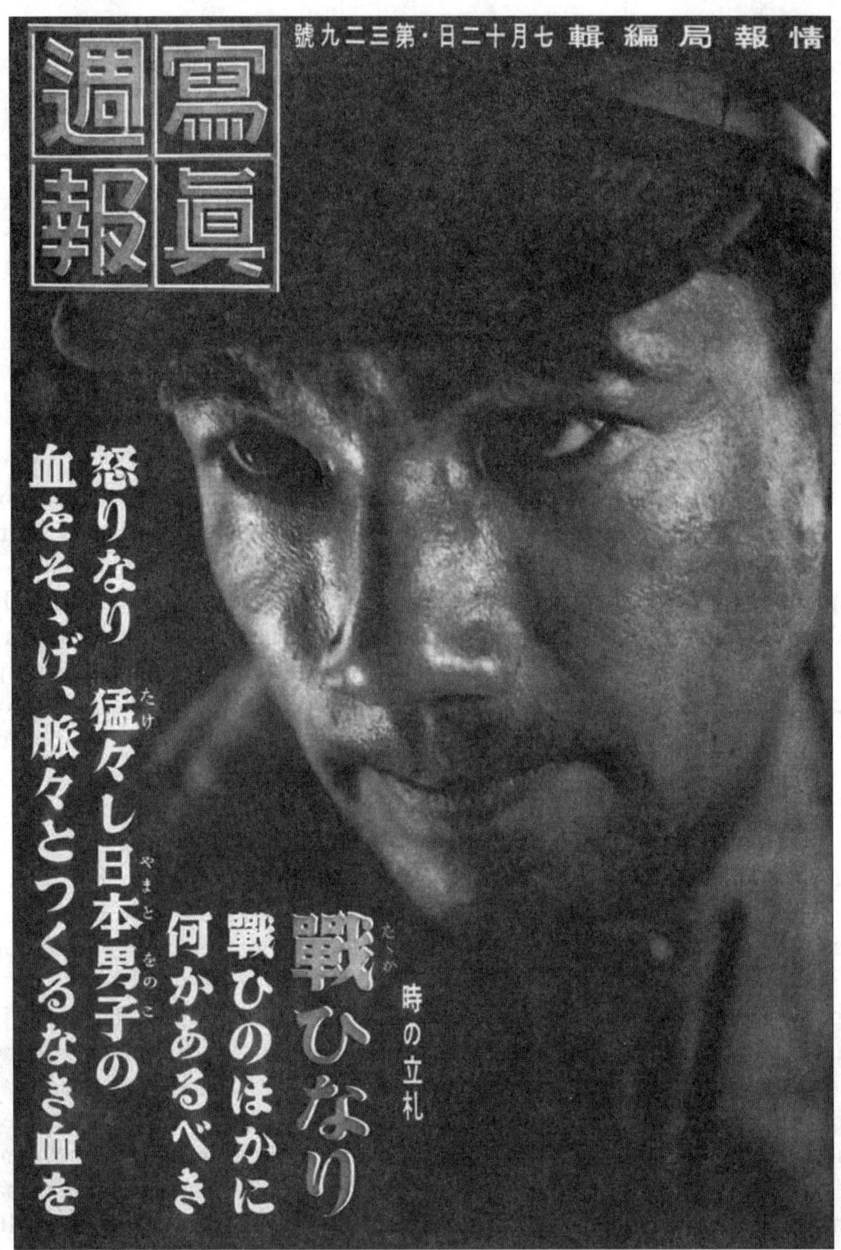

1. *PWR* 329, 12 July 1944. In 1942, *PWR* began carrying the "Signboard of the Times," a full-page message to cut out and display as a poster. Initially, it appeared on the inside front cover, but here is on the front cover. This one says, (from right to left, the first line printed in red ink): "*This is a fight*. What should there be besides fighting? Anger. Pour forth the blood of Yamato's ferocious men, the blood that flows without end."

This 11¾-by-16½-inch cover, with its larger-than-life photograph of a soldier's face, appeared at the height of the Battle of Saipan. The absence of contextualizing background imbues this powerful picture with an unsettling intimacy. The fierceness of the facial expression is heightened by the extreme close-up, the dramatic lighting, and the unusual angle placing the soldier almost on top of the viewer, as if being overtaken in hand-to-hand combat. The enemy would wither before this "anger." This media image of a common soldier, transformed into a modern-day samurai, differs remarkably from that of five or six years earlier.

Media coverage of Japan's military involvement in China in the early 1930s gave little reason to suppose that these escapades would intrude upon civilian life. The Asahi Corporation's special correspondents, following in the tracks of the Kwantung Army, Japan's major force in China, produced photographic "special reports" on the Manchurian Incident (18 September 1931), the Shanghai Incident[4] (28 January 1932), and the Jehol Skirmish[5] (3 January 1933). In each case, one issue described how the problem arose and the next how it was resolved. Media coverage of these events assured the public that their military, unrivaled and unbeatable in Asia, acted only when provoked and out of necessity. By 1937, Asahi, with its own news airplanes, was the media outfit most capable of covering the movements of the Japanese forces in Manchuria and China, although a rival newspaper and publishing giant, the Mainichi Corporation, established a competing force of China correspondents and a *China Frontline* magazine in 1937. The Cabinet Information Section (later upgraded to an Office and finally a Bureau) launched *Photographic Weekly Report* in February 1938.

2 and 3. The Manchurian Incident of 18 September 1931, in which "Chinese guerrillas" (actually, secret troops of the Japanese Kwantung Army) blew up part of the Japanese-run Southern Manchurian Railway, created the premise for retaliatory campaigns and the Japanese takeover of Manchuria.

(left) *Photographic Report on the Manchurian Incident* 2, 20 November 1931. The second of two Asahi journals describing the Manchurian Incident. Troops guard the tracks against further attacks. By the time this second report hit the newsstands, the fighting was over and most of Manchuria had been seized.

(right) *Manchuria Incident Pictorial*, 18 October 1931. Published by *Jiji Shinpō* as an insert to the Sunday edition of "Cartoons and Reading Matter," this cover is a collage of photograph (the soldiers on a stone embankment) and drawing (the sky, the clouds, the Japanese flag). The covers typify the contents of both magazines, primarily photographs of Japanese troops marching or posing in front of landmarks. There are no photographs of battle or of destruction.

The Kwantung Army's seizure of Manchuria was completed only two months after the Manchurian Incident began. In 1931, the three Tokyo- and Osaka-based media giants, Asahi, Mainichi, and Yomiuri, had no access to the front and their coverage of the Manchurian Incident was mostly a rehash, relying on information and photographs supplied by the army. But in January 1932, when fighting erupted in Shanghai, Asahi's reporters were quick on the scene, photographing the battle as it unfolded. The two issues of Asahi periodicals devoted to the Shanghai Incident provided more graphic, detailed coverage than those issued just four months earlier for the Manchurian Incident. Asahi's reporters took "live-action" shots on the battlefield as well as "after-the-fact," posed photographs (the "banzai" photographs, for instance).

4. *Photographic Report on the Shanghai Incident*, 22 February 1932. The first of two Asahi reports on the skirmishes in Shanghai that broke out between Chinese "agitators" and Japanese marines. The story presented here was that Japan's military acted quickly to protect the "international community," including Japanese, from violent Chinese protests, and that once the rebels had been quelled and order restored, the work of the Japanese military was over. The magazine included many photographs of Japanese marines setting up roadblocks and "guarding" Japanese interests. In this photograph, a Japanese armored car equipped with dual machine guns patrols a Shanghai street. A Japanese marine holds the Imperial Navy flag, proof of Japan's control of the situation.

5 and 6. *Photographic Report on the Shanghai Incident* 2, 20 March 1932. Asahi's coverage of the Shanghai Incident included six photographs of aerial bombardment of urban areas and military objectives in a photoessay called, "Activities of our Navy Air Force." With memories of the destruction of World War I still fresh, the Western powers were shocked by photographs like these, which appeared five years before the aerial bombing of Guernica, immortalized by Picasso's famous painting. The aerial photographs themselves are dramatic evidence of the technological superiority of Japan and its military over what they viewed as a backward China.

(top) p. 17 "Bombing the Enemy at Wusongzhen."

(bottom) p. 18 "Completely destroyed Hangzhou Airfield." Photographs: Navy Air Force.

The Shanghai Incident photographs display the harsh realities of war, including raw scenes of carnage and destruction. During the Russo-Japanese War, woodblock prints conveyed the drama and gore of battlefield action, which was still quite difficult for the camera to capture.[6] Photographs of Russo-Japanese War casualties do exist, but they lack the "real-time" spontaneity of Asahi's Shanghai Incident photographs. So different is Asahi's coverage of the Manchurian Incident from that of the Shanghai Incident that it marks a sea change in news reportage. With Asahi's Shanghai Incident coverage, modern photojournalism had arrived in Japan. We might even claim that this was the first instance of modern war photography.[7] What emerged from the Shanghai Incident was the image of a modern military and its warships, bomber planes, and tanks, with the capability of laying waste to a major world metropolis.

7. *Photographic Report on the Shanghai Incident*, 22 February 1932, pp. 16-17. The entire caption reads, "Jiaojiang Avenue has become a desolate, burnt-out wasteland! Our marines charge over enemy corpses."

This remarkable 21-by-15-inch centerfold presents an unvarnished picture of the horrors of war, including corpses. Japanese politicians and military leaders were surprised by the international outcry over the fighting in China. The Japanese press printed several photographs of destruction worse than this when Shanghai and Nanjing fell late in 1937, but refrained from publishing photographs of the dead, whether Chinese or Japanese.

8 and 9. (top) Russo-Japanese War color postcard, circa 1904-1905. The caption says, "Corpse of an innocent victim of a Russian massacre." No context is provided for this photograph. Interpretation of the caption depends upon the assumptions of the viewer, since grammatically it could mean "Corpse of a massacred innocent Russian."[8]

(bottom) The frontispiece of *The Fuzoku Gaho, an Illustrated Magazine of Japanese Life, Special Edition: Pictures of Subjugating Russia* 10, 10 August 1904. "Lieutenant Yoshii Cutting down Tens of Enemy Soldiers During the Fight at Motian Pass" by Yamamoto Shōya. Two nearly invisible eyes peer out from a mass of blood as a Russian's head is split open by Lieutenant Yoshii's unerring sword. Prints like this owe much stylistically and thematically to ukiyo-e artists who specialized in sensationalized pictures of murderers and ghosts, and the original (printed in color) is gruesome, with deep-red blood covering the Russians and Yoshii's blade and scabbard. This barbaric degree of gore was eschewed by the media as Japan became the "bringer of civilization" to Asia in the 1930s.

The Shanghai Incident yielded the narrative of the first warrior-gods of the Shōwa era. Three young men became the most celebrated example of self-sacrifice of the 1930s, the "Three-man Human Bomb" (*Bakudan san yūshi*) also known as the "Three Human Bullets" (*Nikudan san yūshi*, familiarly, *San nikudan*). As reported in the Japanese news, at 5:30 A.M. on 22 February 1932, these three men of the engineers' corps shouldered a warhead and ran with it into the midst of the barbed wire fences that had cost the lives of thirty-six of their comrades, blowing a path through the Chinese fortifications. According to the army's official citation, "realizing that it would be impossible to light the warhead once they had implanted it in the barbed wire fence . . . they decided to

10. "The Three Human Bullets," a 1930s advertising giveaway stamped "Takeda Rubber Boots Shop, Nagano City," put photographs of the three soldiers above an unnamed artist's rendition of their final brave act, carrying a massive warhead toward the Chinese fortifications. The size of this inexpensively reproduced image (11 inches by 13½ inches) made it suitable for framing. The text below the image gave the names of the three soldiers and reprinted the text of the army's commendation of their action.

light it and carry it into the barbed wire."[9] This selfless act of valor allowed the Japanese forces to successfully attack the Chinese. The death of these three young men was exalted as a great example of "Japanese spirit," making a powerful impression on the popular culture of the 1930s. The Three Human Bullets were lionized in film, theater, books, comics, and song.[10] Statues of these heroes were erected.[11] A mid-1930s sculpted bronze panel showing them carrying the bomb can still be seen today on the base of one of the colossal bronze lanterns at Yasukuni Shrine. The cafeteria in the Takashima Department Store in Osaka began serving a "Three Human Bombs Meal" and an enterprising shop began producing "Three Human Bombs" rice crackers.

11-14. *Photographic Report on the Shanghai Incident* 2, 20 March 1932, p. 25. Each of the Three Human Bullets received a full page of coverage in this Asahi-produced magazine, including photographs of family members, the family home, and letters sent from the front. These photographs pertain to Eshita Takeji, who is pictured top left.

(bottom left) Beneath Eshita's portrait is a family photograph: "All of them together [in the army] for the sake of the nation. The deceased Eshita (in hunting cap) with his brothers."

(top right) "[Asahi] Moji Bureau Chief Kamata presents the deceased Eshita's family with consolation money from the Asahi Company." Japanese custom dictates that relatives, friends, neighbors, and coworkers make a donation of money to the family of the deceased, ostensibly to offset funeral expenses.

(bottom right) "Mourning the spirits of the three heroes. Kobe." A makeshift shrine put up by a patriotic citizen of Kobe.

The wartime narrative of these heroic figures was subsequently questioned. Eyewitness accounts made public after the war claim that these young men actually were sent to their deaths. Ordered to blow up the barbed wire fences, they took a warhead out of its box only to find that it had an unusually short fuse. When they tried to take it back, their superior officer yelled at them and they had no choice but to use the bomb to blow a hole in the barbed wire. The short fuse did not leave them enough time to escape. At best their death was an accident, at worst a blunder that the army covered up by turning it into a tale of glory. The public was told that these soldiers acted voluntarily. This tale of military valor reinforced the military ethos of dying for the nation and never enduring the humiliation of being captured. A Captain Kuga Noboru, who was returned to Japan in a prisoner exchange in February 1932, "committed suicide to atone for his capture," and thereafter, "officers who survived capture were often openly pressured to commit suicide."[12]

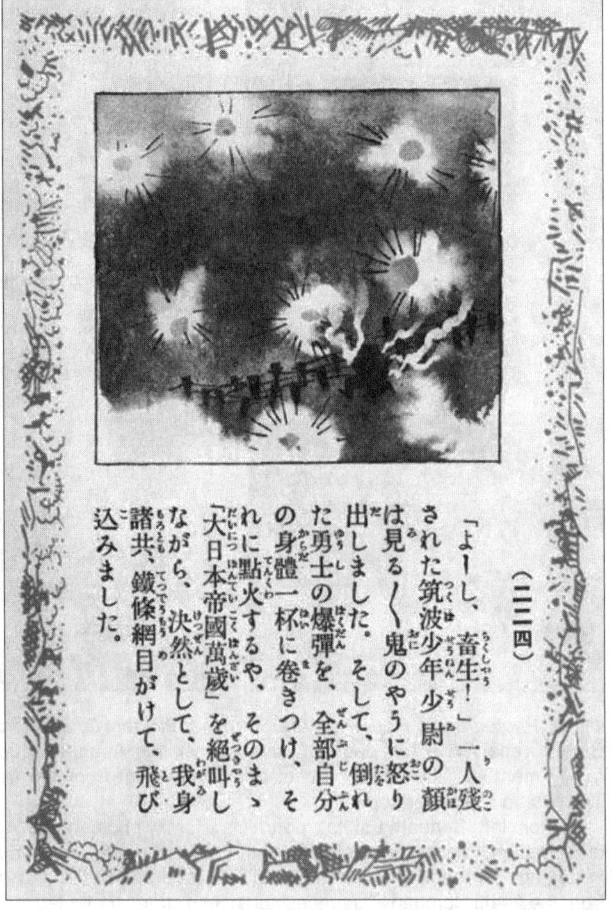

（二二四）

「よーし、畜生！」一人残された筑波少年少尉の顔は見る〳〵鬼のやうに怒り出しました。そして、倒れた勇士の爆彈を、全部自分の身體一杯に巻きつけ、それに點火するや、そのまゝ「大日本帝國萬歳」を絶叫しながら、決然として、我身諸共、鐵條網目がけて、飛び込みました。

15. Contemporary publication data lists *Manga Human Bullet*, by Kiyohara Hitoshi, as a *dōwa* ("fairy tale" or "juvenile story") published in April 1932, and the reading level is appropriate for upper elementary students. The final five pages (pp. 224-228) are reprinted here and on the following page. Page 224 is reproduced in its entirety to show the Rorschach-like decorative border of tanks, cannons, and fences appearing on each page.

Having completed many military exploits, the young protagonist of *Manga Human Bullet*, Boy-Major (*shōnen shōsa*) Tsukuba's last act of bravery is to single-handedly imitate the Three Human Bullets. "Fairy tale" elements are present in the youth's superhuman abilities and in the use of imaginative proper names: the fortress, Akahanayama ("Red Nose Mountain") and General Konbō ("General Club," the Indian club used in calisthenics). Boys who grew into adolescence on a steady diet of patriotic textbooks and comic book and digest versions of military exploits were ripe for recruitment by the time they were of age.

"'Okay, you bastards!' Anger like that of a demon showed on the face of the sole survivor, Boy-Major Tsukuba. Wrapping his body completely around the bomb of the fallen hero, he lit it, and shouting, 'Great Japanese Empire, Banzai!' he resolutely dashed into the barbed wire with the force of his entire body, charging at full speed."

16. “Soon, there was a great explosion that shook the heavens, shredding the sturdy barbed wire that had up to then had caused the deaths of so many brave soldiers. The objective of clearing a path had been achieved. The orderly flew like an arrow to the main camp. ‘What is it? Yes, it’s been blown up . . . yes, he really did . . . he did a great job.’”

17. “When General Konbō heard of the tragic end of Boy-Major, a large tear rolled down his face, which was twitching with tension. Later that night, a battalion of foot soldiers made a brave attack, and fierce hand-to-hand combat developed. And Akahanayama, known around the world to be an impregnable stronghold, was completely captured by our army.”

18. “Oh, Boy-Major Tsukuba Tarō, you have died in battle. The nation-protecting deity Boy-Major has turned into dust. But his many military exploits, his extremely loyal and unparalleled spirit, will never perish throughout eternity, so long as there is a Japanese Empire, and so long as there is a world. Boy-Major will live on forever.” The illustration depicts a monument to Boy-Major.

19. The final page has no text, only this illustration of Boy-Major, whole again. He is as immortal as the many Warner Brothers’ characters of the 1930s (and much later), destined to be destroyed over and over again in five-minute animated cartoons.

Conscription relied heavily on taking sons from large farming families inured to hardship and deprivation, and some of them viewed the glorified account of the Three Human Bullets with cynicism. In January 1932, just as the Shanghai Incident was unfolding, the novelist Shimomura Chiaki wrote "Touring Famine-Struck Regions: A Report on the Ghastly Conditions in the Northeastern Farm Villages." Shimomura interviewed an old man who said, "And this year has been one of the worst famines. This means next year the poor farmers will dry up and starve to death; they will die

20-22. Three ca. 1938 humorous postcards from a brightly colored series called "Military Manga," describing soldiers in the Second Sino-Japanese War. While these soldiers are brave and loyal, the ironic humor is at the expense of the "noble warrior" promoted by the army and the government.

Within each postcard, captions read from right to left.

(top) "A Mountain of War Trophies." First Soldier: "Banzai, banzai!" Second Soldier: "Banzai, banzai!" Third Soldier: "Say, this would be good for cutting up a pig." The third soldier's comment notes the crudeness of the enemy's weapons, more suitable to butchering animals than fighting a modern war. Showing soldiers with a "mountain" of war booty hinted at plunder.

(middle) "Mourning a Brother-in-Arms." First Soldier: "There's nothing else on this battlefield, I'll have to make an offering of snowballs." Second Soldier (crying): "And the enemy's probably going to swipe them." The offering of snowballs on a grave, not the usual rice cakes (or a bowl of rice or cup of sake), was pathetic, and the comment about the theft of offerings, which suggests that battlefield graves were routinely desecrated, would have upset families of fallen soldiers.[13]

(bottom) "Magnificent Entrance into [Censored] Town." First Chinese Man: "Pansai! Pansai!" Japanese Soldier: "Banzai! Banzai!" Second Chinese Man: "Nippon Pansaai, Pansaai!" Depicting Chinese using pidgin Japanese placed an ugly emphasis on differences between "Asian brothers" whom Tokyo hoped to unite in a common cause against Western imperialism.

in the fields. Some will end up hanging themselves. Damn it all! One of my sons is in Manchuria as a soldier. I sent him a letter the other day telling him to fight bravely for our country and die on the battlefield like a man. Then, you know, we'll get some money from the government, and our family will be able to survive the winter. Families with daughters can sell them [to brothels or mills], but we have only boys. So this is the only way I can sell my son . . ."[14] Small wonder, then, that popular culture of the 1930s often treated the harsh realities of military life with irony and light humor.[15]

23-25. Three mid-1930s brightly colored, humorous postcards from the series, "Military Manga: On Leave," published by Matsumura of Kanda, Tokyo. The humor in this series relied on irony: these soldiers' conduct "on leave" is undisciplined, irresponsible, even unmanly. The government's efforts to humanize the soldier's image did not include this kind of behavior.

Within each postcard, captions read from right to left.

(top) "Sword Play." Soldier: "He's too much for me. Help! Help!" Boy: "Come closer and I'll cut you. Tonight, my trusty blade thirsts for blood." The boy recites a clichéd phrase from samurai movies. The sword (emblazoned with the Chrysanthemum Seal) was as good as a warrior's soul; to place this weapon in the hands of a child was not only dangerous, it was unpardonable, as was prancing around in front of it, pretending to be scared.

(middle) "Cherry Blossom Viewing." Children: "How funny! Mr. Soldier is drunk." First Soldier: "Come on, you're a soldier. Pull yourself together." Second Soldier: "Ooh, ooh, I can't drink any more." Third Soldier: "Hey, who said anything about making you drink!" All too familiar in reality, drunken soldiers were an embarrassment to the army.

(bottom) "Health." Soldier: "I'm about average for a soldier of the Japanese Empire." Woman: "Well, young man, the color in your cheeks certainly does look healthy." Boy: "For an Ethiopian, that is." These soldiers' faces are a deep brown color. Likening Japanese soldiers to Ethiopians (a "primitive" people overrun by Fascist Italy in 1935) contradicted Japan's self-appointed role as the "big brother" who "civilized" Asia.

Picture postcards are among the most important sources presenting a wide variety of unofficial and official images of soldiers through the 1930s. The market for military-theme postcards was large; communication between soldiers and their families and friends depended upon correspondence. Postcards were convenient because (unlike letters) the censor need not open them to examine their messages. Postcards with military themes often came with the military frank preprinted on them. Military humor is, of course, nearly universal, but depictions of soldiers in embarrassing or compromising situations would become very scarce in Japan once the Pacific War began.

The Manchurian experiment had resulted in Japan's condemnation by the League of Nations and estrangement from its neighbors. The Lytton Report to the League, completed in 1933, demanded the immediate withdrawal of Japanese troops from Manchuria and China. The report enraged ultranationalist elements in the military, and Japan withdrew from the League. Military and civilian leaders clashed over China policy, which was at an impasse as the 1930s dragged on. This impasse ended with a dramatic showdown, the February 26 (1936) Incident. Unlike the incidents of a few years earlier, this one was staged in the center of Tokyo.

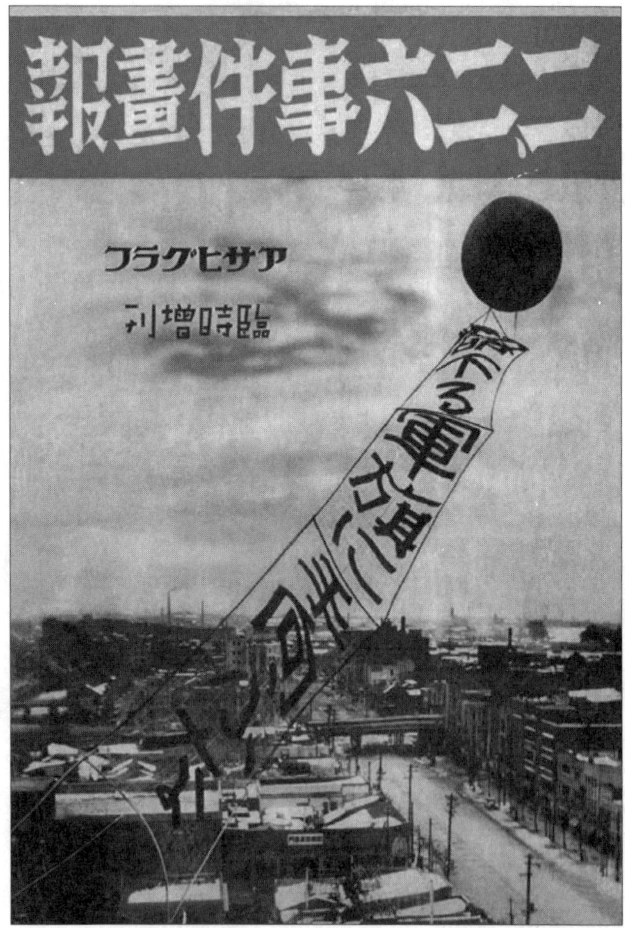

26. *February 26 Incident Pictorial Report*, 25 July 1936. Asahi issued this magazine-format special report upon the announcement of the trial results of the February 26 Incident mutineers. The contents included portraits of the targeted political and business leaders and photographs of the homes in which they were attacked, including the addresses. It also included photographs of their mourning families at their funerals. The bulk of the magazine was devoted to photographs of the confusion in Tokyo as streets were closed off and people were stranded while troops secured the city under martial law. The front cover, pictured here, shows a balloon the rebels raised with the message, "It's no use resisting the Army Flag!"

The events of 26 February 1936 involved two garrisons of mutinous army officers blockading the government district of central Tokyo and proclaiming a "Shōwa Restoration" that would do away with contentious party politics and return direct rule to the emperor. Squadrons from the mutinous ranks stormed the residences of several prominent government and business leaders, carrying out assassinations in the early morning hours. Martial law was declared and troops poured into Tokyo; they called a blackout, and surrounded the rebel soldiers. After a week-long standoff with no sign of the emperor joining the rebellion, the rebels surrendered. In April, a court martial, closed to the public and the media, took place and seventeen instigators were sentenced to death. They were executed by firing-squad in July. Many of the men found guilty had their sentences commuted; they were smuggled out of the country to Manchuria, where they continued their military careers. Top secret documents made public after the war reveal that this incident was also manufactured: the instigators of the "Shōwa Restoration" were acting on orders from high within the military command. The Shōwa Restoration was a failure, but the military bid to take control of the civilian government was a success.

27 and 28. *February 26 Incident Pictorial Report*, 25 July 1936. The sight of troops and armored cars rolling down familiar streets of Tokyo (instead of Shanghai) must have been as shocking as the initial rebellion. These events and their media coverage drove home the point that Japan was tilting toward a government and national policy dominated by the military. Previous "Incidents" had familiarized Japanese with pictures of their country's military personnel and weapons in action in distant China, but now they were confronted with images of their capital as a battleground filled with Japanese soldiers and war matériel.

(top) p. 16. "Fukuyoshi-chō, Akasaka. Troops taking the place of police; the activities of the marines."

(bottom) p. 18. "The activities of the marines' tanks. In the vicinity of Tamura-machi, Shiba Ward."

The outbreak of the China Incident[16] (usually referred to today as the Second Sino-Japanese War) on 7 July 1937 (coincidentally, Army Day in Japan) required a rapid increase in conscripts, and suddenly men in uniform were everywhere in Japan: in the streets, on the trains, in movies and stage reviews, in the news. In the first months of the war, the print media sent forth an onslaught of special reports. Fierce battles and Japanese victories made for brisk copy. Periodicals from this time are unanimous in their patriotic support of the war effort. However, as we shall see, the imagery used

29. *Asahigraph* (29:26), *China Battle Front Photographs* 23,[17] 29 December 1937. "Fall of Nanjing." Japanese troops 150 feet in front of Zhonghua Gate, Nanjing, on 12 December 1937.

to patriotic ends is remarkably different in the late 1930s. If neither military nor home front was prepared for the exigencies of a protracted war in 1937, they would be by the end of the decade. Military service was still portrayed as a rite of passage, a chance to learn to shoot a rifle and use a bayonet, establish lifelong friendships,[18] collect souvenirs, compile a scrapbook, perhaps see a different part of the world, and then come home and start a new life with savings and severance pay. Such routine military service came to an end when the war in China became "long term" in 1938.

30. *Asahigraph* (29:26), *China Battle Front Photographs* 23, p. 4. "In the all-out assault, Commander Hasegawa approached Zhonghua Gate, and at 12:10 P.M. on 12 December, the Engineers Corps of the Yamada Detachment risked their lives to blow up the gate, succeeding in destroying the southern gate, allowing our fierce crack troops to quickly enter the city and plant the Rising Sun flag atop the 70-foot high wall. This photograph, capturing the moment the southern gate was blown up, was taken on 12 December by Special Correspondent Ueno."

31 and 32. *Asahigraph* (29:26), *China Battle Front Photographs* 23, 29 December 1937.

(top, p. 3) "Banzai atop Guanghua Gate, Nanjing. The awaited day has finally arrived. At 1 P.M. on 10 December, the Nanjing General Attack Force's firing stopped. Commander Wakisaka [Jirō], who led the way through the hole blown in the city wall that crumbled under our fierce bombardment, finally took possession of Guanghua Gate at 5 P.M., and amid high emotion, planted the Rising Sun flag atop the highest point on the wall. The photograph shows the Imperial Army shouting 'Banzai!' atop Guanghua Gate." Photograph: Special Correspondent Kojima.

(bottom, p. 5) "The stirring sight of worshipping the imperial palace atop Guanghua Gate, the Imperial Army Flag held aloft. Photographed on 13 December by Special Correspondent Suzuki."

Tradition and modernity, sword and rifle, unite officer and common soldier in worshipping the imperial palace, symbolic source of all military authority, as the sun rises in the morning sky, symbol of Japan in ascendancy.

33. *Weekly Asahigraph Special Report: China Incident Pictorial Report* 11, 27 January 1938. "The Great Rising Sun Flag, catching the wind of the entire Orient, fully unfurls from the rooftop of the National Government Building in Nanjing, the capitol of the foe that opposed Japan. Photograph taken on 17 December, the day of the Imperial Army's parade into the city, by special correspondent Kawamura."

The four characters on the building's façade identify it as "National Government." This powerful photograph, with its high contrast, its provocative perspective, and its asymmetrical composition, anticipates some of the best camera work that would begin appearing in *PWR* from February, suggesting a bold, modern aesthetic capable of elevating the common soldier to the lofty plane of the noble warrior.

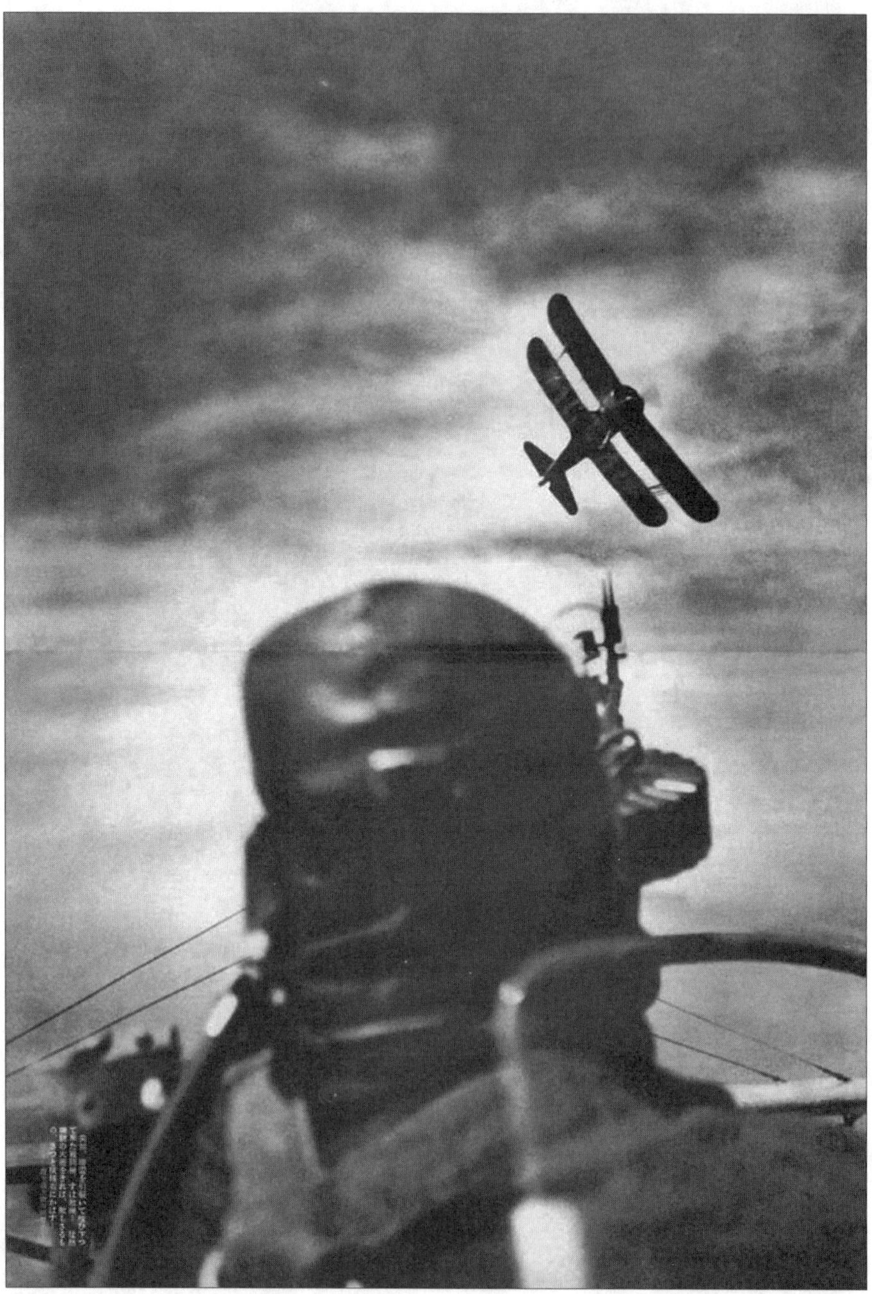

34. *PWR* 15, 25 May 1938, pp. 11-12. For Navy Day, *PWR* printed this photograph of a navy pilot. The caption gives an exciting account of closing in on an unidentified "enemy" (presumably Chinese) fighter plane. This photograph, taken "in midair above the Kasumigaura Practice Field," could only have been shot from the co-pilot's seat, placing the viewer in the middle of the action. The text asks the viewer to imagine the scenario, while clearly identifying it as a practice drill. The caption of this large, two-page centerfold could only be read upright by turning the magazine 90 degrees clockwise, an action simulating the rolling of the aircraft pictured. This innovative use of dramatic photography in *PWR*'s early issues put it on equal footing with the popular, well-established *Asahigraph*.

In 1938, the government took concrete steps to mold the media image of the war effort. Of paramount importance was the new role of the Cabinet Information Office (later, the Cabinet Information Bureau [CIB]), which held a policing authority over the realm of publishing. As a consortium of information agencies within the government, the CIB was the largest source of news stories, especially regarding the war.[19] However, the CIB's activities were proscriptive as well as prescriptive. Besides issuing detailed guidelines to publishers,[20] the CIB made suggestions to publishers that were all but commands. Through *Photographic Weekly Report* and other publications, the CIB served as the government's mouthpiece during the war, not only disseminating information but also creating its own news in the form of government directives to the population.

When *PWR* first appeared on the newsstands on 12 February 1938, its content and layout owed much to rival photographic news digest *Asahigraph* (the format and size of which were strikingly similar to the American magazine *Life*, which *Asahigraph* predated by thirteen years). Photography was made the standard of news reportage by *Asahigraph*, and it was lent greater authority by the government-published *PWR*. The photographs of the two magazines have much in common, but stylistically, the photographs of *PWR* also demonstrate a shift away from the detached and "objective"

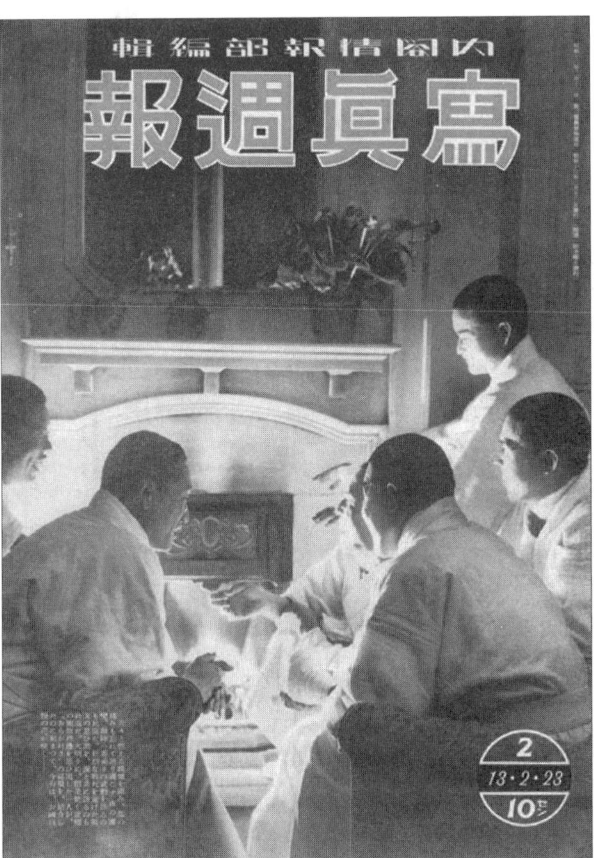

35. *PWR* 2, 23 February 1938. "Huddled around the warm glow of the fireplace, they forget the pain of their wounds and pass the night in a fireside conversation. Here they talk about military valor, about who was first to ride into the enemy camp. And here they tearfully speak of the memories of comrades-in-arms who bravely died in battle. The firelight reminds one of them of being back home around the sunken hearth that is kept burning with twigs and branches, and he introduces the group to the song, 'My Village,' which begins, 'This evening, the flowers are blooming, the pride of this land . . .'" Photograph: *PWR*.

In covering the China war, *Asahigraph* included several photographs of resting soldiers, sleeping in makeshift quarters or bathing in a Chinese bathhouse. *Asahigraph*'s coverage was contextualized with reportorial information. This image lacks context, leaving the place and the subjects unidentified, allowing the reader to fill in the details about "here"—an imaginary, indeed a psychological, locale. *PWR* sidestepped logic and aimed at provoking an emotional response with a dexterous interweaving of text and image, each of which contained vital clues to a narrative larger than the sum of its parts: the Japanese soldier is brave, selfless, and loyal, and also as human and down-to-earth as any village lad.

viewpoint of staid news photography, and a preference for bold lighting and extreme angles dramatizing the subject matter. Evident in *PWR*'s photographs of the war, and of soldiers in particular, is a thorough editing process weeding out potentially negative messages about Japan's men in the field and the sacred quest in Asia.

In the first year of *PWR*'s publication, the magazine's writers and photographers refined the print media's image of the Japanese soldier to more closely fit the military's objectives and the national ideals. At the same time, *PWR* was clearly concerned with the home front's perceptions of the life of the Japanese soldier. Several *PWR* articles in 1938 and 1939 focused on the physical and psychological well-being of soldiers. In fact, the first appearance of soldiers in *PWR* was on the cover of the second issue, where soldiers recuperating from battle wounds were shown seated around a fireplace (figure 35). The scene conveys the message that the nation was repaying these men who had made sacrifices for the nation. In portraying soldiers as ordinary, vulnerable human beings, *PWR* was preying upon the sympathies of the home front.

36. *PWR* 4, 9 April 1938, p. 1. "Battle History of the Imperial Army: Revisiting the Blood Shed by our Revered Forefathers." One of *PWR*'s first goals was to explain the China war to the home front. This entire issue of *PWR* was a special report on the history of the army from its inception in the early Meiji era through the Sino-Japanese and Russo-Japanese Wars, Japanese involvement in World War I and Siberia, and finally in Manchuria and China. Placing the China war within the framework of past conflicts rationalized and legitimated it in terms of the destiny of the Japanese Empire, at the same time demonstrating the great progress the military had made in a mere seventy years. The photograph is identified as "The Military Review that took place at Hibiya Grounds [Tokyo] right after the Southwestern War, 3 November 1877."

The text accompanying the photograph reads, "Japan, which is now undertaking a deed of unprecedented greatness on the Chinese mainland (*Shina tairiku*), only lets blood flow righteously, for peace and justice. Let's now concentrate on reviewing the image of our forefathers, when they clutched their swords and took up their rifles. Army Ministry." The grainy 1877 photograph offers a point of comparison with the technological advances in the mass media. For photographs of military reviews of the 1930s and 1940s, see Chapter 1, figures 5-10.

PWR 4 featured an unusually lengthy article aimed at improving the public's perceptions of the daily life and actions of the Japanese soldier. This article showed new recruits handling the latest equipment (such as the machine gun) and stressed the camaraderie between seniors and juniors, perpetuating an image of boot camp at odds with the majority of firsthand accounts of those who survived the brutality of basic training in the Japanese army.[21]

37-40. *PWR* 4, 9 April 1938, pp. 15-16. One of *PWR*'s early goals was assuring the home front (and future recruits) that life was good in the army. A six-page article titled "Look Lively! Rookie Soldiers of the [China] Incident," brought the lengthy article "History of the Imperial Army" up to date by following new recruits through their daily routine. "In Camp," the first two pages of "Look Lively!" described the morning routine. Sequentially, this layout begins with the top left photograph (reveille) and proceeds clockwise to top right (waking up and dressing), then to bottom right (breakfast) and bottom left (morning roll call).

(top left) "Piercing the still air of the early morning, reveille sounds. 'Iron Discipline' is a crisp melody, conjuring up the martial spirit. At 5:30 every morning at the army camps throughout the nation, our young soldiers jump up to greet the new day. The shadow of a cloud crosses the golden bugle as rose-colored light begins to dye the Eastern skies. Today the weather's good again! 'Wake up! Wake up!' sounds the reveille."

(top right) "Reveille! These guys can't lie in bed hugging the alarm clock. The new recruits throw off the blankets with the image of a dream they were seeing just moments before still lingering in their unopened eyes. 'Hey, don't stick your leg in my trousers!' 'Oh, Squadron Leader, sir! Pardon me, sir!' And yet, these wartime rookies' attitude is such that in just two minutes they are composed and ready for roll call."

(bottom right) "Begin eating! They blow on the steaming miso soup served with boiled rice mixed with wheat. The rookies are growing like young oak trees on three meals a day, which they eat with gusto. 'Wow! This morning there are eggs and fermented soy beans!' Their tough willpower and bullet-like flesh is conditioned by such ample nourishment."

(bottom left) "Crisply saluting hands. Eyes fixed straight ahead, filled with respect and trust. The hand salute is snappy, the eyes sparkle."

41-45. *PWR* 4, 9 April 1938, pp. 17-18. "In the Field," pages 3 and 4 of "Look Lively!" showed the military training rookies undergo in the course of a typical day. This crucial training would prepare them for combat duty. The layout is clockwise, beginning at top left.

(top left) "Their step and maneuvers are still not in line, but *hup*, *hup*, their army boots hit the ground with a powerful rhythm. *One, two. One, two.* In no time at all, even these new recruits will form perfect lines as a part of the parading ranks, demonstrating their heroic form as they march down the avenue."

(top right) "On the offensive, they must jump across criss-crossing trenches."

(center right) "Showing the spirit of the infantry, our world-renowned army, they attack! Facing an actual battle, they will grip the trigger so firmly as if to crush it, and with a scream, kick their way through barbed wire and advance. The smiling faces of young soldiers—their smiling faces show that they have resigned themselves and are able to die, a smile on their face, for the sake of the nation."

(bottom right) "The enemy army rushes forward like angry waves, and even the barrel becomes hot as he fires, fires, fires, mowing them down. The light machine gun, which fires two hundred rounds per minute, is equal to fifteen or sixteen rifles, and holds a strong attraction for the new recruits."

(bottom left) "Their fighting spirit congeals on the points of their rifle-bayonets. Fingers firm on the trigger, looking ahead, the sight of friends who have fallen on the battlefield of the [Asian] continent flickers before their eyes. (Hey, rifle! I wish I could load you with real bullets right now! [They think to themselves.]) Their manly vow is to score a '100 percent' success on their shooting practice behind the embankment."

46-50. *PWR* 4, 9 April 1938, pp. 19-20. “When Drills Are Over,” pages 5 and 6 of “Look Lively!”, concludes the day with exercise, study, and free time. Sequentially, this layout proceeds clockwise from the top left picture, which is both the starting and ending point of the article.

(top right) “After drills, they have physical conditioning—they stretch their arms wide, and take deep breaths, while the smell of supper mysteriously fills the air. Their stomachs groan audibly. The mind wanders, the pace of the drill quickens, and that’s exactly when the squadron leaders admonishes, ‘Hey, you! Wrong!’ Please take time to study this photograph.”

(bottom right) “From now on, war is scientific war. Weapons have increased in variety. The amount of time spent studying the specifications of automatic firearms has also increased. These eyes watch intently, not missing the movement of one spring of the light machine gun, ears listening to every word of their senior’s explanation. When will the time finally arrive for these recruits to hold this light machine gun and let it spit fire at the enemy and shoot them dead?”

(bottom center) “‘At the time they attacked Nanjing, the army advanced with pieces of leather tied around their bare feet.’ ‘What are you talking about?’ ‘Their boots were worn out, shredded like rope.’ With the day’s lessons over, they spend the time before supper at ease, brightly polishing their army boots, pondering their seniors’ tales of hardships, and thinking about how feet are the top priority for the infantry. These once-new boots have already taken on individual character. Pretty soon, these boots, too, will be all grown up.”

(bottom left) “And so ends another day of growing and becoming, through communal living bound in friendship and a [military] framework strong as iron, a member of the invincible Imperial Army and an outstanding member of society. After 8 o’clock roll call, they might write a letter to someone back home, but soon it’s lights out. They can sleep soundly—their bodies tired from the day’s lessons, they quickly fall into a deep sleep, and whatever dreams they see, a smile graces their sunburned cheeks.”

(top left) “The noble spirit of the Imperial Army is seen in the firm, unmoving posture. At the order of ‘Attention!’ the new recruit shows he is reliable, he doesn’t move a muscle. Isn’t his burning spirit apparent in his lips and eyes?” The placement of this final image suggests it is the result of military training, the ideal soldier ready to serve the nation and the emperor.

Subsequent issues of *PWR* printed articles about soldiers, some apparently designed to dispel specific "rumors." For example, a photoessay showing Japanese soldiers with Chinese children is the home front companion piece to a barrage of Japanese pamphlets in English, Dutch, and French, denying Chinese and Western journalists' accounts of Japanese atrocities against Chinese, such as the iconic 1937 photograph of a crying Chinese baby on the platform of a bombed Shanghai railroad station.[22]

51 and 52. *PWR* 47, 11 January 1939, pp. 4-5. "Wuhan Lullaby" shows soldiers as civilizers restoring order and morality, and as colonizers (introducing Japanese toys such as the small Boy's Day paper carp dangled in front of the baby's eyes). The text is an exposition of Bushido, the noble warrior's "code of honor."

(right page) The text is the soldier's interior monologue. "When I stop to think, already many leisurely months have passed since the Wuhan Invasion Force entered the city and began patrolling it . . . already almost half a year has passed since the happy shouts of summer could be heard. Half a year has passed by as if in a dream, and here is another page in my life, as I play with a paper balloon together with these Chinese children who have come out to enjoy the winter sunshine."

(left page) (Interior monologue:) "On the continent they wear padded clothes, and for the first time it occurs to me how fortunate Japanese children are. Just about now, back in my home town, a bitter winter wind is probably blowing, and people are warming themselves in the *kotatsu* (sunken hearth) cooking vegetable stew. On this desolate battlefield on the continent, an abandoned child wrinkled up its nose and eyes, which were red from crying. There's not much the war-toughened hands of a soldier can do for this baby. Of course, the refugees are to be pitied, but only cold-blooded parents could do such a terrible thing! We cannot possibly understand their emotions."

(Unseen narrator:) "These solders used milk and a toy to calm the baby, and although it was a little timid and afraid, they took it back to the refugee assistance center in the town. This is the new version of the Lullaby of the Continent." Photographs: *PWR*.

PWR articles showed the Japanese soldier being treated well in life and in death, and treating the enemy with respect. Examples of these are the photoessay of an in-camp performance and of a battlefield memorial service. Japanese soldiers and their families were deeply disturbed by the suspicion that the cremated "remains" of fallen soldiers returned to Japan contained something other than the actual remains of the deceased. Often, the greatest duty of a "war buddy" (*sen'yū*) was to ensure, if his fellow soldier died in the service, that at least a piece of his body or a personal effect be returned to the family. Remains of the dead are important for the Buddhist funeral service that transforms an impure corpse into a purified (benevolent) ancestor. Personal effects are placed within a family altar kept in the home, and religious rites meant to assure that the deceased rests in peace are carried out for several years (typically, thirty-three) after death. When such rites cannot be performed, the spirit is thought to wander between this world and the next, and can become a malevolent force.

53. *PWR* 44, 14 December 1938, p. 1. "A Cold Winter Wind on the Battlefield." These noble warriors keep their promise to a fallen comrade after his death.

The text reads, "It is lunchtime. Again today, the soldiers have crossed their rifles over the remains of their comrade-in-arms (*sen'yū*) and placed the first serving of rice before him as an offering. They are too poor to also lay flowers. 'He really liked salmon. When there was salmon in the rice porridge, you could see how much he liked eating it.'

"A soldier, thinking about the friend who was unable to savor the fall of Wuhan, tenderly sets down a fork for him. On the First of December, the wind is cold on these soldiers' cheeks. Already a month and a half has passed since Wuhan fell." Photograph: *PWR*.

54-56. *PWR* 44, 14 December 1938, pp. 2-3. "A Handful of Tears for a Warrior." The wooden stave marking the grave says: "Grave of an unknown Chinese soldier." The text pertains to all three photographs (numbered clockwise from top right) and reads,

"Even after capturing Wuhan, the Imperial Army has not slackened its pace in pursuing the fleers, smashing the defeated Chinese army wherever they run, and scoring many military successes. The enemy has retreated from Changsha and from the Liyang region, by way of land and by way of water, and a recent battleground on the continent was littered with the countless bodies of tens of thousands of dead Chinese soldiers.

"They have vanished like the dew on the battlefield, the corpses of these dead enemy soldiers who will take up arms no more and speak no more, and only the wind, to no avail, smells raw and alive. It is merciless, and pitiful beyond words.

"Having found a few minutes of free time, our officers and men have erected this grave to an unknown Chinese soldier, and brought Chinese POWs here to put their hands together before the offerings of wildflowers . . . thanks to the [morally] beautiful, meticulous humanity (*nasake*) of the Japanese warrior (*bushi*), the soul of the fallen enemy soldier is now resting in the earth."

This photoessay contains several layers of meaning, the primary being that the Japanese soldier (here referred to as *bushi* rather than the usual *heitai*) is inheritor and guardian of the samurai ethos of Bushido, a loosely codified *jus in bello*. Although the rank and file of the army came mainly from peasant stock, the modern Japanese soldier embodied the noble traditions of his spiritual forebears and like them, he treats the enemy dead with respect. A second, unsubtle subtext wordlessly renounces Chinese and international accusations of Japanese atrocities in China. And from both of these messages comes a third—that Japanese on the home front need not worry about the spiritual well-being of the soldier on the front, who may be battle-hardened and war weary, but who has not lost his humanity and will therefore always be "a member of the invincible Imperial Army and an outstanding member of society," as promised in "Look Lively!"

57-62. *PWR* 46, 4 January 1939, pp. 8-9. "Exploding with Laughter: Camp Talent Show, Guangzhou." Army life included good, clean, Japanese fun. The layout mimics a theater floor plan; the photographs are numbered and the captions begin in the top right corner and move across the three arched rows.

(top row, right corner, p. 8) "1. What soldiers want most, after food and sleep, is—laughter. What we might think is the simplest and dullest entertainment makes the soldiers feel a hundred times better. The [unnamed] Platoon, Guangzhou Street Patrol, put on an original show they created and performed on a small stage at the front."

(top row, left corner, p. 9) "2. In the garden of the masterless [i.e., abandoned] house of some Chinese, a makeshift stage has been put up. The stage is made from beer crates, the curtains from the soldiers' good-luck flags. The first performance to bring on the warriors' applause was the continental version of a kagura dance, 'Getting Rid of Chiang Kai-shek.'"

(middle row, right, p. 8) "'3. Now, why is it that 'Naniwabushi' always has the most fans? Don't laugh at me. My kimono's got the crest of the world-famous invincible Japanese army.' This comic tale (rakugo) is Soldier Second Class Tōraiken Hiromaru's *A Record of the Way to Bias Bay*."

(middle row, center, pp. 8-9) "4. Concert for violin and harmonica. These two, who only knew of the camp performance three days ago, secretly bought the violin and the harmonica from a Chinese second-hand store."

(middle row, left, p. 9) "5. The program has finally advanced to the major attraction, *The Lullaby of Akagi*. The backdrop is a tent, the temporary stage is put together from signboards, the actors' wigs are made of black cloth and horse tail hair—but the swords are bona fide, genuine articles."

(bottom row, pp. 8-9) "6. Laughter, which knows no bounds, arises spontaneously among them all, from the platoon leader down to the first-class soldier. And yet, just a month ago, the men who became famous on this stage were the heroes of the [censored] Platoon that gained renown for the fierce mopping up operations along the northern bank of the Zhu River." Photographs: Ōyake Sōichi.

63. *PWR* 153, 27 January 1941, p. 31. "From Our Personal Albums." This entire issue of *PWR* announced that it had been "edited by the troops." It included two pages of photographs and sketches taken from soldiers' scrapbooks. Many soldiers sent to China kept scrapbooks during their tour of duty. These scrapbooks were sometimes quite artistic and literary, other times the crude repository of exotic souvenirs and curiosities. Some soldiers' private photographs recorded abuses and even atrocities. This article bolstered the notion that life in the army was an adventure. Notice the photograph in the center of the bottom row with the painted sign, "Down with Chiang Kai-shek, Assist [continues out of frame]."

PWR refined the image of the Japanese soldier in print media with photoessays depicting soldiers' training, lifestyle, actions, spiritual and physical well-being, and the goals and guidelines defining battle. What emerged was the soldier as human being and the soldier as superhuman. A similar effort on the part of *PWR*'s editors and artists weeded out images of soldiers (such as those seen in other publications) that did not fit the mold, a process requiring two or three years because there were 16,788 different active periodicals registered in Japan in 1937, although this number would be reduced to 13,556 in 1941, 10,420 in 1942, 3,081 in 1943, and just 942 in 1944.[23] When the CIB began publishing *PWR*, the image of the "ideal" soldier was not set. For instance, in 1938, *PWR* still accepted commercial advertising such as the "crossover" patriotic advertisement for Meiji caramels (figure 64) incorporating a cartoon of a child playing soldier. Later in the war, *PWR* employed some of Japan's most famous cartoonists, who depicted soldiers as the CIB saw fit. Other magazines would come to realize that their survival depended upon taking cues from the CIB and its flagship publication, *PWR*, designers of the "look" of the soldier, and the "look" of the war.

64. *PWR* 36, 19 October 1938, inside back cover. This advertisement for Meiji caramels, a candy still on the market today, incorporated a cartoon by "Shio." The humor pokes fun at a backward Chinese (identified by the Chinese Nationalist insignia on his helmet) who had never seen a gas mask before. In reality, there is nothing humorous about the use of poison gas, and with gas masks being distributed by the tens of thousands in Japan, making light of an ill-fitting mask ran counter to the government's objective of civilian air defense. Cartoons, scarce in the early issues of *PWR*, were a regular weekly feature from 1942 until the end of the war. The frames read from top to bottom, beginning at top right.

(1) "Oh my gosh! I'm starting to cry. It must be poison gas." (2) "I better put on my gas mask." (3) "It's a little too big for me." (4) Chinese soldier: "Yow! It's a monster!" Boy: "Charge!" (5) "They thought I was a monster and they all ran away." (6) "I put the medal I received on my mask."

65 and 66. (left) *Weekly Asahigraph Special Report: China Incident Pictorial Report* 9, 5 December 1937, back cover. "An advancing soldier, dangling from his neck two chickens bought at the house of a Chinese family." Photographs like this suggest alternative interpretations, and were sometimes reprinted by Chinese, with very different captions, and included in anti-Japanese tracts. Indeed, for Japanese troops, often forced to "live off the land" when on maneuvers, to have "bought" this or other food from a Chinese family would have been rare. The international community roundly condemned Japanese atrocities in China once reports from the Battle of Shanghai began to appear in the world's newspapers in the autumn of 1937.

(right) *PWR* 44, 14 December 1938. The accompanying text is in the form of a dialogue between a cameraman for the Cabinet Information Section (which would become a Bureau in 1940), and a typical soldier. "Cameraman and soldier at the front on the [Asian] Continent. Soldier: 'Oh, are you going to take a picture of me while I'm eating . . . uh, well, is this all right?' Cameraman: 'Yes, that's fine, stay just the way you are.' (Seeing the cameraman's armband) 'Say, you're with the photographic crew from the Cabinet Information Section.' 'Yes. I'm with *Photographic Weekly Report.*' 'Gee, you don't want to take a picture of a battle-worn guy like me.'" Images like this one from the early stage of the war offered photographic "proof" that the boys at the front in China were eating well because they were being supplied with provisions. This soldier eats rice from his mess kit, rather than a Chinese family's chickens. Comparing this photograph of a soldier's dinner to *Asahigraph*'s suggests this plump-cheeked soldier might be a model sitting in a suburban Tokyo field.

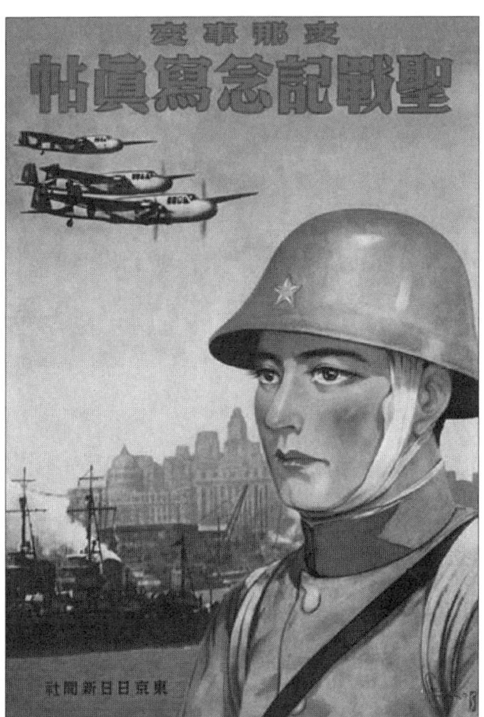

67 and 68. (left) *Commemorative Photographic Album of the Sacred War, the China Incident*, 1 July 1938. This magazine-format newspaper insert appeared on the first anniversary of the outbreak of the China war. The front cover reproduces a full-color collage that is part photograph, part drawing. The highly romanticized, feminized soldier with ruby red lips, large eyes, and bright red cheeks, was drawn by Iwata Sentarō (1901-1974), an artist famous for his "beautiful women" pictures (*bijinga*), and may have been inspired by the Takarazuka all-female troupe of performers, who staged musicals recreating heroic battles in China. This fanciful collage brings together the key elements of the Battle of Shanghai: the naval bombardment from the port, the Shanghai skyline, the Japanese navy air force planes that dropped bombs on the city, the soldier. The collage lacks a unifying narrative, though, depending on Iwata's beautifully drawn soldier for its visual appeal.

(right) *PWR* 21, 6 July 1938. The vertical banner announces, "First Anniversary of the China Incident," while the caption explains that "On the front cover is the official new uniform." Photograph by Kimura Ihee. The first close-up image of a soldier to be placed on a *PWR* cover was this youth with handsome features, reminiscent of the beautiful lad (*bishōnen*) who was a stock character of late Edo period kabuki plays and popular romantic novels, a character women dote on. He holds his rifle-bayonet upright, in the posture of a sentry, but he turns away from the field he patrols and peers directly into the camera and into the eyes of the viewer, one human being to another.

69 and 70. (left) *Weekly Asahigraph Special Report: China Incident Pictorial Review* 24, 15 November 1938. "Invasion of Hankou Commemorative Issue." This brightly colored drawing of a Japanese soldier owes much to social realism and proletarian art, which was fashionable among Japanese leftists in the 1920s and 1930s. In this treatment of a charging soldier, the legs are in an impossibly high leaping action and the facial features are exaggerated by fierceness. The smoke-filled battle scene is narrative in quality: a full-scale battle, with charging troops and planes overhead, is under way, and this soldier carries a Japanese flag for good luck, which drags behind him like a tail. The image invites the viewer to imagine an exciting story about bravery on the front as a soldier leads the charge into the enemy line.

(right) *PWR* 20, 29 June 1938, p. 23. "Charge! The Sacred War Brightens East Asia." This (originally color) poster commemorating the first anniversary of the China Incident was reproduced on a smaller scale in black and white as the inside back cover of *PWR*. This charging soldier displays a certain restraint: his facial features are barely discernible, and his crouching run shows both urgency and a respect for the enemy's bullets. Whether he is moving to attack or performing reconnaissance is unclear; all that matters is that as he advances, his movement mirrors that of the Japanese flag, and he therefore advances the national cause. The field could be clouds of dust on the battlefield, or clouds in the heavens where the spirits of warrior-gods reside. The lack of a specific site invites the viewer to meditate upon and internalize the values at play—loyalty, patriotism, self-sacrifice—values that support Japan's national greatness (kokutai) and the destiny of the Yamato race as world leaders.

A state of permanent war was realized in Japan less than a decade after the Manchurian Incident. The culmination of the militarization of Japanese government and society was General Tōjō Hideki's appointment as prime minister in October 1941.[24] He served simultaneously as prime minister, army minister, and home minister. A nation engaging in permanent war required a strong military and a carefully constructed and controlled image of the soldier. The "noble warrior" of the late 1930s was no different from his Meiji era forebears in waging war only for the sake of "peace and justice," but he now fought for longer periods of time, not only as a combatant but as an invader and occupier, a colonizer and civilizer—indeed, as an ambassador of the Great Japanese Empire. His comportment off the battlefield was as important in advancing Japan's foreign policy as was his valor in battle.

By 1940, with the Japanese press in its fourth year of covering permanent war, military service was more than just a rite of passage; it was nearly a prescribed way of life for able-bodied men. The exception became the norm as tours of duty grew longer and physically fit men could be called up for a second tour of duty. Young men and even men nearing middle age might only temporarily return to society, if they returned at all. Japan's servicemen were as loyal and brave as ever, of course, and the machismo they displayed as the decade began, their "fighting spirit," burned just as brightly at decade's end, but its light was no longer merely the mark of Japanese manhood, it was the badge of honor of the "noble warrior" engaged in "holy war." The soldier was the prototypical citizen in Japan at war, and as such his actions and attitudes were expected to embody the highest ideals of the nation. The same logic applied to the home front, which was expected to emulate the soldier. The figure of the noble warrior became a powerful tool in domestic policies and programs mobilizing the entire nation, as the men, women, and children on the home front became "the people behind the man behind the gun."

Notes

1. After the fall of the Qing Dynasty in 1911 and the establishment of the Chinese Republic in 1912, Japanese writers frequently referred to China as "Shina." For centuries, the Japanese referred to China as "Chūgoku," employing the same characters used by the Chinese. *Kōjien*, a standard Japanese dictionary, states that "'Shina,' derived from 'shin,' is the word foreigners use when referring to China. It first appeared in Buddhist scriptures in India, and was used in Japan from the mid-Edo period until the end of World War II." This pedigree notwithstanding, in Japanese, "Shina" is a pejorative word, associated with the colonization of China by the Western powers and the troubled period of Sino-Japanese relations, from World War I to the end of the Pacific War. Today, the word is occasionally encountered in Japan, where it conjures up nostalgia for the early Shōwa era. ("Shina soba" is "old-fashioned ramen.") Throughout this book, wherever "China" appears in translation, the Japanese is "Shina," just as a "Chinese" person is a translation of "Shinajin." For a detailed analysis of Japanese notions of "Shina," see Stefan Tanaka, *Japan's Orient: Rendering Pasts into History* (Berkeley: University of California Press, 1993).

2. The Japanese government announced the end of the China war when a puppet state was established in 1940 under Wang Jingwei, although the war in China truly never abated, reaching a new crescendo of violence in 1944. From the Chinese perspective, the War Against Japanese Aggression ended with Japan's surrender in 1945. John Dower notes that the Japanese government's official figure for Japanese deaths in the China war from 1937 to 1941 totaled 185,647. See *War Without Mercy: Race and Power in the Pacific War* (New York: Pantheon, 1986), p. 297.

3. Several historians have noted that the war in China was not well received on the home front, despite the outpouring of patriotic sentiment. "Toward the end of 1933, national policy remained in flux, with Manchukuo undigested and enthusiasm for the war beginning to wane" (Herbert P. Bix, *Hirohito and the Making of Modern Japan* [New York: HarperCollins, 2000]), p. 273. The Japanese people "found little exuberance in trudging off to fight the Chinese. Not only were people preoccupied with internal matters, but they also knew that there had been little provocation and that Japan's more likely enemies were to be found elsewhere. The lack of exhilaration among the public helps explain why the government labored so hard at spiritual mobilization and why the movement, from start to finish, had such a humorless mien" (Thomas R. H. Havens, *Valley of Darkness: The Japanese People and World War II* [New York: Norton, 1978]), p. 12. When the mastermind of the February 26 Incident, Kita Ikki, was executed "On August 19, 1937, . . . the Japanese people shared his spirit of bitter cynical fatalism" (David Bergamini, *Japan's Imperial Conspiracy* [London: Panther, 1971]), p. 659. Ienaga Saburō notes that several prominent intellectuals, some moderate Diet members, and Japanese communists questioned the reasons and goals of the war. See *The Pacific War, 1931-1945* (New York: Pantheon, 1978), pp. 86-87, 110-111, 116-121.

4. This Incident, manufactured by the Japanese navy, resulted in fierce fighting with heavy Japanese losses. It began when a group of Chinese supposedly attacked a group of Japanese Nichiren priests on 18 January 1932 in Shanghai. This prompted the Japanese navy to land marines from its Shanghai Fleet on 28 January. They quickly engaged China's Nineteenth Route Army. Heavy fighting ensued, and the navy had to call upon the army for reinforcements. All-out war between Japan and China was narrowly averted when a cease-fire was negotiated, through the offices of the British, on 5 May.

5. Also known as the Shanhaiguan Incident. Japanese troops occupied Shanhaiguan, the entrance to Jehol Province, on 1 January 1933. Two days later, a Japanese soldier was allegedly hit but a bullet fired by a Chinese from atop the Great Wall. A Japanese armored train forced its way through the tunnel in the wall, and troops followed, killing thousands of sleeping Chinese in Shanhaiguan. The Kwantung Army occupied all of Jehol Province by the first week of March.

6. Japanese coverage of the Sino-Japanese and Russo-Japanese Wars employed illustrations drawing upon the stylistic traditions of ukiyo-e. At the time, photographs were still uncommon in the mass media because printing technology made high-quality mass reproduction prohibitively expensive. John W. Dower, in his "Introduction" to Japan Photographers Association, *A Century of Japanese Photography* (New York: Pantheon, 1980), notes that at the time of the Russo-Japanese War, "elaborate woodblock prints were still a major medium through which the war was presented to the Japanese public" (p. 12). Kaneko Ryūichi concurs: "Photographs had not yet risen to [the] prominence [enjoyed by woodblock prints] during the wars with China and Russia, largely because they were unable to capture the scenes of intense battle that could be depicted by woodblock prints," (p. 187). See "Realism and Propaganda: The Photographer's Eye Trained on Society," in Anne Wilkes Tucker, Dana Friis-Hansen, Kaneko Ryūichi, and Takeba Joe, *The History of Japanese Photography* (New Haven, CT: Yale University Press, 2003), pp. 184-194.

7. One researcher of war photography claims that the Spanish Civil War, "coinciding with the establishment of the great picture magazines of the thirties, was the first war to be extensively and freely photographed for a mass audience, and marks the establishment of modern war photography as we know it. It was also the first modern war in which foreign involvement was critical. Whether to intervene in Spain was a question theoretically tied to public opinion, at least in the foreign democracies, and since this opinion was informed at least as much by images as by texts, the press photographs of the Spanish Civil War can be understood as weapons rather than simple illustrations" (Caroline Brothers, *War and Photography: A Cultural History*, [London: Routledge, 1997], p. 2). The assertion that photographs were crucial weapons in molding public opinion worldwide certainly holds true for the production and reception of Japanese and Chinese photographs covering the conflict that began in Manchuria in 1931.

8. The Japanese text reads, "Rokoku ryōmin no gyakusatsu shitai."

9. A slightly different version of these events appears in the English translation of Ienaga. "Lest censorship make the war seem vague and far off, the government churned out fabricated stories to drum up enthusiasm. The famous Three Human Bombs of the Shanghai fighting was a notorious example. Three engineer soldiers were accidentally killed by a short fuse on a charge they set. Intelligence operative Tanaka

Ryūkichi concocted the story that the men had wrapped explosives around themselves and died heroic deaths in a valiant assault on the enemy." See *The Pacific War*, p. 102. We may never know if the men were sent out with explosives charges that went awry or if they managed to light a massive missile like that pictured in figure 10. We do know that they acted on orders and that the official version of events was a fabrication designed as a cover up of a botched military operation and a ploy to buy public sympathy for dubious military goals in China. As a media event, the Three Human Bullets has a modern-day parallel in the equally cynical and mendacious story that made friendly fire victim Corporal Patrick Tillman a war hero of Afghanistan in 2002.

10. NACSIS lists seven books about the Three Human Bullets, all published within a year of the event, not including the *Manga Human Bullets* described in this chapter.

11. Saza-chō, in northern Nagasaki Prefecture, was the hometown of one of the three heroes, Kitagawa Susumu, and is still home to the "Three Human Bullets Memorial." See Chapter 9, figure 12, for a statue of the Three Human Bullets at Seishō Temple on Atagosan, Minato Ward, Tokyo.

12. Bix, *Hirohito and the Making of Modern Japan*, pp. 251-252. Ienaga cites the 1908 law criminalizing surrendering on the battlefield. "It was absolutely forbidden in the Japanese army to withdraw, surrender, or become a prisoner of war. The 1908 army criminal code contained the following provisions: 'A commander who allows his unit to surrender to the enemy without fighting to the last man or who concedes a strategic area to the enemy shall be punishable by death.'" Furthermore, "The Field Service Code, issued in 1941 over Tōjō Hideki's signature as army minister, contained the injunction 'Do not be taken prisoner alive'" (*The Pacific War*, p. 49).

13. One former soldier recollects the sorry state of soldiers' remains returning to Japan in 1942, and the dilemma posed by boxes with decedents' names on them but no remains inside. "Unable to face the greater sadness of families with no remains inside the boxes and believing that the heroic war dead would rest in peace better, we decided to take a few fragments of remains from other boxes. All the while fearing that it was wrong to deceive the bereaved families, we divided the fragments of bones into different boxes, our hands trembling" (Frank Gibney, *Sensō*: *The Japanese Remember The Pacific War* [Armonk, NY: M. E. Sharpe, 1995], pp. 34-35).

14. Mikiso Hane, *Peasants, Rebels, and Outcastes: The Underside of Modern Japan* (New York: Pantheon, 1982), p. 126. Hane notes this account was published in *Tsuchi to Furusato, VII*: 12off. (1976-1977), part of a collection of different authors writing on the difficulties facing Japanese farmers in the early twentieth century. As a proletarian writer, Shimomura Chiaki (1893-1955) was particularly interested in recording the lives of the downtrodden. No earlier published version of Shimomura's account has been located. Such a work surely would have been all but unpublishable until after the war.

15. Barak Kushner describes humorous *rakugo* routines centering on life in the military at this time. See *The Thought War: Japanese Imperial Propaganda* (Honolulu: University of Hawai'i Press, 2005), pp. 89-90.

16. Also referred to as the Marco Polo Bridge Incident or the Second Sino-Japanese War, it began when Japanese and Chinese troops exchanged shots on the outskirts of Beijing. The earliest Japanese reports on this affair dubbed it, "The North China Incident" (Hokushi jiken). A cease-fire was reached almost immediately, but a fresh incident occurred on the night of July 29, when Chinese troops killed two hundred Japanese residents in a small city near Beijing. Japan began an all-out invasion of Shanghai on 13 August. The Battle of Shanghai was fought fiercely for nearly three months. By mid-November, when Chinese Nationalist forces had withdrawn, three square miles of the city had been reduced to rubble and a quarter of a million Chinese were dead. Japanese casualties totaled nine thousand dead and thirty-one thousand wounded.

17. Asahi simultaneously published two periodicals that covered the China war. The first was the weekly *Asahigraph*, first published in 1923 and anticipating the size, layout, and use of photography of the American magazine *Life*, published thirteen years later. Kaneko suggests that the format of *Asahigraph* may have been patterned after the *New York Times Midweek Pictorial* ("Realism and Propaganda: The Photographer's Eye Trained on Society," in Anne Wilkes Tucker, Dana Friis-Hansen, Kaneko Ryūichi, and Takeba Joe, *The History of Japanese Photography* [New Haven, CT: Yale University Press, 2003], p. 188).

In July 1937, the weekly *Asahigraph* began carrying a subtitle, *Pictures of the War Front in China* (*Shina sensen shashin*), and this subtitle was numbered, so that weekly *Asahigraph,* volume 29, issue 26, is also titled *Pictures of the War Front in China* number 23. The weekly *Asahigraph / War Front in China* continued to carry domestic news, popular interest stories, movie reviews, and comics. A second Asahi periodical devoted entirely to the China war was called *Weekly Asahigraph Special Report: China Incident Pictorial Report* (*Shūkan Asahi rinji sōkan: Shina jihen gahō*); it appeared as frequently as the war news warranted, at intervals of from five days to three weeks, from 1937 to 1940. The first two issues were called *North China Incident Pictorial Report* (*Hokushi jihen gahō*); the third, *Japan-China Incident Pictorial Report* (*Nisshi jihen gahō*); and from the fourth, the name became *China Incident Pictorial Report.*

18. Because Japanese military units comprised recruits from the same locale, men from one village or county often served together. The three human bombs were all from northern Kyūshū, for instance. Hino Ashihei's semiautobiographical novel *Wheat and Soldiers* (New York: Farrar and Rinehart, 1939) provides many insights into the local color that flavored soldiers' interactions within one unit. Local and regional rivalries were often reflected in units competing against each other for the greatest glory.

19. The Foreign Ministry, which oversaw the Japanese Press Corps (Dōmei Tsūshin) maintained its independence from the CIB, producing its own publications regarding foreign affairs, most notably the domestic monthlies *Dōmeigraph* (*Dōmeigurafu*) and *Dōmei Global Weekly Report* (*Dōmei sekai shūhō*). It also oversaw the production of several foreign-language publications designed to further Japan's cause overseas. The army and navy maintained their own information agencies, which funneled their photographs and news stories to the public through Dōmei and the CIB. Each published its own books about the war, detailing battle histories and cataloguing the artwork produced under their auspices. In army-occupied areas, the Army Information Corps produced its own publications for local residents, including newspapers and magazines (usually printed in Japanese and the predominant language of the occupied land).

20. Ienaga writes, "The Cabinet Information Committee's [i.e., Bureau's] notice entitled 'The Treatment of News about the Present Situation' informed the media that: 'It is expected that you will exercise self-restraint and not print statements that in any way damage our national interests or impair international trust.' Examples were: 'Antiwar or antimilitary opinions or news items that reduce civilian support for the military'; 'articles that might give the impression that our foreign policy is aggressive'; 'in reporting the views of foreign newspapers, especially the Chinese press, articles which slander Japan, articles contrary to our national interests, or opinions which approve or affirm such negative statements, and items which may confuse the general public's understanding of issues.'" See *The Pacific War, 1931-1945*, p. 100.

21. Ienaga (*The Pacific War, 1931-1945*, pp. 52, 187) and Gibney (*Sensō*, p. 24) partly blame the brutality of boot camp, one of the formative experiences of Japanese soldiers, for the prevalence of atrocities they committed. For first-hand accounts of the severe treatment of recruits and junior soldiers, see Haruko Taya Cook and Theodore F. Cook, *Japan at War: An Oral History* (New York: New Press, 1992) p. 42; Midori Yamanouchi and Joseph L. Quinn, trans., *Listen to the Voices from the Sea* (Scranton: University of Scranton Press, 2000), pp. 34, 49, 53-54, 76; and Gibney, *Sensō*, pp. 27, 28, 30, 31, 41-43, 53, 54.

22. This photograph could not have been published in wartime Japan, but its widespread distribution in the West (and in Western colonies in Asia) meant Japanese travelers might see it. Kushner states this photograph reached an audience of 136 million in just a few weeks through its publication in *Time*, its distribution through the International News Service, and newsreels. See *The Thought War,* p. 211, n74.

23. Gregory J. Kasza, *The State and the Mass Media in Japan, 1918-1945* (Berkeley: University of California Press, 1988), p. 224.

24. Many historians prefer the term, "the Fifteen Year War" (1931-1945), because they analyze the events of 1931 and 1937 as part of the same Japanese expansionist war that led to Pearl Harbor. The primary sources presented in this chapter certainly can be interpreted as supporting this viewpoint. Nevertheless, the Japanese mass media began to report on the China war as an ongoing engagement in 1937, in contrast to the brief "Incidents" of the early 1930s. For instance, prior to 1937, *Asahigraph*'s coverage of current events paid little attention to the military between "Incidents," and in examining issues from the first six years of the 1930s, there is no narrative of an ongoing military struggle in China or in Asia. Therefore, the present study follows the contemporary Japanese media in dating permanent war from 1937.

4. A PEOPLE UNITED IN SERVING THE NATION

In the autumn of 1937, the Japanese government reluctantly admitted that the fighting in China had become a protracted war, and made projections to conclude it within three years. These plans required a wide-reaching expansion of governmental control and a sweeping reorganization of society that would allow Japan's resources to be concentrated on the war effort. One of the central planks of this reform was the Citizens' Total Spiritual Mobilization movement (Kokumin Seishin Sōdōin),[1] launched in September 1937, a program that lasted for three years. Another was National Total Mobilization (Kokka Sōdōin), inaugurated in 1938, legislation allowing the government to requisition human and material resources for the war effort. Collectively, these and other policies of social reorganization were called "the New Order," (Shintaisei) which was promulgated on 3 November 1938, a holiday marking the Meiji Emperor's birthday. The New Order's success in regimenting the people behind the China war is debatable, but in conjunction with economic policies such as rationing and the banning of many "luxuries," it achieved a transformation of civilian life in three short years. This transformation was guided by an information revolution orchestrated by the government. The New Order paved the way, psychologically, for the radical changes to come in the months leading up to Pearl Harbor and the war with the West.

1. *PWR* 1, 16 February 1938, p. 2. A Railway Ministry poster promoting Citizens' Total Spiritual Mobilization, reproduced as the inside front cover of the inaugural issue of *PWR*. The vertical slogan in the upper right says, "Worship *kami* (gods), revere ancestors." The photograph reminds the viewer that Japan is the "Land of the Gods (kami)." The inverted L of half of a *torii* (gate) is reflected in the strong L of a tree branch above it. Together, they form a protective frame around the children in the distant field, and draw a strong visual link between the world of men and the world of kami and nature. This typical landscape scene is given a distinctively Japanese stamp by the prominence of the *torii*.

Government moves to more closely control information began in 1936 with the establishment of the Cabinet Information Committee (upgraded in 1937 to a Division and in 1940 to a Bureau [i.e., the CIB]).[2] Its first periodical appeared in November 1936, bearing the generic title, *Weekly Report* (*Shūhō*). The foreword of the first issue stated that the purpose of publishing the journal was "to ensure that the content and purport of the policies inaugurated by the Government are widely disseminated to the general citizenry and correctly understood by them." In February 1938, *Weekly Report* was joined by a second CIB-issued news periodical, *Photographic Weekly Report* (*PWR*, *Shashin shūhō*). *Weekly Report* was all text and no illustration, while *Photographic Weekly Report* was mainly pictures with a minimum amount of text.

A panoply of patriotic programs, movements, and laws loosely fell under the government's rubric of "service to the nation" and "supporting the war." Boosting Production Service to the Nation, Increasing Crops Service to the Nation, and Student Volunteer Corps Service to the Nation are just a few examples. While most of these lacked well-defined objectives, the government effectively deployed them to browbeat the citizenry in order to render them pliant and cow them into submission. Indeed, the brilliance of the Day of Service to the Nation was that its vagueness and malleability meant it was readily adaptable to the need of the moment. When the army was engaged in a particularly fierce battle, the Day of Service to the Nation would begin with early morning prayers for victory at the neighborhood Shinto shrine, perhaps followed by

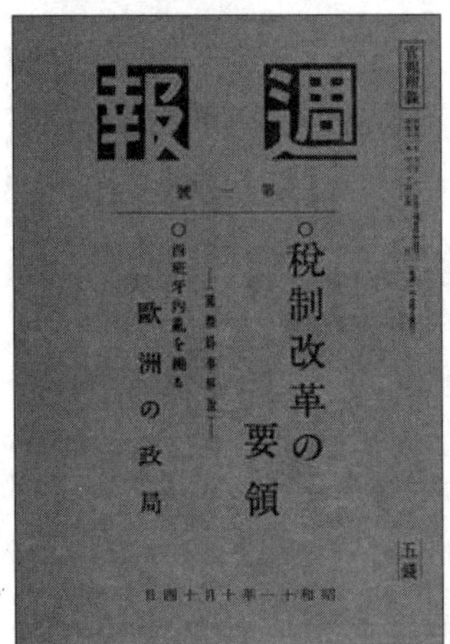

2-4. (left) The front cover of *Weekly Report* 1, 14 October 1936, with headlines about tax system reforms and European politics in light of the Spanish Civil War. This staid appearance changed little in nearly nine years of publication. When the China war began in July 1937, *Weekly Report* included small (3-by-4-inch), grainy photographs. Photographs disappeared from *Weekly Report* once *PWR* appeared in February 1938.

(middle) *Weekly Report* 41, 28 July 1937, p. 1. The first photograph to appear in *Weekly Report*. "Troops Occupying Beijing Raise the Rising Sun Flag."

(right) *Weekly Report* 41, 28 July 1937, p. 4. "Soldier on Patrol at the Front."

5 and 6. (top) *PWR* 23, 13 July 1938, p. 2. Attractive young women, wearing Western dresses and sporting permanent waves (which would be banned later that year), hold up copies of *Weekly Report* and *PWR*, the "National Policy Pamphlet and National Policy Graphic." This advertising image was reproduced on posters and postcards.

(bottom) *PWR* 25, 3 August 1938, p. 23. Yamaguchi Katsuichi of Nagoya submitted this winning entry in a readers' contest to design a poster to advertise *PWR* and its sister publication, *Weekly Report*. The two magazines have been rolled up to look like gun barrels. Beneath the barrel with *PWR*'s logo is written, "National Policy Graphic, 10 sen a copy" and beneath *Weekly Report*, "National Policy Pamphlet, 5 sen a copy." Over seven hundred twenty entries were received in this first CIB-sponsored poster contest. During the three years of the Spiritual Mobilization Movement, *PWR* encouraged the public to participate in the creation of promotional images, challenging them to demonstrate their grasp of the government's goals. Once *PWR* quickly won a large following, the CIB no longer promoted its sales.

7. *PWR* 1, 16 February 1938. The inaugural issue of *PWR* was released to coincide with the anniversary of the Founding of the Japanese Nation (Kigensetsu, 12 February) by mythical emperor Jinmu. The cover photograph, "Singing to Mount Takachiho," is credited to the Railway Ministry, the International News Photography Federation, and the talented Kimura Ihee. This photograph announces the magazine's home front target with an image of schoolchildren singing the "Patriotic March" (the sheet music with a drawing of Mount Fuji on its cover) against the background of Mount Takachiho, site of Emperor Jinmu's descent from the heavens. The mid-air photograph of Takachiho places these children above the clouds, as if they were on the wing of an airplane, making the location of the overall photomontage the viewer's mental connection of the two images. This bold, sophisticated use of photomontage defies gravity in order to create a seamless bond between the mediated world of print media (the sheet music) and photographic "reality" (Mount Takachiho, the schoolchildren), and between print media and home front action (the children sing a patriotic song to Mount Takachiho, which appears suspended in the air beyond, above, and beneath them). These relationships linking patriotic children to "peerless" Fuji and primordial Takachiho suggest that *PWR* not only reflects the truth, but is the truth.

writing comfort letters to and making comfort packages for soldiers. When rice became scarce, the Day of Service to the Nation became a day without sake. So numerous were the government's wartime programs and policies and so onerous their names and slogans, that describing them one by one would be a tedious chore. However, in examining the pages of *PWR*, four distinct (but overlapping) areas of wartime domestic policy can be identified: first, maintaining physical fitness and health, the building block of a strong work force and civilian air defense; second, preparing the home and the family for air raids and training for civilian air defense; third, filling the military's war chest by increasing the level of national savings through purchases of insurance and government bonds, and by making sacrifices—forgoing luxuries, being thrifty, using ersatz or replacement materials, organizing the family and community efficiently, donating goods to precious metals and scrap drives, performing volunteer war work; and fourth, obeying authority, fostering the correct mental attitude toward the war effort, and being a model member of the Yamato race in all situations and at all times.

8. *PWR* 1, 16 February 1938, pp. 12-13. "Radio Calisthenics. The Rising Sun Flag. Mount Fuji. The healthy rhythm of junior citizens exercising in the midst of Nature (*daishizen*). Training the body. Uplifting the mind. Growing up tall and healthy. Oh. The youthfulness of Japan. The strength. This leap [forward]!" This photograph, "exclusive to this publication," curiously notes it has been "Approved by the Tokyo Kenpeitai." The unnamed photographer framed Fuji's peak dramatically off center, like many famous ukiyo-e. The staccato phrasing is evidently meant to reflect the children's thoughts while exercising. This centerfold of schoolchildren exercising on a hilltop facing Mount Fuji appeared in the first issue of *PWR*, the cover of which displayed a photomontage of schoolchildren singing to Mount Takachiho (figure 7).

Photoessays in the first issue of *PWR* announced the agenda of training the bodies and the minds of the population. The government inaugurated the "Citizens' Total Spiritual Mobilization" movement, and the "Day of Service to the Nation" was made the venue for spiritual mobilization. The lofty names of these programs disguised their lack of substance, but as the war progressed, exigency dictated how this precious time would be spent. Initially, the Day of Service was once a month and citizens were told to pray for victory at a Shinto shrine, since spiritual superiority was Japan's "secret weapon." A core component of spiritual mobilization was physical fitness, and people were encouraged to exercise to the beat of Radio Calisthenics (*Rajio taisō*)[3] broadcasts. *PWR* 24 (7 July 1938) included a broadsheet insert giving step-by-step instructions for the nationwide Radio Calisthenics demonstrations scheduled for Army Day (7 July), along with sheet music for the official tune by Horiuchi Keizō.

The radio was new, modern, and exciting in the 1930s, playing a vital role in disseminating information and uniting the population in common purpose and action. Like boot camp, the goal of Radio Calisthenics was conditioning the body while disciplining the mind and subjugating individual will to authority. Photographs of many individuals synchronized into one collective movement by the rhythm of Radio Calisthenics underscore this point. Radio Calisthenics became a tool of mass mobilization, mass organization, and mass psychology. When an entire neighborhood or village turned out at the appointed time to perform Radio Calisthenics, those who failed to participate were viewed with suspicion, especially when one group vied to outdo another in demonstrating patriotic fervor through exercise.

9. *PWR* 181, 13 August 1941, p. 17. "Twenty Thousand People Perform Radio Calisthenics. Kudanshita, Tokyo."

"Early on the morning of 1 August, approximately twenty thousand residents gathered on the grounds of Yasukuni Shrine in Kudanshita, where the souls of heroes sleep, and vigorously participated in the Radio Calisthenics Rally to Train the Mind and Body for Public Service toward the Development of Asia. They lead the vanguard on the first day of this session of the Citizens' Mental and Physical Training Movement for improving the physiques of citizens on the home front. This event was jointly sponsored by the Health and Welfare Ministry and by the Tokyo Prefectural, Tokyo Municipal, and National Radio Calisthenics Associations."

10 and 11. *PWR* 24, 7 July 1938. (top, pp. 12-13) City dwellers train on the beach, while country folk (image included in the article, but not shown here) train in the field or in the middle of the main street. Young or old, male or female, the movements are identical—and the same as those of GIs.

(bottom, p. 12) On Army Day, citizens and soldiers bent and flexed in unison to the beat of the same music printed beneath both photographs.

Air defense preparations began in Japan in 1928, when Osaka and Tokyo held their first drills, which made little impression on the population. Photographs of Japanese aerial bombardment of Chinese targets during the Shanghai Incident of 1932 (figures 5 and 6 in Chapter 3) carried conflicting messages for the Japanese civilian air defense program. On the one hand, these images showed the devastation of air raids; on the other hand, they demonstrated that Japan was master of the skies in Asia. When the Second Sino-Japanese War began, however, Japan needed to prepare for the possibility of an air attack from China or the Soviet Union. Japan's densely packed urban areas were particularly vulnerable to fire, since most buildings were wooden. The government therefore passed the Air Defense Law in October 1937. It did little more than order local governments to establish offices and committees that would provide the infrastructure through which the Home Ministry in Tokyo educated the public about air raid safety. The government devised a number of programs aimed at raising awareness about the hazards of aerial bombardments and poison gas attacks. The government's concerns about air safety were funneled through the CIB, and became "news" when *PWR* and other magazines created photoessays and articles detailing the dangers of air raids, the necessary preparations, and government directives and ordinances. The government's position on air defense was firm insistence on two fundamentals: civilians were responsible for defending their own homes and neighborhoods in the event of an air raid, and civilians were not to flee in the event of an attack but to stay and extinguish the fire.

12. *PWR* 14, 8 May 1938, p. 10. One photograph from an article, "The Police Protect the Imperial Capital during the [China] Incident," shows a policeman fitting a Tokyo family with gas masks.

In the late 1930s, citizens of France, Great Britain, and Germany made similar preparations. No one knew if poison gas would be used in another war, as it had been during World War I, and as Japan was doing (unbeknownst to the public) in its war against China. Being informed and prepared was the duty of every citizen and an important aspect of serving the nation.

PWR 29 explained the government's earliest directives for air defense, which amounted to little more than seeking safety in ferroconcrete buildings, such as schools, and the "duck and cover" formula. The article explained the proper response in different settings: the city block, the park, in a field, at home. The same issue carried an advertisement for gas masks manufactured by a private firm "under the approval of the Army Scientific Research Laboratory," and also featured Home Ministry photographs of different air defense equipment, including buckets, shovels, reed mats, cisterns of water and sand for fighting fires, and room-size cellophane bags and masking tape for securing homes against poison gas (figure 17). In 1942, households were required to have a minimum set of this equipment or be fined.

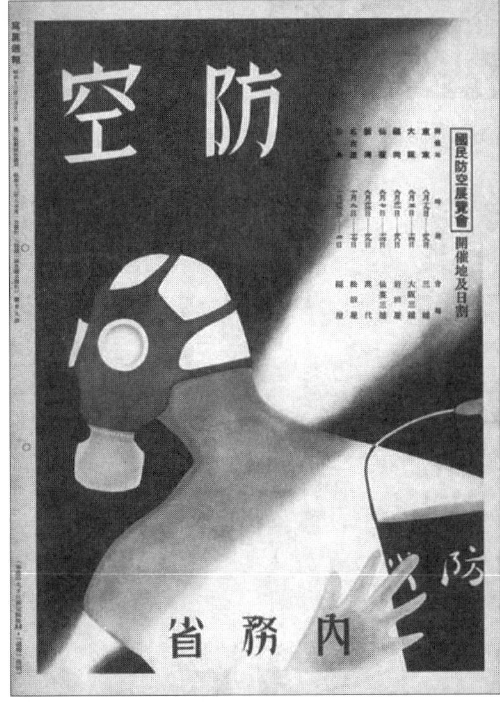

13 and 14. *PWR* 29, 31 August 1938, a special report on air defense.

(right) The front cover used a black and white photograph against a background color of bright fuchsia. "Oh! Air raid! A Women's Fire Defense Supervisor responds with determination when the siren wails. We ourselves must protect the country, we are being counted on to put on our gas masks and charge into the raging flames and the poison gas. Model: Tachibana Mieko of the Tōhō Theater." Photograph: CIB.

The apron and sash bearing the title, "Women's Fire Defense Supervisor," are the uniform of one of the women's patriotic associations with a nationwide organization and membership. The selection and naming of an actress as a model was very unusual in *PWR*. Hara Setsuko and other actresses frequently appeared in the advertisements in *Asahigraph* (see Chapter 5, figure 5), but *PWR*, with its focus on the home front, used average citizens and unknowns in its photographs.

(left) The back cover reproduces (in reduced dimension, and printed here in black and white) a Home Ministry poster announcing the schedule of a Citizens' Air Defense Exhibition touring major department stores in seven of Japan's largest cities, evidence of the cooperation between business and government. The mannequin-like, stylized figure in the poster is ultra-modern and in keeping with the high art-deco fashions of the late 1930s. Government posters did not prefer artwork like this, which would quickly disappear from *PWR*.

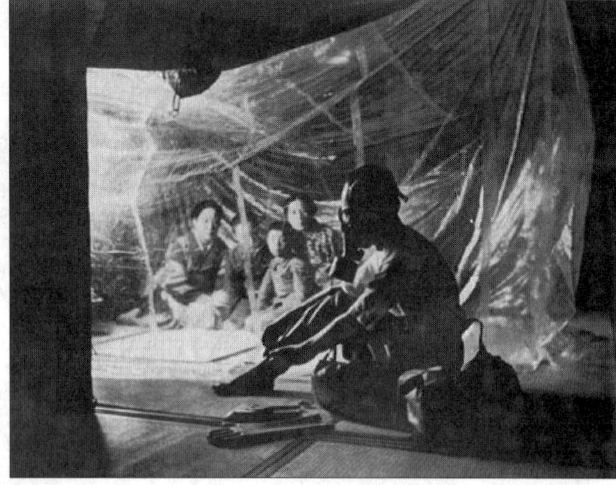

15-17. *PWR* 29, 31 August 1938, p. 8. What to do, and what not to do, when at home and the air raid siren sounds.

(top) "'Oh, no, it's the air raid siren!' If the man of the house starts rushing around looking afraid, then the frightened family follows him outside, looking up to the skies, their hearts racing with anxiety and curiosity. Were a bomb to fall in their vicinity, such a family that does nothing to prepare is just asking to be completely annihilated."

(middle) "To make matters worse, fear has made them lose their cool, and this is what they do. Let's be more careful and do what is normal under the circumstances: put things in their proper places, so that all the highly flammable things are in one place and all the important items are in another, keeping to a minimum any damage from a fire."

(bottom) "When the air raid siren sounds and there is no air raid shelter or air raid dugout nearby, prepare for a gas bomb. Children and the elderly take cover in the evacuation room, prepared in advance by completely stopping up any cracks or holes with paper. Those who are physically fit secure their gas suits and gas masks to their bodies, and guard the home. The cellophane anti-gas tent shown in this photograph will do for the time being, but gas masks are absolutely necessary to be thoroughly prepared against poison gas and the fire from a bomb." Photographs: CIB.

Two other photographs in this series show mother and father covering glass windows with straw floor mats (*tatami*) and clearing away removable sliding doors (*fusuma*), while older sister leads the younger siblings to the closest air raid shelter.

18-21. *PWR* 29, 31 August 1938, p. 5 and p. 7. The top two photographs are from the "In the City" air raid scenario (p. 5), the bottom two from "When Out in the Open" (p. 7).

(top) "When there is a building nearby with a basement, walk in an orderly fashion along the side of the building, and go into the basement. A basement may be unsafe without proper air defense preparations, so take appropriate action after listening carefully to the leader's precautions, and always be informed about evacuation procedures."

(second from top) "When riding on a train or in a car, follow orders from the authorities. When you come to a stop, take shelter in a nearby building. If there is no place to take shelter, hide under a bench. Never stick your head out of the window, or exit a moving vehicle."

(third from top) "When in an open field with no trees to hide behind, make use of a low-lying area or a ditch. However, panicking and 'sticking your head in the sand and leaving your tail uncovered,' like these two, won't do."

(bottom) "When a bomb falls and explodes, it burns in a funnel-shape, so if you are outside of its burn line, you will not be harmed. If possible, find a place lower than the surface of the ground and lie down." Photographs: CIB.

Citizens' Air Defense (*Kokumin bōkū*), a monthly magazine edited by the Military Authority for Central Japan, was launched on 24 July 1939, just days before World War II erupted in Europe. It gave detailed scientific analyses of everything pertaining to air defense equipment and air raid tactics; its advertisements for fire trucks suggest it was read by fire fighters. Images of the destruction that rained down on London during the Battle of Britain put the Japanese on notice that a better air defense program and more substantial bomb shelters were needed. All manner of civic groups began building community shelters according to plans supplied by the government, which admonished the people with terrifying visions of death and destruction from air raids, and chastised them with the voices of dead soldiers.

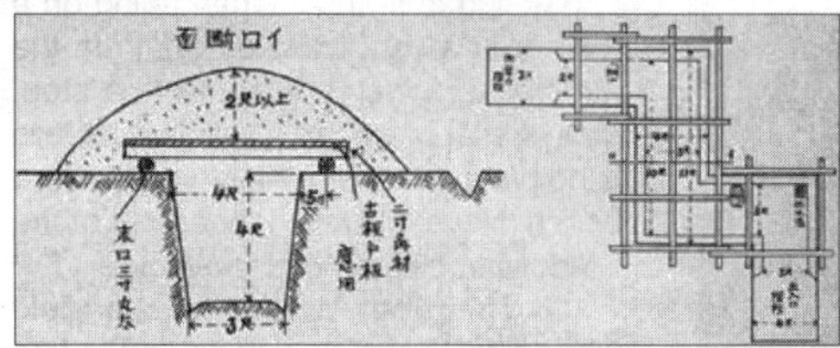

22-24. *PWR* 136, 2 October 1940, pp. 6-7. "The Neighborhood Association Bomb Shelter, Nakano, Tokyo." The women's brigade builds an air shelter under the supervision of Mr. Fujii, who shows them how to make the measurements and use shovels. Evidently, these women can spare ten hours in one day and perform hard manual labor.

(top left) The blueprint and cross-section for the community underground bomb shelter with exits on both ends of its zigzagging tunnel.

(bottom left) "It takes forty people, organized into four squads of ten people, ten hours to complete this air raid shelter accommodating a family of twelve. 'Well, how is it in there?'"

(right) "The air raid shelter is already 70 percent done, and the shovel is starting to get heavy and the breathing rough. 'Heave, ho! Catch your breath later!'" Photographs: Wakamatsu Fujio.

25. *PWR* 136, 2 October 1940, pp. 4-5. "If There Were an Air Raid on a Japanese City" at an imaginary "Shōwa-machi Crossing" and a fictitious Asahi Department Store during the early evening. The cutaway shows an underground air raid shelter (probably a subway station). The chilling text has been translated in its entirety. Illustration by Suzuki Gyōsui.

"One bomb is a direct hit on a corner of the lavishly built ferroconcrete Asahi Department Store, exploding thunderously as it smashes through all eight floors. Some 20 meters [65 feet] of the sales floor surrounding the epicenter are obliterated on all eight floors, and the wooden shops separated from the Asahi by the streetcar, like the Fuji Fruit Store on the corner, are mercilessly and completely destroyed, the fierce flames and explosion killing everyone inside.

"Another hit! This time, it explodes near the streetcar on the street in front of the main entrance to the Asahi Department Store. It is probably another 250-kilogram [550-pound] bomb. Automobiles in front of the store are blown four stories high by the blast. The streetcar is beyond recognition, of course, and the people running for cover on the street, as with all of the people within the entire circumference of 100 meters [328 feet] of the epicenter of the blast—in other words, everyone as far away from it as the Fuji shop—all of them meet a vicious end from the force of the blast or from shrapnel.

"The underground water pipes, gas pipes, and communications lines are destroyed. The air raid shelter in Taishō-machi, only 5 meters [16 feet] away from the explosion, is probably demolished, with everyone inside dying immediately. The [underground] air raid shelter beneath the Fuji shop is safe.

"Still it continues. Next an incendiary bomb punctures the roof of the two-storey chicken restaurant [right foreground], shooting up fierce pillars of flames 5 meters [16 feet] high. It is a 10-kilogram [22-pound] petroleum-based bomb. Look out! If left untended, it will become a huge fire! All of the members of the Shōwa-machi Neighborhood Association rush out of the air raid shelter, where they were taking refuge. They set up a bucket brigade, using water they prepared in advance, and desperately douse the flames. Less than thirty seconds elapse after the incendiary bomb fell and they begin their quick work. If the people of the Neighborhood Association hesitated for even a moment to rush to the scene, the situation would be much worse, but because they do not wait for the fire trucks to arrive, the fire is contained."

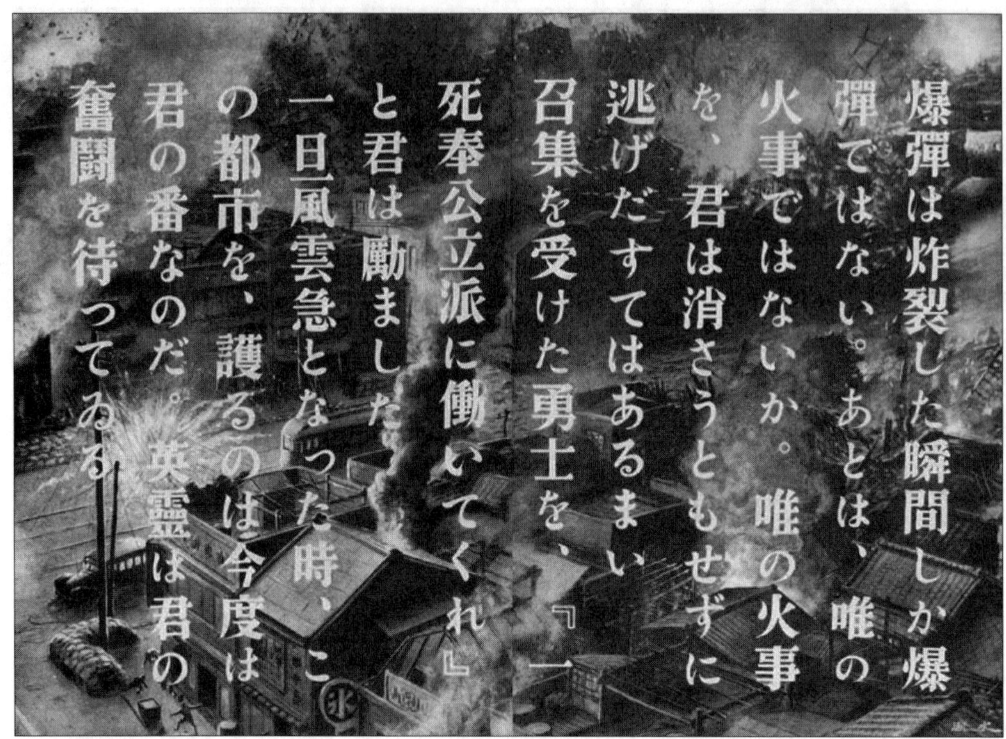

爆弾は炸裂した瞬間しか爆弾ではない。あとは、唯の火事ではないか。唯の火事を、君は消さうともせずに逃げだすてはあるまい召集を受けた勇士を、『一死奉公立派に働いてくれ』と君は励ました。一旦風雲急となった時、この都市を、護るのは今度は君の番なのだ。英霊は君の奮闘を待ってゐる

26. *PWR* 184, 3 September 1941, pp. 2-3. This two-page, poster-size message uses the voices of fallen soldiers to coerce the home front to do their part for air defense: "A bomb is only a bomb in the moment it explodes. After that, it is only a fire. And you wouldn't run away without trying to put out a mere fire, would you? You encouraged the brave warriors who were drafted, telling them to 'do your best job for us, so that your death serves the nation.' And now that the situation has grown serious, it is your turn to guard this city. The souls of fallen heroes are waiting for you to join the fight." Illustration: Suzuki Gyōsui.

The military operations in China were very costly, and with no end in sight to the China war, the government took several measures to fund the campaign. Government spending rose an astounding 2,000 percent from 1937 to 1944, most of it funded by Bank of Japan bonds.[4] The gross national product was increased through trade, with exports and imports both reaching a record level in 1940, and industry was shifted away from products unnecessary to the war effort and toward heavy industry and munitions. A related concern was funding the war, which the government achieved through a steady rise in inflation and through the increase of capital in the form of war bonds, insurance policies, and government savings programs. The goal was to increase the total amount of national savings, an ever-higher target reached through aggressive bond drives and nearly compulsory savings accounts, such as the Citizens' Savings Fund and postal savings, both monitored by the government and collected through different patriotic associations. Large withdrawals from these accounts required permission.

The opening paragraphs of a lengthy article in *PWR* 18 (15 June 1938, pp. 2-17), a special issue about "Serving the Nation Through Savings," tied the home front's savings drive to the soldiers at the front:

The brave, loyal officers and men of the Imperial Forces, who have made numerous noble sacrifices, continue the fight. They have already opened the way for our nation to achieve its highest mission, but the future is still full of many possibilities, and therefore we citizens must harden our unwavering determination in preparing for a long-term war.

If we now failed to supply the emperor's troops fighting at the front with all of the provisions—such as weapons, munitions, and medicine—that they need, or if the economy of we citizens on the home front weakened through inflation, then what would happen to Japan?

Were we to fail to pay attention to the government's loudly calling upon we citizens to "Serve the Nation through Savings," then such insecurities would take shape and become reality. In order to prevent this from happening, from this very moment today, we citizens should all join the "savings war" by taking up the rifle of savings and putting on the uniform of thriftiness.

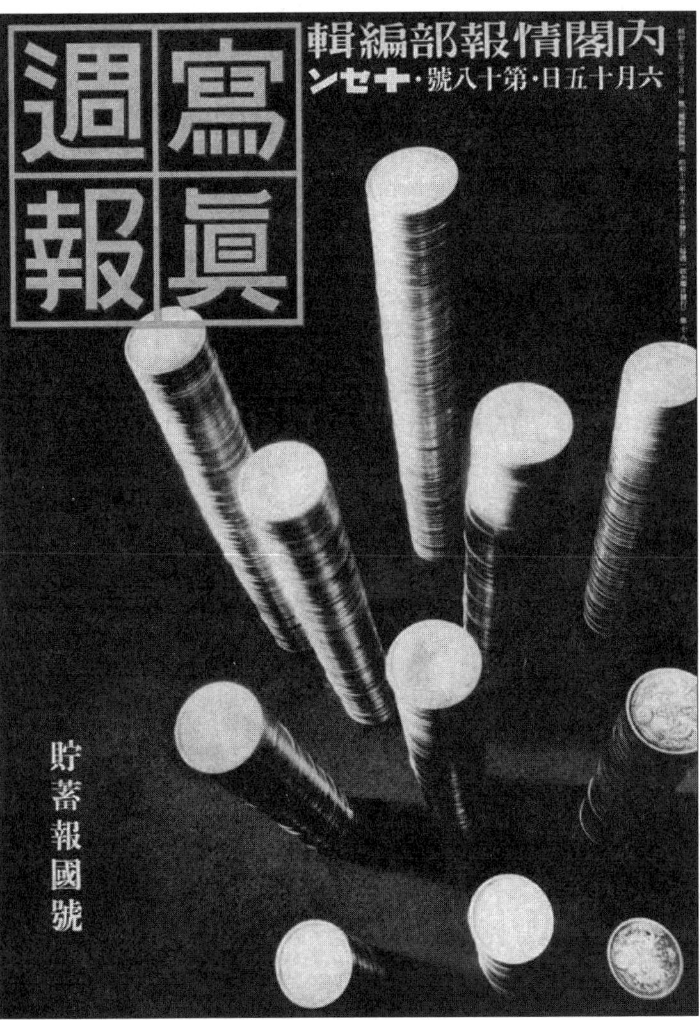

27. *PWR* 18, 15 June 1938. "Serving the Nation Through Savings." This compelling cover photograph carried no caption, its message clear: small coins add up to make large savings.

The silver 50-sen coin seen here was equivalent to about 15 US cents at the exchange rates of this time, although the coin was about the size of a quarter dollar (one hundred sen made one yen). The average daily wage for most types of labor was between 2 and 3 yen per day for men, depending on the industry. Women earned about 50 to 65 percent of men's wages. The average daily wage for a miner or transport worker was 2.3 yen for men, 0.96 yen for women. Those employed in light industry and manufacturing made less, those in heavy industry more. One of these stacks of about one hundred sixty coins had a value of 80 yen. All together, the average male laborer's annual earnings are represented in this picture. Photograph: *PWR* Exclusive.

Most issues of *PWR* contain an advertisement for some aspect of savings, insurance, or bonds, and some issues contain two, so there must be at least two hundred fifty different full-page advertisements in this publication alone. Financial institutions encouraged citizens to deposit savings, insurance companies hawked all manners of insurance against fire or battlefield death, and the government sold postal annuity funds and a variety of bonds in different denominations. Cosponsoring all of these efforts was the Finance Ministry. Many patriotic themes are explored in these advertisements, which must have been a boon for graphic artists during this era of photography.

The artwork of these posters drew upon universal themes: remembering the sacrifices of the men at the front, doing one's duty as a member of the group, investing in the future of the nation, and building a better world. No sooner would a national savings goal be reached than a new goal and a new campaign would be announced, so that the average family, which was depositing 11.6 percent of its annual earnings into savings in 1936, was saving 21.5 percent of its earnings in 1944, while the cost of living rose more than 20 percent each year between 1939 and 1945.[5] The standard of living sank as the consumer output fell from 136.5 percent in 1937 to 102.7 percent in August 1940 (on a par with the steady average of 100 percent reached in the early 1930s) to 40 percent in 1941, and a mere 17 percent by March 1945.[6]

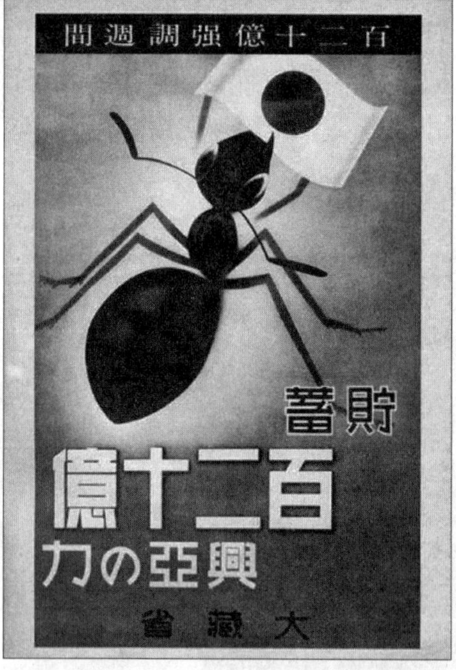

28 and 29. (left) *PWR* 73, 12 July 1939, inside front cover. A typical family and the slogan "One Hundred Million, One Mind." At bottom is the claim that "Ten Billion in Savings Comes from Insurance," a message from the Federation of Insurance Companies, the Finance Ministry, and the Commerce and Industry Ministry.

(right) *PWR* 122, 26 June 1940, inside front cover. A Finance Ministry poster announcing the goal of 12 billion yen in national savings. "The Power of Developing Asia." The selfless worker ant is industrious, indefatigable, and loyal to its group, and therefore an appropriate symbol of the Japanese citizen.

When war spread to the Pacific, the goal of national savings ballooned to 23 billion yen for 1942, and 27 billion yen for 1943. Japan's early victories in the Pacific were reflected in new confidence in war bond advertisements, which favored imagery of victory (Chapter 7, figures 56-58). By 1945, this goal had more than doubled again, reaching an astronomical 60 billion yen. With families struggling to survive in the final months of the war, bond campaigns were replaced with a lottery. *PWR* 372 (11 June 1945, p. 7) carried an article about the first series of the "Winning Ticket" lottery, explaining that "winning" signified both "winning the war" and "winning the lottery." These 10-yen "Winning Tickets" were put on sale in early July and fifteen days after the unspecified number of tickets were sold, a drawing determined the winners of the cash prizes. The first-prize winner received 110,000 yen, nine second-prize winners 10,000 yen, ninety third-place winners 1,000 yen, nine hundred fourth-prize winners 50 yen, and 19,100 fifth-prize winners 10 yen. Prizes had been given before, but not on this scale. For instance, in 1943, with the purchase of eleven two-yen "bullet bonds," the purchaser received one raffle ticket for an unspecified number of 1,000-yen first prizes. A few weeks after the surrender broadcast, the Bank of Japan announced it would not honor war bonds, and with currency devalued after the defeat, lottery winnings also became worthless.

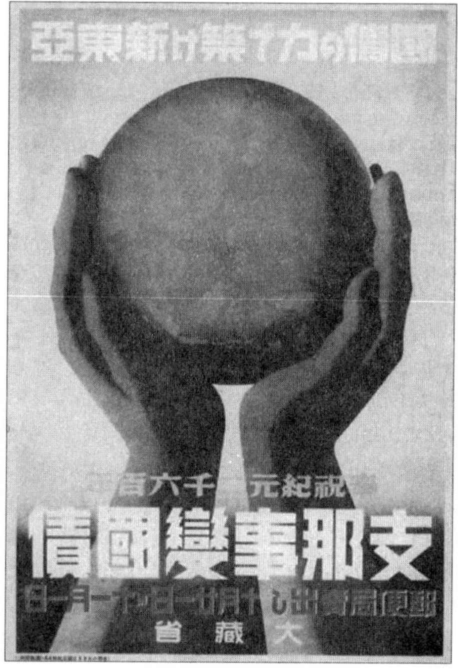

30 and 31. (left) *PWR* 103, 24 February 1940, back cover. Finance Ministry poster for China Incident Government Bonds: "For the Men at the Front—Ammunition! Food! Thermal Insulation!" A fallen soldier's cap towers over a pagoda representing China.

(right) *PWR* 137, 9 October 1940, back cover. Finance Ministry poster for China Incident National Bonds Commemorating the 2,600th anniversary of the founding of the nation. The simple, powerful design of a pair of hands holding the world with Asia turned toward the viewer reinforces the message across the top: "The Power of National Bonds Builds the New East Asia."

32 and 33. *PWR* 197, 3 December 1941. (right) Front cover. "The amount of savings we Japanese citizens must strive to meet this year was set at seventeen billion yen. If we divide that amount among all one hundred million citizens, then each one of us must have 170 yen in savings. We will have to firmly tighten our belts and save, and the boy who, instead of wasting his allowance, has pooled it so he can buy a mini-bond from the lady at the tobacco store, does so for the sake of the nation." The original cover is a black and white photograph with the bond colored gold.

(left) Back cover. This poster for "China Incident Government Bonds" with its prophetic image of an aerial bombardment was displayed the week of the Japanese blitzkrieg attack on Pearl Harbor. The motto on the bomb literally says, "This one bomb, this one bond," or more colloquially, "Every bond buys a bond."

The prevalence of war bond advertisements in 1945 must have been oppressive. With very few items available for sale, advertising became meaningless, besides which the government limited the amount of printed space allotted to commercial advertising. In 1938, "luxury" items (in fact, non-essentials were all considered "luxuries") began disappearing from store shelves and commercial advertising from magazines. By 1943, the number of advertisements and their size had been reduced to 30 percent of the 1937 level, and this figure would be halved in 1944 and then halved again in 1945, so that in the final year of the war, government-related advertising accounted for over 90 percent of all advertising space, while advertising space was at 8 percent of its 1937 level. Conversely stated, the amount of print space given to commercial advertising in 1945 represented a little less than one percent of the 1937 level.[7]

Savings, frugality, and substitute materials were important aspects of the new economic order. In 1938, the government banned permanent waves for women and closed dance halls. Taxi rates were hiked by a new tax, forcing people to use public transportation and thereby saving precious fuel. A nationwide system of rationing began.

These were among hundreds of new measures the Diet legislated in 1938 in an effort to maximize the contribution of Japan's gross national product to the war effort. Still, greater cooperation was needed from the public. On 1 August 1940, the monthly "Day of Service for Developing Asia" was promulgated. (In 1942, it was moved to the eighth of the month to commemorate the outbreak of the Pacific War.) All citizens were to show their support for the war effort by forgoing "luxury" items, such as alcohol, tobacco, and meat, by volunteering for war work, and by participating in scrap drives. The progressively straitened circumstances both prescribed behavior appropriate to wartime and proscribed "unpatriotic" behavior, as every day came to resemble a day of public service. In conjunction with the government's "7 July" (Army Day) ban on many luxury items, the "Luxury Is the Enemy!" (*Zeitaku wa teki da!*) campaign was launched, the brainchild of a brilliant adman and student of the psychology of advertising, Miyayama Takashi.[8] This highly successful public relations campaign unleashed housewives into the public arena, which they policed and censured.

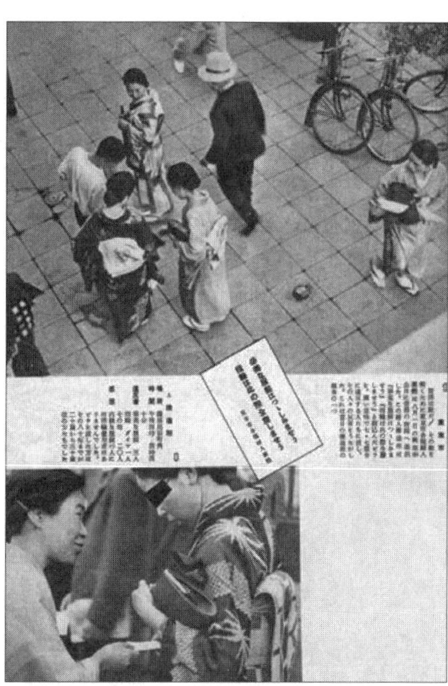

34 and 35. (left) *PWR* 129, 14 August 1940, p. 21. "From Eastern to Western [Japan], Beginning 1 August, the Day of Public Service for Developing Asia." Members of a women's patriotic association patrol the streets as part of the "Luxury is the Enemy" campaign. On a corner of Owari-chō, in Tokyo's posh Ginza District, a member hands out a note (center) to a stylish young woman (her eyes inked out to protect her identity); the note reads, "Let's refrain from ostentatious clothing. All rings are banned." The text states, "in a forty-five minute period beginning at 4 P.M., twenty-four offenders (*ihansha*) were spotted. Their offenses were: too fancily dressed, three; sporting a diamond ring, one; unspecified offenses, twenty. Eighty percent of the offenders were between the ages of twenty and thirty."

(right) *PWR* 153, 29 January 1941, back cover. This full-page advertisement for Federated Credit Unions advising, "Put Home Front Savings in the Credit Union," features a battalion of housewives in *monpe* (peasant trousers) carrying a "Down With Luxury" banner. The dramatic setting, reminiscent of a cinematic backdrop, could be dawn or dusk, city or countryside. They move forward with a samurai's swagger, confident of their mission.

36 and 37. *PWR* 132, 4 September 1940, pp. 18-19. "Sayonara, Luxurious Couple. Photograph courtesy of Tōhō Film Studio." Probably the actress Tachibana Mieko (see figure 14). The same couple in "before" and "after" attire.

(top, p. 18) Here is a well-dressed couple who lead an "extravagant" lifestyle. The caption admonishes, "In our country, the people used to be slaves to luxurious dress, but that era is over." Examples of their extravagances follow.

Man: 18-karat gold tie tack, French cologne, slick imported hair oil "unsuitable for our hair," custom-made Oxford shirt, silver belt buckle, 19-jewel Hamilton wristwatch, white lambskin suede shoes, platinum and aquamarine ring, English imported pipe, Shetland wool suit imported from London.

Woman: collar from distant Kyoto, Saga silk brocade handbag, "200-yen sash costing more than a man's monthly salary, 50-yen fawnskin sash-lifter, 30-yen sash clasp," gold and silver threaded formal kimono costing "the same as five everyday kimonos," custom-made socks, enamel footgear, platinum pearl ring, gaudy red nails, lace handkerchief, French perfume, "Alden facial foundation, Dolare rouge, and Coty lipstick—the stuff of 'Western dependency-ism.'"

(bottom, p. 19) And here the same couple is in step with wartime strictures, yet still quite fashionable. "Completely stripped of extravagance.[9] In wartime, let's lead lifestyles befitting wartime. Certainly this war is not only a problem for politics to solve."

Man: "Freshly washed hair needs no Bay Rum or cologne. A dab of Japanese pomade applied to cowlicks." Italian or German synthetic-blend suit, Japanese all-weather shoes, easy-care necktie and collar, practical hat.

Woman: No flowery headgear hiding the hair's natural beauty. Synthetic sash need not be washed separately. Mother's hand-me-down purse. Kimono made with domestic dyes in black, gray-blue, or purple—"of these colors, choose the appropriate one by age." Long-lasting footgear and socks. "A healthy woman's nails are naturally pink," so no nail polish. "Cosmetics that do no more than bring out the face's natural beauty. Trust Japanese cosmetics and apply lightly to accent a healthy beauty. Painted faces are passé."

Substitute materials took the place of metals, rubber, and petroleum products that were particularly valuable to war production. The home front had to make do with replacement foodstuffs, leaving the most substantial provisions for the men at the front. Meeting the demand for staple crops meant reducing the production of meat, fish, soy beans, rice, alcohol, and sweets, which could rarely be found at any price from 1943 until the end of the war. From early 1942, all rationed rice was unpolished, so that the nutrients in the husk were not lost. While unpolished (brown) rice is more nutritional than polished (white) rice, modern Japanese had come to prefer the look, texture, and taste of white rice—a "luxury" most of their peasant ancestors seldom enjoyed. By 1944, even brown rice was becoming scarce, and in 1945 the population was threatened with starvation. The standard ration for civilians was maintained at 2.3 *go* (11.6 ounces) of rice, or 1,160 calories per day, by substituting inferior staple foods, and even this ration was reduced by 10 percent in July 1945, when the food rationing system went into failure. The real picture of wartime hunger is seen in the plummeting production of fruits and vegetables, which by 1945 had fallen to 57 and 70 percent, respectively, of their 1940 level, and the disappearance of edible fats and sugar from the diet.[10]

38. *PWR* 129, 14 August 1940, p. 20. "From Eastern to Western [Japan], Beginning 1 August, the Day of Public Service for Developing Asia." The caption reads, "In Sapporo, Hakodate, and other cities of Hokkaidō, not only are the department store cafeterias using no rice, they are gladly using rye and udon noodles, and other substitute foods they are calling 'Developing Asia foodstuffs,' which are well received." The sign above the counter reads, "Substitute Foods for Sale Here."

Other photographs in this article showed people enjoying substitute foods in other regions of Japan, including "Kyoto residents lunching on delicious-looking sushi in a department store cafeteria, but made without rice, instead using potatoes as a filling." Even these "substitute foods" would mostly vanish from cafeterias in the spring and summer of 1944.

The first of a series of US embargoes against Japan went into effect in 1940, in response to Japan's occupation of Indo-china. Japan, dependent upon US exports of metal for airplane- and ship-building, immediately launched nationwide scrap drives. Even prior to that time, the government was collecting precious metals, such as platinum and gold, for which a flat rate was paid. In April 1940, *PWR* used a series of photographs of scrap drives in Germany, Italy, England, France, and Sweden to encourage citizens to donate.

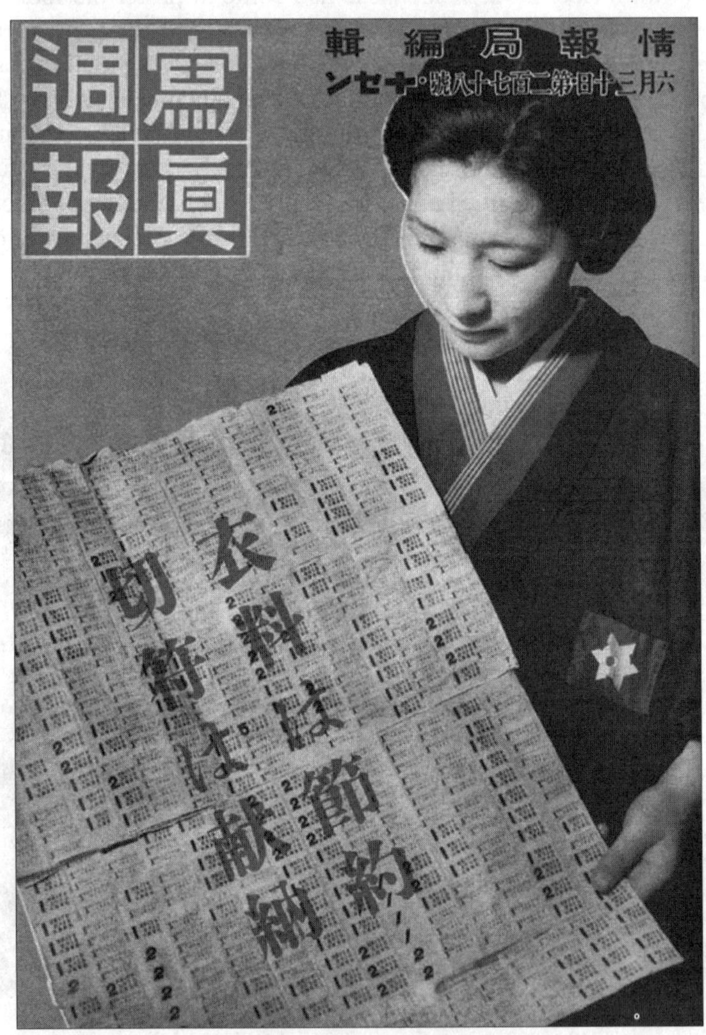

39. *PWR* 278, 30 June 1943. This woman wears the badge of the Japanese Patriotic Women's Association The slogan says, "Be Thrifty with Clothing. Donate Ration Tickets."

"Almost eight hundred clothing ration tickets on a sheet as large as a newspaper. Anyone can donate clothing ration tickets, which is one of the kindest and quickest ways to perform service to nation. Men, women, children, let's donate our clothing ration tickets and advance toward victory."

By spring 1942, even a washcloth or length of string required a ration coupon. With the toilet paper ration set at three sheets per person per day, the Buddhist newspaper *Chūgai Nippō* published Nagahisa Gakusui's timely article, "The National Defense Lifestyle and Urinating and Defecating" (27 and 29 April 1945).

Every country is making a breakneck effort to secure the metal resources wartime requires. In our nation, we are steadily realizing the expansion of iron manufacturing facilities, making use of the iron deposits in the Greater East Asian Co-Prosperity Sphere, but this still is far from enough. To finish building the nation's high-level air defense system, we need to utilize the metal resources lying dormant in storage in our country. Therefore, on 1 April, public offices and social organizations launched a special scrap metal drive. From large items like iron doors down to small items like metal ash trays, all will help the nation when the blast furnaces send them to the front. If every family gathered the metal clasps from one pair of tabi socks, nationwide they would amount to 4.5 metric tons [4.96 tons] of brass, which would be a great help to the nation. Won't all of you in every family think of ways to donate as much metal as possible? (*PWR* 165, 23 April 1940, p. 1)

40-42. *PWR* 165, 23 April 1940. "Dig Up the Lode in the Streets—in Offices, Shops, and Homes." Citizens of other nations were participating in metal drives and so was the Japanese government. Now it was up to the citizens of Japan.

(left, p. 1) "Germany. 'Today is metal collection day. These birthday presents, they can go . . . just like the grandma in the poster says, "I, too, will help Hitler, the Führer."'"

(top right, p. 7) "Go take a look at the Home Ministry. The sound of a hammer echoes through the spring air. A worker sweats as he removes the iron railing."

(bottom right, p. 7) "The Commerce and Industry Ministry is in the middle of removing metal filing cabinets. 'Say, these are heavy.' 'Well, we'll only have wooden ones from now on.'"

43 and 44. *PWR* 151, 15 January 1941, pp. 4-5. An article titled "A Family of Bells Leaves the Temple and Reenters Society"[11] describes the collection of metal fittings and ornamental fixtures from Buddhist temples.

"What is the point of temple bells that are never even rung once, just hanging there uselessly? And too many unused incense burners, candlesticks, and the like heaped together only become the playground of mice and the home of spiders. How much better for them to 'return to society' as iron and brass. The people handing them over to be made into cannons and ammunition are really helping the nation. Temples and churches, too, must 'tuck up their robes' [i.e., roll up their sleeves] to build an air defense nation, and they have hopped on the scrap drive bandwagon collecting unneeded Buddhist altar fittings and hoarded items."

The Japanese text is quite specific in excluding Shinto shrines from scrap drives. The article does not name the temple. Photographs: Yoshida Sakae.

Public institutions and social and religious organizations, including temples, churches, and schools, were easy targets for scrap drives. Thousands of Buddhist objects, some centuries old, were melted down during the war.

The National Total Mobilization Law gave the government the authority to control the distribution of raw materials needed for the war effort, which affected nearly every aspect of Japanese manufacturing. Substitute materials used in manufacturing meant products often broke or wore out quickly. *Sufu*, short for the English phrase "staple fiber" (*sutepuru fibā*), was usually used to describe viscous rayon and everything made from it. By association, anything made of synthetic materials was called *sufu* during the war, and the word quickly took on a second meaning: ersatz, inferior production, poor quality.[11] Glass and ceramics were the usual replacements for metal goods, and these easily chipped and broke. Durable plastics were also used, but less frequently because of the scarcity of the petroleum products needed in their production.

45 and 46. *PWR* 115, 8 May 1940, p. 6. "Even Mr. Ninomiya Is a Substitute Item."

(left) "Good Morning, Mr. Ninomiya." Schoolchildren at an elementary school in Okayama City greet the ceramic statue of Ninomiya.

(right) "Many Ninomiyas in the shed diligently studying." An army of ceramic Ninomiyas in various states of completion.

Bronze statues of Ninomiya Sōtoku, paragon of schoolboy virtue, could be found in most elementary schoolyards before the war. The bronze was melted down for munitions and replaced with ceramic statues made of *bizen-yaki*, one of Japan's famous old kilns, still located today in Okayama Prefecture.

47-51. *PWR* 133, 11 September 1940, pp. 20-21. Photographs by Kikuchi Matasaburō from an article describing the Movement to Emphasize the Daily Use of Substitute Materials that began on 10 September. Plastics, glass, and ceramics were the usual replacement materials, although the article also showed pipes, baseballs, and a man's hat made from soybeans.

(clockwise, from top right)

Drum and shamisen, raw silk replacing the customary dog-hide and catgut heads.

Seiko watch with an acrylic back cover, allowing the mechanism to be seen.

The Japanese Chamber of Commerce's Seal of Approval for products made with "Quality Substitute Materials."

Brazier and fish-grilling plate made from ceramics, not steel.

Zippers made from celluloid.

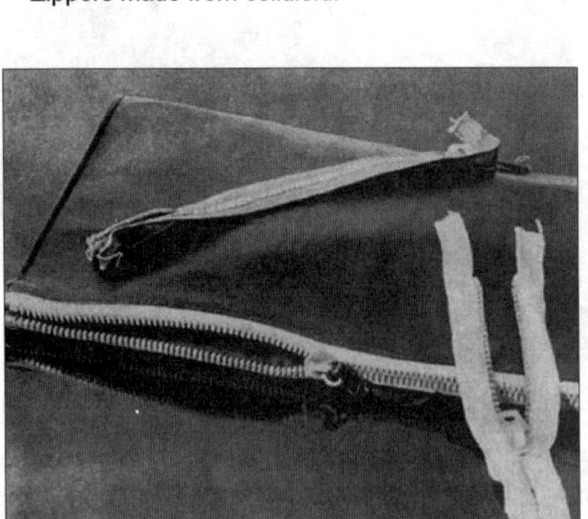

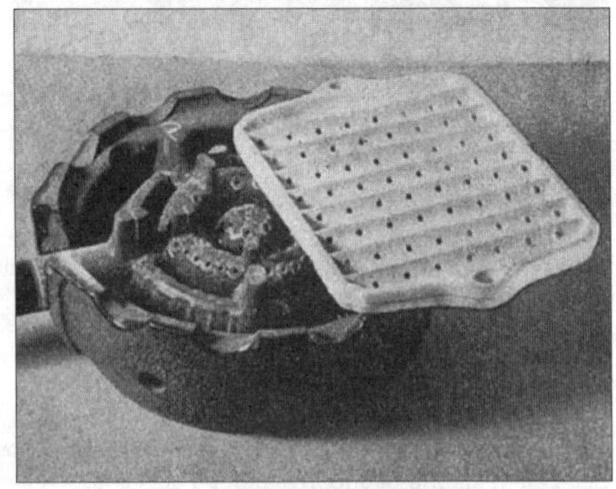

On the home front, mental preparation for protracted war meant guarding against the enemy's ideological weapons while fostering the proper attitude toward Japan's military and its goals. Proper attitude and alertness, the duty of every citizen, were directly linked to the war effort. "Service to the nation," when performed insincerely, could adversely affect morale and ultimately, production. Therefore, morale-boosting, ostensibly the highest goal of the Citizens' Total Spiritual Mobilization Movement, harbored a deeper agenda: creating patriotic citizens who cheerfully obeyed orders and also policed their communities.

From early in the China war, *PWR* carried stories about the propaganda (*senden*) produced by the United States, France, Great Britain, and Germany during World War I, as well as printing articles about two major ideological warfare[13] exhibitions, the first in 1938 and the second in 1940. Both examined contemporary propaganda from Italy, Germany, and the Soviet Union, and also anti-Japanese material produced by Nationalist China. The Second Ideological Warfare Exhibition is frequently invoked as an early triumph of Japanese modern commercial design, reflecting the department store venue

52. *PWR* 1, 16 February 1938, p. 14. "Materials From the [First] Ideological Warfare Exhibition at Takashima Department Store, Nihonbashi, Tokyo. The nation's development depends upon its citizens having sound ideas. Ideological war is being fought in every corner of today's world in peacetime and in wartime, as a diplomatic war, an economic war, and an armaments war, and whether a nation is strong or weak, victorious or defeated in that battle, determines that nation's fortunes. The CIB's purpose in presenting this Ideological War Exhibition is to provide a complete picture of the ideological war fomenting within and around the empire and to raise awareness of its seriousness, while also promoting the Japanese spirit of 'United for the Nation' to deal with and triumph over these attempts by foreign countries to wage ideological warfare."

These materials pertain to the battle of ideas waged by the Chinese. The two Chinese Nationalist posters at top criticize the terms of the Shimonoseki Peace Treaty of 1895, the one at center left heralds the new Chinese Republic. At lower right is an anti-Japanese essay written by a female Chinese student as part of patriotic education, and at lower left, a bomb hidden inside a flashlight. This exhibition had 1.3 million visitors in Tokyo alone and toured nine cities, including Seoul.[14]

as well as the skill of the graphic design staff who worked on this famous exhibit. Part of this exhibition was an abstruse analysis of ideology that seemed to recommend closing the pathways to the mind against negative stimulus.

> What Is Ideological Warfare?
>
> The mind is the fortress of the state. If the mind wavers, several thousand tanks lose their power, and tens of thousands of the sacrifices we have made are wasted. Ideological warfare attacks the mind. Ideological warfare, in time of peace, in time of war, on the battlefield, on the home front. The ideological war being fought in the midst of our everyday lives, is a war without armaments. However, everything becomes a weapon in the ideological war
>
> Bullets of light
> Bullets of sound
> Bullets of color
> Bullets of paper
> Bullets without form.
>
> We are all warriors in the ideological war, shouldering the destiny of our nation. The rise or the fall of Japan will be decided by our mental outlook. (*PWR* 104, 21 February 1940, p. 22)

53-55. *PWR* 104, 21 February 1940, pp. 22-23. "Second Ideological Warfare Exhibition" at Takashima Department Store in Nihonbashi, Tokyo.

(top left) "Our ancestors, with their Japanese spirit, kept winning the ideological war. Here is one of them, Prince Shōtoku."[15] The article suggests reflecting on "how our forefathers won the ideological wars" of the past.

(top right) Foreign propaganda tactics seen through cutouts spelling "PROPAGANDA."

(bottom) Wall display of photomontages of propaganda from European countries embroiled in World War II. The poster of a saluting Hitler was an example of positive propaganda.

As the fighting dragged on in China, popular attitudes toward the war were of paramount concern to the government, which initiated several programs to foster the proper mentality. Mass events were the building blocks of the psychology of home front morale; unity through common action reinforced a sense of national identity. This was true of Radio Calisthenics and even more so of events with strong religious overtones. Participation in mass events demanded little of citizens, while non-participation might have dire circumstances.

PWR invited readers to take a hand in shaping the image of the home front. In the first three years of publication, *PWR* sponsored poster contests and conducted reader surveys. The rationale for the "Readers' Photographs" column, an almost weekly feature from 1938 until 1942, was explained in the initial request for submission.

> This magazine's basic philosophy is assisting the public's "photographic service to the nation," making available as much space as possible to cameramen using the latest technology. Any subject relevant to raising awareness at home and abroad, or to propagating[16] national policy is fine: in the street or in the field, or the factory, the home, or school, wherever the home front is fulfilling its vow. Why not shoot scenes of the Total Spiritual Mobilization Movement, or interesting juxtapositions of the season and social conditions? (*PWR* 21, 6 July 1938, p. 23)

56. *PWR* 74, 19 July 1939, p. 2. "The Second Anniversary of the Sacred War. As the noon siren blared on the day of the anniversary, the One Hundred Million all bowed their heads in prayer for victory."

Moments of silence were not shown again in the pages of *PWR*. Prayer for victory was encouraged, of course, on the monthly Day of Service for Developing Asia. Although not identified here, the place is immediately recognizable as Ginza, Tokyo. A landmark since 1933, the Hattori Clock Store with its famous clock tower, in the distant left of the photograph, is still standing today.

Photographers of all stripes were pleased to see their work in print, and *PWR*'s staff of professional photographers often mimicked "amateur" work, dissolving the barrier between the authority of a government publication and its audience of citizens.

57-60. *PWR* 97, 3 January 1940, p. 34. "New Year's Day and a Day of Public Service for the Development of Asia." A photoessay following a typical family through the series of New Year's holidays, this page depicting New Year's Day. The oldest son's narration highlights wartime virtues: uncomplaining frugality, industriousness, loyalty, and patriotism. These candid shots, which might be mistaken for readers' snapshots, are the work of *PWR* professional Yoshida Sakae.

(top left) "We leave Mom behind to watch the house, and the whole family begins the New Year by getting up early and praying at our tutelary Shinto shrine."

(top right) "The first to be offered the New Year's meal is older brother, who is serving at the front. His portion is left in front of his picture" (in a place of honor in the tokonoma, or alcove).

(bottom left) "We exchange New Year's sake and greetings. We all gain a year at New Year's,[17] so this year I'm thirteen."

(bottom right) "We greet the kids from next door. We'll all go to the school's New Year's ceremony. The kadomatsu decoration is small because of the national emergency, but the Rising Sun flag we put on display stands tall and proud." Photographs: Yoshida Sakae.

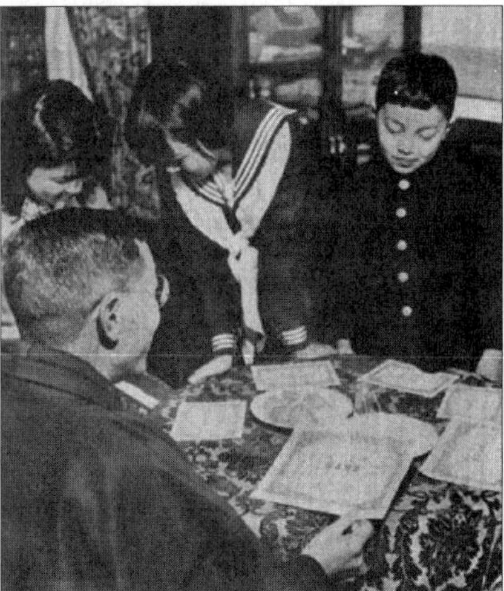

61-64. *PWR* 97, 3 January 1940, p. 35. "New Year's Day and a Day of Public Service for the Development of Asia." The continuation of the photoessay following a typical family through the New Year's holidays, this page being the Day of Public Service, narrated by the oldest son.

(top left) "I listened to the principal's talk about the 2,600th anniversary of the founding of the nation and enjoyed the ceremony. On my way home, I saw father at the shrine exchanging greetings with neighbors because he sent no New Year's cards this year."[18]

(top right) "Every month, we send three care packages to older brother and other soldiers at the front. What better way to spend the third[19] than preparing the year's first care packages?"

(bottom left) "Since there won't be any visitors calling this year, Dad can really relax. We even dragged him into a game of *sugoroku*[20] and beat him at it."

(bottom right) "On the evening of the Seventh, Dad called all of us into the living room and presented us with war bonds for New Year's gifts. The way we spent New Year's shows we are fighting an economic war, too. Smiling, we promised to put our bonds in a safe place." Photographs: Yoshida Sakae.

In wartime Japan, even the most basic actions became an expression of the greatness of the Yamato race and by extension, national destiny. The Education Ministry made films showing the proper etiquette for eating Japanese food, the correct angle at which inferiors and superiors bow to each other, and even the right way to mount a staircase.[21] Manners were more than just a sign of civilization, they were the mark of racial superiority. A Health and Welfare Ministry article in *PWR* 127 (31 July 1940, p. 18) enlightened the people about walking properly because

> Although our nation has the responsibility of leading the Axis in East Asia, we see some of our compatriots walking down the road with a slovenly stride, like the people of a defeated nation, and quite unbecoming for this race leading the Axis in East Asia. Now is the time that we Japanese must stick out our chests, and energetically, with a dignified step, rise to the call of this sacred work!

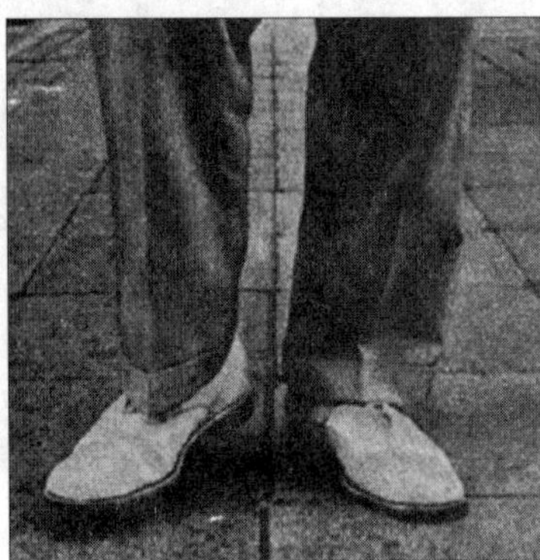

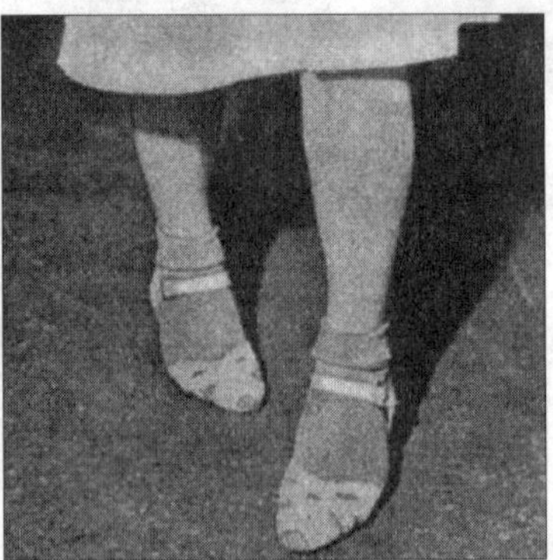

65-67. *PWR* 127, 31 July 1940, p. 19. "Walking Correctly Improves Health." The article explains the added benefit walking correctly: "A person with a slovenly gait usually takes one hundred steps of 65 centimeters (26.5 inches) each per minute, walking 4.5 kilometers (2.8 miles) in an hour. A person with an energetic, correct gait takes 125 steps of 80 centimeters (31.5 inches) each per minute, covering 6 kilometers (3.7 miles) in an hour, which is 1.5 kilometers (0.9 mile) farther and clearly more efficient." Photographs: Senba Tōru.

(top) "They move with a smooth and powerful rhythm, members of the Marunouchi Building's Walk to Work Movement."

(bottom left) "Many men walk with the toes pointed out, like a penguin with a crab's thighs. No one can say this is the proper way for human beings to walk."

(bottom right) "It may be feminine, but walking with the toes pointed in is terribly unhealthy and particularly unsightly with Western dress."

After the New Order was promulgated and the drab "citizen's uniform" came into being, fashion also became an expression of the "right attitude." For men, the uniform consisted of simplified military fatigues (figures 71 and 72), and for women, a wraparound half-kimono top over baggy peasant trousers (*monpe*; see figures 35 and 39). Wearing the citizen's uniform made no statement per se, but failing to do so, or dressing unconventionally, sent a powerful message of dissent. With no other clothing being produced during the Pacific War, people wore the citizen's uniform out of necessity.

Citizens might do everything the government asked—perform volunteer work, buy war bonds, practice air defense, forgo luxuries, donate scrap and other resources, wear the citizen's uniform, send care packages to soldiers, and guard against foreign propaganda—yet not have the proper outlook on the war. They might view the war as unnecessary or meaningless, as an imposition upon their lives, as a hardship to be endured. If so, the government had failed to convince them of the importance of the war. The demands of the war were to be met gladly because each sacrifice connected the citizen to a sacred struggle that was the fullest expression of the destiny of the Yamato race and of national pride. Conversely, those Japanese who demonstrated "uncitizenlike" (*hikokuminteki*) behavior weakened home front morale and sent a negative message to the men risking their lives on the front lines. Cheerfulness was the duty of every citizen. Together with an eagerness to obey orders, it was the surest sign of a "healthy mind" capable of continuing to win the ideological struggle that Japan had been engaged in for well over a millennium, since Prince Shōtoku's time.

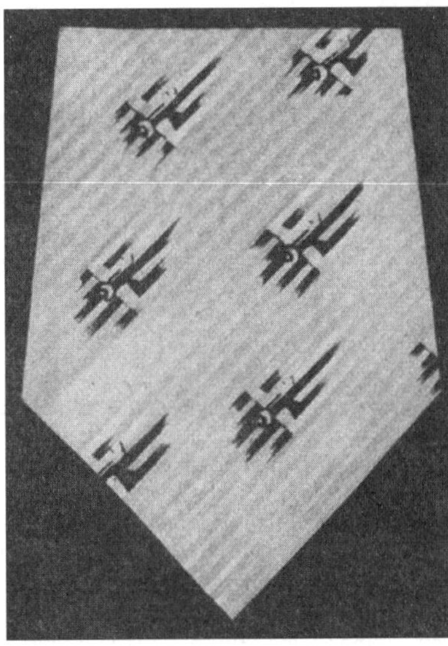

68 and 69. *PWR* 178, 23 July 1941, p. 24. The winning entries in a contest to design fabric with an aeronautical pattern that would "dress up" the citizen's uniform.

(left) Necktie made of silk cloth with a stylized pattern of airplanes in flight, by Ishikawa Torashirō of Tokyo.

(right) Kimono or *monpe* fabric with airplanes by Maekawa Kiichirō of the Design Department of the Takashima Department Store, Kyoto.

70. *PWR* 162, 2 April 1941. "Special Report: The Smile Movement." The caption takes the form of an imaginary dialogue, perhaps between the reader and the people in the photograph.

"'What are all of you so happy about, from the executive and the office manager down to the typist and office boy, did you all just get your salaries doubled overnight?'

"'It's hard to talk to someone like you who is always thinking in such miserly terms. Our company motto is "Smile while you work." If everybody had a sour face and was disagreeable about their work, then our productivity would suffer, but smiling makes us happy—smiling meets the current situation head on, because the Japan of tomorrow will be big enough to have space for everyone.'"

The "Special Report" contained readers' cartoons of smiling citizens and soldiers, happy to serve the nation. During the Pacific War, the "Smile Movement" would be revived as the "Grin and Bear it" campaign (see Chapter 5, figure 37). Upon first glance, this image seems to be a crowd scene, but it is actually a photomontage, in which the central figure, with the appearance of an executive, is a little too large to be in proportion to the children surrounding him.

When the Total Spiritual Mobilization Movement concluded in 1940, home front mobilization entered a new phase. A nationwide network was built that directly connected the people to the government. Two organizations were launched almost simultaneously, one modeled after the Nazi Party in Germany, the other drawing upon the Japanese concept of family (*ie*).[22] The first model was a superstructure represented by the Imperial Rule Assistance Association[23] (IRAA, *Taisei yokusankai*), the second an infrastructure represented by the nationwide system of Neighborhood Associations (*tonarigumi*). *PWR* 141 (6 November 1940, p. 5) explained the connection between the two and their purpose:

71 and 72. *PWR* 150, 8 January 1941, p. 17 (left) and p. 19 (right). Two pages from an article on the activities of the Imperial Rule Assistance Association (IRAA), formed in October 1940 under the second Konoe cabinet as a means of realizing the New Order's goal of "streamlining" society for better efficiency in wartime. With the dissolution of political parties under the New Order, the IRAA was meant to be an interface between citizens and government, along the lines of the Nazi Party. The IRAA oversaw the activities of many other citizens' groups, including the Neighborhood Associations, women's associations, and associations for serving the nation. The IRAA was dissolved in May 1945, when it was folded into the Citizens' Volunteer Army. Note in the middle photograph on the right the simplified military fatigues that clothe citizens in the garb of soldiers.

The photograph at left bears a slogan, "A New Year of Construction, Realizing Our Pledge," and shows the influence of Russian Constructionist design. The line of IRAA members (identified by their sashes) stand out against the flat background photograph of a crowd.

The IRAA movement has already turned on the switch for rebuilding a new Japan and completing a new Great East Asian order which, writ large, is the construction of a new world order. The IRAA is, broadly speaking, the New Order movement, which will, in a word, place we One Hundred Million into one body under this new organization that will conduct all of our energies and abilities for the sake of the nation. Aren't we all mentally prepared to be members of this new organization, and, as one adult to another, without holding our superiors in awe or being preoccupied with the past, cast aside all private concerns in order to perform public service? Under the IRAA are regional town, village, and neighborhood associations, let's convene council meetings and advance the activities of this organization.

73 and 74. *PWR* 141, 6 November 1940, pp. 4-5. "Helping Each Other Across the Fence: Let's Convene Neighborhood Association Councils."

(top) A dotted line shows the boundaries of the Neighborhood Association for the Seventh Squadron of Matsunoki-machi, Suginami Ward, Tokyo.

(bottom) "At the first meeting of the Neighborhood Association Council, our defenses were up and we couldn't communicate well, so it went badly. But once we were done with announcements of notices from above and started discussing matters directly connected to all of our lives, such as community storage space for firewood and a community vegetable garden, things came together. Recently, the prejudices that come from having different occupations have disappeared, and we speak frankly and make progress."

In contrast to the IRAA, the Neighborhood Association meets in a member's home and participants wear everyday clothes. They sit in a circle because each member is an equal. Smaller photographs introduce the individual members: Mr. Yamamoto, of the electronics store; Mr. Iiboshi, a patrol officer; Mr. Kuriota, a driver; and Professor Shirai of the animal husbandry section of the Agriculture School, Imperial University. This commingling of public workers, a store owner, a blue collar laborer, and a professor gives a picture of interaction and cooperation across economic and class lines that was probably more an ideal than an accurate reflection of social reality.

The Home Ministry laid out four objectives of the Neighborhood Associations:

> 1. To organize inhabitants of cities, towns, and villages according to principles of neighborhood solidarity so as to enable them to perform the tasks common to their locality, in consonance with the basic principles for assisting the Throne.
> 2. To function as a basic structure for training and molding the moral life of the people and for realizing their spiritual union.
> 3. To function as agencies for enlightening the people on the purposes and objectives of national policies, so as to facilitate the smooth operation of national administration.
> 4. To function as local control units of national economic life, thereby enabling the successful operation of controlled economy and giving full play to measures for the stabilization of the people's living.[24]

Government directives and ration tickets were distributed by the Neighborhood Association, which was responsible for air defense. Each Neighborhood Association was like a team, in which strong members had to compensate for weak members to ensure compliance with government orders and objectives. The Neighborhood Association in particular became a powerful tool of social organization, encouraging self-policing. By the outbreak of the Pacific War, four years of effective social programming had mobilized the people, uniting them through service to the nation. The effects of this mobilization were seen most dramatically in the lives of women and children.

Notes

1. An early researcher of Japanese propaganda offers this summation of the goals of the Total Spiritualization: "The propaganda aims of the Movement for National Spiritual Mobilization Movement [*sic*] were threefold. First, the object was to secure total unification of public will through appeal to patriotism. Patriotism and loyalty were spelled along the lines of subordination of individual whim to the perfection of the State. Second, increase in war production was sought. Increased effort from each subject would augment the stringent controls over production embodied in the articles of the National Mobilization Law. Third, the attempt was to gain wholehearted support for aggression. This meant redefining the 'China Incident' into language compatible with the lofty ideals of Japan perpetuated by the educational system." See Hideya Kumata, "Spiritual Mobilization—the Japanese Concept of Propaganda," in *Four Working Papers on Propaganda Theory* (n.p.: University of Illinois, January 1955), p. 10.

2. From the early Edo period, the Tokugawa shogunate had censored all publications it deemed harmful to its integrity and governance. Notorious among its many prohibitions was publishing commentary upon current events; this resulted in the most famous kabuki plays being set in the Japanese middle ages, even when the actions described closely paralleled incidents fresh in public memory. The Meiji oligarchs inherited this understanding of the importance of censorship from the shogunate. Whatever its claims to enlightenment, the Meiji government saw no reason to dismantle censorship, only to bring it in line with their goals. It therefore became a tool not only for smiting politically dangerous or subversive writings but also for eliminating those works that might offend late Victorian bourgeois sensibilities with frank discussion of mores. A thorough treatment of this topic is Jay Rubin, *Injurious to Public Morals: Writers and the Meiji State* (Seattle: University of Washington Press, 1984). From Meiji times, the office of the censor had been housed in the Home Ministry as part of its policing duties. The Cabinet Information Bureau—a consortium of military men, politicians, and civilian technicians and professionals—made rules not only for censoring matter it deemed counter-productive, but also for prescribing the kind of material of which it approved.

3. Radio Calisthenics were developed by the Health Office of the Communications and Transportation Ministry (forerunner of today's Japan Post) in 1928 as a means of encouraging the people to build stronger bodies and maintain health. The program became a regular part of school curricula in the 1930s. The familiar tune, usually played on a sole tinny piano, can still be heard today reverberating through the streets and mountains of Japan, since this basic exercise regimen remains in use at schools and in some factories and company offices. Even now, PTA associations and Neighborhood Associations find the daily 6 A.M. Radio Calisthenics to be an effective antidote to juvenile delinquency during summer vacation. When a scratchy old recording is blasted over the regional public address system (the same system used to warn of an impending natural disaster), it has the intensity of a reveille bugler. According to an All Japan Radio Calisthenics Association survey conducted in 2004 with a 62 percent response rate, 76.4 percent of all Japanese elementary schools have some form of Radio Calisthenics program. The first "Radio Calisthenics Rally for Ten Million People" was held in 1962, and has been an annual summer event since then, hosted by large stadiums in every region of Japan. "Radio Calisthenics" became "Calisthenics for Everyone" (*Minna no taisō*) in 1999, just in time for the new millennium. See www.rajio-taiso.jp/research/index.html.

4. Thomas R. H. Havens, *Valley of Darkness: The Japanese People and World War II* (New York: W. W. Norton, 1978), p. 94.

5. Ibid., p. 94.

6. Ibid., p. 95.

7. Nanba Kōji, *"Uchiteshi yamamu": Taiheiyō sensō to hōkoku no gijitsusha tachi* (Tokyo: Kodansha, 1998) p. 60.

8. Ibid., p. 53. Ironically, Miyayama, had made his name in advertising Club (Kurabu) brand cosmetics.

9. Throughout this article criticizing the use of imported goods, "luxury" (*zeitaku*) is frequently written in katakana, as if it were a loan word and not originally part of the Japanese language.

10. See B[ruce] F. Johnston, with Mosaburo Hosoda and Yoshio Kusumi, *Japanese Food Management in World War II* (Stanford: University of California Press, 1953), pp. 150, 159-160. Ienaga Saburō (*The Pacific War, 1931-1945,* [New York: Pantheon, 1978], p. 193) notes that the Health and Welfare Ministry's nutritional standard for a male adult performing medium hard labor was 2,400 calories and 85 grams (3 ounces) of protein a day in 1941, but dropped dramatically to 1,793 calories per day and 60 to 65 grams (2.1 to 2.3 ounces) of protein in 1945.

11. The title, literally translated, would be "World-Returning Ceremony for a Family of Temple Bells." In Buddhism, becoming a nun or monk requires "leaving the world," that is, renouncing society and its worldly trappings. Before returning to live in society, a ceremony was conducted officially releasing the monk or nun from vows.

12. The pejorative sense of the word is borne out in its usage in US surrender leaflets produced by Japanese POWs, and dropped by plane on Japanese cities.

13. The Japanese term is *shisōsen. Shisō is* literally "thought," "idea," or "way of thinking," although *Nihon no shisōshi* is "Japanese intellectual history." Japan's battle against ideas was initially aimed specifically at sophisticated systems of thought—philosophies—especially communism, communist ideology, and the Comintern. Indeed, this battle against the spread of communistic thinking was the rationale for the Anti-Comintern Pact Japan entered with Nazi Germany in 1936. With the outbreak of the Pacific War, the many guises of Western liberalism became the target of the ideological war.

14. Nanba, *"Uchiteshi yamamu,"* pp. 42-43. Nanba provides his source as *Naikaku jōhōbu—jōhō senden kenkyū shiryō dai hachikan* (Cabinet Information Bureau—Information and Propaganda Research Sources, Volume 8).

15. Prince Shōtoku (574-622), an early Japanese intellectual, studied Buddhism and Chinese thought. Japanese tradition credits him with writing the so-called Seventeen Article Constitution and establishing a nationwide system of Buddhist temples. The article does not describe Shōtoku as facing any particular "ideological struggle." Presumably, his ability to adapt the tools of civilization, borrowed from China, to the Japanese model scored a "victory" for the nascent nation.

16. The Japanese original is *senden suru* ("to propagate"). *Senden* can be "propaganda," "advertising,"

"dissemination," or "promotion," and at the time carried no negative connotation. Indeed, it is worth recalling that the original meaning of "propaganda" in Latin, "to spread," was often used in connection to the positive work of spreading the faith, hence the Vatican's Congregation de Propaganda Fide (Sacred Congregation of Propaganda), established in the seventeenth century to disseminate Catholicism among the peoples missionaries encountered in Asia, Africa, and the Americas. Today, somewhat like the checkered reputation of "advertising" in the West, the use of *senden* is more ambiguous.

17. In the traditional manner of determining age, all Japanese became one year older on New Year's Day, regardless of the day on which they were actually born. Reading between the lines, the narration is criticizing the Western custom of singling out someone on his or her birthday with a party and presents, which was a symptom of the Western disease of "individualism."

18. The tradition of sending New Year's cards was well established by this time. The Post Office began issuing special New Year's stamps in 1936. However, in 1940, the government asked that people refrain from sending New Year's cards and from making New Year's visits, as one means of supporting the troops through frugality. In the Christian West, these measures would be the equivalent of canceling major Christmas celebrations and not sending out Christmas cards.

19. On the third day of the New Year, one traditionally does the year's "firsts." These usually reflect hobbies or customary activities, such as first calligraphy of the year, first game of chess, and first flower arrangement, and so on.

20. *Sugoroku* is a board game resembling chutes-and-ladders popular in Japan at New Year's since at least mid-Edo times. The images on *sugoroku* draw upon themes from popular culture and are often arranged by a system of ranking (actors, courtesans, sumo wrestlers, famous places) or by a progression (post stations on a highway, current events). The playing board in this photograph has scenes of China or Manchuria, probably following Japanese victories.

21. See *PWR* 166, 30 April 1941, pp. 18-19, for stills from educational newsreels on how to properly eat, climb stairs, and pray at shrines. Japanese bureaucracy was not alone in this regard. For instance, the US Office of War Information produced a number of posters with suggestions linking personal hygiene and habits to the war effort. The National Archives in Washington, D.C., contain World War II posters addressing nearly every topic imaginable: "A Blood Test for Everyone. Syphilis Strikes 1 in 10 before 50" (ARC Identifier 513716); "At Night Walk Facing Traffic. Wear or Carry Something White" (ARC 513884); "Avoid Sunburn. Use protective ointments. It's smart to stay on the job" (ARC 513898); "Beat the Skin Game. Wear Clean Clothes. A Shower after Work." (ARC 513942); "Don't Smoke in Bed!" (ARC 514164); "For Our Patrons' Health, Use a Fork, Don't be a Butterfingers" (ARC 514292).

22. Like the imperial family, the concept of *ie* ("family" or "home") existed from ancient times. It was a major force in organizing feudal society, with its samurai clans and its tightly knit agricultural communities. The concept was appropriated and manipulated by the Meiji oligarchs in their creation of a modern nation-state.

23. Ienaga writes that "A 'new political structure movement' was planned and the Imperial Rule Assistance Association (IRAA) was established in October 1940. It was not comparable to the mass parties of Germany or Italy and was not very effective in organizing or mobilizing the populace." See *The Pacific War, 1931-1945*, p. 112.

24. From the English-language CIB publication *Tokyo Gazette* (4:7, January 1941) p. 260; quoted in Hideya Kumata, "Spiritual Mobilization," p. 18.

5. WARRIOR WIVES

The Japanese word for "home front" literally translates as "behind the gun" (*jūgo*), a phrase conveying the harshness of civilian life in wartime Japan. With the number of draftees rising in 1931, and especially after 1937, Japanese women and families endured growing hardships. In some villages, virtually no men of draft age remained, the burden of farming falling on women, children, and the elderly. The government's tight control over nearly every aspect of industry, information, education, and society affected women as drastically as it did men. For the first time in Japan's modern history, women's lives were directly linked to war. It was total war. In the process, many of the small freedoms women had won in the 1920s and early 1930s were eradicated and women's social roles and responsibilities were redefined. By the time that the war in China had expanded to the Pacific in December 1941, Japanese women had become vital cogs in a lean, well-oiled war machine. Although women had almost no place in the Japanese military, the government rapidly created new infrastructures that drew them into the war effort while the media transformed the popular image of Japanese womanhood from delicate, submissive, and meek to strong, determined, and capable. Of course, before and during the war, women were cautioned against losing feminine charms and beauty, even as they assumed combat roles, a tension aptly summed up in the phrase "Warrior Wives." The stronger the media image of women during the war, the more powerless women were to determine their own fates.

1. *Asahigraph* (39:1), 1-8 January 1941. "The Rising Sun Flag Dyes the Hearts of the One Hundred Million," by an unidentified artist, graces this full-color cover. Mother and young son are hoisting the flag for New Year's, a task usually performed by the man of the house, who must be a soldier at the front. Morale-boosting is the patriotic duty of the home front.

This lushly printed image is not without an erotic element, as the woman displays a bit of the nape of the neck, considered to be one of a Japanese woman's most attractive features, especially so when viewed from behind (*ushirosugata*). Such beautifully dressed women, and such beautifully printed magazines, would nearly disappear from the home front within two years of this publication.

During the war, women were expected to shoulder heavier responsibilities while continuing to honor conservative social values. A woman was a chaste wife, nurturing mother, diligent homemaker, and guardian of the family's spiritual well-being. Whenever her husband's work required assistance, she was a loyal helpmate in the fields or in the shop. She prided herself on always maintaining her gracious demeanor, whether at home or in public. She accepted these roles uncomplainingly; she was industrious and frugal as a homemaker, and selfless as a wife and mother. Housekeeping in the 1930s was little changed from premodern times, since there were very few appliances or conveniences in the majority of homes. Outside of the cities, few homes were electrified, and throughout the land most housework was done by hand.

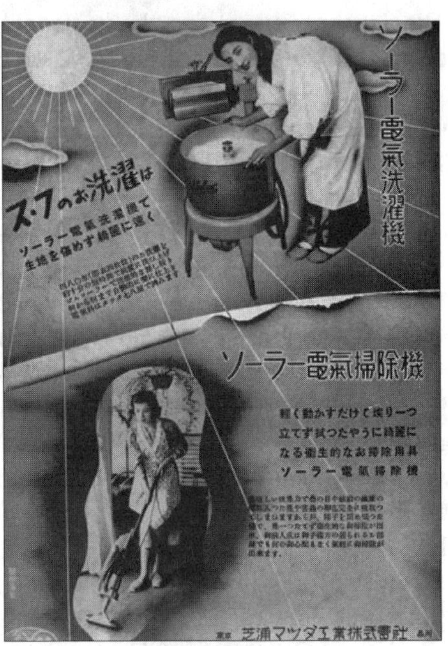

2 and 3. (left) *Women's Club Supplement: "Household Finances During Wartime, Practical Methods to Make over All Types of Japanese Garments,"* 1 November 1938. This special issue is full of patterns for remaking kimono, complete with instructions for dying fabric and actual stencils. This cover shows one attractive homemaker doing so. The magazine is in step with the tighter restrictions on consumption recently announced as part of the New Order. In reality, few women would have had the time to take apart a kimono, die and stencil the fabric, and resew it, as this magazine directs them to. In 1938, it was still unthinkable that Japanese wives could bear arms—those gentle beings kept "inside the house" (*kanai*, the word a Japanese man uses to signify "my wife," literally means "inside the house"; *okusan*, a more general term for wife, literally means "the rear" or "the interior" of the home, that is, the wife's place).

(right) *Asahigraph* (31:3), 20 July 1938, back cover. A rare full-page advertisement for Solar (Sōrā) brand electric appliances manufactured by Matsuda Electric. The electric washing machine is operated by a pretty young woman in kimono and coverall apron like that worn by maids. The vacuum cleaner is modeled by a modern woman wearing the latest fashion.

Advertisements like this were uncommon enough to suggest that these items did not catch on. Obviously, only very wealthy homes would have appliances like these before the war. Most electric appliances would not reach the masses until the late 1950s or after.

The layout of this advertisement likens Solar brand to a bright sun of progress clearing away clouds and liberating women from the drudgery of housework. Very similar graphics would be used a few years later to show the progress of the Japanese army, under the banner of the Rising Sun, in its liberation of Asia from the dark tyranny of colonialism.

Japan was still predominantly an agricultural society until the late 1950s, and most women (and men) spent their lifetimes in farm labor within a patriarchal system. The city-dwellers were, by and large, involved in commerce, manufacturing, or the service industry, occupations in which there was little chance of a woman gaining autonomy. Prewar industrialization had provided some opportunities outside of the home, but only in rare instances did women have careers, support themselves, and live independently of, or as equals to, men. The very few women who did have successful careers usually worked as entertainers (writers, artists, dancers, movie stars, geisha, waitresses), as was the case in the Edo period. Modernization created very few new professions, most of them open only to urban women: schoolteacher, nurse, secretary, sales clerk, telephone operator. The realms of politics, business, and industry remained closed to women, and higher education was viewed as an accoutrement of upper class women.

In the 1920s, the age of Taishō Democracy, women gained a modicum of independence. The fashions—short skirts and bobbed hair—must have felt liberating for women used to wearing layers of kimono and elaborately dressed chignons. Women's groups began to address controversial issues, such as women's suffrage and birth control. As the number of women in the work force increased, women had more money and time of their own. There was a sharp rise in the circulation of popular women's magazines and the number of women earning a living by writing for them. Nevertheless, women had few rights and were defined primarily by their connection to men, whether husbands, fathers, or sons.

4. *Asahigraph* (9:21), 23 November 1927, p. 27. The English caption reads, "Kimono designs, hats and a dress. The dress was made by Madam [Mrs.] Asao Hara, a noted poetess, out of a scarf. The kimono designs are for Geisha parade at the opening of 'Kinza' [Ginza] street, Tokyo." The Japanese caption gives the additional information that the scarf-to-dress idea came from the "Tokyo Women's Fashion Design Institute," as if to say that modern women could not only design their own clothes but their own careers as well, while also gaining renown as poetesses. English captions disappeared from *Asahigraph* in the early 1930s.

5. *Asahigraph* (30:22), 1 June 1938, back cover. A full-page, color advertisement for Lait brand face cream (foundation, *o-shiroi*) featured a smartly dressed young actress, Hara Setsuko (b. 1920), who would not look out of place in any of the world's cosmopolitan centers. The advertisement notes that women can choose among four different, "modern" colors of Lait: flesh tone, light flesh tone, ochre, and white. The prominent use of French ("Blanc de Lait") in the advertisement, as well as the full-length photograph showing the entire fashion ensemble (not merely the face, even this famous one), and the female appropriation of masculine attire (suit with necktie), achieves an air of internationalism and sophistication.

颯爽たり御両人！

ターキーとオリエ山麓のロケ

富士の裾野を駆けめぐる

天晴れ馬上の麗人

6 and 7. *Asahigraph* (29:10), 8 September 1937, pp. 28-29. Two Shōchiku stars on location at Susono at the base of Mount Fuji, filming the talkie "Fatherland," a "war revue" period piece. That an all-female cast portrayed military men meant that, no matter how respectful and patriotic in tone, the film also served to erode the gender roles that the military insisted upon. Placing women atop horses, even for the purpose of movie-making, could have incensed the military, who regularly requisitioned farm animals for service in China. After the war spread to the Pacific, actresses would be limited to roles more in keeping with the aims and realities of the New Order.

8. *Asahigraph* (31:13), 28 September 1938, p. 2. An advertisement for a khaki ensemble by Torie, a haberdasher specializing in fine fabrics and haute couture. This pseudo-military outfit might seem to be in step with the New Order, but in comparison with government prescribed fashions, it is much too chic and, as shown here, has too many expensive accessories (belt, cap, tie, dress shirt, white gloves, boots). The vogue for all things military would fade once home-sewn fatigues became a daily uniform. The text reads, "Men's style—smartly tailored, ideal for activities during times of emergency." One can easily imagine Katherine Hepburn or Marlene Dietrich sporting this suit.

The stagy backdrop of this advertisement appears to be a recently conquered swatch of China, hence the Rising Sun flags and the airplanes.

In preparation for total war, the government quickly co-opted the energy and radicalism of the nascent Japanese women's rights movements and eliminated autonomous women's groups. The government set out on a nationwide make-over mission: Women were to give up permanent waves (outlawed in 1938) and other vestiges of a "decadent" Western lifestyle, and comport themselves in a manner befitting a nation making tremendous sacrifices in order to fight for lofty ideals such as "Asia for Asiatics." When the representatives of liberated Asian peoples were called to Tokyo, it would be a national disgrace if the women of Japan were gussied up in imitation of Hollywood movie stars, and the government was determined to halt such shameful conduct that flew in the face of the ultimate sacrifices being made on the battlefield by Japan's brave sons.

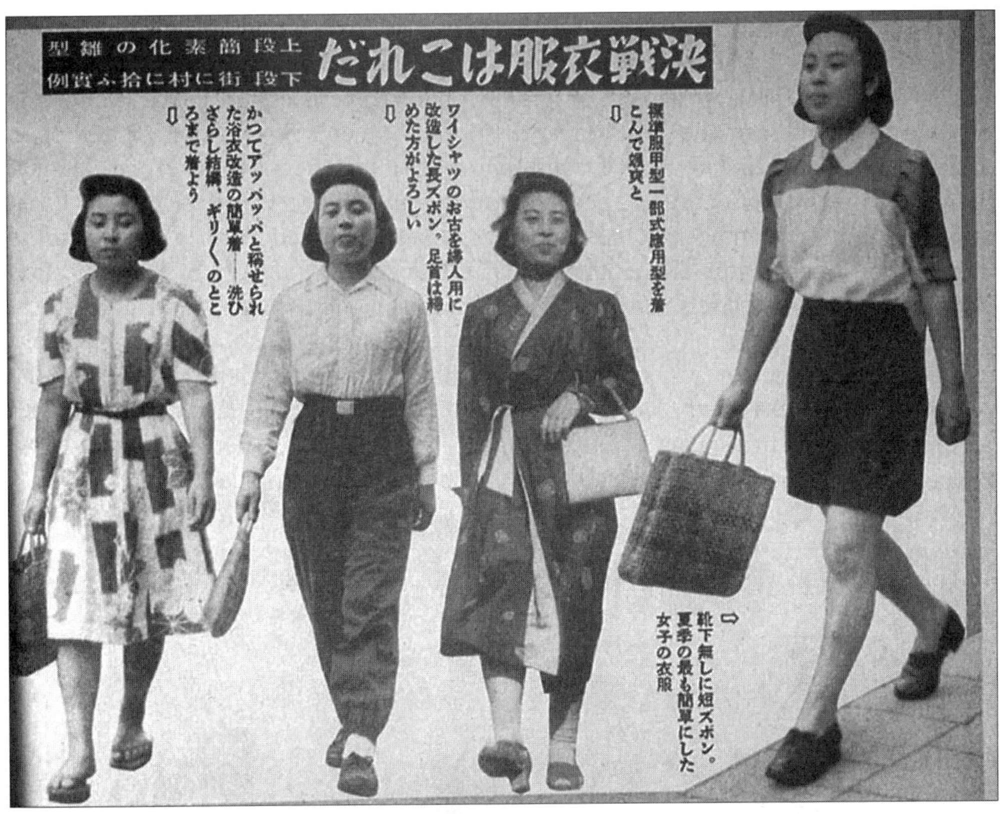

9 and 10. (top) *PWR* 279, 7 July 1943, p. 16. "This Is Wartime Clothing." Government-approved fashions to sew at home (from existing articles of clothing) stressed practicality, modesty, and conformity, virtues reflecting Japan's "ideological" war with the selfish, hedonistic, individualistic West. "Going stockingless is most practical for summer," the article advises. The ensemble second from the left, consisting of refashioned men's pants and men's white dress shirt, would have been shocking in chauvinistic wartime Japan had not the government proposed it. These clothes, frumpy by comparison to the lavish kimono and smart Western outfits already seen, are still more stylish and daring than the baggy, waist-hugging monpe and androgynous fatigues of the "citizens' uniform" (figures 24, 25, and 36).

(bottom) *PWR* 270, 5 May 1943, p. 7. Frugal femininity was promoted in articles like this one. "The beauty of Japanese women is surely not found in thick layers of cosmetics. Besides, if you knew that last year, the cost of rouge and powder came to 170 million yen—well, cosmetics would certainly disappear from the battle for the home front." The article was hardly presaging the disappearance of cosmetics; by this time, they were already almost impossible to find for sale at any price in Japan.

The government directed women's roles in the war effort through women's patriotic associations, which lost their autonomy in early 1942 through government-forced merger. Three of the largest of these groups claimed membership in the millions at the time of the merger: the Great Japan Patriotic Women's Association (Dai Nippon Aikoku Fujin Kai, founded in 1901, with four million members), Great Japan National Defense Women's Association (Dai Nippon Kokubō Fujin Kai, founded in 1933, with nine million members),[1] and the Great Japan Federated Women's Association (Dai Nippon Rengō Fujin Kai, founded in 1931 under the auspices of the Education Ministry). From these and smaller women's groups, the government formed the Great Japan Women's Association (Dai Nippon Fujin Kai), making membership compulsory for all married women over the age of twenty. Although translated here as "woman," the word *fujin* in Japanese refers to a married woman, a "wife" or "lady," a word that connotes not only gender distinction but a woman's place in a patriarchal society. The Great Japan Women's Association received orders from Japan's male military leaders.

11. Officers of the Great Japan National Defense Women's Association, as seen in a commemorative album printed for one local branch of the organization in January 1942, just before its merger into the Great Japan Women's Association. The president of the organization, Mutō Nobuko, is pictured top center. As a soldiers' assistance organization, they had a military officer serve as their general manager, Lieutenant-Colonel Tanaka Minoru of the army (pictured bottom left). Soon the hierarchy would be reversed, with men directing these groups.

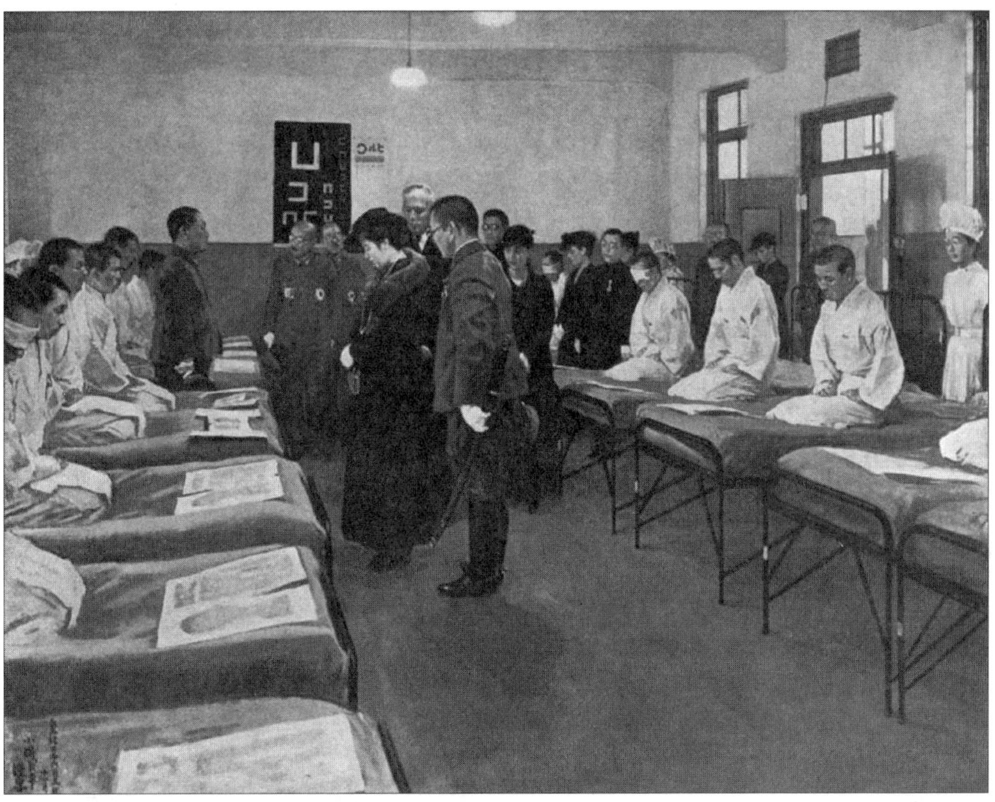

皇后陛下 帝都四箇所に行啓 決戰下銃後女性敢鬪の姿を親しく御覽遊ばさる

12 and 13. (top) "Her Imperial Highness the Empress Visits the Army Hospital," a painting by Koiso Ryōhei signed and dated December 1943, here reproduced from *Great East Asia War Art, Volume II*. The work is very faithful to a photograph that appeared in *PWR*. The wounded soldiers, even those who appear to be very ill and have bandaged eyes, sit in formal posture with heads bowed before the empress. Her close proximity to common people, even the sick and wounded, is in striking contrast to her husband, the undefiled god-emperor.

(bottom) *PWR* 274, 2 June 1943, p. 2. This article about the empress' review of women's war work places her at the symbolic helm of the female war effort. When performing these "feminine" duties (such as visiting the sick and injured), the empress appeared without the emperor. She wears a Western-style dress and hat, her usual attire for public appearances. The official dress code for emperor and empress comprised a variety of kimono for Japanese rituals and a variety of Western suits for these more "modern" roles of the monarchs adapted from the constitutional monarchies of Europe, roles designed to create public personas for them as codified in Meiji times.

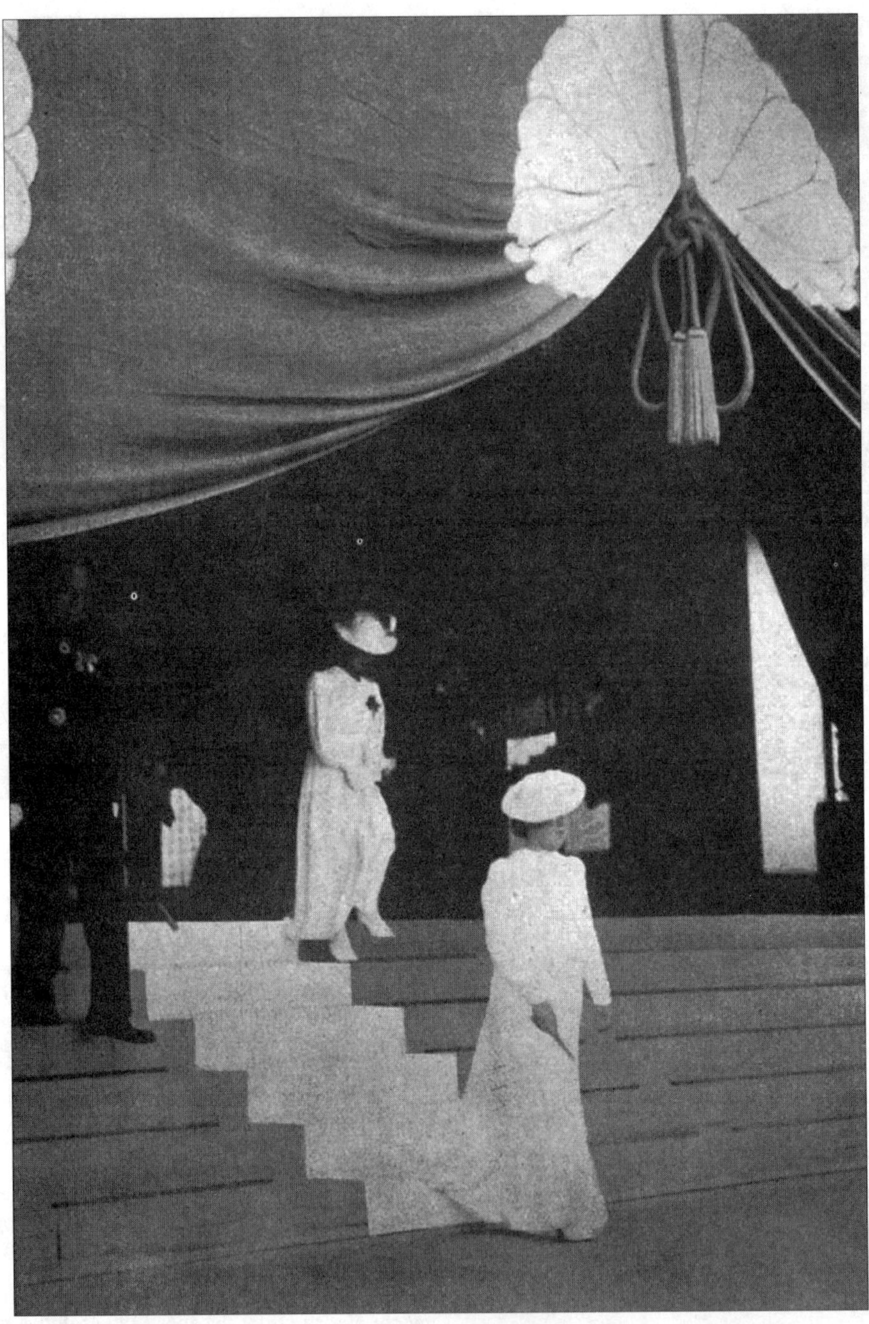

14. *History Pictures* 354, November 1942, p. 3. "Both of Their Imperial Highnesses Offer Prayers to the Heroic Spirits at Yasukuni" was the title of two similar photographs, one of the emperor and the other of the empress, descending the stairs of Yasukuni Shrine after taking part in the autumn ceremony enshrining war dead. Photographs of the emperor and empress together at Yasukuni never appeared in the wartime press, and the empress' Yasukuni visits never appeared at all in *PWR*. *History Pictures*, a magazine with content very similar to contemporary British tabloids, often printed photographs of the many members of the Japanese nobility. Photographs of the empress at Yasukuni were regularly seen in *History Pictures*.

The activities of women's organizations, for years semi-governmental in character, did not undergo a radical change under male leadership; their activities simply became mandatory and more far-reaching, thanks in part to compulsory membership. The government's goal, in mobilizing women and determining women's lifestyles, was to create warrior-wives who would fully support the war effort. Upon its creation in 1942, the Great Japan Women's Association became the strongest link between women, the government, and the war effort.

Any nation at war expects its citizens to provide the most basic matériel of the war effort, personnel, and Japan was no different. The government encouraged women to marry and start families as soon as possible, and to make their selfless devotion to their families the model for their sons' sacrifices on the battlefield.[2] Eligible young women were praised for taking furloughed soldiers and sailors as husbands, sometimes having only a week of married life together before the man left for the front, often going to his death. The Great Japan Women's Association busied itself with motherhood education programs. One of the few social improvements made during the war years was the establishment of day-care centers. It was not enough that healthy young women served the nation by having children; they were expected to leave child-rearing to older women in day-care centers while they manned the war factories.

15 and 16. *Japanese Woman*, February (left) and September (right) 1943. The official monthly magazine of the Great Japan Women's Association often placed images of archetypical on its cover. Here we see two sides of wartime womanhood: the loyal wife, knitting a soldier's socks at home, and the air defense warrior, keeping her family, her neighborhood, and her nation safe against the threat of air raids. (The title was written left to right [in Western fashion] in the February issue, later from right to left [in traditional Japanese style].)

17-19. The duty of every able-bodied, adult woman was to bear children and raise them to be responsible citizens. As we shall see in the Conclusion, the media credited the Japanese woman's spirit of self-sacrifice with fostering selfless valor in their warrior-god sons.

(top left) *PWR* 218, 29 April 1942, p. 17. The Healthy Citizens Campaign of 1-8 May: "Multiply! Strong Children, Strong Citizens." The graph's curve projects the population of Japan's Home Islands from seventy million in 1930 to one hundred million in 1960. The collage implies that today's babies are tomorrow's pilots and munitions makers.

(top right) *PWR* 337, 6 September 1944. Five-year-old boy triplets, full of martial spirit. The "Signboard of the Times" reads, "Lively, lively, strong and sturdy [we grow], / Receiving august blessings from His Imperial Highness. / This is the strength of a people uncramped. / Let's use this strength to shoot down the enemy." The inset is a photograph of the boys that had appeared in an earlier issue of *PWR*.

(bottom) *PWR* 338, 13 September 1944. Childbearing was every woman's first duty, but war work was not to be neglected. This warrior wife seems to have found the perfect balance between the two, sewing soldiers' gloves while nursing her child. The "Signboard of the Times" reads, "At the end of a narrow lane, / The tedious work of making gloves / Is important work. / These innumerable, anonymous efforts, / Make the airplanes fly, the ships run."

Many women found themselves single parents, their husbands serving in the military or, worse still, dead. With the entire nation facing hardships, the press paid little attention to the plight of war widows, although one article in *PWR* 84 (27 September 1939, pp. 8-9) describes a colloquium devoted to helping widows adjust to raising children on their own. The article advises the children: "You must listen to your mothers now," naming these women as the authority figures in their households. While remarrying was a possibility for these women, few men would want to take on the burden of providing for stepchildren. Widowed mothers were forced to rely in part on the good graces of extended family to make ends meet.

20 and 21. (left) *PWR* 137, 9 October 1940.

As all Japan celebrated the 2,600th anniversary of the founding of the nation, this cover photograph of a widow visiting her soldier husband's grave, was a sobering reminder of the price of national greatness and the pursuit of empire. The caption takes the form of the widow's thoughts before the grave.

"The night sky grows light in a new era in Japan and overseas. So much has changed since three years ago.

"'Dear, [the goal of] your sacrifice is now truly being reached,' [so thinks] the widow who places an offering of a bouquet of the seven flowers of autumn. Today, the refreshing winds of a new season blow away the sadness in her breast." Photograph: Umemoto Tadao.

(right) *PWR* 125, 17 July 1940, p. 1. "Holding Their Orphaned Children, They Stand on the Teacher's Platform." These war widows who have just completed their teaching certificates visit Yasukuni Shrine to announce to their dead husbands' spirits that they will raise their children while taking on their new profession as teachers. Teaching would allow these widows to support themselves and their children without remarrying, an opportunity not afforded most women. Widows rarely appeared in the pages of *PWR* during the Second Sino-Japanese War, and even less so after their numbers increased dramatically after the outbreak of the Pacific War.

Women were also essential to Japan's efforts to colonize Taiwan, Korea, and, later, Manchukuo (Manchuria). Japanese business concerns established Japanese settlements throughout the Manchurian countryside, where Japanese families lived like landed gentry, often enjoying a lifestyle unattainable in Japan, complete with Manchurian servants and tenant farmers. The Japanese men who made their fortunes in Manchukuo were eager to have families. A brisk matchmaking business placed eligible young women from Japan in Japanese settlers' Manchurian homes. The government wholeheartedly encouraged emigration to Manchuria.

22-27. *PWR* 125, 17 July 1940, pp. 20-21. A two-page spread about "The Young Women Who Have Gone to Manchukuo." On 10 July, two young women from each prefectural young women's youth group were sent to Manchukuo as "female agricultural warriors." Since they were chosen from girls' high schools, these were intelligent young women.

(right page, top right, p. 20) Raising rabbits.

(right page, top left) They enter the training camp marching, carrying before them the Japanese and Manchurian flags.

(right page, bottom) Using sickles to harvest wheat.

(left page, top, p. 21) They sincerely perform their morning prayers.

(left page, bottom right) They attend a lecture by Katō Shūji, principal of Japan Citizens' High School.

(left page, bottom left) In the hour after finishing drills and before lights out, they write happy letters to their families back home in Japan.

Boosting morale was an important role for the people on the home front, and this duty fell largely upon women. As part of the spiritual mobilization movement, women were told to pray for victory, and to write encouraging "comfort letters" (*imonbun*) to and prepare comfort packages (*imonbukuro*) for soldiers. Care of the Buddhist and Shinto altars in a Japanese home usually fell upon the housewife, and by extension, women were usually the guardians of a family's spiritual well-being.

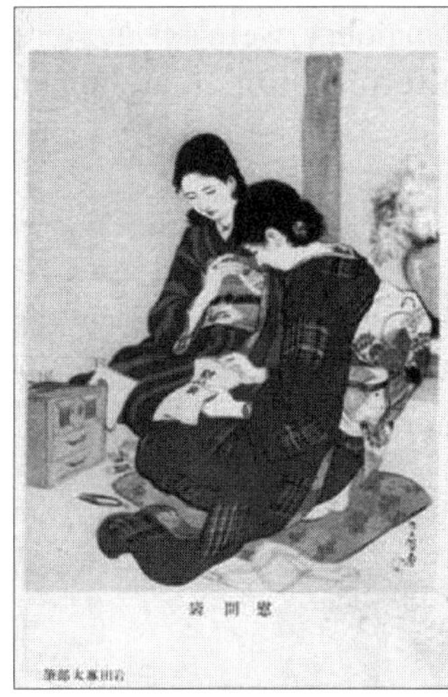

28-32. Five postcards, ca. 1935, from a set printed by the Patriotic Soldiers' Relief Fund, each reproducing a patriotic painting by a famous living artist. They all illustrate the same dynamic of morale: desirable, beautiful women produce it, and men receive it. These women are dressed in very showy kimono, one sign that these were printed before the "national emergency" of 1937.

(top row) "Praying for a Soldier's Fortune" by Takabatake Kashō, "[Making] Comfort Packages" by Iwata Sentarō, and "Soldiers with Comfort Packages" by Tomita Chiaki.

(bottom row) "[Writing] Comfort Letters" by Takenaka Hidetarō and "[Reading] Comfort Letters" by Tada Hokuchō.

One aspect of "morale" was reminding the men on the battlefield of the women waiting for them back home. Japan did not trumpet images of scantily-clad women, indeed, such images virtually disappeared from the mainstream wartime press. Pin-ups were very rare in wartime Japan, in which the ideological war with the West was couched in terms of Western "decadence" and "immorality." From the captured personal affects of Japanese soldiers, we know that they often kept photographs of a wife or sweetheart, and occasionally a contraband erotic picture, although soldiers who were found with such could face ridicule or hazing by their officers or seniors. Nevertheless, Japan's hard-working, chaste maidens were always presented as pretty, even in the grimmest days of the war, offering proof that Japanese spirit was undeterred by hardship and deprivation.

33. *Asahigraph* (29:10), 8 September 1937, p. 30. This advertisement for Okasa, a female "hormone" concoction, claims to be effective in guarding against fatigue while also "protecting youthfulness." The bared breast in shadowed silhouette, the features of the face attractive but indistinct, invites the viewer to imagine becoming this woman, or being with this woman.

Risqué or suggestive pictures of women, with the exception of the "primitive" inhabitants of occupied lands, would disappear after a 1938 ban on lasciviousness in media. The censor bureau enacted the ban in order to make the media more responsible for maintaining a sober mood in keeping with the war in China. From 1937 to 1945, the media showed less and less female flesh, as women disappeared behind censorship and beneath layers of padding. By contrast, male flesh became commonplace in coverage of Japanese soldiers in China and during the Pacific War. It was *PWR*, not the private press, that treated the male body as the raw material with which to express wartime ideals and goals.

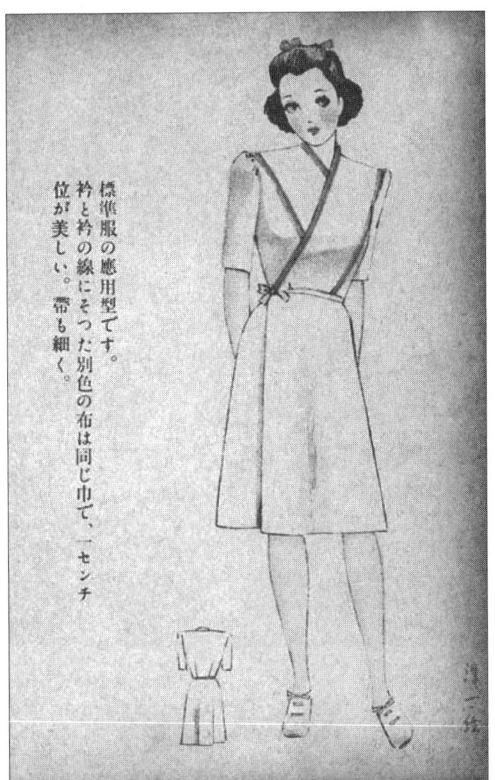

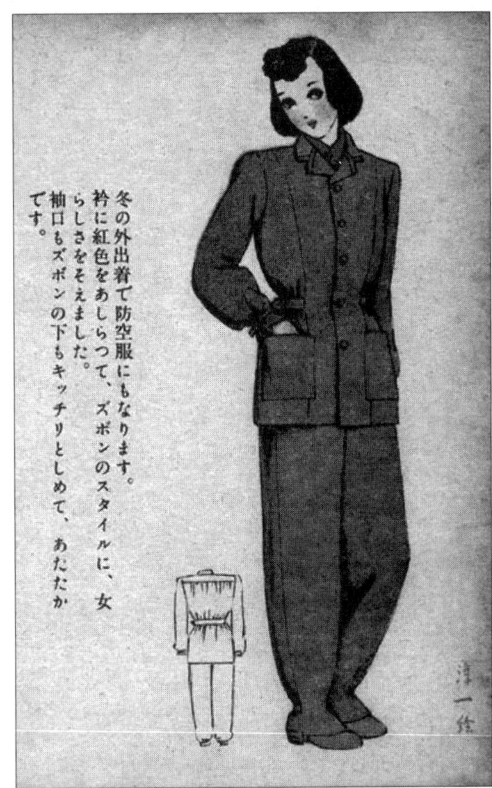

34 and 35 (left). Ca. 1940 fashion postcard, with drawing by Nakahara Jun'ichi,[3] published by Nihon Sosakusha, Tokyo. Marked on reverse, "care letter" for soldiers. Hundreds of postcards like these were printed during the China war, meant to be sent to soldiers. This rather racy costume looks like a nurse's uniform, although in reality, a nurse's uniform was much less revealing (see figure 70). The text claims that this one-piece dress "conforms to the [government-issued] standard of dress," and advises that "a one-centimeter [roughly, ½-inch] strip of edging, in a different color, is attractive, and the sash should be thin, too." The red and white colors are patriotic, of course.

(right) A postcard from the same series by Nakahara. "This outdoor wear for winter also serves as air raid clothing. A touch of red at the collar and the style of the pants embellish them with femininity (*onnarashisa*)." As is much in evidence in woodblock prints, red undergarments for women were very popular throughout the Edo period and after.

36 and 37. (left) *PWR* 151, 15 January 1941. Morale-boosting with battledores, New Year's 1941. This New Year's issue featured three beauties—a Japanese woman in the center flanked by a German and Italian—representing the Axis powers, each holding a battledore[4] with an Axis leader on it: Konoe, Mussolini, and Hitler. Having the Japanese woman holding Mussolini, the Italian holding Hitler, and the German holding Konoe, visually reinforced the image's message of solidarity. Representations of Hitler and Mussolini were uncommon in the Japanese wartime press.

The Japanese woman wears formal kimono (not the modern, fascist-inspired "citizens' uniform"). Here, even as she represents Japan's place in the Axis, she is still the receptacle of "traditional" Japanese culture, especially at New Year's, one of Japan's most important holidays. They hold battledores, a wooden paddle used in an ancient Japanese New Year's game resembling badminton.

(right) *PWR* 354, 10 January 1945. Morale-boosting with battledores, New Year's 1945. The "Cheerful Fight" (i.e., "Grin and Bear It") campaign. As Japan neared crisis in the final months of the war, women were still responsible for home front morale, to "keep on smiling" through devastating air raids. These women are decked out in their holiday finest, nothing better than drab fatigues, the "citizens' uniform." The woman third from left sports a rather flowery-patterned *monpe*, probably tailored from an old kimono. (Monpe were baggy all-purpose peasant pants; the word was also used for Western-style women's work pants. See *PWR* 79, 23 August 1939, p. 8.)

In contrast to *PWR*'s 1941 New Year's cover (or the New Year's 1941 *Asahigraph* cover, figure 1), here we see the toll of three years of the Pacific War: the absence of color and quality in printing (even at New Year's), the dramatic change in women's fashions, and the growing sense of isolation Japan must have felt as the war in Europe entered its final phase and the Allies approached the Japanese homeland.

In addition to the Great Japan Women's Association, the Neighborhood Associations constituted a powerful, nationwide network that mobilized women for the war effort. There was some overlap, in that Neighborhood Associations also depended on women to carry out air defense, self-policing activities, praying for victory, and morale-boosting, in addition to the vital task of ration distribution. Directives to the Neighborhood Associations came from a male bureaucracy within the centralized government's Home Ministry. The Neighborhood Associations were the backbone of wartime social infrastructure. Surprisingly, the nationwide system of Neighborhood Associations only came into being in 1940, although the informally organized predecessors had roots extending back to Edo times.

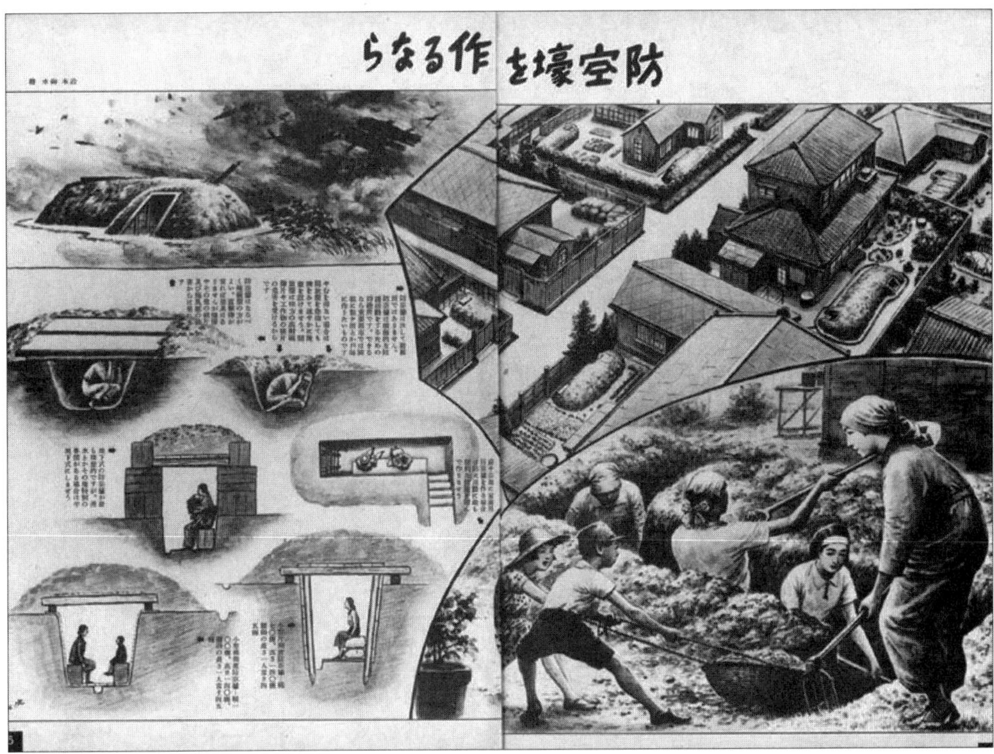

38. *PWR* 184, 3 September 1941, pp. 4-5. "How to Build an Air Raid Shelter." The responsibility for air defense fell heavily upon women. These are government instructions for building a backyard air raid shelter. It is dug, fortified, and operated by women, with the assistance of children, not men. The artist was one of Japan's best-known illustrators, Suzuki Gyōsui.

39-41. *PWR* 288, 8 September, 1943, p. 9. "Don't Stop Extinguishing the Fire: Bucket Brigade Competitive Meet in Osaka." A Neighborhood Association practice drill for air-raid prevention took the form of a bucket brigade competition.

(top left) A man oversees the women's training.

(top right) Before the competition begins, these warrior-wives in their air defense uniforms "fall in."

(bottom) Bucket brigades like that pictured here were, in reality, almost futile from the moment that napalm was used in the carpet-bombing of Japanese cities in early 1945.

War mobilization hinged both on promoting positive behavior and attitudes. Actions that ran counter to the war effort were ridiculed, chastised, and, in extreme cases, reported to the authorities. Government policy stressed the survival of the group over that of the individual and by emphasizing the homogeneity of the Japanese race as "children of the emperor . . . one in mind, many in body." As has been noted, the Day of Service to the Nation was one tool for regimenting the home front, especially women. The popular press rigidly defined wartime gender roles. Since all able-bodied men were supposed to be at the front, images of civilian men became nearly obsolete during the war. The media expressed little sympathy for the plight of women on the home front, who must have increasingly felt the pressures of taking on the work of men in addition to their own work, and of living in a police state, their every move scrutinized. The home front psychology, as revealed in contemporary private diaries and letters, quickly become one of self-censorship. A few examples from the mainstream press illustrate the psychological pressure on women, not only to conform but to outdo each other in showing patriotic fervor. Mechanisms of control penetrated the community. Thus women had to fear that a neighbor-informant might report a moment of lapsed patriotism, say, buying a few extra foodstuffs on the black market. Cartoons were particularly effective in castigating behavior deemed emblematic of "female" weaknesses: covetousness, vanity, indulgence.

42 and 43. *PWR* 251, 16 December 1941. Candid camera-style photographs from the article, "Here There Is Plenty to Spare for War Savings" targeted examples of women's unpatriotic behavior.

(left, p. 7) A well-dressed woman bearing armloads of packages (probably for the approaching New Year's holidays). The caption nearly accuses her of treason: "These days, such a street scene is extremely rare, but the camera only captures reality. Such a person should be sent to America." Photograph: Yoshida Gijūrō.

(right, p. 8) "There is no argument for the absolute need for a permanent. For the hair, it is the heart, not the shape, which is important. You will be praised as a pretty flower because you have donated the time and money [required for a perm] to the nation." The government banned perms in 1938 because they wasted resources and were contrary to "Japanese" values. The women's eyes in this uncredited photograph have been disguised, as if they were criminals.

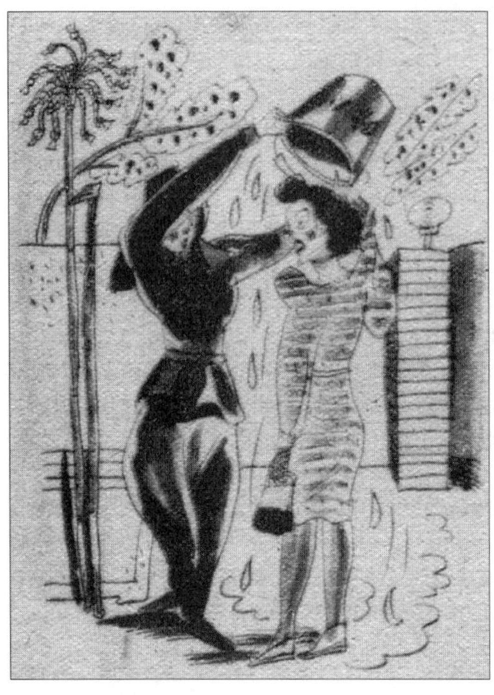

44-46. Cartoons were particularly effective tools for ridiculing inappropriate attitudes and behavior.

(top left) *PWR* 272, 19 May 1943, p. 23. "Wash Her Clean," by Emoto Eiichi, a cartoon with dialogue.

Older sister: "Don't you know what day this is?"

Younger sister: "It's Sunday."

Older sister: "It just so happens to be air defense uniform day, so what's with that American get-up? Brace yourself, I'm going to use this air defense water to wash away the enemy character of your mind!"

This drawing of an air defense uniform is more flattering to the figure than in reality.

(top right) *PWR* 208, 28 January 1942, p. 23. This cartoon about hoarding by Koizumi Shirō had no caption, and needs no explanation.

(bottom) *PWR* 204, 21 January 1942, p. 23. "Put it Out!" The title of this cartoon by Emoto Eiichi refers to both the smoking cigarette and the glaringly inappropriate behavior. The cartoon enumerates the wrongs of this denizen of a Ginza café: "(1) Ratted hair piled high, (2) fox fur stole, (3) bright red lipstick that makes her look like a cannibal, (4) smoking even though she's a woman, (5) legs crossed in imitation of a Yankee." The righteous indignation expressed here betrays more than a hint of misogyny and envy.

During the Second Sino-Japanese War in the late 1930s, women were expected to support the war effort by boosting morale, forgoing luxuries, participating in scrap drives and war bond drives, and keeping the home in good order. With more men drafted after Pearl Harbor, women were called upon to replace them on the home front. Before 1941, many women, especially in urban areas, already had some sort of job that brought in extra income, either in a cottage industry (taking in sewing or washing, for instance), an extension of the family business, or outside of the home. However, if these jobs were in businesses deemed "nonessential" to the war effort, the business itself, part and parcel, might be closed by government order (this happened to dance halls in 1938 and cabarets in 1944). Rationing of foodstuffs, restrictions on consumption, and special "luxury taxes" meant that restaurants and cafés could hardly operate, let alone turn

47-50. *PWR* 242, 14 October 1942, pp. 20-21. "Even Schoolgirls Have Taken off Their Uniforms [and Changed into Monpe]," an article extolling the volunteer harvest work of girls from Shirane High School in Niigata Prefecture. The Education Ministry's regional office granted the girls time off to work the fields.

(top right) "These maidens are cheerful all the time. Even when exerting themselves at work they are unaccustomed to, [they are thinking,] 'That's right, the joy of performing service [to the nation] makes it even more fun.'"

(bottom right) "The maiden squadron's dignified march toward the field, led by a banner proclaiming 'Donating Labor as Service to the Nation.' As they continue their service of sweaty labor, these girls receive splendid [physical] training, too."

(top left) "Those who cut, those who carry, those who hang the sheaves on the rails—their feelings are all in harmony, they find the work enjoyable and they make progress."

(bottom left) "Babysitting the [local] children falls into their hands. Their cheeks glow, watching after them as if they were their own younger brothers and sisters."

a profit. The government thus effectively corralled the urban female work force into war work, stressing that it should be performed as volunteer service to the nation (e.g., without pay). And in the countryside, where every hand was needed to plant and harvest, women bore the brunt of agricultural labor, even pulling plows through the fields after draft animals were requisitioned by the military.

Ironically, the government that frowned upon women having careers of their own was now recruiting them to fill a variety of "soft" jobs for which men were no longer required, jobs that had been reserved for men up to this time. The pages of *PWR* carried several articles showing women filling in for drafted men. Members of Japan's socialist movements, who had fought to open the Japanese workplace to women in the 1920s and early 1930s and were arrested and made to recant their personal convictions, must have cast a cynical gaze upon the many government-created "female firsts" appearing in the wartime press. And if these "female firsts" seemed to signal an easing of gender stereotypes where women are concerned, they only increased the pressure placed on men to serve in the military.

51. *PWR* 285, 18 August 1943, p. 16. A photoessay about high school girls' volunteer war work called "We Won't Be Beaten by Any American or British Girls" describes a recent labor directive prohibiting men from having "easy" jobs. Schoolgirls have filled communications jobs left vacant by men, such as postal carriers. The article points out that these girls are not afraid of working in the heat since they "won't be beaten by men" either. The article urges girls to think of this as volunteer service to the nation rather than an occupation.

⇨
いざ出動ですが女は身だしなみが第一――ちょっと鏡でパフをたゝく濱田さんのゆかしさ

52-56. *PWR* 205, 28 January 1942, pp. 20-21. A photojournalistic spread on (presumably the first) female bus drivers in Tokushima City, Shikoku. Even as women made inroads into the male workplace as "temporary replacements" for conscripted men, chauvinism hardly diminished in the first year of the Great East Asia War.

(counter-clockwise, from top right)

(top right) The twenty-one-year-old Miss Hamada behind the wheel of a Tokushima city bus.

(top left) "Fueling up for the morning run. The bus burns charcoal, which she has to stoke herself."

(middle) "She never forgets that she must look attractive, because she does have her pride as a woman of Japan."

(bottom left) Drivers waiting for their run. "Miss Hamada and the other female bus drivers busily knit, while their male coworkers play *shōgi* [a Japanese form of chess]."

(bottom right) "The female bus drivers pass their lunch break in a sewing class offered by the bus company at their dormitory."

The article says nothing about dormitory life. Before and during the war, many companies employing unmarried women forced them to live in company-owned and operated dormitories (ostensibly, in order to protect their chastity). Room and board was deducted from pay, leaving these women little discretionary income, which may explain why they "busily knit" and sew while their male coworkers pass the time playing games.

57-59. These three covers of *PWR* tell the official version of the evolution of women's war work and the changing face of the warrior-wife.

(top left) *PWR* 206, 4 February 1942. A man instructs a woman, wearing a housewife's apron, in the use of an industrial sewing machine.

(top right) *PWR* 314, 22 March 1944. "Leave the Munitions-making to Us." A female munitions worker wearing a voluminous uniform (the padding was probably for protection from the cold as well as from injury or air raids) needed no supervision.

(bottom) *PWR* 320, 10 May 1944. A team of female mechanics builds an airplane. The image is, of course, reminiscent of Rosie the Riveter. The "Signboard of the Times" says, "Those who scoffed and said, 'Ha, the likes of women!' now take a look at how skillful they are." The admonition is directed at those who scoffed that a woman was incapable of doing a man's job, and is a taunt to male factory workers.

寫眞週報
情報局編輯
十月六日・第二百九十二號・十セン
女性もあげて決戰へ

60. *PWR* 292, 6 October 1943. "Women Also Take up Arms in the Decisive Battle."

The caption says, "Military training for the students of Taizhong's Number One Girls' High School.

"Just because women are serving in the armed forces of the enemy countries of America and Britain does not necessarily mean that the goal for Japanese women is to train to become soldiers. However, in order to crush the enemy's impossible dream [of victory], all Japan is now striking as one body and the entire team will be distributed in the fight.

"There can be no distinction now between the front line and the home front and similarly, there can be no distinction between men and women throwing themselves into the cause of the national emergency. The will to pick up the rifle-bayonet, aim it at the enemy's chest, and plunge it in—all fifty million Japanese women must have that determination."

While the front cover and its caption seemed to say that women would be assigned combat roles, in fact this was not the case at all, and the inside contents of this magazine showed women joining the workforce to replace men called up for duty. The image of women holding rifles may have been meant as a warning: if women did not do more to boost wartime production and replace men in the workforce, they might have to take up arms. At this time, the formation of the Women's Volunteer Corps was more than a year in the future.

舵手も機関士も
わたしらで
熊本縣天草島

61 and 62. (top) *PWR* 292, 6 October 1943, pp. 6-7. A two-page spread highlighting the jobs women could fill as replacements for conscripted men. The right page shows some of the "light" work prohibited to men, and now open to women: waiter, chef, greeter, crossing guard, ticket taker, streetcar conductor, elevator operator, hat check, barber. The left page shows more demanding work women could perform, in this case toiling in munitions factories and in coal mines, dangerous professions that paid slightly higher wages. Women who took such jobs were paid from 65 to 80 percent of men's salaries for comparable work and experience.[5]

(bottom) *PWR* 290, 22 September 1943, p. 14. An article about a twenty-one-year-old Miss Sugimoto, a female ferry captain, probably a "female first" created by wartime exigencies. The article's title stresses female competence: "Leave the Steering and the Boiler Room to Us." Miss Sugimoto's sense of purpose is clear, her words reflect, "the true spirit of a woman of the empire" when she says (in her Kumamoto dialect): "We need all the men on the front line of defense. So even though it's tough for us, we women will work hard to keep the boats moving." The accompanying article states that eighty women were working in ship's boiler rooms.

63-65. *PWR* 292, 6 October 1943, pp. 8-9. "Even the Women of the Enemy Country, America, Have Been Mobilized" shows three examples of American women at war work: (from left to right): railroad worker, munitions work, and airplane technician. The article focuses on the need for greater mobilization of Japanese women. Conspicuously absent is any mention of American women in the armed forces, no doubt because the Japanese military was not ready to suggest that women could be, or should be, admitted into its own ranks. The tone of the article is condescending: "Everybody thought that America was a place where Yankees make merry with jazz, wallow in sports, and are the laziest people on earth, but with the outbreak of war, they have changed their tune . . . From girls to housewives, they fill the war factories . . . And we must beat back those Yankees with our own hands." These photographs probably first appeared in an American magazine (*Life* was one common source) and reached Japan via Europe, although they are uncredited here.

Japan concurred with Nazi Germany: in the fascist model of society, a woman's role was primarily that of mother and homemaker, and gender distinctions were to be maintained in wartime, to the degree possible.[6] Unlike the United States, Great Britain, Australia, and Canada, the Japanese military had little use for women in any official capacity, other than military nurse, although one patriotic women's group campaigned for the formation of a women's volunteer corps in 1937.[7] A rare article in *PWR* 53 (22 February 1939, pp. 10-11) extolled four nurses who died serving in the China war. In the late 1930s, as Japanese society was transformed to total warfare, the Japanese military recruited a few prominent women writers as part of its Pen Corps (*Pen butai*),[8] also toying with the idea of female pilots. The potential of these new roles for women was left untapped. The military's procurement of thousands of women from colonized and occupied regions to stock frontline brothels forced these so-called "comfort women" to endure horrific abuse. The wartime press was silent about this institutionalized abuse of women, which the public first learned of during the 1946-1948 war crimes trials.

As the war situation deteriorated, the Women's Volunteer Labor Corps (Joshi Teishin Kinrō Tai) was established in 1944. It expanded women's responsibilities and called upon women and girls to fill jobs in munitions and in heavy industry left vacant by male conscripts. Many women worked outside the home before the war, but the nature of war work was quite different: its purpose was to serve the nation, not to increase the family's earnings. Primary allegiance was to state authority, rather than to familial authority. For instance, during the war, mothers were encouraged to send children to day-care facilities and to allocate the precious resource of their time and energy to the war effort. Only a "selfish" woman would devote all of her time to her children.

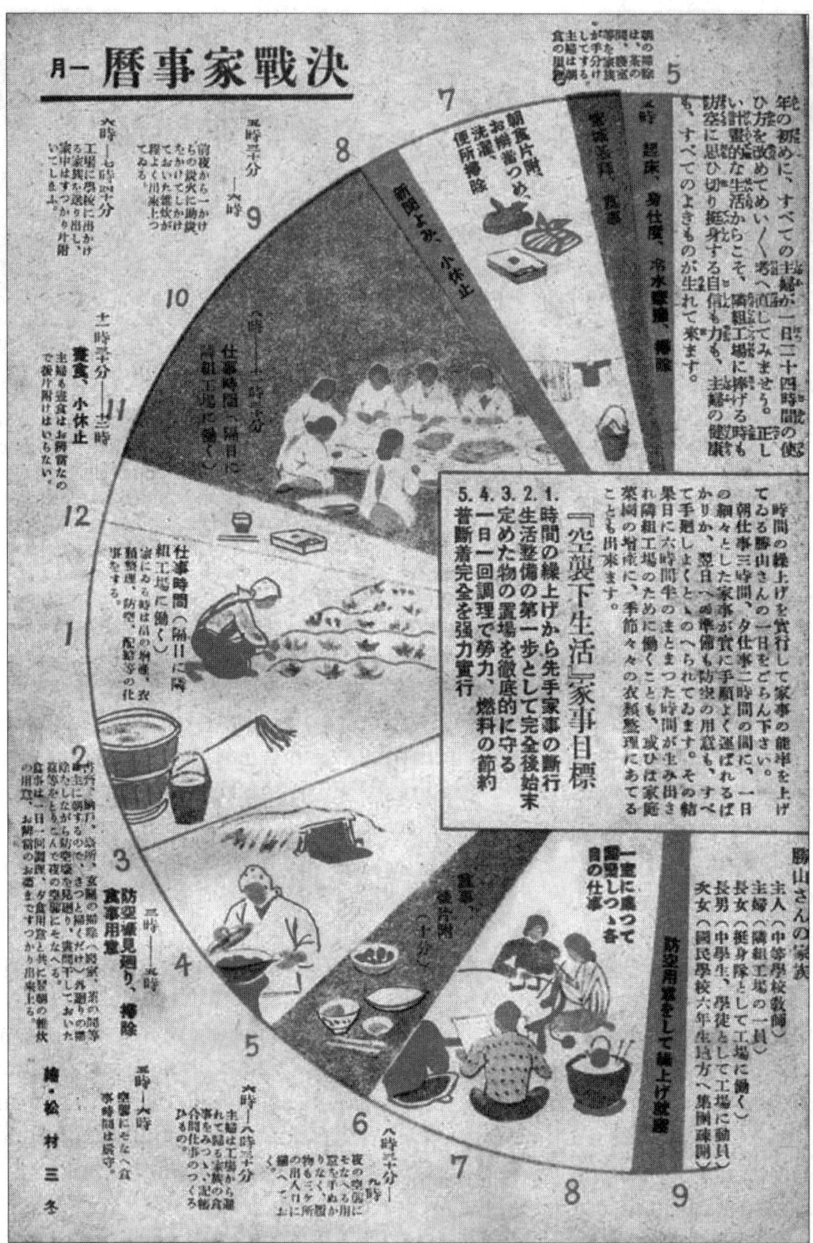

66. *Women's Companion* (39:1), January 1945, back cover. "Decisive-Battle Housework Schedule for January." Patriotic women's groups convened a colloquium to determine how women could balance being good homemakers and mothers as well as productive war workers. The result, this "decisive battle" schedule, was proposed for a typical mother in a family of five. The schedule begins at 5 A.M. and ends at 9 P.M. and allows for two rest periods, fifteen minutes between 7:45 and 8 A.M., and thirty minutes to eat lunch, read the newspaper, and rest. In this scheme, the wife is not only responsible for all of the cooking and cleaning (with few or no electrical appliances or modern conveniences), but does six and a half hours of war work per day in manufacturing or agriculture. The final chore, before lights out at 9 P.M., is checking to make sure that the home's air raid preparations are complete. The attractive fan-shaped graphic, credited to Matsumura Mifuyu, squeezes sixteen hours into a semi-circle—a mere six hours on the face of a clock.

67 and 68. (top) *PWR* 5, 16 March 1938. Female members of the Youth Aviation Club in 1938. This is one of a handful of *PWR* articles addressing the idea of women fliers. These women only trained with gliders and did not pilot aircraft. The article may have been prompted by a 1937 article in *Asahigraph* showing women in a flying club taking off in gliders. *PWR* 64 (10 May 1939) had an article on German "air girls" (flight attendants) for Lufthansa.

(bottom) *PWR* 264, 24 March 1943, pp. 20-21. A two-page spread on middle-aged Osaka women in gliders. The article made no direct connection between women fliers and the military, and did not propose that women actually pilot motorized craft. Of course, by this time, Japan desperately lacked airplanes for trained pilots and had none to spare for noncombat roles.

69 and 70. (left) *Asahigraph* (31:20) *China Battle Front Photographs* 69, 16 November 1938, p. 22. "With the Rising Sun Flag over the Enemy Capital, I Am Unable to Hold Back Tears" is the title that Hayashi Fumiko gave to her photoessay as a special correspondent for the Japanese army in China. Her photographs are rather typical amateur shots of soldiers in the field and at rest.

A very successful writer, Hayashi (1903-1951) was one of two women recruited by the Cabinet Information Bureau for the twenty-two-member "Pen Unit" (*Pen butai*),[9] sent to China in order to raise public awareness of the war—a 1930s version of the "embedded reporter." Hayashi included this photograph of herself with her camera aboard an unidentified transport ship on the Yangtze, presumably on its way to Wuhan.

Once Japanese society had been successfully mobilized for total war, the Pen Unit lost most of its raison d'être. After the outbreak of the Pacific War, some conscripted male writers were sent to Indonesia, the Philippines, and other occupied areas as part of the propaganda corps attached to the army. Women were not drafted and so women writers were not sent abroad by the military after 1941.

(right) *PWR* 230, 22 July 1942. The cover announces, "Special Report: Constructing Great East Asia." A Japanese nurse takes time to teach Japanese to an Indonesian girl. Curiously, *PWR* printed far fewer articles about Japanese nurses than about nurses of other nationalities, including Taiwanese, Philippine, and Vietnamese nurses caring for Japanese troops. The message seemed to be that Japanese women could best serve the war effort by staying at home. This is a rather unusual image of a Japanese nurse acting as a colonizer.

With Japanese forces in full retreat across the Pacific, and with invasion imminent, the government began to prepare for total mobilization of Japanese society. From 1944, able-bodied women were trained (as civilians) as part of the bamboo spear policy to defend against invasion. Only after the loss of Okinawa did the Japanese government promulgate the Volunteer Military Service Law (Giyū Heieki Hō), on 23 June 1945, conscripting all women between the ages of seventeen and forty into a National Volunteer Combat Corps (Kokumin Giyū Sentōtai), commonly called the National Volunteer Army (NVA) in the English-language *Nippon Times*. The Great Japan Women's Association was dissolved and its members redistributed into the NVA, which was to assist (and take orders from) the military in the event of an Allied invasion of Japan. Female troops were not inducted into the army or deployed before the war ended.

71 and 72. (left) *PWR* 265, 31 March, 1943, p. 9. Barefoot middle-school girls practice kendo. Martial arts training for women was becoming commonplace, mandatory even, by 1943, as the Japanese government began to ponder the role of civilians, including women, children, and the elderly, in repelling the anticipated invasion of the Japanese archipelago.

(right) *PWR* 269, 28 April 1943, p 3. "Training Mothers to Be Healthy Soldiers." During the annual "Citizens' Health Campaign" (1-10 May, formerly one week, but at this time, ten days), housewives train with bamboo spears. The site is a local temple yard, and it seems that cherry petals have scattered across the ground. When women did see battle on Saipan and Okinawa, they were expected to fight with whatever they could find: bamboo spears or farming tools. The lot of women who saw actual combat was a far cry from the glorified media image of the warrior-wife.

In preparation for total war, men who controlled the government and the military imposed their ideas about gender upon women: how women should act and dress, and even what they should think. This was, without a doubt, an expression of chauvinism. The military's largest goal, however, was not to denigrate women, but to mobilize them. Crucial to this aim was instilling an unquestioning obedience. Many Japanese feminists embraced mobilization,[10] if not subordination. Of course, after 1937, and particularly in 1944 and 1945, with the formation of the National Volunteer Army, the gendered division of labor eroded. As the war situation worsened, women were expected to perform their "traditional" roles as well as to replace men on the home front and even, in the event of invasion of the homeland, in battle. In the final year of the war, the government promoted a powerful image of the Japanese woman on the home front, her fierce resolve equal to that of a front-line soldier. These fierce images of attractive young women with fine features and unblemished skin are evocative of enduring notions of female beauty. Even so, these wartime pictures of female strength and determination must have been empowering in unintended ways. They anticipated the new freedoms and rights that Japanese women would strive for in the postwar years.

73. *PWR* 333, 9 August 1944. The "Signboard of the Times" says "Fretting over the future course of the war only pays lip service to worry. And that's being [an idle] onlooker. As for me, I'll do it. In order to win, I'll do anything. I'll bring about victory with my own two hands!"

The map behind the young woman shows Saipan, the first piece of Japan's prewar territory to fall into enemy hands. The fierce fighting on the island was just ending as this magazine hit the newsstands.

In the final year of the war, this fierce image of a competent, determined, powerful woman emerged, in sharp contrast to the image promoted at the beginning of the war. This larger-than-life, 11½-by-16¼-inch close-up is the female counterpart to the soldier on the cover of *PWR* 329 (12 July 1944; see Chapter 3, figure 1).

This is the woman who would survive the war, receive the vote and a range of civil and economic rights under the occupation, and continue to multitask in order to rebuild Japan into the world's second largest economy. Of course, she is descended from generations of tough, hardworking women, but in the modern period, she meets some of her largest challenges in the final years of the war.

Notes

1. Figures for patriotic women's associations membership cited in Chizuko Ueno, *Nationalism and Gender*, translated by Beverley Yamamoto (Melbourne: Trans Pacific Press, 2004), p. 17.

2. Chizuko Ueno, *Nationalism and Gender*, pp. 20-21.

3. Nakahara Jun'ichi (1913-1983) gained fame in the 1930s for his illustrations for *Girls' Club* (*Shōjō kurabu*). He is best remembered today for his highly influential manga of the 1950s through 1970s.

4. Highly decorative New Year's battledores became popular in the Edo period, when famous kabuki actors or courtesans were a favorite motif.

5. The *Orient Year Book, 1942* (Tokyo: Asia Statistics, 1943, p. 208) states that in 1941, the average daily wage for transport workers was 2.5 yen for males and 1.44 yen for females, for mining workers 3.39 yen for males and 1.45 yen for females. *The Japan Year Book, 1938-39* (Tokyo: Foreign Affairs Association of Japan, 1939) provides the following figures for 1937 average daily wages: hosiery-knitter: male, 1.98 yen, female, 0.75 yen (p. 755); maker of matches: male, 1.12 yen, female, 0.62 yen (p. 756); day-laborer: male, 1.51 yen, female 0.79 yen (p. 756). The same source cites average daily wages for farm work in 1936 as follows: farm workers by the year: male, 0.50 yen, female 0.35 yen; by the season: male: 1.00 yen, female, 0.80 yen; by the day: male, 0.89 yen, female 0.67 yen (pp. 756-757).

6. For instance, Prime Minister Tōjō, in an address to the Diet in October 1943, stated that "due to the fact that the female draft would cause the collapse of the Japanese family system[,] we shall not institute it at the present time" (quoted in Chizuko Ueno, *Nationalism and Gender*, p. 41).

7. Chizuko Ueno, *Nationalism and Gender*, p. 18. Ueno writes, "It is reported that an increasing number of young women came forward volunteering to go to the war front, but the authorities announced that they would not allow this."

8. Donald Keene writes in *Dawn to the West: Japanese Literature in the Modern Era, Fiction* (New York: Holt, Rinehart, and Winston, 1984), that when the Pen Unit was formed in August 1938, "so many writers wished to join that not all could be accommodated" (p. 927). For a brief description of the Pen Unit's activities in China, see *Dawn to the West*, p. 929.

9. Hayashi had been to China in December 1937 as a *Mainichi Newspaper* correspondent and "was proud to be the first Japanese woman inside Nanking [Nanjing] after its fall that month." In 1938, Hayashi "was so irritated that the *Mainichi* had chosen her rival, Yoshiya Nobuko, to cover the fall of Hankow [Hankou] that she leaped aboard the first *Asahi Shimbun* truck she saw in the fighting zone, and thus had the added distinction of being the first Japanese woman to set foot inside that city after its fall" (Keene, *Dawn to the West*, p. 1143). Zeljko Cipris notes that Hayashi was evidently unimpressed by China: "In her book *The Battlefront* [*Sensen*] she concedes that Chinese territory (which she openly wishes to annex) is desirably fertile and sporadically enchanting, yet insists that its 'filthy soil,' muddy rivers, and landscape resembling 'a heap of rotten fruit' cannot compare with the 'purple hills and crystal streams' of her homeland." See Hayashi Fumiko, *Sensen* (Tokyo: Asahi Shimbunsha, 1938), pp. 15, 108, 196, 200. See Zeljko Cipris, "Responsibility of Intellectuals: Kobayashi Hideo on Japan at War," [unpaginated], n22, in *Japan Focus*, available at http://japanfocus.org/products/details/1625.

10. In her chapter titled "The War Responsibility of Ordinary Women," Chizuko Ueno summarizes Kanō Mikiyo's *Jūgo shi* (*The History of the Home Front*), noting that "it is clear that the female masses did not necessarily take a negative view of the war. Women's participation in the public sphere, made possible by war, was both exhilarating and brought with it a new identity for women, and this is remembered as a feeling of spiritual uplift. Among women's historians, it was Murakami Nobuhiko (1978) who first pointed out the liberating aspect of the war, and Kanō also comments that 'women being on the "home front" was one form of women's liberation'" (*Nationalism and Gender*, p. 38).

6. JUNIOR CITIZENS

In a society waging total war, children are not excluded from the march of events or exempted from the demands of the nation. Indeed, childhood is the period of preparing for war and training for battle, as children may be called on to make direct contributions to the war effort. Children everywhere had similar experiences during World War II; nevertheless, Japanese children were mobilized on a scale far beyond anything attempted in the United States, Great Britain, or even the occupied nations of Europe, perhaps surpassing even Nazi Germany.[1] Mobilization transformed children's lives: prior generations of boys and girls studied in primary schools, but after the educational reforms of the New Order, "junior citizens" (*shōkokumin*) trained in "Citizens' Schools" (*kokumin gakkō*), ready—and often, eager—to join the war effort full-time upon graduation at age thirteen. For those who continued their education, middle school offered advanced training in the specialized skills the military needed most.

As the war situation grew dire, the family unit buckled under growing demands for increased "national service" and "sacrifice" for the sake of the nation-as-family (*kokka*).[2] Many fathers were absent from the home, serving at the front or conscripted as wartime laborers. Japanese government sources state that 185,647 Japanese soldiers died in China between 1937 and 1941, and during the same period a similar number returned to Japan wounded, some permanently maimed. Fatalities increased dramatically during the Pacific War, when another 1,555,308 soldiers and sailors died,[3] leaving widows at the head of single-parent families and placing a strain on the resources of the extended family.

In June 1944, with the threat of air raids looming, the government announced a general evacuation of children. Hundreds of thousands of urban children were separated from their parents and sent to the countryside to live in government-supervised makeshift barracks. The total mobilization of Middle School students followed in August 1944. And the curriculum for all students for the school year beginning in April 1945 was simply "total mobilization." "Education" consisted of little more than long hours of bare-handed labor in agriculture or a munitions factory. These "junior warriors" had their own junior emperor, in the form of Crown Prince Akihito. They had their own weekly newsmagazines, which depicted children functioning with a minimum of adult supervision in a world of total, permanent war. Under these conditions, the family all but ceased to be and childhood innocence—indeed, childhood itself—frequently became a fatality of the war.

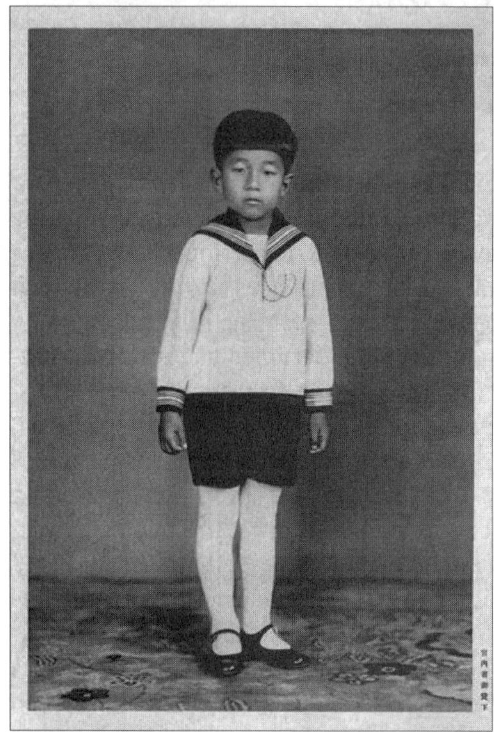

1 and 2. *PWR* 98, 10 January 1940. (right, inside front cover) Children in the plaza before the imperial palace. The text offers birthday wishes. "On the felicitous 23 December 1939, may the Crown Prince greet his sixth birthday hale and hearty. We are aware of the profound significance of his plan to diligently apply himself to studies as a first-level student at the Peers' School in April of the 2,600th year since the foundation of the empire."

(left, p. 1) Crown Prince Akihito, dressed in a boy's sailor suit. For junior citizens, a junior monarch. The layout, placing these two photographs on facing pages, creates proximity between worshipers and worshiped. Photograph: Imperial Household Ministry.

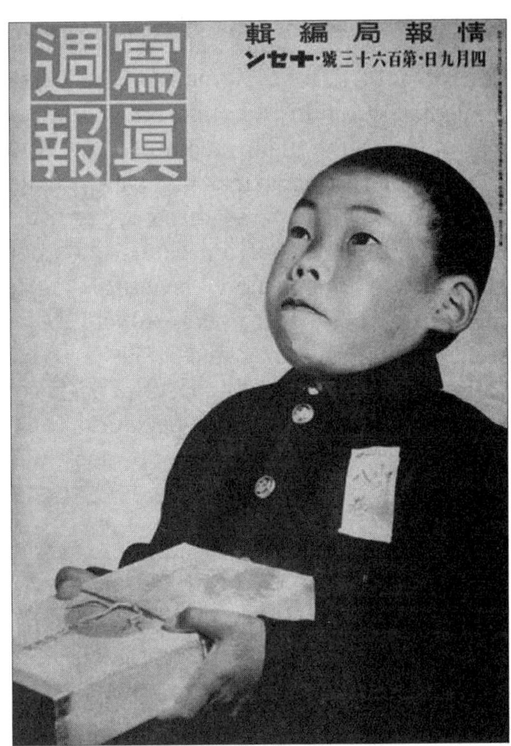

3 and 4. *PWR* 163, 9 April 1941. (right, front cover) "The bereaved children who receive sweets from the empress cry tears of gratitude at this sign of imperial kindness. Such a father has such a child: 'First I will report to father's spirit the wonderful gift from the empress . . . and I will continue in the footsteps of my father who is gone forever, and become a fine adult who will bring no shame to my father's name.' That is his manly vow."

Empress Nagako oversaw the distribution of sweets to the families of fallen soldiers. Images like this one taught children the wartime ethos of sacrifice and service, while also connecting them to the waging of war and to the imperial family. Photograph: Yoshida Sakae.

(left, p. 1) "His Imperial Highness the Crown Prince's Commemorative Visit to the *Mikasa*." Appropriately, the crown prince appeared in the same issue of *PWR*. He is photographed wearing the school uniform of the Peers' School, where he was a second-grade student. The *Mikasa*, flagship of the combined fleet during the Russo-Japanese War, was put on exhibition permanently in 1926 and is still on display at Shirahama, Yokosuka, site of the former Imperial Naval Headquarters and today a US naval base.

A steady program of militarization cultivated by the state from the Meiji era forward laid the groundwork for mobilizing children. The Imperial Rescript on Education (1890), frequently cited as the first enunciation of this goal, commands, "should emergency arise, offer yourselves courageously to the State; and thus guard and maintain the prosperity of Our Imperial Throne coeval with heaven and earth."[4] Meiji era children's magazines and pulp novels retold stirring tales of Japan's military heroes of the past as well as of the soldiers and sailors of the Sino-Japanese and Russo-Japanese Wars. The story of "Three Human Bullets" of the Shanghai Incident (1932) was almost immediately retold in comic book form (see Chapter 3, figures 15-19). Noma Seiji, who founded the giant media concern Kodansha in 1909, made a fortune publishing boys' and girls' magazines that were a major force in steering children's minds toward militarism.[5] When the government turned its attention toward mobilizing children, it copied several pages from Kodansha's book of tricks: the Education Ministry made children's textbooks more "beautiful" and "picture-book like," and used patriotic, even militaristic artwork for such subjects as arithmetic. *PWR* articles aimed at children used simpler language and added syllabary to any complex characters beyond the elementary-school reading level. *PWR* incorporated features meant to educate younger readers, in particular a back-page quiz called "Reviewing This Week's Issue: What Did You Learn?," presented as a set of questions with page numbers for answers.

5. *PWR* 159, 12 March 1941, pp. 4-5. An article in *PWR* introduced "New Text Books for Citizens' Schools."

"Finally, from the new school year in April, the name of primary school has been changed to Citizens' School, and compulsory education extended to eight years. And as you all know, elementary education must be faithful to this new age in which the substance of civilization is being renewed. Some of the new textbooks for the first and second grades of Citizens' School, which all of you have been waiting for, are finally ready. They are much more beautiful than the books you have been using. They are just like picture books."

At top is a reading text and at bottom, arithmetic, for first grade. The article also explains that the paper for children's schoolbooks was made in part from recycled clothes.

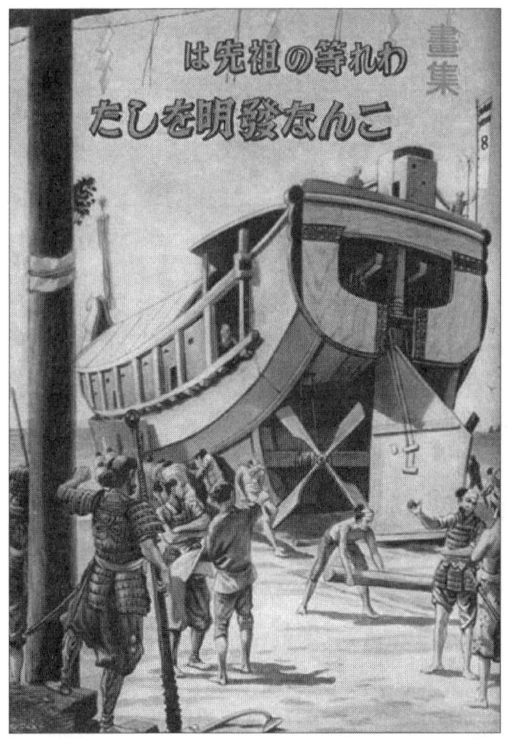

6-8. Kodansha juvenile magazines[6] invited children to imagine military exploits of the past, present, and future.

(top left) "Inventions of Our Ancestors. The World's First Screw Ship," drawn by Yanagawa Gōichi. This sixteenth-century ship with two propellers, "the pride of sea-power Japan," supposedly traveled to China and the South Pacific.

(top right) *Loyal, Brave Japan*, a separate volume of *Boys' Club*, appeared in August 1937, one month after the China war began. It contained a foreword by General Araki Sadao, who also supplied the calligraphy for the front cover as a sign of his "approval" of the book, and was a compilation of recent stories of "beautiful" and "righteous" battlefield death.

(bottom) "Spherical Tank," a drawing by Iizuka Reiji, in a series of fantastic inventions of future warfare. The United States was reported to be developing the tank.

9-11. *PWR* 159, 12 March 1941, pp. 18-19. "Children's Patriotic Paper Theater."[7] The government organized its own Patriotic Paper Theater Association and distributed its materials in schools and through the IRAA's "Children's Councils" and other civic organizations. The storyteller has temporarily set up in the tokonoma of a well-to-do house (top), the meeting place of a Children's Council. (Displayed in the tokonoma is a scroll honoring Hachiman, the deity most closely associated with war.) The story cards included text and dramatic instructions, enabling a good storyteller to engage children and draw out their responses. The rapt faces of the children (middle) attest to this. Children's Councils were another important aspect of mobilizing children, giving them the opportunity to play at participating in patriotic social organizations such as those their parents surely belonged to. An example of a few paper theater panels round out the article (below; also see Chapter 12, figures 18-21).

12. *Great East Asia War Picture Book: The Battle of the Philippines*, pp. 24-25. This 1944 children's book, with text by Ueda Hiroshi and illustrations by Tanaka Saichirō, was edited by the Army Information Division. The accompanying text, "Surrender of the American Soldiers," reads,

"9 April. The enemy on the Bataan Peninsula finally begged to surrender. They understood that, no matter how good a base they had, no matter how many troops and how much ammunition they had, they were no match for the Japanese army.

"An envoy bearing the message of surrender rode in a car draped in a white flag. Afterward, there must have been tens of thousands of prisoners of war who followed. All of them looked relieved that their lives had been spared, but from the perspective of the Japanese army, it was a truly strange sight to behold.

"From ancient times, the Japanese army has never surrendered to a foe. There has never been a single soldier whose life was so dear to him that he became a prisoner of war. In his final moments, he did the manly thing, because,

"'There is not a single one of us who has not made the resolve to commit *gyokusai* [death for honor] for the sake of the emperor.'

"The difference between the Japanese army and the American army is clearly manifested in this resolve. And isn't this also the reason that the Japanese army is stronger than any other?

"The beautiful Rising Sun flag was planted on the Bataan Peninsula soon after."

During the war, children were expected to perform volunteer service and make sacrifices for the nation on a par with adults, and many were happy to do so. Most patriotic programs were designed to allow children to directly participate or to imitate adult roles in them, just as they were encouraged, in the first years of the war, to "play" soldier and nurse. Radio Calisthenics, for instance, cut across all age groups and levels of society. So did victory gardens, scrap drives, and guarding against spies and other suspicious characters. The small sacrifices made by children, such as participation in scrap metal drives, were an inducement to adults to make greater sacrifices. Children were an effective tool in every aspect of war bond drives: in advertising, in sales, and as a targeted customer group, since low-denomination "pint-size bonds" (literally,

13 and 14. (left) *PWR* 2, 23 March 1938, p. 19. "Strong Bodies, Kind Hearts." The caption is partly in the form of children's dialogue.

"Our Dads and older brothers over in China can't be beat. 'My brother's a platoon leader.' 'Well, my aunt's in the Red Cross.' The February wind, the ice in the street, it's nothing to us. Forget about having a snack, don't be mean, play together nicely. With strong bodies and kind hearts, we are the Japan of tomorrow."

These photographs, amateurs' prize-winning entries from the pro-military monthly *Land of Cherry Blossoms* (*Sakura no kuni)*, use dramatic lighting and angle for a distinctly "modern" affect. "Casual" snapshots like these would be solicited by *PWR* for its regular feature, "Readers' Photographs," which it printed from 1938 to 1941.

(right) *PWR* 146, 4 December 1940. The cover reminds the people of the 12 billion yen goal for national savings. The caption reads, "Everybody, let's save money. Grandmother and Grandfather, Mother and Father, Older Brother and Older Sister, even Takehiko and Hato, little by little, we're going to save 12 billion yen—and do you know why? Because it's '12 Billion Yen for New East Asia.' With a population of one hundred million, how much will that be for each of us . . ."

"bean bonds," *mame saiken*) were marketed to children. War bond and soldier's life insurance advertisements often featured children. Since war bonds were an investment in the future of the Japanese nation and people, children were a persuasive force in bond marketing.

Children were also important in morale-boosting. They sent comfort letters, drawings, and comfort packages to soldiers, which usually required some degree of adult supervision. Civic and community groups also provided children with the opportunity to imitate adults' wartime roles, convening "children's councils" patterned after Neighborhood Association Councils. *PWR* 155 (12 February 1941, p. 17) carried an article on an East Asian Children's Council (Tō A Jidō Taikai) convened in Hibiya, Tokyo, on 1 February 1941, with child representatives from Thailand, Mongolia, Manchuria, China, and Japan delivering speeches. Boys represented four countries, and a girl represented China. The event, co-sponsored by the CIB and the Tokyo Municipal Government, brought together two hundred fifty non-Japanese Asian children living in Tokyo and six hundred fifty Japanese children from Tokyo schools, included a theatrical performance by boys and girls in native costumes, and concluded with everyone giving a "banzai" cheer, led by Nagai Ryūtarō, Director of the Imperial Rule Assistance Association. The purpose of the East Asian Children's Council was to promote Asian unity, under the direction of "older brother" Japan.

One of the core elements of the New Order was the reorganization of education. In 1940, elementary schools were renamed Citizens' Schools. The new education stressed "spiritual training" and physical education, as well as service to the nation. The military wielded enormous influence in determining the curricula of Citizens' Schools, which found numerous ways to make education patriotic and assist the cause of militarization. Art lessons produced patriotic calligraphy and pictures for home and public display, while composition was an opportunity to write on patriotic themes such as "Constructing Great East Asia." Science and mathematics lessons incorporated "hands on" experiments in raising (and harvesting) crops and livestock as part of the home front's "production boost." Children raised rabbits, which were skinned for their pelts and made into thermal gloves and caps for Japan's elite pilots. *PWR* 158 (5 March 5, 1941, pp. 18-19) included an article on a classroom that built and flew its own glider.

Of the Citizens' Schools' many contributions to the war effort, none was so great as the regimentation of children into ranks of junior soldiers directly connected to the military leadership through the Imperial Rule Assistance Association and later, the various branches of the military. This linkup was completed in 1940 as part of the New Order, and went into effect with the school year beginning in April 1941 when children began attending Citizens' Schools. The transition from traditional curricula to militarized education paved the way for the dissolution of the classroom itself in August 1944 for middle schools and April 1945 for Citizens' Schools. Junior citizens became junior warriors in fields, in factories, and on the front lines in the battle for the Home Islands. The Education Ministry lost its autonomy in determining school curricula, and by 1944, the army and navy was flooding second- and third-grade classrooms with picture books that were little more than slick recruitment brochures.

15-22. *PWR* 159, 12 March 1941. This issue of *PWR* was devoted to "Children and the Current [Wartime] Situation." Several photographs from this photoessay (on this and the facing page) describe the proper attitude of junior citizens, willing to do without and make sacrifices for the good of the nation.

(this page, top) "'Ichirō, you've got your ransel (backpack) and student cap on. Isn't it too soon? Citizens' School doesn't start until 1 April.' 'Yeah, I know, but Citizens' School will be brand new for us first graders, so me and Haruko are rehearsing.'"

(this page, bottom, p. 1) "'I'm a first grader at Citizens' School. I've got all my books and I can't wait to start. Can I read? Sure, I can read. *Red morning sun, red morning sun*. Right, Mom?'"

(facing page, top left, p. 2) "We are [Imperial] Rule Assistance [Association] kids."

(facing page, top right, p. 2) "Third-grader Saburō's mother took him to the sake-seller's house, where he borrowed Hikari's old schoolbooks."

(facing page, center left, p. 3) "The Saitōs' Kimi is graduating from sixth grade this year. Since she has two overcoats, she is making a gift of one to her neighbor Yoshiko. And Yoshiko is giving her old textbooks to Kimi's younger sister Fumiko."

(facing page, center right, p. 3) "'Hey, Gen. Aren't you too little for that?' 'Well, since you're graduating, older brother . . . and isn't it usual for a uniform to be too big?' Say, he's right. If it's a little too big, the tailor can make it fit."

(facing page, bottom left, p. 3) "This year, the tatami-mat maker's Haru is a first grader in Citizens' School, so her mother is determined to put aside two yen every month in student savings toward Haru's wedding."

(facing page, bottom right, p. 3) "'Come here, Kazuo.' 'What is it, Mother?' 'Look at this. Your father put aside 500 yen in China Incident Government Bonds to commemorate your starting school. Isn't it wonderful? You'd better study hard.'" Photographs: Yoshida Sakae.

私たちは翼賛のこどもたち

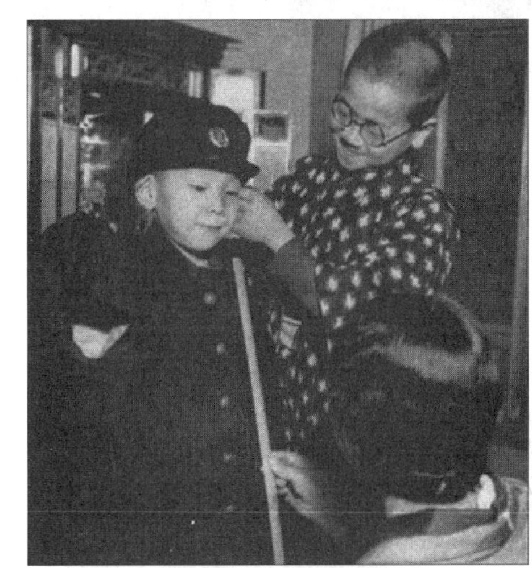

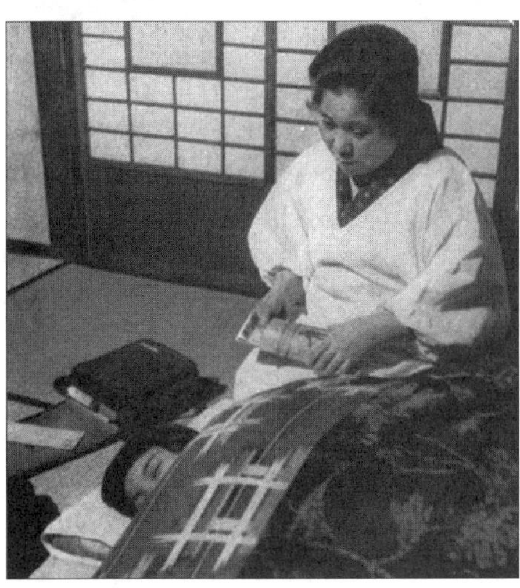

23-25. *PWR* 159, 12 March 1941, pp. 6-7. "Youth Are the Advance Army Shouldering Responsibility for Japan." This article describes the new vocational and military training at specialized high schools. For girls, cooking and housekeeping courses. For boys, horticulture, fishing (top), operating heavy machinery (bottom right), as well as military drills (bottom left). Most of these young men would be drafted before the war ended. Photographs: Umemoto Tadao.

PWR's articles focusing on children and children's concerns did something that children's magazines and general interest magazines (like *Asahigraph*) could not: they placed children at the center of national attention, linking their lives to national policy and the fate of the nation. Indeed, children appeared on the front cover of the inaugural issue of *PWR* (Chapter 4, figure 7). When the military made education one of its priorities, so did *PWR*, paving the way for mobilizing young citizens who would become the Youth Work Corps, the Youth Agricultural Volunteers, the Youth Air Corps, and the young soldiers and sailors of the immediate future. Many of the upper elementary school boys reading and appearing in *PWR* in 1938 would go to war in 1945, all of their memories having been formed in the years of "Incidents" and political assassinations, never having known Japan to be a peaceful, stable society.

Playing soldier and nurse may have familiarized children with military roles, but it did not necessarily militarize children. This was also true of Radio Calisthenics and the many kinds of "service to the nation" in which children could participate and which constituted important facets of children's socialization in wartime. In order to militarize children, the government initiated and augmented programs and events simulated military discipline and battlefield behavior. *PWR* 88 (25 October 1939) contained two photoessays describing programs exposing children to army life, one aimed at adolescent boys in their early teens, the other at boys and girls under the age of ten.

26. *PWR* 88, 25 October 1939, pp. 14-15. A photograph from an article, "Standing Their Ground at the Foot of the Mountain [Fuji], The Student Cap Brigade: Drills Commemorating the Fifteenth Anniversary of the Inauguration of Military Education Exercises." Military training programs like this one were already well-established before the Manchurian Incident and the mobilization of Japanese society began in the 1930s.

The caption reads, "Their screams shaking the mountain, the bayonets of both [student] armies clash in hand-to-hand combat." The combat was simulated, of course. Photograph: Umemoto Tadao.

27-28. (this page) *PWR* 88, 25 October 1939, pp. 14-15. "Standing Their Ground at the Foot of the Mountain, The Student Cap Brigade: Drills Commemorating the Fifteenth Anniversary of the Inauguration of Military Education Exercises."

Images like these still had a novelty element to them in 1939, but by 1944, with several youth training programs in place, they would be commonplace as pressure was placed on Japanese adolescents to enlist in the military and assume combat roles. Many would fight in the Pacific War. Photographs: Umemoto Tadao.

29-31. (facing page) *PWR* 88, 25 October 1939, pp. 16-17. "Pint-size Soldiers for One Day."

The article says, "Children are always drawn to strong soldiers, likable soldiers, so they had their mothers and older sisters take them to the soldiers' camp to get a taste of a day in a soldier's life."

(facing page, top left): "Boom! A terribly loud sound echoes across the grounds. The children quickly cover their ears with both hands. 'Wow!' The children peer into the barrel of the smoking cannon, and gasp with awe."

(facing page, top right) "The small squad that gathered before the main gate at 9 A.M. entered camp full of energy, holding commemorative flags just like the real thing. For each boy with a military uniform and a saber, there was a proud girl standard-bearer."

(facing page, bottom) "These toddlers and kindergartners form a motley squad, but the drill sergeant, who likes children, teaches them the proper way to salute. 'Uncle, how is this?'" Photographs: CIB.

一日だけの豆兵隊

祝一日入営
祝一日入営混成隊

At the outset of the war in the Pacific, children could participate in the euphoria by playing board games (see Chapter 4, figure 63, for an example) that allowed them to track the advances of Japanese troops or taught the basics of air defense. Japanese children, like children in other parts of the world, pasted miniature flags and bombs on a map of the Pacific. Of course, children in Allied countries did not receive a special ration of candy to celebrate the fall of Singapore, as Japanese children did. When the school year began in April 1943, large numbers of children were taken out of the classroom to work in factories producing war matériel. From their early teens, children were expected

32 and 33. (left) *PWR* 74, 19 July 1939. "Give Up Summer Vacation." The caption took the form of a schoolgirl's essay or diary entry.

"It was a sultry day, the cicadas' singing. Buzz. Buzz.

"Sweat rolled down our cheeks as we sewed the deep crimson crosses onto the white uniforms. But the heat was no problem for us, because our labor service to the nation gives expression to our boundless gratitude for the courage of the [nurse-] warriors who wear the white uniform.

"At some point, Miss 'A' felt so thankful that she pressed the white uniform to her breast and started to softly hum the tune, 'The Cannon Fire Is Not Far Away.'

"The summer vacation classroom was filled with a pure, clean feeling." Photograph: Suzuki Minoru.

(right) *PWR* 279, 7 July 1943. "These boy Production Warriors had one of their occasional days off, so they worked, until they were black with dirt, in the garden they made of the empty lot next to the factory. Usually, these boys are exhausted after a day spent in the noise of greasy machines. What a pleasant change to spend the day outside in the sunshine, recalling the fields of their hometown and the smell of the earth as they pass the day swinging their hoes.

"'Summer has finally come.'

"'They must be really busy back home, and worried about us, too.'

"'We're holding up fine.'

"'Yeah. And it's back to work tomorrow.'"

to work like adults and to replace working men recruited and sent to the front. There was little time for games when part of the burden of air defense fell upon children. With US bombing squadrons stationed on Saipan in the summer of 1944, study hours shrank as students labored in fields and munitions factories. And when the war approached Japan's Home Islands in the spring of 1945, posters and magazine stories romanticizing life in the armed forces encouraged boys age fifteen to eighteen to enlist as "volunteers." Denied the possibilities of education and a career, adolescents who faced grim choices—join the military and face danger, or stay behind and face malnourishment and exhausting labor—must have grown up in a hurry.

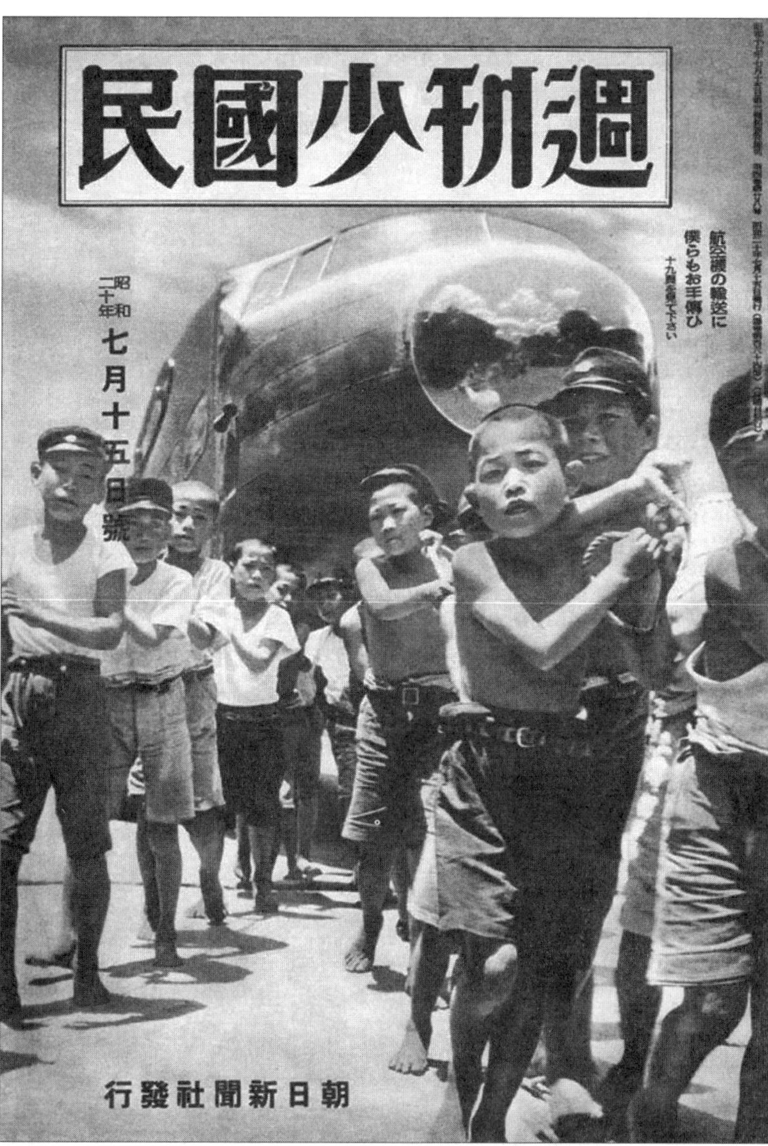

34. *Weekly Junior Citizen* (4:28) 15 July 1945. "We Boys Will Help Transport This Airplane Fuselage."

When the school-year began in April 1945, all students were to devote themselves to total mobilization. Replacing the classroom was the field or factory. These junior citizens were reduced to beasts of burden.

The accompanying article says, "The whole student body of a Citizens' School devote themselves to transporting this fuselage. The strong sun of early summer beats down on the gleaming silver fuselage, beneath which two ropes are tied, the students forming two lines and taking their places. The copper-colored shoulders are small but full of power. 'Heave, heave.' They move forward at the teacher's command. The large fuselage moves ahead in fits and starts. The day is near when this airplane will fly, carrying afar the brave warriors and we boys' dreams."

From the summer of 1944, large-scale evacuations of schoolchildren from urban areas often separated them from parents, siblings, and relatives. Once evacuated and living barracks-style in temple buildings and school grounds, these children were dependent upon their teachers, who determined their daytime activities, oversaw the distribution of their rations, and monitored their living quarters. In these circumstances, children were not merely "junior citizens" but "junior warriors" in agriculture and manufacturing. As the war situation grew desperate, progressively younger students were mobilized to do war work, while adolescent boys were corralled into camps that trained them to become communications soldiers, tank drivers, or pilots. In one sense, these children were virtually slaves, while in another, they were given nearly as much autonomy and independence as adults had during the war. The model for this new generation was evacuee par excellence Crown Prince Akihito, who appeared in *PWR* twice in 1944. He had already appeared several times in *PWR*, always without his family, as if, from the moment of his divine birth, he emerged into the world an independent being.

35 and 36. (top) *Dōmeigraph* 291, July 1943, p. 11. This photograph did not appear in *PWR*, although *PWR* 303 certainly described the occasion (see figure 37). The caption here reads, in part, "The heroic image of His Imperial Highness inspecting a navy aircraft at the Kasumigaura Naval Training Center."

(bottom) *PWR* 321, 17 May 1944, p. 3. The second of two photographs of Crown Prince Akinomiko [later, Akihito] appearing in *PWR* in 1944. Here, he and his fellow classmates pay a visit to Kashima Shrine in Ibaraki Prefecture, northeast of Tokyo. The shrine is dedicated to a mythological warrior. Photograph: Imperial Household Ministry.

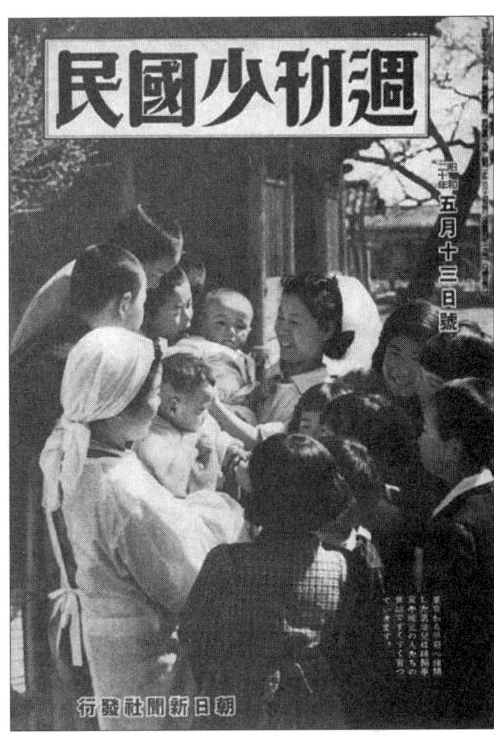

37 and 38. (left) *PWR* 303, 5 January 1944, p. 3. "The Crown Prince Greets His Twelfth New Year." The seemingly self-reliant crown prince, always pictured alone or with attendants (but never with his own parents or siblings) was the evacuee par excellence and the perfect example of the wartime child in his purity and in his many virtues and interests, especially in his thinly-veiled desire to join the fight. Here he is dressed in his school uniform, with schoolboy cap and satchel, in an unidentified location. The main portion of the text reads,

"[Crown Prince] Akinomiko is of a bright disposition and his wholesome growth continues, which is the greatest source of pleasure for Their Imperial Majesties the Emperor and Empress and the imperial family, and of limitless joy for we one hundred million citizens. His Highness, presently enrolled in the fourth year of first-level study at the Peers' School, applies himself diligently to his studies while undertaking tours in every region of each kind of school and armaments factory. He takes a particular interest in the construction and operation of model airplanes. News leaked out that on 1 May of last year, he visited the Navy Air Force corps in Kasumigaseki and Tsuchiura, where he boarded some of the navy's airplanes and recalled the brave battles of heroes at the front." Photograph: Imperial Household Ministry.

(right) *Weekly Junior Citizen* (4:19), 13 May 1945. "Infants evacuated from Tokyo to Kōfu thrive under the care of evacuated schoolchildren and local people." With no school curriculum, older children were expected to take on adult roles wherever possible, in this case, helping run a day-care for infants and toddlers. By 1945, many Japanese children were being raised in government-run facilities, without family members to advocate on their behalf.

39. *PWR* 289, 15 September 1943, back cover. “The Sky Is the Final Battlefield. Flight Crew Training Center. Now Recruiting Students.” One of many advertisements that appeared late in 1943 from the newly created Air Force Bureau, recruiting boys ages eleven to thirteen for its five-year full course and ages sixteen to nineteen for its one-year pilot training course.

In 1944, the government forcibly merged and downsized many newspapers and periodicals. Decreasing paper allotments and the loss of color printing gave the remaining wartime publications a drab, uniform appearance. Children's publications, were an exception. That they were still printed in lush colors attested to the importance the government assigned them, and children, in continuing the war effort.

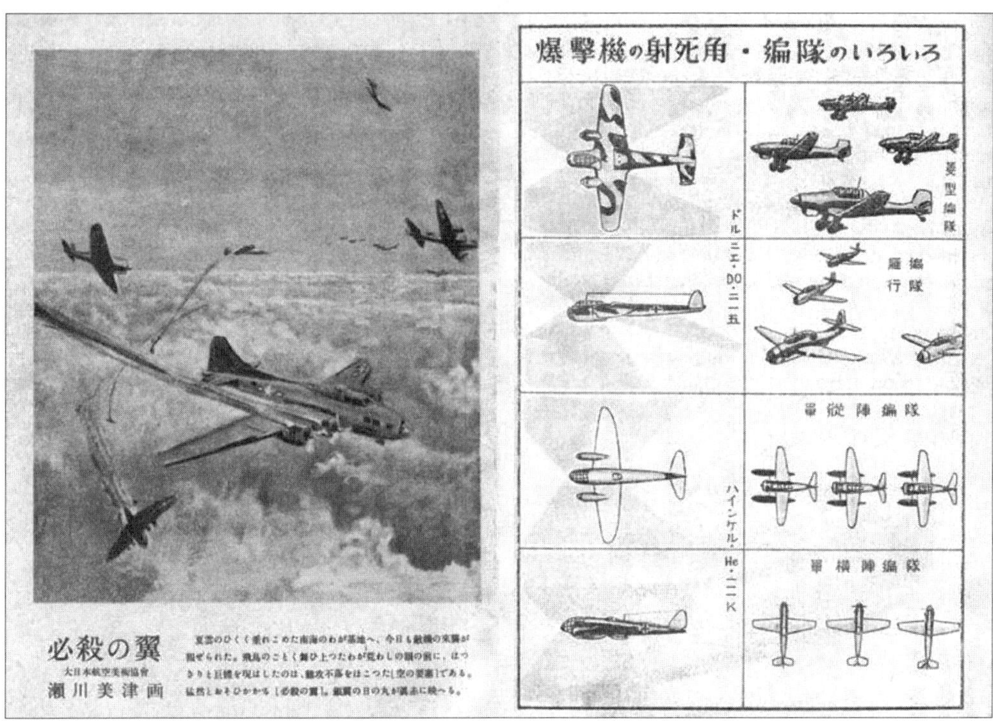

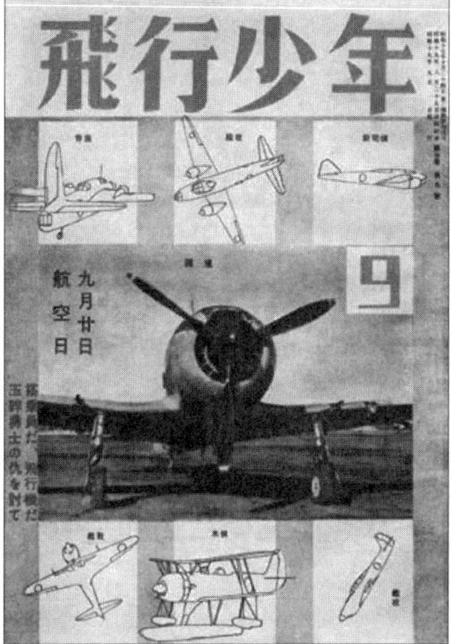

40-42. The Great Japan Aviation Federation edited and published *Aviation Boys* as an enticement to youth to enroll in the Federation's flight school. As late as autumn 1944, no expense was spared to make this an attractive publication. *Aviation Boys* carried articles on the latest aeronautical technology, gave accounts of imaginary dogfights, and described the entrance exams and training of Japan's "junior pilots."

(top right and left) pp. 2 and 3 of *Aviation Boys* (7:10), October 1944. (right) Duotone diagrams of bomber-fighter planes and (left) a color drawing of US airplanes being shot down in a large-scale dogfight. The cover of this issue carries the patriotic message, "You boys' power will win the war, by determining the outcome of the battle for the skies."

(bottom) *Aviation Boys* (7:9), September 1944. The multicolor cover shows both a photograph and diagrams of airplanes against a chartreuse-striped background, asking its readers to imagine that "I'm a crew member! It's an airplane! We will shoot down the foe of the brave soldiers who committed *gyokusai*."

43. *Communications Soldier on the Seas*, January 1945. The Personnel Office of the Department of the Navy printed two hundred thousand copies of this recruitment picture-book, with every page in gorgeous, full color.

"The Importance of Communications," a foreword to the book by Lieutenant-Commander Koizumi Yoshio, stated, "The navy is recruiting youths aged fourteen to twenty for specialized training in the Naval Communications School in preparation for the final battle." The back page of the book contained a "Message to Mothers" encouraging them to let their boys enlist. The text of this picture book was printed entirely in katakana syllabary, the reading level of first- and second-graders.

The story encourages younger brother to emulate older brother and become a volunteer communications soldier. Younger brother's world is one unpopulated by adults, the eldest role model being older brother. The front cover shows older brother, graduated from school and now a junior communications soldier, with younger brother, who vows to follow in his footsteps.

44. (p. 1) Younger brother and his smaller siblings turn on the radio. The text here is entirely their dialogue.

"'It's the Warship Parade March [announcing a naval victory]. I wonder if older brother keyed in the message.'

"'No, he's still in [communications] school.'"

The following six pages, with two-page illustrations, of *Communications Soldier on the Seas*, is a fine example of the suasive power of illustration, especially when beautifully drawn and colored. Younger brother narrates the story.

45. (pp. 2-3) "I'm doing the same thing as older brother is." The poster behind the children is an actual recruitment poster for adolescents.

46. (pp. 4-5) "A Day at School. Older brother had no difficulty entering school. He really applies himself and won't be beaten by anyone. But the most important thing to him is communications."

47. (pp. 6-7) "The war results of Hawaii [the Pearl Harbor attack] were transmitted by wireless. Every day, older brother is learning the transmission code."

There were no advertisements in major publications recruiting girls for military training, although *PWR* did print an article in 1941 describing girls training for (eventual) maritime service. While the government encouraged women of child-bearing age to raise as many healthy "junior warriors" as physically and economically possible, adolescent girls were evidently being considered for military service prior to motherhood. All Japanese females, including schoolgirls, were expected to be physically fit and to pull their own weight during the war, by boosting production of crops, munitions, and the matériel needed for the war effort. The media did not shy away from reporting, though, that girls were fighting on the front in the final phase of the war. *Weekly Junior Citizen* contained an article lauding the fighting spirit of Okinawan girls recently evacuated to the Home Islands ([4:26], 1 July 1945, pp. 7-8). The article included photographs of four interviewed girls who provided graphic details about how they prepared to fight the invading enemy. They trained at home with bamboo spears and practiced karate and judo.

48. *Weekly Junior Citizen* (4:24), 17 June 1945. The cover announces, "Junior Citizens in a Farming Village." The inside article, "Junior Citizens Fight Gallantly in a Farming Village," describes children's efforts in the drive for increased agricultural production.

The article says in part, "In Kawato village, Niigata Prefecture, the land known formerly as Echigo and famous since then for its rice, 'farming village education' is thriving. These schoolchildren refuse to be outdone by adults, doing splendid work and striving to increase production so that we will win this great war."

"Farming village education" is one euphemistic reference to the suspension of classroom education in April 1945 and the total mobilization of children. We can infer from the text that these children were evacuated to Niigata. These girls do not seem accustomed to the hard labor of turning over the mud of the flooded fields prior to planting rice seedlings. Photograph: Sugano Yoshikatsu.

49. *PWR* 180, 6 August 1941, p. 16. “School This Summer.” The caption says, “The midsummer heat reaches 30 degrees Celsius [86 degrees Fahrenheit], but that is nothing compared to the scorching heat at the front. The norm these days for healthy young students, and even youngsters at Citizens' School, is to abandon the idea that because school is out, it is all right to be physically unfit and while away the summer at play. Now, summer vacation is a meaningful time, the time of training the body.”

These girls of Hikawa Citizens' School in Tokyo perform “physical training” at their school every morning at 9 A.M. School curricula shifted from physical fitness to physical training, preparation for the physically demanding roles children would play late in the war. Wartime mores saw nothing improper or immodest in bare-chested girls; since their bodies were pure, they need not cover them from the elements (heat and cold) that toughened them.

50-52. *PWR* 177, 16 July 1941, pp. 2-3. "Girls of the Sea, the Yokosuka Maritime Girls' Troop in Training."

The article reads, in part, "Although they are still girls, they have cast aside mischievous dreams and romantic notions, looked squarely at the reality of wartime Japan, and come to know the ocean and defy it. These are the girls of the Yokosuka Girls' School Maritime Girls' Troop, who twice a week board the destroyer *Kasuga*, where they compete with the seagulls [as seafarers] and continue their training on deck."

(top left) "The future of maritime Japan rests on the tip of the staff she holds aloft—this is the glory of the Maritime Girls' Troop."

(top right) "Lifestyle on board the ship requires a knowledge of tying ropes."

(bottom) "They hold their oars upright, waiting for the order to begin rowing, as rough waves beat the sides, rocking the lifeboat."

In the final months of the war, children's magazines printed photographs of adolescent boys training for combat and about to leave on suicide bombing missions. Articles describing the "birth of the Special Attack Forces" and the glorious suicides of the military commanders on Okinawa filled the pages of these magazines. As the Japanese people braced for the impending US-led invasion of Allied forces, the so-called Final Battle for the Home Islands (*Hondo kessen*), much of the burden of defense was clearly to fall upon the "small but strong shoulders" of Japan's youth. Those boys and girls who were born around 1930 had grown up in a society almost constantly at war during their preschool years, and thereafter engaging in a permanent, total war, all-pervasive and all-consuming. How very natural, then, for fifteen- or sixteen-year-olds who knew no other way of life, to leave behind their homes and families to eagerly, happily, join the war effort and even to accept certain death with "cheerful, smiling faces." Effective utilization of children shows both how complete Japan's "total mobilization" was, and how thorough the indoctrination.

53. *Weekly Junior Citizen* (4:27), 8 July 1945. "The Sharp Spirit That Slices in Two with a Single Stroke."

The related article, "A Camp for Warrior-Gods," says, "With the Final Battle for the Home Islands near at hand, our thoughts fly to the Special Attack Forces pilots at the distant front. In a ground battle, what works best is the 'cutting-in tactic'[8]—to bury the arrogant enemy, the only thing to do is introduce them personally to the cutting edge of the Japanese sword. At this base for warrior-gods, each type of tactic that begins as the morning dew still clings to Mikamine in Sendai, Miyagi Prefecture, reflects the genius of the Imperial Army and forms the foundation of exterminating the enemy and achieving victory."

MIlitary training schools, such as the Sendai Junior Officers' Training School in Mikamine, were an important source of military leaders. By the spring of 1945, these schools and their training programs became the model for preparing all children for combat, in anticipation for an Allied invasion of Japan.

Today, Mikamine is a suburban park famous for its cherry blossoms. A memorial plaque marks the site of the former military school.

54. *PWR* 341, 4 October 1944. The "Signboard of the Times" says, "Wings that soar to heaven, / Iron Bulls (Testugyū) that kick up a hot wind. / Compare our deeds to Fuji's lofty peak, and we grin. / We rise to the national crisis. / Army Junior Soldiers. / Off we go, We boys, too." The messages ends by reminding the reader, "The volunteer recruitment period is until 31 October."

The caption says, "Suppressing their desire to be at the front, the youth tank crew undergo hard training. Today, from between the clouds the sacred peak of Fuji watches over these young men as they train." Following the loss of Saipan, *PWR* devoted lead articles to the military training of adolescents. The Testugyū youth tank troops were held in reserve to protect Japan's main island in the event of Allied invasion.

55. *PWR* 345, 1 November 1944. The "Signboard of the Times" carries the message, "The blood splattered in a decisive battle / Bathes the young cheek. / He is a blossom leading the way in exterminating the enemy. / Naval Volunteer Corps, / We boys are following you." The "blossom" is a reference to the scattered cherry blossoms, frequently likened, in Japanese poetry and art, to men who die heroically in the prime of youth.

The caption explains that "Flexing their arms, strength pours from these sailor trainees of the Takeyama Naval Corps. These boyish faces are full of driving spirit that will rise up and shoulder responsibility for the navy during the Decisive Battle [for the Home Islands]."

56 and 57. (this page) *Weekly Junior Citizen* (4:29), 22 July 1945. "They Take Off Smiling," a cover article about juvenile kamikaze pilots.

(facing page) *Weekly Junior Citizen* (4:29), 22 July 1945, p. 2. "Five Minutes Before Take-off," an article describing the ritualized send-off of an adolescent pilot on a suicide mission. The article says, "The Special Attack Forces camp is cheerful. Completely cheerful. In the shade of green trees, when these youthful members of the Special Attack Forces take a short break from their hard training, they smile and in a second everything becomes cheerful. One day in this cheerful camp is presented to you by the cameras of two *Asahi Newspaper* special correspondents, Anakura and Tomishige."

(facing page, from top to bottom) 1. "The pilot has worked hard with the maintenance crew, so together they form a circle and sing to their hearts' content." 2. "Their song now over, the pilot leaps into the center of the circle and dances with an amusing movement." 3. (a short dialogue) "'Mr. Soldier, I want you to have this.' 'Why, thank you, miss.'" 4. "It would not do if, at the moment of impact, his stomach was empty—so he munches down a large rice ball."

The narrative here suggests a nearly sacrosanct ritual send-off for these teenagers about to become warrior-gods. Japan's reserves of spiritual energy would supposedly offset any technological advantage or superior force the enemy might possess.

出撃五分前

特別攻撃隊の基地はあかるい。底ぬけにあかるい。綠の木蔭も、猛訓練の一ときをそこに憩ふ若々しい特攻隊員がにつこり笑へばたちまちあかるくなる。あかるい基地のある一日を、宍倉富重兩報道班員（朝日新聞特派員）のカメラによつてお傳へしよう。

1 苦勞を共にして來た整備員たちと圓陣をつくつて思ふ存分歌ふ

2 歌ひ終れば、圓陣の中に立つて身ぶり面白くをどり拔く。

3 突入のとき腹がへつては…と大きなおむすびをほゝ張る

4 「兵隊ちやん、これあげまちゆ」「やあ、ありがたう お嬢ちやん」

Notes

1. At this time in China, children in their early teens engaged in warfare, especially in guerrilla situations.

2. The Japanese word for "nation," *kokka*, is composed of two characters, "nation" (*kuni*, nation or land) and "family" (*ie*, family or home). This concept of the nation as one household, with the emperor in the role of father of the nation, featured prominently in wartime rhetoric. The people were expected to unite for the sake of the nation and the emperor, and being overly concerned about the welfare of one's own biological family was seen as "selfish" and even unpatriotic. For instance, a dead soldier's relatives—his parents, siblings, wife, and children—were expected to show no sadness, anger, or resentment over his death, which served the higher good of the national family and the emperor.

3. Fatalities for the China war and the Pacific War cited from John Dower, *War Without Mercy Race and Power in the Pacific War*, 7th ed. (New York: Pantheon, 1993), p. 297.

4. William Theodore deBary, ed., *Sources of Japanese Tradition* (New York: Columbia University Press, 1958), pp. 646-647.

5. Mikiso Hane writes in *Peasants, Rebels, and Outcastes* ([New York: Pantheon, 1982], p. 75) that "Perhaps it could be said that Noma, more than any other single individual, was responsible for fostering militaristic thinking among Japanese youths by oversimplifying issues and glamorizing Japanese military exploits. In this respect he was not simply adapting to the times but helping to chart a course of events. The profound influence that this magazine [*Shōnen Kurabu, Boys' Club*] had on the minds of the young led some critics to contend that his magazine had a greater impact on them than did prewar school textbooks. In 1935, *Shōnen Kurabu* enjoyed a monthly circulation of 500,000."

6. Publication data unknown. These two illustrations (figures 6 and 8) are from an individual's self-bound compilation of articles from boys' magazines from about 1937. Internal evidence suggests the most likely source to be *Boys' Club*.

7. Paper theater (*kami shibai*) appeared in the early 1930s and was an instant hit with children. This form of entertainment, employing story cards, began as a sales device used by candy or toy peddlers to attract young customers. The government was quick to recognize and exploit the potential of this medium: it was inexpensive, easily transported, interactive, and weighted heavily toward image rather than text.

8. The text is unclear on exactly what the "cutting in" strategy entails, whether it is a method of using a sword or (more probably) a troop tactic in the field, perhaps of ambushing the invader.

7. "NOW THE ENEMY IS AMERICA AND BRITAIN!"

Relations between Japan and the Western imperial powers had been strained for several years prior to the outbreak of the Pacific War.[1] When the "long anticipated day" finally arrived and the war began, it came as both a matter of course and a shock to the ordinary citizen, long accustomed to the posturing of Japan's military. The Japanese press had been performing a delicate balancing act for some years, on the one hand presenting a façade of peaceful diplomacy with Japan's neighbors, including the Western powers, while on the other suggesting that this fragile status quo might be upset at any moment, plunging the Asia-Pacific region into war. On 8 December 1941 (7 December in the Western hemisphere), when the declaration of war and the military's attacks on Western bases and colonies throughout Asia were simultaneously announced to the Japanese public, the gravity of the event must have been difficult to grasp, even as city streets buzzed with newspaper extras and radio announcements, and handbills and hastily made posters screamed a new slogan: "One Hundred Million, Now the Enemy Is America and Britain. Slaughter Them!"

1. *Asahigraph* (38:4), *Great East Asia War Report* 4, 21 January 1942, p. 23. A full-page advertisement for Chimori, a vitamin and hormone concoction, with two slogans behind the ripped Stars and Stripes: "Slaughter Them! America and Britain, They're Our Enemies" and "Advance, One Hundred Million, with Raging Morale."

This was the first issue of *Asahigraph* to bear the subtitle, "Great East Asia War Report." The three preceding issues, some with other subtitles, were counted as the first, second, and third "Great East Asia War Reports" after the fact.

The mass media and the government, as seen in preceding chapters, had been actively preparing the population for a greater national and racial destiny since the Total Spiritual Mobilization Movement was launched in 1937. In December 1940, a year of celebrations came to a close and the second phase of the "realization of kokutai" also ended. The new year, 1941, ushered in a new phase of national destiny in which Japan's New Order in Asia would elevate Japan's status from a regional power to an international one. The major obstacle to realizing Japanese national destiny was Western imperialism in Asia. Japan had fought alongside the Allies in World War I, but tensions between Japan and the Western powers had been mounting steadily since the 1919 Treaty of Versailles, which failed to satisfy Japanese demands. The Washington Naval Conference of 1921-1922 set stricter limits on the tonnage of the Japanese navy than on the three other participants (the United States, Great Britain, and France), leaving the Japanese military disgruntled and restless. Insult was added to injury in 1924, when the US Congress, pressured by wealthy Californians, passed legislation excluding Japanese immigrants from the United States. Japan's actions in Manchuria and China confounded and infuriated the Western powers, and armed conflict seemed imminent on more than one occasion, such as when the Japanese sank the US patrol boat *Panay* on the Yangtze in 1937. After Japan seized Indo-china in 1940, the United States expanded its navy and moved its forward command to Pearl Harbor, Hawaii, actions that Japan interpreted as a challenge and a threat to its ambitions.

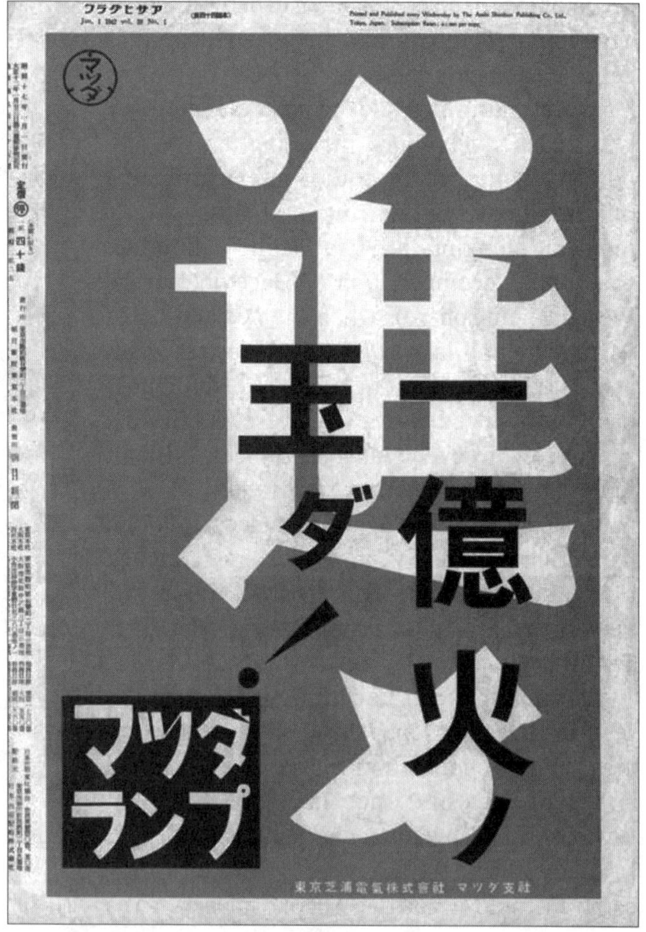

2. *Asahigraph* (38:1-2), 31 December 1941 and 7 January 1942, back cover. A full-page advertisement for Matsuda Lamp Company with an early Pacific War slogan, "Advance, One Hundred Million, with Raging Morale." This strikingly modern word-collage places "Advance" in large white font on a red field, with the rest of the phrase juxtaposed in black in the foreground. The black box at lower left with white letters identifies "Matsuda Lamp."

3. *PWR* 152, 22 January 1941, p. 1. "We Are Steadfast in Our Resolve. Entering Boot Camp at Yokosuka [Naval Base]." Three new sailors tour the battleship *Mikasa*.[2] "From tomorrow, they will be members of the illustrious Japanese Imperial Navy. When they think of what they will do to guard the Pacific, a manly smile floats across their faces." This seven-page article has a detailed explanation of why 1941 will be a critical year in which "the rising tensions in the Pacific must be decided. Japan's goal of liberating Asian peoples and creating a Greater East Asian Co-Prosperity Sphere is being blocked by America and Britain's interference. The two nations want to keep a firm hold on the profits they reap from their interests in Asia."

While the language here is inflammatory, it is also vague. In retrospect, this article all but declares war on the West some eleven months before Pearl Harbor, but a number of commentators, Japanese, American, British, and others, had been predicting war in the Pacific since the days of the Russo-Japanese War. The Japanese home front reader would have had great difficulty in discerning the military's course of action from this article.

Japan signed the Tripartite Treaty in 1940, casting its lot militarily in the Axis camp. With Great Britain the sole source of resistance to the Nazis and Fascists in Western Europe and with a neutrality agreement with the Soviet Union secured, Japan felt confident in seizing French Indo-china "in the name of the Axis," ostensibly to ensure that the Vichy regime was honored there. Japan moved swiftly in the autumn of 1940 to take over Indo-china. The remaining Western imperial powers in Asia—Great Britain, the United States, and the Netherlands—while alarmed by this course of action, were very wary of the onset of hostilities in Asia while Europe was in tumult. Diplomatic pressure on Japan failing to effect a withdrawal of Japanese troops, Roosevelt froze Japanese assets in the United States on 26 July 1941 and on 1 August, joined by the Dutch and British, announced an oil embargo against "aggressor states" including Japan. The embargo drastically hampered Japan's ability to continue its military operations in China and maintain its military presence in Asia, because war factories depended upon tin, rubber, and oil from the Dutch East Indies (Indonesia), and petroleum products and iron ore from the United States. The Japanese press described this boycott as a threat to Japan's rightful interests in Asia.

4. *PWR* 154, 5 February 1941. The lead article, "The American Navy Today," describes the threat to Japan of the expanding American fleet.

"With the pull of a single switch, the newly minted destroyer *Meredith* slips into the sea like a living creature.

"'For American honor and for peace'—such flowery rhetoric is worn out. At Boston and at every naval shipyard across America, they are putting into action with frightening momentum the plan to increase their large navy to a total of seven hundred ships."

The USS *Meredith* (DD-434) was launched on 24 April 1940 from Boston Shipyard. It participated in the Doolittle Raid on Tokyo in April 1942. It was sunk near San Cristobal on 15 October 1942 by bombs from Japanese aircraft during the Battle of the Solomons. Of a crew of about three hundred, less than one hundred survived its loss.

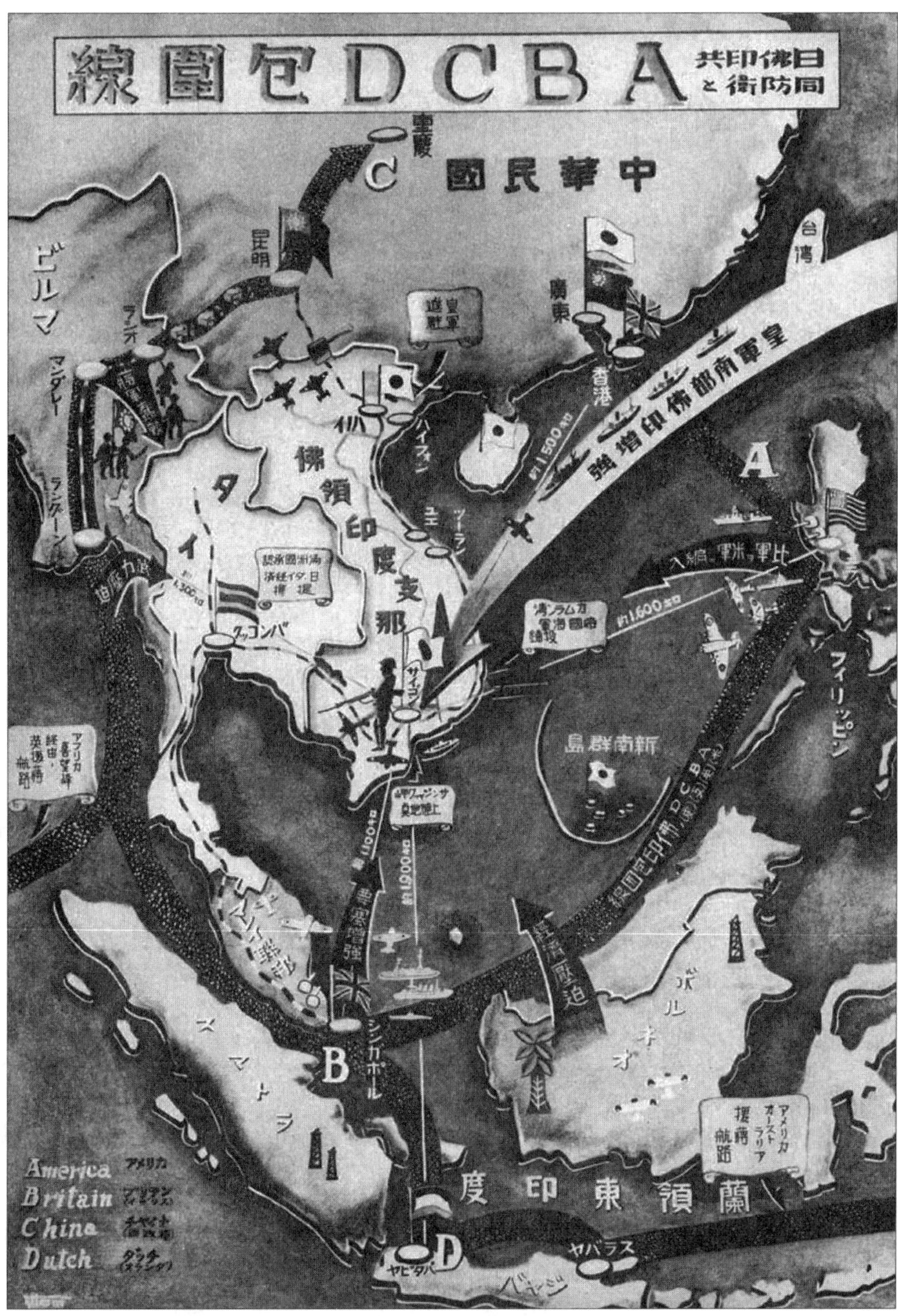

5. *PWR* 181, 13 August 1941, p. 1. The ABCD (American, British, Chinese, and Dutch, as explained in the lower left corner) blockade against Japanese troops in Indo-china, represented by a black line. Japanese troops entered Indo-china in 1940, claiming the colony in the name of the Axis powers after France's capitulation to Nazi Germany. The map shows the Western colonies and their resources, with black arrows from the Philippines, Dutch East Indies, British Malaya, and Borneo indicating the flow of resources to Chiang Kai-shek's Chongqing government. The white arrow shows the route of Japanese supplies to Indo-china.

The Imperial Rescript Declaring War against the United States and Great Britain was printed in every Japanese newspaper on 8 December. The justification for the war was found in the following passage:

> It has been truly unavoidable and far from Our wishes that Our Empire has now been brought to cross swords with America and Britain. More than four years have passed since China, failing to comprehend the true intentions of Our Empire, and recklessly courting trouble, disturbed the peace of East Asia and compelled Our Empire to take up arms. Although there has been re-established the National [Wang Jingwei] Government of China, with which Japan has effected neighborly intercourse and cooperation, the regime which has survived at Chungking [Chongqing], relying upon American and British protection, still continues its fratricidal opposition. Eager for the realization of their inordinate ambition to dominate the Orient, both America and Britain, giving support to the Chungking regime, have aggravated the disturbances in East Asia. Moreover, these two Powers, inducing other countries to follow suit, increased military preparations on all other sides of Our Empire to challenge us. They have obstructed by every means our peaceful commerce, and finally resorted to a direct severance of economic relations, menacing gravely the existence of Our Empire. Patiently have We waited and long have We endured, in the hope that Our Government might retrieve the situation in peace. But our adversaries, showing not the least spirit of conciliation, have unduly delayed a settlement; and in the meantime, they have intensified the economic and political pressures to compel thereby Our Empire to submission. This trend of affairs would, if left unchecked, not only nullify Our Empire's efforts of many years for the sake of the stabilization of East Asia, but also endanger the very existence of Our nation. This situation being such as it is, Our Empire for its existence and self-defense has no other recourse but to appeal to arms and to crush every obstacle in its path.[2]

The Rescript Declaring War, written in a turgid, formal prose, laid out the rationale behind Japan's preemptive strike against the Western powers in Asia. In plain language, there were four reasons that the war was "unavoidable": first, the United States and Great Britain were aiding Chiang Kai-shek's regime in Chongqing, frustrating Japan's efforts to pacify to the region; second, they had initiated an economic embargo against Japan that would cripple the economy (including the ability to wage war); third, the "increased military preparations" seen in the enlargement of the US navy (beginning in 1940) and moving its Forward Fleet to Pearl Harbor in October 1941; and fourth, the exhaustion of diplomatic means to resolve the deadlock in negotiations between Japan and the United States, due to the Western powers' "showing not the least spirit of conciliation" and "unduly delay[ing] a settlement." In effect, the West had put a stranglehold on Japan's economic and military ambitions (the "ABCD blockade") while fortifying its own military presence in the region. The longer this situation continued, the more vulnerable the Japanese position. Japan had to strike or fall to its knees.

The initial reports that came pouring in to the Imperial High Command on 8 December must have seemed too good to be true. Pearl Harbor was taking a severe beating from Japanese torpedoes and bombs. Hong Kong was under attack. Singapore, Davao, Wake, and Guam had all been hit by Japan's navy planes. For some weeks, similar reports filled newspapers and magazines, but all the while, the people were fed a steady stream of slogans, jingoistic messages, and stock images of Japan's military might. No images of the attack on Pearl Harbor or its results were published until January 1942.

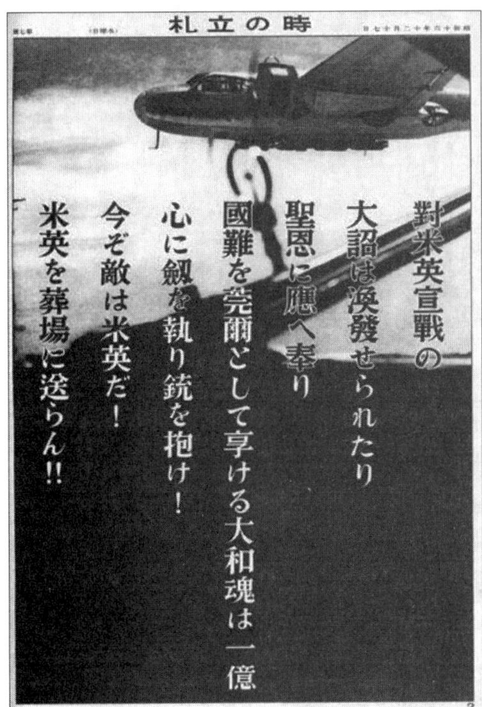

6 and 7. *PWR* 199, December 17, 1941. This issue of *PWR* appeared on the newsstands some days prior to its publication date, that is, around 13 December, and therefore was the first weekly news journal to describe the outbreak of the Pacific War.

(right, front cover) "One Hundred Million! Now the Enemy Is America and Britain!" Photograph: Navy Ministry.

The caption (printed on p. 23) reads, "Finally, we have opened fire! The day has finally arrived for the world to take account of the real value of the Imperial Navy, girded with battle-hardened veterans.

"Remember the indignity of the bombardment of Bakan [Shimonoseki] seventy-seven years ago by the combined naval forces of England, America, Holland, and France.[3] At the dawn of the [Meiji] Restoration, they made their own beds, which they must now lie in, and today the great sword of justice hangs heavily over the heads of the rough and rude enemy.

"Boom! A cannon fires, and finally a new world history begins."

Taken together, the caption and the cover photograph suggest that these battleships fired upon the US Pacific Fleet at Pearl Harbor, which was not the case. The raid was conducted by carrier-based airplanes. The photograph was probably taken during a naval review, such as that held annually on Navy Day.

(left, p. 2) The "Signboard of the Times" carries the message, "The Imperial Rescript Declaring War against America and Britain has been decreed. Responding to this expression of the Imperial Will is the Great Yamato Spirit, which accepts the national crisis gladly and makes the minds and hearts of the One Hundred Million hold the sword and grip the rifle! Now the enemy is America and England! Send America and England to their graves!"

As with the cover photograph of warships, this photograph of airplanes flying in formation is probably a stock image taken from files, unrelated to the attack on Pearl Harbor.

8 and 9. The first larger-than-life hero of the Pacific War was Admiral Yamamoto Isoroku,[4] mastermind of the attack on Pearl Harbor, the linchpin of the larger Japanese blitzkrieg on Allied strongholds throughout Asia and the Pacific on 8 December 1941.

(left) *PWR* 199, 17 December 1941, p. 2, carried this full-page photograph with an article, "Admiral Yamamoto at the Helm," meant to reassure the public that Japan's military leadership had embarked on a course certain to result in even greater victories.

(right) *Asahigraph* (37:26), *Annihilation of America and Britain Report* 1, 24 December 1941. *Asahigraph* put the national hero, Admiral Yamamoto, on its front cover with the slogan "Slaughter America and Britain, Our Enemy! Advance! One Hundred Million with Raging Morale!" In comparison to the *PWR* photograph, the *Asahigraph*'s is a grainy enlargement. Neither publication contained photographs of the attack on Pearl Harbor, instead reprinting stock photographs of naval maneuvers and articles describing the navy's prowess.

In Japan, the Japanese navy was the only source of information (including photographs and later, newsreels) of the Pearl Harbor attack, but the information was not immediately released, leaving the private news organizations in a quandary. *Asahigraph* (37:26), (24 December 1941) carried a subtitle on its front cover, "Annihilation of America and Britain Report 1," but the entire issue contained only one photograph of the "annihilation," an aerial view of the bombardment of Hong Kong. The following double issue (38:1-2), (31 December 1941 and 7 January 1942) for New Year's also contained only one recent photograph, a Japanese navy image of the sinking of HMS *The Prince of Wales* and HMS *Repulse*. Finally, *Asahigraph* (38:3), (called *Surrender of Hong Kong Report* 1, 14 January 1942), published images of Pearl Harbor, the same photographs printed in *PWR* 202 (7 January 1942) with slightly rewritten captions. (Some of these photographs were released on New Year's Day and appeared in the 1 January 1942 issue of Japanese newspapers.) *PWR* had scored a "scoop" against *Asahigraph*, with one of the most sensational stories of the twentieth century. We can only speculate about whether the CIB deliberately withheld the navy's photographs of Pearl Harbor, waiting to release them as a New Year's gift to the nation during the one week that *Asahigraph* was not issued (due to its annual New Year's "double issue").[5] Regardless of the motivations, or lack thereof, surrounding the release of these historical photographs, in January 1942 *PWR* emerged as the leading newsweekly for information on the new war, freshly supplied by military cameramen on the front lines of Japan's blitzkrieg. *PWR* enjoyed an inside track on news that the private media companies did not.

10. *PWR* 200, 24 December 1941, pp. 4-5. "Shattering the Dawn Skies, the Air Raid on Pearl Harbor, 8 December." Two-page centerfold illustration by Matsuzoe Ken.

"On 8 December, the Imperial Navy undertook a devastating air-raid against the American fleet at Pearl Harbor as well as other naval, air, and ground forces stationed there, with great battle results.

"Battle Score: Three US battleships, *Oklahoma*, *West Virginia*, and *Arizona*, sunk; four battleships severely damaged. In addition, many enemy aircraft hit and destroyed."

Matsuzoe, an illustrator who worked for Kodansha's hugely popular juvenile magazines (see figures 6-8 in Chapter 6), creates a scene of the attack that places more than thirty warships in one bay, when in fact, the US Pacific Fleet was docked on one side of Ford Island in mooring formation (two rows of four ships each), with many other ships docked on the opposite side of the small island. Clearly, the artist was not concerned with the geography of Pearl Harbor and Ford's Island. Four ships are shown receiving direct hits (hence the water plumes), in effect collapsing the action of the first wave of the attack from forty-five minutes into one frozen moment. The dive-bombers in the foreground seem to be on a near-collision course.

Matsuzoe's drawing is itself a narrative of all of the events of the attack—dispensing with logical and even historical accuracy for the sake of sensationalism. While the scene is full of excitement and action, it is a work of fancy rather than an illustration of the historical events of 8 December (7 December local time in Hawaii). This portrayal belongs in a juvenile comic book of adventure stories, not in a news report, and certainly not as a record of historical fact. Ironically, *PWR*, responsible for making the photograph the foremost medium of news reportage in mid-twentieth century Japan, relied upon an inaccurate and rather old-fashioned drawing, not a photograph, to announce one of the pivotal events of twentieth-century history.

11 and 12. (top) *PWR* 202, 7 January 1942, p. 3. "Great Heroism! The Battle to Completely Annihilate Pearl Harbor, Hawaii." *PWR*'s first article on the "Pearl Harbor Air Raid" was a photoessay that followed the mission of the Navy Air Force from carrier take-off to the bombing of military objectives at Pearl Harbor, and then the return to their carriers. Here, the text reads, "Determined to fight to the finish, the plane points toward the heavens, toward the great deeds of such a day as this, the day of the air raid on Hawaii. The plane gets a send-off from the deck of the [censored] carrier, carrying with it the real departure [i.e., a new beginning, the start of the war] that will occur when explosions reverberate through the predawn darkness high above the Pacific."

This and the following photographs of the Pearl Harbor attack were credited to the Imperial Navy's Hawaii Air Raid Squadron.[6]

(bottom) This photograph[7] of Japanese planes taking off for Pearl Harbor was not included in either PWR or *Asahigraph*'s coverage of the Attack on Pearl Harbor, but was included in Dōmei's *Photo Almanac for 1942* with the English caption "The Japanese naval air-raiders are marching upon [i.e., advancing toward] Hawaii."

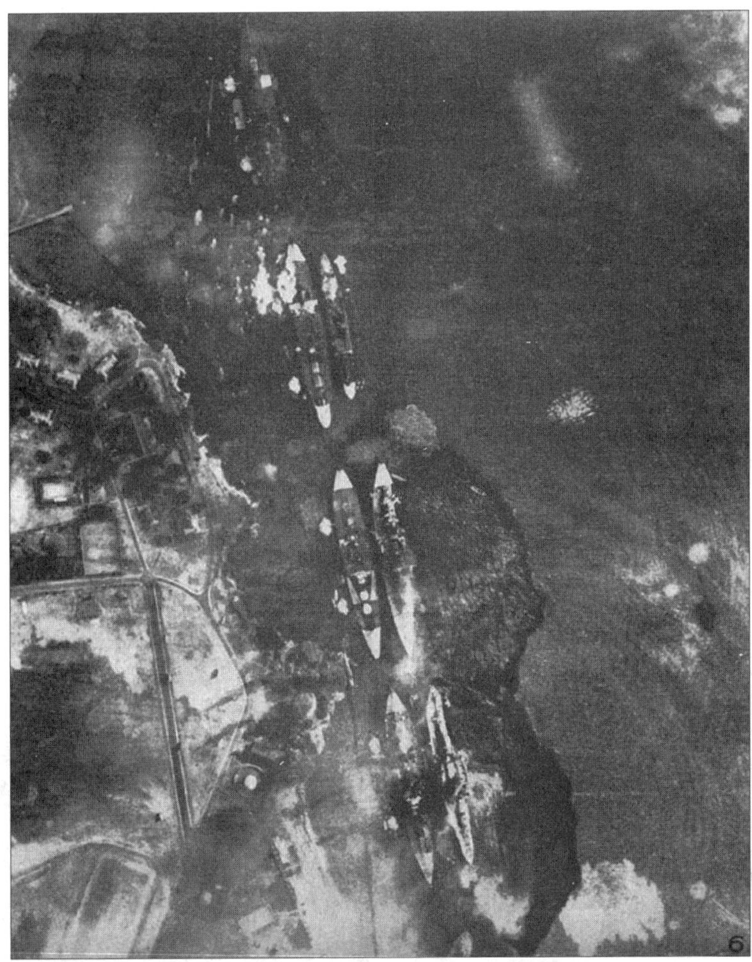

13. *PWR* 202, 7 January 1942, p. 6.[8]

"Looking down directly over the capital[9] ships of the US Pacific Fleet. On the right, or outboard side, oil leaks out from the damaged hulls of the bombed ships. The trail left by a torpedo runs like a white line from the very center of the right side of one ship [USS *Oklahoma*], sending up a plume of water. The ships are in two rows; in the right row, the ship in the center [USS *West Virginia*] and that at the bottom [USS *Oklahoma*] received several direct torpedo and bomb hits; their hulls are twisted and listing. In the left row, the uppermost ship [USS *Nevada*] was directly hit by a torpedo and is leaking oil, the second [USS *Arizona*] received a direct torpedo hit, and the third [USS *Tennessee*], just after this photograph was taken, was hit by a bomb that exploded its powder magazine." Actually, the *Tennessee*'s magazine did not explode, but the *Arizona*'s did.

Two ships not mentioned here are the USS *Maryland*, clearly visible at the bottom of the first row, and the *Vestal* (not one of the eight ships of the Pacific Fleet), outboard to the *Arizona*. Both the *Maryland* and the *Vestal* were hit by bombs; the *Vestal* was beached. The seventh vessel in the Pacific Fleet, the USS *California*, was moored beneath the *Maryland*, just outside the photograph's frame. It, too, was bombed and damaged. And the eighth fleet ship, the *Pennsylvania*, was in dry dock nearby, where it was damaged by bombs.

Dōmei's *Photo Almanac for 1942* printed this photograph, showing more of the image at the bottom of the frame, with the caption "United States capital ships are miserablly [*sic*] crushed under our relentless bombings. Left upper [portion of the photograph]: The Oklahoma class about to sink leaving a whirlpool of fuel oil on the sea surface. Middle left [portion of the photograph]: The California class and the Maryland class. Lower [portion of the photograph]: The Pennsylvania class and the Maryland class."

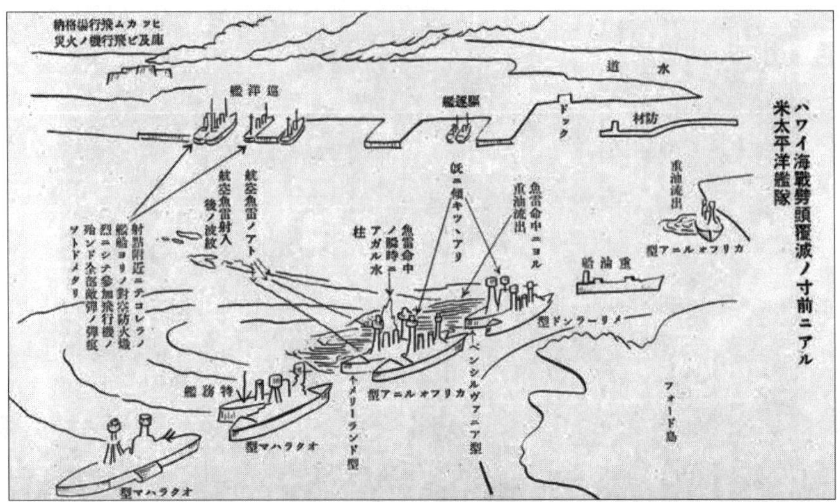

14 and 15. (top) *PWR* 202, 7 January 1942, p. 3. "The Position of the US Pacific Fleet in the moments before the Hawaii Naval Battle sank them." The diagram explains with arrows the work of torpedoes and armor-piercing aerial bombs, stating that two Maryland class, one Pennsylvania class, and one California class ship were sunk by torpedoes, and one California class ship had been hit and was leaking oil. In fact, all eight vessels on Battleship Row were hit and damaged; five were sunk (including the *Nevada*, which was deliberately run aground and sunk in shallow water), the other three sustained heavy damage. Six of these eight would be salvaged, repaired, and returned to action.

(bottom) *PWR* 202, 7 January 1942, pp. 4-5. A two-page centerfold photograph,[10] credited to the Navy Ministry, showing the position of ships on Battleship Row as the raid commenced, one of the most frequently reprinted photographs of the Pacific War. *PWR* gave it no caption, asking the reader to compare the photograph to the diagram.

Dōmei's *Photo Almanac for 1942* gave the photograph this caption in English: "The United States Pacific Fleet just a moment before the Pearl Harbor debacle. By the first bombing[,] Wheeler Airfield is engulfed in huge conflagration. The white line on the water is a torpedo trace. Receiving a torpedo hit, fuel oil streaming from the Pennsylvania class."

16 and 17. (top) The Japanese navy's aerial photograph of the bombing of Battleship Row was an iconic image during the war. It was the image selected for a semi-postal commemorative stamp issued on the first anniversary of the Great East Asia War.

(bottom) The original owner of the magazine below, *Mainichi Great East Asia War Pictorial Report* 13, 8 December 1942, had a keen sense of the historical importance of the Pearl Harbor attack, putting the Battleship Row postage stamp on the front cover of the magazine (issued to commemorate the first anniversary of the war) and having the postage stamp canceled with a special first-anniversary postal cancellation.

The public was encouraged to purchase such keepsakes. The Post Office Ministry issued three commemorative postcards on the second anniversary of the outbreak of the Great East Asia War, each featuring a different work of war art: "Devastating Raid on Pearl Harbor" by Yoshioka Kenji, a painting resembling the photograph in figure 21; "Capture of the Anti-Aircraft Artillery at Wong Neichong, Hong Kong" by Koiso Ryōhei; and "Surrender of the British Army at Singapore" by Miyamoto Saburō, based on a photograph (see figure 35).

18 and 19. (top) Dōmei's *Photo Almanac for 1942* published this famous photograph[11] of a torpedo making a direct hit on the USS *West Virginia* with the English caption "The Japanese naval air-raiders are severely attacking U.S. capital ships around Ford Island in Pearl Harbor." The same photograph appeared in *PWR* 202, 7 January 1942, pp. 6-7, without a caption but with a diagram similar to that of figure 13.

(bottom) Fujita Tsuguharu's 1942 oil painting,[12] based on the photograph, was exhibited in December 1942 at the First Great East Asia War Art Exhibition. Here it is reproduced from plate 1 in the exhibition catalogue, *Great East Asia War Navy Art* (Tokyo: Navy Ministry 1943). It was also printed in a *PWR* article about the exhibition (*PWR* 251, 16 December 1942, p. 3).

20 and 21. *PWR* 202, 7 January 1942, p. 8.

(top) "Take that! Bombardment of the army air force airfield. Although there were still many airplanes left, afterward we wiped them all out with the bombs of a second air raid. Hidden beneath the smoke are many hangars, all of them on fire."

(bottom) "At length, anti-aircraft artillery shells begin to explode [around our planes]. In the midst of their volleys, our squadron of 'wild eagles'[13] calmly returns home in formation. So long, Hawaii!"

The same set of Pearl Harbor attack photographs, which were reprinted in many news publications, inspired several artists' paintings and drawings of the raid. The repetitive coverage of the stunning achievement at Pearl Harbor reflected national pride in a seemingly invincible navy that had scored phenomenal victories against a Western power, breaking the diplomatic deadlock that had hampered Japan's realization of its national destiny. Three weeks after its initial report on Pearl Harbor, *PWR* devoted a second photoessay to the attack in its 28 January 1942 issue, and then reprinted a photograph of the battered shell of the USS *Arizona* from the American press in March. Dōmei Tsūshin reprinted seven of these Japanese navy photographs in its *Photo Almanac for 1942,* and two photographs from the US press showing the aftermath of the attack. Dōmei's English-language article about the Pearl Harbor attack said, "Amidst the admiration of the entire world, the invincible Japanese Navy set up an immortal war history at the dawn on that epoch-making day of December 8, 1941 by destroying the United States Pacific Fleet at Pearl Harbor and her Air Corps on both Wheeler and Hickam Airfields."

22. *PWR* 215, 28 January 1942, p. 7. A few additional Japanese navy photographs of the attack on Pearl Harbor were released late in January 1942.

"Some minutes have passed between the taking of this photograph[14] and the photograph in issue 202 [figure 15]. Of the enemy's capital ships that were pummeled by our torpedoes and bombs, one Pennsylvania-class ship has already sunk, one Maryland-class is on fire, and one Oklahoma-class is billowing smoke from its exploded magazine, resulting in a pathetic state of affairs.

"In this photograph, also visible are what appear to be several rescue ships approaching pell-mell."

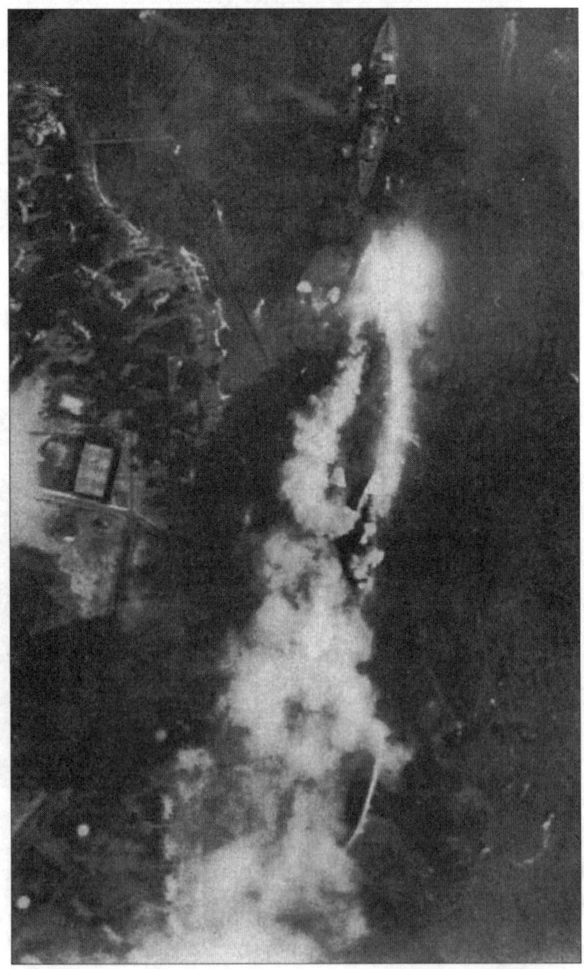

23. *PWR* 212, 18 March 1942, p. 6. "Look! This is the glorious achievement of our warrior-gods, the hull of the battleship *Arizona*, sunk at Pearl Harbor. This photograph is from the enemy side, and was sent from America to London, where it appeared in the weeklies such as the *London News*[15] and *Sphere*. It was cabled here from Berlin."

This photograph appeared in a report on the Nine Pillars of Pearl Harbor, the two-man crews of five midget submarines that were sent on suicide missions. The Japanese navy credited a midget submarine with sinking the *Arizona*. US sources state that none of the midget submarines attained its military objective; all were quickly apprehended and sunk, with the exception of one that was beached by an explosion, presumably a depth charge. The beached submarine contained a surviving crewman, Sakamaki Kazuo,[16] who became the first Japanese POW of the Pacific War. While his capture must have been known to the Japanese military (hence the number of warrior-gods being nine, not ten), his existence was kept secret from the Japanese public until after the war ended.

The devastation at Pearl Harbor represented a major military and strategic victory. The symbolic importance assigned to the raid was clear in the tenor and the extent of coverage devoted to it. The public had good reason to be euphoric over the stunning victories achieved in a few short months as the Japanese military raced across the South Pacific, driving out Western colonial powers and demonstrating that invincible Japan quickly defeated Western nations. For the remainder of the war, 8 December was an anniversary greeted with solemnity; the Day of Service for Developing Asia was moved from the first to the eighth of each month in honor of the outbreak of the war.

Pearl Harbor was one aspect of a multifaceted, simultaneous attack on key Allied positions throughout Asia and the Pacific. Due to the lag in releasing photographs of the raid on Pearl Harbor, the public first saw them while reading about the battle for the Philippines, which was then in full swing. Japan's offensive[17] gave it the advantage, to be sure, and Japanese troops swarmed across Asia. As resistance weakened and Japan's enemies surrendered, one territory after another fell into Japanese hands: the foreign concession in Shanghai was seized on 8 December; and Thailand "surrendered" the same day, after making only symbolic resistance; Guam surrendered on 10 December, Wake Island on 23 December, and Hong Kong on 25 December. In the hopes of sparing the population of Manila from a bloodbath, the Philippine government announced the city would not be defended against invasion. The open city was occupied by Japanese troops on 2 January.

24. "Scene of the Noble Advance of Our Marines Landing on the Northern Shore of Guam," by Ezaki Kōhei (1904-1963), plate 5 in *Great East Asia War Navy Art.*[18]

Lightly defended Guam, surrounded by superior Japanese forces, surrendered on 10 December 1941, becoming the first Western territory to fall into Japanese hands. The event was memorialized in this *nihonga* (Japanese-style) painting. The artist divides his canvas into three sections: ocean and sky, beach, and land, each corresponding to part of the invasion force: the Japanese ships in the harbor, which have brought the invasion force and provided them with fire cover, rendered in light blues and grays; the troops marching along the beach with uniform, fluid movement, in ochre and olive; and the snipers in the foreground who provide cover for the invasion force, in bright yellows and greens, their posture and their camouflage suggesting foliage. The three parts of the canvas, like the three respective military forces, work together in harmony, all aligned toward a common goal that is itself in harmony with the natural, Asian surroundings. Even the ships seem to be a part of the landscape, an extension of the cragged boulders rising up from the water.

The narrative quality of the painting owes much to the picture scrolls and folding screens of Japan's medieval eras, when wealthy samurai would commission artists to create works that commemorated and recorded their own or their lords' military exploits. The artistic success of the painting is evident in a masterful eye for detail in the foreground: the calm but determined expressions on the individual faces of the snipers, the legible code numbers printed on their knapsacks, the leaves of their camouflage, the morning glory mysteriously blooming by the side of the sniper closest to the viewer, the flash of fire emerging from a rifle barrel that exits the canvas to the left.

25 and 26. (top) *PWR* 201, 31 December 1941, p. 7. "Bombing of Hong Kong."

"Key positions in Hong Kong have been bombed and are on fire. Photograph taken from the streets of Hong Kong by the Army Ministry." The accompanying text reads, in part, "The hammer has finally fallen on a century of enemy aggression in East Asia. The enemy boasted that under attack they would not surrender, relying on the final line of defense of their anti-Japanese forces surrounding the city, but the key positions in Hong Kong have already fallen into our hands. Because of the Bushido spirit our army has embodied since the nation was opened [to the West and the modern army was established], twice made a point of asking the enemy to surrender, but the obstinate enemy refused this offer, so there was no choice for our army but to augment its efforts to an all-out assault. In the middle of the night of the eighteenth, our army succeeded in putting down stubborn resistance and under fierce shooting, landed troops on the principal bases, after which, through a battle using 'human bullets' (*nikudan*), we routed the panicked enemy, and finally the Rising Sun flag was raised high over Hong Kong, the port city constructed by England at a great expenditure of materials and time."

(bottom) "Final All-out Attack on Hong Kong Island," by Yamaguchi Hōshun, plate 6 in the Army Art Federation's *Army Campaigns in the Great East Asia War*.[19] It was also reproduced in *PWR* 251 (16 December 1942, p. 4). The painting depicts the "all-out assault" of 18 December. Hong Kong surrendered on 25 December.

27 and 28. (top) *PWR* 201, 31 December 1941, p. 3. "Peerless War Results. Battle of Malay Sea." Photograph: Navy Ministry.

"On 10 December 1941, off the eastern coast of the Malay Peninsula, Britain's Far Eastern Fleet Flagship *The Prince of Wales* and battlecruiser *Repulse* are seen in their death throes, unable to withstand the deadly bombs of our naval aviation squadron's fierce attack. In the foreground, surrounded by white smoke is the *Wales*, suffering from several direct hits from our hawk eyes, and in the distance is the *Repulse* moments before it sank."[20]

(bottom) "Sea Battle Off Malaya" by Nakamura Kan'ichi, 1942, plate 2 in the catalogue of the *First Great East Asia War Art Exhibition*.[21]

When HMS *The Prince of Wales* entered service in April 1941, it represented the latest technology in battleships. It had only been sent to Singapore on 25 October. These were the first two capital ships to be sunk by airpower alone, and their destruction marked the beginning of the end of the era of the battleship's supreme reign on the high seas. Indeed, Churchill and Roosevelt had signed the Atlantic Charter on the deck of *The Prince of Wales* on 12 August 1941, docked off Newfoundland, adding to the symbolic significance of the ship's sinking. Most of the *Wales* crew was saved, but the *Repulse* went down with the loss of some nine hundred souls, most of its crew.

The Battle of the Philippines began with the bombing of Clark Airfield and Cavite Navy Yard on 8 December 1941. Army General Honma Masaharu landed on a small island off the coast of Luzon on 8 December, encountering little resistance. His Fourteenth Army landed on Luzon on 10 December, and most of the island came under his control in the next two weeks. On 20 December, Honma landed on Mindanao, and the march toward Manila began. The Philippine government moved its military forces from Manila and proclaimed it an open city on 25 December. Nevertheless, the Japanese bombed the city prior to entering it on 2 January. With forces of more than one hundred thousand men on each side, heavy fighting ensued through January, but the tide had turned against the Filipino and American defenders, who retreated to the two strong fortresses of the Bataan Peninsula and Corregidor, where they would hold out until 8 May 1942, their tenacity an irritant to the Japanese, slowing the advance southward.

29. "Raid on Clark Airfield," by Satō Kei (1906-1978), plate 9 in *Great East Asia War Navy Art*.[22] Using a tactic that was repeated throughout Asia during the Japanese blitzkrieg, air power on the ground was obliterated in the initial attack on Western bases and strongholds. Without air power and with sea power crippled, the Allied armies on the ground were easy prey for their Japanese pursuers.

References or sources on which the painting is based have not been identified.

PWR 204 (21 January 1942, pp. 6-7) contained an exuberant photoessay describing the capitulation of Manila. The text crowed about the historical importance of the day, and predicted that the Great East Asia War was nearing its conclusion:

> The Rising Sun Flag finally flies over Manila. Our army and navy elite made the first mark when they landed on enemy-held Luzon Island, and 24 days later, on 2 January, the Imperial Forces bloodlessly, triumphantly marched into Manila, cheered by the citizenry.
>
> At the time the war began, the Philippines could expect that Manila would be hit by the fire of our army's attack. But because America—confident about its largest stronghold in the East Asian lands it had seized—boasted that the city was fortified beyond compare, no one could have predicted it would fall into the hands of our army in such a short time.
>
> The surrender of Manila puts a final period on the history of American aggression in Asia, and with the Philippines' return to Asia, the splendid work of establishing the Greater East Asian Co-Prosperity Sphere takes a giant leap forward. And now that the fall of Singapore is only a matter of time, the Great East Asia War—which only began a few months ago—has already jumped ahead to the phase of its resolution.

30. *PWR* 204, 21 January 1942, p. 6. "Showing no signs of fatigue after their noble, fierce battle, a division of the Imperial Army marches into Manila. The excitement of this day, on which American aggression has been completely chased out of Asia, echoes loudly with the sound of their military boots."

31 and 32. *PWR* 204, 21 January 1942, p. 7.

(top) "The Tetsugyū ["Iron Bull" Light Tank] Squadron roars loudly as it advances past the Rizal Monument. The spirit of Rizal, the hero of Philippine independence now sleeping beneath the earth, must be cheering 'banzai' from his heart now that this day has arrived."

(bottom) "The scorched earth policy is a last resort strategy of the weak, and the most sinister crime. These burning enemy ships at the mouth of the Basig River were set on fire by the enemy with his back to the wall. Our army did everything it possibly could to employ a strategy that would spare the beautiful Manila skyline from battle fire, but the tyrannical American army set fire to every part of the city when it retreated and tried to reduce to ashes Manila, this city of the Philippine people." Photographs: Japan Film Company.

On the first two days of the war, the Japanese destroyed most of the British aircraft stationed on Singapore, and on the third day of the war, sank two of Great Britain's largest and most powerful ships, HMS *The Prince of Wales* and HMS *Repulse*. With neither air nor naval support, the "impregnable fortress" of Singapore, while formidable, was vulnerable. The rapid, merciless Japanese advance swept northeast along the Malay Peninsula. British forces under General Percival were soundly defeated at the Jitra line on 11-12 December, and Kuala Lumpur fell one month later. British forces retreated to Singapore, where they were trapped, after Thailand had capitulated to Japan on 8 December and was occupied by Japanese troops. When British, Australian, and Indian troops retreated from Malaya to Singapore, they dynamited the stone causeway connecting the island fortress to the Malay Peninsula. Some one hundred thousand troops of the British Empire now filled Singapore, with Lieutenant General Yamashita Tomoyuki's sixty-five thousand battle-hardened troops stationed just 300 feet across the

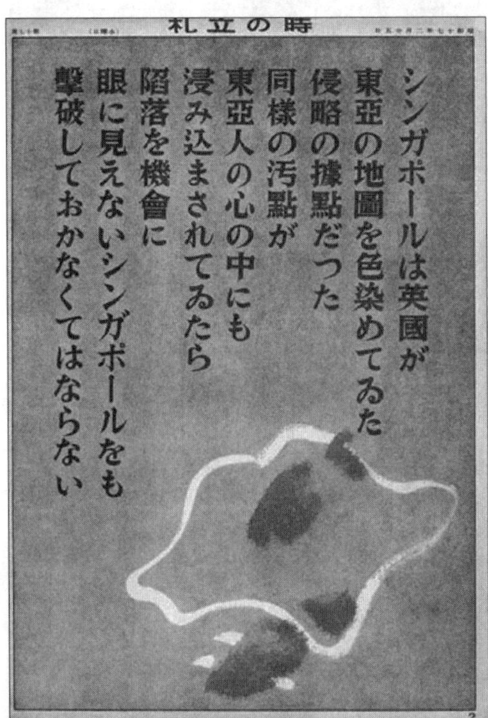

33 and 34. *PWR* 209, 25 February 1942.

(right) "At last, Singapore has surrendered. Oh, the excitement, and yet what lies behind it and quietly overtakes it are our thoughts of boundless gratitude to the army's supreme commander in the region, Lieutenant-General Yamashita Tomoyuki[23] and his soldiers, who since landing at Kota Bharu two months ago have fought their way through horrific heat and thick jungle in fierce hand-to-hand combat. Truly, as the saying goes, 'Under a great general, there are no cowards.' The only words we can say, when we think of these brave warriors who continued the struggle in complete harmony under a bold and fearless general with a prudent, complex strategy, is 'thank you.'"

(left) p. 2. "Signboard of the Times. Singapore was the base from which England invaded, dyeing the map of East Asia with its color. Similarly, because that stain also penetrated into the minds of East Asians, the surrender must be made the opportunity to blow apart that other Singapore invisible to the eye."

Johore Strait. Singapore's population doubled, reaching one million people as refugees fled the fighting in Malaya. A bold and brilliant strategist, Yamashita pressed forward with his attack, never allowing the British to regroup or send for reinforcements. He immediately began bombing and destroying the communications lines between British troops and General Percival's headquarters. Overcrowded and under siege, about two thousand people died each day in Singapore during the bombardment, and with burial of the dead nearly impossible, sickness posed as serious a threat to the island as did the Japanese. Singapore's cannons all pointed to the sea, not to the Malay Peninsula, from which Yamashita continued his punishing bombardment. After only two weeks, Percival realized that not only his troops but civilians as well would suffer a slow and agonizing end, and therefore agreed to surrender on 15 February. Heavily fortified, Singapore was expected to deter Japan's southern advance, and when the defenders—with numbers far superior to the Japanese—surrendered, all sides were surprised. It was the single largest defeat in the history of Great Britain and the British Empire.

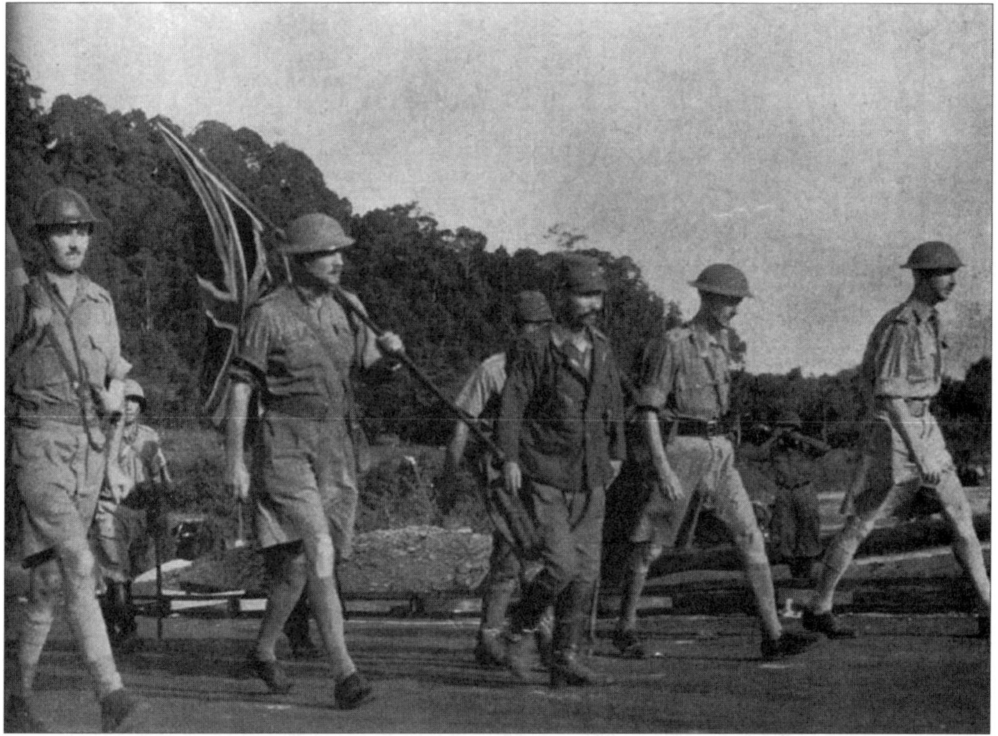

35. This often reprinted photograph was published in Dōmei Tsūshin's *Photo Almanac for 1942*, but did not appear in *PWR*. The *Almanac* printed a short explanation, in English, of the event. "To decide on the last [ultimate] fate of Singapore, a historical meeting took place at 7. p. m. [*sic*] on February 15, 1942 between Lt.-General Tomoyuki Yamashita, Supreme Commander of the Japanese Army in Malay [*sic*], and Lt.-General Arthur E. Percival, Commader-in-Chief [*sic*] of British forces, at the Ford Automobile Company in Bukit Timah. Puzzled by the dauntless Japanese attack, Percival proposed unconditional surrender."

The *Photo Almanac* provided this caption: "Brish [*sic*] Commander Percival surrenders to the Japanese with the white flag." The white flag is cut off by the left margin of the photograph. Percival carried the Union Jack. A Japanese cameraman can be seen to the left of the soldier at the far right of the photograph.

36. *PWR* 210, 4 March 1942.

"The [censored] squadron cheers 'banzai' on the Empire Dock, Singapore.

"After seven days of our attack, Singapore surrendered.

"'Hey, I didn't think they'd surrender so quickly.'

"'And back home [*naichi*] . . . back home, all of you were waiting for us.'

"'Singapore . . . we have even seen it in our dreams.' Now floating before their tear-filled eyes are the faces of their comrades, who died calling 'Singapore.' Oh, Singapore has finally surrendered."

There had been many similar "banzai" photographs in China, and there would be many more as Southeast Asia came under Japanese occupation.

37-39. One of the best-known images of the war was the scene of the signing of the surrender papers that finalized the capitulation of Singapore, an event recorded in images by both the Dōmei Tsūshin Company and the Japan Film Company. Several of the same images were published in newspapers and newsmagazines throughout Japan in February 1942, and again on the first anniversary of the outbreak of the Pacific War. The captions differed slightly from one publication to another. *PWR* 237 (9 September 1942, p. 22) carried an announcement for a Citizens' Film called "Malay Battle Record" that included a scene of Yamashita and Percival at the surrender table.

(top) Published in Dōmei's *Photo Almanac for 1942* with the rather prosaic English caption "The interview between Lt.-General Yamashita and Percival"; *PWR* 210 (4 March 1942, pp. 6-7) gave it the caption, "The fortress of Singapore, which boasted it was impenetrable and would never surrender, was handily defeated. A page in the history of the Great East Asia War that will last forever—Supreme Commander Yamashita at the surrender meeting held at the site of the Ford Company on the outskirts of the city."

Dōmei's *Photo Almanac* published these two close-up photographs of Yamashita and Percival, evidently meant to be the decisive moment in negotiating the terms of surrender.

(middle) The English caption reads, "Lieutenant-General Tomoyuki Yamashita, Supreme Commander of the Imperial Army in Malay." The same *Photo Almanac* carried this Japanese-language caption for this photograph: "Supreme Commander Yamashita barks, 'Unconditional surrender, yes or no?'"

(bottom) The English caption reads, "British Commander Percival in agony." The Japanese caption reads, "Dejectedly, enemy commander Percival begs to surrender."

40. "The Meeting of General Yamashita and General Percival,"[24] by Miyamoto Saburō, 1942, plate 14 in *Army Campaigns in the Great East Asia War.* It was also reproduced in *PWR* 251 (16 December 1942, p. 4). This painting received a prize at the First Great East Asia War Art Exhibition of 1942-1943.

Miyamoto's painting shows details not present in the photograph of the surrender scene: the Union Jack draped in the white flag of surrender, the British helmet laid upside down on the desk. The British commanders look over surrender papers that have disappeared from the desk in front of Yamashita, suggesting that the surrender terms have been dictated by Japan (which, indeed, they were). The composition of the painting makes Yamashita slightly larger than those around him and arranges the others present, Japanese and British alike, like lesser figures attendant upon a deity. Yamashita's firm, strong posture presents a striking contrast to the bent, slump-backed British, just as the Japanese commanders' closed-mouth silence presents a united front against the British, who talk among themselves, evidently trying to reach a decision.

Miyamoto further amplifies Yamashita's strong presence by flattening the space behind him, cleverly accomplished by placing the flags in the room's corner and removing shadows that would give the room limited, mundane dimensions. The table and those gathered around it thus occupy a space both in the world and yet elevated to a higher plane of timelessness and immortality. From the Japanese perspective, the painting was a fitting tribute to a contemporary hero, one who had changed the course of history through his embodiment of the "Japanese spirit" of fierceness, courage, tenacity, and resourcefulness.

Singapore was more than just Britain's military counterpart to America's Pearl Harbor. Singapore was the strongest British fortress in Asia and, along with Hong Kong, represented British economic and political domination. Removing the British presence from Singapore was a major objective in establishing the New Order in Asia. The famous meeting of Generals Yamashita and Percival irreversibly altered the course of history in the Far East, sounding the death knell of the British Empire in East Asia. With the fall of Singapore, little Allied resistance lay between the Japanese and, further south, the Dutch East Indies, New Guinea, and Australia.

41 and 42. (top) *PWR* 210, 4 March 1942, p. 17. An article, "The Parachute Troops are Thriving in the Army" described the parachute attack on Sumatra: "Streaming out of the sky over Sumatra's Palembang oil fields without warning, our army's parachute troops swooped down like hawks over the panicked enemy. As soon as they touched the ground, they stormed over the nearby enemy line. By means of this surprise attack, in a single blow they took control of the central area of Sumatra, the principal island in the Dutch East Indies, which signaled the beginning of the crumbling of the last-ditch line of American, British, and Dutch resistance in the Sunda Island chain."

The caption reads, "Like falling blossoms scattering in a strong wind, one division charges right in to the middle of the enemy camp."

(bottom) "God-soldiers Dropping Down on Palembang,"[25] by Tsuruta Gorō (1890-1969), plate 12 in *Army Campaigns in the Great East Asia War,* glorifies the parachute attack, at the time a spectacular feat demonstrating Japan's strategic ability, military technology, and mastery of the skies over East Asia. This painting was also reproduced in *PWR* 251 (16 December 1942, p. 4).

The Dutch East Indies were now within the sight of Japanese forces. The British commander of Allied forces for the Dutch East Indies, Field Marshall Sir Archibald Wavell, retreated to India, leaving the Dutch to fight alone. Rear Admiral Karel Doorman led a smattering of Allied ships out to engage the Japanese invasion flotilla, in what would be known as the Battle of the Java Sea. The battle stretched across two days, 27-28 February, and was a complete defeat for the Allies, who lost a total of five cruisers and five destroyers. The Japanese fleet sustained no major damage. The fifty thousand defenders of Java were short work for the massive Japanese invasion force led by Lieutenant-General Imamura Hitoshi, and on 8 March the Dutch governor-general agreed to surrender. Meanwhile, Rangoon, capital of Burma, fell to Japanese forces on 9 March. The Americans, British, and Dutch were being driven out of East Asia.

During the spring of 1942, the press gleefully reported on the maneuvers of the seemingly unstoppable Japanese navy as it patrolled a vast expanse of ocean, making raids on Allied positions as far afield as Madagascar, Darwin and Sydney, Australia, and Santa Barbara, California. Every engagement at sea resulted in a Japanese victory and more photographs of Allied ships exploding, on fire, sinking. Dōmei's *Photo Almanac for 1942* summed up the Battle of the Coral Sea (in English) in these glowing (and highly exaggerated) terms:

43 and 44. (left) *PWR* 219, 6 May 1942, pp. 6-7. A two-page centerfold shows the aircraft carrier HMS *Hermes* torpedoed and sinking on 9 April. "The British aircraft carrier *Hermes*, having received direct hits from our sea eagles, is burning fiercely and about to sink straight to the bottom of the Bay of Bengal." Photograph: Navy Air Force.

(right) *PWR* 215, 8 April 1942, p. 18. "Slaughtering the *Exeter*, the Foe of the German Navy at the Battle off the Surabaya Coast," one of a series of four photographs capturing the final moments before the ship sank on 27 February. When the British withdrew from Sumatra, they lent the *Exeter* to the Dutch defenders, who were quickly routed by superior Japanese seapower. Photograph: Navy Ministry.

On May 7 and 8, 1942 the Japanese Naval Forces accomplished the most daring feats ever to grace the illustrious annals of the Japanese Navy in New Guinea waters by blitz-sinking the United States aircraft carriers of the Saratoga-type, the Yorktown-type, a warship California-type, a A-class [*sic*] cruiser Portland-type, and a destroyer and more or less seriously damaging a United States warship of the North Carolina-type, the British warship Warspite-type, the Australian A-class cruiser Canberra-type, the United States A-class cruiser Louisville-type. In this battle the enemy forces lost 98 war planes.

No photographs of the Battle of Midway were published in *PWR*. Issue 226 (24 June 1942, p. 15) did note, in its weekly digest of the war, the outcome of the battle.

On 5 June, a fierce, forceful attack was launched against the enemy's core Pacific base at Midway, halting the reinforcement of the US fleet in the same region. The enemy navy, which suffered from our fierce assault, received heavy damage to its air power and its important military installations.

As of the present time, the following battle results from Midway are clear:

(1) Sunk were one US aircraft carrier Enterprise class and one Hornet class, one San Francisco class cruiser, and one submarine;

(2) Shot down in midair were one hundred fifty enemy aircraft;

(3) important military installations were bombed and destroyed.

In the course of the [Midway] operations, our losses were as follows:

(1) One aircraft carrier sunk, another heavily damaged, one cruiser heavily damaged;

(2) Thirty-five of our aircraft did not return.

45. *PWR* 223, 3 June 1942, p. 3. "Battle of the Coral Sea."

"US aircraft carrier *Saratoga* in a great conflagration shortly before its death throes. The plume of water in the foreground is the trail of a torpedo entering the water and losing velocity." Photograph: Navy Air Force.

Identified here as the *Saratoga*, this is actually the *Saratoga*'s sister ship, the *Lexington*. In the Battle of the Coral Sea, the *Lexington* took several direct hits, caught fire, and was scuttled on 7 May.

While this report of battle results from Midway was not entirely true, it was not entirely false, either. The United States lost one aircraft carrier, the *Yorktown*, and the destroyer *Hammann*. One Japanese aircraft carrier was sunk and another heavily damaged, but two others had to be scuttled. All four carriers—the *Akagi*, *Kaga*, *Hiryū,* and *Soryū*—had taken part in the Pearl Harbor attack. In the final analysis, half of the Japanese navy's striking power was lost at Midway. While it is true that only forty-two Japanese aircraft (not far off from the reported thirty-five) had "failed to return," two hundred eighty planes were entombed with their aircraft carriers, and with them went half of their pilots, among Japan's very best. This heavy loss of aircraft carriers, airplanes, and skilled pilots effectively ended Japan's advance, a fact that was kept secret within the Japanese navy itself and likewise went unreported in the Japanese press, which was still heady with the victories that had quickly accumulated in the first six months of the war.

In six months, the Japanese swept away four centuries of European and American encroachments upon East Asia, although not every campaign went as smoothly as the press would have the citizens believe. The Japanese press glossed over the obvious difficulties of Japanese operations in the Philippines. The Imperial High Command in Tokyo had equated the fall of Manila with the end of resistance throughout the island nation, and moved its Philippine divisions further south. This move frustrated the commander of the Japanese army in the Philippines, General Honma, who had to crush the remaining resistance with inferior troops and reservists. Honma was demoted and placed under Yamashita's command. A comparison of press coverage of the celebrated Yamashita and the nearly invisible Honma underscores the point that Tokyo considered Honma a failure. That Corregidor was continuing its resistance when the war was about to enter its second half-year (especially in light of the swift capitulation of Hong Kong, Singapore, Malaya, and the Dutch East Indies) was evidence of a stubbornness and tenacity out of character with the image of the enemy being formed in the Japanese media, suggesting that the optimistic narrative of the war, one that predicted a speedy settlement with the Western powers, might need some adjustment. Of course, the media's war reports all glowed with one success after another, and the seventy-six thousand American and Filipino defenders who surrendered at Bataan on 9 April (Dōmei's *Photo Almanac* gave the figure as forty thousand) and the thirteen thousand who followed suit on Corregidor on 6 May were called "enemy remnants" rather than "divisions" or "armies." For instance, Dōmei's *Photo Almanac for 1942* contained this description (in English) of the Philippine campaign:

> To swash [smash] one of the key points in the ABCD encirclement campaign against Japan, Japanese naval and military fliers carried out a concentrative attacks [sic] on the Philippines at the outset of the Great East Asia War. On January 2, 1942, only about three weeks oftes [after] the Japanese landing in the Islands, Manila, capital of the Philippines Commonwealth, fell into Japanese hands and enemy remnants who maintained resistance in Bataan, capitulated on April 11. Corregidor, American Stronghold which the United States boasted as practically impregnable, was reduced on May 7 by fighting of sheer bones and muscles, while mopping-up operations in Mindanao were successfully concluded on May 10. With the loss of the Philippines, the citadel of the United States aggression was completely wiped out of the East Asia.

46 and 47. (top) *PWR* 222, 27 May 1942, p. 6.[26] "A group of American soldiers from the underground base at Corregidor surrender, carrying the white flag."

The war digest that appeared on page 9 of this issue gave the figure of 12,495 POWs taken on Corregidor, the majority of them Americans, in addition to six hundred forty dead.

(bottom) Dōmei's *Photo Almanac for 1942* printed this photograph with the English caption "Hands raised and bearing the white flag of surrender[,] thousands of American soldiers pour out of the underground tunnels of Corregidor Fortress to give themselves up to the victorious Japanese."

Only a few seconds seem to have elapsed between this and the *PWR* photograph. The American soldier with his hands up at the front of the cave has now walked past the Japanese soldier with drawn bayonet. Although not originally published side by side in the same publication, the two photographs are clearly part of a series, most likely stills from film footage. Together they suggest the length to which the Japanese military went to create a photographic record of its achievements, attesting to a very real awareness of the lasting historical significance of their actions and of the power of photography to communicate that history. The republication of these photographs in many postwar publications, especially those of wartime enemy America, proves the point.

48-50. *PWR* 222, 27 May 1942, p. 7.

(top) "Meeting between captured enemy General Wainwright (on the left) and other American military leaders and Supreme Commander Honma."

(right) "Our brave soldiers close in on the enemy's position in a pillbox, attacking with a flame-thrower." Flame-throwers were also used by the Allies against Japanese pillboxes and caves when retaking Japanese-held islands in 1944 and 1945.

(bottom) "Enemy General Wainwright broadcasted the unconditional surrender order to remaining US and Philippine troops."

The surrender of American and Filipino holdouts on Corregidor on 6 May 1942 spelled the end of any organized Allied resistance north of Australia and west of Hawaii. Japanese confidence reached new heights and took on new forms of expression. Soiled or desecrated American flags became a symbol of the crushing force of Japan's invincibility. The nude or nearly nude Japanese male, photographed in high contrast to create monumental, almost sculptural images, became the symbol of the spiritual superiority of the Yamato race. Yamamoto, Yamashita, and Tōjō were lauded as the superhuman heroes of the navy, army, and the war cabinet, respectively. The entire nation seemed to have been papered with pictures of battleships, tanks, and bombs, the symbols of military might. For the One Hundred Million on the home front, the photographs of one victorious battle after another, of yet another enemy ship sinking and yet another foreign capital's capitulation, were the compensation for their many years of preparation and "spiritual training" as well as undeniable proof of Japan's invincibility and racial superiority.

51. Dōmei's *Photo Almanac for 1942* included this photograph in its coverage of the Philippine campaign, with no identification of the date or place. This English caption was provided: "American troops fled leaving the Stars and Stripes flag."

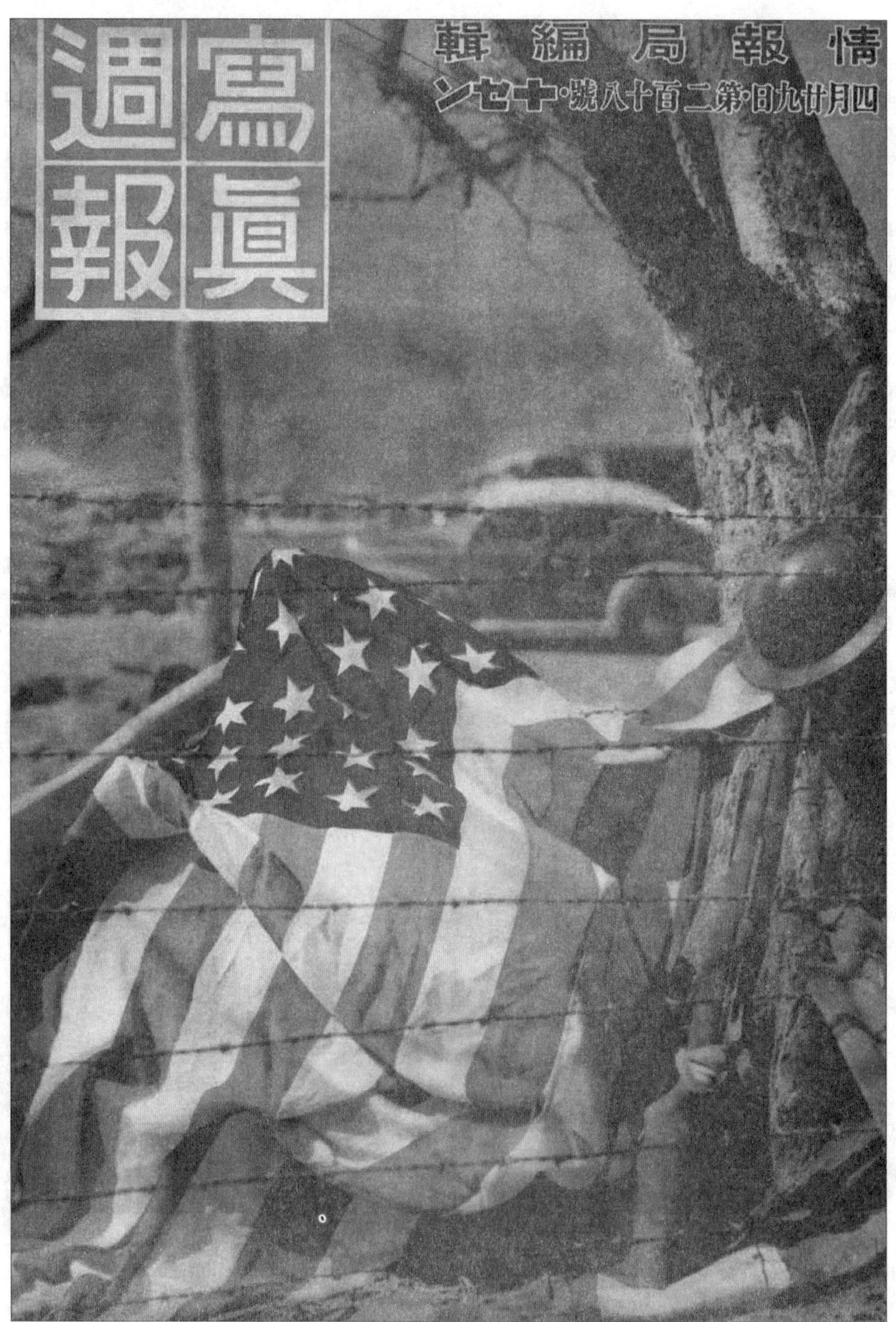

52. *PWR* 218, 29 April 1942.

“The Stars and Stripes flag has dejectedly fallen to the ground at Bataan, transformed into a scrap of tattered rag. Filipinos! Why not use this rag to wipe your feet, muddied by democracy? Let’s put a period to a forty-four-year history of oppression.”

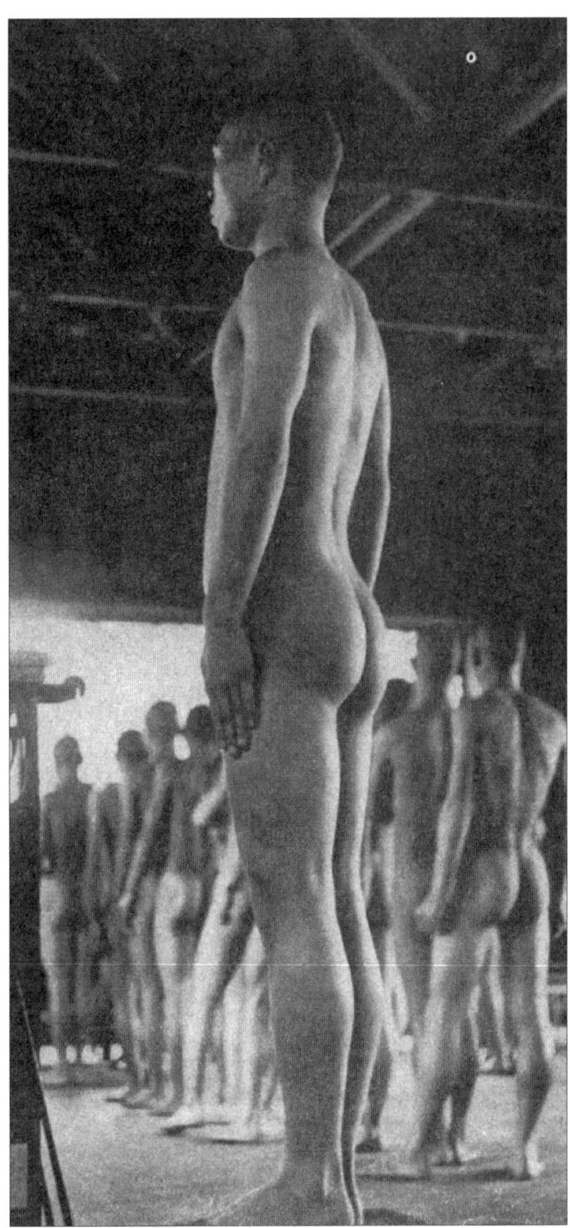

53-55. The male specimen of the Yamato race—perfect in body, sound in mind, pure in spirit—was best viewed from the back. Young men of such sturdy build must have been eating well, despite wartime rations.

(top left) *PWR* 234, 19 August 1942, p. 18. "Students Undertake Maritime Training Aboard the *Azuma*." This photograph is credited to master modern photographer Koishi Kiyoshi (1908-1957).

(bottom left) *PWR* 231, 29 July 1942, p. 2. "Signboard of the Times" No. 36 carried the message: "Above all else, the body is a resource. With a chest like a tank, legs that can even outrun a landmine, and a spirit like a steel-cased bullet, let us, from this time forward, on a wide, vast stage, *forge ahead*."

(right) *PWR* 152, 22 January 1941, p. 6. Sailors waiting for physicals as part of their induction.

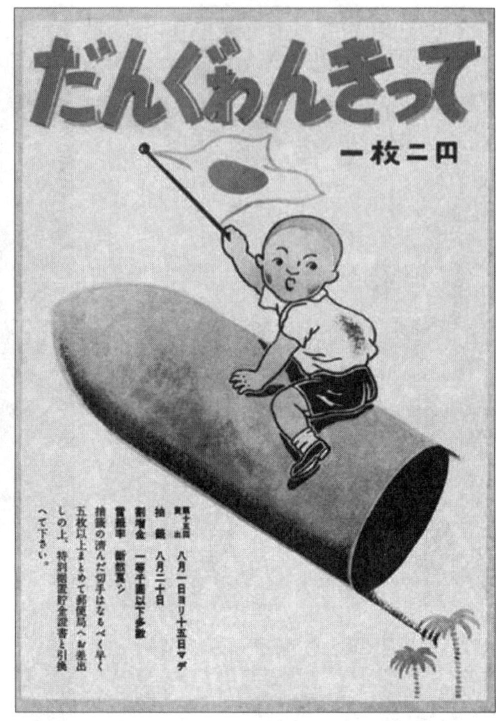

56-58. Japan's early victories in the Pacific were reflected in bold, confident war bond advertisements. These *PWR* back covers, simple in design, are visually arresting. None of these posters cite the sacrifice of soldiers or the duty of citizens, but refer instead to victory. Their appeal is to the ego, not conscience, of the viewer.

(top left) *PWR* 215, 8 April 1942. "Victory. War Expense. National Savings. Great East Asia War Government Bonds." The slogan mimics the coarseness and brevity of military commands.

(top right) *PWR* 283, 4 August 1943. "Bullet Bonds, 2 Yen Each" incorporated the palm trees of the South Pacific. The implications of the artwork's sexual innuendo need no explanation.

(bottom) *PWR* 255, 20 January 1943. "To Cut Through Them [and to Win], Savings. Tōkai Bank, Nagoya."

The text of this clever design employs katakana, which is used in Japanese for writing words of foreign, especially Western, origin, making a pun on the similarly pronounced Japanese and English words, *katsu* ("to win") and "cuts" (in Japanese, pronounced *katsu*).

The fighting in the Solomon Islands began on 7 August 1942, when Allied forces launched an invasion against lightly defended Japanese-held territory, with the conflict heating up on 20 August at Tenaru River. The battle through the dense jungle would drag on for several months, becoming a contest of attrition. The Japanese finally abandoned their efforts to retake the islands in February 1943. This campaign, the first Allied victory against the Imperial Japanese Army, became known in the West as Guadalcanal. The contemporary Japanese press called it the Battle of the Solomons and described it primarily as a series of maritime battles, in which the Japanese navy continued to send Allied ships to their watery graves. If the reports from the Solomons seemed overly optimistic, it was not because the dire implications of Midway had not been forgotten so much as that they had never been acknowledged. As the English-language text of Dōmei's *Photo Almanac for 1942* claimed,

> Taking advantage of the dark night, the Japanese Naval Forces staged a board-by-board battle [that is, fighting strenuously to take each plank of the ship's deck] in Solomon Waters on August 8, 1942. In this first Solomon Battle the Imperial Navy again demonstrated the unerring accuracy and the power of theirs [*sic*] cannon and torpedo attacks by sinking till August 14, 13 enemy class cruisers, 22 destroyers and other minor shipping and heavily damaging a A-class [*sic*] cruiser and 3 destroyers. Fifty-eight enemy planes were also shot down.
>
> The reinforced United States Fleet which attempted a counter-offensive, not having had enough in the failure of the first Solomon Battle, was miserablly [*sic*] shattered once again in the very same waters by the intrepid Japanese Navy between August 24 and Octover [*sic*] 25, 1942. In the second Solomon Battle 30 United States battleships including the aircraft-carrier *Wasp* were sunk or heavily wreck [*sic*] and more than 519 planes were shot down or destroyed.

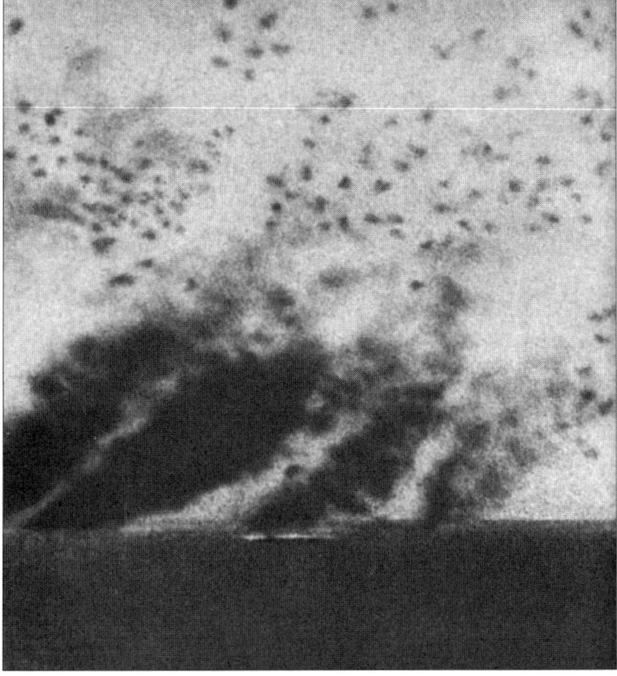

59. *PWR* 246, 11 November 1942, pp. 6-7. "The trend is set! Black smoke rises over the Solomon Sea from the blazing enemy aircraft carrier. The black dots in the sky are from the enemy's anti-aircraft artillery."

60 and 61. *PWR* 252, 23 December 1942, p. 8. "Our 'Sure-Hit, Sure-Kill' Torpedo Attack." Photographs: Navy Air Force.

(top) "15 October, in the southeast Solomon Islands, an enemy ship on the surface, hit and sinking. The enemy vessel, trying to flee, is stopped by the sure-kill torpedoes of our Navy Air Force. The enemy ship, engulfed in thick black smoke and listing heavily, soon experienced a violent explosion that sent it to the bottom. One of the battle results on 15 October from the fight to the death now taking place in the sea near the Solomons."

(bottom) "The end of the enemy aircraft carrier *Hornet* during the Battle of the South Pacific. On 26 October, in the sea north of the Santa Cruz Islands, we pummeled the *Hornet*, which was rendered incapable of launching aircraft. Here it is being guarded by seven escort ships that circle it at top speed as a precaution. In the end, though, the *Hornet* came within reach of our fleet and, while it was being escorted back to port, we finished it off." The *Hornet* (CV8) had performed valiantly in the Doolittle Raid on Tokyo in April 1942.

The first anniversary of the outbreak of the war, which was celebrated on 8 December 1942, was an occasion to give thanks to the emperor whose rescript declared war on the West and to the military who had made many sacrifices in order to accomplish what few had dared dream was possible: they had very nearly freed East Asia from four centuries of Western domination and exploitation. The remarkable progress in securing the wealth of natural resources of Southeast Asia had met with very few setbacks. Some Japanese ships, planes, and troops had been lost, but surely they would be quickly replaced. In April, there had been an air raid on Japan, hitting a few targets in Tokyo, Yokosuka, and Kobe, but it had incurred little damage.[27] American, British, and Dutch military bases had been destroyed, their navies and air forces decimated by Japanese bombs. The Japanese people, the proud Yamato race, now had only to ask what the next step would be for the One Hundred Million in ensuring a more prominent role in global affairs for their emperor, their nation, and their people. In the rarefied air that floated over Japan in December 1942, it seemed quite reasonable to assume that the United States would itself be bombed into submission by Japan's "peerless, intrepid" military.

62. *PWR* 249, 2 December 1942.

"This heroic image of Prime Minister Tōjō, the leader (*sōshi*, führer) of one hundred million citizens, evokes his steel-hard determination to fight through to the end of the Great East Asia War.

"A true-color negative was made through simultaneous tricolor photography, and from that negative four printing plates were created in red, blue, yellow and black, which were used to reproduce the natural color seen here. This is the first such test of the latest offset printing process in one of our country's graphic magazines."

The use of full color on a *PWR* cover was meant to celebrate the first anniversary of the war, to demonstrate Japanese technological advances, and also to honor the greatest hero of the war, Tōjō.

In fact, the first raid on the US mainland took place on 23 February 1942, when a Japanese submarine surfaced off the California coast and lobbed a few shells at oilfields at Golena, south of Santa Barbara Harbor, destroying a pier. The impact of the raid was primarily psychological, putting the West Coast on alert and diverting American matériel toward preventing further attacks. *PWR* 211 (11 March 1942, pp. 6-7) reported on the Santa Barbara raid with typical pomp, printing a stock photograph of a Japanese submarine, a map of the Pacific showing the distance from Tokyo to Santa Barbara, and an exciting text:

63. "Subduing Manhattan," a work of imagination by Kogi Ekan, plate 34 in *Great East Asia War Navy Art*. This statement appeared in the catalogue: "Once our eagles spread their wings over the enemy city, the forest of chalk-white skyscrapers and wharves that they have so proudly built will all shatter and be blown to pieces like leaves falling from trees. While America talks loudly of freedom and humanity, its deeds are on a par with an evil, murdering, savage devil-beast, and the end of this materialist civilization that disguises itself so is a necessity—indeed, it would certainly be divine retribution."

> Bold. Fearless. On 24 February, our submarines crossed 6,000 miles of billowing ocean for the first bombardment of the California coast, which has thrown all of America into a panic. While President Roosevelt, time after time, broadcasts his whining complaints about the battlefield being too far away for America to reach it, our submarines have brought the war to his attention by bringing the battlefield to his front door. Our submarines, without exercising their ability to avoid detection, surfaced right under the enemy's nose. But Roosevelt is deluding [the American people], pretending that this bombardment is merely "a political maneuver on Japan's part."

Through the autumn of 1942, Japanese forces made isolated, sporadic attacks on the West Coast. On 20 June 1942, a submarine shelled the Estevan Point Lighthouse on Vancouver Island, British Columbia. On 9 September 1942, a submarine-launched seaplane dropped bombs near Brookings, Oregon, in an attempt to start forest fires. The Japanese press gave minimal coverage to these attacks, which caused negligible damage. The fire-balloon campaign of 1944-1945, in which large non-motorized balloons were filled with explosives and sent adrift in the Pacific gulf stream, was not reported at all in the Japanese press because of its top secret nature. Of the nine thousand fire-balloons sent adrift, an estimated three hundred reached North America. They failed to set off the intended forest fires, although one killed a picnicking Oregon family.

64. The front cover of *Air Raids on the Continental United States*, by Noyori Shūichi (2nd ed, 1944) used a collage of rather roughly drawn Japanese airplanes dropping bombs upon a photographic image of Washington, D.C. This book, originally published in September 1943, advocated widespread bombing campaigns against major US cities, including Washington, D.C., and New York. The second edition has a new preface dated March 1944 and proposes, at the very least, repeated attacks on the California coastline that would cause massive forest fires and thoroughly demoralize the American population.

Even those Japanese writers and artists (and military strategists) who envisioned the bombing of major American cities did not propose that Japan occupy the United States. Japan's war aims were to drive the United States (and other Western powers) from Asia, and to realize a New Order in Asia that would bring prosperity to the entire region under Japan's leadership. Because the Japanese had countenanced the cultural ramifications of Westernization, with its attendant "polluting" influences of hedonism and individualism, they would have found it absurd to think of "Easternizing" or "Orientalizing" the West. The logic of Japan's war—"Asia for Asiatics"—was firmly rooted in a notion of racial superiority that made Westerners the objects of pity, scorn, and contempt. Now that Japan's military objectives in East Asia had resulted in extraordinary territorial gains, it remained to be seen whether fellow Asians—the junior partners in the Greater East Asian Co-Prosperity Sphere—took to Japan's ideals as quickly as the Japanese hoped they would.

65. *PWR* 208, 18 February 1942, p. 2.

The "Signboard of the Times" printed over a Japanocentric map of the world, carried this message: "Singapore has capitulated, but that only means the time has come to collect dues on the one-hundred-year history of the British Empire's encroachment upon East Asia. And there is still much further to go: Canada, London, Washington."

Notes

1. As early as 1909, the American Ernest Hugh Fitzpatrick's self-published *The Coming Conflict of Nations or the Japanese-American War* (Springfield, IL: Roker), while admitting that "The war between Japan and the United States is only a remote possibility, and likewise the war between Germany and England" (p. 8), foresaw a sea battle between the United States and Japan taking place in the Pacific and resulting in Japan's defeat, but only after Japan had occupied large tracts of the West Coast and a massive battle had taken place in Idaho. It is tantalizing to prognosticate along with Fitzpatrick of the Japanese plan to entrench themselves in a sparsely-populated northwestern United States, where "relying upon the certainty of a naval victory [in the Pacific, they] quickly overrun Idaho, then Utah, making Salt Lake City a military entrepot" (p. 203). *Japan Must Fight Britain*, by Lieutenant-Commander Tōta Ishimaru of the Imperial Japanese Navy (New York: Herald Press, 1936) laid out many of the reasons Japan did indeed go to war against Great Britain—most notably, British domination of international politics to maintain its own imperialist aims, and its economic blockade impeding Japan's designs on southeast Asia. As early as 1914, Major General Tanaka Giichi "urged a preemptive military strike against an increasingly powerful United States" (Frederick R. Dickinson, *War and National Reinvention: Japan in the Great War, 1914-1919* [Cambridge, MA: Harvard University Press, 1999], p. 249).

2. Cited from the Japanese official translation as printed in the *Japan Times*, 8 December 1941, p. 1.

3. In response to the rallying call to "revere the emperor and expel the barbarians" (*sonnō jōi*), in 1863 the Chōshū Clan began firing on foreign ships passing through the Kanmon Straits, the most direct route from the Chinese port cities to Edo (Tokyo). In retaliation, ships from Great Britain, France, the Netherlands, and the United States bombarded Shimonoseki and dismantled the clan's cannonade. Chōshū quickly sued for peace, Japan was made to pay indemnities, and the Straits remained open to foreign ships.

4. A well researched and finely nuanced biography of Yamamoto is Agawa Hiroyuki's *The Reluctant Admiral: Yamamoto and the Imperial Japanese Navy* (Kodansha International, 1979).

5. As with the "Incidents" of the 1930s, *Asahigraph* issued one of its "special reports," *Great East Asia War Pictorial*, on 25 December 1941. In its thirty-four pages (at the cost of 30 sen), it contained only three photographs pertaining to the outbreak of the war, all of them previously published: one of the aerial bombing of Hong Kong and two of the sinking of *The Prince of Wales* and *Repulse*. There were also four small photographs of Japanese troops marching "toward Hong Kong." The magazine included several stock photographs describing Japan's military power and maps of the new battle fronts. This effort was put to shame by *PWR*'s first report on the attack on Pearl Harbor.

6. This is one of many photographs created by the Japanese navy and published in the Japanese wartime press which, through their inclusion in the US National Archives, have been frequently reprinted. The National Archives describes this as a "captured Japanese photograph," record number: 80-G-30549. The US Department of the Navy's Naval Historical Center Web site gives it the identification number NH50603 and the caption, "Torpedo plane takes off from *Shokaku* to attack Pearl Harbor, 7 December 1941." See www.history.navy.mil/photos/events/wwii-pac/pearlhbr/pearlhb.htm. The Destroyer Escort Central Web site includes "the original Japanese caption" in very flowery English, from an unidentified source: "The moment at which the Hawaiian surprise attack force is about to take off from the carrier. On the faces of those who go forth to conquer and those who send them off there floats only that beautiful smile which transcends death . . ." See www.de220.com/Pearl%20Harbor/Pearl%20Harbor.htm for this and other "original captions" to figures 13, 15, 18, and 22. This differs significantly from the English caption to this photograph found in Dōmei's *Photo Almanac for 1942*: "The determined naval fliers are given farewell just before taking off from one of the aircraft carriers for an attack on the United States Pacific Fleet."

7. This image is very similar to National Archives 80-G-182249, a still from a Japanese newsreel.

8. National Archives 80-G-30551; US Naval Historical Center NH 50931.

9. Capital ships were the first rank of warships, especially battleships and aircraft carriers. Evidently, the term did not refer to any particular tonnage or displacement.

10. National Archives 80-G-30550.

11. National Archives 80-G-30554; US Naval Historical Center NH 50930.

12. The exhibition catalogue gives the title, "Pearl Harbor on 8 December." The Tokyo National Museum of Modern Art lists this as one of several paintings on "unlimited extended loan," providing the medium (oil on canvas) and the dimensions (63 by 102 inches). A digitized image of this painting is reproduced on the US Naval Historical Center Web site with this information: "Japanese war art painting, in oils, by Tsuguji Fujita, 1942, depicting attacks around Ford Island. The original painting measures about 2.7M by 1.7M. Courtesy of the U.S. Air Force Art & Museum Branch (their accession # 277.53), 1978."

13. The "wild eagle" (*arawashi*) refers to the pilot, not a make or model of airplane. Japanese press releases avoided detailed technical information, employing a set of interchangeable, clichéd phrases: "naval fliers," "air raiders," "hawk eyes," and so forth. Even the type of plane (bomber, fighter, transport) was rarely mentioned.

14. National Archives 80-G-30552.

15. The photograph appeared in the *Illustrated London News*, 21 February 1942, p. 245.

16. Sakamaki wrote about his war experiences in *I Attacked Pearl Harbor* (New York: Association Press, 1949). He died in 1999 at age eighty-one. For a brief biography, see Burl Burlingame, "WWII's First Japanese Prisoner Shunned the Spotlight," in the 11 May 2002 *Honolulu Star Bulletin*, available at: http://starbulletin.com/2002/05/11/news/whatever.html. Chapter 12 discusses the midget submarines.

17. The contemporary Japanese press explained that Nomura Kichisaburō, the Japanese ambassador in Washington, had delivered an ultimatum to the United States on 20 November 1941 (the second Japanese proposal to lift the oil and steel embargo, commonly referred to as the "B Plan") and that since diplomatic means of settling the two nations' problems had been exhausted, war was declared. The attack on Pearl Harbor was described as an unavoidable, logical course of action, not as a "surprise" attack. Indeed, a similar series of events had led to Japan's declaration of war on Russia in 1904.

18. In the collection of the National Museum of Modern Art, Tokyo. The museum's online database provides these details for the painting: 1942 watercolor on paper, 77 by 107 inches.

19. Now in the collection of the National Museum of Modern Art, Tokyo. Yamaguchi (1893-1971), a recognized master of *nihonga*, achieved a balance between the formal limitations of Japanese watercolor and the demands of modern subject matter. He received the Order of Culture (*bunka kunshō*) in 1965 and received commissions for paintings from the imperial family for the new palace. A museum (*kinenkan*) devoted to his work is in Hayama, Kanagawa Prefecture, close to the Shōwa emperor's summer villa.

20. Dōmei's *Photo Almanac for 1942* printed the same photograph with a Japanese caption stating that the two ships had been spotted by a Japanese submarine and then were attacked and sunk by planes. The same publication's English-language caption, however, told a very different tale: "Britain's East Asiatic Fleet was rubbed out from the world on December 10, 1941, with blitz sinking by Japanese submarines of *The Prince of Wales*, the pride of the British navy, and the *Repulse*, battle-cruiser, off Kuantan, Malay Peninsula." The discrepancy is probably an error in translation rather than an act of disinformation.

21. Another work on "unlimited extended loan" to the National Museum of Modern Art, Tokyo, part of the US "Army Signal Corps Collection." National Archives ID: SC 301094.

22. In the collection of the National Museum of Modern Art, Tokyo. The museum's online database provides this information about the painting: 1942 oil on canvas, 136 by 75 inches.

23. Yuki Tanaka's "Last Words of the Tiger of Malaya, General Yamashita Tomoyuki," is a balanced examination of Yamashita's dubious legacy. See *Japan Focus* (20 September 2005): http://japanfocus.org/article.asp?id=392.

24. The online catalogue of the collection of the National Museum of Modern Art, Tokyo, describes the work as oil on canvas, 71 by 211 inches.

25. In the collection of the National Museum of Modern Art, Tokyo. Their online catalogue provides the following information: "'Japanese Paratroops Descending on Palembang,' 1942, oil on canvas 194.0 by 255.0 cm [76 by 100 inches]." The title uses the word *shinpei* ("god-soldiers"), distinct from *gunshin* ("warrior-gods") in that they were not deceased. Shinpei are godly in that they purportedly enjoy divine protection.

26. National Archives number 208-AA-80B-1.

27. This is, of course, the Doolittle Raid of 18 April, which will be treated in detail in Chapter 10.

8. THE GREATER EAST ASIAN CO-PROSPERITY SPHERE

By the summer of 1942, the Japanese Empire had expanded far beyond the wildest dreams of the Meiji oligarchs of seventy-five years before. Encompassing broad tracts of arable land in Korea, Manchuria, China, Vietnam, Thailand, and Burma; lush, resource-laden islands spread across Southeast Asia; and a vast area of the Pacific dotted with military installations, the Greater East Asian Co-Prosperity Sphere rivaled the Western colonial empires its establishment was designed to destroy. The Co-Prosperity Sphere, Japan's *jus ad bellum*, brought together one billion Asians, under Japanese leadership, in an all-out attack on the West's military, economic, political, and cultural encroachments upon one-quarter of the world's populated surface and one-half of the world's population, constituting the greatest military and cultural challenge to Western civilization since the Mongol hordes decimated eastern Europe.

1. *PWR* 300, 8 December 1943, pp. 8-9. "All of Asia Has Taken up Arms." This collage of the different regional armies being formed throughout the Greater East Asian Co-Prosperity Sphere to combat Western imperialism appeared on the second anniversary of the Great East Asia War. Clockwise, from center bottom: the Manchurian Army (with rifle-bayonets), the Indian People's Army (Sikhs), the Chinese People's Army (charging), the Thai Army (with tank), the Borneo Forces (marching), the Javanese Forces (standing at attention), the Burmese Defense Army (marching toward the camera), the Malaysian Troops (single man standing for review).

The Co-Prosperity Sphere was defined by its contiguous geography, its protection under Pax Japonica, and the inherent "Asianness" of its inhabitants. However, these were tenuous links, at best, between peoples with little else in common. The Co-Prosperity Sphere appeared as a massive bloc on a political map of the world, but at its northern extreme were the light-skinned nomadic herdsmen of the Manchurian highlands, and at its southern extreme were dark-skinned tribesmen in the dense forests of Papua New Guinea. Its western border encompassed the Andaman Islands, its eastern border Polynesia. Within these borders lived hundreds of millions of Chinese, Koreans, Vietnamese, Thai, Burmese, Malaysians, Indonesians, and Filipinos, each people with its own racial, linguistic, cultural, social, religious, economic, and historical distinctions. Many of these groups had been fragmented by ethnic minorities and territorial disputes for centuries. Uniting these one billion Asians in a common purpose was an undertaking fraught with insurmountable obstacles—above all else, communication, as several hundred different languages were spoken throughout the Co-Prosperity Sphere. For the Yamato race, however, nothing was impossible, not even the superhuman achievement of liberating Asia from Western domination and creating a pan-Asian community of nations; from 1942 to 1944, the pages of Japan's newspapers and magazines were filled with images of promise heralding the birth of the new Asia.

朝鮮に志願兵制度生る
京城陸軍志願兵訓練所

2. *PWR* 22, 13 July 1938, pp. 12-13. "Birth of Volunteer Military Service System in Korea: Keijō [Seoul] Army Volunteer Corps Training Camp." Photographs: *Keijō Nippō Newspaper*. The photographs show a dress review. Such articles about Korean and Taiwanese military personnel were uncommon. Few Korean soldiers were genuine volunteers, given the dire economic conditions on the Korean Peninsula, under Japanese rule, and the lack of opportunities for young Koreans. Some were kidnapped by Japanese troops and forced into military service. Korean soldiers were often given inferior positions, such as guarding POWs.[1]

As mentioned in Chapter 2, the rationale for the Greater East Asian Co-Prosperity Sphere was found in the experiment of Manchuria, the model for a new form of empire in which territorial expansion was accomplished without creating a colony from the conquered territory and without politically incorporating it into the Japanese Empire (as was done earlier with Formosa [Taiwan], Korea, and southern Sakhalin). The Japanese invested resources and surplus population into the new state of Manchukuo, building a new nation in an Asian pseudo-wilderness, bringing an urban and industrial form of life to the native population, and giving them modern farms, factories, and cities. The new nation repaid Japanese magnanimity with exports of raw materials and foodstuffs, imports of manufactured goods, and, eventually, political and military support.

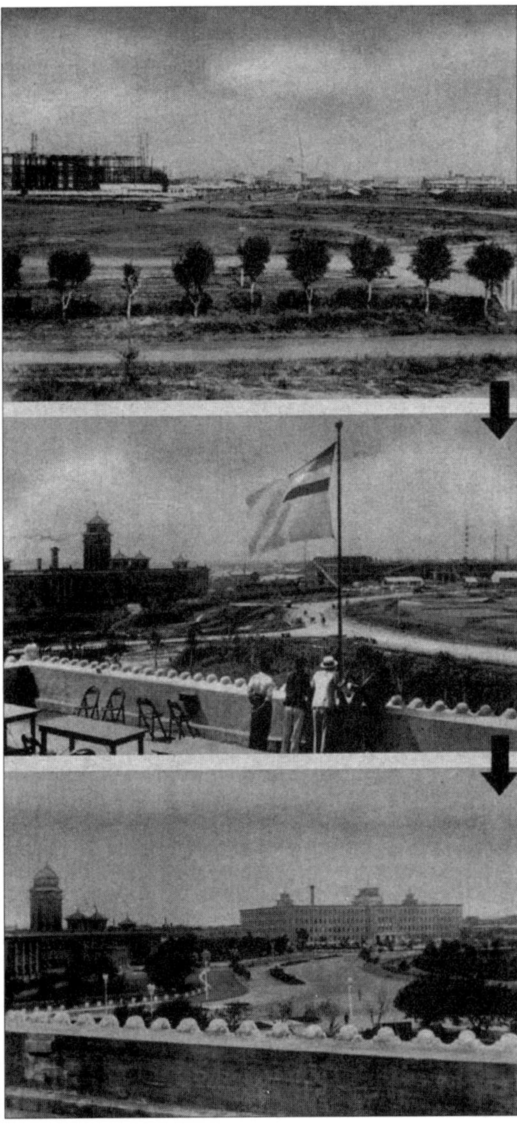

3-5. *PWR* 31, 14 September 1938, pp. 4-5. "Giant Steps in Building Manchukuo." Three photographs of Daidō Plaza in the center of Mukden, the new capital of Manchukuo, show its development in the five years since the new nation was established.

(top) The government building under construction in Mukden, capital of the new nation Manchukuo, 1933.

(middle) Government offices have been built, and the vast circular Daidō Plaza laid out in the center of the new capital city. The Manchukuoan flag flies in the foreground.

(bottom) The same scene at the time of the article, five years later: the miracle of Japanese development, demonstrated upon the *tabula rasa* of the Manchurian plain.

Mukden, known today as Shenyang, is China's fifth-largest city, with a population of 3.6 million.

After three years of fierce fighting in China, the major northern cities had come under Japanese control, and the time had arrived for the "New China" to join the fledgling Japanese commonwealth. In 1940, a puppet state along the lines of the Manchukuoan model was established in northwestern China, with its capital at Nanjing under the leadership of Premier Wang Jingwei. In reality, the Chinese Nationalists under Chiang Kai-shek controlled large areas of China at this time, and most of the world's nations recognized Chiang as China's ruler. The Communists under Mao Zedong had established their own political headquarters in northwestern Yenan. The Japanese government described these as guerrilla and insurgent groups and continued its policy of exterminating them. Within the Co-Prosperity Sphere, Japan's satellite states were given the semblance of political autonomy and therefore the "New China" had its own president, flag, and military forces. Of course, "big brother" Japan reserved a veto power and held real military and economic control.

6-8. (left) *PWR* 97, 3 January 1940, p. 17. "Newborn China's Officers' Training School." Premier Wang (top) inspects troops (the two conjoined photographs at bottom) of the newly established Chinese Central Army's boot camp. The caption uses "Shina" for China.

(right) *PWR* 108, 20 March 1940, p. 1. "This spring, East Asia welcomes a new flag." Wang Jingwei, premier of "free" China, unfurls the new flag in front of a large wall poster of him bearing the slogans, "Promoting Anti-Communism, Making Peace Saves the Nation." Photograph: *Tokyo Nichinichi Newspaper.*

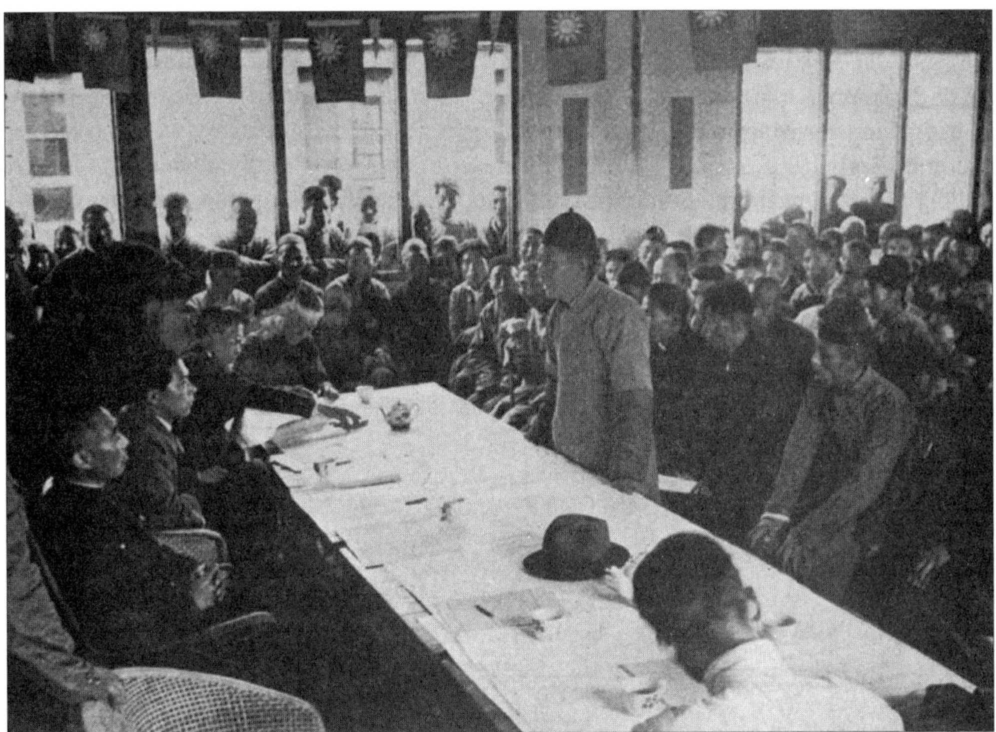

9-11. Dōmei's *Photo Almanac for 1941* gave a glowing account of the "New China" and its military cooperation with the Japanese army. These are the original English captions printed in the *Almanac*.

(top) "Leaders of the 'Model Peace Zones' met in conference."

(bottom left) "President Wang Ching-wei [Jingwei] of the National Government [of China] is on an inspection tour in the 'Model Peace Zone.'

"The National Government of China selected the delta region of the Yangtze River as the first area for the cultivation of the 'Model Peace Zone' campain [*sic*], aided by the Japanese army activities started on July 1 at the delta."

(bottom right) "Children are playing in the 'Model Peace Zone.'"

In 1940, the world's attention was riveted on the Nazi blitzkrieg in Europe. The Japanese, duly impressed by the Nazi war machine, joined the Axis in a military alliance on 27 September 1940, the day after Roosevelt imposed a scrap iron embargo on Japan. Foreign Minister Matsuoka Yōsuke negotiated a nonaggression treaty with the Soviet Union in April 1941. Soon thereafter, Japanese troops were rapidly advancing through southern China toward the border of French Indo-china. The Vietnamese, newcomers to the Co-Prosperity Sphere, quickly learned that membership required more than economic and military cooperation; its cultural dimensions required learning "civilization" from the Yamato race and paying homage to Japan as the leader in Asia. Thailand, a nation that had successfully resisted Western colonization, was now surrounded by the Japanese to the north and the east, and pursued a policy of mollifying Japanese demands while maintaining its independence for as long as possible.

12. *PWR* 126, 24 July 1940, pp. 4-5. "Navy Commander Yanagizawa (second from left, behind the desk) in a meeting with a member of the French Indo-chinese officers' school." This photograph, from the first in a two-part article by Uchiyama Shigenosuke about Indo-china, shows the Japanese in a position of authority as negotiations for the Japanese takeover of the nation proceeded in Hanoi.

13 and 14. *PWR* 127, 31 July 1940, pp. 6-7. "The Supply Route to Liang Shang has Disappeared." Two photographs from an article describing the Japanese takeover of French Indo-china. One major objective, cutting off Allied supply routes to Chiang Kai-shek's Nationalist troops in southern China, has already been achieved, as Japanese troops now patrol the mountainous border. French and Japanese troops appear to be cooperating in these photographs, and the road sign is in French, English, and Chinese characters (legible to Chinese, Japanese, and literate Vietnamese).

15. *PWR* 134, 18 September 1940. "The Flower Girl of Hanoi."

"In the morning, beside the lake of Petit Lac [Hoan Kiem] Park—called the Flower of Hanoi—an Annamese flower girl walks barefoot through the moist morning dew, setting her flower basket beneath the shade of a leafy tree. A gentle breeze stirring in the moments before breakfast invites a lady of this foreign land (*ikoku*) out for a stroll. Her feet stop here and she buys a large bouquet of lotus flowers."

This exoticized text could have been lifted from any Western-language travelogue. The use of the word *ikoku* (strange or different land), rather than the more common *gaikoku* (outside-country) emphasizes the strangeness of the "foreign land," while the lotus is throughout Asia a symbol of Buddhism, a common bond.

This sort of exoticized treatment of a newly acquired territory is typical of the Japanese press's coverage of the lands occupied following Japan's blitzkrieg of December 1941.

16-19. *PWR* 167, 7 May 1941, pp. 18-19. "Co-Prosperity Sphere Youth Learn from the Japan of their Dreams."

"The Thai-French skirmish over Indo-china has ended splendidly, and [Co-Prosperity Youth] have taken a leap forward toward Japan, leader of the Axis in East Asia, which appeals to them. Exchange students from vast Manchuria, Mongolia, dusty yellow China, Thailand with its endless summer, the Philippines, and other East Asian countries have come pouring into Japan this year and started the new school year in the season of cherry blossoms.

"These young male and female exchange students will study in Citizens' Schools, Girls' Schools, and every type of upper-level school, where they will gain a firm understanding of how Japan is righteous (*tadashii*) and how Japan is infallible, and, eventually, they will tell young people in their home countries all about Axis leader Japan."

(right top and middle) Thai exchange students in Japan.

(right bottom) "Thailand is a promising new member of the East Asian Co-Prosperity Sphere. In the home of Thai young women who have come from far away to study here. When they have a break from studying, they learn flower-arranging. From the right, Bunja, Daroon, and Pikul."[2]

(top left) "Omar Yadi from French Indo-china graduated from the business school of a Tokyo university, and is now completing his research on the economic policies of the Tokugawa and Meiji periods, which will be published after he returns to his country. Wu Wenmen, also from French Indo-china, came to Japan last August, and is now enthusiastically studying Japanese at the international student center in Tokyo. In the future, he hopes to make an Annamese-Japanese dictionary. In a dormitory room of the international student center, Omar Yadi (at right) enjoys studying Japanese conversation with Wen (at left)."

(bottom left) "Kariyanta (front row) was attracted to seagoing Japan from the Philippines and is now studying marine courses in Tokyo."

In May 1942, the Japanese military controlled several former colonies, key Allied military positions in Southeast Asia, and half of the Pacific, extending from the Aleutian Islands of Alaska in the north to New Guinea in the south; from eastern India and the Andaman Islands in the west to Guam in the east. The Greater East Asian Co-Prosperity Sphere, which had been little more than an idea two years before, now encompassed over one-eighth of the earth's surface.

Japan could not begin to exploit the resources of these areas without strengthening infracture. Restoring order and rebuilding cities and industries devastated during the invasion became the top priority. This dangerous work was carried out by Japan's military occupiers. In November 1942, the Japanese government created a Great East Asia Ministry with Aoki Kazuo as its first head, charged with the responsibility of overseeing the rebuilding and development of regional economies and the process of uniting Asians of different languages, customs, cultures, and races, thereby preparing them to become full-fledged citizens of the Co-Prosperity Sphere.

20. *PWR* 250, 9 December 1942.

"Shōnan is the gateway to the Southern Regions. This gateway, rebuilt from Western style to pure Japanese style, has the fragrant smell of new wood as its Japaneseness (*nihonshoku*) quickly takes over. Because these policemen who will control the residents living in this new atmosphere are the [local] leaders of the Co-Prosperity Sphere, they require special training. Naturally, the local residents striving to become policemen are receiving strict training in this new spirit, as is reflected in their furrowed brow."

For the first anniversary of the outbreak of the Great East Asia War, *PWR* put on its cover this photograph of new Singaporean police recruits being inspected on their dress code by a Japanese. The camera angle and lens have probably been manipulated to make the Japanese appear a full head taller than the police recruits, although the photograph is cropped at the bottom so that the feet do not show. Photograph: Army Information Corps.

21-26. *PWR* 249, 2 December 1942, pp. 32-33. "Mr. Soldier Gently Takes Us by the Hand and Teaches Us."

"Work—that is what people belonging to the third class do. Well, see for yourself: the Americans, English, and Dutch did nothing themselves but play, and this idea rubbed off on the peoples of the Southern Regions, who they regarded as their inferiors. But once the Japanese army occupied these areas, everything changed. 'These Japanese soldiers, who are so strong in warfare, are in fact really good at and happy to work' [the local people think]. These days, Malayans and Filipinos have come to understand the joy of working, thanks to our soldiers and the staff members of the Military Administration, who have gently taken them by the hand and taught them. Our slogan [in Japan], 'in the workplace, an earnest fight' is already being expressed by the natives of the Southern Regions in their beautiful cooperation in every aspect of constructing [the Co-Prosperity Sphere]." (captions, clockwise from top right)

(top right) "Staff members of the Military Administration have come all the way to this remote region to teach salt-harvesting. Medan, Sumatra."

(bottom row, far right) "'Grip it firmly here and push.' He explains to an Indian how to tan leather at a tannery. Rangoon."

(bottom row, right) "The police who serve on the front line of security, are, literally, being taken by the hand and taught judo. Manila."

(bottom row, left) "'Well, you've really gotten good at it. Okay, tighten it here.' They are repairing broken down cars and clearing them out of the garage one after another. Manila."

(bottom row, far left) "At a hospital, the local young women work hard while learning from Japanese nurses. Shōnan."

(top left) "[Soldier:] 'Got it? Hold the spatula here and put the bean paste inside.' He teaches a girl working for the army how to make delicious bean cakes. Rangoon."

昭南生れて一年

破壊から建設へ

27. *PWR* 258, 10 February 1943, pp. 4-5. "One Year After the Birth of Shōnan, from Destruction to Construction." The first two pages of a thirteen-page article on the first year of Shōnan—Singapore under Japanese occupation.

"Already a year has passed. One year ago, all citizens of Japan kept [a] silent [vigil] and cleansed their hearts, waiting for one announcement. At that time, all Japanese citizens exhibited a sincerity nearing prayer. There was no faking their sentiment. On 15 February of last year, Singapore surrendered, and on the seventeenth, Shōnan was born, and we had our first Victory Celebration of the war. It was an exciting series of events that we will never forget as long as we live. And that excitement has become a new determination for us, to steadily continue the fight to eradicate America and Britain." Photographs: Army Information Corps.

The article reminds the reader of the euphoria following Singapore's surrender, while the photographs describe the destruction and process of rebuilding the war-battered city, with three "before and after" views, the top two sets showing commercial avenues, the bottom showing the port.

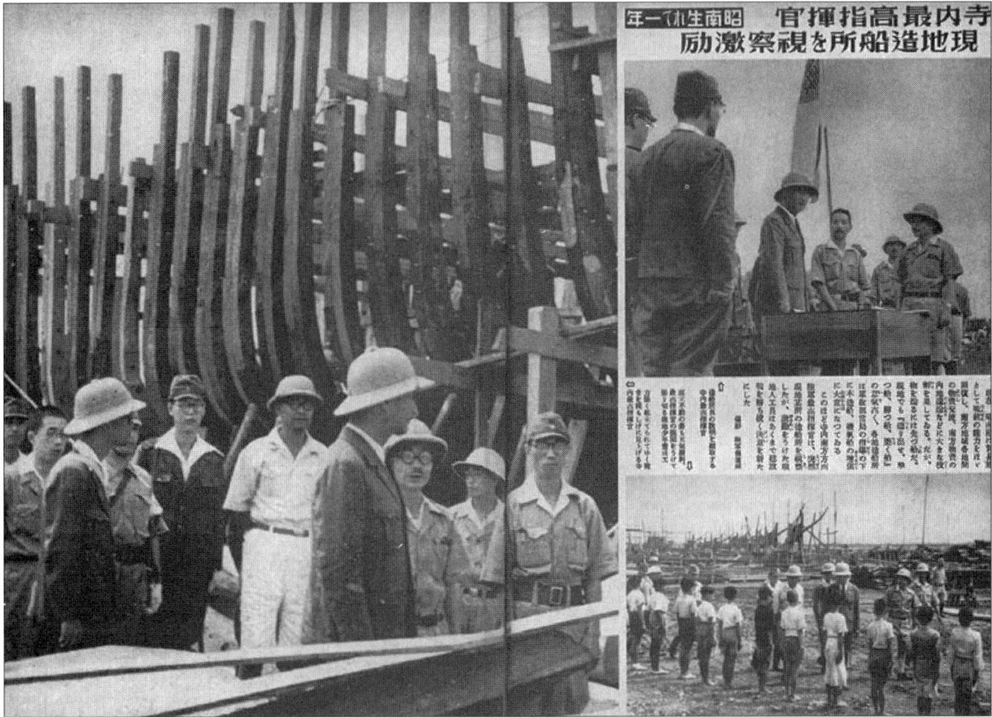

28-30. *PWR* 258, 10 February 1943, pp. 6-7. "One Year After the Birth of Shōnan: Supreme Commander Terauchi Gives Encouragement by Inspecting Local Shipbuilding Facilities."

"At present, Shōnan Harbor has nearly recovered its prewar capabilities and is playing a major role in the flow of supplies to the Southern Regions and in remanding supplies from the Southern Regions to and from the interior. However, in order to transport, there must be ships. Everywhere, on-site spirit is high: 'Ships for shooting [the enemy]. Ships for winning. Ships for building [East Asia].' And in every region's shipyards, under the direction of the regional military authority, they are busily increasing production of wooden ships and motorized craft.

"Supreme Commander of Army Forces in the Southern Regions Terauchi's unannounced inspection of [censored] shipyard renewed the determination of the encouraged local workers to do their utmost to win the construction war."

(top right) "Supreme Commander Terauchi listens to the explanation of the shipbuilders."

(bottom right) "Although standing straight and motionless, these hardworking local construction trainee youths are bursting with energy as they are reviewed by Supreme Commander Terauchi."

(left) "Supreme Commander Terauchi sees how reliably this sturdy keel is being put together." Photographs: Army Information Corps.

31-35. *PWR* 258, 10 February 1943, p. 8 and p. 13. More photographs from the article, "One Year After the Birth of Shōnan."

(top page, right, p. 8) "Newspapers and Traveling Exhibitions Are Flourishing." The caption says, "A large banner with an encouraging message displayed on a busy commercial street." The banner urges support for the war.

(top page, top left) The front page of the *Shōnan Newspaper*, its headline reading, "Greeting the 2,603rd Year Since the Founding of the Empire." This is the New Year's edition for 1 January 1943.

(top page, middle) "Local newspaper reporters steel their determination to use their writing skills to perform public service [for the war] while listening to a lecture by Military Press Attache Ōkubo."

(top page, bottom) "In the batting of an eye, citizens in a Shōnan suburb have flocked around a traveling exhibition." The exhibition displayed a series of posters with war information and slogans.

(bottom page, p. 13) "Paper Theater Gains Popularity in the Streets," another photograph in the series, "One Year After the Birth of Shōnan." This photograph shows a performance in Singapore of "Shōnan is Growing," attended by all ages, from "small children to young adults." The accompanying article employs Malay words transliterated into Japanese katakana, but emphasizes the similarities between Japanese children and those of Shōnan, who reportedly cry out "*Ganbarukurusu!*" ("Kami shibai!") when they see the paper theater man. Another photograph in this article shows a large office with a dozen workers creating paper theater scripts in Malay "under Japanese supervision" and describes paper theater plays used to teach Japanese language to children.

日本女性マニラ先遣部隊から

36-41. *PWR* 266, 7 April 1943, pp. 14-15. "News from the 'Advance Troops' of Japanese Women Sent to Manila." One of the very few articles in *PWR* describing the work of Japanese women in the occupied territories, the text reads,

"We Japanese women who were chosen to be sent to Manila send you our news.

"When we took our first steps after landing and saw the beautiful white city of Manila floating above the line of palm trees, our feeling of resignation changed completely to exhilarating excitement, as if we were walking on air. Some months have passed since then, and day after day, our 'by the book' lifestyle has finally brought us back down to earth. Today we can say that we have really taken ownership of the mission and the work assigned to us.

"The work is ordinary. Our lifestyles are ordinary, too. However, in the course of dispensing with our office duties, we have come to identify with the women of the Philippines and to feel that our modest efforts, one part of the great work of building [the New Order] in the Philippine Islands, are clearly helpful. So we perform our duty gladly and with enthusiasm."

(left page, top) "Midsummer is quickly approaching. Even when the temperature becomes very hot, we continue to process the paperwork. Whether the work is easy or difficult, we ourselves think it deserves considerable physical and spiritual energy."

(left page, bottom left) "It's one thing after another, as the work keeps coming. When we think that our efforts are helping to construct [the Greater East Asian Co-Prosperity Sphere], we realize how very important is each word we type."

(left page, bottom right) "Not just being fit, but healthy—during Radio Calisthenics time, the sound of the piano reminds us of the lives we used to lead, talking face to face with our mothers."

(right page, top left) "Here we are, in front of our quarters. Our motto: 'Our friendship will transcend the workplace. We will practice Japanese music together, believe in and care for each other, protect our chastity, and thereby foster our female virtues and display the true worth of Japanese womanhood."

(right page, bottom left) "Over here [in the Philippines], this is the Ginza. We go out to Escaldo Street to do a little shopping and eat some ice cream."

(right page, right) "Sometimes, on Sunday afternoon, the Filipino women who have become our friends come to visit us." Photographs by Suzuki of the Army Information Corps.

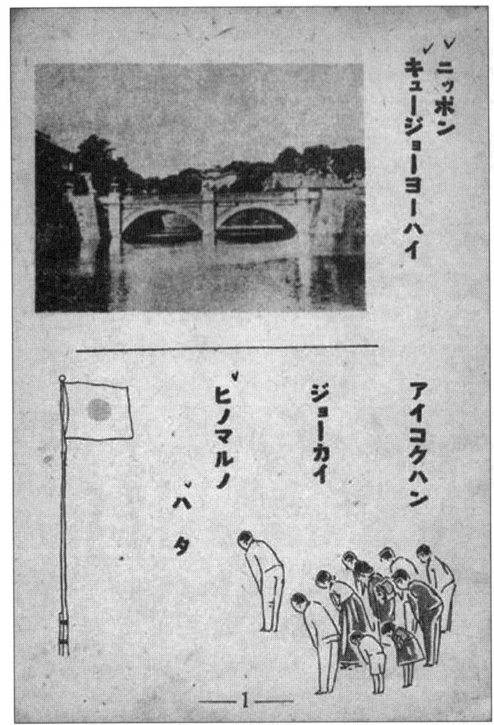

ニッポン
キュージョーヨーハイ

アイコクハン
ジョーカイ
ヒノマルノ ハタ

—1—

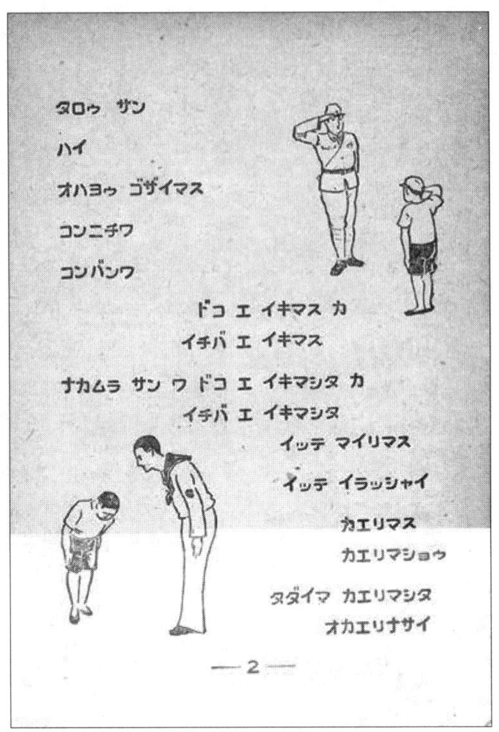

タロウ サン
ハイ
オハヨウ ゴザイマス
コンニチワ
コンバンワ
ドコ エ イキマス カ
イチバ エ イキマス
ナカムラ サン ワ ドコ エ イキマシタ カ
イチバ エ イキマシタ
イッテ マイリマス
イッテ イラッシャイ
カエリマス
カエリマショウ
タダイマ カエリマシタ
オカエリナサイ

—2—

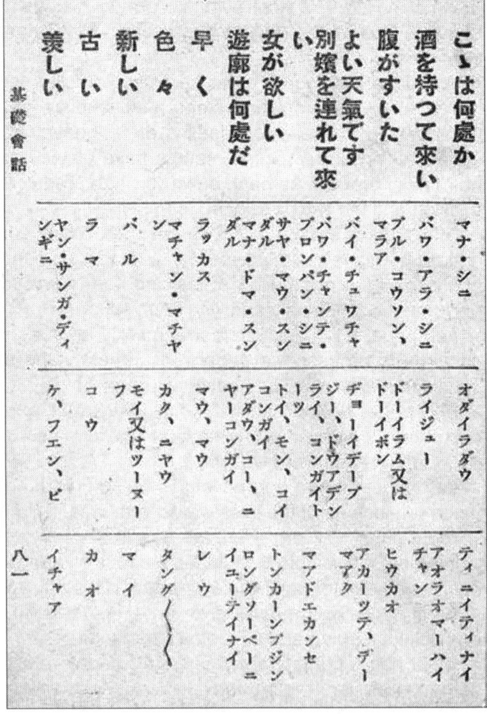

基礎會話

こゝは何處か	マナ・シニ	オダイラダウ	ティニイティナイ
酒を持つて來い	バワ・アラ・シニ	ライジュー	アオラオマーハイ チャン
腹がすいた	ブル・コウソン、マラア	ドーイラム又はドーイボン	ヒウカオ
よい天氣です	バイ・チュワチャ	デョーイデープ	アカーッテ、デー マアク
別嬪を連れて來い	バワ・チャンテ・ブロン・パン・シニ	ジー、ドウアデン ライ、コンガイト	マアドエカンセ
女が欲しい	サヤ・マウ・スンダル	トイ、モン、コイ	トンカーンプジン
遊廓は何處だ	マナ・ドマ・スンダル	コンガイ アダウ、コー、ニ ヤーコンガイ	ロングソーペーニ イユーテイナイ
早く	ラッカス	マウ、マウ	レウ
色々	マチャン・マチャン	カク、ニャウ	タング〳〵
新しい	バル	モイ又はツーヌー フ	マイ
古い	ラマ	コウ	カオ
美しい	ヤン・サンガ・ディ ンギニ	ケ、フエン、ピ	イチャア

八一

42-44. (top left) *National Language* (*Kokugo*), a Japanese phrasebook published in Keijō (Seoul) in 1942. The language level was very basic, the emphasis on patriotism pronounced. On the first page (pictured here), the phrases are "Worship from Afar of the Japanese Imperial Palace" (with a photograph of the Double Bridge) and "Patriotic Group," "Council," and "Rising Sun Flag."

(top right) The "Katakana Society" produced a series of Japanese language books in the late 1930s and early 1940s for distribution among Chinese, Koreans, and Southeast Asians. This typical page includes greetings and phrases about coming and going. The illustrations reveal as much about communication as the text, as a (presumably non-Japanese) boy shows the proper deference toward a Japanese soldier.

(bottom) *Quick Reference to the Languages of the Southern Regions: Thai, Annamese, Malay (Second Edition)*, p. 81. The first edition of this handy pocket translator was published by the "Japanese Soldiers' Publishing Company" in October 1941. This page, from the section on "basic conversation," contains useful phrases translated into Thai, Vietnamese, and Malay (represented in Japanese katakana syllabary), including "Where am I?", "Bring me liquor," "I'm hungry," "It's nice weather," "Bring me a beautiful woman," "I want a woman," and "Where is the brothel district (*yūkaku*)?" This booklet contained no illustrations.

Education and training were some of the largest and most immediate goals the Great East Asia Ministry would eventually inherit from the military governments established in each region. The Japanese language enjoyed little currency in the occupied areas prior to the Japanese occupation. Suddenly, signs and posters written in Nippongo (Japanese), primers and dictionaries, even paper theater and schools, appeared throughout the occupied lands as part of their "Japanification." Schools, in particular, were powerful institutions in spreading the gospel of Great East Asia to local youths, but their limited reach meant innovative approaches to reeducating adults were also needed. Japanese bureaucracy had perfected several programs such as Radio Calisthenics, effective in mobilizing the Japanese home front, that were easily transplanted. Of course, the spread

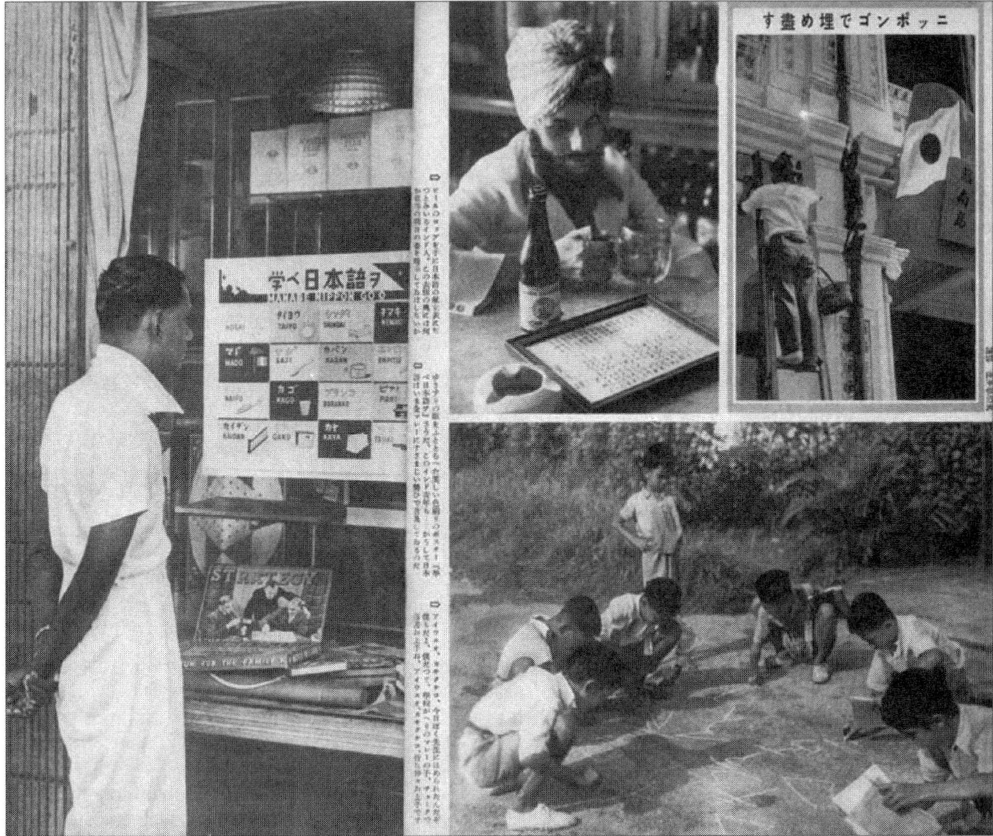

45-48. *PWR* 230, 22 July 1942, pp. 20-21. (clockwise, from top right)

(top right, p. 20) "Plastering Over with Japanese Language."

(top center, p. 20) "With beer mug in hand, this Indian studies a menu written in Japanese. Isn't there some indication of who he will become tomorrow behind his expression?"

(bottom right, p. 20) (The children recite the beginning of the Japanese hiragana system:) "'*A, i, u, e, o, ka, ki, ku, ke, ko*. Today the teacher praised me.' 'Me, too.' 'And me.' Malay children on their way home from school write with chalk very well. *A, i, u, e, o, ka, ki, ku, ke, ko*, all of them really write quite well."

(left, p. 21) "The passerby's eye is caught by the beautiful colors of the poster, 'Learn Japanese.' That's right, even this Indian youth, since Japanese is now spreading through Malaya with a tremendous force." Ironically, an English-language board game called "Strategy," displayed in this store window, is overshadowed by the poster, which has everyday Japanese vocabulary words and corresponding pictures.

of Japanese culture preceded and accompanied the teaching of Japanese language and Japanese values. Many of the newest members of the Co-Prosperity Sphere needed to be taught to develop their Asian spirit and to cast off Western ways; the demolition of symbols of Western colonization went hand in glove with the erecting of memorials to Japanese war dead and construction of Shinto shrines. For a few years, personnel flowed in both directions: Japanese cultural specialists, educators, political and military advisers, and business consultants were assigned key positions in the occupied lands, while promising youths and transitional governmental representatives came to the source of Nipponism to study its finer points.

49. *PWR* 250, 9 December 1942, pp. 20-21. A two-page article, "All over East Asia, the Radio Is Calling out, One, Two Three," describing the spread of Radio Calisthenics.

"In the Philippines, Hong Kong, Java, Guam, and Burma, Radio Calisthenics is now the front line of a movement to make the citizens healthy, just as in Japan.

"'Bathed in the light of the rising morning sun . . .'

"The bright[3] lyrics of the Radio Calisthenics broadcast from Axis leader Japan is bringing together each region of the vast Co-Prosperity Sphere, and now East Asia is, literally, one, as Radio Calisthenics continue to widely promote strong physical conditioning.

"The radio waves distribute the gifts of hope and health—and by all appearance the physiques of the weakly natives (*yowayowashii genjūmin*), will continue to grow stronger, within an equal structure and at the same pace, thanks to the spread of Radio Calisthenics. We can truly say that the foundation of the Co-Prosperity Sphere is being built by Radio Calisthenics."

This photoessay was part of *PWR*'s coverage of accomplishments in Great East Asia on the first anniversary of the war. In the upper right corner is a pamphlet in Japanese and English for "Radio Taiso, Daily Calisthenics on the Air," while bottom right shows the program being broadcast live from Tokyo. The layout of the six photographs, showing "each region of the Co-Prosperity Sphere," reflects the hierarchical relationship described in text of the article, with "Axis leader Japan" represented by men and women in Western clothing in the top photograph in the center column (identified as "Tokyo"). Beneath "Tokyo" is "Manila," then "Hong Kong." In the left column are "Guam," "Batavia," and "Rangoon" [Yangon].

50. *PWR* 250, 9 December 1942, p. 3. "Raffles Is Put in the Museum." The accompanying text reads, "As the symbol of the English invasion of East Asia, the bronze statue of Stamford Raffles stood watch proudly over Empress Place, guarding the British Empire as it prospered through exploitation. But now that Singapore is one of our newly occupied lands and has been reborn as Shōnan, which is beginning to pulsate as a stronghold in our construction of the new East Asia, Raffles has been removed from his throne in Empress Square and tucked away in a corner of the Shōnan Museum as a reminder of one hundred years of English greed.

"Stamford Raffles, while lieutenant-governor of Bencooleen, Sumatra in the early nineteenth century, realized that Singapore would be the best base from which to encroach upon East Asia, so he cozied up to the king of Johore and bought the island for such a pittance it was the same as getting it for free." Photograph: Army Ministry.

The famous statue of Raffles by Thomas Woolner was cast in 1887 to mark Queen Victoria's Jubilee. The colannade surrounding it was built in 1919, when the statue was moved to Empress Place. The colannade, dismantled by the Japanese, could not be found after the war. The undamaged statue of Raffles was reinstalled in its original position, where it stands today.

51-56. *PWR* 264, 24 March 1943, pp. 12-13. "Dedication Ceremony of Shōnan Shrine."

"On 15 February, the splendid day on which the newly born Malaya marked its first anniversary, the protective deity of the Southern Sea, Shōnan Shrine, was dedicated in Shōnan. Local army officers and [Japanese] citizens, as well as local residents, earnestly performed public service in order to complete the construction of the shrine.

"Two days later, on 17 February, a peaceful dedication ceremony, incorporating a colorful celebration, took place. Every [military] unit competed in a martial arts competition performed as an offering to the gods. Army and navy personnel took part in a dedicatory sumo wrestling competition, and there were also performances of traditional Japanese music, short theatrical pieces, Chinese dances, Malayan dances, and a special performance full of Co-Prosperity Sphere color, as offerings to the gods. Local officers and soldiers, as well as local citizens, passed a joyful day, and the entire city of Shōnan was decked out gaily for the celebration."

(clockwise, from top right) Children pay their respects at the shrine.

(bottom far right) "A Japanese child [residing in Shōnan] reads out the 'vow' before the gods."

(bottom right) "The parade of masked fierce warriors from the heart of the interior."

(bottom center) "An interesting part of the celebration was the dance on stilts."

(bottom left) "A large performance [by local residents] in the parking lot."

(top left) "Army and navy brass come to worship." Photographs by Funayama of the Army Information Corps.

57-61. *PWR* 278, 30 June 1943, pp. 16-17. "Japanese and Philippine Children in a 'New Lifestyle' School."

"In response to Prime Minister's Tōjō's announcement of Philippine Independence, Chief Director Vargas sent a telegram of thanks that said, 'We vow to strengthen our determination to give Japan the fruits of our loyal cooperation, earnest in every sense, and to do more to repay the emperor's kindness.' How quickly things change, and what a happy turn of events. Less than a year and a half have passed since Manila surrendered on 2 January last year, and yet the long-awaited independence is being quickly realized after three hundred years of Spanish rule and forty years of American tyranny.

"Recently, under the auspices of the *Manila Newspaper*, the Japanese and Philippine Children's 'New Lifestyle' School opened in a campsite in Balang, about 20 kilometers [12.4 miles] south of Manila. Philippine children shouldering responsibility for the New Philippines of tomorrow and Japanese children raised in the Philippines, about fifty in all, were brought together as compatriots of the new East Asia. To see them becoming friends and training together is to witness with one's very eyes the undeniable progress of Axis leader Japan in building New East Asia."

(right page, top, blackboard and classroom) "Time for Japanese language class. Teacher is pleased with them because they are so enthusiastic that after just one time, they remember a song in Japanese. Their forte is knowing the difference between [the homonyms] *hana* (nose) and *hana* (flower)."

(right page, bottom) "Japanese language class is over, now it's time for drills. The group stands crisply at attention, firmly holding their wooden [practice] rifles. One by one, each receives orders from the group leader, who is their senior. They try to forget about the sweat on their cheeks and backs. . . ."

(left page, top) "The day's lessons over, the campfire burns brightly as the sun sets beyond the hill behind their dormitory. The children join their voices in a broadminded song of Oriental victory."

(left page, bottom left) "Mealtime. Growing children have healthy appetites. The Philippine children seem to be enjoying using Japanese lunch boxes and chopsticks."

(left page, bottom right) "Filipinos and Japanese are children of the sea. These citizens of Great East Asia who will from now on make enormous strides together, hand in hand, undergo rather strenuous training because they must be able to swim."

62-64. Two examples of "Japanifying" the Southern Regions through education.

(top) *PWR* 279, 7 July 1943, p. 8. "Mr. Ninomiya Goes to Jakarta." The text reads, in part, "Gathered around a statue of Ninomiya Kinjirō, an Indonesian teacher explains to the children that they should be good children and study hard, just like Kinjirō." Part of a series of photographs describing the "Southern Regions Growing Brighter and Brighter," in an article describing the civilizing, modernizing light of Japanese influence.

(bottom, left and right) *PWR* 279, 7 July 1943, p. 11. "They Are Becoming Very Good at It: Drawings and Compositions by Students of the Japanese Language School in Pegu, Burma [today, Bago, Myanmar]." Two from a set of six drawings by Burmese students learning Japanese, part of the same series of photoessays describing the "Southern Regions Growing Brighter and Brighter." At left is "Ancient Burmese General Maha Bandoola[4] by Tin Shue (male, age not given)," and placed at right (suggesting a parallel across time) is a "Japanese Soldier, by Mon Mon Mee (male, 14 years old)."

南方はいよいよ明るく逞しく

敵が何とわめかうと東亞でも歐洲でも樞軸陣營の必勝態勢は微動だもしない。北阿戰線やアッツ島は大きな戰局の小さな揺り返しに過ぎなかつた。例へば東亞の現實、新らしい建設を見よ。帝國の必勝不動の態勢が日に強化されればこそ、敵の焦り方も必死になつて來てゐるのだ

殊に第八十二臨時議會で明らかにされた大東亞建設に對する帝國の所信、ビルマの獨立はいふまでもなく、今年中には比島も獨立させ、インドネシア民衆の政治參與まで實現させようといふあのおほらかな大東亞宣言に、敵のうけた打撃は察するに餘りある。開戰以來僅かに一年有半、大東亞共榮圏建設の堂々たる足並に敵の悲鳴さへ聞えるではないか

日本を盟主として急速に進む南方の建設譜、この一連の寫眞を先づ敵に見せてやりたい。そして東亞の新らしい歴史を十分納得させてやりたい

だが、この必勝態勢を切崩さうと、物質力を誇る敵が手段をつくして執拗な反攻を繰返すことも必然である。先づ勝たねばならぬ。武力戰の完勝によつて、東亞の態勢が如何なる手段を以てしても絶對不壞であることを悟らせるのだ。今こそ一億總蹶起、直接戰力の増强に挺身あるのみの秋である

撮影　舟山陸軍報道班員

⇧『どうだいアマン君、新らしく海に飛出す抱負は？』『はいッ、訓練はなか〳〵苦しかつたですが、かうして一人前の船員にしていたゞいたことを本當に有難いと思つてをります。勝つためには船と船乗りが必要です。きつとお役に立ちます』――昭南の現地船員養成所第一回卒業式から

3

65. *PWR* 279, 7 July 1943, p. 3. The first photograph in a set of articles in this issue of *PWR* describing the "Southern Regions Growing Brighter and Brighter." The article describes the many successes Japan has had in building the Greater East Asian Co-Prosperity Sphere and its deleterious effect on enemy morale. The caption is in the form of a dialogue with the young graduate here, named Aman, who is holding a diploma with his name on it, and his nationality, Malay. He wears the tropical version of the citizens' uniform.

"'How about it, Aman, is your ambition to dive into a new ocean?'

"'Well, yes, training was rather severe, but I am very grateful for being made a full-fledged crew member. Ships and sailors are needed in order to win the war, so I am sure I can make myself useful.'

"In Shōnan, at the first graduation ceremony of the Sailors' Training School."

66 and 67. *PWR* 281, 21 July 1943, p. 18. "Tokyo: Exchange Students Are Coming from the Southern Regions."

"The brilliant war results of the Imperial Army have challenged the consciousness of the people of East Asia. The local youths, who have seen with their own eyes the wonders of Axis leader Japan through the supremacy of the scientific technology we have brought to these lands, are filled with a sense of awe and newness.

"'Let's learn from Axis leader Japan' [they think].

"From that time onward, adolescents of the South, who used to be called lethargic and lazy, experienced an awakening of their youthful vigor. And then, once their passion for studying the Japanese language bore lovely fruit, fifty-three young men from Burma, Malaya, Sumatra, and Java were chosen to study in Tokyo, a place they longed for so strongly they were seeing it in their dreams. Crossing some thousands of miles of rough seas, they arrived in the Imperial Capital on 30 June.

"Right away, these Southern youths entered the International Student Association's Japanese Language School on 5 July. After they have spent a year perfecting their study of Japanese, they plan to spend two years at university or at vocational high schools before returning to their homelands, where they will become leaders playing dynamic roles in building the Southern Regions."

(top) "What they see, what they hear—everything teaches them about Japan's strength. The Malayan group is eager to make their homeland like Japan as soon as possible."

(bottom) "With their promised independence close at hand, these fifteen members of the Burmese group are terrifically spirited."

南方から留學生來る　東京

輝かしい皇軍の戰果に東亞人としての自覺を促され、現地にもたらされた我が科學技術の優秀さに、指導者日本の素晴らしさを目のあたりに知つた現地人靑少年は、こみ上げてくる畏敬と親しさを以て

『盟主日本に學ばう』

と叫んだ

この時から、無氣力で懶者だといはれた南の靑少年に潑剌たる若さが蘇つた。そして、まづ日本語の勉强に發した熱意が見事に實を結んで、ビルマ、マライ、スマトラ、ジャワから選ばれた五十三名の現地人若人は、夢にまでみた憧れの東京で勉强できることになり、幾千キロの戰ふ海を越えて、六月三十日帝都に到着した

これらの現地人たちは早速七月五日、國際學友會日本語學校に入學したが、こゝで一年間日本語をみつちり勉强した後、大學又は高等專門學校で二ヶ年の勉學を終へてから現地に歸り、現地人の指導者として南方建設に活躍する豫定である

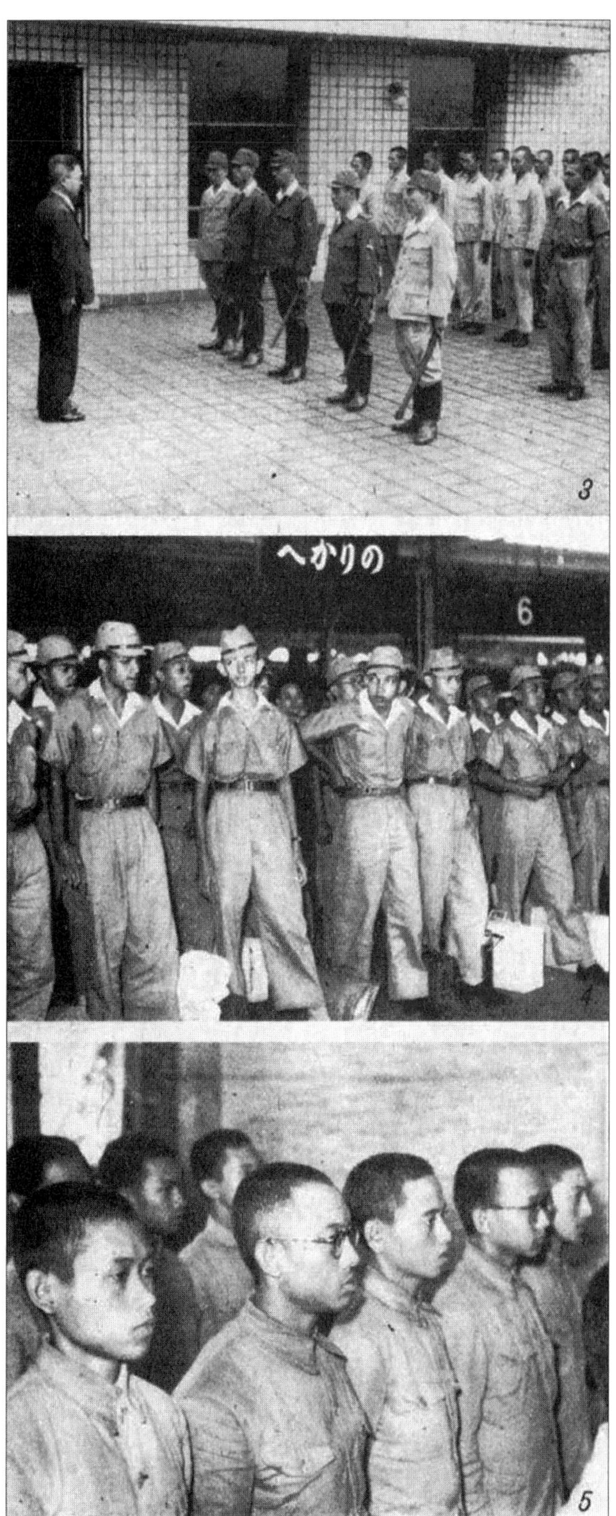

68-70. *PWR* 281, 21 July 1943, p. 18. "Tokyo: Exchange Students Are Coming from the Southern Regions."

(top) "'We are shouldering responsibility for the South.' Hearing the very inspiring words of Great East Asia Minister Aoki, this is the vow they make themselves."

(middle) "The fifteen-member groups from Sumatra and Malaya in their khaki short-sleeve shirts and pants. They are simply stunned by the majesty and greatness of Tokyo, which is beyond what they could have imagined."

(bottom) "Twenty-three members of the Javanese group, who (like the Burmese group) are also wearing the maiden version of their national citizens' uniform. Their firmly pursed lips show their determination."

The war in the Pacific had been launched in order to break the ABCD economic embargo and military stranglehold surrounding Japan. Almost as soon as the Japanese finished "mopping up" operations in the resource-laden areas of Southeast Asia, they began rebuilding oilfields, transportation facilities, and putting the local population to work in factories, mines, and fields. The keystone to the Co-Prosperity Sphere was, of course, economic development: Japan would build up local industries to fuel local markets in exchange for economic, and eventually political and military, cooperation. The swift advance of the Allies across the Pacific meant, however, that the Japanese had precious little time in which to develop and exploit the rich resources of the Southern Regions. By the end of 1943, with the Japanese fleet already in tatters and shipping lines falling prey to Allied attacks, transporting precious war matériel from the Southern Regions to Japan was no longer feasible. Land routes through Japanese-controlled tracts of Indo-china and China proved more reliable, even in the final months of the war, and nearly all of the Vietnamese rice crop was seized and transported to Japan in the summer of 1945, leaving an estimated two million Vietnamese to starve to death. (Allied strategy chose a frontal attack of Japan from the Pacific, leaving the Chinese and, very late in the war, the Russians, to fight Japanese forces in China.)

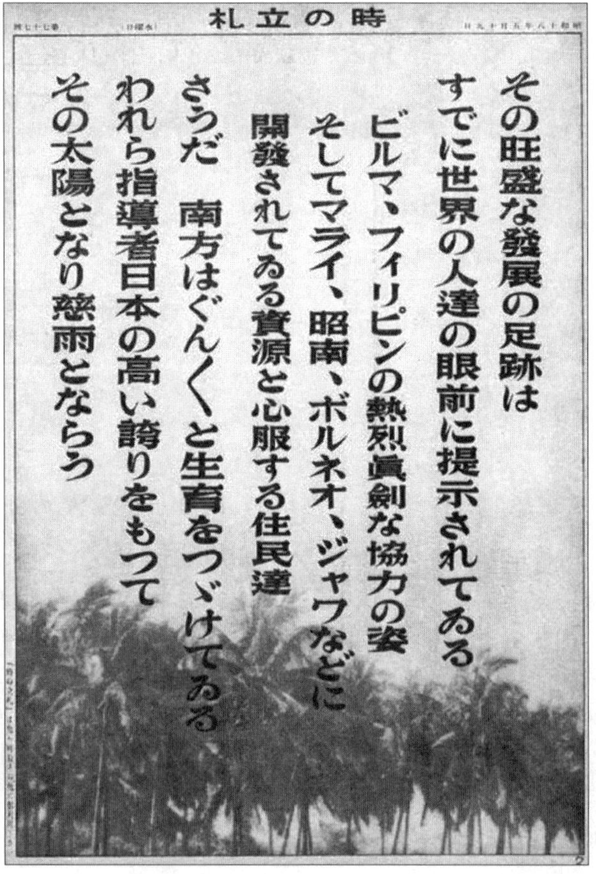

71. *PWR* 272, 19 May 1942, p. 2. "Signboard of the Times."

"The footprints of such vigorous development have already been demonstrated before the watching eyes of the people of the world in the form of the ardent, sincere cooperation of Burma and the Philippines, as well as the resources being developed in Malaya, Shōnan, Borneo, and Java, and the heartfelt respect of the residents there. That's right, the Southern Regions continue to grow rapidly. With our great pride as the leader, Japan, let us become their sun and gentle rain."

The text is written above a stand of palm trees, the all-purpose symbol of the Southern Regions, with their tropical climate. The likening of the Japanese people to ideal climatic conditions ("sun and gentle rain") is a new twist on the shopworn notion of Japan's kokutai being the light piercing darkness throughout Asia.

昭南駅はゴムの洪水

72. *PWR* 247, 18 November 1942, pp. 4-5. "Shōnan Station Is Overflowing with Rubber."

"Even in America, where they are pouring their rich resources into armaments, they are gravely worried they do not have enough rubber, and are said to be strictly rationing passenger vehicle tires. The high volume of rubber manufacturing in the Southern Regions we have occupied accounts for 80 percent of world production. According to figures for 1937, Malaya alone accounts for 50 percent of the world's total output of rubber, producing 461,000 tons, two-thirds of which was exported to America. With our occupation of Malaya, those exports have been completely cut off, and therefore America is in a quandary. Rubber is used in manufacturing armaments such as airplanes, automobiles, tanks, and anti-venom kits, as well as in commercial manufacture of belts, hosiery, and household goods. It has a wide variety of uses. In Japan, this plentiful source of rubber will be put to good use in paints and synthetic fibers, as a replacement for metal, and in new building materials that will replace plaster and wood. The various related organizations and the local Malayan laboratories are making progress with research and ideas, and according to the news from Shōnan, octane from shoe rubber can be made into high-grade petroleum that is just as good as real high-grade gasoline. Presently, steady progress is being made in research leading to greater industrialization."

The photographs show the process of collecting gum from trees, refining it, and drying it. The large photograph at the bottom of the left page shows bales of dried rubber at Shōnan Station.

73. *PWR* 281, 21 July 1943, pp. 12-13. "Panorama of a 1,000-Mile [Vast] Production-boosting Plantation, Sumatra."

"Even in the natural-resources rich Southern Regions, Sumatra's agricultural produce is called a cornucopia, and through the cooperation of the local residents, enormous strides are being made in boosting crop production, playing an important role in the flow of resources from the Southern Regions. Incidentally, when we hear 'Southern Regions' we immediately imagine jungle, but from the first step we take in Sumatra, what first comes to mind is farmland.

"From long ago, due to the good weather and soil, large plantations were made in Shantar, a suburb of Sumatra's capital Medan. Although they are farms, it is a far cry from the wilderness of the interior. The plantations here are from several hundred ares to several thousand ares in size, some as large as 10,000 ares [247 acres]. What we would think of as a township [in Japan] is a single plantation.

"This large plantation, after the Imperial Army's occupation, was renamed Imperial Plantation. In this region, they grow rubber trees, tobacco, and oil palms, as well as sisal, coconuts, cocoa, and various fruit—every type of agriculture is gathered together in one plantation. The fertility of this land is due to the climatic conditions. It is so fertile that upland rice plants thrive with very little care, even without fertilizing, once the seeds have been sown.

"From long ago, in order to make an enormous profit from the specialty products of the Southern Regions, Holland made a large area of 240,000 ares [5,928 acres] into tobacco fields, and of the 1.5 million ares [37,050 acres] of land in the province bordering the eastern ocean, half was taken up by tobacco, rubber, and oil palm plantations, and due to these vast plantations, Sumatra could not be self-sufficient in foodstuffs and was annually importing a large amount of rice from other countries. Since the Imperial Army's occupation, however, our Military Administration Office has for the time being released 60,000 ares [1,482 acres] of tobacco land and had it planted in rice, and with this rice crop, Sumatra will soon be in control of its own self-sufficiency in foodstuffs. The local residents are burning with gratitude and inspiration, and are continuing their fight to boost crop production."

The photographs at the top right show signboards at two plantations declaring them to be under the supervision of the Japanese Military Administration, one a tea plantation, the other tobacco. The remaining photographs show different crops and the processing of palm oil.

ルソン島縦貫鐵道完成す

鐵道は建設促進の動脈である。敵の手に破壊された鐵道を一日も早く復舊することは、占領地の建設に何よりも肝腎なことである

フィリピンのルソン島でも昨年九月、鐵道管理局が設立されると同時に、僅か七十名の邦人職員を中心に比島人を使用して、無殘に破壊された鐵道復舊工事に着手。それ以来機械器具及びその修理設備の不足、雨季の増水、颱風の被害等の様々な悪條件を克服して、工事の進捗に涙ぐましい努力を傾けた結果、豫定より早くマニラ、レガスピー間の復舊に成功、三月二十一日めでたくその開通式が行はれた

比島軍政監部では今後さらに資源の開發に必要な新線を建設し、ルソン島南北縦貫を實現せしめる豫定である

上 比島富士と呼ばれるマヨン山を窓外にマニラからレガスピーに向ふ縦貫鐵道処女列車

下 レガスピーの街を飾る開通記念門

17

74. *PWR* 266, 7 April 1943, p. 17. “Completion of Train Line Crossing Luzon Island.”

“Railroads are arteries accelerating construction. The top priority of construction in the occupied lands has been restoring, as quickly as possible, the rail service destroyed by enemy hands.

“As soon as our Army Administrative Office was established on Luzon Island in the Philippines last September, it set to work rebuilding the railroad so cruelly destroyed. Making use of many Filipinos and a core of seventy Japanese staff, and since then—despite deplorable conditions due to a lack of machinery, tools, and repair equipment, the floods of the rainy season, and damage due to typhoons—as a result of a tremendous effort that brings tears to the eyes, extraordinary progress was made and the Manila-to-Legaspi section was completed ahead of schedule. A joyous ceremony reopening it took place on 21 March.

“The executive officers of the Philippine Army will hereafter build rail lines necessary for the development of resources, and are planning a line that will cross Luzon Island from north to south.”

(top) “Mount Mayon, called the ‘Philippine Fuji,’ could be seen out the window on the maiden trip crossing from Manila to Legaspi.”[5]

(bottom) “A gate commemorating [the maiden trip] displayed in a Legaspi street.”

Economic cooperation also meant that the finance and banking industries came under Japanese control. Japanese military authorities issued paper money for nearly every occupied region, and citizens were forced to trade in the old currency for the new. Coin metal became another "resource" the Southern Regions supplied, with silver and gold filling the coffers of the Bank of Japan. With Japanese controlling the local industries, workers were paid in occupation banknotes and coerced to receive a portion of their pay in "savings" or in war bonds.[6]

75-78. *PWR* 263, 7 March 1943, pp. 12-13. "We Can Depend upon Java, too, for Rising Sun Savings." Beneath the title at top right, a mother and child hold a savings book. The photograph illustrates the word "depend," which in the title is written with the characters for "rely" and "mother."

"The goal of citizens' savings for 1942 is 23 billion yen, and with the forty-fourth period under way in the first three months of this year, only 5 billion yen of that goal remains. Soon, we will reach the finish line. Well, take a deep breath, give another push, and we will easily surpass the 23 billion yen mark, so this year we should be able to break the 27 billion mark without any difficulty.

"The encouraging news from Java is that, 'Japan (*naichi*) doesn't have a monopoly on savings!' The Javanese feel a deep gratitude toward the Imperial Army, and local residents, under the slogan of 'For the Sake of Building Asia Raya (Great East Asia),' are very enthusiastic about their thriving savings program. They enjoy filling their savings books little by little, which strengthens their determination to see the Great East Asia War through to victory."

(right page, bottom, p. 12) "Across 6,000 kilometers [3,728 miles], they are joined by the same sentiment: Savings Build Asia." (The sign says in Malay and in Japanese katakana, "Savings Build Asia.")

(left page, top, p. 13) "Group savings at the Jakarta dry cell battery factory. The tremendous joy of the factory workers is apparent as each holds a Rising Sun Savings Book."

(left page, bottom left, p. 13) "The Jakarta Savings Office, teeming with business even in the morning."

(left page, bottom right, p. 13) "'I'm no good at making deductions for savings'—why, that's ridiculous, just look at our friends in Java who willingly participate." Photographs: Army Information Corps, Java Section.

The Southern Regions fired the imagination of Japanese entrepreneurs, providing them with the *lebensraum* to dream and entertain visions of grandeur. What better way to link together the peoples of the Co-Prosperity Sphere, stimulate investment in local economies, and make money than to build a trans-Asian express train? Such visions were not completely lost with the end of the war. Japan would complete its bullet train (renamed Shinkansen) just in time for the 1964 Olympics.

特急昭南行

79. *PWR* 242, 14 October 1942, pp. 12-13. The cover story of this issue of *PWR* was the seventieth anniversary of the establishment of the Japan National Railway (today's Japan Railway [JR] system). This article describes the proposed "Shōnan Express" that would run from Tokyo to Singapore, and reads in part, "Imagine. 'We're on our way,' we say with bag in hand, boarding a train that goes to Shimonoseki, Keijō [Seoul], Mukden [Shenyang], Beijing, Canton [Guangzhou], Hanoi, Saigon [Ho Chi Minh City], Bangkok, and finally, without ever having gotten off, we arrive in Shōnan. Wouldn't that be wonderful. . . and yet, this wonderful dream could very possibly come true during our lifetimes.

"Indeed, the planning is already under way for the Shōnan Express train.

"As you can see yourself from this map, the tracks will run from Tokyo to Shimonoseki, Keijō, Mukden, Beijing, Hankou, Canton, Hanoi, Saigon, Bangkok, and Shōnan. But one problem is the gaps in the railroad between these cities, and another is the difference in the gauges of these railroads in Japan, Korea, Manchukuo, China, Indo-china, Thailand, and Malaya, but as soon as these two issues have been resolved, the first Tokyo-made bullet train (*dangan ressha*) will travel directly to Shōnan." Text: Abe Teiichi.

The photograph at top right shows the Fuji Express (with Mount Fuji-shaped emblem) at Tokyo Station, and the small photograph at bottom right shows Shōnan Station. The map indicates existing railways (the solid black-and-white checked lines) and proposed construction (the broken lines).

As previously mentioned, the establishment of the Greater East Asian Co-Prosperity Sphere marked a shift away from the older model of territorial expansion, insofar as Japan's goal in "liberating" Asia from Western imperialism was defined by creating "independent" and "self-sufficient" nations from occupied lands. The bold offensive the Allies launched in the Pacific in the summer of 1942 provided further incentive for Japan to create independent nations in Southeast Asia that might offer armed resistance to the Allies and impede their advance toward Tokyo.

In 1943, the Japanese Diet, led by Prime Minister Tōjō, passed legislation granting Burma and the Philippines their independence. When the new leaders of both countries were brought to Tokyo to meet with Japanese leaders and address the Diet, they received extensive press coverage. Prime Minister Tōjō himself had already conducted an inspection tour of the Southern Regions, including the Philippines, in spring of 1943. In preparation for their admittance as full-fledged members of the Co-Prosperity Sphere, the regional Japanese military administrations trained the prospective nations' fledgling armies and navies, which were expected to fight alongside Japan in the war against Western imperialism. Burma and the Philippines held solemn independence ceremonies and large public celebrations, events commemorated by Japanese artists. Behind the scenes, however, Japanese troops, administrators, and business executives remained firmly in charge. The newly minted independence quickly tarnished, even among the most enthusiastic of Japan's local supporters.[7]

80. "The Burmese Independence Ceremony" by Koiso Ryōhei, reproduced as a color postcard of a work featured in the exhibition, "Illustrations of Army Operations in the Great East Asia War." The independence ceremony took place in Rangoon. Ba Maw, standing on a dais before the new Burmese flag, is sworn in as the new head of state. The Burmese and Japanese flags, hanging side by side in the upper right of the painting, suggest a partnership of unity and equality. This painting closely resembles a photograph appearing in *PWR* 286, 25 August 1943, pp. 4-5.

ビルマに獨立の喜び近く

ビルマの防空も隣組で

81 and 82. (left) *PWR* 259, 17 February 1943, p. 3. "The Joy of Burmese Independence Is Near."

"Following our announcement, Ba Maw was all smiles about 'Burmese Independence,' and vowed before the people that [Burma] would make full strides as one jewel in the crown of the Co-Prosperity Sphere. The citizens raised their right hands along with him, showing their joy in moving forward together."

Tōjō had announced Japan's intention to grant independence to Burma on 28 January 1943. Ba Maw became Burma's first Head of State and Government on 1 August 1943. One of his first official acts was to have Burma declare war on the United States and Great Britain.

(right) *PWR* 284, 11 August 1943, p. 6. "Neighborhood Associations Are Responsible for Air Defense in Burma, Too." Preparing Burma for independence, Japan trained the new Burmese army and mobilized civilians. The accompanying article by Oguro Seiichi describes the organization of the Burmese Air Defense Administration, which learned the "air defense theory" of "bucket brigades" from the Japanese model.

(right page, top) "The scenario is that fire has spread to the house next-door. The members of the Neighborhood Association rush to the scene to help fight the fire."

(right page, bottom left) "When the practice air raid siren sounds, a member of the Neighborhood Association demonstrates how he will intensely watch the skies for enemy aircraft."

(right page, bottom right) "Burmese look at the burnt shell of an enemy [Hawker] Hurricane shot down by our ground-based anti-aircraft artillery."

83-85. *PWR* 272, 19 May 1943. "Prime Minister Tōjō Visits the Philippines," was a five-page article illustrated by several photographs. The rationale of the visit was provided, as follows. "On 5 May Prime Minister and concurrent Army Minister Tōjō visited the Philippines, where operations are still under way, returning to Tokyo on 9 May. The purpose of this historic Philippine visit was to inspect military conditions and the status of the military government there, as well as to have heartfelt talks and informal conversations with Director General Vargas and other leaders of the Interim Government, and to directly interact with the Philippine people to seek their sincere cooperation in building East Asia."

(top, p. 3) "Exchanging a firm handshake at his first face-to-face meeting with Director General Vargas, who came to greet him."

(bottom left, p. 4) "Filipinos filled Luneta Park [Rizal Park today] for the Philippine Citizens' Rally to Express Gratitude, and their ears clearly heard, through each fiery word uttered by Prime Minister Tōjō, the greatness of Axis leader Japan, and the righteousness of Japan's leadership."

(bottom right, p. 5) "Inspecting the Philippine Police Academy, he approached the cadets and gave each of them personal advice: 'You're holding the rifle the wrong way.'" Photographs: Army Information Corps, Philippine Section.

東條總理比島を訪問

3

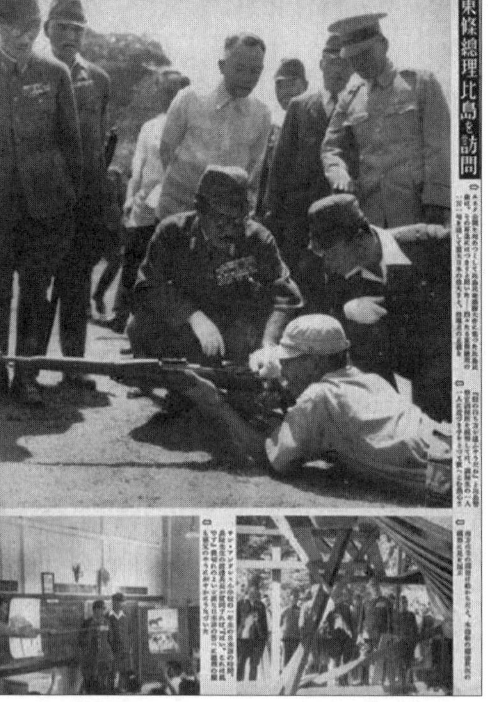

東條總理比島を訪問

86 and 87. (left) *PWR* 263, 17 March 1943. “The reaffirmation by Prime Minister Tōjō at the beginning of the reconvened Diet of the anticipated granting of independence to the Philippines has boosted the determination of the Philippine people to pour forth their precious sweat in cooperating with Japan. This past 8 February, in Manila’s Luneta Park, the Citizens’ Rally of Gratitude [toward Japan] took place. The citizens’ elaborate parade down the city’s main avenue expressed their fervent wish [for independence], receiving thunderous applause.” Photograph: Army Information Corps, Philippine Section.

(right) *PWR* 295, 27 October 1943. “The smile of Dr. Jose Bey Laval, first President of the Philippines—it is also the smile coming from the hearts of twenty million Filipinos who have been liberated from a four-hundred-year history of oppression.

“Since the provisional Philippine government was organized in January of last year, Dr. Laval has served as justice minister and home minister. And when the Philippine Independence Committee was formed, he became its chairman, pouring his energy into drafting the constitution, and now has been appointed the first president of the reborn Philippines. He is a thorough pro-Orientalist (*tōyōshūgisha*), and from early on attacked America’s hidden agenda. At fifty-three years old, he is in his prime.”

88. "Year 2,603 of the Empire: In Commemoration of the East Asian Conference," a painting by Fukuda Shinsei. The artist's lengthy inscription, upper right corner, reads, "At the convening of the Greater East Asian Conference in 2603, Philippine President Laval came to Japan and visited our Army Chief of Staff, His Excellency Sugiyama [Hajime], and they exchanged a historic handshake." Plate 74 in the *Second Great East Asia War Art Exhibition Catalogue*.

The occupied lands were not all on the same track for Japanese-sponsored independence. The Vichy-led French Colonial Administration was left in place in Indo-china, although the Japanese military held de facto power. Only when Nazi Germany lay in ruins in the spring of 1945 did Japan demand that the deposed Vietnamese emperor, Bai Dao, proclaim Indo-china's independence from France. The Allies began pushing the Japanese from the islands of the Dutch East Indies in late 1943, preempting the nominal self-rule promised by Tōjō in a speech made in Gambir, Jakarta, on 7 July 1943. Beginning within months of the Japanese invasion, Indonesian revolts against the Japanese were persistent and deadly, even as Sukarno, Hatta, and Kyai Bagus Hadikusumo were brought to Tokyo and decorated by the emperor on 10 November 1943, in conjunction with the Greater East Asian Conference. These setbacks notwithstanding, Japan's hope that Asians would join the fight against the Allied offensive remained alive as late as the spring of 1945, when the Free India Army dispatched by Subhas Chandra Bose's Free India provisional government was still being touted as a force that would drive the British from India. Had an armed uprising gained momentum in India, it might very well have changed the course, if not the outcome, of the war.

89 and 90. (left) *PWR* 234, 19 August 1942. "These deep-set eyes gaze steadily at the enemy position. In these sturdy arms holding the bomb is the steely awakening of Asia. And all the more serious is the training of this Indian artillery soldier who is aiming for total independence." At Shōnan, photograph: Army Information Corps. This photograph was reprinted in several wartime publications.

(right) *PWR* 298, 17 November 1943.

"This is Subhas Chandra Bose, leader of the Free India provisional government, which is off to a strong start.

"This is the profile of the forty-seven-year-old Bose, whose entire life down to the present day has been spent in the struggle to overthrow British aggression and to free India, who has never stopped to reflect upon the sacrifices he has made to further that cause. And now he has a once-in-a-century opportunity to form a provisional government under the immeasurable generosity of the [Japanese] Empire, and the day fast approaches when he will lead the advance troops of the [Free India] national army as they begin their pursuit of overthrowing British aggression.

"His body is full of martial spirit, and in his ambition to save his 380 million compatriots, he will gladly give his life." Photograph: Army Information Corps, Malaya Section.

91-93. *PWR* 280, 14 July 1943, pp. 4-5. "Forced to Take up Arms for the Goal of Indian Independence."

"Finally the autumn has arrived in which India will take up arms and rise up. Subhas Chandra Bose, former speaker of the parliament and warrior of Indian independence, has come to Japan from Europe, where he was given asylum by Germany. He is now in Shōnan preparing for a giant, historical stride from East Asia toward the war of Indian independence. While in Shōnan, he attended the Federation Conference for Indian Independence convened there on 4 July, and took over the responsibilities of the chairmanship of the Indian Federation from Bihari Bose, and immediately made an epochal proclamation of his intention to form a Free India provisional government, asking that the total energies of all Indian people be transformed into war power, and resolved to move forward in annihilating the British Empire."

(large photograph, bottom) "In order to attain their independence, they have no choice but armed resistance . . . and the spirit of the Indian Army is already reaching the sky."

(left page, top) "The tank corps hammer the soul [of India] into the machinery of modern warfare."

(left page, bottom) "In the burning heat, they continue their 'dead hit' thrusts." Photographs: Army Ministry.

The article's insistence that Indians have been "forced" to armed resistance is a criticism of and challenge to Mohandas Gandhi's policy of nonviolent protest and his willingness to work with Great Britain during the war.

The apogee of the Co-Prosperity Sphere was the November 1943 Greater East Asian Conference, presided over by Prime Minister Tōjō, with the announced theme of "One Billion Asians United for Victory!" The cornerstone of the conference was the Greater East Asian Declaration, by which all member-nations agreed to cooperate for the increased prosperity of all Asia in a spirit of racial equality. Seven Asian leaders were in attendance at a mass rally that filled Hibiya Park in Tokyo, where each made a speech pledging support for the Co-Prosperity Sphere. Conspicuously absent from *PWR*'s coverage of the proceedings, though, were representatives of the Dutch East Indies (Indonesia), Malaya, Singapore, and Indo-china (Vietnam).

94. *PWR* 298, 17 November 1943, pp. 8-9. "Spitting Pure Fire. The Great East Asia Mobilization Citizens' Rally."

The article reads, "The curtain was lowered on the historic Greater East Asian Conference on 7 November. The Great East Asia Mobilization Citizens' Rally, an unprecedented majestic celebration drawing the participation of one hundred thousand filling the chrysanthemum-fragrant large square of Hibiya Park in Tokyo, further strengthened we one hundred million citizens' resolve to complete the incredible accomplishments in East Asia. After the resolution of gratitude to the Imperial Army and Prime Minister Tōjō's clarification to the nation and those abroad of the position of the Great East Asia Combined Advance Army, and passage by common assent of the resolution to bring to completion the Great East Asia War, each of the national delegates gave a rousing address to the crowd that fired the determination of the One Hundred Million—no, the One Billion—to 'continue to shoot' the Americans and British 'and not desist.'[8] The roar from the rally immediately confounded the Americans and British."

Had one billion Asians been armed, trained, and deployed against the Allied advance, they certainly would have "confounded" Japan's enemies. The announcement of Asian unity was met with indifference and skepticism in Washington and London.

95 and 96. *PWR* 298, 17 November 1943. "Mobilizing the War-power of One Billion Asians. Convening the Greater East Asian Conference."

(top, pp. 4-5) "At 9:50 A.M. on 5 November, the curtain was raised on the Greater East Asian Conference. All assembled were in agreement in recommending that Prime Minister Tōjō take the chairman's seat. No sooner had this historical meeting been convened than the proceedings began. Participating nations spoke in *iroha*[9] order, following the speech by the empire's representative, Tōjō."

(bottom, p. 3) Seven "heads of state" who attended the Greater East Asian Conference. Tōjō occupies the place of honor in the center, which is reflected in the caption identifying them. "Center: Japanese representative Prime Minister Tōjō Hideki; (starting from Tōjō's immediate right) the Chinese representative, President of the Executive Yuan and Chairman of the National Government Wang Jingwei; the Manchukuoan representative, Prime Minister Zhang Zhonghui; and the Burmese representative, Prime Minister Ba Maw; (starting from Tōjō's immediate left [i.e., the hand holding the sword]) Wan Waithayakon of Thailand, Philippine President Jose P. Laurel; and the acting head of the provisional government of Free India, Subhas Chandra Bose.

Short-lived though it was, the Co-Prosperity Sphere forever changed the political map of Asia. In some cases, the Japanese defeat of Western colonial powers and Japanese military occupation became a catalyst for solidifying pre-existing independence movements, as was the case in Indonesia and Burma, while in other cases, including Vietnam, Cambodia, and Laos, it precipitated years and decades of armed conflict. Of course, organized resistance movements were active in most of these areas for decades prior to the Japanese invasion. In the case of the Philippines, the very harsh Japanese interlude hardly altered the process of independence scheduled by the United States decades earlier. Among those peoples gathered under the aegis of the Co-Prosperity Sphere, probably the Thais suffered the least. Thailand, a self-sufficient and autonomous nation prior to Japanese occupation, was best equipped to appease the Japanese overlords and countenance their demands.

The Japanese media's image of the home front was largely unchanged by Japan's occupation of Southeast Asia. Far from challenging Japanese notions of racial superiority, the media's presentation of Southeast Asia under the Co-Prosperity Sphere reinforced preconceived notions of the destiny of the Yamato race and Japanese spiritual superiority. This was apparent in every type of comparison made between Japanese and their Southeast Asian "Others"—whether the people and culture in question were determined to be similar to or different from Japanese, and whether the comparisons were of indigenous cultural products to Japanese products or between Japanese cultural exports and Japanese originals.

Japan, writ large, was not only the leader of the Co-Prosperity Sphere but the standard by which other lands, their peoples, and their cultures were measured. Thus, Japanese geography is the norm by which Mount Mayon becomes the "Philippine Fuji." The language employed clearly establishes a hierarchical relation, insofar as the two mountains are not described on equal footing as sharing a similar conical shape. Fuji would never have been described as the "Japanese Mayon." Similar analysis, when applied to other images in this chapter, reveals the same hierarchy in which Japanese soldiers and civilians loom large and appear taller in photographs than their Asian "little brothers and sisters." Japan's "bright" and "shining" cultural, social, and political constructs (Nippongo, Radio Calisthenics, paper theater, statues of Ninomiya, Citizens' Schools, Rising Sun savings accounts, Neighborhood Associations) were transplanted to Southeast Asia in order to shed light on this dark region that had long languished under the shadow of backwardness and Western domination.

The Japanese media created an image of strong male soldiers and political leaders of the Southern Regions, giving a face, sometimes a very charismatic one (Ba Maw and Bose) to the new member-countries, and marking a radical departure from the human imagery chosen by the Japanese press to represent the colonial possessions of Taiwan and Korea, which were typically symbolized by either children or attractive young women, but very rarely by men and probably never by male leaders. When Korean army recruits appeared in the Japanese press, they were shown taking orders from Japanese officers. Similarly, the strength of these new Southeast Asian leaders only reflected the even greater strength of the leader of leaders, Prime Minister Tōjō of Japan.

97 and 98. (left) *PWR* 258, 10 February 1943. The street sign reads, “Shōnan Municipal Swimming Pool.” The first week of February is midwinter in Japan, though Singapore is balmy. The Greater East Asian Co-Prosperity Sphere had thus spread to all climates. The contrast here is fascinating because from their early enunciations in the ninth and tenth centuries, Japanese literature and art have celebrated phenomena associated with the climate and change of seasons particular to Japan (often in contradistinction to the received poetic and artistic traditions of China). The suggestion of swimming outdoors in February would be as bizarre in Tokyo as it would be in Boston, but with the new *lebensraum* of the Co-Prosperity Sphere, perhaps Singapore would one day become a winter paradise for Japanese.

(right) *PWR* 268, 21 April 1943. The untitled text is self-explanatory. “One day, a Care Unit[10] arrived at the army’s recuperation facility in Kuala Lumpur, Malaya. The soldiers, frustrated by boredom, were themselves surprised by how much the sight of a Malay girl and an Indian girl wearing Japanese kimono cheered them up. They must have been reminded of childhood friends frolicking around their hometowns, or their younger sisters.” Photograph by Hirayama of the Army Information Corps.

This cover uses color to communicate subtle messages about Asian unity, sacrifice, and identity. The black and white photograph of the two girls is placed against a bright cherry pink background, coinciding with the season of the cherry trees’ blossoming in Japan.

Regardless of the Japanese government's pretensions of racial egalitarianism in the Co-Prosperity Sphere, exoticized images of the Southern Regions appeared in the Japanese press during the war: naked New Guinean and Andaman Islanders of both sexes and all ages, Lao women with neck-stretching bands, women of Borneo handling large snakes, and bare-breasted women of Bali. *PWR*, the government's official newsweekly, published few images that would provoke laughter, disbelief, or antipathy toward the peoples of the Southern Regions among Japanese readers, but more sensational magazines, such as the monthly *History Pictures*, eagerly printed photographs of the unusual. (*History Pictures* also included many pictures of the Japanese imperial family and the nobility.)

99. *History Pictures* 353, October 1942, p. 3. "Working Women of Bali, Going Together to Shop in the Village."

"The peaceful island of Bali is in the middle of the Sunda chain, east of Java. Not only is the weather extremely pleasant, the women know nothing of the drudgery of work. They are healthy and full of vitality, and cheerfully busy themselves with their housework, going about half-naked both day and night. In the photograph are native women and girls of today, who still carry baskets on their heads and go barefoot, wrapping their bodies in a single brightly colored sarong, always smiling cheerfully. They are on their way to the *pasar ikan* [literally, "fish market," that is, a produce market] to buy fruit."

This Japanese account of a tropical Shangri-la could have been lifted, word for word, from a Victorian-era travelogue. Originally printed in heavily saturated full color, the image is garish.

If Balinese women walking bare-breasted to market were novel, more so were Philippine policewomen and Thai women naval officers. The unarmed Philippine policewomen appearing in *PWR* 279 (7 July 1943, pp. 6-7) were only shown directing traffic, but they nevertheless belonged to a profession still closed to Japanese women. Such articles, while uncommon, suggested that women in some of the countries occupied by Japan had more career choices than did women in Japan, but we can only speculate as to how such articles were interpreted by Japanese women and men on the home front. Articles with exotic or novel images of women rarely made explicit comparisons to the Japanese status quo.

100. *History Pictures* 358, March 1943, p. 15. "The Hard-working Prosperity Sphere: The Thai Navy and Its Female Officers."

"The navy of Thailand, a new [member helping] build [the Co-Prosperity Sphere], has the motto: 'Nation, Courage, Honor, Training,' and its leadership spirit is seen in strenuous training that continues to burn like a fire day and night, and while in partnership with Axis Leader Japan, is staunchly protecting the pride of Thailand." The photographs (numbered 1-4 in the original) are, clockwise, from top right:

(1, top right) "The main cannons of the Thai Battleship (name censored)."

(2, bottom right) "The unfurled flag of the same battleship."

(4, bottom center) "Briskly marching students of the female officers' training school."

(3, left) "Thailand, reflecting upon the situation in the world, in December of last year opened a female army officers' training school. The female army was allowed to enter the school after being selected from among numerous volunteers, and they cut a gallant figure in their dark brown shirts and long pants and smart caps, letting us know that 'We women are warriors building the Co-Prosperity Sphere.' Among the hard-working, they are truly hard-working."

Articles illustrating the Japanese Military Administration's benign view of other religious traditions were at once complimentary and condescending. An article in *PWR* 254 describing the Muslim celebration of Puasa in Malaya and Sumatra went to great lengths to find parallels between Muslim and Japanese religious rituals. Superficial though these comparisons were, they appealed to the sympathies of the Japanese on the home front and took a very tolerant view of the difference of the Other. Given the horrific suffering inflicted upon the peoples of Asia by the Japanese military, it would be some consolation to find that, at the very least, Japanese society became more tolerant and accepting of differences through wartime exposure to the diverse cultures and peoples of Asia. One very surprising photograph of a heavily tattooed Ainu woman printed in *PWR* 346 in November 1944 (figure 103) suggests that this may have been the case. A much more plausible explanation, however, is that as the war situation became desperate for Japan and the government applied greater pressure upon all of the peoples under Japanese rule to make larger sacrifices for the war effort, in Japan as well as in the occupied lands, a show of tolerance toward difference was meant to ease complaints. Notions of Japanese racial superiority, bound up in discussions of identity, national origin, and cultural and ethnic uniqueness, have proven to be quite resilient in the postwar years.

101 and 102. *PWR* 254, 13 January 1943, pp. 14-15. "New Year's in the Southern Regions: Muslim Festival of Thanks. Malaya and Sumatra." The article, in its entirely, is translated here.

"This Puasa, a festival of thanks and sacrifices, was the first to be held under military rule. The festival received the generous support and understanding of our local [Military Administration] Office and was the most peaceful ever for Muslims in Malaya, Java, and Sumatra.

"Puasa is part of a Muslim ritual of fasting and performing austerities, and making pilgrimage to the Holy land of Mecca, and the celebration at the end of the month of fasting is the most fun, just like New Year's in Japan.

"On this day, good boys and good girls wearing their very best clothes attend local ceremonies, offering their prayers to the far-off Holy land of Mecca, and vow before God (kami) to entirely cooperate with the Japanese Imperial Forces."

(left) "The faithful extend both hands toward Heaven and bow down to earth to give thanks to God and make their vows for the coming year."

(right) "Small girls who are usually naked look just like their older sisters. They are thrilled to be wearing shoes and jewelry, and donning their finest robes." Photographs: Army Information Corps.

103. *PWR* 346, 8 November 1944, p. 3. This photograph was one of several in an article describing the Hokkaidō ceremony marking the enshrinement at Yasukuni of 20,197 warrior-gods on 22 October 1944. The caption simply reads, "An Ainu grandmother cries because of the vastness of imperial kindness," but it is still extremely significant in light of the Japanese government's aggressive policy of forced assimilation of the Ainu people in the preceding seventy years. The Ainu woman, with visible tattooing around her mouth, is in the bottom left corner of this photomontage.

Notes

1. To this day, the government of Japan has refused to recognize these Korean soldiers as veterans of the Japanese army and to extend benefits to them. In a particularly bizarre twist of fate, Korean and Taiwanese soldiers who died during the war were enshrined at Yasukuni, although their families do not receive pensions the Japanese government pays to Japanese bereaved family members. The Japanese government has refused to honor the wishes of Koreans to have their relatives disenshrined from Yasukuni. See William Underwood, "Names, Bones, and Unpaid Wages (2): Seeking Redress for Korean Forced Labor," (posted on *Japan Focus*, 17 September 2006), available at: www.japanfocus.org/products/details/2225.

2. The names of these foreign students have been reconstructed from Japanese syllabry in the article.

3. John Dower finds a connection between the "light" shined upon East Asia and the purity of the Yamato race. See *War Without Mercy: Race and Power in the Pacific War* (New York: Pantheon, 1987), pp. 203-233, especially pp. 212-215. In my survey wartime publications, the light of Japan's civilizing efforts is seldom attributed to any particular source, but occasionally it is described as emanating forth from radiant kokutai, one aspect of which is the Japanese people; another, the emperor; and the third, the Land of the Gods (Japan). As a system of thought, kokutai represents a powerful emotional appeal

to the notion of racial superiority.

4. Maha Bandoola (also romanized Bandula, 1780-1825) was a leader of armed resistance against British imperial forces. After he was killed in battle, the British successfully colonized Burma. In translating this article, too, the students' names have been approximated from Japanese kana in the original.

5. The comparison of Mount Mayon to Mount Fuji was also reflected in a commemorative postage stamp issued during the Japanese occupation of the Philippines, with Fuji pictured higher than Mayon. See H. Byron Earhart, *Fuji, Icon of Japan* (forthcoming).

6. There has been at least one major court case in Japan brought by Hong Kong residents who claim they were forced to convert their prewar savings into Japanese-issued currency and military scrip, which the Japanese government has refused to honor after the war. The suit was rejected by a Tokyo court in 1999. See "$11 Billion Claim Rejected by Japanese Court" in the *South China Morning Post*, 18 June 1999.

7. For instance, Dr. Ba Maw and Major General Aung San, leaders of the Japanese-sponsored "independent" Burma decorated by Hirohito in 1943, were already organizing resistance against the Japanese presence in Burma before the "sham independence" was declared in 1943. Biding their time, they rose up in armed revolt against the Japanese in March 1945. See Frank N. Trager, ed., *Burma: Japanese Military Administration, Selected Documents*, 1941-1945 (Philadelphia: University of Pennsylvania Press, 1971), pp. 12-18. Ken'ichi Gotō describes resistance to Japanese occupation and domination in Burma, Indonesia, the Philippines, and Thailand. See "Cooperation, Submission, and Resistance of Indigenous Elites of Southeast Asia in the Wartime Empire," in Peter Duus, Ramon H. Myers, and Mark R. Peattie, eds., *The Japanese Wartime Empire, 1931-1945* (Princeton, NJ: Princeton University Press, 1996), pp. 295, 298-300.

8. A reference to the Uchiteshi Yamamu ("Continue to Shoot, Do not Desist!" Or more colloquially, "Keep up the Fight!") campaign of March 1943, discussed in Chapter 9.

9. *Iroha* is the customary ordering of hiragana, adopted from a poem traditionally attributed to the Shingon patriarch Kūkai (774-835). Generations of Japanese students learned the *iroha* system, and it was also used in assigning order to items in a list (as with alphabetical order). Since the late nineteenth century, the *iroha* system has gradually been superseded by more logical models, in part the work of Western linguists.

10. The Japanese term is *imon butai*, distinct from *ianpu*, "comfort women" (the euphemism for forced prostitutes). From these girls' ages, it is very unlikely that they were "comfort women." The word *imon* ("care" or "comfort") is also found in the Japanese words for comfort letters (*imonbun*) and comfort packages (*imonbukuro*).

9. UCHITESHI YAMAMU: "KEEP UP THE FIGHT"

The single largest public relations campaign of the war centered on Army Day (10 March) in 1943, which was observed throughout the Japanese Empire with several events and the slogan, *uchiteshi yamamu*. Literally translated, the slogan means "Continue to Shoot, Do not Desist,"[1] but a more colloquial translation would be "Keep up the Fight" or "Stay on the Offensive." This classical phrase from the eighth-century *Kojiki* (*Record of Ancient Matters*) was attributed to Emperor Jinmu, mythological founder of the Japanese Isles and putative ancestor of the wartime emperor. During a drawn-out campaign to subjugate the Japanese isles, Jinmu rallied his troops with this phrase, which he made into a song (*uta*).[2] The phrase was pregnant with meaning, conjuring up the sacred origins of Japan; the sanctity of the imperial throne; the connection between the emperor, his loyal subjects, and the land; and the "never surrender" ethos of the samurai and Japan's modern military. It also suggested a parallel between the first emperor's military leadership and the reigning emperor as commander-in-chief, and likened the military struggle leading to the foundation of ancient Japan (that is, Yamato) to the war that expanded the Greater East Asian Co-Prosperity Sphere into a Japanese global empire.

The 1943 Army Day poster is still frequently referred to today when describing the "look" of the war: sleek, minimal, active, powerful, and realistic. The poster had a print run of fifty thousand copies; these were distributed across Japan at the end of February. At the center of this nationwide campaign was a mammoth billboard-size enlargement of the poster that was displayed on the side of a theater, an eight-story building on a commanding corner in the heart of Tokyo.[3] The huge poster, with a total area of 3,559 square feet, became the backdrop of the staging arena for a parade and bond drive. Photographs taken in front of the gargantuan poster made it one of the iconic images of wartime Japan. The events continued across the city. A downed B-29 was displayed in Hibiya Park. The American and British flags were painted on the busy street crossing at Ginza 4-chōme so that pedestrians could "stamp out" the enemy as they crossed the street, reminiscent of Edo period *fumi-e* ("stepping-on pictures") of Christ and Christian symbols that Japanese suspected of practicing Christianity were made to step on as a renunciation of faith.[4]

The Uchiteshi Yamamu Campaign's barrage of optimistic jingoes, dramatic posters, advertising gimmicks, bond drives, and parades with military bands all formed the sugar coating on a bitter pill: a program of total warfare at a time when Japan's military situation had sharply deteriorated. The Uchiteshi Yamamu Campaign provided the context for the government's extracting greater cooperation and greater sacrifice from the home front. The final vestiges of civilian life would be systematically erased in the coming year. Of course, the ideological groundwork for total warfare had been laid out five years earlier with the New Order, and cultivated with heavy doses of "One Hundred Million" programming aimed at eradicating any lingering resistance to the government's policies. The seeds of blind obedience and fervent nationalism were ready to bear fruit, and as part of its special report on the Uchiteshi Yamamu Campaign, *Photographic Weekly Report* 262 (10 March 1943) devoted a series of several full-page photographs tying the home front's response to the campaign to the battle front.

1 and 2. Two Army Day events staged in front of the colossal Uchiteshi Yamamu billboard mounted on the Japan Theater (Nihon Gekijō) Building in the Yūrakuchō Theater District of Tokyo: at left, a Bullet Bond Drive (*PWR* 264, 24 March 1943, p. 17); at right, a military band plays marching music (*Asahigraph* [40:12], *Great East Asia War Report* 64, 24 March 1943, p. 11). The uncredited *Asahigraph* photograph at right is a fine documentary image, but its vantage point looks down on the proceedings from a distance and the accompanying text merely describes the martial music stirring the crowd's patriotic feelings. The photograph maintains the division between military action (the poster's soldier about to hurl a grenade) and the passive reaction of civilians, just as the poster and the crowd occupy different planes. In this sense, the *Asahigraph* photograph is passive and fails to convey the largest goal of the Uchiteshi Yamamu Campaign: greater war effort and greater sacrifice on the home front. The photograph at left (uncredited here) is one of Umemoto Tadao's masterpieces. Umemoto shoots from street level and leaves the band's audience in the background, while his framing places the soldiers of the poster between the bond purchaser and seller, establishing an interactive relationship and suggesting a narrative. He focuses on linking the imagery of battlefield action and home front results of the Uchiteshi Yamamu Campaign: a well-dressed woman buys war bonds from student volunteers. The photograph translates the campaign's goals into results, with everyone participating in the war effort: soldiers and civilians, adults and adolescents, those with money and those without. For Japan to win the war would require placing more soldiers at the front, in turn made possible by home front production of matériel and capital. Military band concerts, while good for morale, would not win the war. Umemoto's brilliant photograph has been reproduced in several postwar books describing life in wartime Japan, where it conveys the atmosphere of total war and the sinister nuance of government coercion of civilians.

3-5. *PWR* 262, 10 March 1943, pp. 1-3.

(top) The front cover photograph (p. 1), supplied by the same Yamabata photography firm that designed the Army Day poster, showed a soldier "in the moment before attacking . . . his fighting spirit evident in his firm grip on his weapon. Before his eyes there is no life or death, there is only 'uchiteshi yamamu,' which is itself the cry of the men of Yamato whose entire bodies and entire spirits gush forth with their blood in service to the emperor." Even his fingers are tensed with anticipation.

(bottom right) The first inside page of the magazine (p. 2), at this time reserved for a "Signboard of the Times" message, simply says, "uchiteshi yamamu" in increasingly larger type, an extremely effective graphic design in Japanese, suggesting that the slogan's imperative grows stronger and louder with repetition.

(bottom left) Page 3 shows an adolescent student of the Army Junior Officers' Training School reading out the "Vow to Serve as a Formidable Shield" by the side of the stone fence leading to the palace. The text explains that in this time of national emergency, the men of Yamato defend their land like a formidable shield and adds that "We see 'uchiteshi yamamu' taking shape in this youth's posture." The small black box to the right of the text bears the uchiteshi yamamu slogan.

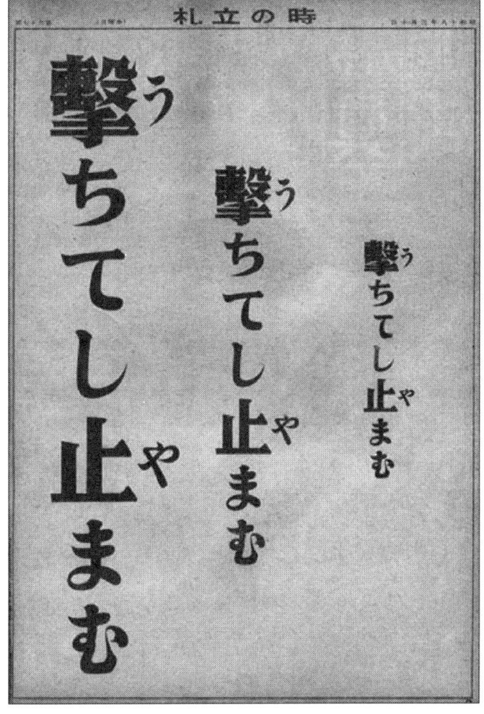

時の立札

撃ちてし止まむ

撃ちてし止まむ

撃ちてし止まむ

6-11. *PWR* 262, 10 March 1943, pp 4-9. (this and facing page) Six more full-page photographs from the same issue of *PWR*, representing the Uchiteshi Yamamu Campaign, each bearing the slogan in a black box in the bottom right corner of the page.

The first three photographs are uncredited.

(this page, top, p. 4) "We Must Shoot Them!" gives an overview of the rapid advances of the first months of the war. This photograph serves to tie the men fighting the war to the effort on the home front.

(facing page, top left, p. 5) "I Still Have One Arm" describes the zeal of a triple amputee soldier who now works in a munitions plant. "Although I've given both of my legs and an arm in the service, I still have this left arm. And even if we [Japanese] were to give both arms and both legs in the service, as long as we are alive, our hearts would beat loudly with 'uchiteshi yamamu.'" The article provides no details about the circumstances in which this soldier was injured.

(facing page, top right, p. 6) The vital role of children in the war effort is illustrated by this boy who makes ball bearings for airplanes. He proudly wears a Rising Sun headband, showing his support for Japan's cause. When village neighbor Sabu became a fighter pilot, the boy promised that he would help make the plane Sabu would fly. Now that Sabu has shot down two enemy planes on his first day out and is a hero, this boy can share Sabu's glory.

(this page, bottom, p. 7) "Cultivating the Land with Fighting Spirit" demands that "all 5.6 million farmers take on the attitude of uchiteshi yamamu" and double the amount of crops. Here, a peasant couple hauls firewood. Photograph: Umemoto Tadao.

(facing page, bottom left, p. 8) "An Over-the-Head Water Bomb" shows a "strong young female fire defense warrior" in action. "The fighting spirit of uchiteshi yamamu represents the One Hundred Million's victory preparations, our inclination to thoroughly practice [air defense] and absolutely protect the imperial throne and this imperial land." Photograph: Katō Kyōhei.

(facing page, bottom right) "Bringing to Life Her Dead Husband's Will" shows a war widow correcting her sleeping daughter's "uchiteshi yamamu" calligraphy, all the while thinking to herself, "Am I not the happiest person in Japan to be able to instill in my child the 'uchiteshi yamamu' spirit willed to her by her father, who died for his country?" Her deceased husband's photograph is displayed in a place of respect in the recessed alcove (tokonoma). Photograph: Senba Tōru.

撃ちてし止まむ
なほ残る片手あり

撃ちてし止まむ
兵器は俺が造る
6

撃ちてし止まむ
頭上の水彈
8

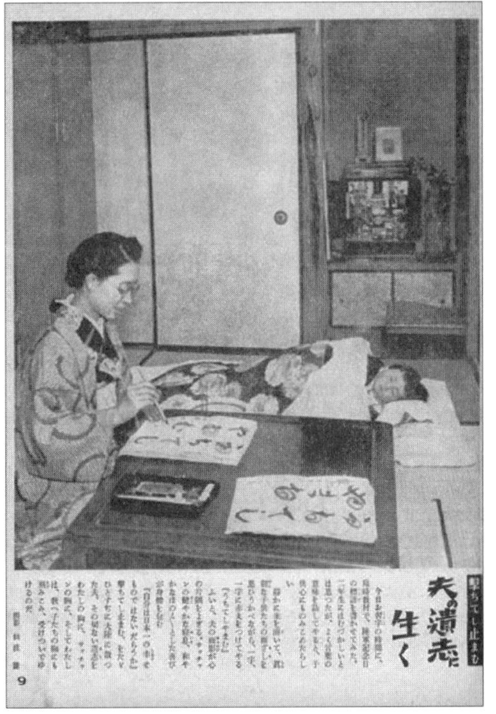
撃ちてし止まむ
夫の遺志に生く
9

三勇士の後をつぐ

10

兵農一如の闘魂

11

12 and 13. *PWR* 262, 10 March 1943.

(left, p. 10) "Follow the Three Heroes." Schoolgirls clean a statue of the "Three Heroic Bombers" (Bakudan San Yūshi, commonly referred to as the Three Human Bullets [Nikudan San Yūshi]) in the precincts of Seishōji[5] in Shiba, Tokyo. The article makes a connection between the children and the three human bombs. "This is the twelfth year since the Shanghai Incident [of 1932], and the children who were then sitting on their mothers' knees drinking milk are today upper-level students at Citizens' Schools." And in a few more years, these students would themselves be soldiers, or perhaps nurses. The text includes an oddly tactile, almost erotic description of the students' work: "With buckets and rags, they began washing the dust off the heroes' bodies . . . carefully, carefully, they touch the hero's shoulder, they touch his knee, and their tender young hearts awaken and swell with the thought that their solemn Yamato spirits will follow in the footsteps of these heroes." This photograph is uncredited.

(right, p. 11) "The Fighting Spirit of Soldiers and Farmers is One and the Same." The last in a series of ten full-page photographs in *PWR* representing different aspects of uchiteshi yamamu. A farmer, identified by his straw hat and jacket, practices attacking a dummy with a bamboo spear. The mayor of his remote village in rural Niigata Prefecture suggested such practice to all villagers the year before. This is the same farmer as in figure 9, who has taken advantage of time on his way home from hauling firewood. The message of uchiteshi yamamu has come full circle, from the soldier at the front (on the front cover) to the farmer in the remote countryside. This credited photograph is another of Umemoto Tadao's famous and frequently reprinted masterpieces.

14 and 15. *PWR* 262, 10 March 1943.

(left, p. 12) A full-page cartoon for children to color, by Yokoyama Ryūichi (1909-2001).[6] Yokoyama's famous schoolboy Fukuchan gives an ogre a kick that sends him sailing. The small Asian boy on the left, his hat suggesting he is Indonesian, carries an uchiteshi yamamu banner. The caption reads, "This ogre is a red ogre. He wears an English flag for his belly band, and an American flag as his loincloth (*fundoshi*). Think carefully about this as you color with your crayon." These colored pages were displayed on neighborhood bulletin boards. Yokoyama's Fukuchan series was reprinted by US propagandists and used in surrender leaflets (printed in the form of newspapers). Yokoyama complained, half in jest, that he never received a dollar in royalties from the United States for all his wartime services. On his eighty-fifth birthday, then US ambassador to Japan Walter Mondale personally presented him with a blanket-sized check for one dollar.

(right, p. 13) Another cartoon for children to color, by Ishikawa Shinsuke (1906-1995). "This enemy soldier is a green ogre who has taken a human form. He has the English and American flags for armbands. After you have asked your mother and father, color him with your crayons."

Placed side by side, these two cartoons reveal different attitudes toward children and war. Yokoyama's "enemy" is a childishly drawn ogre, familiar from folk stories. His Fukuchan wears clogs and a schoolboy cap, and his defeat of the enemy is achieved symbolically, with a good kick. Ishikawa's enemy is a large-nosed, lanky-limbed Westerner, his grim-looking schoolboy wears a military helmet, and his defeat of the enemy requires slicing him in half with a sharp sword. The "red ogre, green ogre" pair is found in Japanese folklore. These are the only two instances of coloring pictures for children printed in *PWR*.

16 and 17. *PWR* 264, 24 March 1943, p. 22. "Army Day in the Imperial Capital." Photographs taken by *PWR* readers in Tokyo, demonstrating home front efforts to boost morale as part of the Uchiteshi Yamamu Campaign.

(top) "Stepping on the Enemy Flag on the Way to Work." The caption reads, "Stomping out the enemies America and Britain. The enemy flags were drawn on the crosswalk of Ginza 4-chōme, and the men and women passing by completely rubbed them out." Photograph: Matsuda Banzō, in Tokyo.

(bottom) "We Children are also 'Keeping up the Fight.'"

"'I colored this one.'

"'I put mine up over there.'

"The children, who did their very best at coloring the cartoon pages [in *PWR* 262, figures 14 and 15], went around the neighborhood putting them on display." Photograph: Kohashi Tatsuo, in Tokyo.

The Cabinet Information Bureau was responsible for disseminating the government's war aims to the home front and boosting morale. In this regard, the CIB was charged with the same mission as the US Office of War Information and Germany's Propaganda Ministry. While the CIB certainly controlled the design and look of domestic media products, they themselves only created a fraction of it, most notably in their flagship publication, *Photographic Weekly Report*. A thriving advertising and commercial design industry served as the locus of visualizing public relations campaigns. These advertising professionals were not merely cogs in the media machine, they were its engine, even while the CIB remained firmly in control of their efforts.

Commercial artists were not the only ones to find a bonanza in war work; fine artists received commissions to paint large canvasses commemorating highlights of the war, and all stripes of writers could support themselves through assignments to create material promoting the Co-Prosperity Sphere or with stipends from governmental agencies. Nearly all of Japan's artists and literati served the war effort, most voluntarily, some reluctantly. Of course, Japanese were hardly exceptional in this regard; American writers, artists, and film directors all played key roles in supporting the war effort.

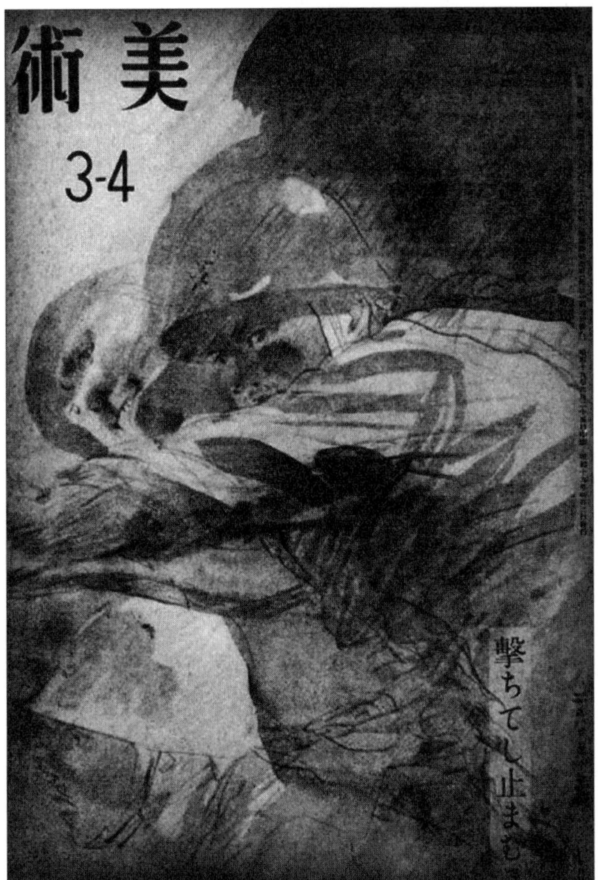

18. *Fine Arts*, New Series 3, March-April 1944.

This cover illustration, by Tamura Kōnosuke (1903-1986), shows a Japanese soldier overpowering an Allied soldier. The soft hues and delicate lines of this pencil and watercolor drawing are better suited to birds and flowers than to the harsh work of killing with one's bare hands.

While bearing the Uchiteshi Yamamu slogan on the cover lower right, the contents of this magazine included illustrated articles about Delacroix and a painting of Saint Ursula by Tintoretto as well as "War Power and Fine Art" and "Craft and the Wartime Lifestyle."

Originally called *Watercolor*, this trade journal of *nihonga* artists, through a series of government- imposed magazine consolidations, became *New Fine Arts* in 1941 and then *Fine Arts* in 1943. The magazine was published consecutively from 1905 to 1992.

Photographic Culture (*Shashin bunka*) published a self-congratulatory article on the construction of the three-story high uchiteshi yamamu poster (figures 1, 2, and 20), an article providing a clinical report on the wartime work of professional advertising and graphic designers. The article is silent on the concept and motivation of the poster, perhaps assuming they needed no explanation, but also leaving the impression that for those working in commercial design, selling war was no different than selling chocolates, light bulbs, or soap.[7] The manufacturers of these "luxury" products had been their major clients before the war. Due to government strictures, few manufacturers could continue to advertise their products through the darkest months of the war.

19. *Asahigraph* (40:12), *Great East Asia War Report* 64, 24 March 1943, back cover. A full-page, two-color advertisement for Tō Lamps featured "uchiteshi yamamu" in a beautifully stylized font, printed in a transparent red over a photograph of a light bulb. The product is shown larger than actual size. The sleek, modern design of this advertisement could easily have come from the same studio that produced the uchiteshi yamamu Army Day poster. The phrase beneath the light bulb says, "Strive on to Victory! Save electricity, save light bulbs."

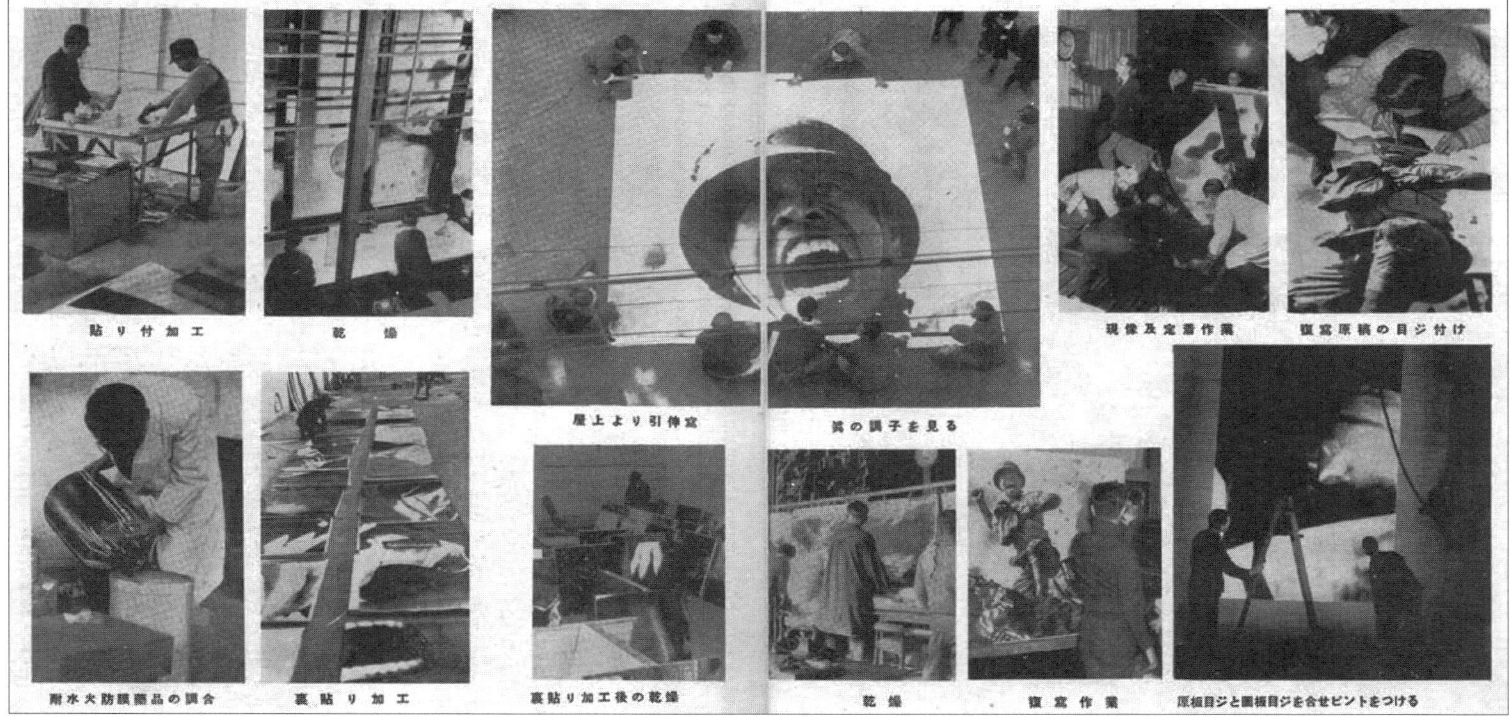

20. This article by Yamabata Yōsuke in *Photographic Culture* ([26:4], April 1943, pp. 9-10), describes the work of the Yamabata Photoscience Laboratory[8] in creating the Army Day poster and billboard. The poster consists of a Bauhaus-inspired photomontage showing two soldiers on the offensive, one hurling a hand-grenade, the other about to charge the enemy. The US flag has fallen during a hasty retreat, reminiscent of photographs popular a year earlier, when the Philippines fell into Japanese hands (see figures 51 and 52 in Chapter 7). The crisply pressed uniforms, the row of perfect white teeth, the faces expressing both the fierceness and steely determination of battle, the dramatic lighting—all are the signature of a professional advertising firm. On closer inspection, these two men seem to be one and the same model. The article uses photojournalism to describe the creation of the billboard. The article provides precise instructions for constructing the wall-size photograph, including the lenses, exposures, and developing fluids used, but no information on the poster's concept or the purpose of the campaign.

21 and 22. (left) *Photographic Culture* (26:4), April 1943, p. 8 The original photomontage from which the mammoth poster was created. The American flag has been thrown to the ground.

(right) *Asahigraph* (40:10), *Great East Asia War Report* 62, 10 March 1943. A soldier about to attack, featured here as part of the first Uchiteshi Yamamu Campaign. The same model, shot from slightly different angles, appears in this photograph, the right side of the photomontage used in the mammoth poster, and the cover of *PWR* 262 (seen in figure 3). The inside story in *Asahigraph* described an increased military effort, including reports on training adolescents in tank warfare.

By design, slogans are compact, pithy, and easily remembered. Through repetition, their messages enter the psyche and may even influence our decisions. As a phrase, "uchiteshi yamamu" could boast an exalted pedigree and divine authority, but its grammar was antiquated and outdated. Its clipped ending with the classical negative particle "*mu*" gave it the sound of a barked military order, harsh on the tongue, although a popular song was created around the slogan in 1943. For such a phrase to gain popularity and function as a slogan required reproducing it ad nauseam and posting it everywhere the eye turned. In March 1943, the CIB "requested" that all magazines, regardless of content or target audience, print the slogan on their cover. With Tōjō serving concurrently as Prime Minister, Army Minister, and Army Chief of Staff, the CIB's "request" to have the Army Day slogan printed on every magazine cover was hard to ignore. The manner in which publishers accommodated this request is something of a barometer of government control of the free press as well as of the media's grasp of the government's wartime goals. Some magazines did little more than copy the official images for the campaign, others used stock patriotic images. Some trade and special interest magazines dutifully placed the slogan on their front covers without adding content addressing the campaign or its meaning.

23 and 24. (top) *History Pictures* 359, April 1943. This cover showed a soldier in northern China melting ice for drinking water. The slogan "uchiteshi yamamu" is preceded by the words "A fierce fight to the death." The image is appropriately martial, if strangely out of season. By April, only Japanese soldiers stationed in the Aleutians would be deep in snow. While sporadic fighting continued unabated in China, the decisive battles were taking place thousands of miles away in the South Pacific. Showing a sympathetic image of soldiers' hardships was one way of encouraging greater home front sacrifices.

(bottom) *Women's Companion* (37:3), March 1943. *Women's Companion* is one of the oldest and most popular women's magazines, still published today. The March 1943 cover of bright plum blossoms (by Okamura Togyū) displays the uchiteshi yamamu slogan in its upper right field. This issue contained no articles about the war or about the slogan, although it did devote a page to a report on the success of bond drives.

Uchiteshi Yamamu was a well-organized publicity campaign, attesting to the extensive influence of the military (in this case, army officers determining publishing policy) within the CIB, even as the CIB was at the height of its powers. The CIB held a prepublication meeting with the editors of major publications on the sixth of the month (the Rokunichi Kai), and this is the probable forum for launching the Uchiteshi Yamamu Campaign. Several newsmagazines used the slogan on one or even a series of cover photographs, illustrating the "attack to the end" theme on the home front and the battlefield. Manufacturers were quick to jump on the bandwagon, and "uchiteshi yamamu" was stamped on cigarette cases, lighters, and pocket knives (perfect items for soldiers' comfort packages). There was an "uchiteshi yamamu" game that enjoined children to compete in shooting the greatest number of enemy soldiers.

25 and 26. The March 1943 covers of the Kodansha juvenile magazines *Boys' Club* (30:3) and *Girls' Club* (21:3) carried the uchiteshi yamamu slogan in small black script (written vertically in the upper right on each cover). "Charge," a painting by Matsuno Kazuo, graced the cover of *Boys' Club*, which contained several articles on the uchiteshi yamamu theme. An article by Colonel Yahagi Nakao explained the importance of winning the war as well as the meaning of the phrase used by Emperor Jinmu to encourage his troops to continue to fight, despite setbacks, and ultimately prevail. A story of the fight in the South Pacific by Major Ōba Yahei, "Destroy America and England. Shoot the Enemy of our Fallen Heroes!" would have filled any adolescent with fighting spirit. Several such articles in *Boys' Club* were aimed at turning boys into soldiers.

Takizawa Hiroyuki's cover painting for *Girls Club* is titled "The Day of Plums," that is, 3 March, traditionally Girls' Festival when a girl put her dolls on display. We see two dolls behind this girl on a small shelf, and the uchiteshi yamamu slogan is written over the dolls. The girl is arranging a vase of plum blossoms. Without the slogan, which is quite unobtrusive, the cover seems far removed from the war. However, the issue contained several articles related to the war. There is a lengthy explanation of the uchiteshi yamamu slogan as well as an article on children and air safety. Despite the martial spirit of these magazines, neither explained to children what their role was in the Uchiteshi Yamamu Campaign.

One magazine that initially failed to participate in the Uchiteshi Yamamu Campaign was *Chūō Kōron*, the vanguard of Japanese intellectual publications.[9] Having been deeply involved in the Marxist debates of the 1920s and 1930s, the magazine came under close scrutiny and ran afoul of the censor on several occasions. In January 1944, five of its editors were arrested by the Yokohama Thought Police and detained without trial. Other arrests followed in a widening dragnet of some sixty intellectual writers. The detainees were severely beaten, and three *Chūō Kōron* staff members were beaten to death. In July 1944, the Cabinet Information Bureau demanded that the magazine "voluntarily" dissolve for "hindering thought control."[10] The army interrogators justified this severe punishment by fabricating a plot to revive the Japan Communist Party and attributing it to the editors. A hasty trial of the detainees took place between 29 August and 15 September 1945, before Allied occupying troops had dismantled the wartime legal system, and suspended prison sentences were handed down for violating the Peace Preservation Law.[11] *Chūō Kōron* resumed publication in 1946 and is today one of Japan's most important intellectual magazines.

In retrospect, the contents of wartime issues of *Chūō Kōron* hardly seem out of step with the war effort. Each issue contained articles discussing different aspects of the war and its economic, social, and cultural implications. While none of these articles reflects negatively on the war effort, in the desperate, paranoid atmosphere of wartime Japan, it must have seemed like heresy to discuss the war effort rather than merely parrot the government's unchanging message of "certain victory." For instance, the magazine dared to publish articles about "Overcoming the National Crisis" in December 1943, in an issue devoted to the second anniversary of the outbreak of the war. That the same issue reprinted the imperial rescript declaring war must have only appeared to be a half-hearted attempt to appease the censor. Some of the "evidence" of *Chūō Kōron*'s antipathy toward the war was the magazine's failure to put "uchiteshi yamamu" on the front cover of its March or April 1943 issues. Indeed, the magazine had printed its title in a stylized Roman script as "Tyuo Koron" until May 1943 (figure 27) and written its volume number from left to right (rather than the traditional Japanese order of right to left), but these signs of Westernization disappeared from the August 1943 issue. At the same time, English loan-words disappeared from the titles of all publications; for instance, *Sunday Asahi* (*Sandē Asahi*) became *Weekly Asahi* (*Shūkan Asahi*).

Pressure from the CIB left its mark on *Chūō Kōron*. In the magazine's final months of wartime publication, "uchiteshi yamamu" appeared on the cover in March, in larger font in April, and in red in the final, July 1944, issue (figure 30). The anti-intellectual antagonism of the military forced *Chūō Kōron* to become a "consolidated magazine" (*sōgō zasshi*) in April 1944. The final issue was a slim sixty-four pages, even though it was a "double issue." A typical issue of *Chūō Kōron* in 1942 had two hundred fifty pages or more. Famous in the first fifty years of its existence for publishing provocative new writing by Japan's leading literary luminaries, fiction completely disappeared from the magazine in 1943 and 1944. The military took a particularly dim view of reading for any purpose other than to learn information or skills vital to the war effort or to boost morale and patriotic fervor.

27-30. Four front covers of *Chūō Kōron* display subtle clues to the magazine's problems with the censors.

(upper left) The May 1943 edition had already appeared when the editors were called in for a "consultation" with the censors about the lead article, "A New Approach to the China Problem and [Changing] Our Attitude." At issue were the magazine's left-leaning tendencies prior to the war and its lack of support for the war effort, as evidenced in its failure to place the uchiteshi yamamu slogan on its March or April 1943 covers.

(upper right) After consultation, the editors put the slogan on the March 1944 cover at center right with a short explanation: "The front is waiting. For guns. For planes." The magazine dropped its romanized title (*Tyuo Koron*, as seen on the May 1943 cover), and began writing the month and volume number (seen bottom center beneath the large vertical magazine title) in the traditional Japanese order of right to left.

(bottom left) In April 1944 the uchiteshi yamamu slogan was slightly enlarged. "Consolidated Magazine" appears in a box, upper right corner.

(bottom right) In July 1944, "uchiteshi yamamu" was written in white letters in a solid red box.

31 and 32. (left) *Dōmeigraph* (11:3), March 1943. Edited by the Foreign and Communications Ministries, *Dōmeigraph* was partly financed by the CIB. It focused on overseas news. The cover of the March 1943 issue showed a soldier patrolling northern Manchuria, and neither this cover nor the following month's printed "uchiteshi yamamu." The March 1943 issue duly placed the slogan in a caption beneath a photograph of a February festival at Yasukuni Shrine. Evidently, as a governmental publication devoted to foreign news, *Dōmeigraph* was exempted from home front morale campaigns.

(right) *Dōmeigraph* (11:4), April 1943, p. 17. The by-now obligatory photograph of the colossal Army Day poster did not appear in *Dōmeigraph* until its April issue came out on 31 March. The caption reads, "We certainly will win! Renewed determination on Army Day."

The slogan "uchiteshi yamamu" was used again to commemorate Army Day in 1944, although the campaign had been scaled back dramatically. Many magazines revived the slogan on their front covers, but without the mammoth poster and events accompanying the 1943 campaign, it failed to have much impact. The surrender of Italy, the retaking of some islands by the Allies, and the strain on Japanese civilian life must have given the second Uchiteshi Yamamu Campaign the unappealing aura of stale leftovers. Curiously, while Navy Day was also marked with ceremonies and special issues of magazines, it never became the center of a massive public relations campaign, despite the extraordinary naval victories of the war's first months. In 1945, *PWR* devoted a cover to Army Day (361-362, 7 March 1945), with a photograph of a young soldier and a terse message: "Always think only of winning. Give everything to winning. That is what our ancestors did." The same issue nowhere printed the "uchiteshi yamamu" slogan; it carried a grim report from Iwo Jima, attesting to the dire war situation. Coincidentally, the horrific firebombing of Tokyo and Yokohama occurred on Army Day in 1945.

33-35. *PWR* 312, 8 March 1944, pp. 1-3.

(top) The front cover (at this time, numbered p. 1) for Army Day 1944 says "Army Day" without the "uchiteshi yamamu" slogan and features an Army Air Force pilot. Only airplanes would stop the Allied advance

(bottom right, p. 2) The "Signboard of the Times" message reads, "At the time of the Mongol invasion, the Sino-Japanese War, and the Russo-Japanese War—our ancestors, in those times of national emergency, raised a war cry. Listen carefully, and you can hear that same tide of blood, roaring: 'National emergency has come. Continue to shoot, do not desist.'"

(bottom left, p. 3) These boys of the Sendai Army Junior Officers' Training School are reading aloud the Imperial Rescript to Soldiers and Sailors, promulgated in the Meiji era. The white text against the black background calls for public outrage similar to that of forty years before (at the outbreak of the Russo-Japanese War), at the conclusion of the "fight to the death" in the Marshall Islands.

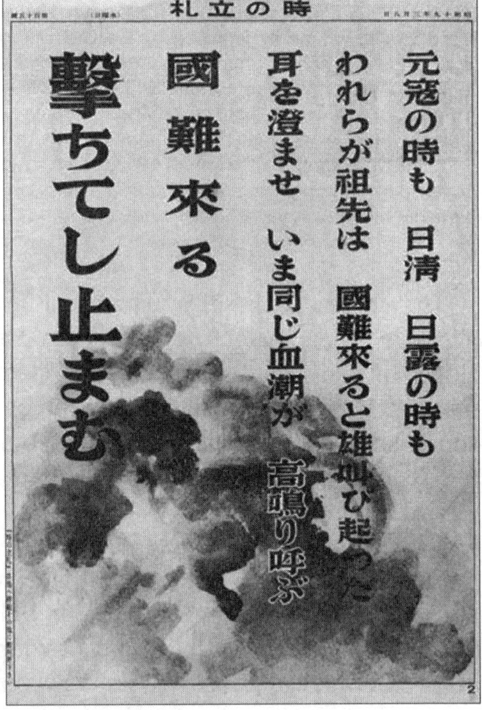

36 and 37. (left) The monthly news digest *Monthly Yomiuri* (2:3) for March 1944 put a photograph of a statue of the imperial loyalist Kusunoki Masashige (1294-1336) on its cover with the uchiteshi yamamu slogan. Kusunoki, who lost his life in a failed bid to restore the imperial throne to political power, was resurrected as a national hero after the Meiji Restoration of 1868. That he lost his life and failed in his mission hardly mattered; his actions had been loyal and correct, and history had proved him right some six centuries after his death.

(right) *Asahigraph* (42:9), *Great East Asia War Report* 113, 8 March 1944. A soldier, with a look of determination, is featured here as part of the reprised Uchiteshi Yamamu Campaign of 1944, when "banzai" suicide charges were being carried out in the fight for the Solomon and Marshall island chains. His fierceness and loyalty to the emperor and the cause of national greatness made the modern soldier the descendant of such glorious samurai of the past as Kusunoki.

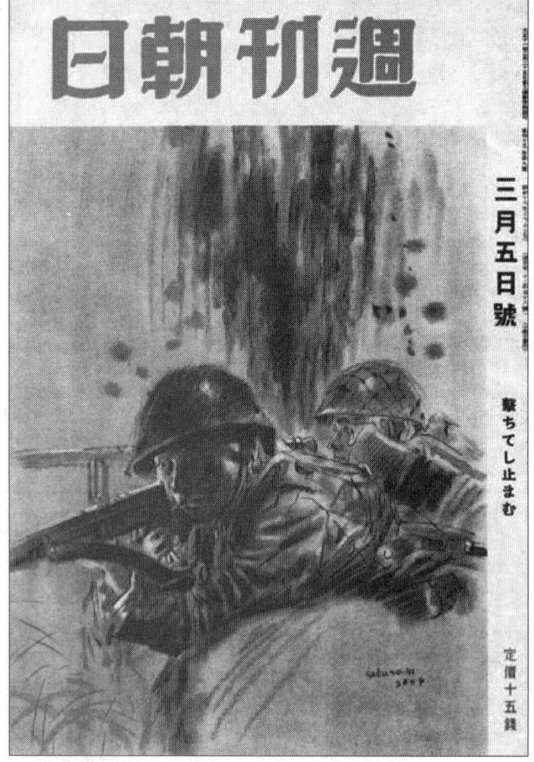

38 and 39. (top) *History Pictures* 307, March 1944. The banner beneath the magazine's title reads, "Keep Shooting Down the Ugly, Malicious Enemy" and incorporates "uchiteshi yamamu." The banner along the bottom reads, "The Autumn of the Rise or Fall of the Land of the Gods, Japan." The caption to the cover photograph is "Our Anti-aircraft Camp on [censored] Base in the South Pacific." Inside the magazine are four photojournalist spreads devoted to "uchiteshi yamamu": "Guarding the Frozen Northern Border"; "Our Wild Eagles, Fighter Pilots Before Taking Off"; "The Fruits of War before our very Eyes"; and "Defending the Islands of the Pacific."

(bottom) *Weekly Asahi* (45:9), 5 March 1944. "Uchiteshi yamamu" appears vertically along the right margin. The drawing is signed "Saburo" in roman letters, the work of Miyamoto Saburō. Originally a middle-brow general interest magazine called *Sunday Asahi* (*Sandē Asahi*) until 1943, the contents here are entirely devoted to the war, especially in the Pacific.

Any assessment of the Uchiteshi Yamamu Campaign must recognize that beneath the public relations rhetoric lay a burgeoning crisis confronting the war effort and the Great Japanese Empire. This crisis was impending defeat. Of course, with the war in Europe still raging, the outcome in Asia was far from predictable. Anything might happen: the fickle American public might tire of war; the Soviet Union might turn against its ally, the United States; or a divine wind might once again save Japan from an invading fleet. Those in power knew that the tide of war had turned decidedly against Japan as early as the summer of 1942, but this fact had to be hidden from the public if morale and order were to be maintained. There was too much at stake—not only the territorial gains in Manchuria, China, and the resource-rich Southern Regions, but the sovereignty of Japan itself.

40. *PWR* 312, 8 March 1944, p. 19. "With the Wings of Uchiteshi Yamamu," a cartoon by Ishikawa Shinsuke. The caption says, "The enemy is trying to break down the door to our South Pacific. The only thing that will kill this ogre is increased airplane production." The imagery departs from the usual depiction of the horned American (or English) "ogre," which here is a ferocious beast resembling a bear. The South Pacific is represented by a rather Western-style fortress made of blocks of stone, while Japanese airplanes have sprouted arms and legs, reminiscent of the personification of everyday objects popular in manga of the late Edo period. The airplanes are used metaphorically to hold a door shut, rather than to fly over the wall and bomb the enemy ogre-beast. The caption delivers a clear message, although the cartoon itself is a somewhat confused image, anticipating the ramming missions of kamikaze air attacks, which would first be launched in October of 1944.

By 1943 the military leadership was desperate, as Japan was in full retreat across the Pacific and facing acute shortages of troops, planes, ships, labor, and matériel of all kinds. Student conscription began in the second half of 1943 to help fill the depleted ranks of the military. The fate of a nation—and a people—hung in the balance between the first and second Uchiteshi Yamamu Campaign. Although the war factories were in operation around the clock, Japan was deficient in the raw materials of heavy industry and lacked both infrastructure and transport lines with the occupied southern lands.

The Uchiteshi Yamamu Campaign and the Yokohama Incident were two sides of the same coin, an attempt to create a state of total war mobilization, one in which all citizens harbored the same thought of giving their all for victory and those suspected of not doing so were tracked down by the Thought Police. While the Uchiteshi Yamamu Campaign was mostly forgotten after the war ended, it did form an important chapter in the history of Japanese graphic design. The men who devised this ultra-modern advertising blitz emerged from the war physically unscathed, ready to resume the places they had made for themselves at the forefront of the Japanese advertising and commercial design industry. Their experience conducting nationwide public relations campaigns during the war would be invaluable in the coming age of broadcast advertising. None of them were purged during the Occupation, and as the Japanese economy reemerged from the ashes, they found themselves leading major advertising and public relations firms,[12] some of which are among the largest and most influential in the world today. If Japanese modern design was born in the 1930s, it came of age during the war, and without missing a beat, quickly dominated the postwar advertising world. From this perspective, the Uchiteshi Yamamu Campaign was victorious.

Notes

1. Kodansha's *Encyclopedia of Japan* (Tokyo: Kodansha, 1993) translates the phrase colloquially as "Attack to the End" (Vol II, pp. 1416-17). Cook and Cook translate the phrase, "We'll never cease to fire until our enemies cease to be!" (*Japan at War: An Oral History* [New York, The New Press: 1992], p. 67). John W. Dower translates it "roughly" as "Fight to the Bitter End!" (Japan Photographers Association, *A Century of Japanese Photography* [New York: Pantheon, 1980], p. 20). All of these translations convey the sense of the original.

2. The full translation of the original text is Donald L. Philippi (trans.), *Kojiki* (New York: Columbia University Press, 1977).

3. A massive photomontage (7½ feet high and 60 feet long) of Japanese scenery and culture was constructed at the Paris Exposition of 1937 under the direction of Hara Hiromu, a preeminent Japanese graphic designer. The photomontage is reproduced in Nanba Kōji, *"Uchiteshi yamamu": Taiheiyō sensō to hōkoku no gijutsusha tachi*, p. 40. A mammoth photographic wall poster showing Mount Fuji from across Suruga Bay was constructed for display at the Japanese Pavilion at the 1939-1940 New York World's Fair as part of the theme, "the Architecture of Tomorrow." An *Asahigraph* article states the work was done by a team headed by a man identified only as Tanba, assisted by Kobayashi and Harada of Rokuōsha. Fuji was chosen because it was the "symbol" (*shinboru*) of Japan. See the photoessay in *Asahigraph* (31:22), 30 November 1938, pp. 16-19. The mural has been widely credited to the famous graphic designer Yamana Ayao. For instance, Nanba (*"Uchiteshi yamamu,"* p. 45) quotes Yamana's published reminiscences describing his reasons for choosing Fuji's natural scenery for this colossal photograph.

4. For an example of similar denigration of the Japanese flag by a US officer, see the illustrations between pages 90 and 91 in Major Damon "Rocky" Gause, *The War Journal of Major Damon "Rocky"*

Gause (New York: Hyperion, 1999).

5. Seishōji is located on Atagosan, in today's Minato Ward. The statue was dismantled shortly after the war ended, and today only one-third of it is still on site.

6. Yokoyama appeared in an article, "The Surprise Attack of the Cartoon Entertainment Brigade" in *PWR* 161 (26 March 1941, pp. 18-19), in which he was shown drawing caricatures of wounded soldiers recuperating in the Military Hospital in Kiyose, Tokyo. Yokoyama speaks about his experiences as a cartoonist during the war in an interview included in Cook and Cook, *Japan at War: An Oral History*, pp. 95-99, and also describes his visit to GHQ shortly after the war's end to demand royalties (which was denied), pp. 471-472.

7. There is a sizable body of literature in Japanese investigating the evolution of professional propagandists, nearly all of whom worked in advertising and design firms before the war and quickly adapted their skills toward the creation of propaganda for the home front and the occupied areas. Two of the best sources are Nanba, *"Uchiteshi Yamamu,"* and Tagawa Seiichi, *Sensō no gurafizumu: kaisō no "FRONT"* (*War Graphism: Reminiscences about FRONT*, Tokyo: Heibonsha, 1988). Gennifer Weisenfeld also explores the connection between Japanese modern design, advertising, and war propaganda in "Touring Japan-as-Museum: *NIPPON* and other Japanese Imperialist Travelogues" (*Positions: East Asia Cultures Critique* [8:3], Winter 2000, pp. 747-793).

8. Nanba writes that Kanamaru Shigene took the photograph used in this poster, which was constructed by Nihon Gunji Kōgei (*"Uchiteshi Yamamu,"* p. 165). Nanba does not mention Yamabata's role in its creation. The Yamabata Photoscience Laboratory may have employed Kanamaru and worked with Nihon Gunji Kōgei in the construction of the mammoth billboard, but no connection has been established.

9. According to Hatanaka Shigeo, the editor of *Chūō Kōron* at this time, "In 1943, all Japanese magazines were asked to place the slogan 'Uchiteshi yamamu!' . . . on the cover of their March issue to commemorate Army Day. People who'd be excited by something like that wouldn't be reading *Chūō Kōron*. But I knew there'd be a big fuss if we didn't put the phrase in someplace [*sic*], so we printed it just after the editorial. That wouldn't do! We were the only magazine that didn't obey instructions" (quoted from p. 67 in the extensive interview of Hatanaka in Cook and Cook, *Japan at War: An Oral History* [pp. 64-68, 222-227]). Hatanaka, speaking more than forty years after the war; provides many insights into the Yokohama Incident. For a penetrating analysis of the Marxist debates in Japan in the 1920s and 1930s, see Germaine Hoston, *Marxism and the Crisis of Development in Prewar Japan* (Princeton: Princeton University Press, 1986).

10. The Yokohama Incident began in September 1942 but did not directly affect *Chūō Kōron* until the following year. The editors of *Kaizō* and *Nippon Hyōron* were also rounded up in the same dragnet, and *Kaizō* was also ordered to disband. By all accounts, this was the most severe and far-reaching instance of press censorship during the war. Gregory Kasza writes in *The State and Mass Media in Japan, 1918-1945* (Berkeley: University of California Press, 1988), "the Yokohama Incident was not typical of press policy under the New Order. It is, rather, the softer image of the consultation meeting that symbolizes the dominant pattern of state-society interaction" (p. 231). For a more detailed account of the Incident, see *The State and Mass Media in Japan*, pp. 229-231.

11. Janice Matsumura advances a convincing argument in *More Than a Momentary Nightmare: The Yokohama Incident and Wartime Japan* (Cornell East Asia Series, number 92; Ithaca: Cornell University Press, 1998) that accusations of Communist sympathies were the pretext for a crackdown on influential writers and journalists associated with the Shōwa Research Association, which had close ties to the first Konoe Cabinet of 1937-1939. This group advocated a cautious approach to the war in China and did not support the spread of the war to the Pacific. The final chapter of the Yokohama Incident has yet to be written, as surviving relatives of some of the convicted journalists have sued the government for a retrial, citing coerced confessions. In a 2005 ruling, the Tokyo High Court upheld the Yokohama District Court's 2003 decision to allow the retrial. See "Retrial over Wartime Free-speech Crackdown Ok'd" in the 11 March 2005 *Japan Times*. The same article claims that four defendants died in prison during the war and that Asahi newspaper staff were among those arrested. However, on 20 January 2007, the Tokyo High Court dismissed the appeal because the five defendants had been granted a general amnesty. The final hope for clearing the initial charges of 1944 rests with the Japanese Supreme Court. See Setsuko Kamiya, "'Yokohama Incident' Appeals Dismissed," *Japan Times*, 20 January 2007.

12. Nanba meticulously traces the careers of several influential graphic artists, commercial designers, photographers, and journalists from prewar positions in the private sector through their war work for various branches of the propaganda machine and finally to major postwar advertising and public relations

10. FACES OF THE ENEMY

Dehumanization and demonization of the enemy is a phenomenon occurring everywhere in wartime. In the Japanese media, it was evident to some extent throughout the war, particularly in ridiculing and vilifying the Allied leaders, usually in the form of caricatures of Roosevelt and Churchill.[1] Even so, the media had no set image of the enemy as a people or as individuals, and upon them were projected a panoply of sentiments: amity, distrust, sympathy, condescension, outrage, fear, and hatred. The actors in this puppet-play were usually real men and women—foreign visitors to Japan, foreign residents arrested and tried as spies, and combatants and civilians captured in East Asia during the first six months of the war.

The media's changing view of the enemy reflected the Japanese government's shifting attitude toward and reevaluation of the Allied threat. Several competing images of the enemy existed simultaneously in the media in the first year of the war, but by the time Saipan had fallen into enemy hands, a fixed, monolithic image became dominant. The foe threatening the Yamato race, their sacred land, and their god-emperor became an evil, loathsome, barbaric monster. The carpet-bombing of Japan's cities confirmed that the foe was a "bastard-demon," the epithet favored in the final year of the war.

1. "Maltby with a Sun Tan" by Ihara Usaburō, plate 78 in the catalogue of the Second Great East Asia War Art Exhibition. Major General C. M. Maltby, commander of British forces in Hong Kong, was captured when he surrendered Hong Kong on 25 December 1941.

Painted between 1942 and 1944, little in Maltby's expression conveys his status or experience as one of the highest-ranking POWs of World War II, other than the patch over his pocket with the number one on it, suggesting he was POW No. 1. The portrait becomes a work of war art in the context of the historical circumstances of its creation. While the wartime press expressed contempt, tinged with pity, for the enemy who chose the ignominy of surrender, a viewer today, Japanese or otherwise, might see no such sentiment expressed in this work of art.

During the Second Sino-Japanese War, *Asahigraph* and *PWR* avoided publishing photographs of Chinese enemy soldiers or their military or political leaders, which might have only aroused suspicions in the West or be put to use by the Chinese press in its anti-Japanese imaging war. The Japanese media instead focused on positive images from China showing the wonderful progress being made under Japanese guidance. These positive images were in turn part of the Japanese government's imaging war against the Western powers, one aimed at winning over Westerners to the Japanese cause in Asia.

The Chinese enemy rarely found his way into the pages of Japan's photojournals. The front cover of *PWR* 35 (12 October 1938) is one exception, appearing when Japanese exasperation with the tenacious General Chiang Kai-shek was at a feverish pitch. This very unusual cover is a photograph of a papier-mâché effigy, reportedly part of an anti-Chiang rally in Jinan, China. Chiang bears the dubious honor of being the only enemy leader to appear on *PWR*'s front cover. Caricatures of Chiang (usually depicted as a lackey of Churchill and Roosevelt) only became common in the mainstream press after the Allied embargo prompted a backlash of anti-ABCD rhetoric. Another exception is seen in a *PWR* article about a Chinese "terrorist"[2] who threatens the social stability of the "good people" of China who were happily working with Japan to "construct the New Asia."

2. *PWR* 35, 12 October 1938. The vertical phrase at left announces, "Here is Chiang Kai-shek!"

The caption says, "Well, well. Here is Chiang Kai-shek, ready for the funeral pyre.

"While our brave soldiers are unifying the world, this Chiang Kai-shek deludes the [Chinese] people with outlandish, crude words. He deceives the people with reckless statements such as 'Oppose Japan and Save the Nation,' and 'Cooperating with the Communists Saves the People.' This Chiang Kai-shek will put all of China to the torch and kill tens of thousands of Chinese people in order to be its sole dictator. Burning and rending [the country] apart is still not enough to satisfy this Chiang Kai-shek." The photograph is credited to "the CIB, at an anti-Chiang demonstration in Jinan."

3 and 4. *PWR* 175, 2 July 1941, p. 26. Two photographs from an article about the apprehension of a "terrorist" (*tero hannin*) in Hankou. The article demonstrates the Japanese method of "pacifying" occupied areas of China. The photograph at right shows the military police in Hankou receiving a telephone call about a "terrorist" on the loose. At left, the arrest of the "terrorist" following a dragnet of Hankou's streets. This issue of *PWR* appeared on the fourth anniversary of the China Incident.

Racism was omnipresent in the Japanese press during the war. After all, the entire war was couched in terms of the destiny of the Yamato race. As seen in preceding chapters, the media's descriptions of the superiority of the Japanese people was unwaveringly consistent. And while the Japanese media image of the Yamato race was monolithic, its attitudes toward other races were surprisingly malleable. Some factions of the Japanese military and government were enamored of Nazi Germany, but Nazi notions of subhuman races were not universally accepted by Japan's ideologues, even during the eight months between the conclusion of the Tripartite Pact (October 1940) and the Nazi invasion of the Soviet Union (June 1941), when Japanese infatuation with Germany was running at a high. Japanese skepticism of Nazi notions of race were in part due to the Japanese having themselves long been the recipients of prejudicial treatment at the hands of Westerners. In particular, the Jewish question was answered with ambiguity and with widely divergent responses. While some Japanese militarists parroted Nazi rhetoric about Zionist conspiracies, others openly welcomed and assisted Jewish refugees and saw them as an asset to the Japanese Empire.

An analysis of the media reveals a conflicted view of Westerners, especially Americans, in the years immediately preceding the Pearl Harbor attack. Of course, a current of anti-American (and anti-Western) sentiment had been present in the Japanese press since the country had been forcibly opened in the mid-nineteenth century, but it escalated after the Japanese invasion of China in 1937. Both the United States and Japan made efforts to ease their strained relations, such as when the USS *Astoria* made a goodwill call on Tokyo in April 1939. From looking at the photographs of smiling US sailors in the pages of *PWR,* few would have thought that two and a half years later, the two nations would be bitter enemies. Both sides made good use of the opportunity to tout the goodwill mission as a sign of improved relations across the Pacific.

5-10. *PWR* 105, 28 February 1940, pp. 18-19. "Shanghai's Palestine."[3]

"The Jewish refugee camp established in the Yangshupu district of Shanghai under Japanese Imperial Army jurisdiction, where some two thousand five hundred refugees lead modest but comfortable lives under our kind protection, is the very image of their original homeland, Palestine.

"Since last autumn, Jewish refugees who are looking for a paradise in which to start life anew, full of a spirit of revitalization, have been seeking out the section of Shanghai we are patrolling. Their numbers, already exceeding ten thousand, are concentrated in the Yangshupu district. They are repairing damaged Chinese houses and building a bustling Jewish town, opening newly refurbished restaurants, sundry goods stores, cafés, haberdasheries, millineries, and so forth. The majority of them still do not have reliable employment. In particular, those who have only just moved to Shanghai face difficulties, and so they are being housed in the refugee camp, where they receive three meals a day.

"Through the kindness of the Imperial Army, this refugee camp was built last spring making use of Chinese houses. Since then, thanks to financial support from charitable organizations around the world, the refugees have been living as a self-governing, self-supporting community with a leader chosen from among themselves. Our important work to build a New Order in East Asia, which they have seen with their own eyes, resonates with their fervent wish for a new life, and they hope to be able to repay our kindness by leaving behind their refugee status as quickly as possible and cooperating in our plan to build the continent [i.e., further develop China]."

(top row, right) The kindergarten and elementary school employs "people who were teachers in Europe."

(top row, center) The large cauldron in the cafeteria kitchen.

(top row, left) The large dining hall in the cafeteria.

(bottom row, right) A cobbler's shop, one of the many new small businesses run from within the camp.

(bottom row, center) The bakery of the cafeteria, which feeds some six thousand five hundred people.

(bottom row, left) Inside the men's dormitory on a rainy day. Photographs: Suzuki Minoru.

11 and 12. *PWR* 62, 26 April 1939. When Japanese Ambassador to the United States Saitō Hiroshi (1886-1939) died suddenly in Washington, D.C., President Roosevelt sent the USS *Astoria* to Tokyo to repatriate his remains, a show of respect that duly impressed the Japanese.

(top, p. 12). "After the sailors finished their visit to Yasukuni Shrine, they crammed in to a lively luncheon held in their honor by the city of Tokyo at the Seiju Garden in Fukagawa."

(bottom) *PWR* put the *Astoria*'s visit on its front cover with the banner "The *Astoria* Links Japanese and American Goodwill."[4] The photograph shows the march of the Japanese honor guard accompanying Saitō's body from the ship. At the bottom right, leading them, is Captain Turner of the USS *Astoria*. According to the caption, the Japanese Navy Band played Chopin's "Funeral March."

The *Astoria*, which participated in the Battle of Midway, was sunk on 9 August 1942 during the Battle of the Solomons. Photograph: Katō Kyōhei.

13-15. *PWR* 62, 26 April 1939, pp. 12-13. Crew members of the USS *Astoria* enjoy sight-seeing in Tokyo.

(top) "The sailors were invited to an Asakusa review hall. All of them applauded wildly at the gorgeous dancing of the beautiful Japanese girls."

(bottom left) "Cherry blossoms, cherry blossoms. A sailor drawn to the cherry blossoms gently presses his lips to the petals."

(bottom right) "Getting off of the wood-burning buses at the Kaminari Gate of Asakusa Temple, they strolled down the Nakamise shopping lane to worship before Kannon [in the Temple's Main Hall]. With surprise in their eyes, they looked up at the world's largest paper lantern [hanging in the Kaminari Gate]." Photographs: CIB.

While these photographs are typical tourist snapshots, the captions contain a distinct subtext on gender. The male American sailors seem to encounter a very feminine, inviting Japan imbued with sensual overtones.

In the Japanese wartime press, the first major anti-Western publicity campaign, called "Guard Against Espionage" (Bōchō), was launched in 1940 alongside the New Order. During the campaign, the press gave spine-chilling details of foreign spies active in Japan, some of them described as attractive women posing as tourists. Soon, everything foreign was equally suspect and tainted. As an article in *PWR* 229 (15 July 1942) warned, "Worshipping foreigners (*gaijin sūhai*) is the first step toward behavior that sells out the nation." Japanese drawn to Western culture were portrayed as disloyal, and the arrest of a Catholic priest on spying charges cast all Christians, including Japanese, in a bad light.[5]

16 and 17. *PWR* 168, 14 May 1941.

(right) This *PWR* cover, with its shadowy figure borrowed from a Hollywood B-film, carries the simple message, "Secrets, Secrets, Don't Leak Secrets." The overlaid lines of phrases, typed in English, heightens the ominous atmosphere. An inside article described one convicted British spy as typing alone in his room at odd hours.

The caption says, "As the arms war, the economic war, the propaganda war, the ideological war, and the configuration of modern war are all becoming more complex, sure enough, the stealthy activities of spies collecting secret information are becoming more artful. A snippet of careless conversation, a little scrap of paper—they sparkle in the eyes of a spy. Therefore, the role we play as warriors of secret-protecting is all the more important."

This issue of the magazine carried a lengthy article on the Kobe Spy Incident.

(left, p. 3) "The Kobe Spy Incident. What sort of espionage did he do? The central figure in the Kobe Spy Incident, the Englishman Woodfield Peters." The photograph is of Peters; the large map of Japan was "found in his possession."

18-23. *PWR* 168, 14 May 1941, pp. 2-3. This article gave a detailed account of Vincent Peters's life in Kobe.

(top row, right) "Peters's passport and permit to stay in Japan." The name on the passport is Mr. Vincent Oswald Woodfield Peters.

(top row, center) "Peters's seven tools. Items in his possession—the extremely cautious Peters carried packed in his valise cooking utensils, always ready to flee at any time or hole up if under siege."

(top row, left) "The exterior of the Fuji Apartment at Shimo Yamate Dōri 2, Kobe, where Peters lived for four months."

(bottom row, right) Two photographs surrounded by a border show Peters's landlady and the room he rented, with a demonstration of his mysterious "hanging milk bottle" habit. The small inset article is called, "Hanging Down a Milk Bottle," which is explained in the text:

"Kishimoto Masako (age forty-nine), landlady at 2-44 Yamamoto Street, Kobe, Peters' apartment until he was arrested aboard the *Taiyō-maru*, talks about him. 'Peters said he worked in trade. He would always leave at 9:10 in the morning, and then come back shortly after noon, then go back out around 1:30 P.M., returning home at 5 P.M. He was very meticulous about the times of his coming and going. He didn't seem to have any friends, but he was cheerful and personable. Still, there were things that struck me as suspicious. He was always typing in the middle of the night. And also, he was buying milk, and he must have arranged it with the deliveryman, because every morning he would hang the bottle by a string from the second floor. One morning I asked him why he did such a strange thing, and he replied that he just didn't want to be a bother to everyone. He was very careful with money, and in everything he was extremely cautious. His meticulousness gave off the smell of a spy."

(bottom row, center) "Interior view of the room at the Fuji rented by Peters."

(bottom row, left) Fujikawa Kumaji, age forty-nine, manager of the Fuji Apartment, where Peters also lived for a few months.

24-30. *PWR* 229, 15 July 1942, pp. 8-9. "Behind the Robes of a Priest, the Eyes of a Spy." An article about a thirty-nine-year-old French Canadian from Quebec, given the pseudonym Martin Fisher, who was arrested in Hokkaidō on 29 December 1940 on suspicion of collecting sensitive information. He was sentenced and on appeal given a three-year prison sentence on 8 November 1941. Among the evidence presented against him was that he received money from Canada, collected picture postcards from every region of Japan, was in possession of a good camera, and received letters in French. A lengthy article described him as a master of disguise, having "perfected the guise of a Dominican priest." This article appeared in conjunction with "Guard Against Espionage Week," 13-19 July.

(right page, top right) The criminal Martin Fisher, now imprisoned in Hokkaidō, for spying.

(right page, top left) The many picture postcards he collected.

(right page, bottom right) An incriminating letter that came from Canada, supposedly containing his orders in coded language.

(right page, bottom left) Celebrating mass.

(left page, top right) The church in Hakodate, Hokkaidō, where Fisher was first assigned.

(left page, top left) A student named Sasamori, from Sanbon-machi, Aomori Prefecture, who talked to officials about Fisher's suspicious activities.

(left page, bottom) A camera he received from one of the faithful.

PWR's thirteen-page article on Vincent Woodfield Peters and the activities of spies in Japan, while one of the longest single articles printed in *PWR*, barely hinted at the military secrets Peters allegedly passed on to British intelligence. Peters's trials were reported, the first of which handed down an eight-year sentence, reduced to five years on appeal. This was further appealed to the Supreme Court.[6] *PWR* failed to mention that British subject James Melville Cox, a Reuters correspondent rounded up along with Peters, died mysteriously in police custody.[7] Peters's landlady, with her intimate knowledge of his comings and goings and his suspicious behavior, had sounded the alarm for the One Hundred Million: foreigners might pretend to be nice, but their friendliness might mask evil intentions. Peters's trial, magnified through the lens of the press, became the trial of all English-speaking foreigners in Japan. And Martin's conviction cast doubt upon the Christian church and its Japanese adherents. The effect of these arrests on Japan's foreign community was chilling. Japanese sympathetic to foreigners or associated with them through work or business came under suspicion.

With the outbreak of the Pacific War, the image of the enemy underwent a major transformation. The press now referred to the United States and Great Britain as the conjoined BeiEi (linking the first Sino-Japanese characters for Beikoku and Eikoku, America and Britain). The two nations were frequently represented by Roosevelt and Churchill in the guise of a greedy banker and a plundering pirate who put selfish interests and hedonistic desires ahead of the welfare of their own people and the Asians they exploited. The United States was Japan's major adversary in the war, and accordingly, Roosevelt was most frequently targeted by Japanese caricaturists. Old Glory, the most emotionally potent of American symbols, was singled out for unusually harsh treatment: the flag was regularly drawn backwards by cartoonists, photographed fallen on the ground, and painted on the crosswalks of city streets so that the One Hundred Million could trample it as they went about their business (see Chapter 9, figure 16).

Cartoons offer fascinating insights into the psychology of the Japanese war effort, and with the outbreak of the Pacific War, *PWR*'s back page began to carry a weekly feature of small, single-panel cartoons, usually focusing on a theme. These small cartoons were windows into Japanese ideas about the war. The majority of these cartoons addressed the liberation of Asia and civilian participation in the war effort, although in the first months of the war, several cartoons, such as those on the theme, "America's Lament," ridiculed the morale of American enlisted men and war workers who lacked "fighting spirit." POWs in particular were seen as beneath contempt. Images of POWs from the first year of the war reflected a peculiar amalgam of incredulity, pity, scorn, and glee, as if the Japanese themselves did not know what to make of them.

Yet even as Allied fighters and war workers were ridiculed for their poor performance at the outset of the war, the Allied sailors and soldiers who gave their lives for their countries were shown a modicum of respect in the press, evident in the black funereal band placed around photographs of sunken enemy ships and their crews (see Chapter 7, figures 23, 25, and 44). The press attributed this respect to Bushido, a Japanese form of chivalry, which required the victor to pay homage to the enemy dead. The other side of the Bushido coin was that those who did not fight to the death were reviled.

31-33. (top) *PWR* 207, 11 February 1942, p. 23. "Shrimp and Snapper," by Yoshigaki Seiten. "These shrimp couldn't catch a red snapper. These 'long-arms' shrimp are in a panic, having snagged their own chins." The humor here depends upon word-play and a knowledge of Japanese culture. Red snapper (*tai*), a fish served at celebrations (New Year's, weddings, and so on), here signifies a victory. "Long-arms" (*tenaga*) is a deformed human being with impossibly short legs and long arms, usually pictured carried by Long-legs (*ashinaga*), a companion with short arms and long legs. Long-arms and Long-legs function by working together. Here, Long-arms Churchill and Roosevelt (competitive, individualistic creatures) are unable to cooperate, and therefore the snapper eludes them. The word-play is found in the word "shrimp," which in Japanese is pronounced *ebi*, a pun on the English letters A and B, which stand for "America" and "Britain." The two Allied leaders were often caricatured as pirates, parasites living by plunder and exploitation. While the cartoon is implicitly critical of Western values (individualism and imperialistic capitalism), its sophisticated humor is specific to Japanese culture.

(middle) *PWR* 210, 4 March 1942, p. 23. "The Fire Has Gone out in the Fireplace," by Koizumi Shirō. Roosevelt laments, "Having spoken of others' shortcomings, my lips feel very cold in the Asian wind, and I can't have a fireside chat with Americans or with people in other countries." Behind him loom large shadows identified as "labor disputes" and "strikes," while his broken-down chair is labeled, "Loss of credibility." He is trying to kindle a fire and burn a crucifix, its significance unclear: it may show a loss of faith in the Christian deity, or perhaps be the grave marker of Roosevelt. This cartoon, one example demonstrating keen awareness of trends in US politics and culture, cites a famous haiku by Matsuo Bashō.[8]

(bottom) *PWR* 338, 13 September 1944, p. 23. "Divine Punishment," by Ishikawa Shinsuke. "Now is the time to put the eight-headed serpent to the sacred sword." A young Asian couple, labeled "small countries," hide in the grass as a Japanese soldier prepares to cut off the head of a giant snake with Roosevelt's face. The human-eating snake has left behind a pile of bones. The cartoon draws upon one of Japan's oldest recorded mythological tales, "The Serpent with Eight Heads."[9]

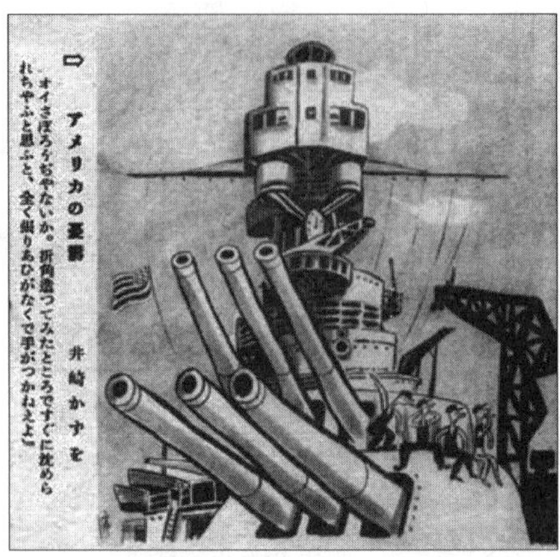

34-36. Three cartoons about low morale. The first two illustrate the theme "American Melancholy." These cartoons suggest that Americans are individualistic and pragmatic to a fault and would rather save their own skins than engage in a losing battle for the sake of their own pride or national honor. In the first stage of the war, as the Japanese blitzkrieg unfolded, the prevailing stereotype of Westerners was that they were egotistical, selfish, and debauched, given over to hedonistic pleasures. Note the inversion of the American flag, the canton (the field of stars) being in the third, rather than the first, quadrant.

(left) *PWR* 203, 14 January 1942, p. 23. "The 'Spirit' of the American Sailor," by Ōno Shūzō.

"Huh. All of the money's gone to the side of Japan's winnings. What kind of game is this?"

(top right) *PWR* 203, 14 January 1942, p. 23. "American Melancholy," by Izaki Kazuo.

"Hey, you guys are laying down on the job."

"Well, when we think about all the trouble we went to building those ships, only for them to be sunk, we know they can't compete, and we lose our concentration."

(bottom right) *PWR* 206, 4 February 1942, p. 23. From a series of cartoons called "Great East Asia War Cartoon Diary," by Ishikawa Shinsuke. The caption says, "American POWs, in the mood to travel, under escort." Presumably, they smile cheerfully because they have saved themselves and not died fighting. That an officer would lead his men into captivity, not into battle, was unthinkable and unpardonable to the Japanese mind.

This cartoon owes much to the form of manga perfected in Edo times, in which the drawing conveyed much of the message. Indeed, this cartoon, with its reverse-orientalist humor, really needs no caption at all: For decades, Westerners traveled to "exotic" Japan and, led by Japanese guides, traipsed through the countryside (represented here by Mount Fuji), some of them writing blatantly racist travelogues. The only such travelers to Japan during the war were POWs. Not until very recently have Japanese been able to easily tour Europe and the United States. With prewar resentment of US exclusionist policies running high, cartoons like this must have felt exhilarating, serving as balm for old wounds.

37 and 38. (top) *PWR* 203, 14 January 1942, p. 23. Another cartoon on the theme "American Melancholy." Satō Toshio titled his cartoon "This Is No Movie," a commentary not only on the cultural dimensions of the conflict in the Pacific, but also on racial stereotyping in Hollywood, where roles for Japanese men were limited to villains and servants. (The late 1930s' sleuth Mr. Moto, on the other hand, was portrayed by a Caucasian actor.) The director supplies the dialogue: "If this were a movie, we could reshoot this scene. Oh, Cut! Cut!"

The physical stereotypes here predate this war, harkening back to earlier encounters between Japanese and Westerners.

(bottom) *Tokyo Puck* (5:26), 1 April 1910, p. 3. This humor magazine, borrowing its name from the famous English publication, printed captions in English and Japanese. The cartoon, "It's a Coward by Dog That Barks," implies that Americans are all talk and no fight. Here is the original English-language caption:

"War, it is a relic of barbarous days, and not a thing which the up-to-date taylor-made [*sic*] gentlemen of American style would dare to tackle. On the other hand, these young fellows in Japanese dress, quiet and unpretentious as they may look, only give them the word and then . . ."

The graphics compare Japanese and Caucasian physiques to canine breeds, noting that the larger, louder dog is not always the better fighter. Wartime rhetoric described Westerners' long, spindly limbs as ill-matched to the squat, solid build of the Japanese male.

Photographic Weekly Report, true to its name, showed a heavy bias toward photographs, which were essential in forming the image of the enemy. The first photographs of the enemy to appear in *PWR* after the outbreak of the Pacific War were those of US Marines recalled from Shanghai in late November 1941. These photographs were given sarcastic, humorous captions when they were published days after Pearl Harbor. The spectacular Japanese blitzkrieg of the early months of the war resulted in the capture of tens of thousands of prisoners-of-war. Since surrender was unthinkable to the Japanese military man, photographs of the enemy POWs were proof of the inferiority of Westerners, who cared more about their own survival than about personal or national honor.

39-41. *PWR* 199, 17 December 1941, pp. 7-8. Three photographs from an article, "American Influence Has Been Driven out of Shanghai."

(top right) "On the pier, a brass band made up of refugee children plays 'Auld Lang Syne' for the departing Fourth Marines,[10] who are unaware that it is really their funeral dirge." The message on the sign appears backwards because it is held up for the departing Marines on board to read and has been photographed from behind.

(top left) "When it was decided the Marines would be recalled [from Shanghai], there was a group wedding for twenty-one couples in one day, for Yankee girls and Shanghai girls, however . . . " Japanese women would never have been shown crying in public when taking leave of their soldier-husbands.

(bottom) "'Hey! Can you hand me my gun? I forget it somewhere over there!' This marine seems to have forgotten how to fight, too." Photographs: [Army] Information Corps, China Section.

42. *PWR* 202, 7 January 1942, p. 18. This is the first photograph of POWs to appear in *PWR*. It illustrated a report on the surrender of Hong Kong. The caption says, "Unable to endure our army's fierce attack, these English POWs gave up. Truly, here is the image of England (*Igirisu*) with its tail between its legs."

The brutal treatment of Allied POWs during the Pacific War marked a major shift in the attitudes of the Japanese press (and military) since World War I, when German POWs were held in Japanese camps. During the Russo-Japanese War, Russian POWs were shown every courtesy, even leniency, and many kindnesses.[11] During the Pacific War, the press published photographs of POWs that lend themselves to many interpretations today, but few contemporary Japanese would have detected in them any sign of the brutal treatment of POWs so well documented elsewhere.[12] Of course, the same press that reported only positive accounts of POWs' treatment also described them as unworthy of the same. As an article in *PWR* 218 (29 April 1942, p. 6) bluntly proposed, "Let's look at the images of the defeated [Westerners] spread out here. And then let's think about why they have become this way. They were the world's wealthy. Proud of having the highest material civilization. Their golden rule was freedom and individualism, but their wives and children were more important to them than [their duty to] their country."

Over two hundred thousand POWs were captured in the first four months of the war, a figure swelled by an additional eighty thousand when Bataan and Corregidor surrendered shortly thereafter.[13] The sheer numbers of POWs meant that treating them in accordance with the stipulations of the Hague and Geneva Conventions would have required an outlay of resources that the Japanese military was loathe to release from its war coffers, especially after suffering through Allied embargoes. Brutal treatment and forced labor reduced the outlay of expense as well as the number of POWs; by war's end, one in four had died and those who were liberated from the camps often required months of care to return them to health.

43. *PWR* 213, 25 March 1942, pp. 6-7. "A Pathetic Scene of Shamelessness—Two Hundred Ten Thousand Enemy POWs."

This short article, translated in its entirety, emphasizes differences between Allied and Japanese soldiers. Photographs of hordes of POWs spoke more loudly about Western cowardice than did cartoons.

"This photograph of POWs taken during the Battle of Singapore barely shows a fraction of them. Among the many remarkable fruits of war our side has reaped since the war began are over two hundred ten thousand POWs. In less than four months, many times the number of enemy soldiers [pictured here], on encountering danger to themselves, regardless of appearances and reputation, immediately laid down their arms and came crawling into our camp [begging for mercy]. And of course, among them are several officers of every rank, men who had heavy responsibilities.

"What a picture of shamelessness. For the officers and men of the Imperial Army, it goes without saying, and for we Japanese [civilians], too, the very thought of [surrender] is physically impossible. But before we spit on them and yell, 'Shameless creatures (*yatsu*)!' we are checked by the humane feeling of pity . . . After all, if we stop and think about the situation, somewhere in a corner of our hearts remains a feeling akin to the perspective and way of thinking of our fellow human beings who, up to this time, were under the control [of the British]. Of course, the proud image of the officers and men of the Imperial Forces who give their 'one life to the nation,' when compared to this ugly photograph, ought to make [these POWs] take a long, hard look at themselves."

The caption says, "The Indian soldiers, on the other hand, may be happy [to be POWs] . . . The Australian soldiers are probably thinking about returning home right away and having a nice drink of liquor . . . Among the English soldiers, there must be some who feel shame, but they are unable to give their lives for the land of their ancestors." Photograph: Army Information Corps.

何を語る俘虜の横顔

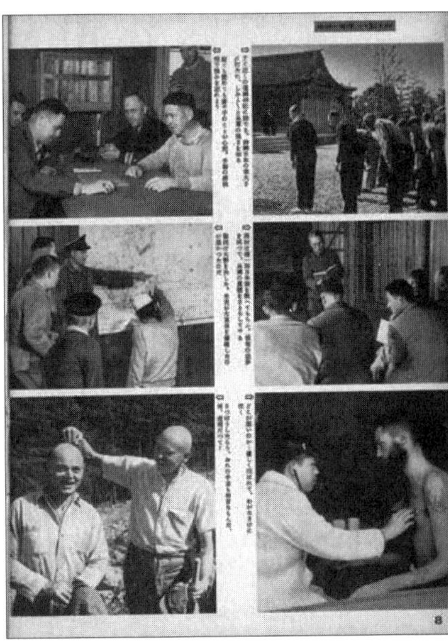

44-50. *PWR* 218, 29 April 1942, pp. 6-8. "What Do They Tell us? POW Profiles. The POW Camp at Zentsūji, Kagawa Prefecture."[14] A series of photographs describing POWs held in Japan and their daily life in a camp set up in a Buddhist temple complex. Conspicuously absent here is any form of work, although photographs in this article (not included here) show the POWs preparing their own food and hoeing a field.

"Some three hundred eighty POWs are being held at the Zentsūji POW Camp, of whom forty-nine are officers. Most of them were taken at Guam. An account of their usual daily schedule is as follows: Rise at 6 A.M., roll call at 6:20, cleaning until 7:20, Breakfast at 7:30, one hour of exercise after 9 A.M., lunch at noon, announcements and bulletins at 2 P.M., one hour of exercise after 3 P.M., supper at 6 P.M., roll call at 6:20, lights out at 9 P.M."

(left page, p. 6) Notable POWs, clockwise from top right: "General Keene, Air Force Commander on Wake Island; navy doctor Thatcher, the famous American optician; Sergeant Taylor, a former platoon commander; Captain Haviland of the sunk *Penguin*; Vendekar, captain of a Dutch submarine; Major Bowden, an English pilot shot down off the coast of Codabal; Thompson, an Australian pilot who was shot down; McMillin, the former governor of Guam and the oldest of the POWs at age fifty-four." The photograph in the center shows the entrance to the camp, guarded by a Japanese sentry.

(right page, top right, p. 8) "They pray at the nearby Gokoku Shrine. Awestruck by the greatness of Japan, Land of the Gods, they quietly come to know the strength of the Imperial Army." In 1940, Gokoku shrines, which existed in Japan for centuries, were placed under the jurisdiction of Yasukuni, serving as local centers for patriotic Shinto during the war.

(right page, center right) "They receive Japanese language lessons once a week from a camp officer. Peeling away their nightmare, they are made to realize the true meaning of the Imperial Army."

(right page, bottom right) "'Where does it hurt,' he asks gently, and the POW weeps at our kindness."

(right page, top left) "Waking and sleeping, they worry about their wives and children. They forget their worries playing chess on a handmade board."

(right page, center left) "The course of the war was decided by America and Britain's wrongful invasion of East Asia."

(right page, bottom left) "'Nice and clean, isn't it? My handiwork's not bad. What, you think it's choppy?'"

51-54. *PWR* 235, 26 August 1942.

(clockwise, from top right)

(top right) The cover article was "Even POWs Perform Service to the Nation, by Building Shōnan Shrine." The cover photograph was explained by this text: "The sacred bridge gracing the approach to Shōnan Shrine is nearly complete. This prisoner of war, enduring the scorching heat, mindlessly moves the paint brush. He forgets about the miserable defeat of his own country and faintly feels something majestic, something Japanese—perhaps that feeling amounts to being sincerely convinced that the history of the New Asia should be this way."

(bottom right, p. 5) Pouring concrete.

(bottom left, pp. 4-5) The pedestrian road leading to the shrine, with the sacred bridge.

(top left, pp. 4-5) The pillars of the shrine.

The article identifies these POWs as British and Australians. Photographs: Army Information Corps, from the Construction Site of Shōnan Shrine.

POWs were featured in cartoons and photographs, as well as in serialized anecdotal accounts in *PWR* such as "A POW in Malaya." War art found rich subject matter in POWs, and several canvases were devoted to panoramas of the defeated. Paintings of POWs are among the most controversial images produced during the war, (despite the majority of them being drawn from photographs), if for no other reason than that they glorified moments of abject humiliation and unchained brutality. The psychological effects of these paintings on wartime Japanese viewers must have been enormous, sweeping away the innumerable slights, both real and perceived, that Japanese had suffered at the hands of Westerners over many decades. By their scale, their skillful execution, and their public nature, these were artworks that enjoined the population to savor the spectacle of the English-speaking world in defeat and decline.

55. "Record of the Ninth of April," by Mukai Junkichi, plate 19 in *Collection of Paintings Recording Army Campaigns in the Great East Asia War*. A short biography of Mukai[15] included in the exhibition catalogue states he was an army artist in the Philippines in 1941 and 1942, implying that this work was drawn from life. The catalogue calls attention to Mukai's use of different colors for the victorious Japanese troops, the "American soldiers who lost the spirit to fight," and the Philippine people who had taken refuge in the jungle and came out to witness "their former oppressors in defeat." The placement of the Japanese guard standing atop wrecked Allied machinery visualizes the common theme that America's matériel strength was no match for the Japanese soldier's superior spirit. The POWs seem to march out of the left and right fields of the frame of the painting, suggesting an infinite line, while the dark foreground enjoins the viewer to watch the march from the elevated perspective of the guard. This work, which also appeared in *PWR* 251 (16 December 1942, p. 5), records the first day of the infamous twelve-day "Bataan Death March."

On 23 July 1942, Japan and the United States exchanged one thousand five hundred diplomatic corps and foreign nationals from each side at Lourenço Marques (today's Maputo), Mozambique. US Ambassador Joseph Grew and members of the US diplomatic corps, as well as members of the foreign press, were among the one thousand five hundred enemy nationals who left Japan.[16] The Japanese media took a benign view of the exchange, which would suggest that, for all of the enmity and ill will between the two nations, diplomacy still existed on some level, at least as long as Japan was winning the war. A second exchange of foreign nationals took place in Portuguese Goa in September 1943, to little media fanfare.

56. "End of the Road for the American Troops in the Solomon Sea"[17] by Fujita Tsuguharu (1943, oil on canvas), reproduced from the *Second Great East Asia War Art Exhibition Catalogue*. It also appeared in *PWR* 302 (22 December 1943, p. 2).

Fujita paints a very grim scene, citing a genre of nineteenth-century Western romantic painting, a small crew adrift in the ocean.[18] Originally, this genre described, allegorically, the universal human condition of needing spiritual guidance. Viewers who identified with the drifting men were thereby encouraged to find faith. Fujita treats the enemy as individuals, rather than as a horde. Each man's posture and expression reveals a different attitude toward his final hours of life. Some seem to recoil with fear and horror at the sight of circling sharks, others seem to have sunken into disbelief or resignation, while one, with a bandaged arm, stands tall with an air of determination, rather ironic given his circumstances. From the vantage point of the present, Fujita's citation of this romantic theme seems multivalent—both sympathetic and mockingly cruel. As an artist who had lived for many years in the West, Fujita may have secretly identified with and felt sympathy for the enemy. However, in the context of Japanese wartime rhetoric, that military men clung to life and were so ill-prepared to die with dignity could only invite unflattering comparisons between Western selfishness and Japan's Bushido code, and Fujita's painting certainly lends itself to this interpretation.

57-59. *PWR* 236, 2 September 1942. The cover story is devoted to the repatriation of Japanese from North and South America.

(top) "The *Asama-maru* docks at Yokohama harbor bearing the white cross" [of a hospital ship].

(bottom right, p. 2) *PWR* carried a lengthy article on the returnees, "A Different Fatherland, a Beloved Motherland: The People Who Returned from the Americas on the Exchange Ship." The article says, in part, "taking their first steps inland from Yokohama are Ambassadors Nomura, Kurusu, and Ishii, who immediately boarded a waiting car and headed to the imperial palace to pay their respects on this felicitous occasion."

(bottom left, p. 4) A full-page photograph showing the joy of families reunited with their loved ones returned from enemy countries in North and South America.

The Japanese image of the enemy underwent an ugly transformation following the Doolittle Raid of 18 April 1942. Sixteen B-25s were launched from the deck of the USS *Hornet*, about 700 miles south of Tokyo. Ten of the B-25s dropped bombs on Tokyo, mostly destroying steel plants, fuel refineries, a train station, and a dock. Some bombs hit a school, a hospital, and a residential area. Yokohama, Nagoya, and Kobe also received some damage. Some ninety factories were damaged in the raid, fifty people were killed and another two hundred fifty wounded. Most of the B-25s landed in China and their crews made their way to safety. A few of the fliers were killed making difficult landings, and eight were captured by Japanese forces in China.

本土空襲の米機乗員

天人ともに許さぬ暴虐

非軍事施設を盲爆

60-62. *Mainichi Great East Asia War Pictorial Report* 12, 8 November 1942, pp. 4-5. "The American Crew That Conducted the Air Raid on the Home Islands. Murderous Bombing That Neither God nor Man Can Forgive." *PWR* did not print photographs of the Doolittle pilots. Mainichi, a publishing giant, printed these photographs in its monthly war pictorial in an article describing the military tribunal in which these bomber crew members were found guilty of committing crimes against humanity.

(right) This uncaptioned photograph is of Lieutenant George Barr, navigator of crew 16 (plane 40-2268) of the Doolittle Raid.

(middle) Uncaptioned here, Carroll V. Glines (*Doolittle's Tokyo Raiders*, p. 311) reproduces this picture with the caption, "Lt. Hite . . . being led blindfolded from a Japanese transport plane after being flown from China to Tokyo." Glines states that the crew was flown to Tokyo on 20 April.

(left) The caption simply says, "The crew of an American airplane [airplane 40-2268 of the Doolittle Raid] who have fallen into our hands." Unidentified here, they are, from left to right, Lieutenant William G. Farrow (pilot), Captain Jacob DeShazer (bombardier), Lieutenant George Barr (navigator), Sergeant Harold A. Spatz (engineer-gunner), and Lieutenant Robert L. Hite (co-pilot). Farrow and Spatz were executed, while the remaining three crew members, sentenced to life terms, were liberated at the war's end.[19] The B-25 (at top of the page) is identified.

The Japanese government had been educating the public about air safety for nearly a decade, but the government and the defenders of the homeland were caught unawares by this daring raid. The press cast the enemy in an entirely new light following the raid: he was now despicable and inhuman, the cold-blooded killer of innocent children and hospital patients. The fate of the eight captured fliers was of considerable concern to both the Japanese and the American press. In Japan, a new law was quickly enacted so that the fliers could be legally tried and punished:

> Those crew members of enemy craft that conduct air raids against areas under control of the Great Japanese Empire and fall under our jurisdiction, in the event they have committed atrocities or crimes against humanity, will be tried by military tribunal and sentenced to death or severe punishment. (*Mainichi Great East Asia War Pictorial Report* 12, 8 November 1942, pp. 4-5)

The eight ill-fated fliers were tried and found guilty, sounding a warning to Allied flyboys to expect no mercy if captured.

> Announcement by the Information Chief of the Imperial High Command
>
> As a result of the interrogation of captured crew members of the US planes that conducted the air raid on the mainland of the Japanese Empire this past 18 April, a military tribunal has shown that they committed crimes against humanity. Severe punishment must now be handed down.
>
> Proclaimed by the Defense Minister, 19 October 1942 (ibid.)

Japanese newspapers and photojournals published "testimony" (from interrogations) presented at the trial of one of the gunners,[20] who was accused of strafing civilian targets, including a school:

> In Tokyo and other places, they deliberately bombed and firebombed non-military facilities, such as hospitals, schools, and homes, and killed noncombatants, in particular innocent children at a Citizens' School. They confessed to doing so, according to their interrogations, presented as testimony at the trial: "There were many children playing in the schoolyard of a Citizens' School, and I suddenly felt the urge to let those little Japs (*kono Jyappu domo*) have a taste of fire, so I quickly dived down and we strafed them with our guns," he testified. By his own admission, he says that he bombed them out of hatred [of Japanese], although they were completely innocent children. How can we help but say that God and man can scarcely forgive such evil, which these crew members acknowledge as normal conduct for them? (ibid.)

The media's account of the motivations of the Doolittle raid also sent a message to the home front: the enemy would show Japanese, even children, no mercy. This message was reinforced by *Life* magazine's nearly simultaneous publication, on 6 April 1942, of photographs of Manzanar, one of the earliest and largest of the Japanese-American internment camps. Japanese stationed in Europe with the diplomatic or press corps must have kept a close eye on the US media, because American photojournals became a major source of evidence of the white man's hatred for people of color. Several such photographs from the US press were reprinted in Japan during the war, some with their original English-language captions.

ぼくらの友達を射殺した米機の仇はきっと討つぞ

63-66. *PWR* 267, 14 April 1943, pp. 6-7. "We Will Have Revenge on the American Planes That Shot to Death Our Friend." An article about a Tokyo school bombed by the Doolittle Raid one year earlier, quoting the testimony of the gunner who "felt the urge to let those little Japs have a taste of fire." The article continues, "At [censored] Citizens' School in Tokyo, where innocent victim Ishide Minosuke was felled by enemy bullets, their indignation—not one bit diminished since that day—has congealed into the desire of the entire student body to fight the war. These darling children are burning with the wholehearted desire to completely shoot down the American planes and avenge the death of Ishide, and those who graduated this year unanimously decided to help boost our war power as youth warriors building airplanes. They are now gallantly flexing their muscles in the army, navy, and private sector airplane factories.

"For those students still enrolled, air raid drills are a curriculum bringing to life the victim's sacrifice, and they demonstrate the determination to shoot down and annihilate America and Britain in their lessons. We see that innocent determination in a composition written by a classmate of the deceased Ishide:

"'Upon the First Anniversary Memorial Service for Ishide Minosuke,' by Suzuki Eisaburō Second Year, Upper Level, [censored] Citizens' School, Tokyo.

"'The sky! The sky! That clear expanse of blue is the sky of righteous Japan!! The sky of the airplanes of righteous Japan!! Yet suddenly, on 18 April, the enemy planes of the devil (*akuma*) appeared in the sacred sky, shot Ishide, and fled. It's too bad [they got away]. What a pity. Minosuke, cut down by the devil's blade, what a pity. Surely, surely, there will be vengeance. Otherwise there will be no end to the indignation raging in my heart! How quickly the days pass, already it is the first anniversary of Minosuke's death. Again today I will clean Minosuke's grave and swear before his spirit, "I will continue to shoot them, I will continue to shoot them" [uchiteshi yamamu]. In no time, we will [graduate and] become members of society, and then, I will go into the Air Force I dream of. Oh, I cannot wait for the day I fly.'"

(far right) "Behind the watchful eyes looking at the sky is a fiery rage: 'Just try to come, American planes.'"

(top left) "They intently study the enemy plane recognition chart. 'This is the ugly plane' the older student tells them, indicating a North American[21] with his pointer."

(bottom center) "His [Minosuke's] *kaimyō* [a Buddhist name given to the deceased] of 'Hiun Jūgeki Zenshi' ['Misfortunate Rifle-shot Virtuous One'] and pathetically new memorial stone silently accuse the enemy, America and Britain, of their atrocities."

(bottom left) "As 18 April approaches, memories of their classmate Ishide float before their eyes, and their hearts are filled with hostility toward the enemy."

67-70. *PWR* 229, 15 July 1942, pp. 18-19. "The American Government Carries Out Forced Relocations. Our North American Compatriots Await the Day of Victory." The poor quality of the images is due to their having been "transmitted by wireless from Berlin to Tokyo." They are credited to *Life* magazine.[22] The brief article is translated here in its entirety.

"Although they were citizens up to the moment the war began, Nisei (second-generation Japanese) residing in America were done this inhuman disservice, along with their fathers and mothers, as soon as the war began. They were forcibly moved to the foothills of the Sierra Nevada Mountains, deep in the California interior, where they are suffering in barracks they built with their own hands.

"Ever since [the United States passed] legislation prohibiting Japanese from owning land and excluding Japanese from immigrating, Nisei have risked their lives protecting the land their parents developed with their bare hands. Although they swore on their very lives their allegiance to America, when the curtain lifted at the beginning of the war, America's attitude toward them was far from what they had expected. There's no mistake about it: the rights of citizenship that America gave to these Nisei were rights they could enjoy in name only. Japanese (*hōjin*) residents of America and Nisei who had no say in the matter of being moved to the isolated interior are now taunting America for its injustice by writing over and over on the walls of the chilly camp, the word 'shame.'"

(topmost) "Our compatriots, forced to quickly build their own barracks at the foot of snowy mountains."

(top left) "Our compatriots take what they can carry to the hastily built barracks."

(middle left) "Loading essentials onto a car, they head for the isolated internment camp."

(bottom left) "Makeshift homes in the camp bear little resemblance to the pleasant lives they led before the war."

マニラの敵國人收容所

71. *PWR* 230, 22 July 1942, pp. 8-9. "Manila's Internment Center for Enemy Nationals." Part of the Santo Tomas University campus was made into this infamous internment camp,[23] here described in contrast to the US internment camps for Japanese-Americans.

"In this war, every nation has built a number of camps corresponding to the number of POWs and enemy nationals. Regarding the treatment of POWs, there are international agreements in place, but regarding the treatment of resident enemy foreign nationals, there is still no such agreement, and every country is worrying about how to deal with them.

"Here are photographs showing the daily life of the over three thousand enemy foreign nationals of America, Britain, and other countries being held in the camp on the campus of Santo Tomas University in Manila. In the section of the campus provided for them, no restrictions are placed on them, and they are supplied with ample food, clean beds, and even recreational equipment. Under our supervision, they are allowed to self-govern their own lifestyle. They can lead carefree lives pursuing their individual pleasures and their personal liberties. Really, for them, adjusting to such a lifestyle should not require much effort. And if they are not truly grateful for such extraordinary treatment shown them by our warriors' sense of humanity, despite their being enemy foreign nationals, then they deserve punishment.

"However, when we compare the feelings of the American and British people detained at the beautiful university campus in Manila to those of our citizens detained in barracks deep in the Sierra Nevada Mountains, we see the enormous difference between the one group, who let us hear them laughing with self abandon when their ancestral land was defeated in war, and the other who, hearing whispers on the wind of their ancestral land continuing to fight and continuing to win, joyfully cheer, 'Banzai!'

"When there must be war, it should be won, a fact we are silently made to realize when visiting the enemy foreign national detention center."

72. *Global Knowledge* (16:6), June 1943, p. 48. "Tyranny and Atrocities in America."

The Detroit race riot of 20-21 June 1943 must have touched a sensitive nerve among Japanese, themselves the victims of prejudice in the United States, where exclusionist legislation passed in 1922 essentially put a halt to Japanese immigration. This short article, translated here in its entirety, does not mention that thirty-four people, twenty-five of them African-American, were killed in thirty-six hours of unrest; nor does it translate the large billboard. The source of the photographs is not named.

"Recently, America has fallen into an acute housing crisis. In Detroit's suburbs, several housing units are being built, which are advertised as available to rent to the general public. Negroes (*niguro*) are also supposed to be able to rent these apartments, but despite their best efforts to negotiate [with city hall], they are not allowed to move in. After some time, the situation finally erupted into a riot so violent that the mounted police were called out. They drew their pistols and shots were fired to put down the riot. This is America, which hollers about freedom and equality every time it opens its mouth. What can we say about this actual incident of tyranny and atrocity but 'you demon-bastards.'"

The second year of Japan's war against BeiEi, America and Britain, saw offensive turn to defensive. The Doolittle Raid remained an isolated incident, but the wholesale slaughter of Japanese troops was under way. The government was frustrated by military setbacks and the press fixated upon American racist policies against its citizens of Japanese descent and African-Americans. On the Japanese home front, shortly before the Uchiteshi Yamamu Campaign was launched, the entire nation was purified by purging every last vestige of enemy influence: English-language signboards, product labels, and music originating from the English-speaking countries of the world. *PWR* 257 (3 February 1943) was devoted to this purification campaign. Every instance of "enemy culture" was to be erased from daily life. Packaged products with labels incorporating English were still luxury items for many Japanese, and the home front was now to do without them, ostensibly because they "reeked of the enemy." *PWR* had accepted advertisements for items brandishing English on their labels in its first two years of publication, and even in the weeks before the war began, *PWR* titled an article about Tokyo girls bringing presents of toys and books to farming villages, "Santa Claus [Santa Kurōsu] Comes to a Farming Region." By 1943, such days were long gone.

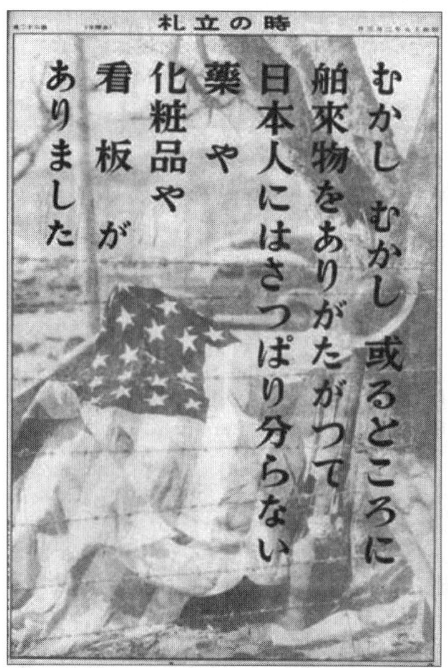

73 and 74. *PWR* 257, 3 February 1943.

(right) "Completely Erase Every Trace of America and Britain." In the window of the "CHINATOWN" brothel a sign proclaims in English: "50 Sen Only! For the Fair Girls' Service. The [illegible] bright and sentimental saloon is the highest restorative for the weary!" The caption reads, "With its signs written horizontally, what on earth is this shop selling? This shop is not in London or New York, but right here in our very own Japan. Who do they think their customers are? While we are in an eat-or-be-eaten war with America and Britain, why should we allow the existence of a business with such signage and décor, prostituting itself to America and Britain?"

(left, p. 2) "Signboard of the Times 62. Once upon a time, there was a place where imported items were gladly received, and there were medicines, cosmetics, and shop signs completely unintelligible to Japanese." The same photograph was used for the cover of *PWR* 218 (see Chapter 7, figure 52).

75. *PWR* 257, 3 February 1943, pp. 4-5. "Let's Deploy American and British Records [in the War Effort]."

"With American and British jazz still ringing in our ears, and American and British images still reflected in our retinas, our bodies still reek of American and British odors. Therefore, in order to win against America and Britain, we must stop prostituting ourselves to the enemy, wash out our ears, rinse our eyes, and cleanse our hearts. As unpolluted Japanese, making a fresh start is our top priority."

The two-page collage includes two photographs of people turning in records of "enemy music" and two cartoons. In the upper right corner, Roosevelt leads a band with the US army insignia on the drum. Mortar shells seem to be launched from the bells of the musical instruments. At bottom left, an archetypical father uses records for bayonet practice as mother and son urge him on.

The cartoons and photographs are set upon a smashed Victor Japan record of Leo Reisman and Orchestra playing W. C. Handy's "St. Louis Blues." A stylishly dressed couple fall into the chasms of the shattered record.

This issue of *PWR* contained a four-page list, arranged by manufacturer and serial number, of one thousand one hundred records of enemy music to be handed over to the authorities. Among the banned songs were "Auld Lang Syne," a tune known in Japan as "The Firefly's Light," with Japanese lyrics. This tune, still popular in Japan today, is often played a few minutes before businesses, bars, and restaurants close for the night as an announcement of closing time.

76. *PWR* 257, 3 February 1943, pp. 6-7. "Let's Eradicate Every Trace of America and Britain from Shop Signs."

"These are certainly not shop signs in New York or London. No, they are displayed on the streets here in Japan. Although we are now fighting against America and Britain, our cities are inundated with these horizontal [English-language] signs . . . is it not necessary to put an end to signs that curry favor with America and Britain?"

The caption describing the column of "before and after" photographs at far left says, "The local council decided to remove all signs of America and Britain from Yokohama's Benten Street, formerly a shopping street catering to American and British customers, and repainted all of the signs with nationalistic slogans. Here are some examples."

Two shops (top and bottom) have had their signs replaced with the slogans "Great East Asia Fights on to Victory" and "Keep at it, the Enemy Is Desperate."

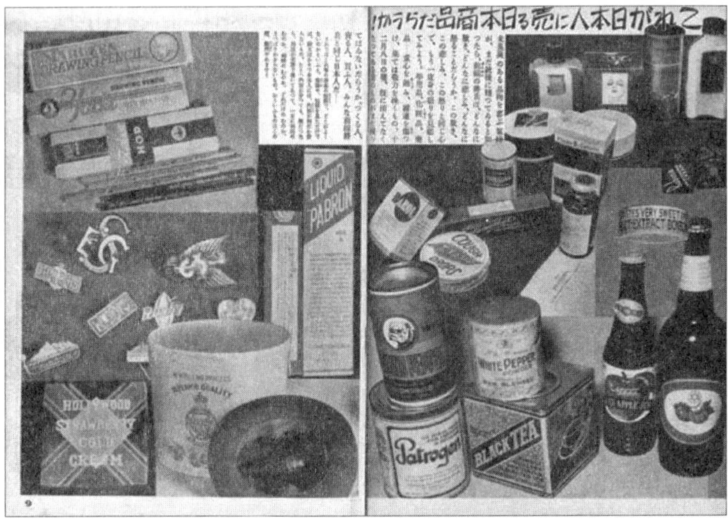

77 and 78. (top) *PWR* 257, 3 February 1943, pp. 8-9. "If the troops fighting at the front knew that even now there are people on the home front who feel happy to have items that reek of America and Britain, imagine how shocked, saddened, and angered they would be. With the same shock, sadness, and anger, take a look around you for these items. School supplies, cosmetics, pharmaceuticals . . . like a rot on innocent young minds, like a stain on wifely virtue, they hamstring our war power, these things that should have disappeared on the morning of 8 December, but are somehow still here. And the people who make them, the people who sell them, the people who buy them, are just as Japanese as the men on the front are . . ."

On both pages are various food products, pharmaceuticals, and cosmetics, while at the top of the right page are pencils and in the center of the page are a collection of lapel pins, most of them probably from extracurricular activities. The products include several brands still in existence today (Bulldog, Nikka, Pablon, Maruzen, Tombow), and some items that were advertised in *PWR* in its first years. In reality, these items had mostly disappeared from store shelves by this time.

(bottom) *PWR* 25, 3 August 1938, p. 23. Meiji, a major foodstuffs company, advertised Western foods with English-language labels in *PWR*. This half-page ad was for "Milk Oats" (*miruku ōtsu*) oatmeal, at a time when dairy products were luxury items rarely consumed by most Japanese, especially in rural areas.

病院船うらる丸がうけた
米機鬼畜の所業の跡
17

79. *PWR* 272, 19 May 1943, p. 17. "Scars on the Hospital Ship *Ural-maru* (Uraru-maru),[24] Attacked by American Planes, the Handiwork of the Demon-bastards."

"Crying over their defeats, America and Britain are exhibiting their barbaric nature, even making illegal attacks on hospital ships. On 29 October 1942 it was the *Ikaru-maru*. Since the beginning of this year, seven ships [have been attacked]: on 4 January the *Arabia-maru* (Arabiya-maru), on 30 January the *America-maru* (Amerika-maru), on 4 March the *Manila-maru* (Manira-maru), on 3 April the *Ural-maru*, less than two weeks later on 15 April the *Fusō-maru*, and on 25 April the *Buenos Aires-maru* (Buenosu Airesu-maru).

"The *Ural-maru* was attacked by a Boeing B-17 about 7.5 miles SSW of Bechangi Point in the South Pacific. Despite the *Ural-maru* having the proper designations and being painted according to international treaties, the enemy planes deliberately circled and confirmed the ship's status, only to savagely attack it. A hole 5 meters [16 feet] in diameter was opened in its third hold, which was riddled with more than one hundred shell marks and two hundred bullet holes. Four holes were opened on the second deck, twisting the beams of the hospital rooms and shamelessly forcing out the war dead. This photograph shows only a small part of the fresh damage done at that ghastly hour.

"The incomprehensibly cruel disservice done to our compatriots residing in America, the atrocity of brutally strafing to death innocent schoolchildren at the time of the [Doolittle] air raid, using tanks to crush to death the wounded heroes of our army on Guadalcanal[25]—there are more incidents illustrating the demon-bastard nature of the enemy than we can count, absolutely more than can ever be forgiven."

The Japanese media reported that several Japanese hospital ships were strafed and attacked by US planes in the first months of 1943. This latest atrocity was added to the growing list of incidents that showed the "demon-bastard" nature of America. Even these incidents, however, would pale in comparison to what 1944 would bring. With the fall of Saipan, Japan braced for attacks on the Home Islands. Blood-curdling tales of American barbarity and extreme cruelty toward Japanese, alive and dead, served as warnings to Japanese everywhere: better to die fighting against the American monsters than to die a humiliating, excruciating death in their hands. A few months before the Battle of Saipan, *Asahigraph* printed some of the most vicious press attacks on America. In this regard, *Asahigraph* outdid *PWR* in the final year and a half of the war.

80. *Asahigraph* (42:8), *Great East Asia War Report* 112, 1 March 1944, p. 3. This article, "Shoot! These Demon-Bastards! A Close Look at Atrocities Committed by the Enemy, America," appeared at the time of the second Uchiteshi Yamamu Campaign. The front cover reprinted the Uchiteshi Yamamu slogan and an even larger one proclaiming, "Shoot! The demon-bastard America!"

This article explains that the phrases "Kill you Jap? Kill the Jap!!" are "the way they say 'kill Japanese.'" The caption identifies the map at the top as Rabaul, copied directly from the pages of *Life* magazine, in which the repeated use of the word "Jap" is clearly visible. In the center is "Our evil enemy Roosevelt, who frets over the 'implementation' of the East Asian general counter-offensive, because he is aiming at a fourth term in office as president."

At the bottom of the page are the "Three men [leading] the enemy, America's, counter-attack." From right to left: Admiral Halsey, Admiral Nimitz, and General MacArthur.

Asahigraph's in-depth report on American atrocities began by presenting evidence, from the American press, of American's hatred of Japanese:

> The enemy, America, has turned to a fierce, large-scale counter-offensive, citing the general consensus, which is that animosity and hatred toward Japan is running rampant. [America's] leaders, too, at the time the war broke out, swore to "wipe the Japanese off the face of the earth"—[this boast] is not merely propaganda (*senden*), it is the unattainable goal they cherish at the bottom of their hearts.
>
> We cannot forget that they [America's leaders] have made use of every available opportunity to drill slogans inciting hatred of Japan and Japanese into the hearts of the masses.
>
> "Buy Bonds, Kill Japanese," "Save Paper, Kill Japanese," they say.
>
> And the masses call Japanese "Japs," and "Yellow Monkeys."[26] In their daily conversation, in place of "good morning," they now mouth the words, "kill you Jap."
>
> The photojournal *Life*, which boasts a circulation of four million, published a photograph of a helmeted human skull atop a destroyed tank with the explanation, "Japanese army bones placed on top of an incinerated Japanese army tank by the American army." In the 30 November 1943 edition of the *New York Daily News*,[27] an editorial brazenly proposed, "If poison gas is a weapon that inflicts mortal damage, then we should use it against Japan."
>
> Who was it that bombed and shot at a hospital ship? Who was it that despicably killed our wounded soldiers on Guadalcanal by placing them beneath the tread of a tank and running them over?
>
> Let's look directly at the cruel, barbaric nature of demon-bastard America, and let our fighting spirit and martial determination burn bright as fire. To lose this war would mean that Japan would certainly cease to be.
>
> Shoot! These demon-bastards!! (*Asahigraph* [42:8], *Great East Asia War Report* 112, p. 3)

The same article commented acerbically on the internment of people of Japanese ancestry in the Allied nations, particularly in the United States, while noting that the Bushido code of honor bound the Japanese military to treat internees justly and leniently.

> [Cordell] Hull, Secretary of Defense of the enemy, America, in agreement with British Foreign Secretary [Anthony] Eden, made an announcement about the "Japanese army's barbaric acts" toward enemy POWs and detainees, issuing general mobilization orders for American and British newspapers and radio stations to inaugurate a massive propaganda campaign slandering Japan.
>
> For our part, based on the ancient Japanese code of Bushido, we treat enemy POWs justly and noncombatants as leniently as possible, which has been common knowledge worldwide since the time of the Russo-Japanese War. Nevertheless, the enemy is perpetrating baseless propaganda and making of it a convenient excuse for indiscriminate bombing of the Japanese Home Islands.
>
> In light of their slander and fabrications, how do they explain the persecution of Japanese interned in the enemy lands?
>
> One example is enough to answer the question. Upon the outbreak of the Great East Asia War, eighteen thousand Japanese living in Davao, in the Philippines, were forced at the gunpoint of American soldiers into American military facilities, where they received only a daily handful of rice and salt. The number of Japanese who were massacred there reached fifty-six.[28]
>
> The more than two hundred thousand of our compatriots in the United States struggling to live in internment camps are oppressed by the American military and the American authorities. Since the war began, six Japanese men and women residing in California have met their ends at the hands of mob violence, and three other Japanese have been similarly injured. However, despite our side lodging protests on three occasions, American authorities have, to this day, put off arresting the culprits. (*Asahigraph* [42:8], *Great East Asia War Report* 112, p. 7)

Asahigraph's litany of US atrocities revived the *Life* magazine story of April 1942 about Japanese internees in American camps, adding to it photographs from an International Red Cross report. This time, a small piece on US attacks on Burmese villagers was included, illustrated by a photograph of a fleeing, naked child that anticipates photographs of the Vietnam War a quarter-century later.

81-85. *Asahigraph* (42:8), *Great East Asia War Report* 112, 1 March 1944, pp. 6-7. "The Enemy Continues Its Maltreatment of POWs, and Persecutes our Interned Compatriots."

(right page, top) "Japanese (*hōjin*) living on the West Coast of the United States held in internment camps in the interior. Photograph from *Life* magazine."

(right page, bottom right column) "Our compatriots, forced to collect firewood at an internment camp in the American interior. Three photographs from the official journal of the International Red Cross."

(right page, bottom left column) "[top] Deep in snow, an internment camp for Japanese in Canada. [bottom] Cramped quarters of an internment camp in New Zealand." These two photographs are not credited.

(left page, top) The slogan "Uchiteshi Yamamu" is at far left. The English-language title is copied exactly (even the type font) from *Life* magazine, as is the caption beneath this photograph: "Morning wind sends dust swirling down Owens Valley as first Jap internees carry their luggage to dormitories where they will live till [*sic*] end of war." A Japanese caption is added to this: "Japanese residing on the American West Coast, who have been sent to this camp in the interior, carry heavy luggage."

(left page, bottom) "They Even Persecute Innocent Natives." The caption says, "Burmese Living Along the Border Chased Out." The short inset article explains, "The American, British, and Indian Armies teeming along the Burmese-Indian border are diligently working at a counter-offensive campaign, forcing the natives living along the border to flee and massacring those who are friendly toward the Imperial Army. These natives are forced to flee with nothing but the clothes on their backs, driven across the feverishly hot, steep, disease-infested Arakan Range into India. How long will it be before these native people, whose eyes have been filled with scenes of bitterness and hatred, can return to their homes?"

Reeling from the loss of Saipan, in August 1944 the Japanese media seized upon an infamous *Life* magazine "human interest" photograph as proof that US troops' hatred of the Japanese led to desecration of the dead. The *Life* photograph claimed to show the skull of a dead Japanese soldier with a note carved into it by a marine, who sent it to his sweetheart. The Japanese press may have intended the *Life* photograph to serve as an indirect explanation of the mass civilian suicide at Saipan, since it conveyed the message that the fate of those captured alive by the "demon-bastard Yankees" would be too horrific to contemplate.[29] The underlying racism inherent in such trophies—in which human remains were treated no better than hunting trophies, souvenirs, or grotesqueries—needed no explanation to Japanese audiences familiar with the limited and demeaning roles historically assigned Asians in Western societies and as reflected in Western culture, Hollywood films in particular. The press widely disseminated this *Life* photograph, which appeared in the *Asahi Newspaper* on 11 August 1944 (p. 3) under the caption, "Completely Slaughter the American Ogres."

When air raids came to the Japanese Home Islands, they were received stoically as confirmation of the inhuman, barbaric nature of the American enemy. The objective not to harm civilians, stated by General Curtis LeMay and printed by the US military in leaflets dropped over Japanese cities, was contradicted by the numbingly horrific reality witnessed on the ground. The incendiary attacks on large urban areas were scientifically designed to create firestorms trapping and incinerating people by the tens of thousands. During the war, the Japanese press never released air raid casualty figures, but from the scale of destruction evident in the photographs printed in *PWR* and *Asahigraph*, thousands of deaths could be assumed. (Air raid photographs appear in Chapter 12.)

86. *PWR* 335, 23 August 1944, p. 2. This infamous photograph originally appeared in *Life* magazine (16:21), 22 May 1944.[30] *PWR* placed a black funereal border around the photograph as a sign of respect. The caption is translated here in full.

"The sacred bones of our brave heroes should be enshrined at Yasukuni, but once they have fallen into the hands of the devil-bastards, they tragically become the ideal souvenirs for [the GIs'] girls. Roosevelt, who was pleased to receive a paper cutter carved from a sacred bone [of a fallen Japanese soldier], had to return it after being roundly rebuked by public opinion. There's no point in mincing words: The Yankees are revealing their true nature, that of devil-bastards. All we can do is vow to go over to the US mainland and take back these sacred bones."

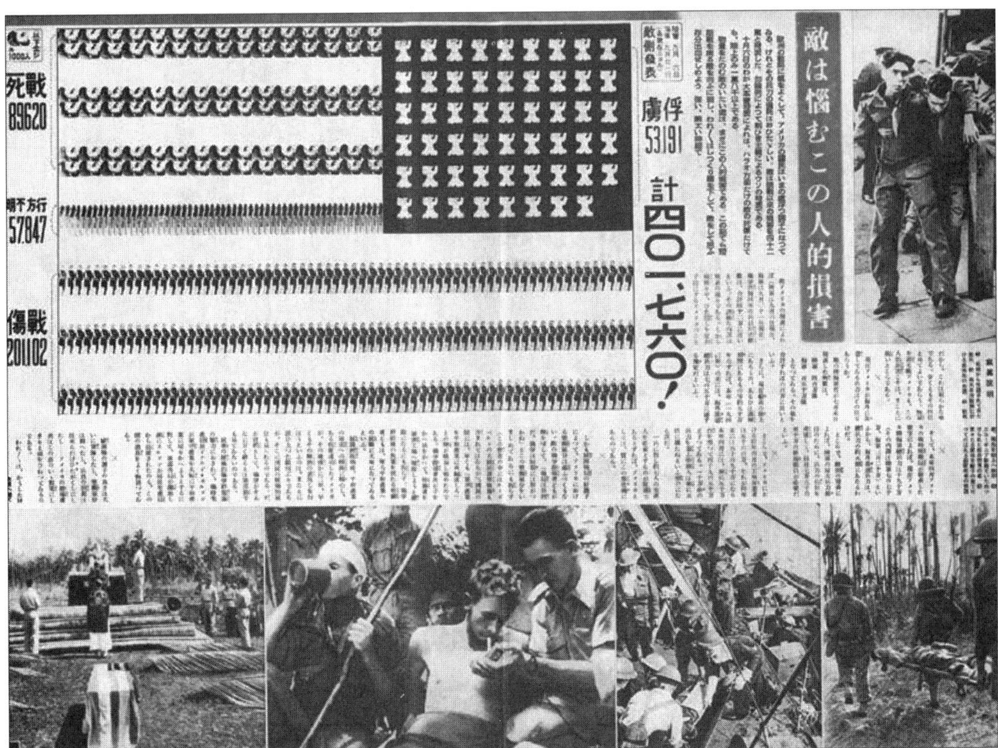
敵は悩むこの人的損害

戦死 89620

行方不明 57847

戦傷 201102

俘虜 53191

計 四〇一、七六〇!

87-92. *Asahigraph* (43:16), *Great East Asia War Report* 145, 18 October 1944, pp. 8-9. "The Enemy Is Worried by These Casualties." The article reads, in part:

"The American people have a good feeling about the war in Europe, and these days they are buoyant. However, they are suffering tremendous losses of military personnel. The [American] enemy announced that since the war began, they have suffered four hundred twenty thousand casualties. Of course, the announcement is a lie because, depending on the case, they use a discounting principle (*waribikishūgi*) [to lower the numbers].

"According to an announcement made on 6 October by our Imperial High Command, in the Palau region alone, enemy casualties have been above eighteen thousand since they landed there.

"The enemy, calling for [an increase] in the amount of matériel, is already suffering from these personnel losses. In this regard, when we take on such an enemy who grows impatient even when fighting a short-term war, we know that we should dig in and make the enemy bleed to our heart's content. We, with our strong nerves of steel." The photographs are all of US soldiers.

(clockwise, from top right)

(top right) "Soldiers being sent back from the front line."

(bottom row, far right) "Transporting the wounded on a front in the South Pacific."

(bottom row, right) "War dead and injured being loaded onto a ship."

(bottom row, left) "Battle fatigue is evident among soldiers being pummeled on the New Guinea front."

(bottom row, far left) "Funeral for enemy war dead, their palm-frond wrapped corpses piling up one after the other."

(top left) An inverted American flag made of personnel losses. The "stars" are made of POWs (numbering 53,191), the symbol being a man on his knees with his hands in the air. The "stripes" are, from top to bottom, deaths (89,620), represented by a casket and cross; missing-in-action (57,847), represented by a man with a veil covering his face; and wounded (201,102), represented by a man with a bandaged arm and leg.

93. *Asahigraph* (44:11), *Great East Asia War Report* 165, 14 March 1945, p. 5. "The Bleeding of the Enemy Escalates; American Forces Suffer Unprecedented Personnel Losses in their 'War of Quantitative Strength' (*butsuryō sakusen*)." This article relates official US military reports released in the spring of 1945 admitting that US fatalities in World War II had reached one hundred sixty-eight thousand, a figure forty-three thousand higher than the total number of US fatalities suffered in World War I. The article argues that the "war of quantitative strength" waged by the United States depended on deploying superior numbers of men and materiél to bring the war to a quick conclusion, a strategy destined to fail because the American public would not tolerate the high loss of life. The article quotes "Associated Press reporter with the US army Edmund Waite who, reporting on the high price being paid in blood, stated that 'In the three days since the commencement of the Iwo Jima Campaign, the US Marines are losing three men every minute,' which has thrown American citizens into a state of extreme anxiety." The article concludes that "The US military, which has encountered a torrent of bloodshed running from Attu to Iwo Jima, will give the citizens the impression that [the Battle of] Iwo Jima is a victory, supposing they can seize the island, but they will be unable to avoid even greater casualties if they continue to fight against Japan. The casualty rate will upset American citizens' will to continue the war, and the military may not be able to smooth over the public's unrest."

(top) "Row after row of graves of American war dead in Tobruk, [North] Africa."

(bottom right) "American and British wounded being sent from the front in northern Italy."

(bottom left) "The hot sand of the South Seas stained by the vile blood of fallen American soldiers." This famous image, published in *Life* on 20 September 1943, was the first to break the American taboo against publishing photographs of the dead during World War II.[31]

By the spring of 1945, the ordinary Japanese citizen had no reason to doubt that all of the faces of the enemy had merged into one—that of an unspeakably inhuman, bloodthirsty beast. Those Japanese on the home front who lived to tell of the wanton, calculated torching of entire neighborhoods and cities surely harbored the desire to see the monster bleed, and this bloodlust was answered with photographs of dead US servicemen. One of these published photographs was a clear violation of the Hague and Geneva Conventions prohibiting desecration of the enemy dead. If the Japanese media had demonized and dehumanized the enemy, especially America, in the first years of the war, then it was a demonic and inhuman face the United States showed the Japanese home front in the final months of the war. Not until the Occupation was well under way would the people of Japan see a different side of Americans.

94. *Asahigraph* (44:18), *Great East Asia War Report* 168, 5 April 1945, p. 11. "Grave of the Despicable Planes." The caption to the gruesome photograph at the top of the page simply states, "These enemy crew members met a terrible death, having been crashed into by one of our 'body-ramming' heroes."

At this point in the war, kamikaze planes sometimes rammed B-29s in midair. The photographs on the bottom half of the page show debris and wreckage of an unidentified American bomber, presumably that carrying the two dead fliers. The article gives no information about where this crash took place or who these dead fliers were. Their corpses are presented merely as evidence of the article's inflated claim that "recently, on the average 50 percent or more of the enemy raiders in each raid are being shot down or damaged."

In this author's examination of thousands of Japanese wartime photojournals, this is the only instance of a published photograph denigrating the enemy dead.

Notes

1. The standard work on this topic, John Dower's *War Without Mercy: Race and Power in the Pacific War* (New York: Pantheon, 1987), gives detailed analysis of Japanese caricatures of the enemy (pp. 234-261). Although hundreds of caricatures of Roosevelt and Churchill were created during the war, this chapter (in keeping with this book's selection criteria) does not treat them at length because Japan's photojournals and newspapers devoted little precious space to Allied leaders and caricature. The photographic medium, assigned the role of documenting and recording the war, took precedence. Furthermore, in striking contrast to its American counterpart, from early in the war the Japanese press created and published many photographs of captured enemy combatants and civilians. Of course, photographs never made the cartoon (or, more broadly, artwork) obsolete or superfluous.

2. The Japanese here is *tero hannin*, the word for "terrorist" being an English loanword, anticipating the postwar trend to apply English words to social problems such as the homeless (*hōmuresu*).

3. For more information on the well-documented Jewish community in Shanghai see Marvin Tokayer and Mary Swartz. *The Fugu Plan: The Untold Story of the Japanese and the Jews During World War II* (New York: Paddington Press, 1979); and David Kranzler, *Japanese, Nazis, and Jews: The Jewish Refugee Community of Shanghai, 1938-1945* (New York: Yeshiva University Press, 1976).

4. The United States was repaying a Japanese diplomatic gesture. In 1926, the Japanese government repatriated the body of US Ambassador to Japan Edgard A. Bancroft on a Japanese battleship.

5. Wilfred Fleisher (*Volcanic Isle* [New York: Doubleday, Doran: 1941], pp. 125-126) notes that at the same time, the Japanese Christian leaders of the Salvation Army in Japan were arrested and only released on the proviso they sever ties with the British Salvation Army, no longer receive financial support from abroad, and repatriate all foreigners in their employ. The crackdown on Christians led to a "reform" of Christian churches in Japan, which could no longer belong to non-Japanese entities.

6. Otto Tolischus notes that Peters was sentenced to five years in prison for violating the Military Secrets Protection Act in February 1941, evidently the result of the appellate trial. See *Tokyo Record* (New York: Reynal and Hitchcock, 1943) p. 11. No documents have come to light regarding Peters's fate.

7. Donald Read, in *The Power of News: The History of Reuters, 1849-1989* (New York: Oxford University Press, 1992) concludes that Cox most likely committed suicide. Wilfred Fleisher, longtime publisher of the *Japan Advertiser* (later the *Nippon Times* and *Japan Times*), writing in 1941, provides an account of Cox's death suggesting that hallucinogens were used to induce a suicidal state. Fleisher notes that the Japanese press did report on Cox's death, reproducing the "suicide note" Cox composed while in police custody, which Cox's wife and the British Embassy found to be highly suspicious (*Volcanic Isle,* pp. 307-310). According to Bergamini, fourteen of the fifteen Britons arrested on espionage charges were released and expelled from Japan (*Japan's Imperial Conspiracy* [London: Panther, 1972], p. 720).

8. The haiku of Bashō referenced here is: *Mono ieba / kuchibiru samushi / aki no kaze* ("Speaking of [people's] shortcomings, the lips feel cold, in the autumn wind." In other words, if we criticize others, we end up alone.) In this cartoon, the poem becomes *Mono ieba / kuchibiru samushi / Ajia no kaze*: Roosevelt, having spoken critically of Asia (that is, Japan), has lost his supporters in light of the crushing defeats of the early months of the war.

9. *Yawata no orochi*, translated by Basil Hall Chamberlain as "The Serpent with Eight Heads" in Hasegawa's series of *Japanese Fairy Tales* (Tokyo, 1886).

10. The Fourth Marines were stationed in Shanghai in 1927 to protect American interests in the International Settlement. They were ordered to evacuate on 10 November 1941. They left Shanghai on 27 and 28 November and were reassigned to the Philippines, where they became defenders of Corregidor. Their current home base is Okinawa.

11. One example is Eliza Ruhamah Scidmore's *As the Hague Ordains: Journal of a Russian Prisoner's Wife in Japan* (New York: Henry Holt, 1907). Scidmore's account of her Russian husband's time as a POW in Japan, illustrated with photographs of actual POW facilities, fairly glows with praise for the very civilized Japanese.

12. The best overviews of abuses of Allied POWs are Gavan Daws, *Prisoners of the Japanese: POWs of*

World War II in the Pacific (Scranton, PA: William Morrow, 1994); and Laurence Rees, *Horror in the East: Japan and the Atrocities of World War II* (New York: Da Capo, 2001).

13. These figures for captured Allied personnel include Indians, Filipinos, and other Asians, many of whom were released by the Japanese and not held in camps. Dower (citing the Tokyo Judgement in *War Without Mercy*, p. 41) notes that 27 percent of 132,134 Westerners taken prisoner by the Japanese died in captivity.

14. For additional information on the POWs held at Zentsūji, see the highly informative Web site of Roger Mansell, Director of the Center for Research, Allied POWs Under the Japanese: www.mansell.com/pow_resources/camplists/osaka/Zentsuji/zentsuji.htm. The Web site includes five photographs, some from a wartime German publication now in the collection of the National Archives, and a complete roster of the men held at Zentsūji confirming these names and ranks: Campbell Keene, Commander, USN; Sergeant Jacob Eugene Taylor, CWT, USN; James W. Haviland, Lieutenant, USN; William E. Bowden, First Lieutenant, RAF; R. Thompson, First Lieutenant, RAAF; George J. McMillin, Captain USN and Governor of Guam. Additional information on POWs at Zentsūji can be found in Joseph Rust Brown, *We Stole to Live* (Cape Girardeau, MO: privately printed, 1982).

15. Born in Kyoto, Mukai (1901-1995) studied art in Europe in the late 1920s. Today he is remembered for his "life work" (begun in 1945), an artistic recording of Japan's diminishing number of traditional thatched-roof farmhouses. His atelier in Setagaya Ward, Tokyo, is now a museum devoted to this "life work," with a Web site providing a biographical sketch and information (in English) on his postwar work: www.mukaijunkichi-annex.jp/main_e/index.htm. The Web site is silent about his war art.

16. *New York Times* correspondent Otto D. Tolischus, repatriated aboard the *Asama-maru*, gives a vivid account of the voyage in *Tokyo Record*, pp. 381-404.

17. In the collection of the National Museum of Modern Art, Tokyo, the work is on "indefinite extended loan" from the United States, one of many works of Japanese war art from the US National Archives.

18. Mark H. Sandler offers an insightful discussion of this work in "A Painter of the 'Holy War': Fujita Tsuguji and the Japanese Military," in Marlene J. Mayo and J. Thomas Rimer, eds. with H. Eleanor Kerkham, *War, Occupation, and Creativity: Japan and East Asia, 1920-1960* (Honolulu: University of Hawai'i Press, 2001), pp. 188-211. Sandler notes that "I am not alone in recognizing Fujita's debt to a corpus of celebrated shipwreck pictures by French Romanticists. Tanaka Jō, in his biography of Fujita, points to Gericault's *Raft of the Medusa* (1818-1819) and Delacroix's *Bark of Dante* (1822) and *Shipwreck of Don Juan* (1841) as likely sources for the Solomon Sea painting. Curiously, Tanaka fails to mention the most obvious model for the work, Delacroix's *Christ Asleep during the Tempest*" (p. 204). Regarding the Solomon Seas painting, Sandler provocatively asks, "Who is this embattled man, uncowed by his predicament, with features that are neither purely Caucasian nor Japanese?" Sandler posits the "possibility that Fujita privately projected himself [as the standing man] among the disciples in a painting celebrating victories by the 'divine soldiers' of Japan" (p. 204). Such an interpretation would have been unlikely among the contemporary readership of *PWR*, of course. In the English tradition, too, there are also several possible sources for Fujita's Solomon Seas canvas: John Collier's 1881 painting *The Last Voyage of Henry Hudson*; early nineteenth-century lithographs of Captain Bligh cast adrift by mutineers; and most directly, Frank Beard's late 1890s allegorical "Adrift," which places a worried old man in an oarless boat in a sea marked "Agnosticism" pursued by a shark labeled "fate," itself suggesting a commentary on Delacroix that Fujita may have cited here with his shark-infested waters.

19. See Carroll V. Glines, *Doolittle's Tokyo Raiders* (New York: Van Nostrand Reinhold, 1981), pp. 305-312, for Barr's account of their mission, and pp. 342-377 for details of their captivity and the war crimes trial of their handlers. For photographs of these crew members, see pp. 306, 311, and 372. DeShazer became a missionary and returned to Japan, where he spent over thirty years. One million copies of his account of his wartime experience, "Watakushi Wa Nippon No Horyo Deshita" ("I Was a Prisoner of the Japanese," Bible Meditation League, 1948), were printed and distributed in Japan. According to the Doolittle Raiders Remembered Web site MSN Group (www.doolittleraid.com/raiders.htm), DeShazer and Hite are among fourteen surviving Raiders at the time of this writing (April 2007).

20. The trial transcripts attribute this "testimony" to Farrow. See Carroll V. Glines, *Doolittle's*

Tokyo Raiders, p. 350.

21. North American built the P-51 Mustang. Doolittle's raiders employed sixteen Boeing B-25s.

22. These famous photographs by Dorothea Lange appeared in *Life* magazine (12:14), 6 April 1942.

23. J. E. McCall's first-hand account, complete with cartoons, humorous poems, and important historical documents, *Santo Tomas Internment Camp: Stic in Verse and Reverse, Stic-toons and Stic-tistics* (Lincoln, NE: Woodruff, 1945), gives the total number of internees at 6,874 (p. 66) of whom three hundred ninety died during the war, most from malnutrition and attendant illnesses (pp. 137-146).

24. The ill-fated *Ural-maru* was torpedoed by the USS *Flasher* off the Philippine coast on 27 September 1944. All but three hundred of two thousand three hundred people on board perished. It was converted to a troop transport ship in 1942, later being used as a hospital ship. When sunk, it was being used as a transport ship.

25. Images of tanks, bulldozers, and steamrollers exterminating Japanese troops can be found in wartime Hollywood films. See Michael S. Shull and David Edward Wilt, *Hollywood War Films, 1937-1945* (Jefferson, NC: McFarland, 1996), p. 233.

26. The text here uses characters for "Yellow Monkey" (*kiiroi saru*) and provides syllabry (*furigana*) reading, "Yellow Monkey" (*ierō monkii*). The phrase "Kill you Jap" is printed entirely in katakana (*kiru yū Jappu*), to which a Japanese explanation is provided in parentheses: "*Nihonjin yarō o korosu ka.*"

27. "We Should Gas Japan," the cited *New York Daily News* editorial of 30 November 1943, was one of several articles in the US press urging the government to gas Japanese, even civilians, in violation of the treaty signed by the United States, Japan, and other nations as part of the Washington Naval Conference of 1921-1922. Other articles had more inflammatory titles, including "You Can Cook 'Em Better with Gas," *Washington Times Herald*, 1 February 1944. See n96 in Lieutenant-General Robert G. Gard and Senator Patrick Leahy's Foreword, "History's Revealing Light," to the 1999 Center for International Policy article, "Commander-in-Chief: Contrasting the Presidential Roles in the World Campaigns to Ban Chemical Weapons (1919-45) and Land Mines (1990s)," available at: www.ciponline.org/oldiprcomm.htm.

28. The twenty thousand Japanese residing in Davao were rounded up by Philippine troops on 8 December and forced into guarded makeshift detention centers, from which they were liberated by Japanese troops on 20 and 21 December. Small children were among those who died from deprivation, although an exact figure of deaths has not been found. Ironically, of the 5,027 men conscripted from among the Davao Japanese community, only 374 survived the war. See Lydia N. Yu-Jose, "World War II and the Japanese in the Prewar Philippines," *Journal of Southeast Asian Studies* (27:1), 1996.

29. Wartime Hollywood films were no less inflammatory in their depiction of the horrors that befell captured troops: "*The Purple Heart* left nothing to the imagination. Under no circumstances, the storyline insisted, should an American serviceman be taken prisoner by the Japanese. Other films had already issued that dire warning: *Bombardier*, *Flying Tigers*, *Marine Raiders*, and *Bataan* revealed the consequences of Japanese capture . . . *Operation Burma* lit up the screen with the mutilated corpses of American GIs tortured to death by their enemy" (Robert Fyne, *The Hollywood Propaganda of World War II*, [Metuchen, NJ: Scarecrow Press, 1994], p. 63).

30. The original *Life* caption was, "Arizona worker writes her Navy boyfriend a thank-you note for the Jap skull he sent her." Dower notes that Roosevelt refused the gift of the letter opener (*War Without Mercy*, p. 330, n90).

31. *Life* provided the rationale for publishing the photograph: "Why print this picture . . . of three American boys dead upon an alien shore? Is it to hurt people? To be morbid? Those are not the reasons. The reason is that words are never enough. The eye sees. The mind knows. The heart feels. But the words do not exist to make us see, or know, or feel what it is like, what actually happens. The words are never right. Last winter . . . we told about Bill [who was shot on the beach by Japanese snipers] . . . And we said then that we thought we ought to be permitted to show a picture of Bill—not just words, but the real thing. We said that if Bill had the guts to take it, then we ought to have the guts to look at it. Well, this is the picture. And the reason we print it now is that, last week, President Roosevelt and Elmer Davis and the War Department decided that the American people ought to be able to see their own boys as they fall in battle; to come directly and without words into the presence of their own dead."

11. DYING HONORABLY, FROM ATTU TO IWO JIMA

On 21 May 1943, the Imperial High Command reluctantly announced the death of Admiral Yamamoto Isoroku, whose airplane had been shot down in an American ambush in the Solomons on 17 April. Coming on the heels of the first Uchiteshi Yamamu Campaign, the news was a shock, and this national hero was given a lavish state funeral. Without his leadership, a mood of pessimism settled over Japan. From mid-1943, slogans and buzzwords reflected the fact that the tide of the war had turned against Japan. In headlines and war bond posters, the catchword *kessen* ("decisive battle," the final battle that would decide Japan's victory) was increasingly replaced with the homonym *kessen* ("blood-battle," a desperate fight to the death). A media event was needed, one that would rouse the troops and the home front to a feverish pitch and regain the momentum and morale of Japan's advance through the Pacific and Asia.

1. *PWR* 327, 28 June 1944. The "Signboard of the Times" says (vertically, from right to left): "For us, only the wait was unbearable, but finally the day has come— ATTACK, JUST ATTACK."

The "fight to the finish" (kessen, literally, "bloody battle") campaign announced in the summer of 1944 featured images of ever-fiercer soldiers in mid-action. Surely this photograph was not taken on the battlefield, but is only staged to look that way, with the shouting mouth and the posture of charging reminiscent of the uchiteshi yamamu poster for Army Day 1943.

In June 1943, a media spectacle was made of the first major *gyokusai* (a "banzai" suicide charge), which took place on 29 May 1943 on the Aleutian island of Attu. The Aleutian campaign had been launched almost exactly one year earlier, partly in response to the Doolittle Raid on Tokyo, which the High Command suspected might have originated from bases in the island chain.[1] The Aleutian invasion was also designed as a diversionary tactic to lure the US Pacific Fleet from

2-6. *PWR* 274, 2 June 1943, pp. 17 and 18 (page 18 is on the verso of page 18 in the original magazine).

(left page, p. 17) "In Memoriam. Admiral Yamamoto Isoroku."

(right page, p. 18) "Heroic Images of the Admiral in Days Past."

(right page, top) "Admiral Yamamoto perfecting his bold, brilliant master battle plan." No information is provided about the circumstances of this photograph, frequently reprinted in postwar histories, which (like the other photographs on these two pages) is almost certainly a publicity shot created by the Navy Ministry.

(right page, bottom left) "The admiral in his hotel at the time he was sent to the London Conference."

(right page, bottom center) "The admiral, whose words and actions were one and the same, well wrote the phrase, 'The battlefield always exists.'" The phrase, which colloquially could be translated, "The battlefield is everywhere," is in Yamamoto's hand and is signed and dated by him, April 1935. The phrase describes the samurai's mental state of preparedness.

(right page, bottom right) "The heroic image of the Admiral on deck, keeping an eye on the enemy."

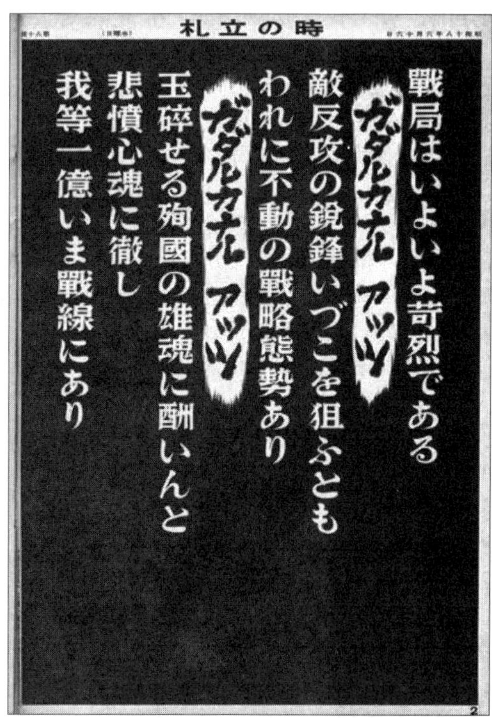

7 and 8. *PWR* 276, 16 June 1943, pp. 2-3.

(right) "Signboard of the Times 80." The small-size poster carries a chilling message: "The war situation has grown fiercer. *GUADALCANAL ATTU*. The Enemy's counter-offensive may sharpen and take aim at some regions, but we are prepared with a strategy of steadfastness. *GUADALCANAL ATTU*. We will repay our debt of gratitude to the heroic spirits who committed *gyokusai* and gave their lives for their country, with the indignation sinking deep into our souls, as now we, the One Hundred Million, form the front line."

This black-and-white poster uses the written character to dramatic advantage. The main text is white lettering against a black background, with the names of Guadalcanal and Attu in a deliberate, crude hand, as if written by a finger in drops of blood. In August 1942, Japanese troops on Guadalcanal had fought with a ferocity that shocked Allied personnel. Of three Japanese garrisons that fought on Guadalcanal, only fifteen men were taken prisoner.

(left) "State Funeral of Admiral Yamamoto." The uncredited photograph is of "the hearse entering the Hibiya burial ground." The article describes the attendance of an imperial proxy and members of the nobility at Yamamoto's funeral. "The emotions of we One Hundred Million who bid farewell to the spirit of the admiral as we remember his extraordinary achievements that shocked the world and daunted the enemy America-Britain, are the profound sadness creeping over us with a chilling sensation. Another emotion transcends that sadness as we are overwhelmed by our firm vow to avenge him by wiping out the enemy."

Midway, leaving Pearl Harbor vulnerable. The campaign began with the shelling of Dutch Harbor, Alaska on 3 June 1942. On 7 June, two thousand five hundred unopposed Japanese troops occupied Attu and Kiska, the two US islands in the Aleutian archipelago closest to Japan. These forbidding islands were of little military significance to the United States, home to an advance listening post for distant Dutch Harbor and a few hundred native Aleuts. As a foothold from which to invade Alaska, however, the Japanese presence was a menace. For Japanese watching the war's progress, Attu and Kiska were two more Rising Sun flags on the northeastern corner of the Asia-Pacific map, a symbolic occupation by Japan of a piece of US territory in the Western Hemisphere.

The Attu garrison had grown to 2,630 men by 11 May 1943, when eleven thousand US troops began landing on Attu amid a naval bombardment of Japanese positions. Admiral Hosoda's three attempts to land supplies failed, due to a US naval blockade. After initial skirmishes along the coast, the Japanese troops retreated to the island's most defensible valley and waited to engage the enemy, who arrived two weeks later. Many of the troops had already perished, and many more were weakened or exhausted after several months on the barren island. Supplies were running out. Colonel Yamazaki Yasuyo, commander on the island, had received word from Tokyo that no reinforcements or supplies were being sent. Surrender was out of the question, and their prospects were grim.

9. *PWR* 228, 8 July 1942, p. 5. *PWR*'s coverage of the Aleutian occupation included this photograph of two captured men who have not been identified. "We interrogated two retreating enemy defenders, Caulfield and John. 'How many residents are there?' 'About ten, but not a single woman.' 'What company do you work for?' 'Not a company, the navy.' 'Do you like the war?' 'No, we hate it.'" Their answers, and their appearance in civilian clothes and heavy beards, would suggest low morale to *PWR*'s readership.

10-14. The occupation of Attu and Kiska was described with the same set of a dozen photographs in many publications. This photoessay appeared in Dōmei's *Japan Photo Almanac 1943*, with captions in English and Japanese. The original English cutline is as follows:

"America's northern air base for raiding Japan Proper was completely bottled up with the landing of Japanese army and naval units on Aleutian Islands on June 7, 1942. The landing operations were carried in difinance [*sic*] of a dense fog and raging waves peculiar to the arctic seas, and the vanguards successfully prosecuted their duties amid the persistent attacks of the enemy planes, to say nothing of the violence of Nature. Above [left] Japanese army units pushing on through the bitter cold wind. Below [left] Machine-guns being carried on sledges. Top [right] Cannon must be carried in pieces. Center [right] A brief rest! Japanese fighters taking a meal with frozen canteens. Bottom [right] Military troops marching in snow-covered Attu Island."

Colonel Yamazaki gathered together his men for a final, all-out assault on US positions. The remaining men, numbering between seven hundred and one thousand, gathered at Chichagof and made a midnight charge. They broke through US picket lines and wiped out a field hospital and quartermaster depot. Half of Yamazaki's men died in the attack, and half—some four hundred or more men—blew themselves up with grenades, scattering viscera and brain across the tundra. Many of the US casualties were men bayoneted in their sleep. Imperial Headquarters received the Attu garrison's final transmission on 27 May, so Japanese intelligence of the battle depended upon US broadcasts. US forces reported finding 2,351 enemy dead on the island. Only twenty-eight Japanese were captured alive. Significant damages were inflicted: one thousand eight hundred US casualties, including six hundred fatalities. In terms of US casualty rates, Attu was the second costliest campaign of the Pacific theater (the costliest being Iwo Jima): seventy-one US personnel killed or wounded for every one hundred Japanese stationed on Attu.

Yamazaki's "invention" of military mass suicide quickly became a cultural phenomenon. Attu was heralded in the Japanese press as an outstanding example of military valor and "Japanese spirit," for which a new word was needed. From the time of the Russo-Japanese War, soldiers who killed themselves in suicidal combat had been called *nikudan*, "human bullets." A euphemism was coined to describe the new extreme of collective self-sacrifice inaugurated at Attu: *gyokusai*. Literally, the word means "a jewel crushed"; in English-language publications produced in Japan during the war, the term was translated as "death for honor."[2] The original phrase comes from classical Chinese sources, where it does not advocate battlefield suicide but simply states that a great man is distinguished from an ordinary one by his devotion to his principles.

A major group of twenty-four artworks devoted to the Attu gyokusai were printed in a 1944 book edited by the Information Division of the Army Ministry, *Picture-scroll: Attu Island Bloody Battle* (hereafter, the *Attu Picture-scroll*), designed for release upon the first anniversary of the suicide charge. The *Attu Picture-scroll* was the first attempt on the part of the government to sharpen Japanese perceptions and attitudes toward mass suicide, providing a narrative with ritual elements that would be copied in subsequent accounts of other gyokusai. The *Attu Picture-scroll* was also the most detailed and articulate expression of the concept of gyokusai generally, as well as the most sustained effort to describe one instance of gyokusai.

The *Attu Picture-scroll* incorporated the work of several artists (all members of the Army Artists' Federation [Rikugun Bijutsu Kyōkai]) working in different media (oil, watercolor, pastel, pencil) and in different styles (*nihonga*, or "Japanese-style picture," and *yōga*, "Western-style" academic picture). The artists who participated in the *Attu Picture-scroll*'s creation were among Japan's most successful fine artists before the war, and with the exception of Fujita Tsuguharu, resumed successful careers in Japan after the war. Most had studied or traveled in Europe and America, and among them were some of the Japanese leaders of modernism in the visual arts. The artworks are reprinted with no notation of the medium or dimensions of the original works, or date of their completion (either 1943 or 1944).

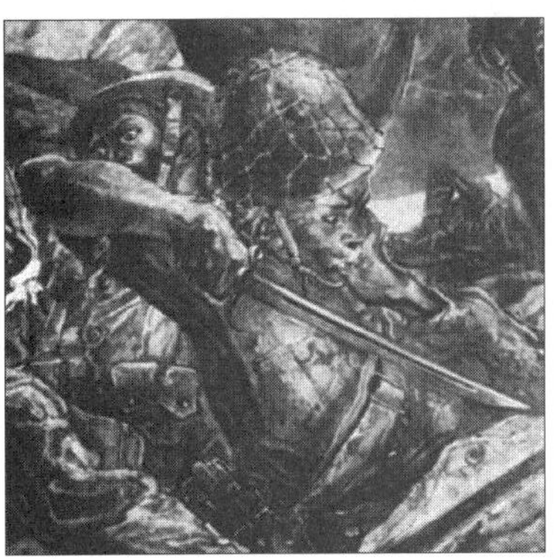

15-17. "Gyokusai on Attu Island," Fujita Tsuguharu (1943).[3]

(top) p. 3 in the *Attu Picture-scroll*. Fujita's epic vision of hand-to-hand combat, undoubtedly one of the masterpieces of Japanese war art, aims at psychological truths at odds with records of the battle, which took place in the US encampment near the beach, surely without waves crashing on rocks behind them. The violently churning seascape suggests a metaphor for gyokusai: wave after wave of warriors crashes jewel-like against the enemy, wearing them down just as the ocean's waves eventually erode even the hardest rock. The palette lends itself to this interpretation, being a nearly monochrome sea of ochre and brown, and further suggesting that all human beings are one Leviathan in the midst of a life-or-death struggle.

(middle and bottom) Enlarged detail from Fujita's "Attu Island Gyokusai" (included as such on pp. 4-5 of the *Attu Picture-scroll*).

(middle) Fujita's rendition of Colonel Yamazaki, calling out not to his men but to the viewer. His is, perhaps, the kindest and saddest face of the men portrayed here. The narrative of the *Attu Picture-scroll* makes his rallying cry, "follow my lead, don't let us die in vain!" Today's viewer may see, in Fuijta's depiction of Yamazaki, an expression of the tragedy and futility of war.

(bottom) Detail of hand-to-hand combat as imagined by the artist. The Japanese soldier's facial features have been transformed by the intensity of battle.

In medieval picture-scrolls, text and illustration play off each other in a flowing, continuous narrative in which neither text nor illustration tells the entire story. This reference to courtly literature gave the modern work an air of authenticity by citing the distant past, and the form allowed narrative elements to speak forcefully, sometimes at the expense of factual accuracy. We do not know what information was available to the artists and writers who worked on the *Attu Picture-scroll*, although it seems they had some information from Allied sources.[4] Even so, in several points the *Attu Picture-scroll* strays from standard postwar histories of the battle for the Aleutians. From a literary and artistic perspective, however, we might argue that its virtues are to be found in the poetic truths and emotional realities it communicated to its contemporary audience.

As Chairman of the Army Artists' Federation, Fujita Tsuguharu contributed the introduction to this volume, in which he explained that the rationale for compiling the book ("under the orders of the Army Ministry") was to convey something of the heroic example of the "gyokusai corps (*gyokusai butai*)" to Japan's young men and adolescents. Fujita, along with another contributor to this book, Miyamoto Saburō, were among a group of artists sent by the army to the Malay Peninsula, Singapore, and Thailand in 1942. Fujita's stirring "Gyokusai on Attu Island" was the first image in the *Attu Picture-scroll*, thereby beginning with the "end" of the story of the gyokusai and setting the solemn tone of the narrative that unfolded in its pages, a story of ordinary men who seized upon extraordinary circumstances and chose to die for honor and the promise of eternal glory.

18 and 19. (top) Attu Island in a photographic frontispiece from *Attu Gyokusai: A Record*, a memorial book describing the Sapporo Communications soldiers who died there as members of the "Gyokusai Corps."

(bottom) Attu Island as depicted in artist Kitō Nabesaburō's "Island of Snow and Ice," illustration 2 in the *Attu Picture-scroll*.

Chichagof Bay, the site of the gyokusai, is across the water at the base of the snow-capped mountains. The picture-scroll artists worked from Japanese military photographs when available, lending their work verisimilitude. None of these artists would have traveled to Attu.

Three illustrations in the *Attu Picture-scroll* (not shown here) describe the Japanese occupation of the island and the establishment of anti-aircraft defenses. The *Attu Picture-scroll* argued that these two Aleutian islands were slated to serve as the US's staging grounds for air raids against Japan, and that by occupying them, Japan's Home Islands were safeguarded against US bombardments. That no US bombs were dropped on Japan after the Doolittle Raid of April 1942 until late 1944 lent some credence to this theory. Takai Teiji's depiction of a Japanese Zero, (refitted with pontoons) shooting down an unidentified "enemy plane" is a highly unlikely scenario, although Japanese planes did harass the US forces landing on neighboring Amchitka Island in the early months of 1943.

20 and 21. (top) "Our Seaplanes Chase away a Great Enemy" by Takai Teiji, illustration 9 in the *Attu Picture-scroll*. Takai (1911-1986) gained renown as a surrealist painter before the war. In the 1950s, he studied "action painting" in the US, where his works were widely exhibited.

(bottom) Sakai Yasuhiro's "Crossing the Snowy Incline" (illustration 4 in the *Attu Picture-scroll*) draws upon photographs, yet offers a more aesthetically appealing image of a snaking line of soldiers stretching from the foreground to an invisible horizon.

Sakai shows the soldiers marching toward, rather than away from, the viewer, a reversal of the photographer's perspective seen in figure 14. The composition draws the eye down the slope, toward the shore, as if an endless line of men were marching, patient but determined, from Japan itself to the furthest corner of the earth.

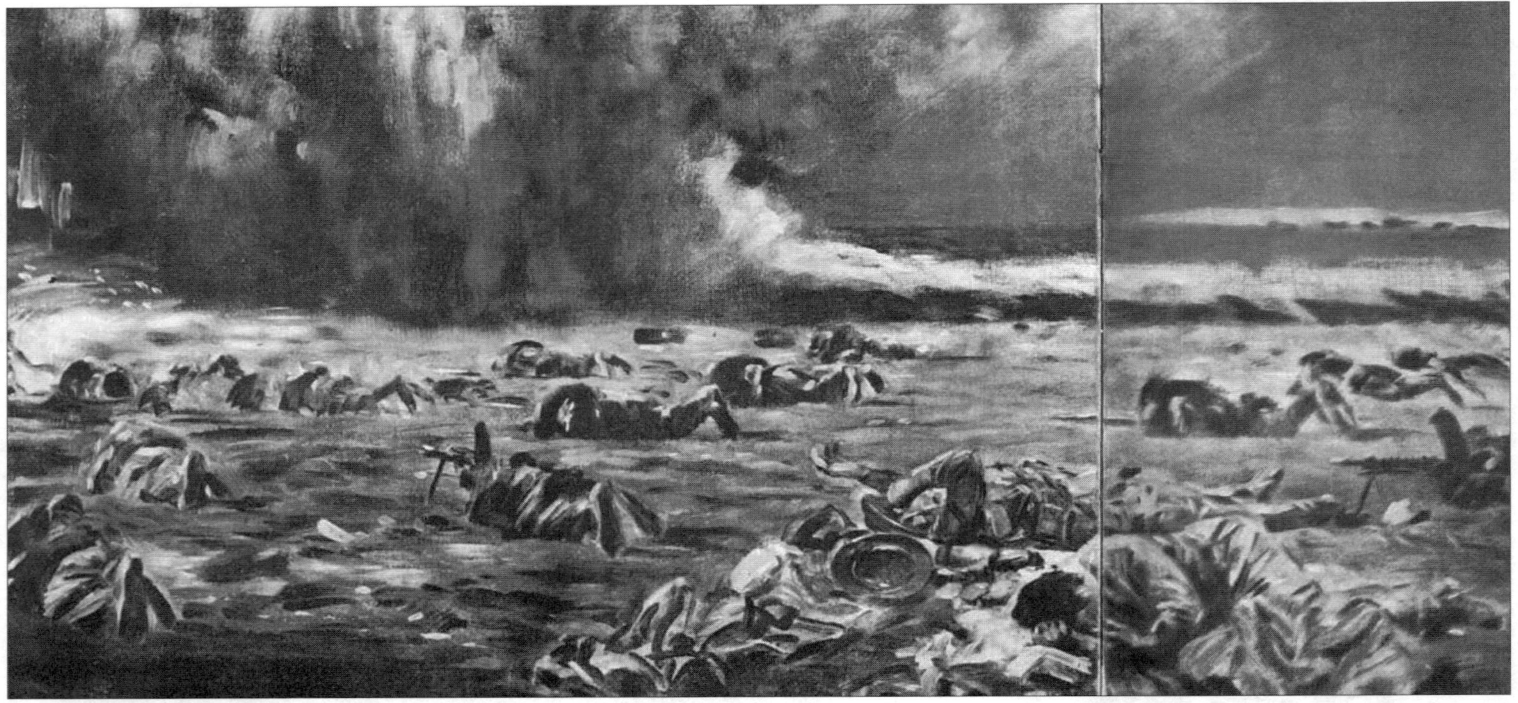

22. “Enemy Battalion Mowed Down on the Waterfront” by Miyamoto Saburō, illustration 11 in the *Attu Picture-scroll*. The accompanying text reads, in part, “Facing the *asura*-like fierce resistance of our brave warriors, the enemy required ten times the manpower to gain the upper hand over our light troop cover. The enemy began to push in on our men from adjacent areas to the north, center, and south. The troops that landed and gathered on the southern escarpment of Massacre Bay were a large force, which our men determined to be the principal enemy force, and against this strong enemy legion, one of our battalions, under cover of night, carried out a night raid of unparalleled courage. They fought all along the line and across to the water front, and without leaving any enemy to flee, mowed them all down. What splendid tales of the fighting spirit of our Imperial Army, who continued to shoot without stopping until the very end, could the bright gleam of their swords have told us, as they walked in the darkness across corpse after enemy corpse?”

While standard battle histories state that US forces did incur heavy losses in the early encounters on Attu, the narrative here draws upon the imagination of the creators of the *Attu Picture-scroll*. Asura, originally a Hindu god, signifies in Buddhism a group of demi-gods protecting the Buddha. These fierce, terrifying spirits are fond of warfare. The religious reference elevates the combatants to the level of deities and their struggle to righteous, holy war against those who would dare attack the Buddha.

23. “Communicating the Generously Kind Imperial Rescript,” by Yamamoto Hikoshiro, illustration 15 in the *Attu Picture-scroll*. According to the accompanying caption, as the time approached to confront the much larger enemy force, Yamazaki read out to all of the defenders of Attu Island an imperial rescript received by radio transmission on 25 May 1943. The contents of the rescript are not described, but it renewed their determination to repay the emperor’s kindness by charging the enemy in an all-out fight to the last soldier. The caption ends with a dramatic device borrowed from theater: “Here we see the entire battalion’s will to fight congealing as the thunder of enemy artillery momentarily mocks the steely voice of Commander Colonel Yamazaki reverently reading out the imperial rescript.”

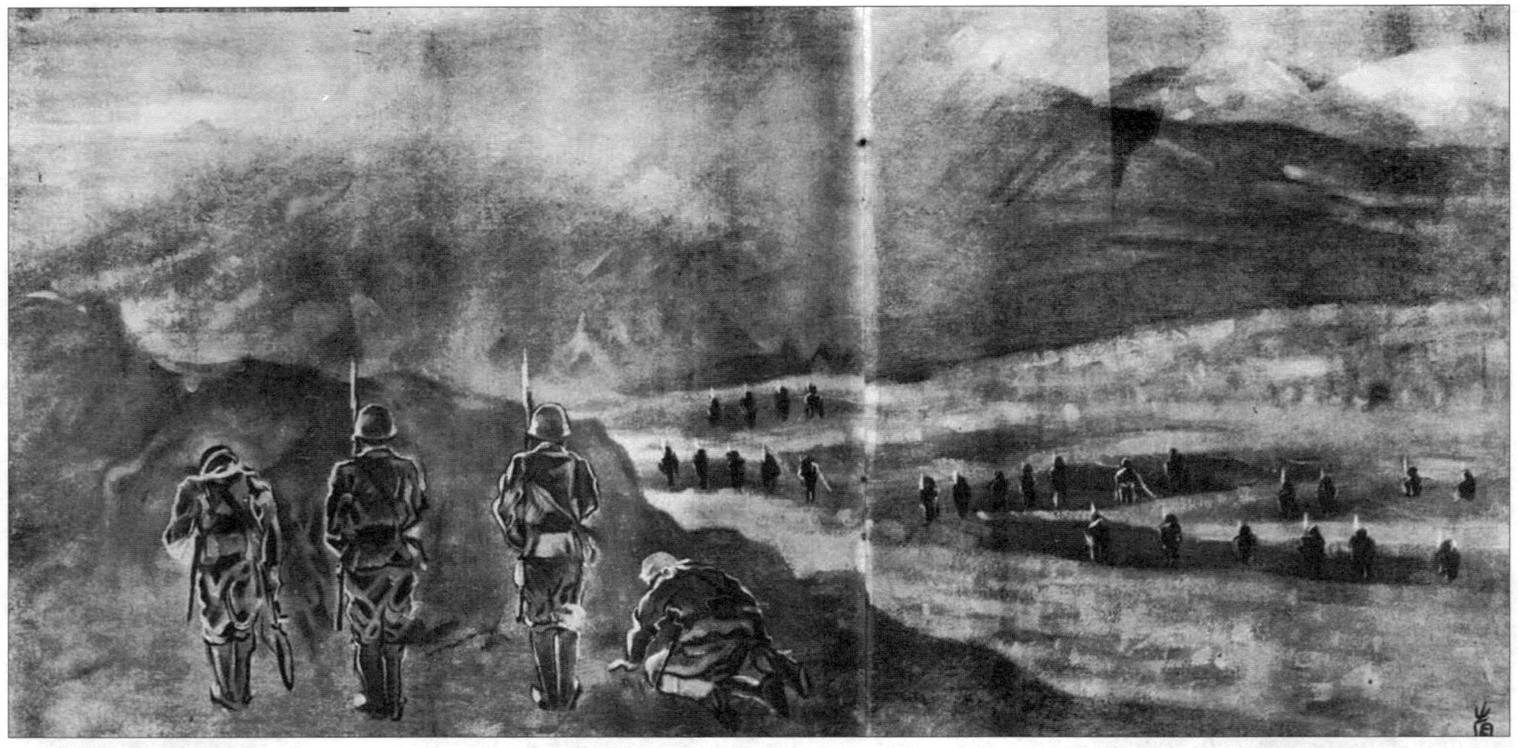

24. “Worshipping the Imperial Palace from Afar” by Enokura Shōgo, illustration 17 in the *Attu Picture-scroll*. In the early hours of 29 May 1943, the men bow and pray to the distant imperial palace as the sun’s first rays appear on the horizon. The caption describes the psychology of gyokusai as well as the connection between the home front observer and the battlefield practitioner: “For all living beings born Japanese, this was a most pious moment. The steely glint of their bayonets and the solemn, pure energy racing through their bodies made their hearts completely ready for the gyokusai that would repay the gift of life they had received.”

25. “Breaking Through the Enemy Line of Defense” by Sekiya Akira (1943), illustration 18 in the *Attu Picture-scroll*. The accompanying text is translated in its entirety.

“In the middle of the night of the 29th, our own Commander Yamazaki gathered together his remaining troops and undertook an extremely heroic human bullet (nikudan) attack that pierced through the enemy’s picket lines and drove on to the main enemy camp at Massacre Cliff.

“Wielding an extremely fine sword forged by a legendary maker, Commander Yamazaki took the lead and those following him all pointed their bayonets forward. They advanced into the very center of the enemy camp, where they carried out their final, horrible asura-like fight. They introduced the shuddering fear of death to the entire enemy army, whose confusion and dismay was beyond panic, and whose resistance completely crumbled. Thus our men achieved their manly act of gyokusai.

“How heroic. How noble. The twenty-ninth day of May 1943 has become an immortal day in the history of the Great East Asia War, one that burns brightly through the incomparable loyalty of our own brave soldiers of the Yamazaki Corps, who showed by example that Jinmu’s Imperial Army knows no regrets, and who achieved a great spiritual victory, a huge military result of the soul.”

Citations of the "Yamazaki Corps" follow Sekiya's illustration, along with a detailed discussion of the significance of the event and the precedent it set:

> The gyokusai of the brave warriors of Attu resulted in the annihilation of an enemy force over four times larger in number, a fact from which we can calculate that, if we one hundred million Japanese citizens resigned ourselves to gyokusai against the enemy, at least two hundred million Anglo-Saxons would be instantaneously wiped off the face of the earth. And since Americans are so practical about numbers, this fact has plunged them into an abyss of fear.
>
> The enemy's fear of gyokusai is most plainly and obviously evident in their actions immediately after Attu in the case of Kiska, from which our defenders had been completely evacuated. From their [hysteria] we can deduce that gyokusai is one of our most advantageous strategies and should be more widely deployed from the north to the south, on every front of the Great East Asia War.

26. "Portrait of Commander Yamazaki" by Matsuda Fumio, illustration 19 in the *Attu Picture-scroll*. This oddly pudgy posthumous portrait of Yamazaki is replete with symbols of his duty and resolve. In one hand he clutches rolled-up papers, perhaps his orders to "defend the island at all costs," in the other he firmly grips his long sword, symbol of the Japanese military man. His posture is that of a man of quiet but fierce resolve, an everyman who, through extreme self-sacrifice, has become a warrior-god and a larger-than-life hero. We see some of Yamazaki's fallen men's spirits rising out of the mist behind him, incriminating those who would not follow their example and "die for honor."

The irony of this portrait is, of course, that it incorporates characteristics and actions only attributable to Yamazaki after his death. The darkly messianic man pictured here could never have posed for this portrait in the artist's studio, only in the artist's imagination.

In fact, the Attu gyokusai altered US plans regarding Kiska, which US intelligence believed harbored as many as ten thousand Japanese troops. Reinforcements were shipped in and the number of troops doubled to thirty-four thousand (including five thousand five hundred Canadians). The air force and navy dropped 754 tons of bombs on Kiska in the weeks leading up to the 15 August invasion. The Kiska campaign cost the US three hundred casualties, including one hundred dead (seventy perished when a navy destroyer hit a mine, others were victims of friendly fire). The securing of Kiska was an embarrassing waste of lives, supplies, and time, for not a single Japanese was found on the island. The entire Japanese garrison of 5,183 men had been evacuated on 28 July. The *Attu Picture-scroll* derisively attributed the Allied debacle at Kiska to hysteria following the terrifying fight to the death on Attu. Yamazaki and his men received thanks as warrior-gods, and the hitherto unknown Yamazaki himself was posthumously hailed as a national hero.

27 and 28. Hashimoto Tetsurō's "Ship Construction Sends Sparks Flying" (bottom) and Kitō Nabesaburō's "The Fight in a Farming Village" (top) (numbers 22 and 23 respectively in the *Attu Picture-scroll*) show how men and women on the home front honored the spirits of Yamazaki and his men by making greater efforts to boost war production. These workers are faceless, anonymous, in contrast to the individual features of the fallen heroes. This treatment of the home front suggests a hierarchy of sacrifice in which the men dying at the front received the highest glory.

If the *Attu Picture-scroll*'s narration of the Attu gyokusai ended with the portrait of Yamazaki, then it would fail to show that he and his men's deaths were not in vain: they must be avenged by the Japanese people's redoubled morale. Consequently, the final four images portray the home front's response to the gyokusai, showing the increase in the production of fighter planes and ships as well as in crops.

The final illustration in the *Attu Picture-scroll* shows student conscripts, draped in Rising Sun flags and bearing aloft their school banners, hurrying to join the fight. University student exemption from military service was terminated in June 1943, and all physically fit men over the age of eighteen became eligible for conscription. The action of the *Attu Picture-scroll* is thus moved forward chronologically, strengthening the bond between Yamazaki's men and the home front, and the recent past and the present of 1944. The final words of the text of the *Attu Picture-scroll* accompany Suzuki's "Student Conscripts": "'Follow the Heroes of Attu'—until the day comes when we have completely annihilated the despicable enemies America and Britain, this slogan must never be forgotten by we one hundred million fellow citizens, not even in our dreams."

29. "Student Conscripts Depart for the Front" by Suzuki Mitsuru, the final illustration in the *Attu Picture-scroll*. Presumably a watercolor, this picture owes much to the dramatized historical style perfected by Jacques-Louis David and other European academic painters of a century earlier. The painting conveys a sense of urgency and purpose metaphorically (as does David's "Liberty Leading the People"), in that it depicts the emotion and force of the student conscripts rather than an actual historical event. Their vast numbers, their rising out of the very earth, likens them to the sacred land of Japan itself. The sun of the Rising Sun flag held aloft has broken through the dark clouds. Clear skies lie ahead thanks to the efforts of the student conscripts having joined the fight.

30 and 31. (left) *PWR* 294, 20 October 1943. "Now Is the Autumn of Students Springing into Action." The caption reads, "Emergency Student Conscription examinations will take place from 25 October to 5 November, and boot camp will begin on 1 December.

"Little time remains before they depart for the front. The students must think about the examinations, then boot camp . . . this decision [to conscript students] was unexpected and so in their tense excitement, it will seem as though, all in a flurry, they will be dashing off [for the front] the next day.

"Wait just a minute, though. Are they prepared for the front, are they physically trained, are they mentally disciplined? Until the bright, sunny day of their departure, not even five minutes in a day will be wasted or spent daydreaming.

This is a student of Waseda University in military training."

(right) *PWR* 299, 24 November 1943, p. 18. "Four Thousand Tokyo University Students Sent Off to the Front." The article states, "The footsteps of these students departing for the front reverberate forcefully through the chilly autumn skies, sending off crest after crest of the vigorously waved caps of currently enrolled students. On the faces of the departing students was a silent determination and a look that said, 'Follow us, lower classmen!'

"Under clear skies the send-off rally of some four thousand students from Tokyo University's Law, Literature, Economics, and Agriculture Departments led the way for universities in the Tokyo metropolitan area. Beginning at 9 A.M. on 12 November, at the auditorium on campus, the entire student body gave an enthusiastic send-off ceremony, and when it ended, the gaitered students departing for the front, with the pure-white school flag in the lead, began to march in formation down the memory-filled lane lined with ginkgo trees. At 11 A.M., they lined up in formation before the Double Bridge leading to the Palace, gave a banzai cheer to the emperor, and then dispersed."

征けこの感激を胸に

出陣學徒壯行會

11

10

32-36. *PWR* 296, 3 November 1943, pp. 10-11. "Go! With Inspiration in Your Heart. The Send-off Rally for Students Departing for the Front."

"On 21 October, the Education Ministry convened a Send-off Rally of Students Departing for the Front in the Meiji Shrine Outer Garden Stadium, where the autumn colors have at last taken on a deep hue. A fine venue, this sacred ground where students from all over Japan, their skills already honed in anticipation of this day, competed in demonstrating their martial splendor. The ardent loyalty of these students of the Land of the Emperor, who do not look back, and the moving sincerity of the citizens seeing them off, which flowed forth like a torrent, made this Send-off Rally an event that, from this day on, will forever be an inspirational chapter in the history of this exciting century.

"We are already repeating to ourselves Prime Minister Tōjō's Rally Speech:

"'I have the same feeling today as our ancestors did when their children first entered military camp and every family and every household held a celebration to send them off. We one hundred million compatriots, with heartfelt respect and gratitude, give you a grand departure and a happy send-off.' And then, as the war situation grows fiercer and fiercer these days, we cannot but be heartened by the words of the young students: 'We, the young students of this age of Shōwa, with the conviction that we must win and in a spirit of 'never surrender,' will fulfill our duty to protect the nation, and leave behind for future generations a lasting legacy of Japan's bright honor."

(right page, top) "Sending off the students were, from right: Education Minister Okabe, Prime Minister Tōjō, and [illegible]."

(right page bottom) "The cheers of the female students sending them off."

(left page, top) "The dignified step of 'annihilating America and Britain,' seen in the procession of marching students departing for the front, with Minister Okabe saluting them."

(left page, bottom left) "Ehashi Shinshirō, student of Tokyo University's Literature Department, enthusiastically reads out a message as the representative of the students departing for the front."[5]

(left page, bottom right) "Okui Shinji, student of Keiō University's Department of Medicine, delivers the rally message as the representative of students attending the rally."

The Japanese media's glorified account of the final charge at Attu, disseminated throughout the homeland and the war front, became the template for repeated mass suicides across the Pacific, initially by military men, later by civilians. The rationale for these banzai attacks was found partly in the high casualty rates inflicted upon a much larger enemy force at Attu. These casualty figures were verified by published Allied reports. If Japanese suicide attacks always resulted in seventy enemy casualties per one hundred Japanese dead, then Japan would win the war through sheer numbers, provided that Japan drew upon a broader base of recruits than did the United States. This morbid algebra influenced strategy in the two final, desperate years of the war. The High Command believed that with over five million troops in the field, if every Japanese soldier killed or wounded one of the enemy before himself being killed, a mounting death toll would dim the American people's enthusiasm for the war and that they would force their government to negotiate a settlement of the war favorable to Japan.

37 and 38. The homes and families of some of the "Yamazaki Gyokusai Corps" were publicly honored. In the autumn of 1943, the Sapporo Communications Bureau published a book, *Attu Gyokusai, a Record*, with rather lengthy vignettes of fourteen of their officers who died on Attu. Each officer's portrait was reproduced, as well as photographs of his calligraphy, home, or surviving family members. The biographies contained much personal information, even about upbringing and "hobbies." At left is Azuma Kaneyoshi, who died at age forty-three (p. 13 in the *Record*). His eulogy notes that his mother died when he was two, that he was an excellent father who raised his children to be "good Japanese," that his hobbies included calligraphy and hunting for seasonal herbs and vegetables, and that he was a decent poet who wrote fairy tales for his daughter. A letter to his daughter is reproduced because it shows his courage and resolve: "Will father return home the same human being as before? Will he return home a more refined and noble person than he was up to now? Or will he return home venerated as a god (kami)? He doesn't know the answer, but in this case [of leaving for the front], his heart is filled with joy and his attitude is absolutely not that of a sissy (*memeshii*)—be sure to tell your Mother this" (pp. 16-17). At right is a photograph of the cenotaph erected in front of his home. The inscription reads, "Home of a Hero of the Attu Island Gyokusai, Azuma Kaneyoshi of the Sapporo Communications Bureau" (p. 19).

Depictions of gyokusai depended upon the skill and imagination of illustrators and news writers, since no photographs of gyokusai were taken by the Japanese. Unencumbered by photographic "evidence" and firsthand Japanese accounts, artists and writers had a freer hand in interpreting (and embellishing) accounts of gyokusai. The deeply patriotic and dramatic nature of gyokusai made it a rather popular subject for artists, whose imagination could go where the camera could not. The achievement of these artists' moving, haunting images of soldiers and civilians "choosing" death over dishonor is all the more remarkable when we consider the stark reality of an anonymous, violent death in a distant, alien land. In 1943, there was no sunny prospect of returning home for rest and relaxation for the Japanese GIs, no dancing with movie stars at the Hollywood Canteen. Not even the remains of Japanese soldiers who ended their lives with hand grenades would return to Japan. Their memories and spirits were all their loved ones had to memorialize.

Some illustrations and texts of the *Attu Picture-scroll* describe the character and emotions of the men who participated in the suicidal charge. Yamazaki, a virtual unknown before the attack, posthumously became a paragon of military virtues. He was resigned to his fate, stoic even, yet happy to be able to lay down his life for the nation; he was fierce when facing the enemy in battle, but fatherly regarding his own men; above all else, his sense of duty and loyalty was unshakable. Even his facial features proved malleable in the hands of different artists seeking to place a different emphasis on the many virtues of the fifty-two-year-old commander. In his composite portrait we see authority, resignation, determination, valor, courage, rage, manliness, paternal affection, and humanity.

39. "Final Communication from Attu," by Sakai Yasuhiro, was exhibited in the Second Great East Asia War Art Exhibition in 1943. Here it is reproduced from the exhibition catalogue, *Great East Asia War Art, Second Series*, p. 10. Sakai achieves an almost photographic realism. The drama of the men in the background approaching the enemy is contrasted with the collected calm of the Communication Corps men, one of whom has a bandaged head.

Just as Yamazaki was immortalized in a number of drawings and paintings, the banzai charge on Attu was depicted in at least three pictures completed within a year of the event. In addition to the two works included in the *Attu Picture-scroll*, a third was shown at the Second Great East Asia War Art Exhibition in 1943. This painting, by Takazawa Keiichi, was titled "Aa, the Yamazaki Corps" and is an interesting counterpoint to Sekiya's and especially Fujita's treatment of the same subject matter. Takazawa presents an almost demonic Yamazaki, eyes bulging and face contorted like one of the fierce asura mentioned in the *Attu Picture-scroll*. His depictions of the American enemy seem to be based on images of British and Australian soldiers, given their drooping mustaches and broader helmets. Takazawa's composition is much more dramatic, the action much swifter than Fujita's sprawling sea of struggling humanity, but his Westerners are little more than caricatures.

40-44. Five faces of Yamazaki hagiography. (clockwise, from top left) An official military photograph, and four artistic reinditions: Yamazaki as depicted in Matsuda's portrait, Takazawa's "Yamazaki Corps," Sekiya's "Breaking through the Enemy Line of Defense," and Fujita's "Gyokusai on Attu Island." The artists' renditions were done posthumously, after Yamazaki had been proclaimed a warrior-god and war hero.

Sekiya (figures 25, 43), Fujita (figures 15, 16, and 44), and Takazawa (figures 42, 45) portray Yamazaki's final charge quite differently. Sekiya has Yamazaki wearing a traditional headband (*hachimaki*), pure white to signify the resolve to fight to the death. But Fujita and Yamazaki envision him helmeted (albeit with distinctly different helmets). All three artists picture him without glasses. Sekiya and Fujita have him wielding a long sword (a very fine one from a famous maker, the *Attu Picture-scroll* text informs us), while Takazawa shows him plunging his rifle-bayonet into the chest of an American. Sekiya's illustration depicts the initial charge through the lines of the US camp, while Fujita's and Takazawa's show the ensuing struggle of some minutes or hours later. Obviously, Yamazaki would not have removed his helmet for the charge through enemy lines only to put it on (over a headband) in the final moments of the gyokusai. These minor discrepancies are fascinating not for what they tell us about the battle itself but for what they reveal of Japanese artists' perceptions of heroes. Yamazaki, the quintessential Japanese soldier, embodies traditional and native values (the long sword, the headband still worn today by Japanese when facing a difficult task, such as final exams) while embracing modern, Western technology (the helmet, uniform, and rifle). His spirit is Japanese although he is dressed in the uniform of a modern military man. If these minor details seem contradictory, no contradiction blemishes the emotional truths each picture tells as part of the larger picture-scroll (and in the largest context of the official narrative of the war): a Japanese dies gladly for honor because the Japanese spirit transcends paradoxes of history (the modern versus the traditional, the native versus the foreign), just as it overcomes seemingly overwhelming odds to score both a tactical and "spiritual" victory. That these three artists pictured Yamazaki and his final heroic actions very differently in no way diminished his stature, but on the contrary, only lent his composite portrait fullness and complexity.

45. "Aa, the Yamazaki Corps," by Takazawa Keiichi. (1943, medium unknown); p. 36 in *Great East Asia War Art, Second Series*. Takazawa views the action from the beach, and therefore the mountains form the background, a reversal of Fujita's perspective.

The Army Art Federation's depictions of the Attu gyokusai may appear realistic (that is, they are works of mimetic art), but these artists shied away from the gruesome reality. While employing different media and styles, they adhered to rules and guidelines set by the CIB and its censors. The effect of these guidelines on graphic representations of battle meant that Japanese soldiers' deaths would not be as brutally depicted as they had been during the Russo-Japanese War (see Chapter 12, figure 2). Instead, the *Attu Picture-scroll* artists and unnamed writers accessed a shared racial identity to create an imagined history of the attack and interpretation of its meaning. Several assumptions, especially those about the unity of the "Yamazaki Corps," do not stand up to scrutiny. The corps did not fight "to the last man," since twenty-eight (by some accounts, twenty-nine) were taken prisoner. (This number represents slightly over one percent of the entire garrison, so it might be dismissed as negligible when summarizing the garrison's final actions.) A larger question about the men's morale is raised by US soldiers' eyewitness accounts of some Japanese chargers sitting down in the middle of the US camp and eating American rations. These accounts of pathos reflect a universal in human nature: how utterly miserable to be facing certain death on an empty stomach after days or weeks of deprivation, cold, and hunger.

The *Attu Picture-scroll* provided more than a template for illustrating heroic death on the battlefield, it proposed a course of action. Attu was the first, but by no means the last, banzai charge. Gyokusai took place repeatedly during the Allied island-hopping that led from Guadalcanal to the Marianas and Palau. There were two gyokusai charges at Bougainville on 30 October 1943, in which seventy-two Japanese troops died. About forty fled rather than charge. At Tarawa, the fight-to-the-death policy was more closely followed during the gyokusai of the night of 21-22 November 1943. In the final tally, of 4,836 Japanese troops stationed on Tarawa, 4,690 were killed. Of the 146 survivors, 129 were Korean laborers, leaving only seventeen of four thousand seven hundred Japanese military personnel, about one-third of one percent, to be taken alive. The Tarawa campaign cost the US marines three thousand casualties. As the US military became accustomed to banzai charges, it became more adept at repelling them. While the frenzied, suicidal attacks were harrowing, they provided the opportunity to engage and kill large numbers of the enemy without having to flush them out.

Some of the largest incidents of gyokusai took place at the end of the Battle of Saipan in July 1944. A Japanese garrison of thirty thousand men was sent to defend the 72 square-mile island and its population of about thirty thousand Japanese colonists. On 15 June, the first of seventy thousand US marines began coming ashore on Saipan's southern beaches, where they encountered heavy resistance. The marines established a camp for Japanese civilians on 23 June, and it soon had a population of over one thousand. The marines continued to push northward toward the tip of the teardrop-shaped island. By 6 July, the battle's outcome was clear, and the leader of naval forces on the island, Admiral Nagumo (who had been task force commander of the Pearl Harbor attack) committed seppuku by slitting open his stomach. His "second" then shot him through the back of the head. That night, thousands of Japanese troops, led by sword-brandishing officers, charged the marines' positions, madly firing weapons and screaming "banzai." The charge lasted fifteen hours. Some of the marines' mortar tubes and machine gun barrels, overheated from repeated firing, were no longer serviceable.

On 9 July, US forces had reached the northern tip of Saipan, where thousands of civilians had sought safety at Marpi Point with the remaining Japanese troops. These civilians, including women, children, and the elderly, were pressured by Japanese troops to participate in gyokusai, in this case nothing like a banzai charge, but grisly death through whatever means were at hand. Entire families were expected to blow themselves to pieces by huddling around a single hand grenade. Others threw themselves to their deaths off the cliffs or drowned themselves in the ocean. The suicides continued for three or more days, despite the marines' efforts with loudspeakers to entice the Japanese to surrender. US eyewitness accounts describe some civilians being physically tossed over the side of the steep cliffs by Japanese soldiers. Most of these "suicides"—by some calculations, as many as 90 percent—were not voluntary, a fact that has only slowly entered the Japanese national consciousness in recent decades. The final death toll was grim: US forces incurred 14,111 casualties (20 percent of the landing force) of which 3,426 were fatalities, while only 921 of thirty thousand Japanese troops were captured

46. *PWR* 330-331, 6 July 1944, pp. 4-5. Miyamoto Saburō's illustration "imagining" the banzai charge of 6-7 July was on the news stands as thousands of Saipanese civilians were dying at Marpi Point. This detail shows about one-third of the 16½-by-23-inch *PWR* centerfold.

The caption reads, "Supreme Heroism! The Saipan 'White Tiger Brigade,'[6] as artistically imagined. Following the officers and men, boys took up weapons and rose to fight. Here, each of our fellow countrymen used his very body to assist in striking at the enemy, thereby keeping the promise that the One Hundred Million fight to the end. Aa, beneath the unceasing artillery fire, how these people must have swallowed iron-hot tears as they fell. And now American soldiers are wallowing like pigs on this island still wet with our countrymen's tears of blood. We must never allow these deaths to be in vain. We One Hundred Million make a vow to the gods: We will smite these hated barbarians and win."

The collage-like blur of activity uses high contrast lighting and distorts the scale of the foreground and background to approximate the confusion and drama of the assault. The placement of the boy-soldiers near a partially destroyed US plane connotes the superiority of Japanese spirit over American matériel.

alive. Most appalling, however, were overall civilian deaths, estimated conservatively at ten thousand, at least one-third of the island's population. While exact figures are unknown, some historians place civilian deaths as high as twenty thousand. When the human cost of Saipan was calculated, US military records indicate exactly 10,258 civilians were taken prisoner.

The press glorified the events on Saipan, heaping praise on civilians and military men alike for their brave gyokusai.[7] These accounts did little, though, to improve public perception of the war's course. Saipan was the first piece of Japan's prewar territory to fall into enemy hands, dealing a psychological blow. More distressing, however, was the knowledge that US airfields on Saipan (once they were built) would extend the B-29's reach to Tokyo. Confirmation that the war had reached a critical turning point came two days after the loss of Saipan, when Prime Minister Tōjō and his war cabinet resigned en bloc.

Very few works of art focused on the horrific, makeshift deaths of thousands of Saipanese civilians. Perhaps the only artist who dared to visualize the event was Fujita Tsuguharu, who produced one of his most famous and poignant canvases, "Our Compatriots on Saipan Remain Loyal to the End,"[8] an inspired and haunting work. In the center of the painting, a group of women and girls huddle together, surrounded by soldiers, many of them wounded and inert. Mothers comfort their children. These women are young and fleshy, reminiscent of Renoir's late period. Yet these women are not preparing their toilette prior to a promenade, they are preparing to hurl themselves and their children over the cliffs to their deaths. The central figure is a woman holding a child in one arm, a pike in the other. Behind her are the cliffs, with one body in mid-fall. She looks in the direction of the enemy, her posture communicating the anguish of being torn between her duty to save her children from the shame of capture and her duty to fight and protect the nation. By focusing on mothers and daughters and conjuring up maternal love, this eerie painting makes a large-scale tragedy intimate and personal. This work glorifies civilian (rather than military) sacrifice, its sentimentality suggesting unnerving questions about the aims of the war and the very survival of the Japanese race.

By mid-1944, the Imperial High Command realized that gyokusai, while an effective tool of psychological warfare, wasted precious seasoned troops and did little to slow the Allied advance toward Japan. A new strategy called *fukkaku*, "digging in" or endurance warfare, was implemented. Instead of gathering together remaining troops for an all-out banzai charge as a campaign neared its end, the new strategy buried clusters of soldiers in dense jungle, or embedded them in caves and tunnels. Each of these guerrilla cells was charged with infiltrating enemy camps and killing as many of the enemy as possible before themselves being killed. The purpose of fukkaku was to bog down the Allied advance toward Japan in a costly war of attrition that would erode US morale and public confidence in the war effort, so that the United States would sue for peace and recognize Japan's control over an Asian empire.

The mainstream press did not note this shift in tactics. Indeed, from the vantage point of the home front, the results were much the same: whole battalions of troops sent to

47. *PWR* 367, 18 April 1945, p. 13. Fujita Tsuguharu, "Our Compatriots on Saipan Remain Loyal to the End."

some forlorn distant place to fight to the death, only to return to Japan as spirits. In terms of overall troop fatalities, there was little difference between the earlier banzai charge, "gyokusai," and the refined strategy of attrition, "fukkaku": rarely were more than 10 percent of the Japanese troops in either type of combat taken prisoner, with overall Japanese fatalities often reaching the ninety-seven percentile. And the fukkaku strategy did not preclude the banzai charge, it merely discouraged its use except as an absolute, last-ditch tactic by weakened or wounded men who might otherwise be captured alive and brought back to health in an enemy hospital. The press continued to laud the suicidal missions of whole garrisons sent to Peleliu, to Iwo Jima, and to Okinawa with the word, "gyokusai."

Fukkaku and gyokusai (in its original sense of the banzai charge) were quite different military tactics, of course, but the successful implementation of fukkaku owed much to the cultural phenomenon of gyokusai, which sensationalized willed death on the battlefield. The publicity surrounding gyokusai attacks increased expectation that the men leaving for the front would return as warrior-gods. From the vantage point of English translation, fukkaku, like gyokusai, was "dying honorably." When viewed from the position of the Japanese soldier on the ground, fukkaku meant a higher probability of suffering longer and dying alone, rather than surrounded by comrades in a massive charge while still (comparatively) robust. The press described all of Japan's fallen soldiers as "brave heroes," but in reality, those who died in small numbers in drawn-out campaigns received less notice than did the larger, more dramatic banzai charges. Being spread thinly over a larger territory did not make surrendering a more viable option for Japanese troops until very late in the war (or after the war's end), since Japanese soldiers hiding nearby might shoot anyone attempting to surrender. Indeed, the stubbornness of these embedded Japanese soldiers is legendary. Some held out for thirty or more years, refusing to lay down their weapons and dismissing as mere disinformation reports that Japan had surrendered and that the war was over.[9]

At the Battle of Peleliu, the Japanese put the new fukkaku strategy into play. The small coral island in the Palau group had an airstrip and was a strategic stepping stone to the Philippines. The US invasion began on 15 September 1944 and dragged on for more than two months, with the island declared secure on 25 November. The ensuing battle turned a tropical paradise into a festering hell as the unforgiving coral made burial of the dead difficult, and insects thrived on bloated corpses. Of eleven thousand Japanese troops, only 202 were captured alive, the rest were slowly annihilated. The cost, however, was enormous: 10,786 casualties among the US marines, of which 2,336

48 and 49. The Mariana Islands were vital to the security of the Japanese Home Islands, and as they fell one after the other—Saipan, Guam, Tinian—the sense of urgency grew. Two very dramatic messages from *PWR* conveyed this sense of desperation, one by photograph and slogan, the other by the artist's hand and imagination. At left, a photograph of camouflaged Japanese snipers with a slogan written over its border that reads, "The Battle for the Marianas is Crucial. We One Hundred Million, with Fateful Determination, Face up to this National Crisis" (*PWR* 333, 9 August 1944, p. 3). At right, a drawing shows a similar scene of Japanese guerrillas in the jungle, but at closer proximity and with movement and drama (*PWR* 337, 6 September 1944, p. 3). The accompanying caption reads, "This fighting spirit Is the One Hundred Million's, too. The fight to the finish of our brave soldiers left behind on Guadalcanal, as imagined and drawn by Tamura Kōsuke." This "imaginary drawing" (*sōzōzu*) places the viewer alongside the men as they move toward a target, presumably to fight to the death. By comparison, the men in the photograph appear static and staged. Very few photographs illustrating the Battle of the Marianas appeared in periodicals, since few pertinent ones were available other than official photographs of the military leaders who died there. During the Marianas campaign in the summer and autumn of 1944, graphic artists served as the eyes of the nation.

50. *PWR* 334, 16 August 1944, p. 3. "Imaginary Drawing of the Last-ditch Fight of the Brave Warriors on Tinian" by Iwata Sentarō. An article called "The Battle of the Marianas in Its Critical Phase" gave a nearly hopeless, but realistic report of battlefield conditions from the Marianas Defense Command, dated 1 August, stating; "1. Since the enemy landed on the main island, we have inflicted heavy losses on the enemy concentration along Akashi and Shōwa Avenues. The front line has contracted in the region north of Akashi, where a fight to the death is under way. 2. On Tinian Island, since the enemy landed in the northern region, although inferior in number our soldiers checked the enemy's southern advance, inflicting heavy losses upon them. However, yesterday, the thirty-first, the enemy broke through our final line of resistance in the southern region and engaged in battle. 3. On Roc Island, we have sustained several days of fierce bombardment from the enemy, but our courageous fighting has prevented the enemy from landing." Tinian was quickly made into a US airbase, and from here the Enola Gay took off on its mission to drop the atomic bomb on Hiroshima.

As with Iwata's 1937 work (Chapter 3, figure 67), these soldiers are beautiful. They wear the headbands of samurai, rather than helmets, linking them to the Bushido code of the feudal past. The short sword is highlighted, while the semi-automatic rifle (in the foreground) is dark and almost obscure, further tying this scene to the past. The fighting spirit of the Japanese race—*yamatodamashii*—transcends time and place.

were fatalities. The "digging in" strategy was extremely effective at Peleliu, where the casualty ratio approached one US troop for one Japanese killed.

The Battle of the Philippines began on 20 October 1944, when four hundred twenty transports and 157 warships under General Douglas MacArthur's command began landing men on Leyte amid a flood of firepower. General Yamashita Tomoyuki, the "Tiger of Malaya," was put in charge of two hundred fifty thousand Japanese defenders. The final major naval battle of the Pacific theater took place between 23 and 29 October at Leyte Gulf. With fuel supplies dwindling, the Japanese ships were sent out with little hope—indeed, little point—of returning. The siege of Manila in January and February 1945 was a month-long killing spree in which cornered Japanese troops slaughtered about one hundred thousand Filipinos. Atrocities like this were not reported on the home front. Indeed, the Japanese defeat there was never quite reported in Japan—resistance was supposedly continuing when the war ended. Some Japanese holdouts in the Philippines surrendered as recently as 2004, after entire lifetimes spent as guerrillas. Organized resistance ended, though, by March 1945. Japanese losses in the Philippines totaled over two hundred thousand. Since the Philippines had become an "independent" nation in October 1943, the defeat was not portrayed as a blow to Japan's sovereignty. Surely the Filipinos were continuing the fight against Western imperialism.

The Battle of Iwo Jima witnessed the most effective implementation of the fukkaku policy. The Japanese used the punishing terrain to advantage, burrowing into the volcanic rock and patiently lying in wait to ambush the enemy. *PWR*'s coverage of

51. *PWR* 364-365, 28 March 1945, p. 2. This photograph of "Lieutenant-General Kuribayashi Tadamichi at the command of his troops on Iwo Jima,"[10] credited to Shishikura of the Information Corps, appeared with his "final telegraph" from the island, which says:

"The final battle is now before our very eyes. On the night of the seventeenth, my officers stood at the head of their men, and as all of them prayed for the victory and safety of the emperor and the nation, they undertook a brave, fierce all-out attack.

"Since the enemy invasion, we have continued to fight robustly against an unimaginably greater matériel advantage that has come from land, sea, and air. The enemy, who we ourselves have been rather glad to take on, were confronted by the courageous fighting of our officers and men, truly the screams of monsters [*kijin*, literally, "demon-gods"].

"Even so, the enemy's persistent, fierce attack felled our men one after another and therefore, contrary to your expectations, we have been forced to relinquish this important land to the enemy, for which I beg pardon and offer profound apologies.

"When I think that without recapturing this island the Land of the Emperor will not be calm for all eternity, then at the very least I vow as a spirit [in the afterlife] to lead the Imperial Army in another attempt [to retake this land].

"Now the bullets are flying, our water has run dry, and as all of us left to fight have come to the point of making our final fight to the death, we think of our gratitude for the emperor's kind benevolence as we, with no regrets, pulverize our bones and crush our bodies.

"Here, we officers and troops, together as one, cheering 'banzai' for the long life of the emperor, bid you eternal farewell."

the battle noted with pride that the US press referred to Iwo as "Hell island." The commander, Lieutenant-General Kuribayashi Tadamichi, had riddled the volcanic island with tunnels and filled its cavities and caves with guerrilla cells. The pride he expressed in his final telegram was not unwarranted: his garrison of twenty-two thousand men endured five weeks of fierce fighting against a force of over seventy-five thousand men, more than three times larger, with vastly superior air and naval power. The human scorecard was again grim: only 1,083 Japanese taken prisoner, with the remaining twenty-one thousand dead; the combined US marine and navy losses of 24,700 casualties including six thousand nine hundred killed. In the space of five weeks, some twenty-eight thousand souls were lost on a 5-square mile deserted island. At Iwo Jima, the Japanese had exceeded a one-to-one Japanese American casualty ratio.

The press worked in overdrive to sugarcoat another bitter defeat, giving the home front a stirring, personal account of the final actions on Iwo Jima written by Kuribayashi himself and sent to Tokyo as a final telegram. Kuribayashi's prose is refined and literate, describing his and his men's final suicidal actions not as gyokusai ("crushing jewels") but with a new, related word meant to convey humility in referring to oneself, *gyokushin* ("crushing the body"). By printing Kuribayashi's telegram, *PWR* gave civilians the privilege of peering inside military affairs, as if they were themselves members of the military elite and privy to its communications. The *PWR* article makes the inflated claim that US forces suffered thirty-three thousand casualties on Iwo Jima from the time of their landing through 16 March. Yet it also dryly notes that Japanese troops have disappeared from Iwo Jima and ends with a terrifying prospect: "The enemy is already beginning to land on the islands southwest of Kyūshū, moving forward with their strategy for the Home Islands. Finally, the time has arrived. How very bright will the glory of victory shine across this Land of the Emperor when we One Hundred Million have entirely become like the brave warriors of Iwo Jima. The real fight is still to come." Kuribayashi (more precisely, his ghost), was passing the torch to civilians through his "final telegraph," reprinted with his photograph in *PWR*.

The Japanese press had dutifully reported each battle as a "victory," although the truth must have been more obvious as the fighting drew closer to the Home Islands.[11] We can hardly imagine what effect undiluted reports of the war's course would have had on Japanese morale. Even if the Japanese public had been presented with incontrovertible proof of the devastating military defeats of 1943 and 1944, the Allied carpet bombings of civilian urban areas only confirmed the message of the Japanese wartime media: Americans were racists who had an irrational fear and unmitigated hatred of Asians, Japanese in particular, and would not stop short of exterminating the Japanese race. The US military's position must have been clear to those transmitting it: until Japan unconditionally surrendered, there would be no mercy, but after the surrender, Japan would be treated with compassion. For those on the receiving end, however, the two propositions seemed contradictory: if the United States really meant to treat Japanese civilians as innocent victims of the military clique, as American surrender leaflets stated, then why were nearly defenseless cities, filled with the elderly, women, and children, being systematically torched?

Japanese strategists knew that banzai attacks were demoralizing for Allied troops (who initially were culturally and psychologically ill-prepared for them), and exploited this weakness, albeit at a terrific cost of life. From the Japanese perspective, gyokusai was a sharp attack not only on Allied personnel but on Allied "values" of individualism and hedonism, for the enemy was such a cowardly lot they routinely chose to surrender rather than fight. In truth, acts of extraordinary courage and cowardice are universal during war. Mass suicide of military personnel and coerced mass suicide of civilian populations, however, cannot be found on all sides of the war, not even among the defeated nations.

While sacrifice is the common denominator of military service, the cultural and social configuration of sacrifice is much more significant than its personal or historical circumstances. The Japanese nation sanctioned and ritualized an extreme degree of sacrifice—mass suicide attacks—condemned by the Allies as lunatic and fanatic. The Allied dismissal of gyokusai masked a palpable fear of a baffling psychology and course of action that Westerners could not comprehend and seemed afraid of seriously contemplating. "Dying honorably" meant that there would be no quick or easy solution to the riddle of ending the war. And so, as horrific and hopeless as the war had already become when the third anniversary of the Imperial Rescript Declaring War against America and Britain was marked, with little fanfare and subdued celebration, on 8 December 1944, surrender was still inconceivable. The press continued to tell the

52. *PWR* 364-365, 28 March 1945, p. 2. This photograph of Iwo Jima, taken from an airplane (the wing is visible upper right) was cabled to Japan. The lines of striation running through the image vertically are the result of very poor printing. The caption says, "We absolutely must win. Let's follow [the example of] these brave warriors."

The severe landscape of Iwo Jima, a heap of punishing ash, was the first moonscape of the war. Coincidentally, it appeared in the same issue of *PWR* reporting on the Great Kantō Air Raid (see Introduction, figure 2). That the image was blurred and indistinct hardly mattered, its message of decimation had already been brought home to Japan by Allied carpet bombing. The picture of Iwo Jima, an island made nearly uninhabitable by the forces of nature, might as well be post-air raid downtown Tokyo. The weapons of modern warfare would create other moonscapes in Japan in the final five months of the war.

people that victory was just around the corner, that increased effort would surely bring about a splendid result. And the government also made the spectacle of gyokusai the means of transmitting to the civilian population the absolute code of Japan's military: no surrender. The wholesale slaughter continued throughout Asia because on the one hand, the Japanese refusal of the terms of unconditional surrender allowed the United States to feel justified in relentlessly punishing an unrepentant Japan, and on the other hand, Japan's military was ready to sacrifice so many lives in the hope of insuring the autonomy of the state apparatus and survival of its emperor.

53. *PWR* 363, 14 March 1945, p. 2. Ishikawa Shinsuke's cartoon cites a Japanese folktale in which a thumb-size samurai kills a giant ogre who has swallowed him whole, by cutting his way out of the ogre's stomach (hence the cloud of gas escaping from the stomach). The caption reads, "The Devil and the Cutting-from-Inside Corps. Keep on stabbing, stabbing, inside his stomach." The ogre, a caricature of a lanky-limbed GI with the head of Roosevelt and ogre's horns, is weighed down with armaments so massive as to make effective fighting impossible. Indeed, his spidery limbs buckle under their weight just before he tumbles to the ground.

Wartime cartoons incorporated visual elements emphasizing the advantages of the typical Japanese physique, with its stout, firm legs placing the body's center of gravity closer to the ground, and the disadvantages of the typical Caucasian physique, top-heavy and awkward with its spindly limbs. This Japanese David-and-Goliath cartoon portrays several truths with text and image. Japan's leaders could no longer deny the US's advantage in terms of armaments and manpower. The ratio of US to Japanese troops engaged in each battle from Attu to Iwo Jima was usually about three (if not four) to one. From the Japanese perspective, the United States would never win the war without disproportionately superior numbers of troops and matériel, because Japanese soldiers were willing to make greater sacrifices than their American adversaries, even to be swallowed alive and (figuratively) consumed by the enemy, if necessary. The cartoon therefore comments upon the efficacy of "dying honorably," represented by the banzai charge (the soldier with sword) and kamikaze pilot (with outstretched arms bearing a lit explosive).

Notes

1. A *PWR* article suggesting this connection between the Aleutians and the Doolittle Raid appeared on the second anniversary of the raid. See "The Enemy Is Coming from the North, too" (*Teki wa kita kara mo kuru zo*), *PWR* 317, 19 April 1944, p. 2.

2. A common source of the phrase is the *Book of the Northern Qi* (636), by Li Baiyao (564-647). John Dower summarizes the key passage thus: "on matters of principle, the man of moral superiority would break his precious jade rather than compromise to save the roof tiles of his home" (*War Without Mercy: Race and Power in the Pacific War* [New York: Pantheon, 1986], p. 231). Morohashi's *Dai kanwa jiten* quotes the *Book of the Northern Qi* as well as the *Nanshi* (*Southern History*) as sources for gyokusai. Morohashi explains, "gyokusai is becoming a jewel and breaking apart. It is said of dying to protect honor and justice, or to further a cause" (Volume 7, p. 793). Morohashi's metaphorical interpretation suggests that the actor assumes the firm quality of the jewel (a rare or beautiful stone, such as jade) rather than of the earthenware roof tile (which is malleable and easily broken). Oda Makoto's novel *Gyokusai* has been translated by Donald Keene as *The Breaking Jewel* (New York: Columbia University Press, 2003).

3. This work and many others, including Fujita's "Compatriots on Saipan are Loyal to the End" ("Saipantō dōhō shinsetsu o mattō su," 1945, oil on canvas, 71 by 144 inches), were part of an "extended loan" to SCAP for a war art exhibition that was planned to tour Japan after the defeat in the fall of 1945. A *Nippon Times* article from 26 November 1945 (p. 2) mentions that SCAP asked Fujita to head up the "Combat Art Section" and organize the tour. For years it was rumored that these works were languishing in the bowels of US military archives, but by 2000 they had been returned to Japan. Some were displayed in a pioneering exhibit at Gallery Kawafune in Ginza, Tokyo, in 2001. The National Museum of Modern Art, Tokyo, is now in possession of Fujita's "Attu Gyokusai" (1943, oil on canvas, 76 by 102 inches) and "Saipan Gyokusai," along with some one hundred fifty works of war art, and has exhibited some of these works since 2002. The museum renders the title "Attu Gyokusai" as "Final Fighting on Attu."

4. In a 2003 online article "Proretaria bijutsu to sensōga ni okeru 'kokumin'-teki shikaku" ("Visualization of 'Citizen'-ness in Proletarian Art and War Pictures"), Kobayashi Shunsuke claims that Fujita Tsuguharu's painting of the Saipan gyokusai relied in part on the battle report published in the 19 August 1944 issue of *Time* magazine, which was translated into Japanese and sent to Japan by a Japanese *Asahi Newspaper* correspondent stationed in a neutral country. See www.e.yamagata-u.ac.jp/~shun/proletar.html.

5. The mass send-off of student conscripts at the Meiji Shrine Outer Garden Stadium, an event given moderate coverage at the time (certainly less so than the Attu gyokusai), became one of the formative events in postwar memory of the war, in large part thanks to the publication of writings left behind by fallen students, *Listen to the Voices of the Sea* (*Kike wadatsumi no koe*), first published in 1949. Indeed, a very poignant account of this very send-off can be found in English painstakingly translated by Midori Yamanouchi and Joseph L. Quinn, which notes that Ebashi's speech was titled "We Certainly Do Not Expect to Return Alive." See Midori Yamanouchi and Joseph L. Quinn, translators, *Listen to the Voices from the Sea* (Scranton: University of Scranton Press, 2000), pp. 135-138.

6. The White Tiger Brigade (Byakkotai) was a group of adolescents from the Aizu Clan who killed themselves when their castle fell during a Restoration-related struggle in 1868. Citing this historical precedent invokes a racial identity of Japanese as a people of extraordinary spiritual resolve, who die fighting rather than surrender.

7. One historian cites an imperial order encouraging civilians on Saipan to commit suicide rather than be taken prisoner: "the order empowered the commander on Saipan to promise civilians who died there an equal spiritual status in the afterlife with that of soldiers perishing in combat. On June 30, the prime minister, war minister, and chief of staff, namely General Tojo, intercepted this order and delayed its sending. It went out anyway, the next day" (David Bergamini, *Japan's Imperial Conspiracy* [London: Panther, 1972], p. 1012).

8. The work is now in the collection of the National Museum of Modern Art, Tokyo. One unnamed contributor to a series of online wartime scrapbooks recalls an exhibition of war art in the spring of 1945 in which Fujita's Saipan canvas was included. The contributor says that as an elementary school student at

the time, he or she was not allowed into a separate exhibit room that included works like Fujita's that were deemed too disturbing for children to view. Nevertheless, the contributor cut out a newspaper reproduction of the famous Saipan work from the *Asahi Newspaper* around the same time. This image is available online. The scrapbook series is called "Shūsen zengo ninenkan no shinbun kirinukichō" (Newspaper scrapbooks from the two years around the end of the war) and the particular article is the third in the series, "Saipantō gyokusai to Fujita gahaku" ("The Saipan Island Gyokusai and the artist Fujita." See www.asahi-net.or.jp/~uu3s-situ/00/50-nen3.html.

9. One famous account by a soldier in the Philippines who continued to resist for thirty years after the war's end is Onoda Hiroo's *No Surrender: My Thirty Years' War* (Tokyo: Kodansha International, 1974).

10. The Japanese Government's Geographical Survey Institute recently announced that "Iōtō," the original reading of the characters for Iwo Jima, had been officially reinstated. In fact, standard Japanese dictionaries have for many decades made a distinction between Iōshima (also Iōgashima), a "Sulphur Island" off the coast of Kyūshū, and Iōtō, the "Sulphur Island" due south of Tokyo that was the site of the massive World War II battle. *PWR* supplied no syllabry for these characters. The juvenile magazine *Weekly Junior Citizen* supplied syllabry for the first two of the three characters (that is, Iō), thereby indicating that the third character be read in the same *onyomi* style: Iōtō. Reiji Yoshida, writing in the *Japan Times*, notes that prewar maps often added syllabry for the characters to yield the reading, Iōjima. See "Iwojima, Site of Fierce Battle, is Officially Renamed Iwoto," in the *Japan Times*, 19 June 2007, available online at www.japantimes.co.jp/.

11. Masao Miyoshi writes that while "No Japanese knew what to expect in the summer of 1945 . . . some diplomats in Moscow and Bern were trying to communicate and negotiate with the Allied Powers" and that there were "abbreviated, but clear references to such efforts in the *Asahi* newspaper even in the first half of 1945. Thus they knew a little about the intentions of the Allies and even of the US-Soviet relations before the spring of 1945. Still, the continual quarrels among the war leaders in Japan made analysis of the news and reports extremely difficult and their transmission to the public nearly impossible. In addition to the harshest information control, there was a shortage of paper, limiting the daily newspapers to two pages, with the minimal tidbits of hard news and proportionately ample propaganda. People were of course told of the latest lost battles but were repeatedly assured of the final victory; and they tried their best to believe the unbelievable." See "Who Decides, and Who Speaks? *Shutaisei* and the West in Postwar Japan," in Andrew Gerstle and Anthony Milner, eds., *Recovering the Orient: Artists, Scholars, Appropriations* (New York: Harwood Academic, 1994), p. 270 and p. 270, n3.

12. THE KAMIKAZEFICATION OF THE HOME FRONT

The loss of Saipan to US forces in the summer of 1944 heralded a maelstrom of death and destruction in the Japanese homeland, previously little touched by US attacks. With the completion of US air fields and bases on Saipan, not only were the Southern Regions of the Greater East Asian Co-Prosperity Sphere prone to Allied attacks, but also the Japanese Home Islands were vulnerable. From the final months of 1944, two new phenomena dramatically transformed the face of the war: massive US air raids on targets in Japan and the deployment of kamikaze pilots—a last-ditch effort to stop the US-led advance across the Pacific toward Tokyo. Facing a profound national crisis, the government preached a jeremiad, calling upon the Japanese people to emulate the kamikaze pilots—to become "kamikazefied" (*kamikaze ni ka suru*, literally, "change into kamikaze") and embody the "Special Attack Force spirit" (*tokkōtai seishin*).

1. *PWR* 353, 3 January 1945. The "Signboard of the Times" on the front cover of the New Year's issue carries the message, "In this new year, although the fierceness of the battle intensifies, our will to fight is unyielding. We One Hundred Million are already kamikazefied. The people of this Land of the Gods renew their will to fight."

Kamikazefication of the home front, down to the last schoolgirl, became the rallying cry in 1945. This girl is tying on a headband with the word "kamikaze" on it. The Japanese plane over her head and the map of the Philippine Islands (site of the first kamikaze mission) suggest the link between the actions of the suicide pilots and the home front.

Nine months of carpet-bombing reduced 60 percent of Japanese urban areas to rubble, including virtually all major cities. The home front was in danger of disintegrating into chaos and squalor. The kamikazefied "children of the emperor" were to meet the chastening punishment of air raids with usual good cheer, just as they had gladly accepted greater sacrifices and deprivation.

In June 1945, the Imperial High Command announced the division of the four main islands into eight geographical regions, each of which would fight alone in the event of an Allied invasion, following the Okinawan example. This plan to fight to the death, called the "Final Battle for the Home Islands" (*Hondo kessen*), was intended as a stern message to the United States: invasion would come at a high price. The government directed civilians on the ground to imitate the suicide pilots' aerial actions, in the event that the Allies landed on Japanese soil. Every man, woman, and child was expected to die fighting to protect the sacred land of the Japan and preserve the imperial throne. The government glorified the civilian gyokusai on Okinawa, calling it proof of the kamikazefied state of the home front. During the three months of the battle, one-quarter to one-third of the civilian population perished, over one hundred thousand lives. (In reality, many deaths were coerced by the Japanese military, a fact not known by the Japanese public until much later.) With each new military and civilian death, the need for vengeance increased and the idea of surrender grew more remote. Witness a 3 July 1945 English-language *Nippon Times* article (translated from a *Mainichi Newspaper* editorial):

> Mainichi is Confident of Final Victory in War, Says All Advantages Will Be on Japan's Side in Battle on the Main Islands
>
> The Okinawa operations, however, have provided me with a source of confidence in regard to the decisive war of Japan Proper. On considering the total armed power our enemy the United States massed at that time, the forces Japan threw in, and the war results, and estimating the armed forces that the United States and Japan will be able to mass against the coming decisive fight, and then considering what war results will be achieved, I am able to say confidently that it will be all right.
>
> A battle fought on the main island will be the final battle. It is impossible to conceive of the battles so far as the present war is concerned. Ours is a race which is possible only in relation to the structure on which its State rests. The day when tht [*sic*] 3,000 year history of our country, a history of a state of oneness between the Sovereign and the people, ends, is the day when our race goes out of existence. Our duty to our ancestors is to die to preserve the fundamental character of our State.

The popular fascination with the extremely courageous, suicidal actions of the Special Attack Force pilots was a cultural phenomenon traceable through the Three Human Bullets of the Shanghai Incident of 1932 (see Chapter 3, figures 10-14), to men of the Russo-Japanese War who killed themselves rather than be captured, to Saigō Takamori, who died by his own hand when his Southwestern War failed in 1877, and to the Aizu Clan's "White Tiger Brigade" (*Byakkotai*) who killed themselves rather than surrender the clan fortress during the struggles surrounding the Meiji Restoration of 1868. Premodern Japanese history also seems to be populated by martyrs,[1] such as the forty-seven loyal rōnin whose suicidal actions in 1701 inspired what is arguably Japan's finest and most enduring dramatic work, *Chūshingura,* which quickly became an iconic work in the canon of Japanese literature in translation.[2] Wartime culture repeatedly invoked such examples of "extreme loyalty" from every period of Japan's history.

2. “Sailors of the *Kinsu-maru* Committing Seppuku,” by Yamamoto Shōya, appeared in *The Fuzoku Gaho, an Illustrated Magazine of Japanese Life, Special Edition: Pictures of Subjugating Russia* 5, 10 May 1904 (illustration tipped in between pp. 10-11). Rather than be taken prisoner, these Japanese sailors destroy military information (the map being shredded at left) and then kill themselves. Although seppuku is, literally, “cutting the belly,” one man opts for a pistol as a more expedient means of ending his life: his shot to the head scatters blood and brain over the upper part of the picture. Although the Japanese media did not publish pictures of Japanese dying (or of their corpses) during the fifteen years of fighting (1931-1945) in Asia and the Pacific, “death for glory” became one of the hallmarks of the war and of wartime culture.

With its establishment in 1869, Yasukuni Shrine became the home of the spirits of Japanese soldiers and sailors who died "in the service of the emperor." Enshrined at Yasukuni as "warrior-gods" (*gunshin*), fallen soldiers and sailors were believed to reside in the afterlife alongside the spirits of the imperial ancestors. The emperor himself presided over the enshrinement ceremonies (see Chapter 1, figures 24-26). Of course, dying in battle and killing oneself on the battlefield were hardly synonymous, but no distinction was made at Yasukuni, which enshrined the spirits of men who never saw combat and died of battlefield disease. As early as the Russo-Japanese War, killing oneself rather than being captured was a laudable action warranting a place in popular culture. Indeed, the classic account of willed battlefield death, *Human Bullets* (*Nikudan*, 1905),[3] is an autobiographical narrative of the Russo-Japanese War. *Human Bullets* was translated into English in 1906, when translations of contemporary Japanese literature were scarce, and went through several printings.

伜は九段の若櫻

靖國神社春の臨時大祭
厳かに執行さる

3

3. *PWR* 270, 5 May 5, 1943, p. 3. "Our Son Is a Young Cherry Blossom [at Yasukuni] in Kudan." The scattering of cherry blossoms, likened to the death of a young man in his prime, is a common theme in classical Japanese literature.[4] Here, a formally attired elderly couple have come to Yasukuni to witness the mass enshrinement ceremony that included their son's spirit.

4. *PWR* 219, 6 May 1942, pp. 20-21. "Listening in at the Altar of Yasukuni." Short interviews of visitors to Yasukuni who observed the ceremony enshrining 15,017 new warrior-gods on 23 April 1942. These Japanese of all ages, from different parts of the nation and speaking different dialects (transcribed in their comments), are brought together by Yasukuni and its spiritual power. No widows were interviewed.

(right page, p. 20) Comments translated in columns, starting at top right:

"I am so grateful to be able to come to the shrine and pray, I can't think of anything else." Yamaki Sawa, age sixty-nine, Hokkaidō.

"As the oldest son, I don't want to do anything to tarnish the reputation of my younger brother." Atsuta Heiichi, age thirty-six, Chiba.

(evidently, the voice of the fallen soldier) "Yoneko, you really came all the way to see me. You've really made your older brother happy." Uchida Yoneko, age seventeen, Hokkaidō.

"This is my first time in Tokyo. Everybody's been showing me around." Kashiwabara Tsunemasa, age sixty-seven, Nagano.

"I think that the gods exist only in Japan." Sugimoto Aisaburō, age seventy, Kyoto.

"I think my son reached a man's goal of sincerity. I'm sincere, too." Maeda Kikuzō, age sixty-five, Shizuoka.

"Me, uh, I'm sure I'll be a strong soldier when I grow up." Hasegawa Ryōichi, age seven, Tokyo.

"I arrived this morning. I am moved by the sight of the giant torii." Shirasaki Matsujirō, age fifty-two, Fukui.

"(Chuckling) My boy must be happy, being deified like that." Yamada Takezō, age sixty-three, Wakayama.

"I'm grateful. I am determined not to be outdone by my [fallen] uncle." Nakazato Chikao, age twenty-eight, Ibaraki.

(left page, p. 21) In columns, starting with the column of two at the right side of the page.

"Just to be able to pray here, I feel so grateful, just like getting over an illness." Murata Manjirō, age sixty-seven, Osaka.

"I came from far away. What can I say, I'm so grateful." Ōshita Kiyokichi, age fifty-three, Kagoshima.

"Sons belong to the nation. All five of my boys are in the service." Ōtake Moto, age fifty-five, Chiba.

"Loyal service is of a piece, they say, and my son's filial piety moves me and makes me happy." Terauchi Kanekichi, age sixty-three, Tochigi.

"It was my second son who died." Nigo Kenji, age sixty-three, Okayama.

"Yeeeess, I came to meet my [dead] son." Iwama Miki, age seventy, Mie.

"I did my best to come meet my older brother. He's a great man." Fujimoto Toshiaki, age eleven, Oita.

"I'm impressed by the kindness of everybody in Tokyo." Uchida Kamekichi, age sixty-eight, Hokkaidō.

"Crying 'air raid' and panicking. I must apologize [for such cowardly behavior] to my dead son." Mima Moto, age forty-eight, Osaka. [This is probably a reference to the still-fresh Doolittle Raid.]

"It was my son's face, healthy and well, just like always, that came floating before my eyes." Hiroki Toshinosuke, age sixty-six, Ibaraki. Photographs: Yoshida Sakae.

The first Special Attack Forces were midget submarine squadrons, which completed several daring missions in the first two years of the war.[5] Their courageous deeds were celebrated in the press, especially their successes at Pearl Harbor; Diego Suarez, Madagascar; and Sydney, Australia. These midget submarine attacks, while carried out with a suicidal resolve, were not suicide missions in the strictest sense, because the completion of the mission did not necessitate the destruction of the battery-powered vessels and their crews. In fact, one two-man crew did manage to return to its mother submarine after carrying out a successful raid during the Battle of Guadalcanal on 17 November 1942. Ironically, the press did not hail these men as heroes because they survived, although they severely damaged a transport ship, the USS *Majaba*.

Of the twenty sailors manning the ten vessels involved in the three famous midget submarine raids, only one survived. This survival rate of one in twenty, or 5 percent, was higher than that for the much larger gyokusai attacks, many of which had a survival rate of about one percent. While the leaders of the gyokusai attacks became national heroes, the hundreds or even thousands of men they led into battlefield suicide remained anonymous in the national press. The Special Attack Forces were treated differently; perhaps the nature of their daring deeds, creeping deep inside enemy-held waters to attack enemy naval bases, captured the imagination. Or maybe it was the idea of a two-man crew in a small submarine destroying a large target, such as an aircraft carrier or destroyer, and killing hundreds of the enemy. The media showered attention upon these men who willingly accepted death as part of their mission, and the posthumous glorification of these midget submarine pilots, their personal effects, families, and hometowns set the stage for the kamikazes.

The first Special Attack Forces mission of the Great East Asia War took place at Pearl Harbor on 8 December 1941. Lieutenant Iwasa Naoji led a squadron of five two-man midget submarines that coordinated their attacks with the aerial bombardment. Each midget submarine was equipped with two torpedoes and a scuttling charge capable of destroying the vessel and crew in the event that its capture was imminent. Released from their mother submarines, they were sent to torpedo, at close range, US capital ships around Ford Island. One submarine, believed to be *I-20*, was intercepted by the destroyer USS *Ward* and sunk around 6:30 A.M., an hour and a half before the air raid began. The two crew members, Ensign Hirō Akira and Petty Officer Katayama Yoshio, became the first casualties of the Great East Asia War. Of the four remaining submarines, two were sunk at Pearl Harbor without having fired their torpedoes. One submarine, *Ha-19*, washed ashore after being damaged, contained one dead crew member and one seriously wounded, unconscious sailor.[6] The wounded man, Ensign Sakamaki Kazuo, became the first Japanese POW of the war. The Japanese public only learned of his existence after the war's end.[7] Detailed information about the midget submarine attacks was concealed from the Japanese public because of its sensitive nature. The fifth midget submarine, *I-16* manned by Lieutenant Yokoyama Masaharu and Petty Officer Ueda Sadamu,[8] radioed a message to its mother ship, "success, success, success," although it may have been reporting on the success of the aerial bombardment rather than reporting a kill from its torpedoes. The Japanese military credited the midget submarine with the sinking of a US capital ship, presumed to be the USS *Arizona* (see Chapter 7, figure 23). To this day, *I-16* remains unaccounted for, leaving open the possibility that it penetrated the harbor and launched its torpedoes, a controversial theory that has gained support in recent years from US Naval Institution researchers.[9]

The nine men who died in the midget submarine attacks on Pearl Harbor, these "Nine Pillars" of loyalty, were posthumously promoted two ranks, given a lavish military funeral, and lionized in the press. They were immediately absorbed into popular culture as the "Nine Warrior-Gods of the Shōwa Era," their example held up as a new standard of courage and self-sacrifice for military men and civilians alike. A seminal four-page article by Navy Information Bureau Chief Corporal Hirade Hideo in *PWR* 212 (pp. 4-7), a brilliant exposition of sang-froid, gave the rationale for suicidal missions and provided a template for the home front's acceptance of them. Hirade begins by describing their

5. *History Pictures* 357, February 1943, p. 12.

"Recently donated to the Navy Hall, this is Honma Shūgaku's portrait of the nine warrior-gods who, at the beginning of the Great East Asia War, penetrated the important base of the American Pacific Fleet at Pearl Harbor, sinking enemy warships as their lives scattered like the petals of nation-protecting flowers."

This painting seems to have the Nine Pillars floating above the site of their attack (and deaths), forming a "protective shield of gods" around Pearl Harbor, rather than their homeland. The insignia on their hats reflects their promotions.

glorious mission without giving any concrete details of exactly what targets they hit, concentrating on their patriotism, loyalty, and courage as they penetrated deep into enemy waters in their midget submarines. He describes them as typical, virtuous young men who became godlike through their suicidal mission.

> These brave warriors were nothing but the most excellent men, having won the confidence of their superiors for some time beforehand and the respect of their juniors who shared their barracks. None of them set their sights on advancing in rank, and none were pleasure-seekers, either. They had no concern for themselves, having cast off the very concept of "ego." Still in their twenties and in the prime of youth, they gave themselves completely, body and soul, for the emperor and the Fatherland, protecting the nation by scattering their lives like petals of manhood in full bloom.

One of the most striking sections of Hirade's article recounts, as vividly as a film script, the Nine Pillars' final moments before leaving for their fatal mission. These anecdotes gave the public an intimate glimpse into the character and psychology of their heroes while also normalizing suicidal actions.

純忠比なし 軍神九柱

特別攻撃隊の偉勳 畏くも上聞に達す

感状 特別攻撃隊

昭和十七年二月十一日

聯合艦隊司令長官 山本五十六

6. *PWR* 212, 18 March 1942, p. 3. "The Nine Pillars, Warrior-Gods of Incomparably Pure Loyalty." In March 1942, the Navy Ministry released the names of nine sailors who died in midget submarine missions during the attack on Pearl Harbor. Each wrote his final words in calligraphy that was reprinted in this magazine article, along with a commendation from Admiral Yamamoto Isoroku, the Imperial Headquarters' official account of their actions, a photograph of the sunk USS *Arizona* (see Chapter 7, figure 23), and an article praising them as young men of exceptional virtue.

The crew members are (in columns, starting at top right):

(first column) Iwasa Naoji, Yokoyama Masaji, Furuno Shigemi.

(second column) Hirō Akira, Yokoyama Shigenori, Sasaki Naokichi.

(third column) Ueda Sadamu, Katayama Yoshio, and Inagaki Kiyoshi.

They ranged in age from twenty-two to twenty-nine and all hailed from different prefectures. Most of them came from rural hamlets.

At Ease as They Departed for Certain Death

Even as they embarked for a place of death, not life, these brave warriors were calm and collected, no different from when they left for one of their regular training sessions.

Just before they left, these heroes gathered together with their war buddies to talk and laugh, and one young hero said, "After the attack is over, I'd like to go ashore and tell those bastards a thing or two," harmlessly taking his pistol out and stroking it. Another hero, having changed into new underclothes, said, "I should go wearing my battle uniform, but it will be hot. Well, pardon me for wearing my fatigues." He calmly went about getting ready. Another hero, hearing one of his war buddies say, "Be sure to avoid any depth charges," responded with carefree laughter. "Are you kidding? Before they have a chance to drop any, we will have opened a big hole slitting the enemy [ship's] belly!" Taking his time to leisurely roll a cigarette, another spontaneously composed a bit of doggerel: "The following day, / I also heard Roosevelt's tearful whining, /As I stood [in judgment] before the King of Hell."

One of the heroes, who liked his sake, was offered these words of encouragement by one of his war buddies: "Produce some big war results, and when you come back, we'll have a good long drink." This made him smile, but not once did he respond with his usual, "Yes, we'll have a drink together." These heroes must have known they should not use phrases such as "I'll be back" and "No matter what, I'll survive."

The heroes then gave their war buddies staying behind pats on the back and a brief pep talk. "Let's stick with it until the very, very end. The next time we meet will be at [Yasukuni] Shrine in Kudan."

The time had finally come for their departure.

Usually, when leaving for the front, a soldier tells his commanding officer, "I will be back," but on that day, these heroes enthusiastically told their COs, "I am now on my way," they did not say, "I will be back."

"I am counting on you."

"You can count on me, sir."

7. *PWR* 212, 18 March 1942, p. 5. "The Special Attack Forces Strike an Enemy Ship," by Matsuzoe Ken, shows a midget submarine torpedoing a US ship on Battleship Row, Pearl Harbor. Strangely, the scene takes place by moonlight, although it was already morning at the time of the attack. The illustration probably refers to the famous photograph taken by a Japanese airplane during the attack (see Chapter 7, figure 15). The photograph has since been forensically analyzed by a team from the US Naval Institute, who conclude that a midget submarine attack was responsible for hits on the USS *West Virginia* and USS *Oklahoma*. This theory remains controversial.

The next section of Hirade's article reconciles suicide missions with the ethos of filial piety. In making an example of the selfless sacrifices made by the families of the Nine Pillars and focusing on the difference between Japanese and American mothers, the text sets a high standard of self sacrifice and stoicism for the home front.

> Such a Mother Has Such a Hero [for a Son]
>
> One fact that must be entered into this illustrious account is that the great spirit of sacrificing oneself and dying for one's country becomes great through the influence of a great mother. As has already been mentioned, all of the heroes were famous for their filial piety. One of the heroes found the most pleasure in spending the whole day with his mother, and whenever he had even a short time off, he would always go home. In such actions we see one facet of the hero. So great is the power of these mothers who so lovingly raised their sons, so great is the spiritual influence of these mothers who, for the sake of their homes, their husbands, and their children, continued to toil with no regrets for themselves, showing that the greatest happiness comes from devoting themselves to others, so enormous was the influence [of their spirit of sacrifice] that it cultivated a great power in these heroes as well. Were it not for these noble mothers of Japan, how would such manly heroes, so pure and loyal, be born?
>
> If we were to compare these heroes to the circumstances of the military men of the enemy, America and Britain, who quickly run away when confronted with such superior adversaries and hope to avoid dangerous situations that might lead to their deaths, we see how completely different are our heroes. We cannot overlook the karmic connection between selfish, hedonistic mothers [of the West] and their [cowardly] children.

The final section of Hirade's article solidifies the link between the actions of the Special Attack Forces midget submarines and the home front.

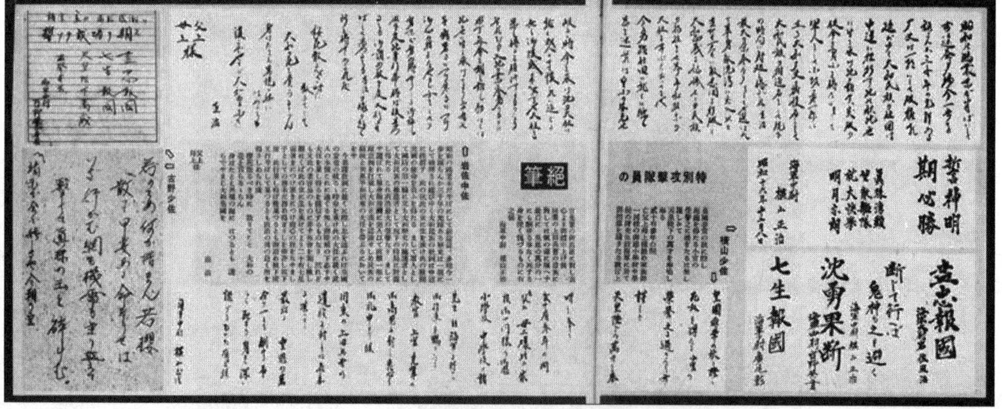
絶筆
特別攻撃隊員の
誓神明
期必勝
盡忠報國
七生報國
沈勇果斷

8. *PWR* 212, 18 March 1942, pp. 6-7. Samurai facing death would leave behind a few words of encouragement as a memento for their loved ones, a custom continued in the modern age. The Nine Pillars' final words were stirring, patriotic phrases such as "Perform Loyal Service to the Nation," "I Pledge to the Gods, We Must Be Victorious," and a repetition of the final words of Kusunoki Masashige, "[I would give] Seven Lives in Service to the Nation." Some of the men's "final words" are written in a very bold hand, probably with brush and ink, while others seem to have been hastily written in pencil on pieces of notebook or scrap paper. The thick black border is a sign of respect for the dead.

The Spirit of "Dying by the Emperor's Side"[10]

No matter how long the Great East Asia War continues, no matter how strong the enemy may become—in the moment the Fatherland needed them, these heroes made a firm decision. They would give seven lives for the nation, no matter how many times they might be reborn in this world, these brave warriors who could be firmly entrusted with protecting the nation. It is truly lamentable that the number of lives they have to give are not as countless as the hairs on one's head.

The heroes of the Special Attack Forces are "battle gods" (*ikusa no kami*) and at the same time, "gods of peacemaking" (*heiwa kensetsu no kami*). For those of us who live in this world after the Great East Asia War ends, it must be a world of lasting peace. And at that time, these "warrior-gods" will become "peace gods" (*heiwa no kami*) Because the destruction of the present moment is not destruction for the sake of destruction but destruction for the sake of peace.

These nation-protecting heroes are the children of we Japanese citizens, our older brothers and our younger brothers. That they clearly demonstrated that the fluid flowing through the veins of we citizens is a tide of blood of incomparably pure loyalty should serve as encouragement to us in times when we have doubts about our role as individuals or when the nation faces a crisis or the country is imperiled. Let me repeat that it is easy to become excited for a while, but difficult to die calmly, especially as we are now only at the beginning of a protracted war.

9. *PWR* 217, 22 April 1942, p. 3. "Joint Naval Funeral for the Warrior-Gods, the Nine Pillars, 8 April, Hibiya Park, Tokyo."

"The funeral for the warrior-gods—the nine pillars of incomparably pure loyalty who will return no more after their participation on 8 December 1941 in the dawn raid on Pearl Harbor, sinking capital ships of the US Pacific Fleet which went to the bottom of the harbor—took place on 8 April, a change only in the month and not the day [of their death]. It took place in Hibiya Park's funeral grounds and was the most serene and dignified funeral in a very long time—since the Naval Funeral of Lieutenant-Commander Hirose. On this day, we one hundred million citizens think of them with a new sense of gratitude, with yearning and admiration, as we send their spirits off to eternity.

"'Go to sea, waterlogged corpses'—the heroic spirits of the nine warrior-gods have flown to the heavens, and are now, as this burial ground is bathed in the bright sunshine and the glory of the Fatherland, already enshrined for all eternity as a fiercely strong shield of gods protecting the nation."

10-15. *PWR* 233, 12 August 1942. Two pages from a four-page article about children, members of Tokyo Youth Groups (under the direction of the IRAA), who formed a Lieutenant Iwasa Admiration Squadron. Squadron Leader Ogura Narinosuke, age sixty-two, and Squadron Assistant Leader Yamaguchi Kōichi, age 33, took seven children from Tokyo on a three-day tour of Maebashi, Gunma Prefecture, Iwasa's hometown, where they visited the home he grew up in (his birthplace) and the school he attended.

"The first unit of the Warrior-God Lieutenant Iwasa Admiration Squadron from Tokyo Youth Groups will travel to eleven birthplaces of warrior-gods. They visited Maebashi, the hometown of the warrior-god [i.e., Iwasa] on 29 July . . . Immersed in the natural environment in which the warrior-god was raised, their hearts were all the more impressed by the greatness of the warrior-god, and they were inspired by thoughts of the warrior-god in his former days [here on earth]."

"His body lies at the bottom of Pearl Harbor, crushed and scattered in youth like the petals of a cherry blossom, but the rays of light he left behind will never burn out, and the 'soul' of the warrior-god, the light that these young people sought in his birthplace, left a deep, deep impression on their young minds."

(left page, top right, p. 17) "When the Admiration Squadron arrived at Maebashi Station, they were greeted by members of the Jōnan Citizens' School Youth Group. Here, Yoshizawa [of the Tokyo group] returns the greeting of their friends at Jōnan School."

(left page, top left) "At the warrior-god's birthplace. The front gate of the warrior-god's birthplace has a sign, 'home of warrior-god Iwasa Naoji,' so they could find it right away."

(left page, bottom) (in the voice of the children) "We met with the warrior-god's parents, and were grateful for the many lessons we received from them."

(right page, top, p. 18) "The group made a firm resolution as they prostrated themselves before the lieutenant's grave, where they listened to the lieutenant's favorite teacher, who taught the lieutenant in fifth grade, talk about the warrior-god's childhood."

(right page, bottom right) "In the memorial to the warrior-god installed at Jōnan Citizens' School, the Admiration Squadron could see many articles associated with him."

(right page, bottom left) "The spirit of the warrior-god having been impressed upon these children's hearts, they received this photograph [of Iwasa when an elementary-school student] as a souvenir that will help them live every day of their lives together with him."

16 and 17. "The Nine Warrior-Gods and Their Birthplaces," a series of paintings by Kumaoka Yoshihiko, was shown in a special exhibition in Tokyo that toured Japan in 1943. Here, the paintings of Ueda Sadamu (top) and his birthplace near Hiroshima (bottom) are reproduced from plate 23 in the exhibition catalogue of *Great East Asia War Art, Second Series*.

Ueda's photograph appears in the upper left corner in figure 6. In this painting (in contrast to Honma's, Figure 5) his hat reflects his rank in life, rather than the rapid promotion he received in death that entitled him to wear the hat with larger insignia.

The painting of the warrior-gods placed the portrait floating above the waves of the ocean, reminiscent of the words to the sailors' farewell song, "Umi Yukaba" ("If I Go to Sea"), a military march with rather plaintive lyrics. The paintings of the warrior-god and his birthplace were displayed in close proximity in the exhibition, reminding the viewer of the role of the warrior-god as a protective deity.

Ueda's midget submarine, launched in the hours before the aerial bombardment of Pearl Harbor began, was perhaps the only one to have succeeded in torpedoing a US ship during the raid.

18. Ueda Sadamu's story was portrayed in *Mother of a Warrior-God*, a 1943 *kamishibai* ("paper-theater"), text by Suzuki Noriko and illustrations by Nonoguchi Shigeru. The final four panels, numbered 19 through 22, are reproduced here sequentially.

Sadamu's parents were poor farmers, but his mother worked hard to send him to university. In panel 19, Sadamu bids farewell to his mother.

"'Mother!' Sadamu called out, taking a few steps to catch up to her.

"'What is it?'

"'Mother, please be sure to take good care of yourself.'

"'Well, that's what I should be saying to you, as your mother.'

"'Mother, you've always worked so hard, without ever taking a break. Please live a long, happy life.'

(Storyteller:) "These were the last words Sadamu would ever say to his mother."

19. Panel 20 shows the midget submarine attack at Pearl Harbor.

(Storyteller) "On 8 December 1941, at the commencement of the war, he volunteered to take part in a raid on the enemy American Pacific Fleet in the naval station at Pearl Harbor, Hawaii. His body was scattered like a flower, while protecting the nation. The name of Chief Petty Officer Ueda Sadamu is on the glorious roster of the nine warrior-gods of the Special Attack Forces. The nine heroes entrusted themselves to their beloved little ships and set their sights on Pearl Harbor. At the time they rushed toward [their objectives], they were something close to gods, sublime and spiritual. Once their manly act of courage and loyalty had been told, the entire citizenry could only weep tears of gratitude."

The storyteller then sings a few verses of "Umi Yukaba" ("If I Go to Sea"), a send-off song: "Go to the Sea, waterlogged corpses. Go to the mountains, corpses pushing up grass. By the emperor's side, there is no death, so I have no regrets."

20. In panel 21, Warrior-God Sadamu speaks from beyond the grave.

"Mother, please be happy. Me and the others, we did it."

(Storyteller:) "Responding to his mother's great love, the child also greatly repaid his debt of gratitude to her. The hard work to which Mother Saku resigned herself, she who had no regrets in working on and on for the sake of [the education of] her precious child, grew vigorously in Chief Petty Officer Sadamu's body, bloomed fragrantly and withered.

"She is a great mother who raised a warrior-god, comparable to the mother of Kusunoki Masatsura, the mother of Yoshida Shōin, the mother of General Nogi."[11]

21. In panel 22, the final panel, we learn who is the greatest hero of all.

"Saku, mother of a warrior-god, is far away from the voices of gratitude and praise, however. Walking across the morning dew of the highland village, she is no different today than she was long ago, still carrying a heavy load of lumber on her back. Some days, she remembers the Chief Petty Officer.

"Noble-minded, kindly, humble is this mother. Such is a Japanese mother who gave birth to one of the Nine Warrior-Gods of the Shōwa Era."

After the Dutch East Indies came under Japanese control, Japanese forces set their sights on Australia. Hostilities began on 18 February 1942 with an air raid inflicting significant damage to the military base at Darwin on the northern coast of Queensland. Sporadic attacks on Australia continued for the next year and a half, utilizing Japanese aircraft, submarines, and midget submarines. Three Japanese midget submarines raided Sydney Harbor on the night of 31 May 1942. One was sunk before it could launch its torpedoes. A second, manned by Lieutenant Matsuo Keiu and Petty Officer Tsujiku Masao, was damaged by a depth charge. The two men killed themselves with handguns

22 and 23. *PWR* 243, 21 October 1942, pp. 2-3.

(right, p. 2) "Signboard of the Times 48." The message, written in a literary style, describes the spirit of sacrifice versified in the navy's send-off song, "If I Go to Sea," and epitomized by the Special Attack Forces: "This life is not my own. / Swallow once, / Follow me / To the bottom of the blue ocean / And I will teach it to you: / This life is not my own."

(left, p. 3) "The Brave Souls of the Special Attack Forces who Raided Sydney Harbor Return to the Fatherland." The caption says, "The exchange ship bearing the remains of the four brave warriors pulls in to Yokohama."

Beside the photographs of each of the four men are their ranks, names, and places of birth. From right to left: Lieutenant Chūman Kenshi, Lieutenant Matsuo Keiu, Petty Officer First Class Ōmori Takeshi, and Petty Officer Second Class Tsujiku Masao.

rather than be captured alive. The third submarine, operated by Sub-Lieutenant Ban Katsuhisa and Petty Officer Ashibe Mamoru, penetrated the harbor, which was filled with Allied ships, and launched both torpedoes. One sunk an old transport ship, HMAS *Kuttabul*, and the other damaged a Dutch submarine. Ban and Ashibe's submarine was not accounted for by Allied intelligence, but the Japanese press reported them dead. The Australians recovered four bodies, which they cremated with full military honors, for which the Australian commander was severely criticized by the Australian public. Australia returned the ashes to Japan via a neutral country.

24-27. *PWR* 243, 21 October 1942, pp. 4-5.

"On 31 May, the Special Attack Forces made a daring moonlight raid, slipping through the heavy dragnet in Jackson Bay outside of Sydney Bay, and scored a great blow to the enemy by sinking one enemy ship moored there."

(right page, top) "The remains of the Four Pillars are solemnly carried from the ship [repatriating them]."

(right page, bottom) "Some of the relatives who have come to receive the remains and tell them 'you really did well.'"

(left page, top) "The remains, borne by family members and old friends, proceed silently past the Marine Youth Corps, who salute the remains with the dipped funerary flags."

(left page, bottom) "Is there anyone, among we one hundred million citizens, who would not weep before the spirit of incomparable loyalty of the four fallen warriors?"

The third midget submarine raid to capture public attention took place on 29 May 1942, when two midget submarines were launched to attack Allied ships in Diego Suarez Bay, Madagascar. The French colony, under Vichy control, had posed a threat to trans-Atlantic shipping and communication, and therefore the Allies had seized it early in the war. The Japanese raid on Diego Suarez Bay was the westernmost attack made by Japanese forces. Two midget submarines took part in the raid, one of which fired both of its torpedoes, hitting and severely damaging the battleship HMS *Ramillies* and also sinking an oil tanker, HMS *British Loyalty*. The crew members, Lieutenant Akieda Saburō and Petty Officer Takemoto Masami, beached their submarine and sought cover on shore. When discovered by royal marines, a firefight ensued and they were killed.

忠烈の武勲燦たり

第二次特別攻撃隊十勇士等の海軍合同葬

28-30. *PWR* 267, 14 April 1943, pp. 4-5.

(right page, p. 4) These ten sailors are the crews of the three midget submarines that attacked Sydney Harbor and the two submarines that attacked Diego Suarez. Four of the men who attacked Sydney Harbor already had their photographs featured when their ashes were returned to Japan. Each man is identified by name, rank, age, and hometown, beside his "final words" written in his own hand.

Right column, from top to bottom: Akieda Saburō, Chūman Kenshi, Matsuo Keiu, Ban Katsuhisa, and Iwase Katsunori.

Left column, from top to bottom: Takemoto Masami, Ōmori Takeshi, Ashibe Mamoru, Takada Kōzō, and Tsujiku Masao. They ranged in age from twenty-two to thirty.

(left page, p. 5) "Joint Funeral Service for the Ten Heroes of the Second Special Attack Forces Squadron."

The press portrayed the young men of the midget submarine Special Attack Forces as serious, self-effacing, brave, loyal, and coming from an ordinary background and typical surroundings. The media were careful to note that these warrior-gods' qualities were common to all Japanese military men and these "heroes" were extraordinary only in that they were given the opportunity to demonstrate the great reserves of courage and loyalty shared by all Japanese, civilians included. Navy Information Bureau Chief Corporal Hirade's *PWR* article credited the heroes' mothers for instilling in them the spirit of sacrifice and loyalty, a theme echoed by the moral at the end of *Mother of a Warrior-God*. Ordinary citizens were inextricably tied to their heroes, a fact brought home by the connection between the fallen men of the Special Attack Forces and their hometowns, by their families' place in the limelight, and by government exhortations to the home front not to forget the debt of gratitude owed to these young men who willingly sacrificed themselves in the prime of life for the common good. Conversely, the glorification of warrior-gods exerted additional pressure upon the men who were called up for suicide missions to follow through, not only for the sake of nation and emperor, but for mother and hometown, too.

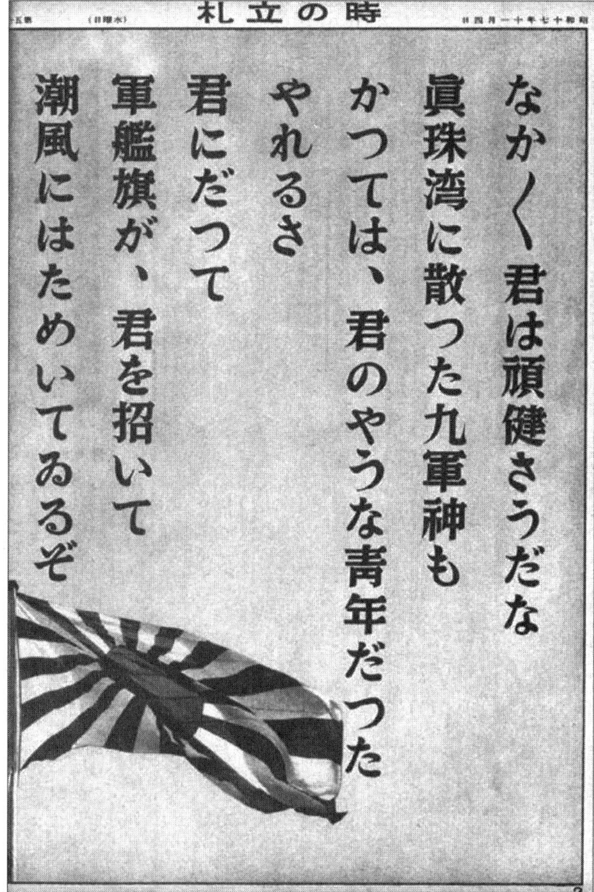

31. *PWR* 245, 4 November 1942, p. 2 (inside front cover). Signboard of the Times 50. "You look like a fine physical specimen. The nine warrior-gods whose lives were scattered [like cherry petals] at Pearl Harbor were once young men like you. You know you could do it. The battleship's flag is calling you, flapping in the salt air."

The message uses the example of the nine warrior-gods of Pearl Harbor to cajole men to join the navy. The message does not explicitly state that men who join the armed forces must become warrior-gods and accept suicide missions, although every soldier and sailor pledged to give his life to emperor and nation upon entering boot camp.

Events of 1943, including the Uchiteshi Yamamu campaign, the Attu Gyokusai and subsequent gyokusai, and student conscription, reflected the deepening crisis in the Pacific. *PWR*, which had boasted that Japan had more than enough aircraft in the early months of the war, was now openly calling for impossible increases in airplane production. Unknown to the Japanese public, the navy, the pride of the nation, had already suffered irreversible losses. Japan lacked the air power to patrol the skies over the Co-Prosperity Sphere and protect the empire. The precious remaining war matériel had to be used wisely for maximum impact while munitions stores were restocked and student conscripts trained. And then Saipan came under attack. A desperate, fierce battle ensued, claiming the lives of thousands of local residents. When Saipan fell in the summer of 1944, the media described the compulsory civilian mass suicides there as gyokusai, thus likening civilian and military mass suicide. *PWR* warned the home front that the time had come to pray and prepare for the worst.

From the summer of 1943 through the summer of 1944, entire garrisons were lost in fierce battles, and the Special Attack Forces faded from public view. When the Battle of the Philippines began, however, the Special Attack Forces made a dramatic reappearance in the press. These were the suicidal pilots about whom so much has been written and who seem to hold a lasting place in the imagination of people in many parts of the world. At the time, the Japanese media bombarded the public with images of the pilots, which dominated *PWR* for the final nine months of the war.

32. *PWR* 330-331, 26 July 1944. With the battle for Saipan in feverish pitch, *PWR*'s front cover carried this photograph of a praying man. The "Signboard of the Times" says,

"Our country is already a battlefield. At the grass roots level, the people will form a human fence to protect this Land of the Gods."

In the spring of 1944, *PWR*'s page size doubled from A4 (8¼ by 11¾ inches) to A2 (11¾ by 16½ inches), and the page count halved (from twenty-four to twelve). This A2-size magazine cover was almost as large as a newspaper page or a small-size poster. *PWR*'s page size returned to A4 in April 1945.

"Double-issues" (like this issue) of *PWR* usually followed a disruption in printing and distribution, often due to an air raid.

The first kamikaze air attacks took place during the Battle of Leyte Gulf on 25 October 1944, although in earlier incidents, Japanese pilots rammed their airplanes into Allied targets in suicidal dives.[12] The first *PWR* article about kamikazes appeared in issue 347 on 15 November 1944, by which time the public was already aware of the nature of the kamikaze missions. The preceding issue, *PWR* 346 (8 November 1944, p. 2) contained an article ripe with hubris, "The Battle of Pursuit, Securing our Opportunity for Victory," describing how in mid-October Japanese air- and sea-power turned back the American fleet, which had menaced Taiwan and Okinawa with air raids prior to invading the Philippines. "This naval battle inflicted severe losses upon the enemy, and undeniably, the beating they received undermined their strategy toward the Philippines." The article noted that the war was now a "three-dimensional war" (*rittaisen*) involving coordinated action on land, sea, and in the air, and that the most precious elements of this new kind of war were matériel (especially airplanes) and time, a word repeated in boldface. The article was full of lofty exhortations to do more for the war effort, warning the public to brace for a second and even a third naval battle off the Philippine coast. Kamikaze's suicidal actions are only alluded to: "On 25 October, our maritime squadron's close-range attacks became the core component of our naval battle."

The wartime press seems to have avoided revealing how the kamikaze squadron was formed. *PWR* gave no account of the organization of the first kamikaze squadron. The *Asahi Newspaper* provides several pieces of the story, however, especially when the headlines are read sequentially from 13 to 25 October, as a ferocious naval battle ensued off the coast of Taiwan, then Okinawa, and finally, Leyte Gulf. Every day front-page headlines boasted of sunk enemy ships, at first indicating the score for the day, and later on the impossibly large cumulative score.

13 October. Taiwan: Superior Number of Enemy Planes, One Hundred Quickly Shot Down. Indiscriminate Bombing of Taiwanese Urban Areas by China-based US Air Force.

14 October. Enemy Air Fleet Crippled. One Aircraft Carrier Sunk, One Unidentified Ship Sunk. One Aircraft Carrier Damaged, One Unidentified Ship Damaged. Enemy Raiders Increase to 1,100 Planes. One Hundred Shot Down. Air Raid again Yesterday on Taiwan.

15 October. Sunk: Three Aircraft Carriers, Three Unidentified Ships, One Escort; Damaged: One Aircraft Carrier, One Unidentified Ship. Our "Certain-Kill" Body-ramming: Even Greater War Results. One Hundred B-29s from the [Asian] Continent. 160 Planes Shot Down. Shelling and Air Raid on Taiwan.

16 October. Total Effort to Annihilate the Enemy Fleet. Twenty-three Enemy Ships Hit. Seven Aircraft Carriers Sunk. In Hot Pursuit of the Beaten Enemy: Greater War Results Expected.

17 October. Death Blow to Enemy Fleet. Thirty-five Enemy Ships Hit. Thirteen Aircraft Carriers, Three Battleships Sunk.

18 October. One Aircraft Carrier, One Battleship Killed. In Total, Forty-two Enemy Ships Sunk or Damaged, Including Eighteen Aircraft Carriers.

19 October. Across the Entire Pacific, High Probability of an All-out Attack by the Enemy.

20 October. Enemy Fleet, Leading Flotilla, Invades Leyte Harbor, Philippines; Our Army and Navy Cooperating in Fierce Battle Now Underway. Air and Sea Battle off Taiwan still Raging. Forty-five Enemy Ships Hit, Including Nineteen Aircraft Carriers and Four Battleships.

21 October. Raiding English Air Flotilla Dealt Critical Blow. Four Aircraft Carriers Hit. Body-ram Scores Direct Hit on Aircraft Carrier: Brave Air Flotilla Commander Admiral Arima Masabumi.

The *Asahi Newspaper* editorialized on 17 October (page 3) that the people should not let the string of victories go to their heads, while printing on the same page a photograph of airplane factory workers going to work "with a bounce in their step," a banner overhead reading, "Great War Results! We, too, Are in Hot Pursuit [of the Enemy]!" The seeming contradiction between extraordinary, positive war results and this cautious, even negative interpretation belied the growing schism between the media's exaggerations and reality. Basking in the afterglow of the war's early victories, the military was not about to diminish its aura of invincibility in Japan's crucial hour of need. The military gave itself a limitless credit line for war results; the balance would be repaid in due time, once it had replenished its stock of armaments and personnel. Of course, the more exaggerated the reports of sunk ships, the more time, aircraft, and pilots would be needed to make the bottom line balance.

The pressure placed upon the military to produce the results that had already become "news" is one factor explaining the extraordinary sacrifices about to be made. The first indication came on 15 October when the *Asahi Newspaper*, describing the report from the Imperial High Command of the preceding day's battle, simply noted that "since 12 October, our air flotilla, encountering fierce resistance from planes launched from a sizable enemy fleet coming from the islands to the southwest and headed toward Taiwan, dealt severe damage to the fleet with a fierce 'certain-death certain-kill body-ramming' attack." Whether the pilots involved had taken off with the intention of crashing their planes into Allied ships was unclear. There had been earlier incidents in which pilots flying badly damaged craft had deliberately crashed into Allied targets.

The 21 October *Asahi Newspaper* gave a face and a dramatic twist to the new "body-ramming" tactic with the death of Admiral Arima, who "of his own accord climbed into the cockpit and took off for battle. Flying several hundred miles' distance over the ocean, he spied a group of enemy aircraft carriers. He withstood fire from enemy Grumman fighters, dodging their resistance, and brilliantly, valiantly, staying at the forefront of the air fleet, advanced to fire, launching his torpedo. Still leading his companion craft, he literally pierced right through the innards of a regular-size aircraft carrier, his heroic body-ram sinking it, as was confirmed from the reports from other wild eagles flying with him."

Reports of incredible war results continued, day after day, with the front page of the 27 October *Asahi Newspaper* revising the total number of sunk and damaged Allied ships to fifty-five, or more than two ships per day. The front page of the same paper carried photographs of the emperor and empress at Yasukuni Shrine, where they prayed to the spirits of the brave warrior-gods to protect the nation. It would seem that these stupendous war results had moved the emperor and empress to give thanks. The *Asahi Newspaper* reported the following day that nine more Allied ships had been hit. Finally, on 29 October, the front page of the *Asahi Newspaper* printed an article about Lieutenant Seki Yukio, commander of the first squadron of kamikaze pilots, "The Heroic Example of God-Eagles will Burn on Through All Ages: The Shikishima Squadron of the Kamikaze Special Attack Forces."[13] The subtitle explained, "The Enemy Fleet Has Been Halted. Certain-Death, Certain-Kill Body-Ramming."

As with Admiral Arima's example, "body-ramming" meant a suicidal dive in an airplane resulting in certain death, which distinguished the actions of the kamikaze airplane from those of the midget submarine Special Attack Forces, which launched torpedoes rather than used their vessels as ramming weapons. Indeed, the 29 October *Asahi Newspaper* carried a separate article, "They Cast Aside Their Lives to Save the Nation, this Attack Force Unrivalled in Japan and Abroad, Using the Most Noble Tactic." The strategy was an intelligent update of gyokusai; the basic idea of body-ramming a superior force was essentially the same, in that one's very flesh was used as a pounding weapon ("gyokusai" was, literally, "crushing jewels") but it was now accomplished at a much higher and more destructive speed as man and machine were fused in a sublime, near-sacred union. In the final months of the war, kamikaze pilots sometimes rammed US superfortresses in mid-air, and at least one survived to tell the tale, according to a *Nippon Times* article of 7 August: "Hero Flier Rams B-29 in Grim Aerial Duel; Escapes Death by Bailing Out in Parachute."

33. *PWR* 347, 15 November 1944. This *PWR* cover displayed the dramatic "final photograph" of Lieutenant Seki Yukio, leader of the Shikishima Unit, one of the first four squadrons of kamikaze pilots. Behind him is a map of Leyte Gulf, where the first kamikaze attacks took place on 25 October 1944. He died in the attack.

The caption obliquely refers to one rationale for deploying the kamikaze, making use of limited resources to maximum effect: "With a direct hit from a single plane, they protect this Land of the Gods. Ah, the Kamikaze Special Attack Forces. Their exemplary loyalty will burn brightly through all ages." Photograph: Onoda, Information Corps.

The smaller caption quotes Seki as encouraging the members of his squadron with the words, "We are not members of a bomber squadron, we ourselves are bombs. Got it? Then follow me." Seki's face is contorted by his fierce resolve, reminiscent of the *mie* pose of a kabuki actor in a samurai role. He is often credited with dealing a deadly fatal blow to the escort carrier USS *St. Lo*, but it was another man in his squadron. Seki hit the USS *Kalinin Bay*.[14]

The five kamikaze pilots of the Shikishima squadron were an immediate sensation. All five had hit US escort carriers, sinking the USS *St. Lo* and killing 114 members of its crew, and inflicting some damage to the *Kalinin Bay*, *Kitkin Bay*, and *White Plains*. The kamikaze wrought significant damage at Leyte. The guns on Allied ships were not designed to shoot from close range and were at a distinct disadvantage when suicide dive-bombers were bearing down on them. Indeed, the tactic was one the Western mind was ill prepared to anticipate, and the Japanese exploited the element of surprise. The guns on Allied ships were quickly refitted to deal with kamikazes. In nine months of activity, 355 Allied ships were damaged by kamikaze attacks, of which fifty-seven were sunk. About three thousand Japanese airplanes were lost in kamikaze attacks, resulting in the deaths of almost four thousand Japanese pilots and crew members.

34 and 35. *PWR* 347, 15 November 1944, p. 2. The first issue of *PWR* to include photographs of kamikaze pilots gave a detailed account of their mission under Fleet Commander Admiral Toyoda Soemu. The article ended with a rousing order to the home front: "With 'the sincerity of a Japanese' (*Nihonjin no magokoro*), let's shoot and chase away the fleeing enemy. Follow the Kamikaze Special Attack Forces! One Hundred Million, march in unison, following them." The article gives a detailed breakdown of the five ships sunk and fourteen damaged by the Kamikaze Special Attack Forces in just five days:

"25 October. Sunk: One medium-size aircraft carrier, one cruiser; damaged: one medium-size aircraft carrier.

"26 October. Sunk: One large-size aircraft carrier; damaged: one large-size aircraft carrier.

"27 October. Sunk: One transport; damaged: one battleship, one transport, one cruiser, one unidentified ship.

"29 October. Sunk: One large-size aircraft carrier; damaged: one large-size aircraft carrier, one cruiser, two unidentified ships.

"30 October. Sunk: One large-size aircraft carrier; damaged: one medium-size and one small-size aircraft carrier, one battleship."

(left) "We Must Follow their Example: The Kamikaze Special Attack Forces." The map shows the proximity of Leyte Gulf to China and southern Japan. The photographs are of the four pilots in Seki's squadron, all of whom took part in the first kamikaze mission on 25 October and hit Allied targets. From left to right: Seaman First Class Ōguro Shigeo, Petty Officer Nagamine Hajime, Petty Officer Tani Nobuo, and Petty Officer Nakano Iwao.

(right) "Shikishima Squadron, take off! The fleet commander, using a crutch, firmly shakes their hands, one by one, encouraging them. The commander is supported by the sub-commander." Photograph: Onoda, Information Corps, in [censored] Base, Philippines, 25 October.

36. *PWR* 347, 15 November 1944, p. 3. "Attack of the Kamikaze Special Attack Forces," as "imagined" by Matsuzoe Ken.

The caption is brief: "Following a member of the squadron who made a direct hit on an enemy aircraft carrier, a Special Attack plane makes a headlong assault and explodes on impact."

The original magazine page is as large as a newspaper, 16 by 11½ inches, and the kamikaze aircraft is clearly visible smashing into the deck in front of the bridge (see detail, below).

Matsuzoe's "imagined" drawing presents a scene that could neither be seen by the naked eye nor captured by the camera, since in the moment of impact between the plane and the aircraft carrier, the explosion would obscure the airplane with smoke and flame.

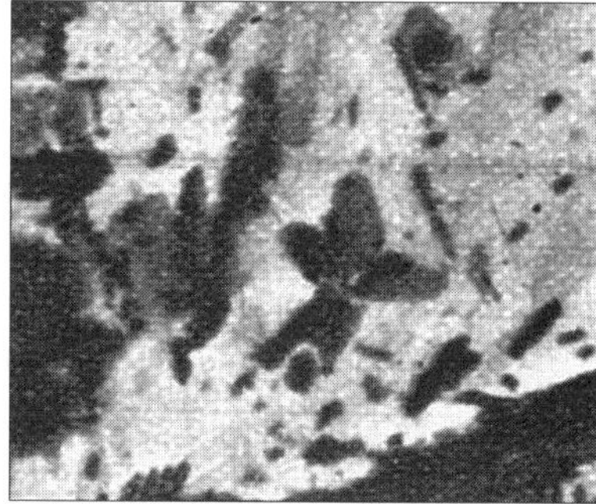

After a kamikaze mission, the names of the dead pilots and their final words would be broadcast over the radio. Fighter pilots enjoyed an esteem of their own during the war, not only in Japan, of course. They were the fittest, the bravest, most talented and intelligent, the finest specimens of the nation's manhood in youthful virility. While kamikaze pilots did return to base if they found no target to strike, when the opportunity presented itself, they had only one chance at inflicting a deadly blow. Their missions were almost always solo, and as such they were quite unusual in Japan, because unlike the collective actions of most soldiers and seamen, when the kamikaze pilots received their orders, they carried them out alone and acted as individuals. In death, too, when they became heroes of the nation, they were honored as individuals. Those characteristics that made them unique—their names, their birthplaces, even their birth homes and their childhood likes and dislikes—were all part of the public image of each. Yasukuni made no distinction between warrior-gods, whether they had died from a cold during maneuvers, by their own hand as part of a gyokusai attack, or whether they had perished when they deliberately smashed their planes into enemy craft (or, more likely, into the ocean when they missed the target). The press, however, did distinguish between those who died as heroes and those who died less noble deaths.

海軍神風特別攻撃隊の三十七勇士

37 and 38. (top) *PWR* 300, 8 December 1943, pp. 36-37. This issue appeared on the second anniversary of the attack on Pearl Harbor. The caption reads, "This one death with which to repay the emperor's benevolence." Here, the image of a pilot's "one death" is duplicated many times over into a mass effort. The neat rows of identical uniforms, the very same salute, the cropping of the photograph to create a borderless pattern suggesting an endless supply of pilots—all serve to efface the individuality of these men.

(bottom) *Mainichi Great East Asia War Pictorial Report* 36, 8 December 1944, p. 10. "The Thirty-seven Heroes of the Navy Kamikaze Special Attack Forces." Arranged by squadron, beneath each man's photograph is his name, rank, and age. Here, each photograph is of an identified individual. In total, nearly four thousand Special Attack Forces pilots and crew would lose their lives in combat.

PWR had set the tone for the popular adoration, indeed, worship, of the kamikaze pilots, with its cultivation of the image of the warrior-gods who had manned the midget submarines. The sanctified air surrounding the kamikaze owed much to Shinto purification rituals, as seen in photographs depicting what were described as the men's final moments on earth. The men wrote their final words in their best calligraphic hand, drank a final cup of sake, sang a farewell song with the compatriots they left behind, and took off. They looked dashing in their perfectly pressed uniforms, aviator's caps, goggles, gloves, and white scarves, white being the color associated with death in Japanese culture. These men might be as "carefree and lighthearted" about death as the midget submarine crews had been, but they would not depart for certain death looking anything but picture-perfect. As media figures, successfully performing their duty required playing this part before the camera. The kamikaze were given star billing on the stage of domestic news, where their last photographs and final words were used to fan the flames of morale.

39-42. *PWR* 348, 22 November 1944, p. 3. "The Kamikaze Special Attack Forces Take Off to Attack." From their inception, the Special Attack Forces were anointed in rituals with religious overtones. These photographs, taken by the Japan Film Company, are probably stills from newsreel footage.

(top right) "The time has come for the Shikishima Squadron to depart. Their compatriots raise their voices in singing 'Off to Sea' (Umi yukaba) and 'The Student Pilots' Song,' probably the last these pilots will ever hear from those who have vowed to follow them."

(top left) "Upon their departure, their commander exchanges farewell cups of sake with Lieutenant Seki and his men. Some say 'I'm off,' others answer, 'Off you go,' these absolutely pure officers and men whose great deeds will live on for eternity. Follow them!"

(middle) "These men, comrades-in-arms, need no words to communicate to each other. Their determination to sacrifice themselves for the sake of the imperiled nation burns hotly in the pure hearts of these five warriors taking their leave of their comrades. Their passion is transmitted to the officers and men who see them off."

(bottom) "These god-eagles have flown, not to return. But their loyalty will continue to burn brightly for ten thousand generations."

43 and 44. *PWR* 368, 25 April 1945.

(left) "With this One Person, Serve the Nation: the Special Attack Spirit."

The small caption says, "Carrying a long-sleeved kimono-clad doll, this Special Attack warrior is in high spirits as he is about to take off." Photograph by Mori of the Information Corps.

This photograph also appeared in *Asahigraph* ([44:17], *Great East Asia War Report* 171, 5 May 1945, p. 2), where it was not part of a montage, and included the faces of all four pilots.

Mementoes from family members or loved ones, such as the beautiful doll, were sometimes taken along on a final mission, strengthening the bond between the dead pilot, as a warrior-god, and the people he left behind. The island behind them is Okinawa, although the fighting there was already mostly over. The collage of photographic elements is strikingly reminiscent in composition to the front cover of the inaugural issue of *PWR* (see Chapter 4, figure 7).

(right, p. 3) The two photographs at the top of the page are from the enshrinement ceremony at Yasukuni Shrine on 24 April, in which were invoked the spirits of 41,318 new warrior-gods. The larger photograph at bottom, credited to Suzuki of the Information Corps, is of a group of kamikaze pilots about to take off. The placement of the photographs of suicide bombers and the enshrinement ceremony at Yasukuni is suggestive of the kamikaze becoming warrior-gods, but this layout may simply reflect the exigencies of the tighter, smaller format of *PWR* in the final months of the war. On the facing page (page 2, not shown here) was an instructive article, illustrated with photographs, on how to make salt at home, another indication of the straitened circumstances Japanese faced in 1945. At this point in the war, with their numbers increasing dramatically, kamikaze pilots appearing in *PWR* were no longer named.

45 and 46. PWR 367, 18 April 1945, p. 13. Works of art from the "Army Artists Exhibition Held at the Metropolitan Museum of Art in Ueno Park, Tokyo, from 11 to 30 April" were introduced to a wider public through the pages of *PWR*.

(top) "The Kamikaze Special Attack Forces Take Off from [censored] Base" by Ihara Usaburō (1894-1976). One of the final iconic images of the war, this painting has been frequently reproduced because its image is readily available through the National Archives. The dark scorch mark at upper right is not part of the original artwork, but is the result of poor quality printing typical of the final months of the war. The painting depicts a scene similar to a famous photograph of schoolgirls holding branches of cherry blossoms and waving farewell to kamikaze pilots taking off from Chiran Base, Kyūshū.

(bottom) "Fierce Fighting of the Banda Squadron off the Philippine Coast," by Miyamoto Saburō, depicts an enemy vessel suffering a direct hit from an Army Air Force kamikaze pilot as a second plane rapidly approaches for a second hit.

Both paintings are part of the permanent collection of the National Museum of Modern Art, Tokyo.

Not all suicide missions were carried out by aircraft. There were also suicide boats, suicide submarines, human torpedoes, and even suicide paratroopers. Suicide boats, human torpedoes, and submarines never figured largely in the pages of *PWR*. They were fewer in number than the airplanes, deployed much later in the war, and held in reserve as secret weapons. The suicide paratroopers made the cover of *PWR*, as did the Kongō Squadron of human torpedoes. *PWR*'s descriptions of these men put them on the kamikaze pedestal.

47 and 48. (left) *PWR* 352, 20 December 1944. The "Signboard of the Times" on this front cover compares the war effort of civilians and suicide parachute troops: "Do not spare anything in the battle for the home front, either. Body-ram them!"

The caption, lower left, says, "The god-soldiers who dropped from the skies over Palembang [in 1942, see Chapter 7, figures 41 and 42] have been redeployed at the decisive battle for Leyte. In high spirits, these warriors of the Takachiho Paratroop Squadron prepare to board, equipped with parachutes heavier than their own bodies, as well as machine guns. At [censored] Base, Philippine Islands." Photograph by Kanazawa of the Information Corps.

The suicide mission handed to these crack paratroopers was to drop on US airfields in southern Luzon and destroy as many airplanes as possible before killing themselves. Some four hundred fifty were deployed, about half of them reaching the ground alive. They succeeded in destroying only two airplanes, a jeep, and a washstand.[15]

(right) *PWR* 356, 24 January 1945. The "Signboard of the Times" reads, "The fierceness of battle approaches this Land of the Gods. Aa, all planes, Special Attack. Say it again: all planes, Special Attack."

The caption (lower left) says, "The Kamikaze Special Attack Forces' Kongō Squadron is about to engage in battle. The base is charged with 'must-kill' energy and even the southern wind rustling the tips of the palm fronds feels cold to the touch." Photograph: Japan Film Company.

The Kongō Squadron were kaiten pilots, their vessels being human-guided torpedoes launched from conventional submarines. It is unclear why they are dressed in pilots' uniforms, caps, and goggles. We can only speculate that this may be a deliberate masking of the nature of their suicide craft.

The media emphasized the close connection between the home front and the kamikaze pilots. Physically, this bond was the airplane itself. People on the home front, the "kamikazes of production," were responsible for building the airplanes used in the attacks, and representative airplane factory workers took turns with kamikaze pilots sharing the front covers of *PWR* in the autumn of 1944 and the spring of 1945. When a kamikaze pilot took off on his final mission, his plane bore aloft the hopes and prayers of the home front. Scoring a victory by sinking a ship meant the pilot had successfully used

49 and 50. (left) *PWR* 348, 22 November 1944.

The second *PWR* cover devoted to the kamikaze phenomenon featured a "Signboard of the Times" message commending the home front's role in the successful kamikaze attacks.

"Today, / We build airplanes. / Tomorrow, / They whip up a sacred wind on the battlefield. / Send them forth: / Airplanes imbued with [Yamato] spirit."

From the context, here the primary meaning of "sacred wind" (kamikaze) is a fierce wind, a whirlwind, like the typhoon that smashed the Mongol invasion fleet. Of course, "kamikaze" here also refers to the Special Attack Forces.

Significantly, the second issue of *PWR* to describe the Special Attack Forces put civilian workers on its front cover, underscoring the strong link between the battlefield and the home front. Indeed, messages like this one pitted the two forces of morale against each other in a mutually reinforcing relationship. Civilians' hard work and the sacrifices they made to build the airplane, as well as the "spirit" pounded into the craft, obliged pilots to make their best effort and score a direct hit. Conversely, the pilots' sacrifice of their very lives in making suicide attacks meant that the workers building the planes owed the pilots their best effort to create aircraft that would produce results.

(right) *PWR* 358, 7 February 1945. "Signboard of the Times."

"The trees of the Land of the Gods / Are becoming the wings of battle / Striking the hated enemy. / Build them! Wooden airplanes."

The caption elaborates, "These workers are in a 'certain-kill battle' to assemble the prototype of a splendid wooden airplane that will not miss an opportunity [to strike] for even one minute or one mile."

These workers appear to be teenagers. All of them wear headbands emblazoned with "kamikaze."

his training, skill, and courageous resolve, and it also meant that the factory workers on the ground had built an aircraft that served its pilot by functioning properly and carrying him swiftly and surely to his target. A kamikaze score was the result of the pilot's sacrificing his life for the emperor, nation, and people, and his sacrifice was reflected in the sacrifices made by those who worked longer hours under greater duress and deprivation to build the planes, and indeed, the hardships endured by the entire nation to boost produce while saving more money to finance manufacturing more airplanes.

51 and 52. The airplanes themselves were national heroes in the final months of the war.

(left) *PWR* 346, 29 November 1944.

"The righteousness of the Land of the Gods explodes at Leyte. Ah, Army Special Attack Forces. You will never fail the Land of the Emperor."

The caption says, "A member of the Fugaku (Mount Fuji) Squadron paints Fuji's sacred peak and a lightning bolt on the tail of his beloved plane." Photograph: Terano, Information Corps.

(right) *PWR* 355, 17 January 1945.

"Signboard of the Times."

"These wings / Having caught the divine wind / And flapping with 'must kill' / Will kill every last Yank-bastard (Bei-yatsu). / Build them, Build them. / And charge their wings / With the prayers and the fury of the One Hundred Million."

The caption says, "With a turn of this phoenix's wings, one of our army's elite stalks its favorite prey. Over the skies of Yunnan." The caption is ambiguous about the target, and it would seem from the photograph and the caption that a dogfight is being described, rather than a suicidal dive, although kamikazes also rammed B-29s. Photograph: Katayama, Information Corps.

53 and 54. The spiritual dimension of the war effort also united home front and battleground. Evidence of Japan's spiritual superiority was found in the extraordinary degree of sacrifice Japanese were capable of stoically enduring, all the while continuing to do their utmost for the good of the nation.

(left) *PWR* 369-370, 9 May 1945. This cover carried no large-print message. The caption is, evidently, the girl's prayer: "Wings. Wings we Japanese have made. Pounded into these wings is the one hope and prayer connecting us all.

"Young Japanese god-eagles leaving today, while putting a period on the end of your own life, protect our beautiful homeland by scoring a perfect hit against the enemy with this plane entrusted with our own lives."

(right) *PWR* 371, 1 June 1945. The "Signboard of the Times" spouts the relentless message of "Certain Victory": "In attire pure and clean, / Cheerfully, / The young gods set off—A great shield of a victorious nation."

The caption at lower right simply says, "A warrior of the Shinbu Squadron of the Army Special Attack Forces prays before his beloved craft prior to his cheerful take-off." The pilot's prayer for a successful, mission prior to his final sortie was an important ritual adding to the kamikazes' allure as spiritually "pure."

The Japanese government was quite aware that Westerners viewed suicidal attacks as illogical and contrary to human nature. In the mind of Japan's military strategists, this not only gave Japan a tactical advantage, but was further proof of the racial superiority that had carried the war effort forward thus far and would see it through to the very end. This point is clearly demonstrated in an article printed in the English-language *Nippon Times* (7 July 1945, p. 3), in which Rear Admiral Kurihara, Vice Director of the Press Section of the Imperial Headquarters, is quoted in an "address to six hundred youths of the Kunitachi High Communications Training Institute." Kurihara's response to Russian and German newspaper correspondents' questioning of the kamikaze policy provides chilling insight into the psychology of Japan's wartime leadership.

Why Japan Will Win War Is Told by Kurihara

Last year, I met foreign news correspondents. At that time the foreigners looked as if they did not understand my talk concerning the Special Attack Corps. A Tass correspondent asked me what our war aims were. "Our war aim lies in the lasting security of the power of our country. We are trying to ensure the lasting continuance of our racial power of existence," I replied. He then said, "You say that you are going to secure the lasting continuance of your racial power of existence, but is not the Special Attack Corps suicide? It is contrary to your war objective." I replied that therein lay the essence of Japan. "To die for the nation is to live," I told him. "The proclamation of the Commander-in-Chief of the Combined Fleet contains the expression 'to live in eternal justice,' which does not signify death but life." "There is no way of translating the term 'to live in eternal justice' into German," said a correspondent, adding that it was "contrary to fact." I replied that the Special Attack Corps was "contrary" to them but that it was "definitely regular" to the Japanese nation.

This spiritual attitude is essential. When every Japanese subject is made fully aware of the fact that to die for the Emperor is to live, then will the Japanese people bring tremendous power into play and greatly add to the Nation's war power. I believe that the greatest war result of the War of Greater East Asia will be the permeation of the special attack spirit into the hearts of the entire nation. The world will be shaken when the time comes for the Japanese people, as true subjects, to bring this spirit into play.

家庭軍事講座

銃剣術の基本

55. *PWR* 348, 22 November 1944, p. 7. "Home Military Forum No. 1: The Basics of the Art of a Bayonet." The first article in a new series, providing practical, explicit do-it-yourself instructions for becoming a civilian combatant in the event of an Allied invasion of Japan's Home Islands.

The boundary between the home front and the battlefield was being eroded both by enemy bombs and government directives to prepare for the invasion of the Home Islands.

Having proclaimed the Battle of Okinawa a success, based upon an assessment of Allied personnel losses, in June 1945 the government announced, "The Decisive Battle for the Home Islands," carving the four main islands into eight regions, each of which would fight as an independent unit for its own survival, along the lines of the Okinawan model, in the face of invasion. "Home-front warriors"—many of them women and children—had proven themselves in combat and auxiliary roles in the Battle of Okinawa. The government ordered the home front to emulate the kamikaze's code of "certain death, certain kill" and began training the population in hand-to-hand combat. Whether facing air raids or battles, home-front warriors were expected to follow the military code of no surrender, even to commit suicide if necessary. When the military fought on Japanese soil, as in the cases of Saipan and Okinawa, those civilians who tried to surrender risked being shot in the back by the troops sent to "defend" them.[16]

手榴弾

56. *PWR* 368, 25 April 1945, p. 14. "Home Military Forum: Hand Grenades." An article instructing civilians in the use of hand grenades, in preparation for the battle for the Home Islands.

Incendiary bombing campaigns against targets in Taiwan and Okinawa began in October 1944. In November 1944, Tokyo came under attack. The initial reaction of the government was to revive the "Smile Movement" with the new name, "Grin and Bear it," and to remind the people of the many years of preparation for such raids. Their air safety organizations, firefighting training, and ever-ready buckets and brooms were now rewarding them with swift action and presence of mind. After all, were they to panic and fail in their duty to protect their families, their homes, their neighborhoods, and the nation, they were hardly worthy of being called Japanese. The case of Nazi Germany, which had surrendered, became another example of spiritual inferiority. *Asahigraph* ([44:18], *Great East Asia War Report* 172, 15 May 1945, pp. 2-3) carried an article that flatly stated, "The Nazi flag has been buried in the ground. Hitler is dead. They gave up like cowards because they were spiritually flawed." The German people had not been willing to give their lives for their Führer or their Fatherland.

An article in the semi-governmental English-language publication *Contemporary Japan*, "Tokyoites under Air Raids" ([14:1], January-March 1945, pp. 75-82), by

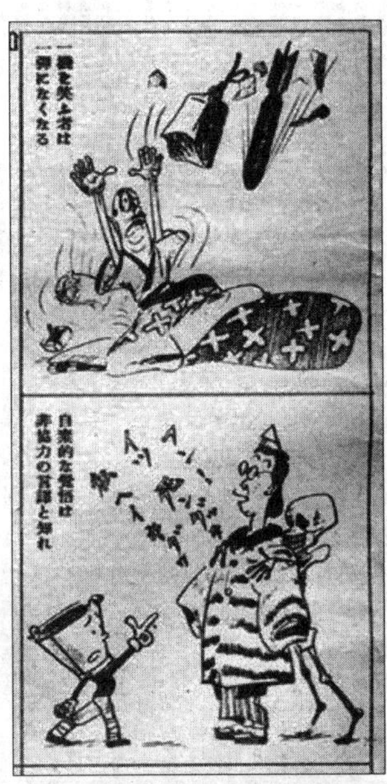

57-59. (left) *PWR* 359, 14 February 1945. Launched at New Year's 1945, the "Grin and Bear It" (literally, "Cheerful Fight") campaign, reminiscent of a very similar "Smile" Campaign of spring 1941 (see Chapter 4, figure 70), was meant to show that even under the duress of air raids and shortages, Japanese morale did not flag. These "junior citizens" were assigned large, adult roles in the war effort. The caption reads, "These student workers can be called the 'kamikaze' of war production."

(right) *PWR* 358, 7 February 1945, p. 7. Two cartoons with rather grim humor about air raids.

(right top) "He who scoffs at 'just one plane' may be killed by 'just one bomb.'" This man did not heed the air raid siren and just stayed in bed.

(right bottom) "Know that when resignation means self-annihilation, it is an uncooperative attitude." A skeleton helps a woman dressed in kimono and geta put on an overcoat, instead of the prescribed protective air raid overalls, hood, and shoes. She defiantly says, "Ha. I don't care when I die, anyway." A bucket (representing fire safety) points at her with a look of concern.

Mitsuaki Kakéhi (as the author romanized his name), depicts air raids as a source of "cheerfulness—a kind of light-hearted buoyancy." This very peculiar article, published around the time of the Great Kanto Air Raid (10 March 1945), is extracted here.

> Believe it or not, the air raid has aroused in us a feeling of cheerfulness—a kind of light-hearted buoyancy—such as we experience when something long expected finally happens. No wonder, we are proving ourselves equal to the situation. [. . .]
>
> Many interest [*sic*] and humorous incidents and episodes are being frequently narrated in connection with the "America no o-kyakusan" (American visitors), and they amply testify to the kind of life the Tokyoites are leading under air raids. For instance, when American bombers penetrate the skies of Tokyo, the Tokyoites, one and all, invariably say, "Well, the 'America no okyaku-san' have come; how sad they have brought us poor presents this time; hope they will bring us something nice next time." They also talk among themselves in many humorous ways about the various phases of the "hit and run" tactics of the raiders. The more humorous among them will often say: "What a pity the American visitors are too quick to drop bombs and get away; they seem to dislike us. They ought to taste our 'defence' hospitality by staying a bit longer."
>
> The most popular name given to American planes is "Teki-san" (Mr. Enemy). It was first used by Japanese soldiers stationed on the South Sea islands. . . . By far the most humorous name given the American sky-raiders is "Bu-san." Because the siren screeches even when a single hostile plane is sighted, the raider has been named "Bu-san" after the sound of the siren, and it is applied collectively, too. This name is especially liked by the children. Their adaptability to the new environment is so mervellous [*sic*] as to be beyond question. Not only have they got used to "Bu-san," but "Bu-san" has become their great favourite. When American raiders in formations or singly appear over Tokyo, it is a usual sight to see children in every locality running about joyfully and shouting: "Bu-san has come, utteshimae (down it)." The children in Tokyo now play in the streets "keikai keiho asobi" (air-alert game) and "kushu keiho asobi" (air-raid alarm game). Interesting to note is that they, after shouting that the bombing has started, take shelter in dug-outs and go out again according to directions given by one of them playing the part of a civil air defence warden.
>
> [. . .] the plight of the innocent victims of civil bombings cannot but arouse our indignation. It has now become a usual method of American raiders to demolish the homes of non-combatants. It would be quite right to say that they are doing so with malice prepense [sic]. Such an attitude not only shows an unpardonable lack of ordinary human feeling, but also exposes a deplorable callous mentality. Dr. Toyohiko Kagawa, famous Christian preacher of Japan and the most passionate lover of humanity, is most indignant, because America who speaks of Christian morality "is today sending warplanes to those very areas where she sent her missionaries to preach the Gospel and to slaughter those very 'sons of God' whom her missionaries baptized." Her bombers are attacking our schools, temples, shrines and churches. Can you call these in accord with the Christian principles? Dr. Kagawa's words: "The second World War in the Orient, is again inflicting upon Christ the agony which he suffered on the Cross."

In the pages *of PWR*, the Japanese people were unfazed by the air raids, which only toughened their resolve to strike back at the enemy. There were no setbacks, no downturns in the war, and with America wasting its resources on carpet bombing campaigns, there would be little war-power left for an invasion of Japan. Thus, every apparently negative development was to be seen in a positive light. The "nocturnal visitors" did the work of leveling whole city blocks, revealing precious land now ready to be plowed and planted in "victory provisions." Living in dugout shelters in the midst of scorched-earth desolation might seem to have economic and psychological drawbacks, but it could boast a level of fire safety hitherto unknown in Japan's cities.

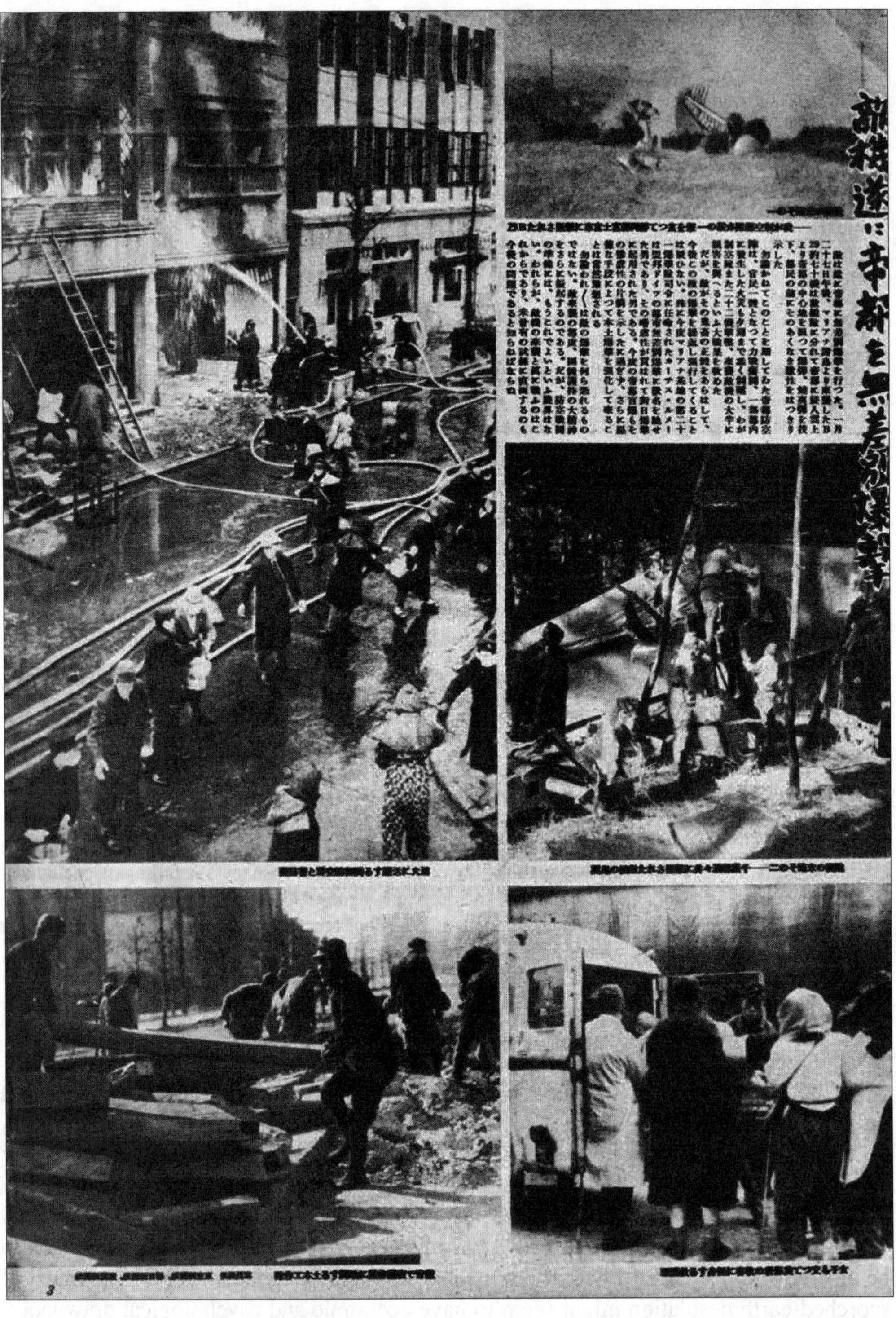
敵機遂に帝都を無差別爆撃

60-64. *PWR* 358, 7 February 1945, p. 3. "Enemy Planes Have Finally Indiscriminately Bombed the Imperial Capital." The article (on the facing page) is justifiably pessimistic, and yet dangerously overconfident, about air raids and the public's ability to contain their damage. The article, which makes no mention of deaths, is translated in its entirety.

"The enemy has finally undertaken indiscriminate bombing of the Imperial Capital. On 27 January, seventy B-29s based in the Marianas came on an air raid, breaking into squadrons and aiming at the center of Tokyo. They dropped conventional bombs and incendiary missiles from above the clouds, clearly showing we citizens their bloodthirsty, inhuman nature.

"Of course, the Tokyo Air Defense Forces were well prepared for this event, and officers and citizens acted as one body in a fierce battle [against the raiders and the fire]. Fire broke out in one part of the metropolis and was quickly brought under control by evening. Our air defense squadron achieved a great war result, shooting down twenty-two of the enemy bombers and inflicting damage on more than half of the raiding force.

"However, the enemy has shown his true form as a demon-bastard, and there is no doubt that such bombings will be repeated and intensified. Especially since Curtis LeMay, commander of the Twenty-First Bombing Fleet based in the Marianas, and a man who has become infamous for his indiscriminate bombing of German cities, has been assigned the task of committing atrocities against Japan by conducting indiscriminate bombing. The recent blind [i.e., indiscriminate] bombing of the Imperial Capital is nothing more than just a small taste of their barbarous nature, and we can easily foresee deeds yet more wicked still as they intensify their bombing of the Home Islands.

"Of course, we are not the slightest bit afraid of enemy bombs. We have already awakened the great spiritual reserves of protecting the national polity (kokutai) in the event of another enemy air raid. Therefore, in order to prepare for another air defense battle, we can never say that we have reached our limit and done enough. Our true battle with enemy air raids is still to come, and we must know that the problem henceforth is confronting our insufficiency in test runs."

(facing page, right column, top): "This B-29 swallowed a 'certain-kill' shell from our Air Defense and crashed near Fujinomiya, Shizuoka Prefecture."

(facing page, right column, middle) "End of the road for despicable fliers, part two—the tail of an enemy plane shot down near Sasai, Chiba Prefecture."

(facing page, right column, bottom) "Women take turns tending to the wounded, devoting themselves to the First Aid Squadron."

(facing page, left column, top) "The Neighborhood Association Air Defense Squad and the Air Safety Forces in action putting out the fire."

(facing page, left column, bottom) "Working through the night, house carpenters battle at clearing away and rebuilding." Photographs courtesy of *Tokyo Newspaper*, *Mainichi Newspaper*, and *Yomiuri Newspaper*.

65. *PWR* 364-365, 28 March 1945. Air raid survivors clear away rubble in what had been a congested Tokyo neighborhood a few weeks before. This double issue of *PWR*, the first to appear after the 9-10 March air raid, contained the famous centerfold of the emperor touring the ruins (Introduction, figure 2). The cover gives planting instructions for different staple crops and the "Signboard of the Times" urges, "Leave no place untilled / Leave no spot unsown / For this Land of the Emperor / Is the mother of victory's provisions."

The accompanying article, "We Must Avenge Ourselves on This Foe" (p. 6), is translated in its entirety.

"As far as the eye can see, a bleak, burnt-out wasteland—in the predawn hours of 10 March, the enemy raided the Imperial Capital, deliberately targeting residential areas, dropping incendiary bombs like rain. Fanned by fierce winds, in one night a vast area was incinerated.

"This was only the beginning. Nighttime bombing raids were conducted against the cities of Nagoya, Osaka, and Kobe, all part of the same goal. Prior to invading our Home Islands, the enemy intends to destroy we citizens' will to fight, and has therefore initiated the most barbarous scorched-earth, genocidal tactic.

"What now burns in the hearts of all Japanese is virulent anger and hatred toward the yankee-devils.[17] Just watch us now, we will be avenged against this foe.

"Because the enemy is coming to torch us, we must not let ourselves be burned, and so we are rapidly evacuating [i.e., and tearing down] buildings. Every structure saved from burning is being transformed into greater war-power.

"The enemy is coming to kill us, and therefore we must not be killed. Everyone left [in the cities] who is nonessential there should evacuate. Every one of us who is left alive will fight to the very end."

66 and 67. *PWR* 364-365, 28 March 1945, p. 6.

(top). This photograph shows the souvenir shops lining the entrance to Asakusa Temple, Tokyo, before the air raid (see also see Chapter 10, figure 15).

(bottom) "Unforgivably, the enemy scattered bombs over schools and hospitals. Such is their true nature, which contradicts human morality and international law. The photograph shows, from the lane of shops lining the approach, Asakusa Kannon, which became a victim of the demon-bastards."

The ferroconcrete shop stalls leading to the temple were rebuilt in 1923 after being destroyed in a fire and earthquake. The wooden Asakusa Temple, a rare survival from the early seventeenth century, was completely lost. Ironically, the 1923 shops now predate the current temple, a ferroconcrete replica completed in 1958. Kannon is the goddess of mercy.

68-70. *PWR* 364-365, 28 March 1945, p. 6. "Even One Day sooner, Return to the War!" is the continuation of the article cited in figures 66 and 67.

(top) "Walking down the chilly, creepy lane, the workers quickly set out for the factory. The sturdy sound of marching feet. Shoulder to shoulder, they vow to take revenge. They will quickly build and send off [war matériel]."

(bottom left) "Burning with anger to avenge our foe, they spur on a freight train. This freight train is stuffed to the gills with matériel that will become tomorrow's armaments for annihilating the enemy. At the factory, they are waiting for it. This enemy-annihilating freight train, which must make a speedy delivery, keeps running all day today." A hand-made poster says, "Get LeMay."

(bottom right) "Air raid victims already walk with the strong gait of having been reborn. Those workers whose factories were burnt down go out and apply for work in other factories. After all, every factory is a Japanese factory, so it does not matter where one works."

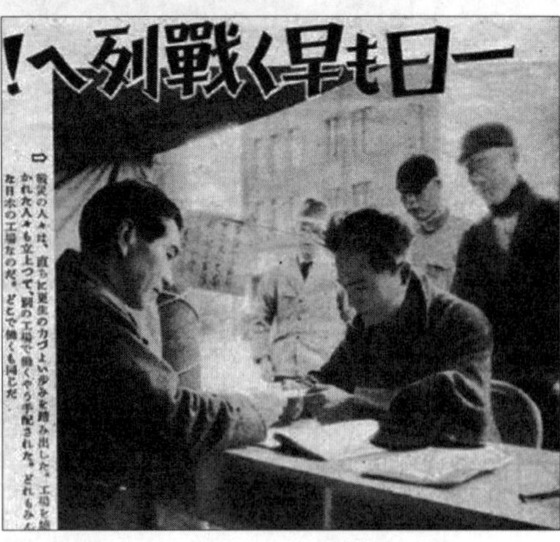

暁とともに起きる

簡易な地窖の作り方

71. *PWR* 371, 1 June 1945, p. 6. An article called "Up at Dawn" shows photographs of a man using a hammer to build a dugout and a middle-aged couple tending their crops in a burnt-out urban area. The small diagram is for "An Easy Way to Build a Dugout." The cheerful text paints an idyllic picture of life in the ruins:

"The quiet song of a smooth, calm, milky-white morning. The beat of a drum approaches.

"Again today, a sun as lively as the drum beats down a greeting upon this village of air raid victims. The door of the opposite dugout opens, and a robust face peers inside the dugout next door. They are surprised to see so many people have come, one after another, for the [neighborhood] meeting, thronging around the drum.

"None of the air raid victims' faces shows even a trace of the dark shadow cast by being burnt out by the enemy airplanes. Their flesh, having been all but stripped naked, is only filled with the firm desire to use every muscle to protect the Imperial Capital and its precious factories, to not let their guard down for even a moment. Their duty lifts their spirits. These people are bound to each other by a real sense of affection for comrades-in-arms and a love of their neighborhood that transcends logical explanations. One voice harmonizes with another, one hand wordlessly takes another. And then, in this wild burnt-out land, the lack of cooperation is filled, and the dugouts are built in quick succession."

壕舎の作り方

72. *PWR* 372, 11 June 1945, p. 14. *PWR* showed how to make the best of living conditions in burnt-out urban areas by clearing the rubble, building dugouts, and planting crops—while continuing to work in war factories. This report on the construction of new dugouts reads like a brochure promoting the splendors of government-subsidized housing.

"The Tokyo Metropolitan Air Defense Bureau, which is building three thousand dugouts in every part of the metropolis, is making public these construction plans as a reference for all of the air raid victims throughout the nation. First off, since the dugout is nearly invisible from the air, it will hardly ever become a target [of air raids]. It really looks like nothing more than a mound of earth, and with a squash patch planted on top of the roof, it will hardly stick out at all.

"The dugout is a half-level beneath the ground, but retains little humidity. Slotted windows on its north and south sides allow for good ventilation by cross breezes. And they provide enough light to work by. The opening is a one-mat earthen floor area that serves as the entranceway, so that when visitors call they can sit on the wooden threshold and take care of business. It is also a good place to put a cauldron so that rice-cooking is easy. The space beneath the six-mat tatami room is open so that dampness does not directly affect it, and this room has ample space for everything—living, dining, and storage."

The photographs show the well just outside the dugout, the stairs leading down into it, and the "ample space" of the "everything" room and its earthen entranceway.

焦土に漲る闘志

逞しき壕舎村

73. *Asahigraph* (44:18), *Great East Asia War Report* 172, 15 May 1945, pp. 10-11. "Champions Brimming with Life on the Scorched Land: A Robust Dugout Village." This *Asahigraph* article describing air raid victims living in the remains of collapsed houses was full of encouraging words and patriotic jingoism. The article is written in part from the perspective of the victims.

"Storehouses reminiscent of old Edo and [the shells of] ferroconcrete buildings sticking up here and there are all that is left of this section of Hongō Ward, where the members of forty-three households continue their lives in dugouts, referring to their neighborhood as (censored) Town, a name based on the original name of the district.

"When the neighborhood they lived in was destroyed, it was Koga Ichirō, an architect, who quickly got on his feet and started calling upon his neighbors.

"'Let's live in dugouts. We have to fix up the land we lived on [and return it] to the way it was before,' he told his neighbors.

"The people, fueled by rage, quickly responded to his suggestion and immediately began drawing up plans to live in the burnt-out area."

The optimistic tenor of this article does little to mask the desperation apparent in the photographs. This very realistic report on makeshift living in the rubble presents a picture different from *PWR*'s government-built model dugouts with their many convenient features.

74 and 75. *Asahigraph* (44:18), *Great East Asia War Report* 172, 15 May 1945, pp. 6-7. One section of the article "Champions Full of Life on the Scorched Land" was titled, "We Must have Revenge for this Criminal Bombardment." At the same time that *PWR* printed artwork glorifying the war effort (figures 45 and 46), *Asahigraph* published these drawings of devastation. The main text of the accompanying article dared tabulate the number of displaced victims, although it was careful not to give the number of dead.

"There have been twelve instances up until April of criminal bombardment of urban areas by the enemy, who is intent on transforming the entire area of the Empire into a burnt-out wasteland, and the number of homes in the Imperial Capital and other cities lost in air raids has surpassed seven hundred seventy thousand, while the actual number of air raid victims has reached 3.1 million.

"Has this criminal bombardment by an enemy who can only be called inhumanly barbaric and genocidal broken our will to fight?

"Never! Never! Absolutely never. We citizens are filled with feelings of indignity and anger, and our indomitable will to fight is now completely focused on making the burnt-out land part of our war power."

Accompanying the article were two artists' drawings of scenes of the ruins left by the massive air raid of the night of 9-10 March.

(top) "The Vicinity of Sumiyoshi-chō, Fukagawa," by Ōta Tenkyō.

(bottom) "The Area Around the Meiji Theater," by Ōta Tenkyō.

76 and 77. *Asahigraph* (44:18), *Great East Asia War Report* 172, 15 May 1945, pp. 6-7. Two drawings by Hasegawa Nakao, illustrating the article “Champions Full of Life on the Scorched Land.”

(top) “The Fukagawa Industrial Belt.”

(bottom) “Night Scene of a War-ravaged Area.”

Japan was dealt an even deadlier blow than the continued threat of air raids when the rice crop for 1945 was projected to be dangerously below average. The cover article of *PWR* 372 (11 June 1945) addressed this new peril with an uncharacteristically frank recounting of unadorned facts. The article described the dire status of rationing and even admitted to "imperfections" in the rationing system. Of course, since everyone depended upon rations to survive, the population was already aware of these "imperfections," but criticizing the government's war programs simply was not done in wartime Japan. Food rations had already been reduced in volume by 10 percent in the spring of 1945, and the nutritional value of rations also dropped significantly.[18]

78 and 79. *PWR* 372, 11 June 1945.

(right) "Let's Give All Our Energy to Increasing Foodstuffs Production." The text of this article begins on the front cover, evidently a space-saving measure.

(rleft page, top left, p. 3) "There's no excuse for making farmers do all the work when they are short of hands, so soldiers have traded their rifles for hoes and will strive to do their best to boost production of provisions."

(left page, bottom left) "What a shame to let nature's gifts go to waste. Even a small strip of land will produce [crops] like these if well tended to."

(left page, top right) "It can be grown—wherever there are workers and sweat. Even in the city's waterways, wheat yields grain."

(left page, bottom right) "This is also the way to bring to life the Land of the Emperor—putting one's spirit into cultivating undeveloped land, and boosting production."

Let's Give All Our Energy to Increasing Foodstuffs Production

> Provisions are the dynamo of the fight. Food is the only thing we must absolutely secure. And that is why the government has implemented several measures aimed at boosting production one level, and hopes to gain the cooperation of the entire citizenry in realizing this goal.
>
> Nevertheless, food supplies are strained and complaints have grown loud. [The shortage] seems to be a fact. Of course, shipments have been disrupted by air raids, and in some respects the rationing system is imperfect. [The shortage] has many causes which have occurred one after the other. Besides, our country's larder was under stress to begin with.
>
> In usual times, rice production in our country, in an average year, is 63 to 64 million *koku*[19] domestically [that is, in the Home Islands]; Korean rice production is 20 million *koku*, and Taiwanese rice production is 1.5 million *koku*, but figures are in the red regarding the amount of rice needed for our domestic diet this year, roughly 78 million *koku*.
>
> Therefore, several million *koku* of foreign rice are being imported,[20] so we should somehow get by, but circumstances have changed drastically since a year ago. Domestic rice production is about the same as in an average year, but figures are bad in Korea and Taiwan, and due to the war, shipments from the Southern Regions and Taiwan cannot be counted on. That leaves Manchukuo. Switching over to a rationing system of Japanese-Manchukuoan provisions, soybeans and millet are being imported from Manchukuo and distributed to everyone [in Japan] in place of rice.

The article concludes on an upbeat note, revealing the "silver lining" to the dark cloud of food shortages:

> Every moment of the war teaches us something about the clothing, provisions, and shelter of this new battlefield lifestyle. This is true where our diet is concerned, too. Mountain vegetables, field grasses, nuts, and seeds that up until now we thought inedible, we now find are a new taste sensation that satisfies our hunger. Diet is itself a discipline *(michi)*. All of us must learn this discipline, reduce [our consumption] this summer, and give our all to increasing food production, while also gladly accepting an austere battlefield diet and splendidly keeping up the fight.

These images of Japan in the spring and summer of 1945 are scenes of a land battered beyond recognition. The cities lay in ruins, the nation's infrastructure was severely damaged, and the people faced starvation. When the final issue of *PWR* appeared in July 1945, the nation was sinking in a seemingly bottomless abyss. Germany had capitulated, and Japan stood alone and nearly defenseless against its enemies. And yet there was no hint of surrender in the press, which continued to insist that the decisive battle for the Home Islands would result in victory. *Nippon Times* articles were full of confidence: "Way to Victory Opened by Okinawa Campaign; Asahi Correspondents See Lesson in Exploits of Special Attack Corps" (3 August, p. 2), Japan "Set to Smash Invaders" (4 August, p. 2), "Nippon Wooden Plane Superior to Mosquito Now Being Produced in Great Mass for Decisive War" (5 August, p. 2). The *Nippon Times* also printed an editorial called "Overcome This Trial" (1 August, p. 2), which admitted that the incendiary bombing campaign had taken a toll, but it also noted that the population was being dispersed from the large cities and the war factories moved underground. Besides, the editorial reassuringly stated, "it is common knowledge that it is impossible to decide the outcome of war with bombs."

Notes

1. *Chūshingura* was one of the first four works of Japanese literature to be translated into a Western language. The first edition of Frederick Dickins's translation, *Chiushingura, or The Loyal League, a Japanese Romance* appeared in 1875; it went through at least five printings by 1910 and was translated into French in 1886. There are at least two other English translations of the work, the most serviceable being Donald Keene's *Chushingura: The Treasury of Loyal Retainers, A Puppet Play* (New York: Columbia University Press, 1971).

2. The theme of dying for a lost cause and its connection to the kamikaze is described extensively in Ivan Morris, *The Nobility of Failure: Tragic Heroes in the History of Japan* (New York: Holt, Rinehart and Winston, 1975).

3. Roger J. Spiller, in his introduction to the 1999 Bison Books edition of *Nikudan*, titled, *Human Bullets: A Soldier's Story of the Russo-Japanese War* (Lincoln: University of Nebraska Press), by Sakurai Tadayoshi (1879-1965), notes that in Japan the book sold forty thousand copies in its first year (p. x) and that Sakurai became a major general in charge of the army's department of propaganda, *shinbun han* (newspaper division) during World War II.

4. Emiko Ohnuki-Tierney provides an excellent overview of this phenomenon in *Kamikaze, Cherry Blossoms and Nationalisms: The Militarization of Aesthetics in Japanese History* (Chicago: University of Chicago Press, 2002).

5. These midget submarines are not to be confused with the Kaiten that appeared in the final months of the war. The Kaiten were sent out on ramming missions, essentially human-guided torpedoes. They have sometimes been called the prototype of today's "smart bombs."

6. *Ha-19* was salvaged and repaired by the United States. During the war, it toured the United States as part of a war bond drive, and can be viewed today at the National Museum of the Pacific War in Fredericksburg, Texas.

7. Sakamaki's existence was made public in a 9 December 1945 *Nippon Times* front-page article, "Lone Survivor of Pearl Harbor Sub Attack Found." A follow-up article on p. 2 of the 19 December 1945 *Nippon Times* released Sakamaki's name. The timing of the article was hardly coincidental. Sakamaki published an account of his mission, *Furyo seikatsu yonkanen no kaiko* (Reflections of Four Years of Living as a POW), (Tokyo: Koenkai, 1947), translated in English and given the sensational title, *I Attacked Pearl Harbor* (New York: Association Press, 1949). He saw *Ha-19* again in 1991, and died in 1999 at the age of eighty-one. For his obituary, see the *Honolulu Start Bulletin*, 11 May 2002, "Whatever Happened To?" by Burl Burlingame, available at http://starbulletin.com/2002/05/11/news/whatever.html.

8. There are at least four variations of Ueda Sadamu's name. *PWR*, making use of the official naval dispatch, provided furigana reading "Ueda Sadamu," the style followed in this book. However, in Donald M. Goldstein and Katherine V. Dillon, eds., *The Pearl Harbor Papers: Inside the Japanese Plans* (Washington: Brassey's, 1993), p. 276, the name is given as Wada Sadamu (which seems to be an error), with the variation Uyeda [Ueda] Tei. And in *Mother of a Warrior-God*, the furigana for the name reads "Kamida Sadamu." In this study, I have followed *PWR*'s rendering of the name for the sake of consistency. It is fairly common for Japanese to have different readings for their given names, less so for family names.

9. The Imperial High Command's official report on submarine operations from December 1941 to April 1942 is inconclusive regarding the success of the midget submarines at Pearl Harbor: "Reliable information on the effectiveness of the midget submarine attack could not be obtained. It was believed that they caused a certain amount of damage to the enemy fleet considering the confusion in Pearl Harbor as witnessed by one or two submarines. A radio message of success from one of the midget submarines and an intercepted plain message dispatched from the United States forces giving general warning supports this belief" (cited in Donald M. Goldstein and Katherine V. Dillon, eds., *The Pearl Harbor Papers*, pp. 276-277). A recent study proposing the success of the midget submarines at Pearl Harbor is "Pearl Harbor—Attack from Below" by Commander John Rodgaard (Ret) et al., in the official publication of the US Naval Institute, *Naval History*, December 1999, available at www.usni.org/navalhistory/Articles99/Nhrodgaard.htm.

10. The final line of a poem by Ōtomo no Yakamochi, "Umi Yukaba," from Japan's oldest anthology of

poetry, the eighth-century *Manyōshu*: *Umi yukaba / mizuku kabane / yama yukaba / kusa musu kabane / okimi no hen / ni koso shiname / kaerimi wa seji*. Cook and Cook translate this as "Across the sea, corpses soaking in the water, Across the mountains, corpses heaped upon the grass, We shall die by the side of our lord. We shall never look back" (*Japan at War: An Oral History* [New York: New Press, 1992], p. 259).The poem was put to song twice, first in the 1880s and again in 1937. The anthem of the Japanese navy, it was the obligatory send-off song for sailors and was quoted frequently at the beginning of the war. This adaptation of a poem written by a courtier of an ancient era to the modern military man drawn from erstwhile peasant stock is another example of the modern Japanese military's appropriation of high culture as historical justification for its existence.

11. Kusunoki Masatsura (1326-1348), son of the better-known Kusunoki Masashige (1294-1336), took up his father's lost cause and died in battle in a failed bid to wrest power away from the shogunate and restore to political power the southern court of the Japanese imperial line. Yoshida Shōin (1830-1859) was one of the philosopher-rebels inspiring the Sonnō Jōi (Respect the Emperor, Expel the Barbarians) Movement, eventually executed for attempting to assassinate Ii Naosuke, a bakufu official responsible for concluding the port treaties with the Western powers. Some of Yoshida's followers rose to prominence in the Meiji government. General Nogi Maresuke (1849-1912), a hero of the Russo-Japanese War, committed seppuku on the day of the Meiji Emperor's funeral in order to atone for the fifty-six thousand young men, including two of his own sons, who died under his command during the war.

12. Denis Warner and Peggy Warner note that a badly hit torpedo bomber deliberately flew into the superstructure of the transport ship USS *George F. Elliott* on 8 August 1942 at Guadalcanal. See *The Sacred Warriors* (New York: Van Nostrand Reinhold, 1982), p. 50, n. 3. US wartime films also depicted suicidal acts by US servicemen. For instance, in *Bataan*, "A fighter rammed his aircraft into a strategic bridge to prevent enemy forces from crossing" (Robert Fyne, *The Hollywood Propaganda of World War II* [Metuchen, NJ: Scarecrow Press, 1994], p. 41). In *Wing and a Prayer*, "In human terms, the price was high to preserve the ship. For Ensign Kevin O'Shea it became a sacrifice for God and country; he rammed his aircraft into the path of a torpedo which was heading straight for the carrier's hull" (Fyne, *Hollywood Propaganda*, p. 5). That fictionalized accounts of suicidal ramming missions were seen in Hollywood films would have only bolstered the idea that in wartime, dying for one's country was "rational" and commendable behavior, albeit under slightly different circumstances.

13. Shikishima was the site of the imperial palace of the Yamato nation in Nara and pre-Nara times.

14. Warner and Warner, *The Sacred Warriors*, pp. 106-108.

15. Warner and Warner, *The Sacred Warriors*, p. 143.

16. Two months after the war's end, the *Nippon Times* (31 October 1945, p. 3) printed army nurse Kure's account of retreating Japanese troops in the Philippines bayoneting Japanese children whom they deemed a liability.

17. Here the text supplies the reading "Yankee" (*yankii*, in furigana) to the pejorative word *kichiku*, a combination of *ki* (demon or ogre) and *chikushō* (beast-born). The word "chikushō" is found in Buddhist scripture, where it indicates living beings whose minds are not moving toward enlightenment and therefore are destined to be reborn as lesser beings—in the case of human beings, beasts, typically, insects or worms. The word is roughly equivalent to "bastard" in English.

18. When the Occupation began, thousands of Japanese were dying of starvation. MacArthur would inherit this food shortage problem, which he solved with emergency shipments from the United States.

19. One *koku* is equal to 180.3 liters (381 pounds). The *Orient Year Book* for 1942 (p. 1720) quotes rice production figures of 65.9 to 69.0 million *koku* for the years 1936-1939. Of the years reported therein, 1926-1939, the lowest production figure is 51.8 million *koku* in 1934, the year of the Tōhoku famine, and the highest is 70.8 million in 1933, the average being about 62 million *koku* (11.8 million tons) for this fourteen-year period.

20. The Japanese military's "importation" of the entire rice crop of Vietnam in July 1945 was responsible for up to two million Vietnamese starving to death.

CONCLUSION: ENDGAME

By 1 August 1945, over sixty of Japan's cities had been devastated by incendiary bombing and the nation's war machine was all but destroyed. According to the media, however, the people's will to fight was anything but diminished by the prospect of an Allied invasion. "Certain Victory" (*hisshō*) was now parsed in terms of a "Decisive War" (*kessen*) for the homeland that would end with the invaders repelled from Japan's shores. Presumably, the Allies would then desist in demanding unconditional surrender, which was unacceptable to the Imperial High Command. The Japanese government was prepared to let more blood flow to protect the national polity and the imperial institution. The covenant between god-emperor and his people was to be kept at any cost.

The Japanese government treated the Potsdam Declaration, issued by the Allies on 26 July, as an affront that Japan would not dignify with a response. A 29 July front-page article in the English-language *Nippon Times*, tellingly titled "Potsdam Declaration to Be Ignored in Japan: Truman, Churchill and Chiang Demand Unconditional Surrender of Japan," tersely noted that "Foreign Minister Shigenori Togo reported the contents of the joint declaration of Truman, Churchill, and Chiang Kai-shek with regard to Japan at the regular Cabinet meeting on July 26. It was indicated that the Japanese Government would ignore the declaration, whatever its nature, and say nothing on it. It was further indicated that things like the joint declaration would not affect in the least the basic policy of Japan which is that of pushing the work of carrying the War of Greater East Asia through to its end." The obstinacy of the government's position was reflected in such editorials as that in the 3 August *Nippon Times* bearing the title, "The Potsdam Declaration, an Example of Wishful Thinking."

The war situation worsened dramatically in three disastrous days, 6-9 August. First, Hiroshima was nearly obliterated by an atomic blast on 6 August, and then on 9 August, a second atomic bomb fell on Nagasaki and the Soviet Union entered the war against Japan, quickly overrunning Manchuria. The Soviets had informed Japan that the non-aggression treaty the two nations had signed in 1941 would not be renewed when it expired on 5 April 1945, but this was far from a declaration of war. The press cautioned that the Soviet advances were to be taken seriously, but downplayed their gravity. A 12 August *Nippon Times* article on various Soviet troop movements across a wide front including Manchukuo, Outer Mongolia, Chosen [Korea], and Karafuto [Sakhalin], highlighted the positive report from Korea that "the Soviet force which crossed the northern frontier of Chosen is very weak."

The first reports on the atomic bombing of Hiroshima were published on 9 August. The *Nippon Times* carried a short article, "New-type Bombs Used in Raid on Hiroshima," providing sketchy details about the small number of planes participating in the attack, which caused "considerable damage to the city quarters." The following day, the *Nippon Times* printed the Home Ministry's "Directions for Defense Against the New Bomb," with the conflicting message that while the still unidentified new bomb "cannot be taken lightly . . . when a new war weapon appears, its effects are usually exaggerated." The Home Ministry's directions to the population were to be on guard against lone airplanes, seek shelter immediately, and protect themselves against the intense heat of the new bomb's blast with blankets or futon.

On 11 August, more details emerged about the deadly affects of the bomb in a protest lodged by the Japanese government through its Swiss embassy stating, "On August 6, an American plane dropped a new type bomb in the city area of Hiroshima and instantly killed and wounded many citizens and destroyed a major portion of the city. The city of Hiroshima is a common ordinary urban community without any particular military defense facilities and as a whole does not possess any characteristics which can be called military objective[s]." The protest argued that using the new bomb was "contrary to international law" and contradicted America's stated policy on "the use of poison gas or any other inhuman means of warfare," the new bomb being "more cruel than any weapon or missile which has been used in the past." The protest concluded that in deploying the bomb, America "committed a sin against the culture of the human race." Therefore, "The Japanese Government under its name and under the name of the entire human race of civilization hereby accuses the American Government. At the same time, it strongly demands that America refrain from using such inhuman weapons." The same front page carried another article, "Total Wartime Effort Asked [of] Japanese Nation: Overcoming of Present Crisis to Defend National Polity Urged by Shimomura."

> With the use of a new-type bomb by the enemy and the unilateral declaration of war by the Soviet Union, Hiroshi Shimomura, President of the Board of Information, urged the 100,000,000 people of the Empire to exert further their total efforts for the protection of Japan's national polity . . .
>
> [Shimomura said,] "The enemy's air raid upon Japan proper has recently become particularly fierce, as he is prepares [*sic*] for a landing operation on Japan [p]roper. Such enemy operations, [o]ur Land, Sea and Air Forces are smashing in their efforts everywhere. We are ready to crush the enemy at one stroke with the spirit of the whole fighting forces being the same as that of the Special Attack Corps.
>
> "In the meanwhile, the people are bearing up well under the attacks and raids of the barbaric enemy, and are advancing bravely with the spirit of serving the Empire. Our enemy has began [sic] to use a newly invented bomb, and is causing to innocent women, children and the aged most cruel casualties[,] never before seen in human history.
>
> "Then on August 9, the Soviet Union which had been in neutral relation with us, joined the enemy rank and after making an [*sic*] unilateral declaration commenced to attack us. Our [f]orces have readily met the Soviet offensive, and will not allow their further advance.
>
> "Yet we must recognize that the worst condition has now come. For defending the final line, for protecting the national polity and the honor of our race, the Government is exerting utmost efforts, and at the same time expects that the people will overcome the present difficulty to protect the [national] polity of the Empire."

Given that Japan was completely surrounded and faced battles on all sides as well as the threat of repeated atomic attacks, Shimomura's call upon the kamikazefied population to rally for the "honor of our race" and protect the national polity attests to the powerful appeal of the narrative of "Certain Victory" and its attendant myths of racial integrity and national greatness, even when facing the spectre of annihilation conveyed by detailed eye-witness accounts from Hiroshima, such as the gruesome scene described in the 11 August *Nippon Times*:

> At a certain national school, children, who had been doing physical exercises in the open without much clothes on them[,] suffered severe burns. The skin was torn off, and they were in agony, though the scorched parts were not bleeding much. Some of them were suffering from water blisters.

Each day's newspaper brought fresh details of the devastation in Hiroshima and the inhuman nature of the "new-type" bomb. The 12 August *Nippon Times* reported:

> The cruel havoc wrought by the new type bomb used by the enemy against Hiroshima is so horrible that it is utterly beyond description. All the buildings within the affected area were totally destroyed and many innocent women and children, killed, writes a *Yomiuri Hochi* correspondent who visited Hiroshima following the raid. The gist of the correspondent's report is as follows:
>
> "Upon entering the suburbs of Hiroshima city, I found that all the windows had been blown out and the [roof] tiles were covered with dust. The trunks of burnt trees were scorched black. Only three buildings, including the Police Station[,] remain [standing] in the city. Making the Police Station their headquarters, Governor Kono and other officials of Hiroshima Prefecture are pushing rescue work. It is very touching to see them working hard without sleep in spite of the fact that they have lost their families. I was also impressed by the complete composure of those citizens who were assisting in the rescue work."
>
> An eyewitness story of the explosion of the new bomb, as told by an old woman, Ai Kono, 61, who resides in the city[,] was reported by the same reporter as follows:
>
> "I looked skyward as I heard the droning of an airplane and saw a black spot floating. At this instant, the spot shed blue and red lights like lightning. No sooner I had become dizzy, than a scorching heat struck my body."

In the following days, the newspapers reported European criticism of the use of the atomic bomb. To cite some *Nippon Times* headlines, "Vatican Press Hits American Employment of New Type Bomb" (11 August), "'Threat to Peace': Outlawing of New Bomb Suggested by [London] Daily Herald" (12 August), "Attlee May Seek Curb on Use of New Missile; Agreement with U.S. on Bomb Use Against Japan Brings Widespread British Criticism" (13 August), "Protest by Japanese on New Type Bomb Lodged through Swiss Government" (13 August), "Swedish Paper Scores Use of Atomic Missile: People Should have been Warned, Undertaking Inhuman, Morgenbladet Says" (14 August). If the Japanese government hoped to shame the United States into negotiating a settlement of the war, the people received not the slightest intimation that the war's end was in sight and they were repeatedly exhorted to keep up the fight.

Finally, an editorial in the *Mainichi Newspaper* commenting upon Cabinet Information Bureau President Shimomura's speech about the "worst condition" of the war (reprinted in the 14 August *Nippon Times*) seemed to signal an imminent change:

> Our people have full knowledge of the crisis confronting the country without any special explanation. The Government clearly says, [the nation now confronts] "the worst condition" . . .
>
> We by no means think that our people are looking unconcernedly at the Government's statement, a statement which reveals its determination to endeavor for tomorrow by stressing the protection of the nation's polity and the maintenance of the honor of the nation.
>
> [This is a]n attitude not to be disturbed at any turn in the situation. This is the attitude of a great people. In our country we have the Imperial Family, eternal and everlasting, and with the Imperial Family as the center, the one hundred million people are united. This is what we call the protection of our national polity and the maintenance of the honor of our race. Should our people allow themselves to disturb their domestic unity, they would have to abandon their glory to live eternally.
>
> Under the Imperial Family the one hundred millions [*sic*] are to have a really domestic unity. At a period of the extension of national fortunes the Japanese people maintained unity well and why not tighten the unity if they enter into a period of reverses?
>
> Man must have time for reflection either as [an] individual or as a race. Development without reflection leads to stumbling. If we are to be given moments for reflection, it must be God's advice. We should never be in despair nor violent. We are a great people.

Conceding that "we are a great people" who would "maintain unity" with the imperial family through "a period of reverses" was as close as the press came to admitting defeat. Of course, the Soviet declaration of war and the deployment of atomic bombs could not be whitewashed as easily as were the series of military defeats in the distant South Pacific. If these "reverses" did spell defeat, then the people were to find solace and purpose in their "tightened unity" with the imperial family, an idea that would find fuller expression in the days to come.

The full significance of the atomic bomb, initially lost in the context of carpet bombing that had decimated more than sixty cities, emerged forcefully on 15 August, when the Rescript to Restore the Peace was announced, Japan surrendered, and hostilities ceased. The carefully crafted rescript[1] explained the Japanese government's official position regarding the resolution of the "Certain Victory" it had pursued for eight years of war beginning in 1937 with the undeclared China war and extending in 1941 to the Pacific War. Were it not for the powerful momentum of "Certain Victory," the rescript itself might have been largely unnecessary. The rescript begins by reiterating the nobility of Japan's war aims and exonerating the government, armed forces, and citizenry from blame for the war's outcome:

> We declared war on America and Britain out of Our sincere desire to ensure Japan's self-preservation and the stabilization of East Asia, it being far from Our thought either to infringe upon the sovereignty of other nations or to embark upon territorial aggrandizement.
>
> Despite the best that has been done by everyone—the gallant fighting of military and naval forces, the diligence and assiduity of Our servants of the State and the devoted service of Our one hundred million people, the war situation has developed not necessarily to Japan's advantage, while the general trends of the world have all turned against her interest.

In other words, it implied, "general trends of the world"—the defeat of Italy and Germany, the Soviet Union's entry into the war against Japan, the rout of Japan's forces, the loss of empire, and the decimation of the homeland—were setbacks unforeseeable when the emperor issued the Rescript Declaring War against America and Britain, but even the combination of these disadvantageous developments did not necessarily spell the immediate end of resistance or defeat for Japan.

> [T]he enemy has begun to employ a new and most cruel bomb, the power of which to do damage is indeed incalculable, taking the toll of many innocent lives. Should We continue to fight, it would not only result in an ultimate collapse and obliteration of the Japanese nation, but also it would lead to the total extinction of human civilization. Such being the case, how are We to save the millions of Our subjects; or to atone Ourselves before the hallowed spirits of Our Imperial Ancestors? This is the reason why We have ordered the acceptance of the provisions of the Joint Declaration of the Powers [i.e., the Potsdam Declaration].

Here, the emperor echoes the media's commentary on the inhumanity of the atomic bomb, thereby claiming the moral high ground and finding a reason for accepting the Potsdam Declaration: to save the Japanese nation from "obliteration" and even humanity from "total extinction."[2] In a word, the surrender is the emperor's gift to the Japanese people and the people of the world. The rescript concludes by laying out the future of the peace.

> We are keenly aware of the inmost feelings of all ye, Our subjects. However, it is according to the dictate of time and fate that We have resolved to pave the way for a grand peace for all the generations to come by enduring the unendurable and suffering what is insufferable.
>
> Having been able to safeguard and maintain the structure of the Imperial State, We are always with ye, Our good and loyal subjects, relying upon your sincerity and integrity . . . Let the entire nation continue as one family from generation to generation, ever firm in its faith of the imperishableness of its divine land, and mindful of its heavy burden of responsibilities, and the long road before it. Unite your total strength to be devoted to the construction for the future. Cultivate the ways of rectitude; foster nobility of spirit; and work with resolution so as ye may enhance the innate glory of the Imperial State and keep pace with the progress of the world.

HIS MAJESTY ISSUES RESCRIPT TO RESTORE PEACE

Joint Declaration of U.S., Great Britain, China and Soviet Union Accepted—Continuation of Hostilities Would Only Mean Obliteration of Japanese Empire

His Majesty the Emperor on August 14 graciously issued an Imperial Rescript to bring the war to an end and to restore peace once again to the world. He ordered the Government to communicate to the Governments of the United States, Great Britain, China and the Soviet Union that the Japanese Empire accepts the provisions of their Joint Declaration.

The full text of the Imperial Rescript follows:

1. *Nippon Times* 16,672, 15 August 1945, p. 1. The language of the rescript, as officially translated, reflected that of the Japanese original: the words "surrender," "capitulate," "failure," and "defeat" are absent from the article and from the rescript.

The government's official narrative of the war ended as it began, with an imperial rescript. Indeed, newspapers reprinted the rescript declaring war on the eighth of every month, "Imperial Rescript Day," the last being 8 August 1945. For the first time, however, via the medium of radio, the emperor spoke directly, in his own voice, to the Japanese people. At noon on 15 August, all Japanese radios broadcast a recording of the emperor reading the rescript of surrender. Never before had the emperor directly addressed his people and publicly set the course of national policy, an event that seemed to herald the dawn of a new era.

The tone and import of the Rescript to Restore the Peace, however, were consistent with the narrative of "Certain Victory." The rescript's wordsmiths prudently avoided words akin to "defeat" and "surrender," finding no fault in Japan's war plan and assigning no responsibility to anyone, least of all the emperor or the imperial institution. The rescript does not countenance the possibility of a more intelligent military strategy or morally or spiritually superior adversary. On the contrary, it reaffirms the national greatness of Japan and racial superiority of the Yamato, who will "endure the unendurable and suffer what is insufferable" in order to save Japan and humanity from extinction, just as the people had "cheerfully" made so many sacrifices for the sake of liberating Asia. "Defeat" was triggered only by Japanese conscience (assisted by the foreign technology of nuclear weapons), since the salvation of humanity remained the moral imperative of the Japanese emperor, his government, and his subjects.

The rescript is thus not the foreordained ending to "Certain Victory," but merely an announcement that the story is "to be continued." The triumphant ending to "Certain Victory" would come when the unified "total strength" of the "one family" of the nation, "ever firm in its faith of the imperishableness of its divine land," had accomplished "the construction of the future" and shone forth the "innate glory of the Imperial State."[3] (To this day, the Japanese government officially commemorates the end of the war on 15 August, not on 2 September, the day on which the Instrument of Surrender was signed by Allied and Japanese representatives on board the USS *Missouri*.) The rescript offered no satisfactory ending to "Certain Victory" and time marched quickly on.

In those very strange days between the announcement of the rescript (15 August) and the arrival of the first Allied occupying troops (26 August), the images of war, and the war of images, underwent a change of guard. *PWR* ceased publication in July, but the lacuna created thereby was quickly filled by the private sector, which continued to publish daily newspapers and weekly photojournals. The first sign of change in the media's tone is evident in the account of the decision to surrender. The *Nippon Times* printed an unsigned editorial on 15 August commenting upon "The Restoration of the Peace," applauding the decision to end the war made by the emperor, "ever solicitous of the happiness and welfare of His subjects" threatened with atomic annihilation:

> Considering the circumstances [e.g., the hostilities] which have prevailed in the past, the decision [to end the war] could not have been easy. But notwithstanding these difficulties, the decision has been made. Considerations of a higher order have prevailed, and rightly so.
>
> It is only proper that the ultimate welfare of the people and the saving of human civilization from extinction should prevail over lesser considerations even if substantial sacrifices should be necessary.

> There is no denying, however, that the future will not be easy. The Japanese people are well aware that their burden will be heavy and that much suffering lies in store for them. But having already suffered grievously from the war, they are resolved to bear patiently the further trials which lie ahead so that they may yet eventually emerge to the enjoyment of a better era.

The editorial smacks of the blind optimism of "Certain Victory":

> Japan has made this decision which will contribute so immeasurably to the future welfare of humanity. How many lives this action will save, how many human hearts will now be able to beat with new hope, how great a burden, both material and spiritual, has been lifted from the backs of millions, can scarcely be imagined.

Of course, had the same concern for saving lives found expression nine months earlier, Japan's cities and their residents would have been spared the US incendiary bombing campaign, several cataclysmic battles in the South Pacific would have been precluded, and millions of people throughout Asia would not have perished. The logic of this altruistic argument rings false in light of the sacrifices required by "Certain Victory" and the Japanese Government's zealous pursuit of empire and flagrant disregard for the lives of people everywhere, including its own citizens.

On the following day, 16 August, the newspapers revealed with astonishing candor that the Japanese and American negotiations of the surrender revolved around concern for one life in particular, that of the emperor—hence the obtuse phrase, "We are always with ye," in the Rescript to Restore the Peace. The *Nippon Times*, in a flash of unintended irony, printed side by side on its front page two articles describing the intricate diplomatic dance leading to the surrender. The larger of the two articles, with the unabashed title "Benevolent Words of Imperial Solicitude Bring Tears to Leaders at Epochal Meet," gave a moving account of the Imperial High Command's deliberations over the Potsdam Declaration:

> With the appearance of the cruel new weapon, the atomic bomb, the united efforts of the Japanese people for the prosecution of the war have been nullified. The powerful destructive power of the atomic bombs which were dropped on the city of Hiroshima on August 6 and on Nagasaki city on August 9, brought about a basic change in the process of the war. All the officers and men at the front and the people on the home front who are imbued with the fierce fighting spirit of the Special Attack Units had to change their ways of fighting, as a result of the use of this super explosive.
>
> All the Japanese cities faced a grave situation of being reduced to ashes and many more harmless Japanese people exposed to the menace of being wantonly killed by the new bombs. It was at this critical moment that His Majesty the Emperor was benevolent enough to have caused His Government to adopt necessary measures to stop the war.
>
> Since August 9, a series of meetings by the Supreme War Conference and extraordinary Cabinet sessions had been held daily for the purpose of devising measures to [accept the Potsdam Declaration] . . . A very important and historic conference was held in the Imperial Palace at 11 [A].[M]. on August 14 in the August presence of His Majesty the Emperor . . . It is reported that His Imperial Majesty was gracious enough to say the following at the Conference:
>
> "As a result of carefully pondering over the general trends of the world as well as Japan's situation, We should like to carry on the policy as has been already fixed [by the Allies], by enduring the unendurable and suffering what is insufferable to atone Ourselves before the hallowed spirits of Our Imperial Ancestors and to save the millions of Our subjects. You may have opinions of your

> own, but the answer of the Allied Nations, We believe[,] recognizes the sovereignty of the Emperor and you all should understand this as We believe. Whatever may happen to Us, We cannot stand to see the nation suffer from further hardships."
>
> All those in attendance, upon hearing these benevolent Imperial Words, burst into tears in spite of the August presence.

This astonishing text contains two contradictions. In one place the primary concern in ending the war is the welfare of the Japanese people, but in another it is vouchsafing the sovereignty of the emperor. And the emperor, believing his sovereignty to be guaranteed by the Allied Nations' answer, implies that he cares not "whatever may happen to Us." These contradictions are more baldly expressed in an adjacent, related article, "Notes Sent by Japan, Allies' Reply Revealed," which printed verbatim the diplomatic exchanges leading to Japan's surrender. The Japanese Government's 10 August note to the Western powers unveils earlier efforts to negotiate a settlement:

> In obedience to the gracious command of His Majesty the Emperor who, ever anxious to enhance the cause of world peace, desires earnestly to bring about an early termination of hostilities with a view to saving mankind from the calamities to be imposed upon them by further continuation of the war, the Japanese Government asked several weeks ago the Soviet Government with which neutral relations then prevailed, to render good offices in restoring peace vis-[à]-vis the enemy Powers.

In the time that elapsed since "several weeks ago," the military sent thousands of young men to their deaths and the media fanned the flames of bloodlust among the home front and its Volunteer Army Corps, while the government was, in fact, attempting to settle the war through Soviet diplomatic channels. This admission was tantamount to exposing the deceptive, manipulative nature of the narrative of "Certain Victory": the Japanese people were continuing to suffer, to die in air raids, and to prepare for a fight to the death on the Home Islands primarily for the sake of empowering the Japanese government's position at the negotiating table so that the "Imperial State" could be "safeguarded" and "maintained." When the Soviet route to peace ended in failure and August brought cataclysmic changes in the war situation, the Japanese Government finally communicated that "it was prepared to accept the Potsdam Declaration under the understanding that the declaration 'does not comprise any demand which prejudices the prerogatives of His Majesty as a sovereign ruler.'"

The article printed the 13 August response of the four nations (the United States, Great Britain, the Soviet Union, and Nationalist China) regarding the sovereignty of the emperor, which stated that "From the moment of surrender, the authority of the Emperor and the Japanese Government to rule the state shall be subject to the Supreme Commander of the Allied Powers . . . The Emperor will be required to authorize and ensure the signature by the Government of Japan and the Japanese Imperial General Headquarters of the surrender terms"[4] and "shall issue his commands to all the Japanese military, naval, and air authorities of Japan and all the forces under their control wherever located to cease active operations, and to surrender their arms and to issue such other orders as the Supreme Commander may require." As for "the ultimate form of the government of Japan," it shall "be established by the freely expressed will of the

Japanese people." The Japanese Government replied on 14 August that "His Majesty the Emperor has issued an Imperial Rescript regarding Japan's acceptance of the provisions of the Potsdam Declaration . . . His Majesty the Emperor is prepared to authorize and ensure the signature by His Government and the Imperial General Headquarters of the necessary terms for carrying out the provisions of the Potsdam Declaration. His Majesty is also prepared to issue his commands to all the military, naval, and air authorities of Japan and all the forces under their control wherever located to cease active operations, to surrender arms, and to issue such other orders as may be required by the Supreme Commander of the Allied forces." Indeed, an imperial rescript was issued on 17 August ordering all Japanese forces to cease hostilities and lay down arms.

The inner workings of Japan's rulers had been shrouded in secrecy long before the war began, and the 16 August *Nippon Times* article describing the surrender negotiations is therefore all the more striking for its candid reporting of such sensitive information. Previously, on those rare occasions when the press printed "Imperial Words," they had not spoken to political issues or matters bearing directly upon the governance of the nation. "Certain Victory" had only one component that the government adamantly insisted upon shielding from the vicissitudes of shifting fortunes: the imperial institution.

The immediacy with which the Japanese government undertook historical revisionism was astounding. By the time that the fifteenth of August had become the sixteenth, the very authors of "Certain Victory" had abandoned and disowned it. Once the integrity of the imperial institution had been guaranteed, the government had no compunction in informing the people that their lives were, at best, a secondary consideration in terminating the war. The 16 August *Nippon Times* article describing the negotiations allows for only one conclusion: peace would have come weeks or months earlier, if the people's welfare had been a higher consideration than the emperor's.[5] However, had the High Command agreed to surrender terms that did not guarantee the emperor's safety, there may have been a violent reaction among the Japanese people, after decades of being conditioned to believe that Japan would cease to be without the emperor.

By publicizing the conditions under which the Japanese government had accepted the Potsdam Declaration, the emperor was, in effect, covertly appealing to his subjects to ensure that SCAP upheld its promise to him while also laying bare the latent threat of public unrest that might result in the abrogation of that promise. The emperor's bid to solidify his people's loyalty was also evident in another instance of "Imperial Words" conveyed to the people through the good offices of his royal relative, Prince Higashikuni Naruhiko, who became prime minister on 17 August. The *Nippon Times* made the happy news its lead article on 21 August: "His Imperial Majesty Asks Government to Brighten up the People's Daily Life."

> When the extraordinary Cabinet Council was opened at 2 [P].[M]. Sunday afternoon [19 August], the Prime Minister [Higashikuni] announced that, being received in audience by His Majesty the Emperor the same day, His Imperial Majesty gave the following most gracious words.
>
> "Brighten up the people's life after the conclusion of the war. For instance, immediately lift the light control and brighten up the streets; hurry the re-establishment of amusement facilities, and speedily abolish mail censorship."

> The Cabinet decided immediately to observe the spirit of the gracious Imperial wish and hurriedly put into effect various measures for brightening up the people's daily life.

If the emperor could not let his people eat cake, at the very least he could let them drink and make merry by "asking" his government to re-establish age-old outlets for frustrations pent up during the long years of wartime deprivation. In August 1945, "brightening" no longer took the form of the morally superior Japanese shining kokutai's light on Asia and liberating the region from oppression by selfish, decadent Westerners, it now referred to the establishment of brothels (e.g., "amusement facilities") throughout the land.[6] If the "Imperial wish" was that the people's lives be bright, such outlets were a thinly disguised bulwark against social unrest in a time of crisis and tumult.

In the two weeks of transition prior to the Occupation, the media also printed shocking, frank reports from the atomic-bomb devastated cities. The *Asahi Newspaper*, on government orders,[7] sent two photographers to Hiroshima and Nagasaki days after the blasts. Some of their photographs were published in the *Asahigraph* on 25 August, perhaps the first uncensored, unstaged, unmediated news photographs to appear in the Japanese press in a decade. As such, they are emblematic not only of the painful birth of a new Japan, but of the price paid for peace. Ironically, it would be some years more before the Japanese press regained the freedom to publish photographs or graphic descriptions of the atomic bombings. The 25 August *Asahigraph*'s photoessay describing the atomic bombings was no more controversial or sensational than many other depictions of wholesale destruction and barren desolation: Attu, Saipan, Iwo Jima, Okinawa, the 64 fire-bombed cities of the Home Islands. The text accompanying the article was a straightforward statement of the scientific facts as known at the time, with none of the personal dimension of the eyewitness accounts of suffering already published in the newspapers. Nevertheless, this issue of *Asahigraph* was suppressed by SCAP under the direct orders of MacArthur, on the grounds that images of atomic bomb damage constituted sensitive information that might reveal military secrets.

SCAP's move to rein in the Japanese press may have been provoked by an avalanche of damaging information about the incendiary and atomic bombings. The 26 August *Nippon Times* (p. 4) carried two different commentaries worth summarizing here for the light they shed on Japanese attitudes toward the war just days before the Occupation began. The first article, "The Sufferings of the People," carried a litany of death and destruction: two hundred sixty thousand civilians dead from bombing campaigns, four hundred twenty thousand wounded, and 9.2 million rendered homeless; and eighty-two cities bombed, over half of them decimated. Among the dead were ninety thousand killed and another one hundred eighty thousand wounded in just two instances of the atomic bomb's deployment. An unsigned article of the same day gave the fearful news that the number of dead in Hiroshima had doubled from thirty thousand three days after the explosion to sixty thousand two weeks later, despite those injured having felt fine in the days after the blast. "The Suffering of the Japanese People" concluded that

> The moral problem of a world which would permit such cruelties to be inflicted upon any people, even under a recognized state of war, is a problem of paramount urgency. Whatever may be the

excuse, however plausible may be the reasons given in justification of any war, it is to be gravely doubted whether any human being has the moral right to inflict such a horror upon an extensive civilian population as has been inflicted upon the Japanese people. Mankind must be spared from any possibility of a repetition of such suffering as the Japanese people have experienced. It is not a matter of statecraft; it is not even a matter of high ideals; it is a matter of simple humanitarianism. The construction of a kind of world in which wars will be impossible is a task to which all nations should bend their utmost.

原子爆弾とは

2-7. *Asahigraph* (44:28), 25 August 1945, pp. 4-5. The lead story in this issue of *Asahigraph* was the Rescript to Restore the Peace, which was praised as "a sign of the great compassion of the emperor for his people," much as had been the emperor's tour of firebombed Tokyo five months earlier. The Rescript to Restore the Peace mentioned "a new, inhuman weapon that threatens all humanity," which introduced the topic of this article, "What Is the Atomic Bomb?" This remarkably balanced report, printed in the week between the announcement of the surrender and the arrival of occupying troops, contained none of the derogatory language or vitriol found in the *Asahigraph* so regularly in the preceding months. The article, which concentrated on a scientific explanation of the bomb, noted that the attacks took "ninety thousand precious lives" and injured twice that number.

(right page, top, p. 4) "Parachute-equipped, remote-controlled dish, said to have been used to record the force of the atomic bomb."

(right page, middle) "Time schedule at the train station. Nothing happened to the white areas, but the numbers and letters were burnt."

(right page, bottom) "Residents of the atom-bombed city of Nagasaki rise up and bravely carry their wounded relatives on their backs."

(left page, top, p. 5) "The tragic state of the city of Hiroshima. Nothing is left, everything was swept away by the fire."

(left page, bottom right) "The terrific force of the atomic bomb's blast blew freight cars off the tracks and onto their sides."

The idea of Japan preaching peace, when its own military leaders had themselves longed to bomb their enemies just weeks before, must have been shocking at the time, and yet sixty years later, whatever shortcomings the Japanese government has had in its dealings with the war's legacy, it certainly has not grown bellicose. The pseudonymous "Japonicus" went further still, making a scathing polemic of his editorial, "Atomic Bomb," which appeared on the same page 4 of the 26 August *Nippon Times*:

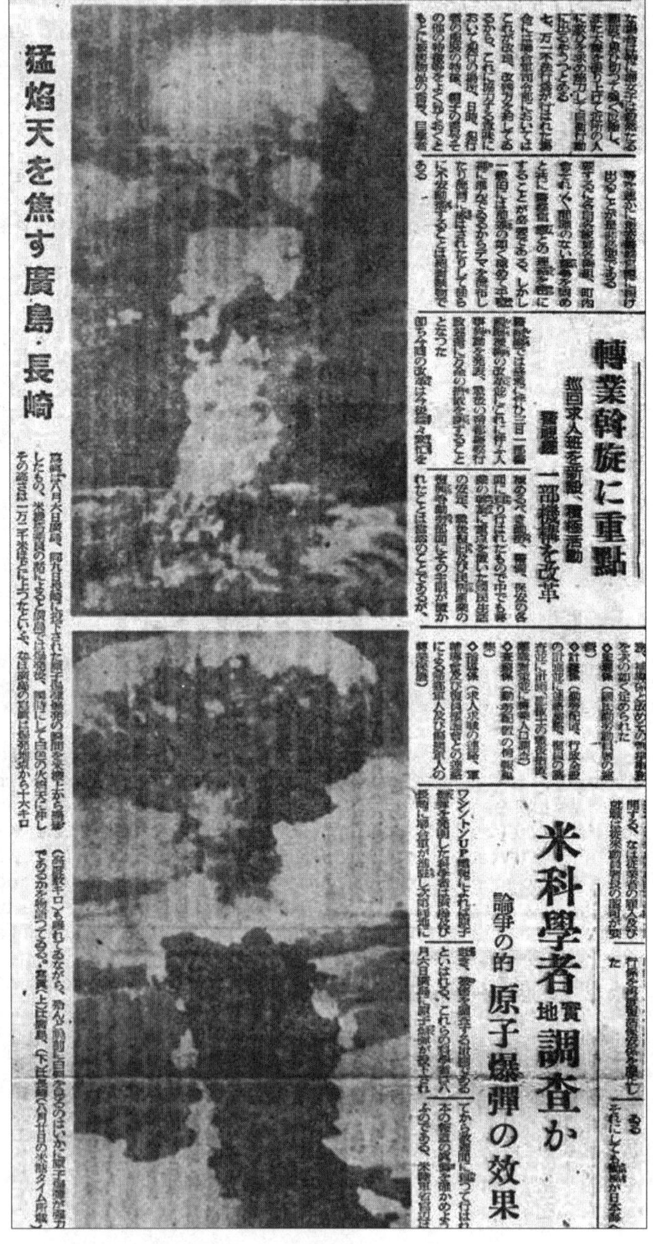

猛焔天を焦す廣島・長崎

轉業斡旋に重點

都區求人班を新設、積極活動

一部機構を改革

米科學者 實地調査か

論爭の的 原子爆彈の效果

8. *Mainichi Newspaper*, Morning Edition, 4 September 1945, p. 2. "Tremendous Fire Lit the Sky over Hiroshima and Nagasaki."

"The photographs were taken by American planes in the moment that atomic bombs were dropped on Hiroshima (on 6 August) and on Nagasaki (on 9 August). According to one of the American bombing crew members, in the moment the bomb exploded over Hiroshima, a white pillar of smoke rose skyward some 12,000 meters [7.45 miles]. The photograph of Hiroshima was taken from a distance of 16 kilometers [10 miles] from the epicenter (with a high [shutter] speed), and yet seeing the pillar of smoke before his very eyes made him realize the incredible power of the atomic bomb. The upper photograph is of Hiroshima, the lower of Nagasaki. Both are reprinted from the 20 August issue of the American magazine *Time*."

Another article on the same page is titled "US Scientists to Conduct Survey on Actual Site [of the Atomic Bomb]. Purpose of their Research: The Effects of the Atomic Bombs."

> The Allied statesmen are reported to have set up in Germany an international military tribunal to try "war criminals," including perpetrators of "war crimes" within the purview of international law. The employment of the atomic bomb with malice aforethought and without any previous notice to destroy a large and populous town in defiance of international treaties and international morality just prior to the opening of the trial of "war criminals" cannot but impress the world at large that there is one law for the conqueror and another law for the vanquished, however fairly the trial itself may be conducted. The severe justice to be meted out to "war criminals" might impress Europeans with awe regarding the might of the victorious Allies, but will surely not help to promote a reverence for justice. On the contrary, it would rather lend further color to the naive philosophy so deep-rooted in the popular mind that after all, Might is Right, [which] is by no means a good omen for the creation of a new world of peace and amity which all mankind certainly desire.

Japonicus raises an excellent point about "victors' justice,"[8] but fails to mention that when it was Japan's turn to mete out justice to the captured crew members of the Doolittle Raid, three of the eight men were executed while another died from maltreatment. In short, Japanese attitudes toward the end of the war (if not the war itself) were taking shape before the Occupation began.

SCAP took control of the Japanese media by the end of August, setting the stage for the Japanese people to be presented with the American-orchestrated photographs of the signing of the Instrument of Surrender, which appeared in Japanese newspapers on 3 September. The following day, Japanese newspapers published the aerial photographs taken by US bombers immediately after the atomic bomb explosions (figure 8). Thus, for Japanese, as for Americans, the approved illustration of the atomic bomb was the American-made, American-mediated photograph that became an abstract icon of the nuclear age—the ominous but tidy mushroom cloud unfurling heavenward and announcing to the gods, including Japan's two million or more warrior-gods (the military dead), America's ascendancy as a global superpower. Those images would be stripped of the destructive power of the bomb that leveled cities and instantaneously took the lives of tens of thousands of civilians on the ground.

As soon as Japan regained its status as a sovereign nation in 1952, the Asahi Corporation published photographs detailing the undiluted horrors of the atomic bombings: faces melted by heat, bodies covered with keloids, and the shadows of vaporized human beings. These two types of bomb images—one from the perspective of vulnerable victims on the ground, and the other from the safe distance of bombers in the air—represent more than just the different viewpoints of vanquished and victor, private-sector media and military- and government-created media: they have come to represent polarities in Japanese and in global thinking about war. Both types of bomb images have become emblematic of twentieth century history.

In striking contrast to the bomb photographs are the images of "Certain Victory," once so potently authoritative and pregnant with meaning, to which no one claims ownership today and which may be appropriated by anyone for any purpose: the explosions on Battleship Row, Pearl Harbor; Generals Yamashita and Percival finalizing the surrender of Singapore; the mammoth Uchiteshi Yamamu billboard; the unnervingly innocent smiles of the baby-faced kamikaze pilots; the emperor and his entourage inspecting the ruins of Tokyo.

"Certain Victory" is, from beginning to end, a tightly constructed, engrossing narrative, replete with the hallmarks of a great epic. It is a romantic tale of noble and powerful forces, of larger-than-life heroes both aristocratic and common, of drama and tragedy of oceanic proportions, and ultimately, of personal sacrifices on a monumental scale. The power of this narrative is its ability to instill in human beings a profound sense of purpose, tapping deeply into it audience's inner reserves of strength and inveigling them to give their lives to assure its outcome. So enduring is the seductive charm of "Certain Victory," with its grandiloquent talk of national greatness and racial destiny, that it retains its fascination among Japanese ultranationalists today. And some Japanese who lived through the war as young adults feel nostalgia for a time in which the noblest of human sentiments seemed to guide the entire nation and every person belonged to a movement much larger than her or himself: the creation of a new national polity and a new world order.

The failings of "Certain Victory," however, become apparent when its version of contemporary events is measured against the actual course of the war and the fate of its victims, Japanese, Asian, European, and American. Furthermore, its powerful allure became a dangerous tool in the hands of Japan's wartime leaders, who applied tremendous pressure upon the people, on the home front and the battlefield, to make the hard realities of a lost war conform to this narrative of racial invincibility, national infallibility, and imperial godliness.

In the harsh light of hindsight, "Certain Victory" is dangerous mythology rather than fact. Let us view again, in this harsh light, one recurring, embarrassing, haunting image of the war. We return to the image with which this book began, that of the emperor inspecting the damage from the Great Kanto Air Raid, because it conveys, in the most obvious and extreme terms, the final result proposed by "Certain Victory"—a gray world in which everything and everyone has been destroyed and only the emperor remained, no longer divine but quite human, small, and ineffectual.

For those who can bear to look unflinchingly at the massive loss of life in this and other wars, these images of destruction on a superhuman scale become a terrifying vision of all that is lost when people allow leaders to rule them through fear, intimidation, and the manipulation of arrogant lies about national greatness and the rectitude of war. If we dare to gaze deeply into this landscape, what we see is the final result of unbridled human folly and unchecked megalomania: a world of destruction and debris, denuded of all life but that of generals without armies, rulers without subjects, and gods without worshippers.

Notes

1. The rescript, based upon Hirohito's words, was drafted by Chief Cabinet Secretary Sakomizu with the assistance of Kawada Mizuho and Yasuoka Masahiro, scholars of the Chinese classics. See Herbert P. Bix, *Hirohito and the Making of Modern Japan* (New York: Harper Collins, 2000), p. 525.

2. From the standpoint of civilian victims, the accusation that the deployment of atomic weapons represented a crime against humanity is irrefutable. For the Japanese wartime government to make this accusation, however, was disingenuous, given the well-documented atomic program pursued by Japanese scientists during the war and the horrific chemical and biological weapons tested and deployed primarily against the Chinese. For the Japanese atomic program, see Walter E. Grunden, *Secret Weapons & World War II: Japan in the Shadow of Big Science* (Lawrence: University Press of Kansas, 2005). For chemical and biological weapons development and use by the Japanese military, see Peter Williams, *Unit 731: Japan's Secret Biological Warfare in World War II* (New York: Free Press, 1989) and Sheldon H. Harris, *Factories of Death: Japanese Biological Warfare 1932-45 and the American Cover-Up* (New York: Routledge, 1994).

3. While many Japanese were well-positioned to take advantage of the changes brought about by sweeping reforms (such as land reforms) made during the Occupation, air-raid victims were, by every account the "losers" in Japan's war, having never received any compensation to speak of, although air raid compensation was established by the governments of Great Britain and Germany within a decade of the war's end. See Hanai Kiroku, "The Remembered and the Forgotten: Slighting the Firebombing Victims of Japan's Pacific War," *Japan Focus* 252, 25 September 2006, reprinted from the *Japan Times* of 28 August 2006; available at www.japanfocus.org. Hanai notes that while Japanese war veterans began receiving pensions in 1954, and the atomic bombing victims began receiving government compensation in 1994, the five hundred thousand victims of conventional firebombing have received at most a few hundred dollars per person per year, even for major disabilities resulting from the fire bombings. As this book goes to press, a suit has been filed against the Japanese Government by 112 victims of the Great Tokyo Air Raid of 9-10 March 1945, who seek a combined 1.23 billion yen in reparations and an apology for decades of unrecognized suffering. The suit states its rationale thus: "There were no differences between soldiers and civilians. The government should recognize that all of Japan was a battlefield at the time." See Jun Hongo, "Civilian Survivors Sue State Over Tokyo Air Raid," in the *Japan Times*, 10 March 2007, available at: http://search.japantimes.co.jp/cgi-bin/nn20070310a2.html.

4. Bix (*Hirohito*, pp. 518-19) states that "To make the Byrnes note more palatable to Hirohito, the army leaders, and Hiranuma, Vice Foreign Minister Matsumoto Shinichi (after discussions with Tōgō), and Chief Cabinet Secretary Sakomizu resorted to mistranslation of several key words in the English text. In the operative sentence, 'From the moment of surrender, the authority of the Emperor and the Japanese Government to rule the state shall be subject to the Supreme Commander of the Allied powers,' Matsumoto changed 'shall be subject to' [*reizoku subeki*] to read "Shall be circumscribed by [*seigen no shita ni okarereu*].'" Whether the emperor was apprised of the government-operated *Nippon Times*' publication of the Byrnes note is unclear, but it may have been a moot point. By 13 August, Bix states, "The latest enemy leaflets were giving the Japanese people both the government's notification of surrender on one condition and the full text of Brynes's [sic] reply to it" (*Hirohito*, p. 526).

5. Bix notes that the deliberation of peace within the Imperial High Command began as early as mid-February 1945. See *Hirohito and the Making of Modern Japan*, pp. 487-490. Bix writes: "The wartime emperor ideology that sustained their morale made it almost impossibly difficult for them to perform the act of surrender. Knowing they were objectively defeated, yet indifferent to the suffering that the war was imposing on their own people, let alone the peoples of Asia, the Pacific and the West whose lives they had disrupted, the emperor and his war leaders searched for a way to lose without losing—a way to assuage domestic criticism after surrender and allow their power structure to survive" (*Hirohito*, pp. 520-521).

6. Bix (*Hirohito*, p. 538) quotes a "Recreation and Amusement Association" official explaining publicly the Home Ministry's establishment on 19 August of these associations as a "dike to hold back the mad

frenzy [of the occupation troops] and cultivate and preserve the purity of our race long into the future." These brothels were used by Allied personnel. There is abundant evidence, however, that the initial flood came from Japanese men, as noted by many Japanese commentators, including longtime observer of Japanese sexual mores and novelist Nagai Kafū.

7. Two staff members of the *Asahi Newspaper* photographed Hiroshima and Nagasaki in the weeks after the atomic bombs. Miyatake Hajime (1914-1985), a photographer for the Intelligence Corps of the Chūbu Military Command, spent three days photographing the devastation in Hiroshima (9-11 August). Matsumoto Eiichi (1915-2004) and Miyatake photographed Hiroshima and Nagasaki from 25 August to 15 September. Their film was confiscated by SCAP, but they kept copies that were published soon after the Occupation ended. Japanese and other published sources generally credit the 6 August 1952 issue of *Asahigraph*, which published Miyatake and Matsumoto's 1945 photographs, as being the first publication exposing the horrors of the atomic bombings. This is true, of course, where the portrayal of human victims is concerned. The Asahi Corporation donated 121 photographs by Miyatake and 157 by Matsumoto to the Hiroshima Peace Memorial Museum in 2005.

8. The definitive study of the dubious legal basis for the Tokyo War Crimes trial is Richard H. Minear's pioneering work, *Victors' Justice: The Tokyo War Crimes Trial,* (Princeton: Princeton University Press, 1971).

APPENDIX 1: ANNOTATED BIBLIOGRAPHY OF JAPANESE WARTIME NEWS JOURNALS

Wartime periodicals fall into two broad categories, those published by various government and semi-government agencies and those published by private-sector news agencies. The "big three" Japanese commercial media conglomerates—Asahi, Mainichi, and Yomiuri—were involved in every area of publishing: newspapers, magazines, books, and monthly news digests. For the duration of the war, daily newspapers, both national and local, were the best and most consistent sources of information. Nevertheless, weekly photojournals dominated the wartime print media, in particular, *Photographic Weekly Report* and *Asahigraph*. A third, significant photojournal was Mainichi's *China Incident Pictorial* (later renamed *Great East Asia War Pictorial*), which was issued irregularly and ceased publication in the spring of 1945.

As the Battle of Saipan raged in the summer of 1944, the war situation grew critical. In a drastic streamlining measure, the government forced mergers of most periodicals, many of which "voluntarily" dissolved. Generally, the rule for mergers was to create one publication that answered the needs (geographically or topically) of the many publications it replaced. Each prefecture was left with one local newspaper, and one special interest journal, such as *Cinema News* or *Fine Art*, was created from several others.

This Annotated Bibliography is limited to select major wartime news journals most directly concerned with current events and the progress of the war, that is, most essential to the narrative of "Certain Victory." Since all of the thousands of periodicals in print during the final two years of the war were required to be linked to the war effort, this list is far from comprehensive, and is hardly representative of the much larger collection from which these bibliographical notes were taken and from which this book was written.

1. *Asahigraph* (*Asahigurafu*). Tokyo: Asahi Newspaper, 1923–2000.
   A. *Asahigraph* (1-220), 25 January 1923–September 1923. Daily. Publication interrupted by the Great Kantō Earthquake.
   B. *Asahigraph* (1-4105), 16 November 1923–15 October 2000. Weekly. New enumeration beginning with volume 1, number 1; serialization denoted concurrently with issues numbered from 1 to 4105.
      i. *Asahigraph* (1:1-29:3), 16 November 1923–21 July 1937. Weekly, 10¼ by 15 inches, 36 pages, 20 sen.

ii. *Asahigraph* (29:4-33:18), *China Battle Front Photographs* (*Asahigurafu: Shina sensen shashin*) 1-112, 28 July 1937–1 November 1939. Weekly, 10¼ by 15 inches, 36 pages, 20 sen (issue 1), 25 sen (issues 2 through 117).

a. *Asahigraph* (29:4-29:6), *Special Report: North China Incident Pictorial Report* (*Asahigurafu tokushū: HokuShi jihen gahō*), 1–3, 28 July 1937–11 August 1937. Weekly, 10¼ by 15 inches, 36 pages, 20 sen (issue 1), 25 sen (issues 2 and 3). Enumerated retroactively as *China Battle Front Photographs* 1–3.

b. *Asahigraph* (29:7-29:9), *Special Report: North China Battle Front Photographs* (*Asahigurafu tokushū: HokuShi sensen shashin*) 4–6, 18 August 1937–1 September 1937. Weekly, 10¼ by 15 inches, 36 pages, 25 sen. The issue numbers are consecutive from *North China Incident Pictorial Report*. Enumerated retroactively as *China Battle Front Photographs* 4–6.

c. *Asahigraph* (29:10-29:11), *Special Report: Sino-Japanese Battle Front Photographs* (*Asahigurafu tokushū: Nisshi sensen shashin*) 7 and 8, 8 September 1937–15 September 1937. Weekly, 10¼ by 15 inches, 36 pages, 25 sen. The issue numbers are consecutive from *North China Battle Front Photographs* (there were no *Sino-Japanese Battle Front Photographs* nos. 1–6). Enumerated retroactively as *China Battle Front Photographs* 7 and 8.

d. *Asahigraph* (29:12-30:5), *Special Report: China Battle Front Photographs* (*Asahigurafu tokushū: Shina sensen shashin*) 9–28, 22 September 1937–2 February 1938. Weekly, 10¼ by 15 inches, 36 pages, 25 sen.

e. *Asahigraph* (30:6-33:12; 33:15-33:18), *China Battle Front Photographs* (*Asahigurafu Shina sensen shashin*) 29–113, 9 September 1938–20 September 1939; 11 October–1 November 1939. Weekly, 10¼ by 15 inches, 36 pages, 25 sen. Holiday or special issues had 52 pages and cost 40 sen. Sequential run interrupted by two issues devoted to the outbreak of World War II in Europe (see next entry).

iii. *Asahigraph* (33:13-14), *Photographs of the Great War in Europe* (*Asahigurafu Ōshū taisen shashin*) 1 and 2, 27 September and 4 October 1939. Weekly, 10¼ by 15 inches, 36 pages, 25 sen. These two issues contained no information on the China war, and interrupt the sequence of *China Battle Front Photographs*.

iv. *Asahigraph* (33:19-37:25), 8 November 1939–17 December 1941. Weekly, 10¼ by 15 inches, 36 pages, 25 sen.

a. *Asahigraph* (33:19-35:18), 8 November 1939–30 October 1940. Weekly, 10¼ by 15 inches, 36 pages, 25 sen. Multicolor front and back covers.

b. *Asahigraph* (35:19-37:25), 6 November 1940–17 December 1941. Weekly, 10¼ by 15 inches, 32 pages, 25 sen. Color removed from covers, pages reduced to 32, evidently in response to total mobilization inaugurated under the umbrella of the New Order.

c. *Asahigraph* (36:1-36:25), 1 January 1941–25 June 1941. Weekly, 10¼ by 14¼ inches, 32 pages, 25 sen. Page size slightly reduced, black and white with the exception of the special double issue for New Year's.

d. *Asahigraph* (37:1-37:25), 2 July 1941–25 June 1941. Weekly, 10¼ by 14¼ inches, variable pages, 25 sen. The distinctive red Asahigraph banner was introduced on 2 July 1941 (37:1), an issue with 36 pages. By the end of July, the page count was reduced to 28, and again in October to 24.

v. *Asahigraph* (37:26-44:24), *Great East Asia War Report* (*Asahigurafu Dai Tō A sensō*) 1–180, 24 December 1941–15 August 1945.

a. *Asahigraph* (37:26), *Annihilation of America and Britain Report* (*Asahigurafu BeiEi gekimetsu*) 1, 24 December 1941. Weekly, 10¼ by 14¼ inches, 24 pages, 25 sen. Enumerated retroactively as *Great East Asia War Report* 1.

b. *Asahigraph* (38:1 and 38:2), 31 December 1941 and 7 January 1942 (New Year's double issue). Weekly, 10¼ by 14¼ inches, 44 pages, 40 sen. Enumerated retroactively as *Great East Asia War Report* 2.

c. *Asahigraph* (38:3), *Surrender of Hong Kong Report* (*Asahigurafu Honkon kanraku*) 14 January 1942. Weekly, 10¼ by 14¼ inches, 24 pages, 25 sen. Enumerated retroactively as *Great East Asia War Report* 3.

d. *Asahigraph* (38:4-40:2), *Great East Asia War Report* (*Asahigurafu Dai Tō A sensō*) 4–54, 21 January 1942–13 January 1943. Weekly, 10¼ by 14¼ inches, 24 pages, 25 sen.

e. *Asahigraph* (40:3-42:12), *Great East Asia War Report* (*Asahigurafu Dai Tō A sensō*) 55–116, 20 January 1943–29 March 1944. Weekly, 10¼ by 14¼ inches, 20 pages, 25 sen. Price increase to 26 sen beginning 7 July 1943 (41:1, *Great East Asia War Report* 79).

f. *Asahigraph* (42:13-44:1), *Great East Asia War Report* (*Asahigurafu Dai Tō A sen shashin hōdō*) 117–155, 5 April 1944–27 December 1944. Weekly, 10¼ by 14¼ inches, 16 pages, 26 sen. Price increased to 30 sen from 1 November 1944 (43:18, *Great East Asia War Report* 147).

g. *Asahigraph* (44:2-44:14), *Great East Asia War Report* (*Asahigurafu Dai Tō A sensō*) 156–168, 3 January 1945–5 April 1945. Weekly, 10¼ by 14¼ inches, 16 pages. 30 sen.

h. *Asahigraph* (44:15-44:24), *Great East Asia War Report* (*Asahigurafu Dai Tō A sensō*) 169–180, 15 April 1945–15 August 1945. Trimonthly, 10¼ by 14¼ inches, 16 pages, 40 sen. Issued on the fifth, fifteenth, and twenty-fifth.

v. *Asahigraph* (44:25-44:38), 25 August 1945–25 December 1945. Trimonthly, 10¼ by 14¼ inches, 16 pages.

vi. *Asahigraph* ("The Asahi Picture News") (45:1-47:14), 5 January 1946–1 May 1947. Trimonthly, 10¼ by 14¼ inches, 20 pages, price steadily increased due to postwar inflation.

vii. *Asahigraph* ("The Asahi Picture News") (47:13-58:15), 4 June 1947–April 1954. Weekly, 10¼ by 14¼ inches, pages vary, price steadily increased. Publication resumed after a one-month hiatus due to currency instability.

viii. *Asahigraph* 1548–4105, April 1954–13 October 2000. Weekly, smaller size, pages vary.

The venerable *Asahigraph* had a long run of over seventy-five years. The early issues of this pioneering photojournal bore on the masthead the English subtitle *The Asahigraph Weekly* and logo, "The Only Pictorial Weekly in the East," and included many bilingual (Japanese and English) captions. In its first six or seven years, the novelty of the photograph gave the magazine sufficient raison d'être; news was a secondary concern at best. Covers began incorporating color in the early 1930s.

Asahigraph came to maturity in the 1930s, striking a balance between popular interest items and current events. When it began featuring reports of the war in China on 28 July 1937, the journal carried a subtitle related to war reportage, eventually being rechristened *Asahigraph China Battle Front Photographs.* Each of these issues was given two numbers, one corresponding to the *Asahigraph* issued serially since 1923 and the other a *China Battle Front Photographs* issue number, which ran consecutively for 112 issues. This subtitle was removed from the front cover of the 27 September 1939 issue (33:13), which was devoted to the war in Europe. "China Battle Front Photographs" returned briefly to the front cover before becoming a smaller, occasional back-page feature. War coverage was downplayed and the magazine gave more space to popular culture in late 1939 and through 1940.

The New Order, with its demands for total mobilization, left its stamp on the *Asahigraph.* As advertising shrunk, so did the page count and the use of color. In 1940 and 1941, *Asahigraph* took on a more somber appearance, reserving the use of color for special issues, such as on New Year's. From July 1941, the front cover sported a red banner with "Asahigraph" in white, its standard look for over a decade. With the outbreak of the Pacific War, *Asahigraph* once again took on a subtitle; first it was *Annihilating America and Britain Report*, then *Surrender of Hong Kong Report*; finally, it settled upon *Great East Asia War Report*, a subtitle it would carry until August 1945. Several subtle changes were made beginning with *Asahigraph* (42:12), *Great East Asia Report* 117, 5 April 1944. The price was raised, the page count lowered, and the covers became black and white. In addition, the explanatory phrase—"gahō zasshi" (pictorial magazine)—was placed before *Asahigraph*, most likely a bid to make the magazine more purely "Japanese." The masthead continued to carry "gahō zasshi" through the end of 1944; the phrase was removed from the New Year's 1945 issue (*Asahigraph* [44:2], *Great East Asia War Report* 156, 3 January 1945). The final issue to carry the subtitle, *Great East Asia War Report*, appeared on 15 August 1945.

At 20 sen per copy, *Asahigraph* was a moderately priced publication in the 1920s. The price rose to 25 sen in the early 1930s. The course of the war was reflected in both the price and page limitation of *Asahigraph*. The price rose to 26 sen (with additional postal tax of 1 sen) beginning with the 7 July 1943 issue (41:1, *Great East Asia War Report* 79). The postal tax was raised to 2 sen from the 5 April 1944 issue (42:13, *Great East Asian War Report* 117), when the title was modified to one that sounded less foreign, and the familiar red *Asahigraph* banner became gray. The magazine was void of color for the remainder of the war. The price was increased to 30 sen (with postal tax of 2 sen) from 1 November 1944 (43:18, *Great East Asia War Report* 147), and again to 40 sen (with a postal tax of 5 sen) from 5 April 1945 (44:14, *Great East Asia War Report* 168).

The 5 April 1945 issue announced on its front cover that the magazine was being issued henceforth three times a month, and this was the first issue on which English-language publishing information (required for overseas mailing) was finally wiped from the back cover. The price rose to 40 sen.

Even in the darkest days of the war, the *Asahigraph* sometimes demonstrated its independent viewpoint. It printed a story by Ishikawa Tatsuzō (*Great East Asia War Report* 134, 2 August 1944); his *Living Soldiers* had caused a censorship scandal in 1938. And it made the opening of the second front in Europe (e.g., following D-Day) front page news (*Great East Asia War Report* 127, 14 June 1944). Also noteworthy is a harsh denunciation of Nazi Germany for losing courage and "giving up" (*Great East Asia War Report* 172, 25 May 1945). When the subtitle *Great East Asia War Report* was removed from the cover on 25 August 1945, the price rose 50 percent to 60 sen, with the postal tax still 5 sen. By this time, the magazine consisted of two large, folded broadsheets that had to be cut apart into pages and assembled by the reader.

2. *Weekly Asahigraph Special Reports* (*Shūkan Asahigurafu rinji sōkan*). Tokyo: Asahi Newspaper.

   A. *Photographic Report on the Manchurian Incident* (*Manshū jihen shashin gahō*) 1 and 2, (date unknown) and 30 November 1931. Issue 2: 10¼ by 15 inches, 30 pages, 20 sen.

   Entirely black-and-white report on the Manchurian Incident, in which "Chinese Guerrillas" (in fact, secret troops of the Japanese Kwantung Army) blew up part of the Japanese-run railway, thereby creating the premise for retaliatory campaigns. Designed like a souvenir or commemorative album, it was entirely photographs and captions, with only one half-page of introductory text. No live-action photographs.

   B. *Photographic Report on the Shanghai Incident* (*Shanhai jihen shashin gahō*) 1 and 2, 22 February and 20 March 1932. 10¼ by 15 inches, 32 pages, 20 sen.

   Two issues about skirmishes in Shanghai between Chinese "gangsters" and Japanese troops. Includes what are presumed to be the first "live action" war photographs in a Japanese photojournal. No use of color in either issue, but more text than the earlier *Photographic Report on the Manchurian Incident.*

   C. *Photographic Report on the Jehol (Rehe) Punitive Expedition* (*Nekka tōbatsu shashin gahō*), 1 and 2, 7 March and 17 March 1933. 10¼ by 15 inches, 32 pages, 20 sen.

   A two-part report on an incident of "Chinese provocation" on the path of escalation from Manchuria to the all-out invasion of 1937. No use of color in either issue, format very similar to *Shanghai Incident* and *Jehol* special reports.

   D. *February 26 Incident Pictorial Report* (*Ni ni roku jiken gahō*), 25 July 1936. 10¼ by 15 inches, 50 pages, 30 sen.

   A one-time "special" describing the failed military coup d'état of 26 February 1936, printed days before the beginning of the trial of the perpetrators. Its contents included photographs of the slain government leaders and their funerals as well as the major figures in the "rebellion." Issued with a tipped-in *Asahi Newspaper* extra announcing the sentencing of the rebellion's leaders.

E. *China Incident Pictorial Report* (*Shina jihen gahō*) 1–35, July 1937–August 1940. 10¼ by 15 inches, 36 pages, 25 sen, issued irregularly like newspaper extras.
   i. *North China Incident Pictorial Report* (*HokuShi jihen gahō*) 1 and 2, 30 July and 15 August 1937. 10¼ by 15 inches, 36 pages, 25 sen. Enumerated retroactively as *China Incident Pictorial Report* 1 and 2.
   ii. *Sino-Japanese Incident Pictorial Report* (*Nisshi jihen gahō*) 3, 30 August 1937. 10¼ by 15 inches, 36 pages, 25 sen, Enumerated consecutively from *North China Incident Pictorial Report* and retroactively as *China Incident Pictorial Report* 3.
   iii. *China Incident Pictorial Report* (*Asahigurafu Shina jihen gahō*) 4–35, 20 September 1937–August 1940. 10¼ by 15 inches, 36 pages, 25 sen. Enumerated consecutively from *Sino-Japanese Incident Pictorial Report*. The issue commemorating the fall of Wuhan (*China Incident Pictorial Report* 24, 15 November 1938) had full-color covers, 66 pages, and was priced at 40 sen.

   Thirty-five special reports devoted to the China Incident, with a minimum of advertising, appeared over the course of three years. The covers were printed in duotone, with blue or red as a second color. These "extras" reported major developments in the Japanese military campaign in China, such as the fall of Shanghai, Nanjing, and Wuhan. They appeared about twice a month for the first year of the war. Issue 25 appeared on 17 December 1938, and issue 33 on 22 October 1939. In the nine months that followed, only two more issues were produced, a reflection of the waning public interest in the China war, which dragged on inconclusively despite several major victories. These specials ceased altogether once Japan announced it had "achieved its objectives" in China in the summer of 1940.

F. *Pictorial Report on the Great Upheaval in Europe* (*Ōshū daidōran gahō*), 1–4, 25 September 1939–1 July 1940. 10¼ by 15 inches, issued infrequently. Issue 1: 66 pages, 50 sen. Issue 4: 34 pages, 25 sen.

   Rather lavish magazines with full-color covers and dozens of photographs of Hitler's war machine and the destruction left in its wake. Issue 1 is an accurate (though Axis-leaning) account of the outbreak of World War II in Europe and the standing of Allied and Axis military might. Issue 4 shows a smiling Hitler "riding into the enemy capitol" of France at the apex of the Blitzkrieg.

G. *Pictorial Report on the Great East Asia War* (*Dai Tō A sensō gahō*), 25 December 1941. 10¼ by 14¼ inches, 36 pages, 30 sen.

   Coverage of the victorious attacks made in the first weeks of the war, with several graphs explaining the results of the attack on Pearl Harbor, but no photographs of the damage.

3. *China Incident Pictorial* (*Shina jihen gahō*), 1–141, 3 August 1937–8 April 1945. Osaka: Mainichi Publishing. Issued periodically at different intervals.

A. *China Incident Pictorial* (*Shina jihen gahō*) 1–101. 3 August 1937–20 October 1941.
   i. *Northern China Incident Pictorial* (*HokuShi jihen gahō*) 1–3, 3–21 August 1937. Trimonthly, 10¼ by 15 inches, 32 pages, 20 sen. Enumerated retroactively as *China Incident Pictorial* 1–3.
   ii. *China Incident Pictorial* (*Shina jihen gahō*) 4–49, 10 September 1937–21 December 1938. Trimonthly, 10¼ by 15 inches, 32 pages, 20 sen. Published on the first, eleventh, and twenty-first.
   iii. *China Incident Pictorial* (*Shina jihen gahō*) 50–85, 5 January 1939–20 July 1940. Bimonthly, 10¼ by 15 inches, 32 pages, 20 sen.
   iii. *China Incident Pictorial* (*Shina jihen gahō*) 86–100, 20 August 1940–20 October 1941. Monthly, 10¼ by 15 inches, 32 pages, 20 sen. Issued on the twentieth.

B. *Great East Asia War Pictorial* (*Dai Tō A sensō gahō*) 1–40, also subtitled and numbered as *China Incident Pictorial* (*Shina jihen gahō*) 101–141, and also enumerated by volume numbers (8 January 1942 [1:1] to 8 April 1945 [9:4]).
   i. *Great East Asia War Pictorial* (*Dai Tō A sensō gahō*) 1–14, (*China Incident Pictorial* 101–115), 8 January 1942–8 January 1943. Monthly, 24 pages, 10¼ by 14¼ inches, 20 sen. Number 2 issued on 25 January 1942, thereafter issued monthly on the eighth in honor of the Japanese blitzkrieg (8 December).
   ii. *Great East Asia War Pictorial* (*Dai Tō A sensō gahō*) 15–30, (*China Incident Pictorial* 116–130). 8 February 1943–8 May 1944. Monthly, 20 pages, 10¼ by 14¼ inches, 20 sen.
   iii. *Great East Asia War Pictorial* (*Dai Tō A sensō gahō*) 31–40, *China Incident Pictorial* 132–141), 8 June 1944–8 April 1945. Monthly, 16 pages, 10¼ by 14¼ inches, 20 sen. Price hike to 30 sen from issue 36 (8 December 1944).

The first issue of *China Incident Pictorial*, initially published as a special edition by the *Osaka Mainichi* and sister *Tokyo Nichinichi* newspaper companies, bore the title *Northern China Incident Pictorial*. From the fourth issue (10 September 1937) the title was changed to *China Incident Pictorial* and the format was standardized. It appeared trimonthly through the end of 1938, bimonthly from January 1939 to July 1940, and monthly thereafter through spring 1945. The monthly appeared on the twentieth of each month, but beginning in February 1942 was issued on the eighth—the anniversary day of the Japanese blitz. Like so many other magazines, the page count was gradually decreased, while the price rose. Mainichi took a practical approach to the decrease in pages and put as many photographs on its covers as possible, wrapping them around from front to back.

The *Mainichi Weekly* complements the better-known *Asahigraph* in its coverage of the war in China. Indeed, the title was exactly the same as Asahi's *Shina jihen gahō* (*China Incident Pictorial Report*, translated slightly differently to avoid confusion). Mainichi sent a team of reporters and photographers to China who created original material. The Mainichi publication had a somber tone: the entire production was black and white (even the cover), and contained fewer photographs of smiling Japanese soldiers, so prevalent in the pages of *Asahigraph* and *PWR*. "Banzai!" photographs are present, but not gratuitous. Mainichi's coverage of the war is gritty and raw; the magazine regularly included photographs of wounded Japanese soldiers, fleeing Chinese refugees, captured Chinese soldiers (many of them mere boys), and destroyed villages and flattened city blocks. The coverage of the fall of Nanjing is particularly interesting as it shows a captured Chinese resistance leader and photos of captured Chinese guerillas, nonexistent in either *Asahigraph* or *PWR*. Over all, the Mainichi publication seems to be less of a government mouthpiece than the Asahi, if no less patriotic.

One significant difference in the Mainichi coverage of the war in China is that where the *Asahigraph China Incident Pictorial* ceased publication in the summer of 1940 (by which time the war was supposed to have ended), the Mainichi continued to publish its *China Incident Pictorial*, albeit as a monthly. The outbreak of war in Europe did not push the China war off the front cover or warrant a lead story. There was no November 1941 issue, and the 8 December 1941 issue could explain little about the outbreak of the war. Issue 102 was published one month later, 8 January 1942, its cover bearing a banner explaining that the "*China Incident Pictorial* is Renamed *Great East Asia War Pictorial*." This renaming was in line with the Imperial Edict declaring war, which explicitly linked the Great East Asia War to the war in China. The Mainichi's nearly seamless coverage offers a more cohesive sense of causality between the China war and the Pacific War and therefore more closely reflects postwar perspective.

From 1942 Mainichi must have had increasingly difficulty sending photographers to the battlefront, but even as late as September 1944, *Great East Asia War Pictorial* published war photographs not seen in *Asahigraph* or *PWR*. And while increasingly strict government control of the press all but ruled out any divergent view, in November 1942 (*Great East Asia War Pictorial* 12) the Mainichi published photos and an article on the trial of captured Doolittle Raid pilots that did not appear elsewhere. Toward the end of the war, the numbering became erratic (the 8 September 1944 issue is called *Shina jihen gahō* 135 and also *Dai Tō A sensō gahō* 34, while the 8 December 1944 issue is called *Shina jihen gahō* 136 but jumps to *Dai Tō A sensō gahō* 36). It probably ceased publication in the spring of 1945 with the government's final consolidation of periodicals.

4. *Domeigraph* (*Dōmeigurafu*), 252–319. Tokyo: Dōmei Tsūshinsha, 1940–1945.
   A. *Domeigraph* (*Dōmeigurafu*) 252–297, April 1940–January 1944. Monthly, 11¾ by 8½ inches, unpaginated but typically 80 to 100 pages, 70 sen. Issued on the first of the month. Issued on the seventh of the month from December 1941, evidently in honor of the day on which Japanese blitzkrieg (in the Western hemisphere).
   B. *Great East Asia Report* (*Dai Tō A hō*) 298–319, February 1944–January 1945. Biweekly, 11¾ by 8½ inches, pages and price unknown. Issued on the first and the fifteenth.
   C. Reprint. Tokyo: Yumani Shobō, 1989–1990.

Dōmei Tsūshinsha (literally, Federated or United News Agency) was founded in 1935 as a modern media conglomerate uniting all news agencies and medias, print as well as radio and film, and was the official press agency of the Japanese Government. Domei's domain was foreign news, and as such the agency wielded tremendous influence through its many publications.

The monthly *Domeigraph* was much less sensational than *PWR* or *Asahigraph*, emphasizing analysis, rather than image. On the one hand, the *Domeigraph* maintained a higher journalistic standard for its coverage of the war, and on the other, it achieved a slick look, in terms of both its advertising and story layouts, suggesting that its staff were keenly aware of the latest international trends in graphic design. The influence of the Russian constructionist school, as seen in the use of photo-collage and extreme angle photography, is more prevalent in *Domeigraph* than in *PWR*. *Domeigraph*'s sophistication was evident in its 70-sen price and its carrying advertisements for luxury items with English names late in 1943, even after *PWR* had lambasted such products and called for their demise that spring. It also included more analysis about the media itself, in articles such as "Japanese-language Newspapers in the Southern Regions" (July 1943). As a "best of" monthly, it could also examine trends in the international situation, giving an accurate, in-depth picture of the Detroit race riots in its August 1943 issue. It also reprinted photos from "enemy" news, including a photograph of Roosevelt and Churchill at the Quebec Conference, damage to the deck of an American aircraft carrier from a Japanese bomb, and a photo of Klu Klux Klan members in the United States (December 1943).

Evidence suggests that *Domeigraph* had at least one earlier incarnation in the 1930s, perhaps as a weekly news magazine, but issues 1 through 251 have not been located in either OCLC/WorldCat or NACSIS. In 1989–1990, reprinted the wartime issues of *Domeigraph*, with the following numbers missing: 253–255, 300, 302, 304, 307, 308, 314–318. From 1938 to 1943, Dōmei Tsūshinsha also published an annual photo almanac with captions in English and, occasionally, other foreign languages. *Domei's Photo Almanac* is a wonderful source of information for researchers who do not read Japanese.

5. *Global Intelligence* (*Sekai chishiki*). Tokyo: Seibundō Shinkōsha.
   A. *Global Intelligence* (1:1-7:6), October 1931–October 1935. Monthly, 7¼ by 10¼ inches. Six issues per volume.
   B. *Global Intelligence*. January 1935–June 1944 (8:1-17:7). Monthly, 7¼ by 10¼ inches, typically 120 to 140 pages, 80 sen. Twelve issues per volume.
   C. *Global Intelligence.* February–May 1946 (1:1-1:4). Tokyo: Seibundō Shinkōsha. Monthly.

Global Intelligence aimed at a higher level of reader and carried more in-depth news analysis, playing *Newsweek* to *Asahigraph*'s *Life*. *Domeigraph* was probably patterned after it. A monthly publication priced at a rather high 80 sen, it carried several pages of photos on better-quality paper and articles introducing international events unusual aspects of foreign cultures. When the Pacific War started, it focused on the cultures of the "conquered lands" in Southeast Asia and even printed photos of bare-breasted beauties. Frequently a world leader appeared on the cover, such as Mussolini in October 1943. A rather unflattering photograph of Admiral Husband E. Kimmel, disgraced by the Pearl Harbor debacle, was placed on the cover of the December 1942 issue, revealing a sophisticated sense of humor unusual in wartime news journals. The page count remained above 100 throughout 1942, with the October 1942 issue featuring "Strife in America and Britain" containing 168 pages and specially priced at 1 yen 20 sen. The front cover of this issue carried a dramatic photograph of white American police restraining and beating an African-American. In 1943, however, the quality and page count of the magazine rapidly declined due to the strictures placed on wartime publications. Also in 1943, the English-language publication data, required for international mailings, was removed from the back cover. The magazine's title had been rendered "The Sekai Tisiki." The magazine ceased publication in autumn 1944. It was revived in February 1946 (with the new series beginning with volume 1 number 1) and at least four issues appeared; its fate thereafter is unknown.

6. *History Pictures* (*Rekishi shashin*). 1-371, June 1913–April 1944. Tokyo: Rekishi shashin kai.
   A. *History Pictures* (*Rekishi shashin*), 1–343, June 1913–December 1941. Monthly, 12 by 9 inches, unpaginated (typically, 20 leaves), 60 sen (price in 1940). Oblong format with artwork and photographs printed in color on one side only and on tipped-in plates.
   B. *History Pictures* (*Rekishi shashin*), 344–371, January 1942–April 1944. Monthly, 11¾ by 8¼ inches, unpaginated (typically, 12 leaves), 60 sen. Oblong format with some full-color illustrations.

A splashy monthly publication with full-color covers as late as the spring of 1944, inlaid full-color plates, and duotone prints throughout, *History Pictures* was probably originally intended as a visual supplement to newspapers in the age when even the most rudimentary photographs were scarce in their pages. At the price of 60 sen per copy, this was a rather expensive periodical, given its low page count. After 1943, the magazine could not include the lavish tipped-in plates and full-color prints that were its hallmark and major selling point. For instance, issues from 1940 and 1941 included reproductions of patriotic woodblock prints by Meiji master Tsukioka Yoshitoshi, and the New Year's 1941 issue included a tipped-in color plate of a painting of Mount Fuji by Yokoyama Taikan, suitable for framing. Full-color photographs of the emperor and of important scenes from the war were also featured. No issues later than April 1944 have been located, and *History Pictures* probably succumbed to the forced merger of magazines carried out in late 1944.

7. *Photographic Weekly Report* (*Shashin shūhō*), 1938–1945.
   A. *Photographic Weekly Report* (*Shashin shūhō*) 1–146, 12 February 1938–4 December 1940. Tokyo: Printing Office of the Cabinet Information Division. Weekly, 8¼ by 11¾ inches, 24 pages, (exclusive of color front and back covers), 10 sen.
   B. *Photographic Weekly Report* (*Shashin shūhō*) 147–375, 11 December 1940–25 July 1945. Tokyo: Printing Office of the [Cabinet] Information Bureau.

i. *Photographic Weekly Report* (*Shashin shūhō*) 147–314, 11 December 1940–22 March 1944. Weekly, 8¼ by 11¾ inches, 24 pages (inclusive of color front and back covers), 10 sen.
ii. *Photographic Weekly Report* (*Shashin shūhō*) 315–365, 29 March 1944–28 March 1945. Weekly, 11¾ by 16½ inches, 12 pages, 10 sen.
iii. *Photographic Weekly Report* (*Shashin shūhō*) 366–375, 11 April 1945–25 July 1945. Trimonthly, 8¼ by 11¾ inches, 16 pages (inclusive of front and back covers), 10 sen. Printed entirely in black and white on two large broad-sheets, each sheet containing four pages on each side printed recto-verso, and each sheet folded in half twice. Published on the fifth, fifteenth, and twenty-fifth.

C. Reprint. Tokyo: Ōzorasha, 1989–1990.

The sister publication of *Weekly Report*, the first issue of *Photographic Weekly Report* (*PWR*) contained many photographs and little text (other than captions). *PWR* went through several modifications in its format, although the sleek, bold stylistic elements, and the emphasis on photography, remained constant. The impact of the cover photograph was strengthened by leaving it uncluttered; its accompanying caption was printed on the inside back cover (usually numbered 23). Only three issues had illustrations, rather than photographs, on their covers. Two were full-color special issues (97, for New Year's 1940; and 175, for the fourth anniversary of the Second Sino-Japanese War, with a drawing by Fujita Tsuguharu); the third was issue 342 (11 October 1944) and featured a violent drawing by Mukai Junkichi of a Japanese soldier on the verge of plunging a sword into the throat of an overcome Allied soldier.

Initially, *PWR* accepted full-page advertisements from the private sector. The back page of issue 2 shows a young beauty touting Fuji film. The government had little use for commercial advertising, which was deemed counter-productive, and by late 1941, *PWR* only allotted advertising space to savings programs and war bond campaigns. Strategically priced at 10 sen, *PWR* sold moderately well until 1940, when readership increased with coverage of the 2,600th anniversary of the founding of the Japanese nation. In the first five years of the magazine, holidays were usually marked by full-color covers and a forty- to fifty-page double issues, which cost 20 sen.

From issue 315 (29 March 1944), the magazine format changed: the page size was doubled and the page count was halved. The larger format could be mailed folded in half, and thus stapling was no longer necessary. (With the outbreak of the Pacific War, the number of staples per copy had already been reduced from two to one.) These "large size" magazines had two- or three-tone photographs on the covers through issue 328 (5 July 1944). The larger page size could accommodate larger-than-life, dramatic head shots.

From 11 April 1945 (issue 366) the magazine went back to the original page size, but with 4 pages printed recto-verso on both sides of two enormous sheets that were folded in half twice to arrive at a 16-page magazine. The "weekly" became a tri-monthly. To compare the bright cover and lavish format of earlier issues to one of these uniformly brownish gray issues of 1945 is itself a commentary on the course of the war. The paper is coarse, the print quality very faint, the pictures dark.

PWR had several features that were introduced and phased out. The magazine had a "readers' photographs" section that appeared in most issues from late 1938 until the outbreak of the Pacific War. The Pacific War saw the introduction of a back page of small-format cartoons and the "Signboard of the Times" message. The latter usually appeared on page 3 (late in the war, appearing on the front cover), relied heavily on a textual message, and was designed to be detached and displayed as a poster.

8. *Weekly Report*, 14 October 1936–August 1945.
   A. *Weekly Report* (*Shūhō*) 1–217, 14 October 1936–4 December 1940. [Tokyo:] Printing Office of the Information Bureau of the Prime Minister's Cabinet. Weekly, 5¾ by 8¼ inches, typically 30 to 60 pages, 5 sen.
   B. *Weekly Report* (*Shūhō*), 218–452, 11 December 1940–August 1945. [Tokyo:] Printing Office of the [Cabinet] Information Bureau. Weekly, 5¾ by 8¼ inches, typically 30 to 60 pages, 5 sen. In its final year, usually 16 pages; price increase to 10 sen from either issue 440 or 441 (April 1945).

The small-format *Weekly Report* was the first publication of the Cabinet Information Committee (CIC), appearing within a few months of its establishment. *Weekly Report* was, from beginning to end, a small-format, modest publication with soberingly plain green covers, priced at a mere 5 sen. When the war situation grew dire, the green on the cover was reduced to a thick, crude, vertical stripe (from issue 372, 1 December 1943), which later became a horizontal swatch (from issue 389), and finally disappeared (from issue 414, 27 September 1944). The format was hardly modified in nine years. When the CIC was upgraded to an office, "Edited by the Cabinet Information Committee" was dropped from the front cover, and when the office was upgraded to a bureau (the CIB), a banner was added to the front cover stating, "Edited by the Cabinet Information Bureau." Special issues, sometimes with large-scale foldout maps, sold for 10 sen. It rarely included illustrations and was utterly devoid of cultural or human-interest stories, its reportage devoted to government policies and legislature. *Weekly Report* was perhaps the final "weekly" magazine to remain a weekly, rather than a trimonthly, in the final months of the war, and was the best source of public information on the workings of the government before and during the war years.

APPENDIX 2: GLOSSARY

ABCD. The Americans, British, Chinese, and Dutch. The three Asian imperial powers that put economic and military pressure on Japan following the invasion of Indo-china in the summer of 1940. Japan was nearly encircled geographically by the Asian colonies of the three powers and by Chiang Kai-shek's forces in China. Anti-ABCD rhetoric began flooding the Japanese press in the autumn of 1940 and reached a feverish pitch in the months prior to the attack on Pearl Harbor. The ABCD stranglehold on Japanese ambitions in Asia was alluded to in the Imperial Rescript Declaring War on America and Britain and cited frequently as a reason for the outbreak of the war.

BeiEi. "America-Britain," or "Anglo-American." An abbreviated, conjoined form of Beikoku (America) and Eikoku (Great Britain) and the most common term used by the wartime press to refer to Japan's enemy. The term is not pejorative or derogatory.

Bōchō. "Guard Against Espionage" (or, more literally "Guarding Secrets"). A key phrase in the anti-espionage campaign of 1940, itself a bid to foment anti-Western xenophobia in the wake of strained international relations. One of many government programs that fell under the rubric of Total Spiritual Mobilization.

Bushido. "The Way of the Warrior." The Japanese fighting man's code of honor and battle-field ethics, closely linked to Japanese notions of "humanity" (nasake) and "sincerity" (magokoro). While Bushido clearly has premodern antecedents, like so many of Japan's "traditions," it was only fully enunciated and codified in the Meiji period, in particular in *Bushido* (1899), the seminal text written and published in English by the Japanese Quaker Nitobe Inazō.

Fukkaku. "Digging in." Warfare of endurance, that is, of attrition, which Japanese forces practiced throughout the Pacific region from late 1944 until the war's end. Indeed, some soldiers embedded deep in jungle interiors, would continue to resist decades after the war's end.

Gunshin. "Warrior-god." The enshrined spirit of a men who died in the emperor's service.

Synonymous with gokokushin, "nation-protecting deity." Yasukuni ideology claimed that the spirits of fallen enlisted men continued to protect Japan in the afterlife.

Gyokusai. "Death for honor." This phrase from a seventh-century Chinese text means "to crush jewels." The media first applied the word to the suicidal charge made on 29 May 1943 on Attu Island by Japanese troops led by Colonel Yamazaki Yasuyo. Several instances of gyokusai followed, until the practice took the form of fukkaku, "digging in." The Japanese press hailed the civilian suicides at Marpi Point at the climax of the Battle of Saipan as "gyokusai." In common English, gyokusai is "a banzai charge."

Hakkō Ichiu. "Eight Corners Under One Roof." According to legends recorded in the *Nihon shoki*, upon conquering all of the tribes in the land, Emperor Jinmu (putative founder of Yamato, the first Japanese nation) announced his sovereignty by claiming to have brought the world ("the eight corners") together ("under one roof"). Although this "world" extended no further than what is today western Japan, the phrase became a justification for expanding Japanese rule over Asia. In 1940, in commemoration of the 2,600th anniversary of the mythical founding of the Japanese nation, a pillar was built in Miyazaki, Kyūshū, in the purported site of Jinmu's palace.

Hikokuminteki. Literally, "uncitizenlike," the meaning is "unJapanese." This adjective was applied to any behavior or attitude that ran counter to the war effort. Today, the word conjures up the secret police and lack of civil liberties accompanying the rise of Japanese militarism in the 1930s.

Hisshō. "Certain" or "ultimate victory." A phrase used for the duration of the Pacific War to reassure the public that Japan would emerge the winner in the struggle against the Western imperial powers. Similar terms, such as kessen, were used interchangeably.

Hondo kessen. "The Final Battle for the Home Islands." Here, *kessen* is "decisive battle." The government insisted that the entire population of Japan would die fighting, if necessary, in this final battle.

Ichioku. "One Hundred Million." The one hundred million subjects of the Japanese Empire (Japan, Korea, Taiwan, and other territories), the population announced by the Japanese government in 1937. The phrase was employed in several wartime slogans, such as "ichioku isshin" ("One hundred million, one mind" [that is, united in purpose]) and "Ichioku hi no tama da" ("one hundred million fireballs" [freely translated, "the raging morale of one hundred million"]).

Imon. "Care" or "comfort," as in imonbukuro ("care package") and imontegami ("comfort letter"). The term should not be confused with comfort women (*ianpu*).

Jūgo. "The home front." Literally, "behind the gun." A term common in the 1930s and the first two years of the Pacific War. It was quickly superseded by words such as "production warriors" and "agricultural warriors" as civilian life disappeared and all Japanese were mobilized.

Kamikaze in ka suru. "Kamikazefication." The government's ultimate goal in mobilization of the citizenry in anticipation of a landed invasion of Japan's Home Islands. "Kamikazefied" citizens were ordered to train for battle and fight to the death against the Allied invaders. The media praised the widespread civilian suicides during the Battle of Okinawa, as an example of kamikazefied society. In fact, most civilian suicides were coerced or forced by the Japanese military on the island.

Kessen. "Decisive battle." The two characters are "decision" and "battle." A word used throughout the course of the Pacific War to denote the coming of "ultimate victory." Each battle Japan fought was decisive since, hypothetically, it might bring about the Allies' defeat and the war's end. The phrase was used most frequently in 1942 and 1943, but had currency as late as August 1945. The word is a homonym (see next entry).

Kessen. "Fight to the death." The two characters are "blood" and "battle," thus a "bloody battle," a fight to the finish. Used interchangeably with *hisshō* ("certain" or "ultimate victory"), especially after the loss of Saipan, the first of Japan's prewar territory to fall into enemy hands. The word reflects the spiritual superiority of the Japanese, who are willing to die fighting.

Kichiku. "Demon bastards." A derogatory term for the enemy, used most frequently after the tide of war turned against Japan. Used as a noun, also as an adjective in longer phrases such as "demon-bastards Yankees."

KōA. "Constructing" or "Building Asia." One of the central tenets of the New Order announced by Prime Minister Konoe Fumimaro in October 1938. Japan's destiny was to shine its civilizing light, under the benevolent rule of the emperor, throughout Asia, resulting in an end to Western imperialism and a new world order.

Kokumin Gakkō. "Citizens' School." A word that immediately calls up wartime Japan. As part of the New Order, Japan's national education system was restructured. Curricula became more militaristic as elementary school children were mobilized. Citizens' Schools, opened nationwide in 1940, were quickly dismantled by the Occupation authorities.

Kokutai. "National Polity." An organic conception of the nation, akin to the leviathan. Volition was assigned to kokutai, and the citizens were expected to answer to its demands. While wartime ideologues (and some postwar historians) have gone to great lengths to elucidate Kokutai, in practical usage it differs little from the utterances of politicians all over the world when they speak of the nation in absolute, anthropomorphic terms, e. g. "America believes in democracy and fights for freedom."

Magokoro. "Sincerity." The etymology of this word is "true heart," that is, "innermost heart," where there can be no disingenuousness. The word indicates honesty in one's intentions and actions. During the war, a "sincere" soldier would willingly accept a dangerous mission and gladly give his life for nation and emperor. Conversely, the Japanese press often described Westerners as "lacking in sincerity" in the negotiations leading up the war, and then in their cowardly manner of fighting once the war began.

Nasake. "Humanity." The common meanings of the word today is "mercy" or "sympathy." During the war, the media used the word to describe the morality and justice of Japanese troops in occupied lands, and thus it connotes "leniency."

Nikudan. "Human bullets" or "Human bombs." Literally, "flesh bullets." Applied to the soldier who himself becomes a weapon, using his very body like a bomb and dying in the process. The word was popularized during the Russo-Japanese War through the bestselling book, *Nikudan*, by Sakurai Tadayoshi. The phrase continued to be used during the Pacific War, but was largely supplanted by gyokusai.

Senden. "Propaganda." The same word is used in everyday parlance for "advertising" or "promotion." *Senden* had positive connotations in Japanese (just as "propaganda" did in Europe and the United States during World War I). In modern Japanese, the loan word "puropaganda" (propaganda) has the negative connotations it does in English.

Shōkokumin. "Junior" or "little citizens." A seemingly innocuous manner of referring to children, the phrase today is still associated with their wartime mobilization. Junior citizens kept the munitions factories operating around the clock and patrolled the skies for enemy airplanes. Thousands of junior citizens became junior pilots, junior sailors, and junior soldiers.

Uchiteshi yamamu. "Keep up the fight." Directly translated, this classical phrase becomes "continue to shoot, do not desist." A slogan attributed to Emperor Jinmu and taken from Japan's oldest collected mythology, the *Nihon Shoki*. The phrase was the centerpiece of a brilliant public relations campaign designed to boost morale as the momentum of the war came to a standstill in the spring of 1943.

Yamatodamashii. "Japanese spirit." Yamato, the name of the land of Jinmu, is an old name for Japan. During the war, *yamatodamashii* meant "fighting spirit."

Zeitaku ha teki da! "Luxury is the Enemy!" A major public relations campaign launched in 1940 under the aegis of the New Order. The word *zeitaku* carries the connotation of "extravagance" or "excess," that is, of wastefulness, and during the war, was applied to everything the government deemed unnecessary to the war effort.

BIBLIOGRAPHY

Agawa Hiroyuki. *The Reluctant Admiral: Yamamoto and the Imperial Japanese Navy.* Kodansha International, 1979.
Bergamini, David. *Japan's Imperial Conspiracy.* London: Heinemann, 1971.
Bix, Herbert P. *Hirohito and the Making of Modern Japan.* New York: HarperCollins, 2000.
Brothers, Caroline. *War and Photography: A Cultural History.* London: Routledge, 1997.
Brown, Joseph Rust. *We Stole to Live.* Cape Girardeau, MO: privately printed, 1982.
Cipris, Zeljko. "Responsibility of Intellectuals: Kobayashi Hideo on Japan at War," posted online at *Japan Focus*, available at http://japanfocus.org/products/details/1625.
Cook, Haruko Taya, and Theodore F. Cook. *Japan at War: An Oral History.* New York: New Press, 1992.
Daws, Gavan. *Prisoners of the Japanese: POWs of World War II in the Pacific.* Scranton, PA: William Morrow, 1994.
deBary, William Theodore, ed. *Sources of Japanese Tradition.* New York: Columbia University Press, 1958.
Dower, John W. "Introduction" to Japan Photographers Association, ed. *A Century of Japanese Photography.* New York: Pantheon, 1980.
——. *War Without Mercy: Race and Power in the Pacific War.* New York: Pantheon, 1986.
Duara, Prasenjit. "The New Imperialism and the Post-Colonial Developmental State: Manchukuo in Comparative Perspective," in *Japan Focus* (30 January 2006), available at http://japanfocus.org/article.asp?id=512.
Earhart, H. Byron. *Fuji, Icon of Japan.* (forthcoming.)
——. *Japanese New Religions, A Bibliography.* Ann Arbor: University of Michigan Press, 1979.
Encyclopedia of Japan. Tokyo: Kodansha, 1993.
Fitzpatrick, Ernest Hugh. *The Coming Conflict of Nations or the Japanese-American War.* Springfield, IL: Roker, 1909.
Fleischer, Wilfred. *Volcanic Isle.* New York: Doubleday, Doran: 1941.
Fralin, Frances. *The Indelible Image: Photographs of War, 1846 to the Present.* New York: Harry N. Abrams, 1985.
Fyne, Robert. *The Hollywood Propaganda of World War II.* Metuchen, NJ: Scarecrow Press, 1994.
Gard, Robert G., Lieutenant-General, and Senator Patrick Leahy. "History's Revealing Light." Foreword to the 1999 Center for International Policy article, "Commander-in-Chief: Contrasting the Presidential Roles in the World Campaigns to Ban Chemical Weapons (1919-45) and Land Mines (1990s)," available at: www.ciponline.org/oldiprcomm.htm.
Gause, Major Damon "Rocky." *The War Journal of Major Damon "Rocky" Gause.* New York: Hyperion, 1999.
Gibney, Frank. *Sensō: The Japanese Remember The Pacific War.* Armonk, NY: M. E. Sharpe, 1995.
Glines, Carroll V. *Doolittle's Tokyo Raiders.* New York: Van Nostrand Reinhold, 1981.

Goldstein, Donald M., and Katherine V. Dillon, eds. *The Pearl Harbor Papers: Inside the Japanese Plans*. Washington, DC: Brassey's, 1993.

Gotō Ken'ichi. "Cooperation, Submission, and Resistance of Indigenous Elites of Southeast Asia in the Wartime Empire," pp. 274-304 in Peter Duus, Ramon H. Myers, and Mark R. Peattie, eds., *The Japanese Wartime Empire, 1931-1945*. Princeton, NJ: Princeton University Press, 1996.

Grew, Joseph. *Ten Years in Japan*. New York: Simon and Schuster, 1944.

Grunden, Walter E. *Secret Weapons & World War II: Japan in the Shadow of Big Science*. Lawrence: University Press of Kansas, 2005.

Gunther, John. *Inside Asia*. New York: Harpers, 1939.

Hane, Mikiso. *Peasants, Rebels, and Outcastes: The Underside of Modern Japan*. New York: Pantheon, 1982.

Harris, Sheldon H. *Factories of Death: Japanese Biological Warfare 1932-45 and the American Cover-Up*. New York: Routledge, 1994.

Havens, Thomas R. H. *Valley of Darkness: The Japanese People and World War II*. New York: Norton, 1978.

Hoston, Germaine. *Marxism and the Crisis of Development in Prewar Japan*. Princeton: Princeton University Press, 1986.

Ienaga Saburō. *The Pacific War, 1931-1945*. New York: Pantheon, 1978.

Japan Revolutionary Communist League. *Zenshin*. Viewable online at www.zenshin.org/.

The Japan Year Book 1938-39. Tokyo: Kenkyusha, 1938.

Johnston, B[ruce] F., with Mosaburo Hosoda and Yoshio Kusumi. *Japanese Food Management in World War II*. Stanford: University of California Press, 1953.

Kaneko Ryūichi, "Realism and Propaganda: The Photographer's Eye Trained on Society," pp. 184-194 in Anne Wilkes Tucker, Dana Friis-Hansen, Kaneko Ryūichi, and Takeba Joe, *The History of Japanese Photography*. New Haven, CT: Yale University Press, 2003.

Kasza, Gregory J. *The State and the Mass Media in Japan, 1918-1945*. Berkeley: University of California Press, 1988.

Keene, Donald. *Dawn to the West: Japanese Literature in the Modern Era, Fiction*. New York: Holt, Rinehart, and Winston, 1984.

Kiroku, Hanai. "The Remembered and the Forgotten: Slighting the Firebombing Victims of Japan's Pacific War." *Japan Focus* 252, 25 September 2006, available at www.japanfocus.org.

Kobayashi Shunsuke. "Proretaria bijutsu to sensōga ni okeru 'kokumin'-teki shikaku" ("Visualization of 'Citizen'-ness in Proletarian Art and War Pictures," 2003). Published online at www.e.yamagata-u.ac.jp/˜shun/proletar.html.

Kranzler, David. *Japanese, Nazis, and Jews: The Jewish Refugee Community of Shanghai, 1938-1945*. New York: Yeshiva University Press, 1976.

Kumata, Hideya. "Spiritual Mobilization—the Japanese Concept of Propaganda," pp. 1-30 in *Four Working Papers on Propaganda Theory* ("Written in Part with the Help of the United States Information Agency under Contract 1A-W-362"). N.p. [Champaign]: University of Illinois, January 1955.

Kushner, Barak. *The Thought War: Japanese Imperial Propaganda*. Honolulu: University of Hawai'i Press, 2005.

Linebarger, Paul M. A. *Psychological Warfare*. Washington, D. C.: Infantry Journal, 1948.

Matsumura, Janice. *More Than a Momentary Nightmare: The Yokohama Incident and Wartime Japan* (Cornell East Asia Series, number 92). Ithaca: Cornell University Press, 1998

McCall, J. E. *Santo Tomas Internment Camp: Stic in Verse and Reverse, Stic-toons and Stic-tistics*. Lincoln, NE: Woodruff, 1945.

Minear, Richard H. *Victors' Justice: The Tokyo War Crimes Trial*. Princeton: Princeton University Press, 1971.

Miyoshi Masao. "Who Decides, and Who Speaks? *Shutaisei* and the West in Postwar Japan," pp. 269-292 in Andrew Gerstle and Anthony Milner, eds., *Recovering the Orient: Artists, Scholars, Appropriations*. New York: Harwood Academic, 1994.

Morris, Ivan. *The Nobility of Failure: Tragic Heroes in the History of Japan.* New York: Holt, Rinehart and Winston, 1975.

Nanba Kōji, *"Uchiteshi yamamu": Taiheiyō sensō to hōkoku no gijitsusha tachi* ["Uchiteshi yamamu": The Pacific War and Media Experts]. Tokyo: Kodansha, 1998.

Ohnuki-Tierney, Emiko. *Kamikaze, Cherry Blossoms and Nationalisms: The Militarization of Aesthetics in Japanese History.* Chicago: University of Chicago Press, 2002.

Onoda Hiroo. *No Surrender: My Thirty Years' War.* Tokyo: Kodansha International, 1974.

The Orient Yearbook for 1942. Tokyo: Asia Statistics, 1942.

Philippi, Donald L., (trans.) *Kojiki.* New York: Columbia University Press, 1977.

Read, Donald. *The Power of News: The History of Reuters, 1849-1989.* New York: Oxford University Press, 1992.

Rees, Laurence. *Horror in the East: Japan and the Atrocities of World War II.* New York: Da Capo, 2001.

Rodgaard, John, Commander (Ret) et al. "Pearl Harbor—Attack from Below." Posted online at *Naval History*, December 1999, available at www.usni.org/navalhistory/Articles99/Nhrodgaard.htm.

Rubin, Jay. *Injurious to Public Morals: Writers and the Meiji State.* Seattle: University of Washington Press, 1984.

Sakamaki Kazuo. *I Attacked Pearl Harbor.* New York: Association Press, 1949.

Sakurai Tadayoshi. *Human Bullets: A Soldier's Story of the Russo-Japanese War.* Lincoln: University of Nebraska Press, 1999. (Reprinted from the first edition of 1907 published by Houghton, Mifflin.)

Sandler, Mark H. "A Painter of the 'Holy War': Fujita Tsuguji and the Japanese Military," pp. 188-211 in Marlene J. Mayo and J. Thomas Rimer eds., *War, Occupation, and Creativity: Japan and East Asia, 1920-1960.* Honolulu: University of Hawai'i Press, 2001.

Scidmore, Eliza Ruhamah. *As the Hague Ordains: Journal of a Russian Prisoner's Wife in Japan.* New York: Henry Holt, 1907.

Shull, Michael S. and David Edward Wilt. *Hollywood War Films, 1937-1945.* Jefferson, NC: McFarland, 1996.

Svinth, Joseph R. "Fulfilling His Duty as a Member: Jigoro Kano and the Japanese Bid for the 1940 Olympics," *Journal of Competitive Sport*, May 2004, available at ejmas.com/jcs/2004jcs/jcsart_svinth_0504.htm

Tagawa Seiichi. *Sensō no gurafizumu: kaisō no "FRONT"* (*War Graphism: Reminiscences about FRONT*). Tokyo: Heibonsha, 1988.

Tanaka Chigaku. *What Is Nippon Kokutai? Introduction to Nipponese National Principles.* Tokyo: Shishio Bunkō, 1936.

Tanaka, Stefan. *Japan's Orient: Rendering Pasts into History.* Berkeley: University of California Press, 1993.

Tanaka, Yuki. "Last Words of the Tiger of Malaya, General Yamashita Tomoyuki." Posted on *Japan Focus* (20 September 2005), available at http://japanfocus.org/article.asp?id=392.

Tokayer, Marvin and Mary Swartz. *The Fugu Plan: The Untold Story of the Japanese and the Jews During World War II.* New York: Paddington Press, 1979.

Tolischus, Otto D. *Tokyo Record.* New York: Reynal and Hitchcock, 1943.

Tōta Ishimaru, Lieutenant-Commander. *Japan Must Fight Britain.* New York: Herald Press, 1936.

Trager, Frank N., ed. *Burma: Japanese Military Administration, Selected Documents*, 1941-1945. Philadelphia: University of Pennsylvania Press, 1971.

Tucker, Anne Wilkes, Dana Friis-Hansen, Kaneko Ryūichi, and Takeba Joe, *The History of Japanese Photography.* New Haven, CT: Yale University Press, 2003.

Ueno, Chizuko. *Nationalism and Gender* (translated by Beverley Yamamoto). Melbourne: Trans Pacific Press, 2004.

Underwood, William. "Names, Bones, and Unpaid Wages (2): Seeking Redress for Korean Forced Labor." Posted on *Japan Focus*, 17 September 2006, available at: www.japanfocus.org/products/details/2225.

Warner, Denis, and Peggy Warner, with Commander Sadao Seno. *The Sacred Warriors.* New York: Van Nostrand Reinhold, 1982.

Weisenfeld, Gennifer. "Touring Japan-as-Museum: *NIPPON* and other Japanese Imperialist Travelogues," pp. 747-793 in *Positions: East Asia Cultures Critique* (8:3), Winter 2000.

Williams, Peter. *Unit 731: Japan's Secret Biological Warfare in World War II.* New York: Free Press, 1989.

Yamanouchi, Midori, and Joseph L. Quinn, translators. *Listen to the Voices from the Sea.* Scranton, PA: University of Scranton Press, 2000.

Yu-Jose, Lydia N. "World War II and the Japanese in the Prewar Philippines." *Journal of Southeast Asian Studies* (27:1), 1996.

INDEX

Numbers in bold indicate illustrations.

About the Author

David C. Earhart received his PhD in Comparative and Japanese Literature and has taught and lectured extensively on World War II and modern Japanese culture. He was born in Japan, where he lived for many years, working as a professional translator and language instructor. He currently resides in Vancouver, British Columbia and is researching *kamishibai* and the mobilization of Japanese children during World War II.